PONYO

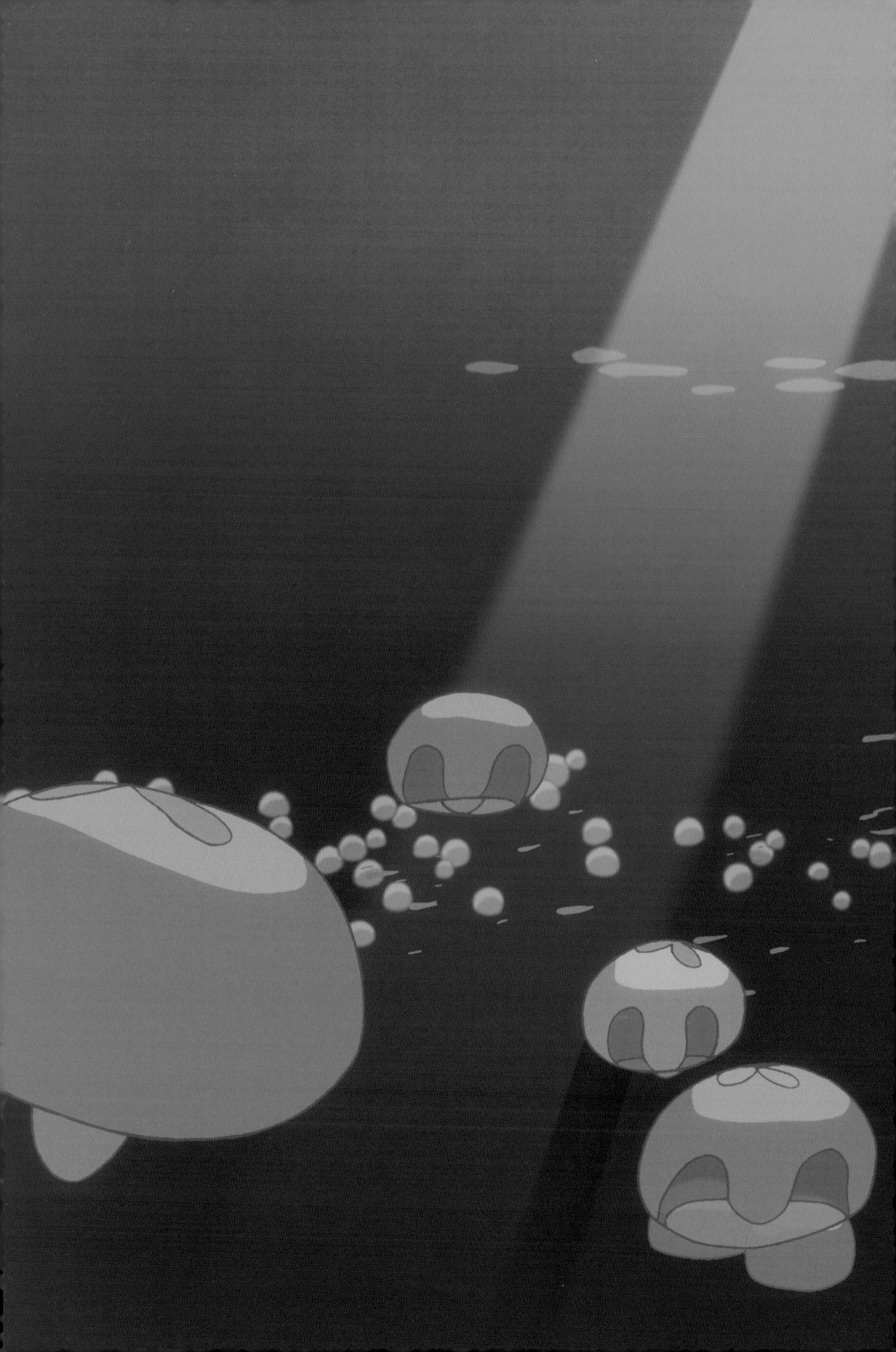

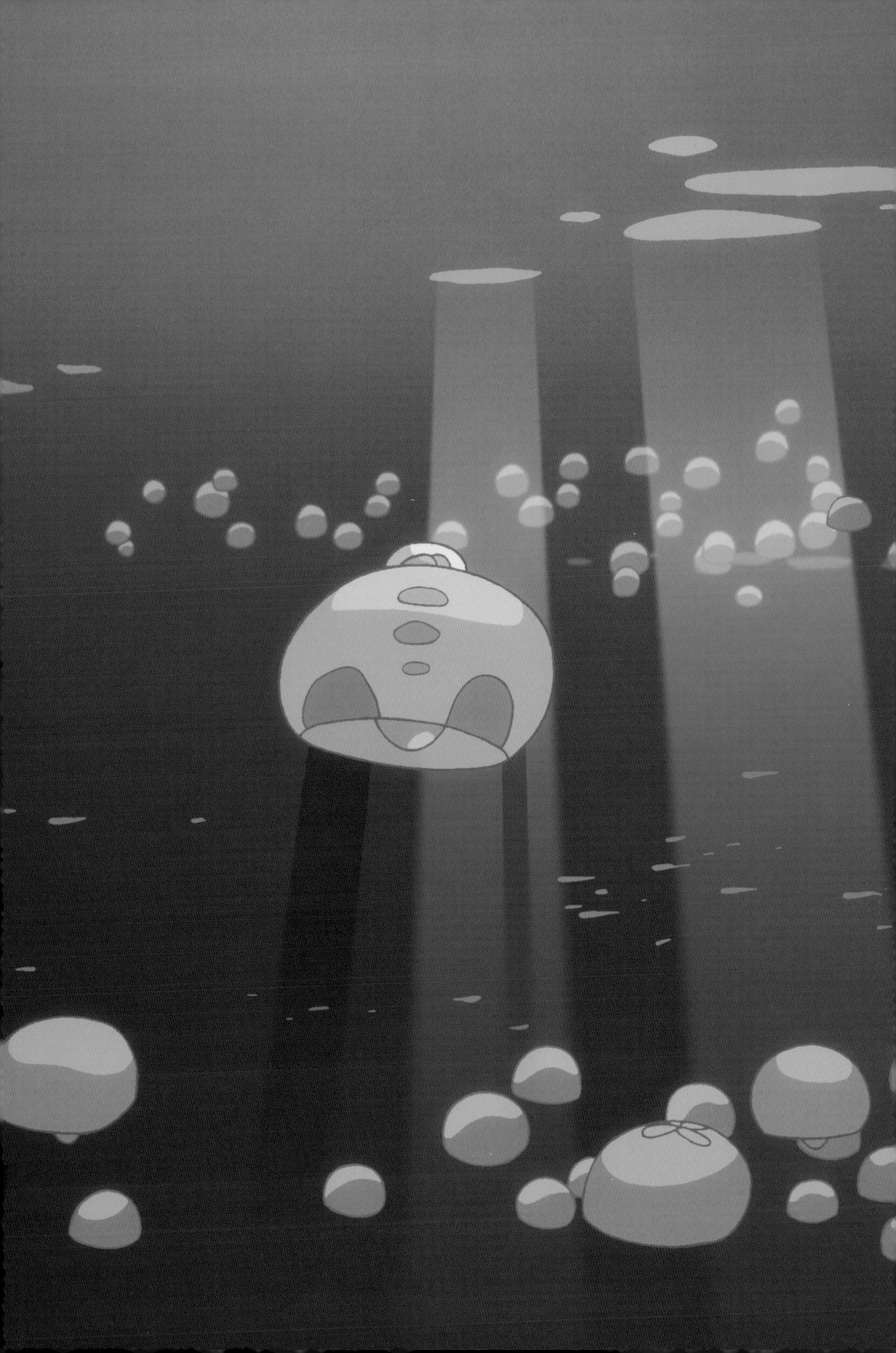

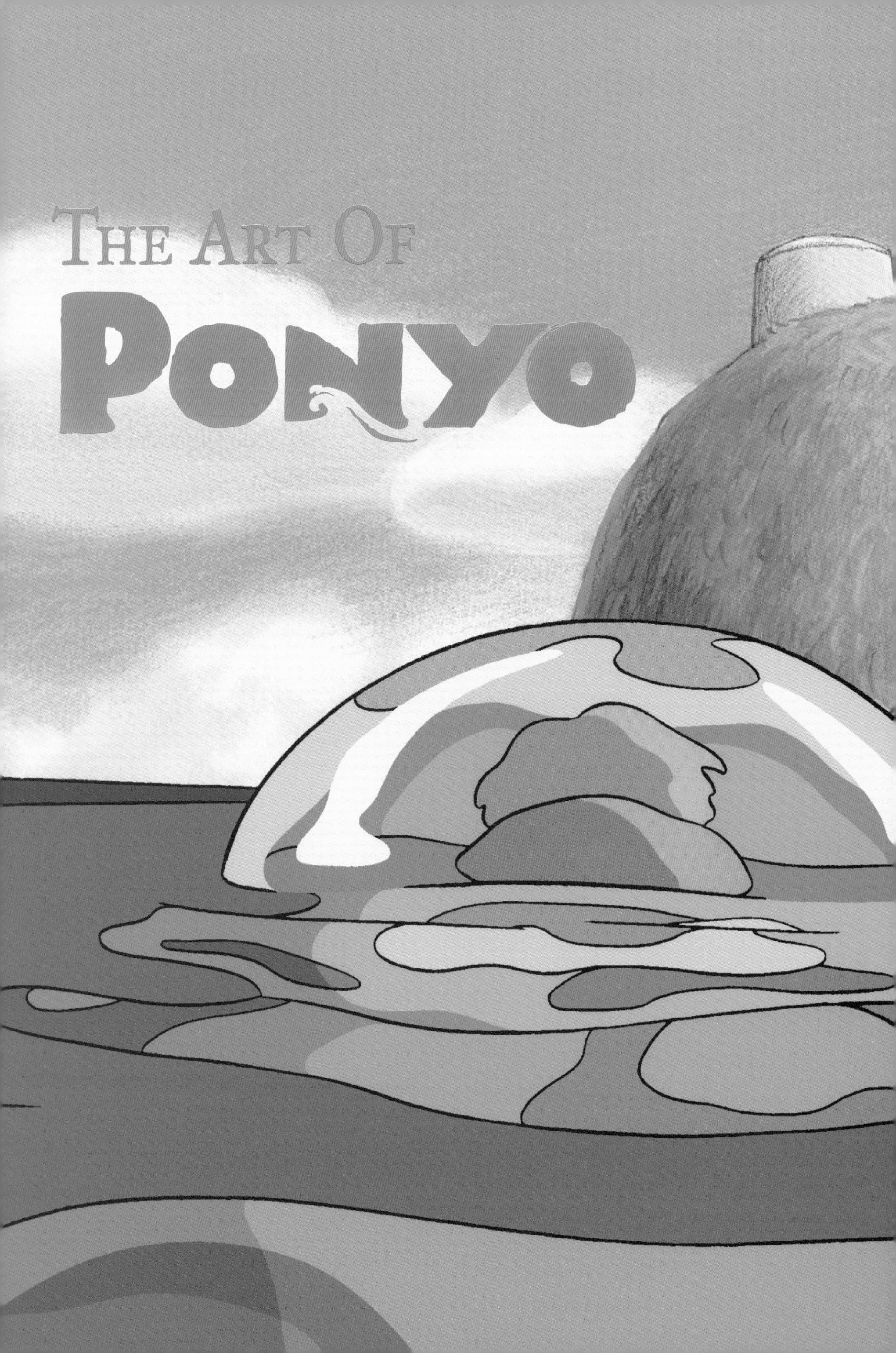
THE ART OF
PONYO

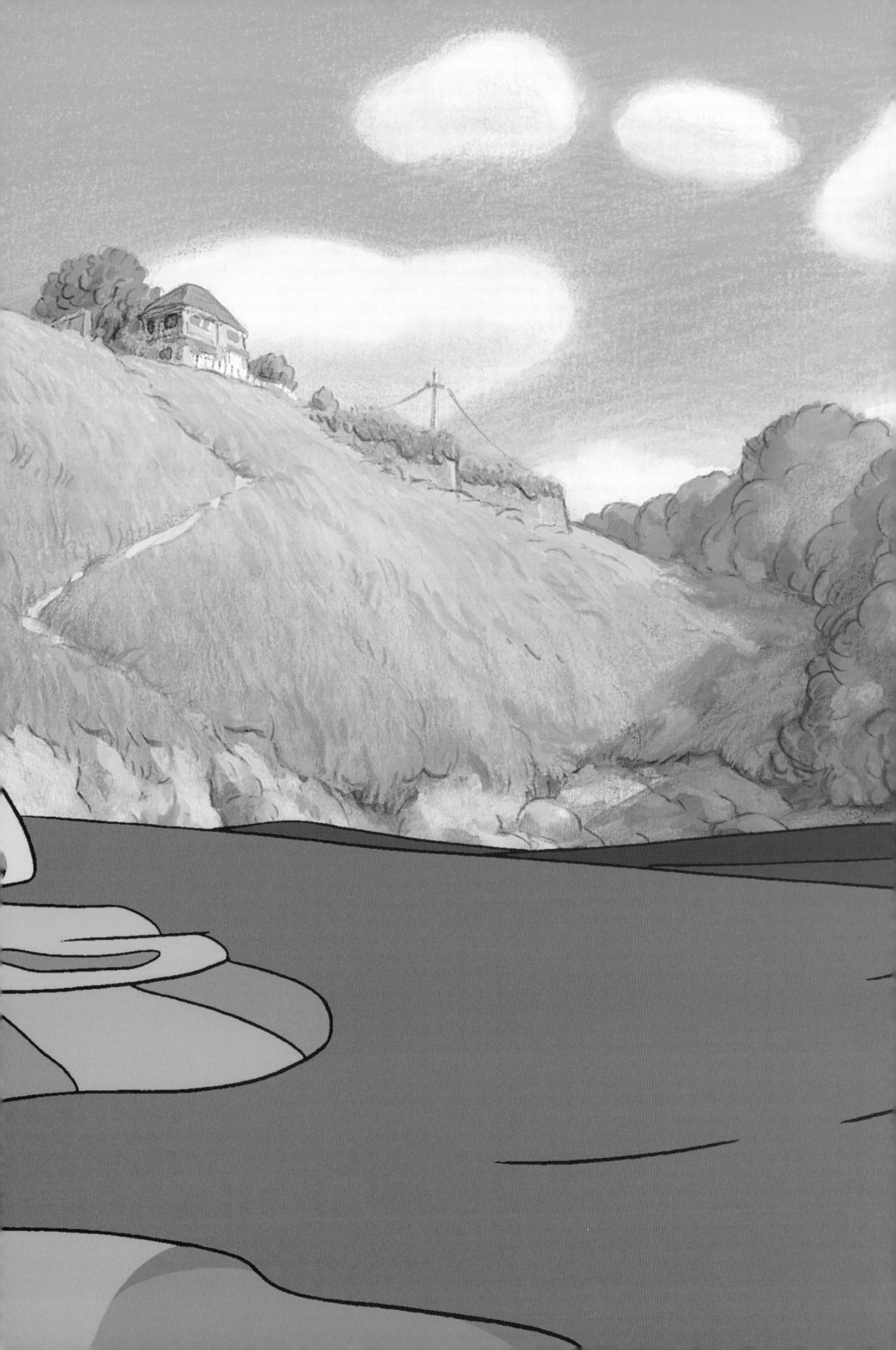

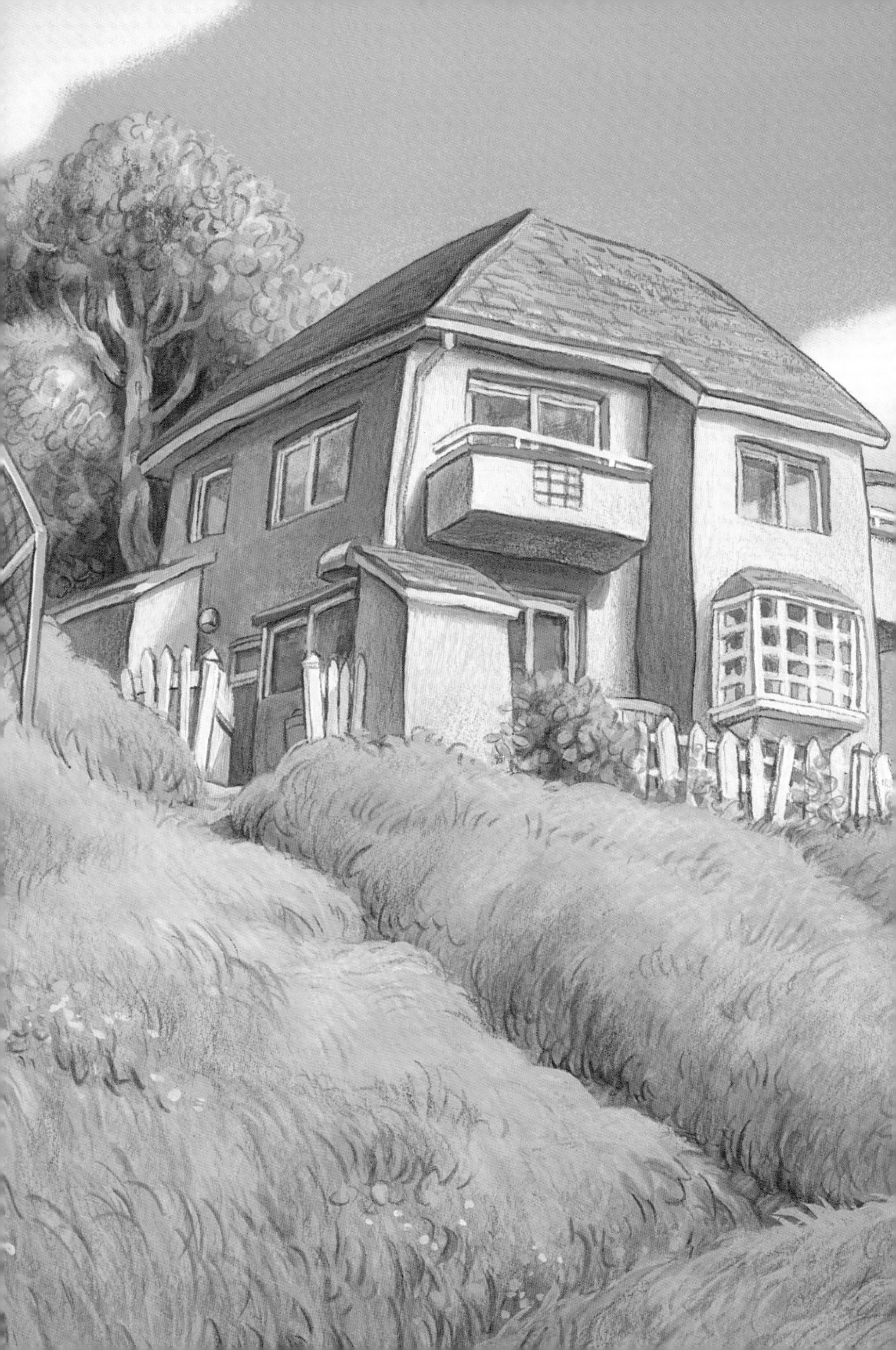

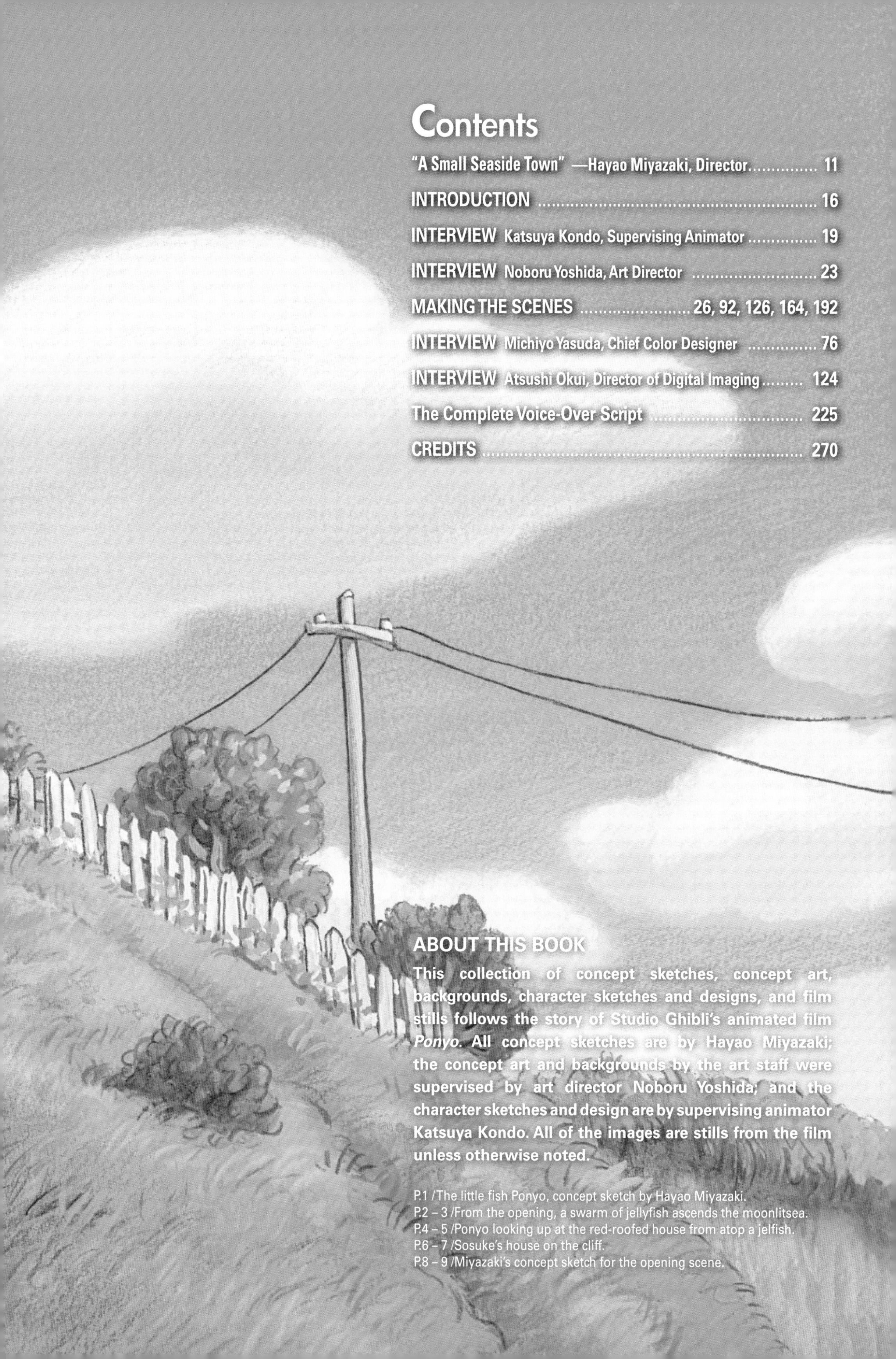

Contents

ABOUT THIS BOOK

This collection of concept sketches, concept art, backgrounds, character sketches and designs, and film stills follows the story of Studio Ghibli's animated film *Ponyo*. All concept sketches are by Hayao Miyazaki; the concept art and backgrounds by the art staff were supervised by art director Noboru Yoshida; and the character sketches and design are by supervising animator Katsuya Kondo. All of the images are stills from the film unless otherwise noted.

P.1 /The little fish Ponyo, concept sketch by Hayao Miyazaki.
P.2 – 3 /From the opening, a swarm of jellyfish ascends the moonlitsea.
P.4 – 5 /Ponyo looking up at the red-roofed house from atop a jelfish.
P.6 – 7 /Sosuke's house on the cliff.
P.8 – 9 /Miyazaki's concept sketch for the opening scene.

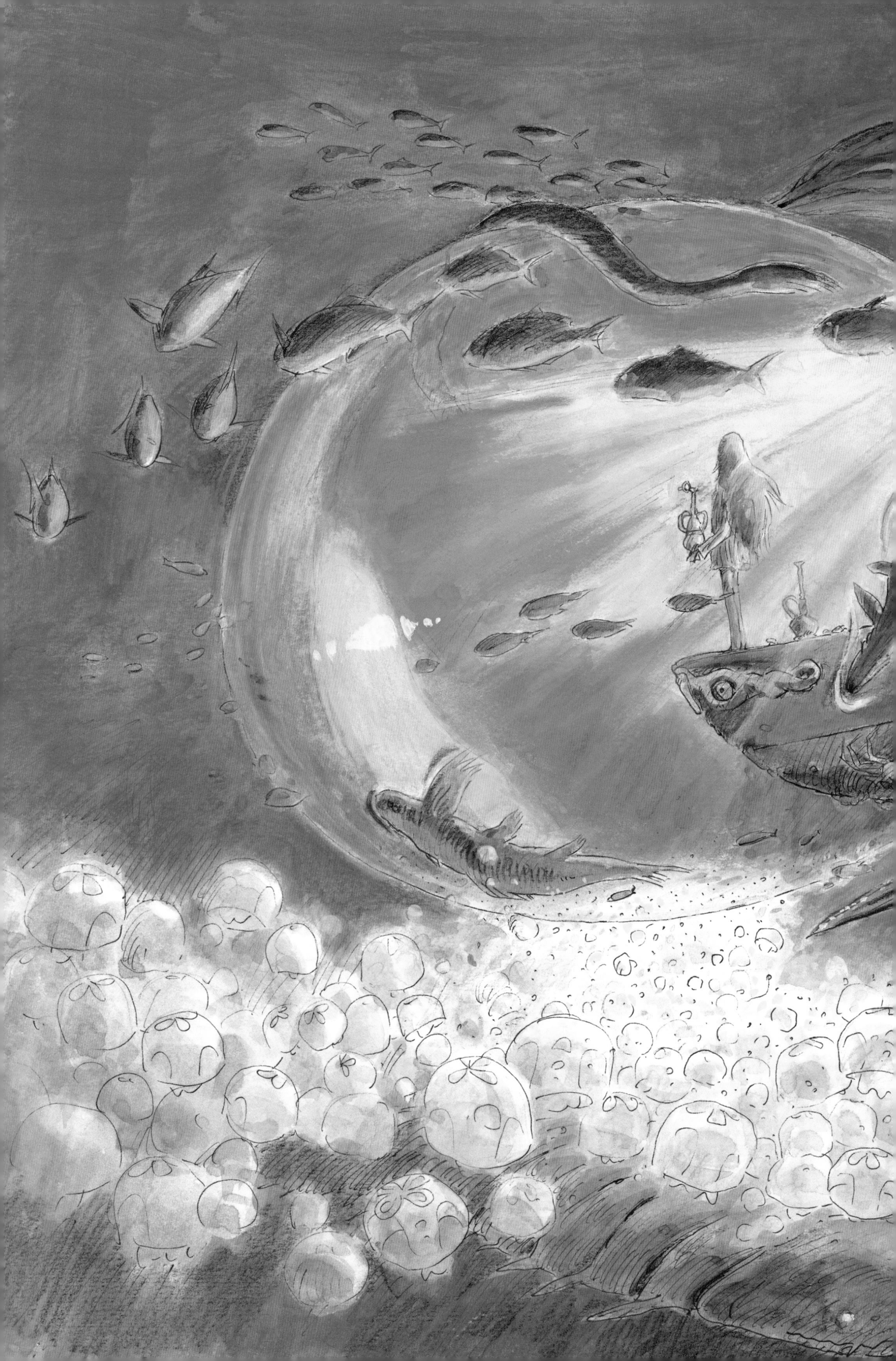

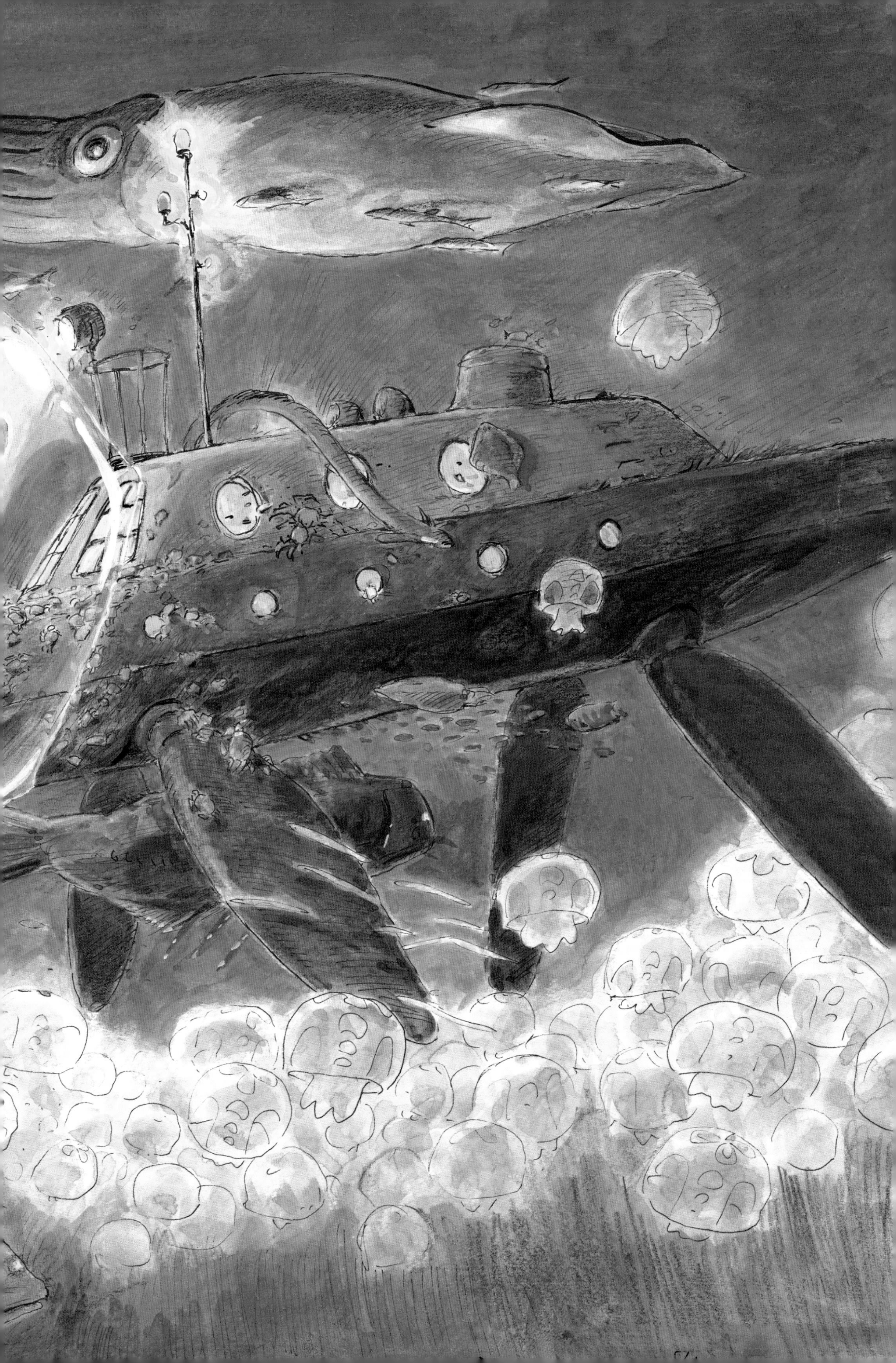

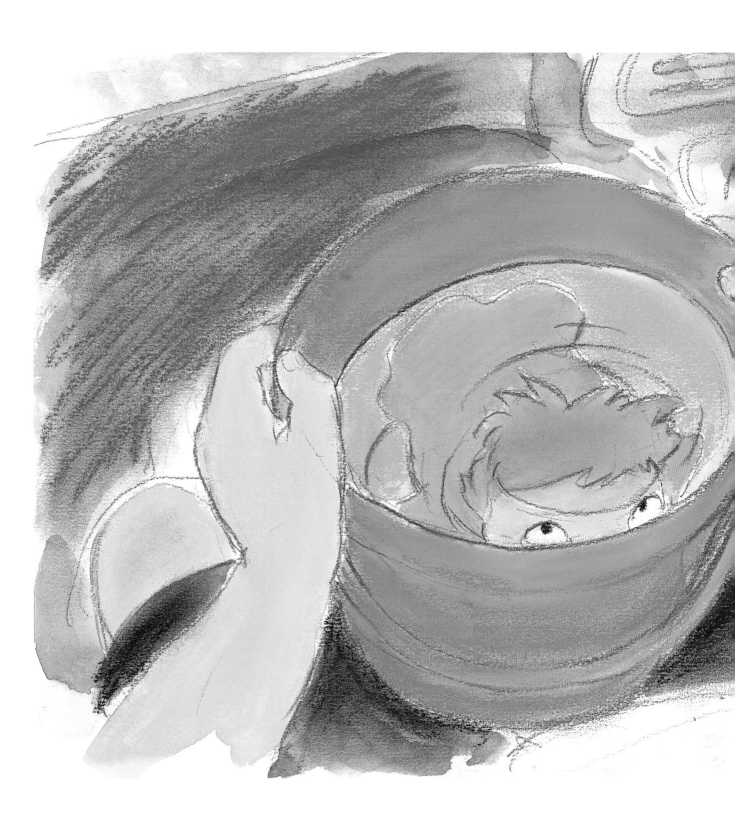

A SMALL SEASIDE TOWN

This is the story of Ponyo, a little fish from the sea who struggles to realize her dream of living with a boy named Sosuke. It also tells of how five-year-old Sosuke manages to keep a most solemn promise.

PONYO places Hans Christian Andersen's "The Little Mermaid" in a contemporary Japanese setting. It is a tale of childhood love and adventure.

A little seaside town and a house at the top of a cliff. A small cast of characters. The ocean as a living presence. A world where magic and alchemy are accepted as part of the ordinary. The sea below, like our subconscious mind, intersects with the wave-tossed surface above. By distorting normal space and contorting normal shapes, the sea is animated not as a backdrop to the story, but as one of its principal characters.

A little boy and a little girl, love and responsibility, the ocean and life – these things, and that which is most elemental to them, are depicted in the most basic way in PONYO. This is my response to the afflictions and uncertainty of our times.

—Hayao Miyazaki

HAYAO MIYAZAKI

Hayao Miyazaki was born in 1941 in Tokyo. He began his career at Toei Doga (currently Toei Animation) in 1963. After working on scene planning and key animation for *Little Norse Prince* (1968), he moved on to A Productions where he was in charge of the story, screenplay, scene planning, and key animation for *Panda! Go Panda!* (1972). In 1973, he, along with Isao Takahata and others, moved to Zuiyo Images. Later, Miyazaki worked for Nippon Animation and Telecom. In that time he was responsible for scene planning and layout on *Heidi* (1974), and animation direction on *Future Boy Conan* (1978), and directed his first theatrical feature with *Lupin III: The Castle of Cagliostro* (1979). Based on his original manga serialized in *Animage* magazine, he wrote and directed *Nausicaä of the Valley of the Wind* in 1984. He left Nippon Animation and Telecom to co-found Studio Ghibli in 1985.

Since then Miyazaki has directed the animated features *Castle in the Sky* (1986), *My Neighbor Totoro* (1988), *Kiki's Delivery Service* (1989), *Porco Rosso* (1992), *Princess Mononoke* (1997), *Spirited Away* (2001), and *Howl's Moving Castle* (2004). *Spirited Away* won the Golden Berlin Bear Award at the 52nd Berlin International Film Festival and the Oscar® for Best Animated Feature at the 75th Academy Awards®, and Miyazaki won the Golden Lion Award for Lifetime Achievement at the 62nd Venice Film Festival.

Miyazaki has also written several books such as *The House Where Totoro Lives* (Asahi Shimbun); *Shuna's Journey, What Is Film?* (conversations with Akira Kurosawa); *Princess Mononoke; Starting Point; Mushime & Anime* (conversations with Takeshi Yoro) (Tokuma Shoten); and *Turning Point* (Iwanami Shoten).

1

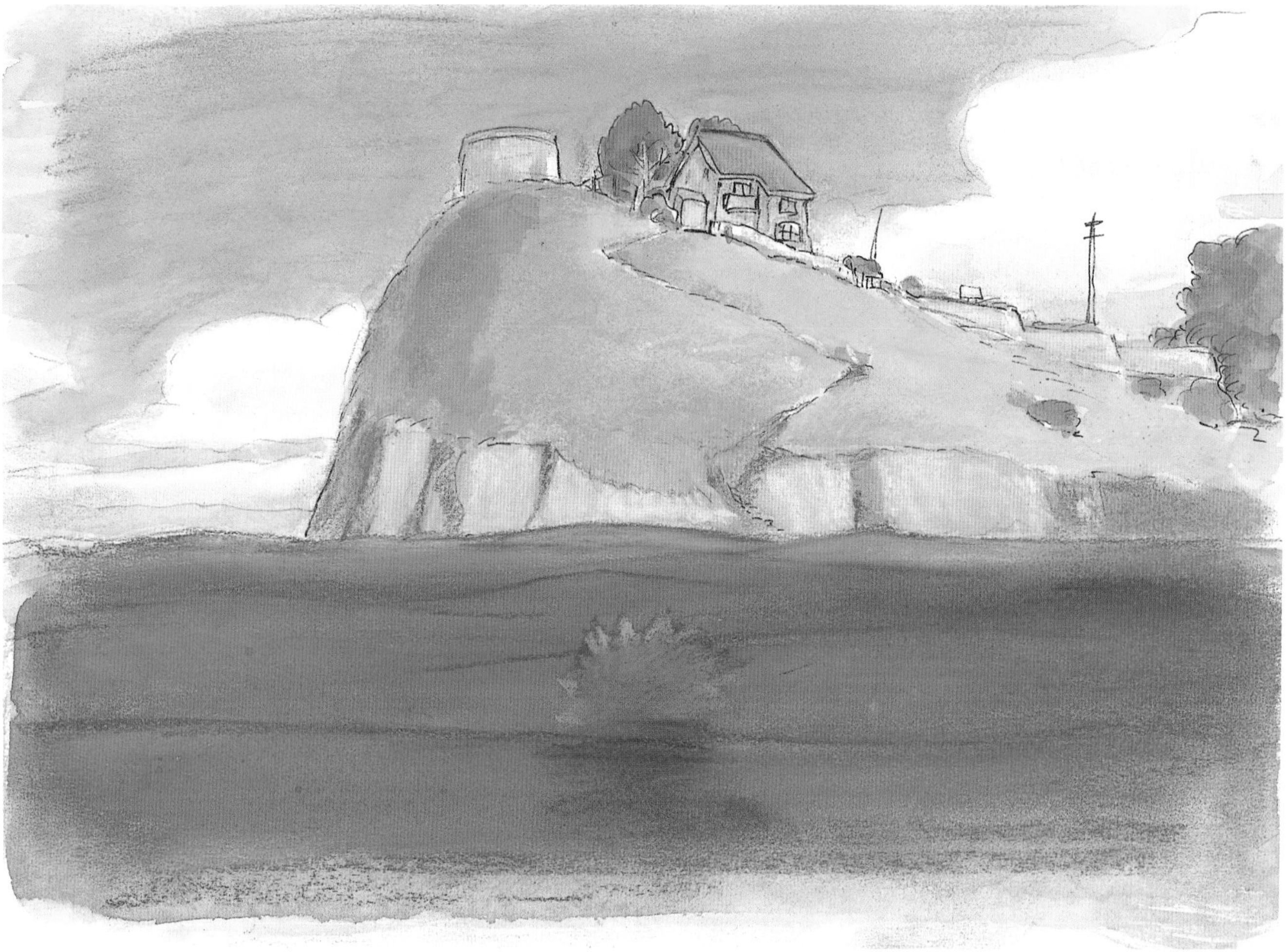

2

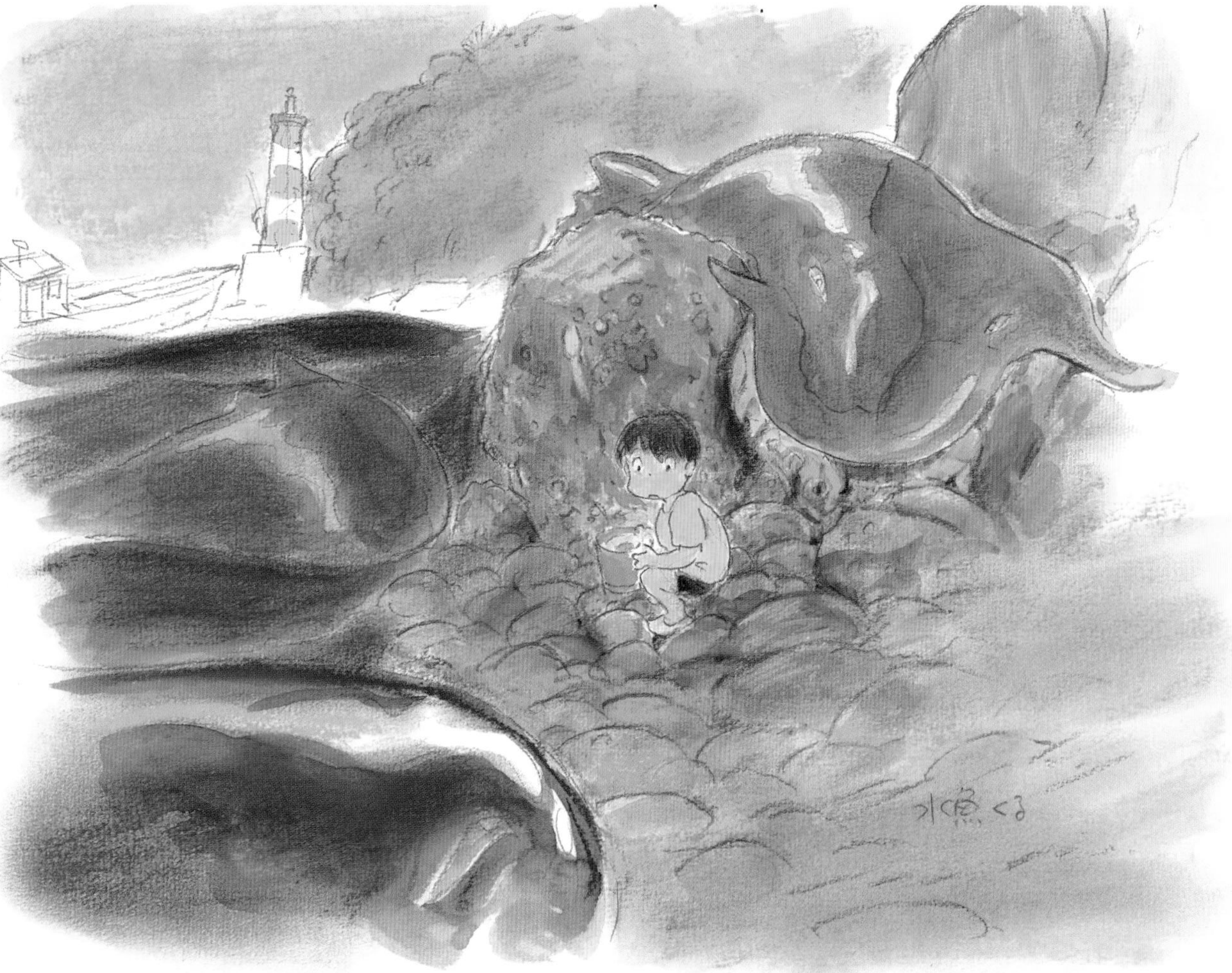

3

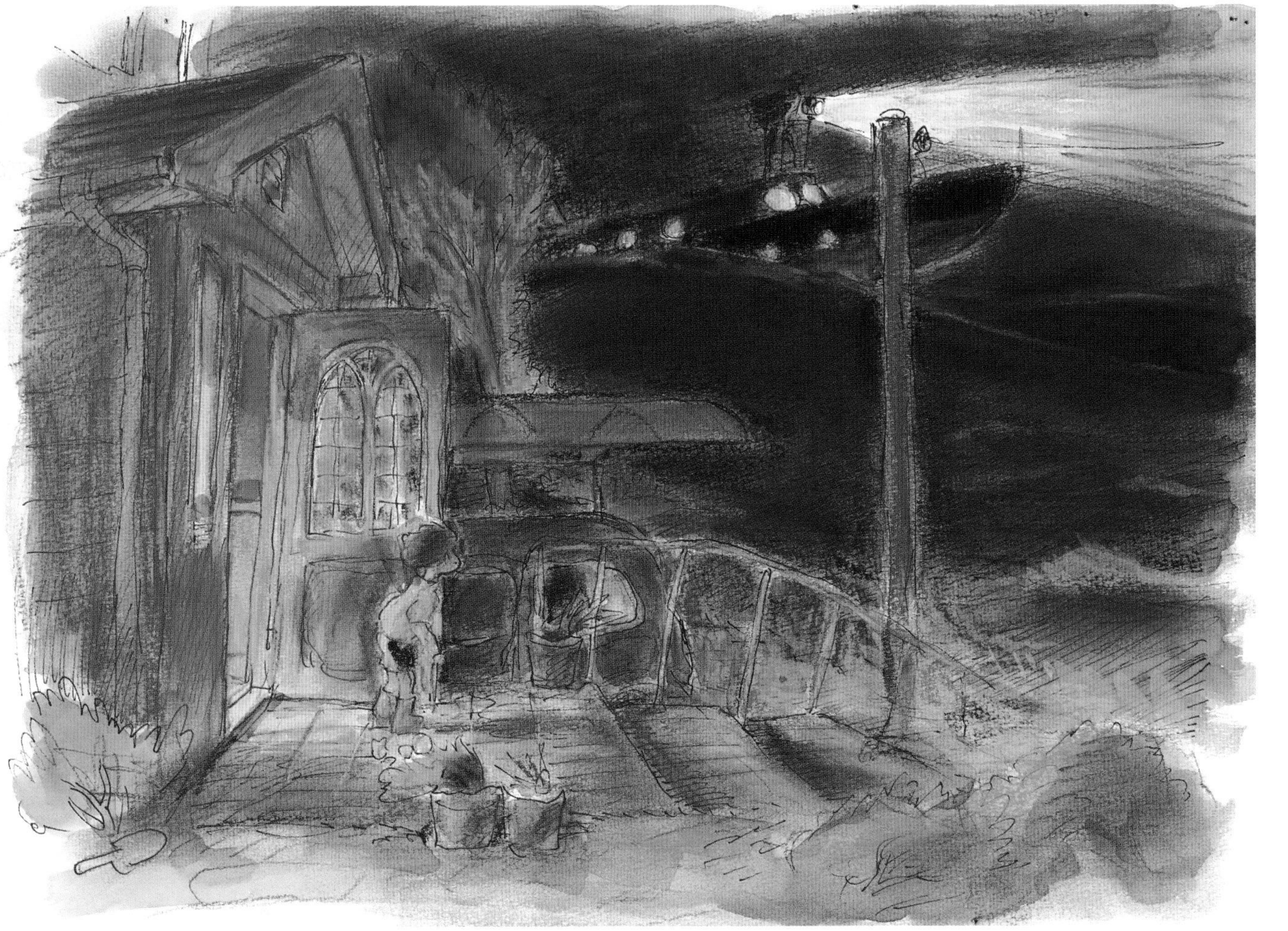

4

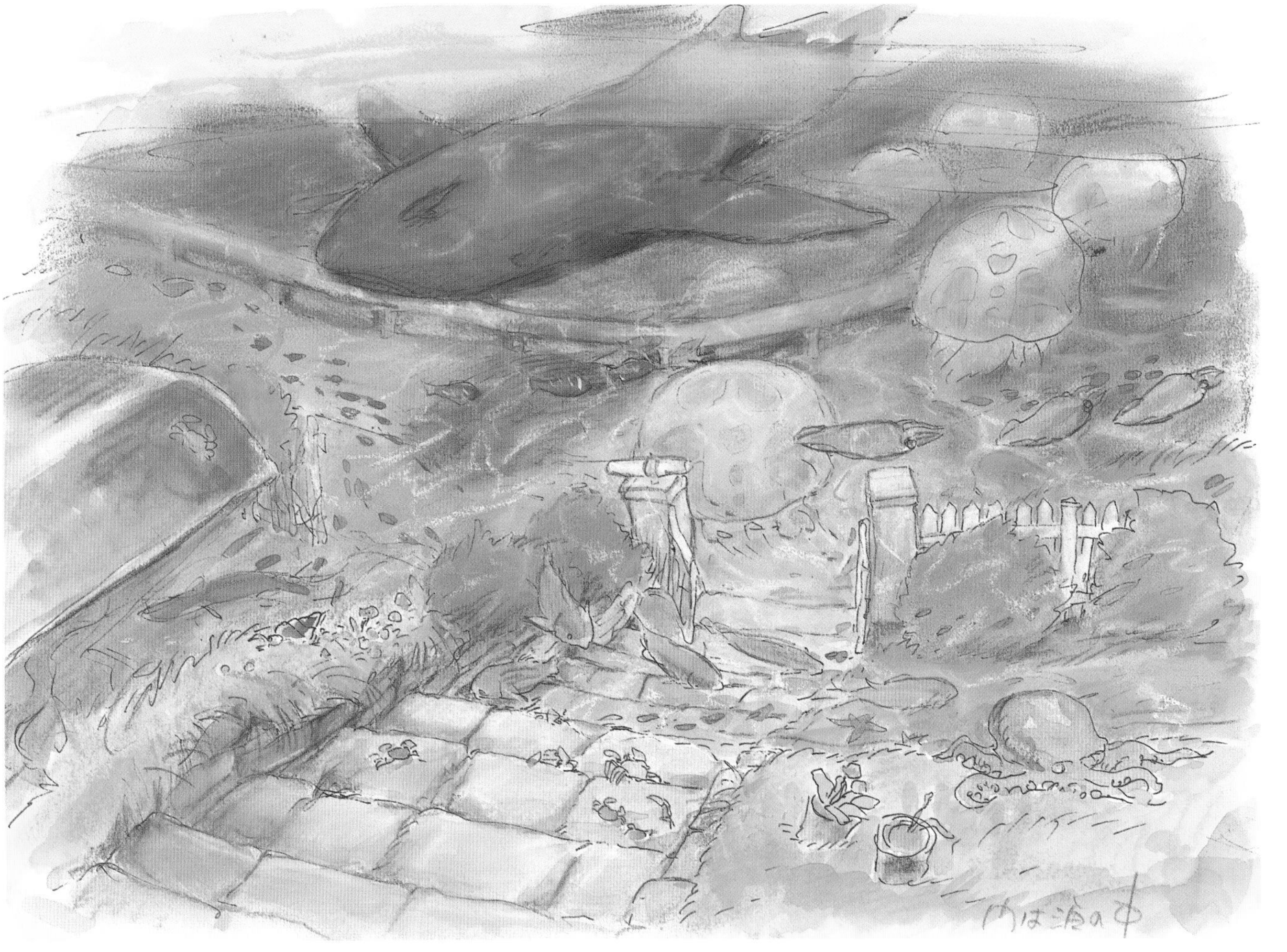
外は海の中

5

水星道が〜〜〜に〜〜と〜に〜〜に〜〜〜〜。

6

7

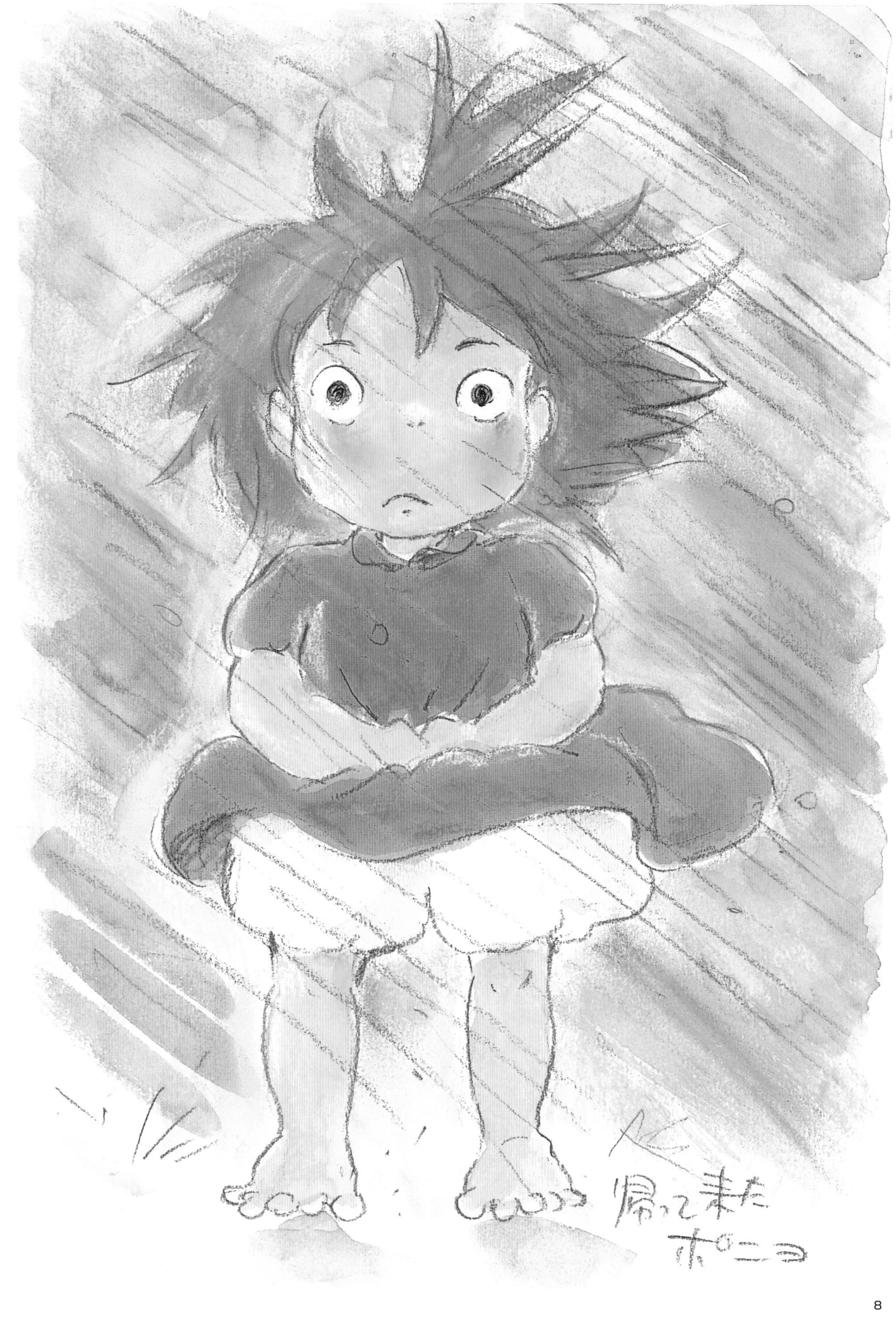
帰って来た
ポニョ

8

1–8 /Concept sketch of Ponyo looking up at Sosuke from a pail—which became the basis for the first promotional poster—and other sketches. Includes scenes not in the film.

INTRODUCTION

Production Synopsis

Ponyo is the first work directed by Hayao Miyazaki since *Howl's Moving Castle* in 2004, and is Studio Ghibli's 15th animated theatrical feature.

Ponyo is an inquisitive little fish who escapes her overprotective father, Fujimoto, and arrives at a port town inhabited by humans. There, she is trapped inside a jelly jar and rescued by a kindhearted boy named Sosuke. Touched by his promise to protect her, Ponyo becomes a human girl using the magic passed on to her by her father, with devastating repercussions in the human world.

The film is written and directed by Miyazaki. Katsuya Kondo served as supervising animator in his first Miyazaki-directed feature since *Kiki's Delivery Service*. Noboru Yoshida, who also worked on *Howl's Moving Castle*, oversaw the art direction; Michiyo Yasuda, who has been involved with Isao Takahata's and Miyazaki's films since the Toho Doga (currently Toho Animation) days, supervised the color design. Atsushi Okui also joined the team as director of digital imaging following his work on *Howl's Moving Castle* and *Spirited Away*. And with the addition of Kitaro Kosaka, Ai Kagawa, Takeshi Inamura, and Akihiko Yamashita as assistant supervising animators, the production team ventured forth fully prepared.

Following the release of *Howl's Moving Castle*, plans for *Ponyo* gradually took shape thanks to a series of animated shorts for Ghibli Museum Mitaka, a trip to the Setonaikai region, a reading of the complete works of Soseki Natsume, and a visit to the Tate Gallery in England. Preproduction began in the spring of 2006. Yoshida and Kondo, who had been involved with Miyazaki on the museum shorts, worked with the director to devise a plan and direction for the project. Their goals in creating *Ponyo* included:

• capturing the delightful motions that can only be rendered through 2D animation by drawing the animation entirely by hand and without relying on overly ornate CGI.

• pursuing the possibilities of animation and art without struggling under the demands of a production schedule.

• showcasing the picture book-quality of Yoshida's background art.

• celebrating the innocence and cheerfulness of a child's world through Ponyo's cuteness.

With these ambitious ideals in mind, the production staff officially went to work in May 2006. Miyazaki continued to draw concept sketches, while Yoshida began working on concept art. After the main staff embarked on a research trip in July, Miyazaki began storyboarding in the fall. Test shots were examined, and key animation began in October. The project was announced in March of 2007. Key animation continued around the announcement of the theme song in December, and the last of the storyboards were completed in January of 2008. Key animation and art were completed in May, culminating in 1,139 shots and 170,000 frames of key animation drawings. The first preview screening took place June 25, and the film was released in Japan in Toho theaters on July 19, 2008.

This book contains the preliminary concept sketches, concept art, background art, and stills used during the production of *Ponyo on the Cliff by the Sea*, and is designed so that the reader can follow both the storyline and the process of filmmaking. We hope you'll read the captions as well as the staff interviews.

Studio Ghibli

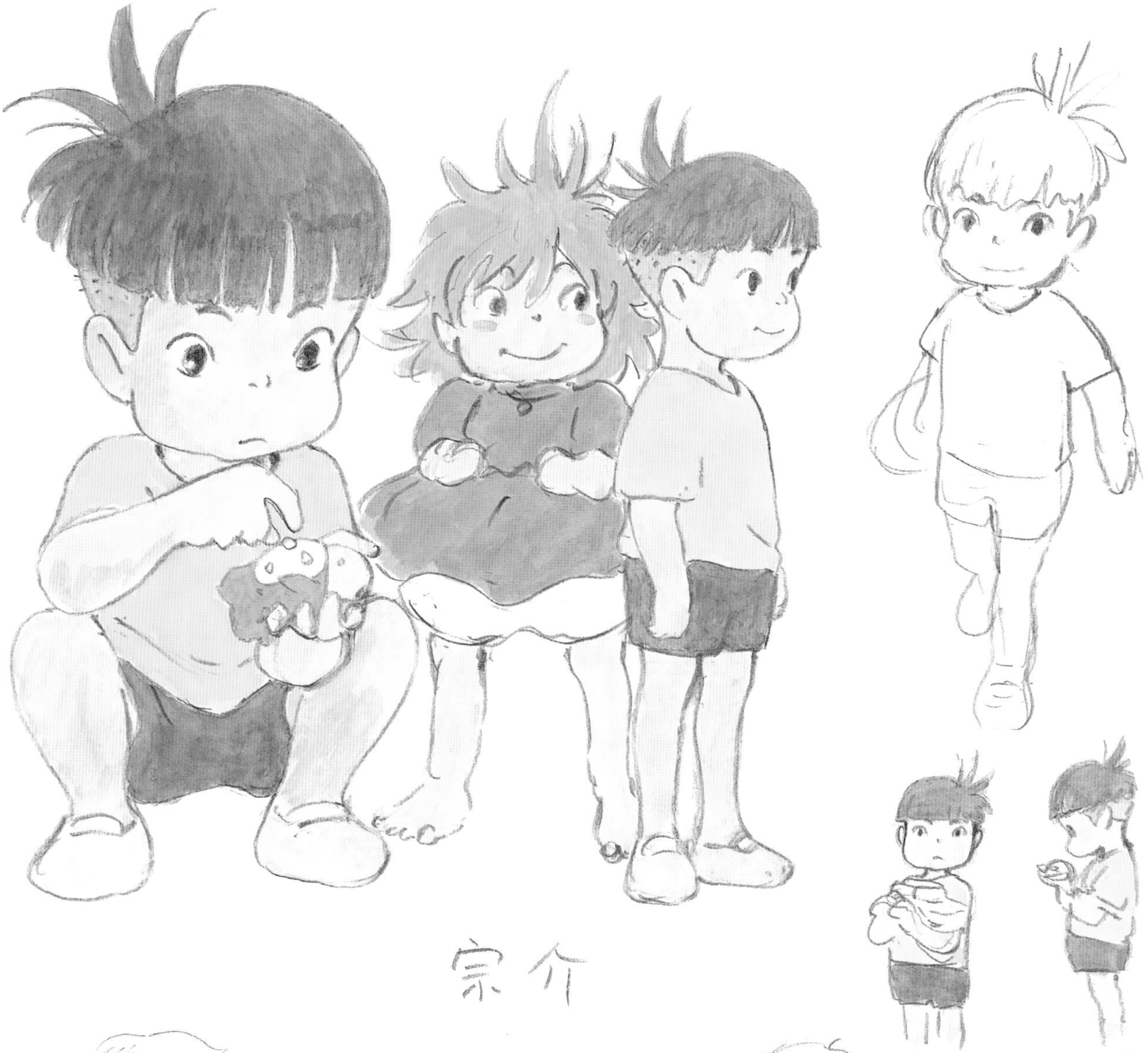
宗介

1

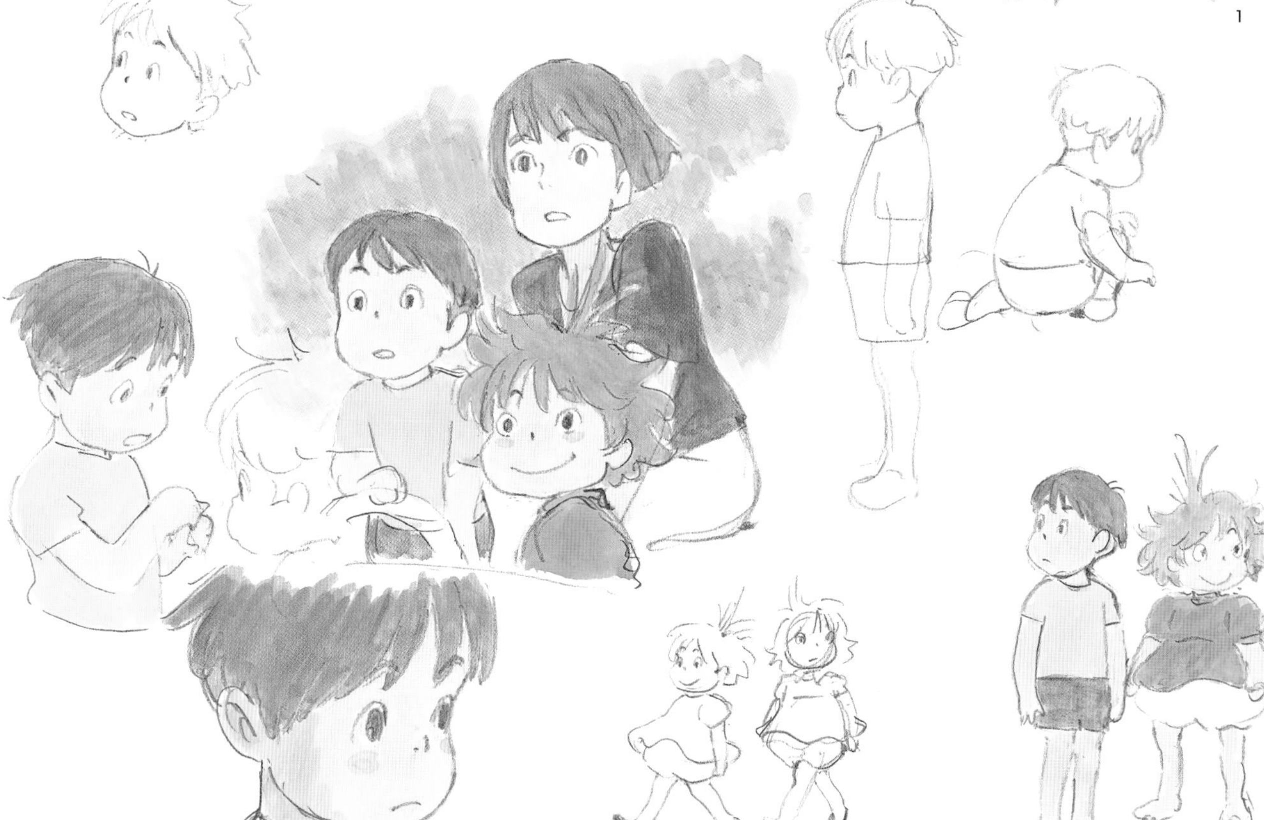

2

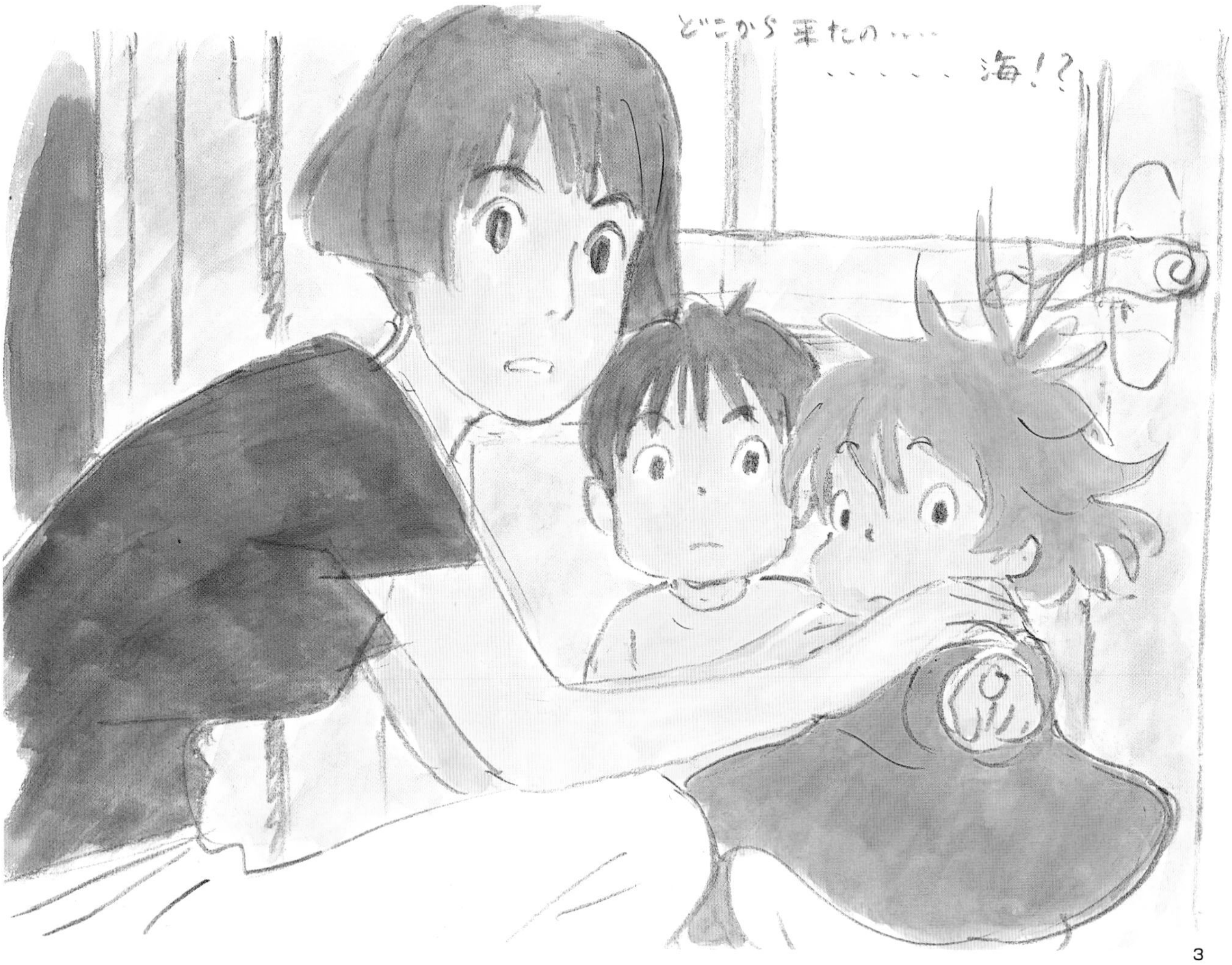
どこから来たの‥‥
‥‥‥海!?
3

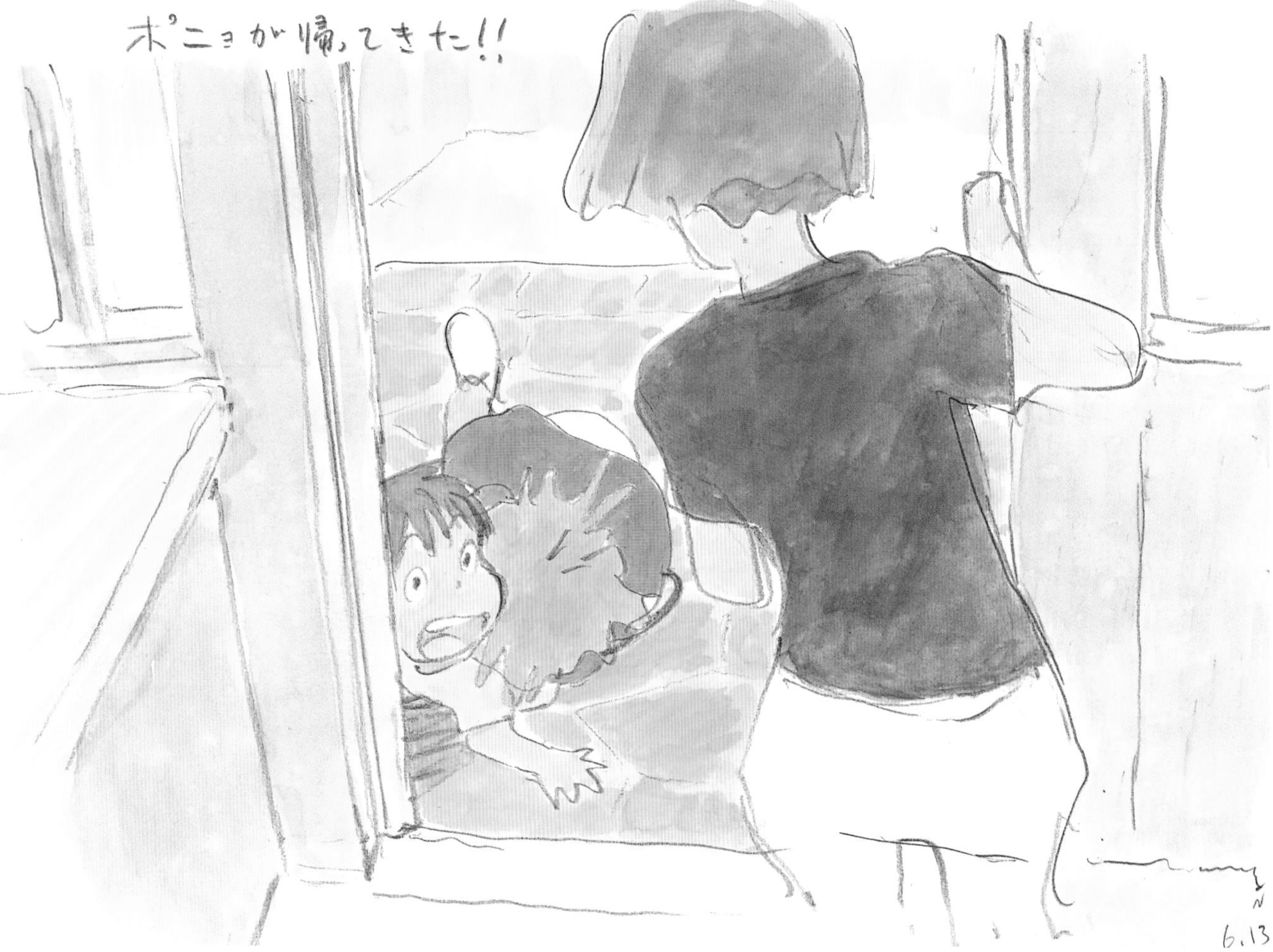
ポニョが帰ってきた!!
4

Katsuya Kondo was born in 1963 in Aichi Prefecture. He began his career at An Apple in 1983, where he was key animator for films such as *Space Cobra* (1983) before becoming a freelance artist. He took part in his first Studio Ghibli project with *Castle in the Sky* (1986). Later he was character designer and supervising animator on *Kiki's Delivery Service* (1989), supervising animator on *Only Yesterday* (1991), and served as character designer and supervising animator on *Umi ga Kikoeru* (Ocean Waves, 1993) as well as providing illustrations for the original novel. He was the animation director on the Ghibli Museum short *House Hunting* (2006). In addition to working as supervising animator on *Ponyo*, Kondo also wrote the lyrics to the theme song.

INTERVIEW
KATSUYA KONDO
Supervising Animator

This time, I placed the greatest emphasis on the layout check.

—It's been a while since you last worked on a Studio Ghibli feature as supervising animator.

Kondo: Yes, that's right. This was the first time working with Hayao Miyazaki since *Kiki's Delivery Service*, so it's been a very long while. But it wasn't because I had left [*laughs*]. A lot of things happened.

—How did you become involved with *Ponyo*?

Kondo: I had been animation director on a Ghibli Museum short called *House Hunting*. It was a project for which Miyazaki had written the story and the screenplay as well as directed. *House Hunting* wasn't too difficult to render—we used simple lines and no dialogue—but it was still fun for kids with the animation alone.

During that production, we talked about whether we could make a film in the same vein: by using solid, simple lines that fully showcased the virtue of drawing by hand. After completing work on *House Hunting*, I got the official offer to work on the next full-length feature. I thought it would be interesting to work on the project as a progression of *House Hunting* with a little more consideration to story, so I answered yes. So it wasn't like the offer to do a feature had come out of the blue. After Miyazaki had come up with concrete plans for the project, we began preproduction.

—Miyazaki drew his concept sketches using watercolor and crayon this time.

Kondo: He started out using watercolor, but colors tend to blur in that medium. Since he had it in his mind to make this a film for kids, he seemed eager to use bolder colors. Then during preproduction he found some pastel crayons and began coloring with them. The colors were so vibrant Miyazaki seemed elated, exclaiming, "This is great, this is great!" For Miyazaki, the idea of using pastels was exciting. And that's why I think the concept sketches turned out differently from previous sketches.

—Did the palette of the concept sketches determine the direction for this film?

Kondo: There was that trend. Many current animated films tend to extract colors or use monotones and subdued hues. I wasn't explicitly working in opposition to this, but I didn't want to use a quiet palette but more vivid colors. With that said, there are a lot of colors to choose from, so I consulted with chief color designer Michiyo Yasuda during the actual production. We elected not to use dull colors and yet mostly steered away from basic primary colors that might come off as crude.

—This time Miyazaki's storyboards were also painted in watercolor.

Kondo: Isn't it great? I think what sets this film apart from previous films is the color design. Rather than creating a story set in a world everyone is familiar with, we had to combine the fantasy and real worlds and come up with a singular worldview filtered through the eyes of a child. That's why I believe the color was necessary. It was probably motivated by Miyazaki's mood too, but it also made things more explicit for everyone involved. It's like having a layer of flesh and features added to a wooden artist's model—having the colored storyboards made it clearer for us and a lot clearer for the ink and paint staff and the key animators.

—So the layout was more complete in the storyboarding stage than is usual.

Kondo: Yes. From a production standpoint, I place the highest importance on the storyboards. They are the foundation. Once in a while, Miyazaki himself might make changes to the layouts during the rough check, even though he drew the storyboards. In the end, I'm the one responsible for the final layout check, so if the fixes were good I would go ahead and make further changes accordingly. But if I thought an expression or a line of a character's body was rendered a little better in the original storyboards, I would change it to be closer to what it was in the storyboards.

—Your title appears as "Animation" in the film's opening credits.

Kondo: That was a title given to me by Miyazaki, and I'm not sure how to interpret that either [*laughs*]. In my mind, I consider myself the supervising animator.

—You also drew the characters for the key animation.

Kondo: As the characters for *Kiki's Delivery Service* were my own, this was the first feature for which I supervised the animation with Miyazaki's characters. I rarely supervise projects for which the character designs are not my own, but since I worked on *House Hunting* with Miyazaki's characters, I've gotten used to it. Since I had his rough sketches in the preliminary stages, I was able to approximate his vision in my drawings. Although, the characters generally ended up looking like my own anyway.

—Can you describe what the work process was like in more detail?

Kondo: As Miyazaki finishes his storyboards, we talk it over with the animators. Then, as I said before, Miyazaki does the rough check on the layouts as the animators work on them. After the animators make the suggested changes, the layouts come to me in the end.

—And that's when the fixes you were talking about took place?

Kondo: This time I placed the greatest emphasis on the layout check. This can be said of previous works, of course, but this might be the first time I placed primary importance on scrutinizing the layouts. I did this for my own sake. There are times when the animators are working on a different track (direction), and I have to steer them back to the right rails. First, I solidify our direction and revise the layouts by focusing on three areas: the relationship between setting and characters' movements, character expressions, and spatial relationships. If I do that, my most important job as supervising animator becomes easier. In any event, I always try to honor whatever is written on the storyboards. Since the layouts checked by Miyazaki contain his instructions for adding more expressive detail, making certain those changes are reflected in the revised layouts for the animators is most important. As long as we have these revised layouts, we know what we're missing or have too much of when it comes time to revising the key animation.

—So then you weren't revising the layouts on *Kiki's Delivery Service*.

Kondo: I wasn't doing the checking at the time. Miyazaki drew the storyboards and obviously did the layout check; when the key animation was completed, he made all the changes himself as necessary. He was doing everything. I placed the greatest importance on the layout check this time because I wanted to ease his load even just a little bit. Although, he never said to me, "It was easier this time" [*laughs*]. While it would be hard to hear him say that the process was the same as usual, I'd like to think that it was a little bit easier this time.

—What guidelines are the most important to follow when you're editing the key animation?

Kondo: Miyazaki always looks at the drawings first. If they're fine, they come straight to me. If he thinks something isn't right, he'll pencil in the changes according to the guidelines set in the layouts. Then I'll firm up and finalize the lines, making sure to reflect his intended changes. As for the rest, I check to make sure the tone set in the layout hasn't been diminished in the animation and make the final revisions if I think it's a little off.

—You have four people—Kitaro Kosaka, Ai Kagawa, Takeshi Inamura, Akihiko Yamashita—working as associate supervising animators?

Kondo: I can handle the workload myself in the beginning, but it gets tough just to finalize the lines on Miyazaki's edits when things start to pick up as production continues. So the assistant supervising animators work on finalizing those lines. It's a tremendous help because the key animations come to me with those revisions already done. After that, all I need to do is revise specific points as needed.

—You took on the formidable task of drawing the animation entirely by hand. Did anything strike you as especially challenging?

Kondo: Because we had to feature the sea as a character, Miyazaki labored over how to render the water. So I pulled back from that and focused on retouching the characters. Characters are absolutely essential to any movie, and Miyazaki understands that. In other words, my job is like applying a glaze or a coat of varnish. It's about bringing out the polish in something that has a beautiful shape. That is the most important part of my job, and so I check the layouts, making slight modifications to a cheek line, adjusting the outline of a shoulder, redrawing the eyes repeatedly because they're not quite right... I think these subtle adjustments are like "makeup" and often the most crucial.

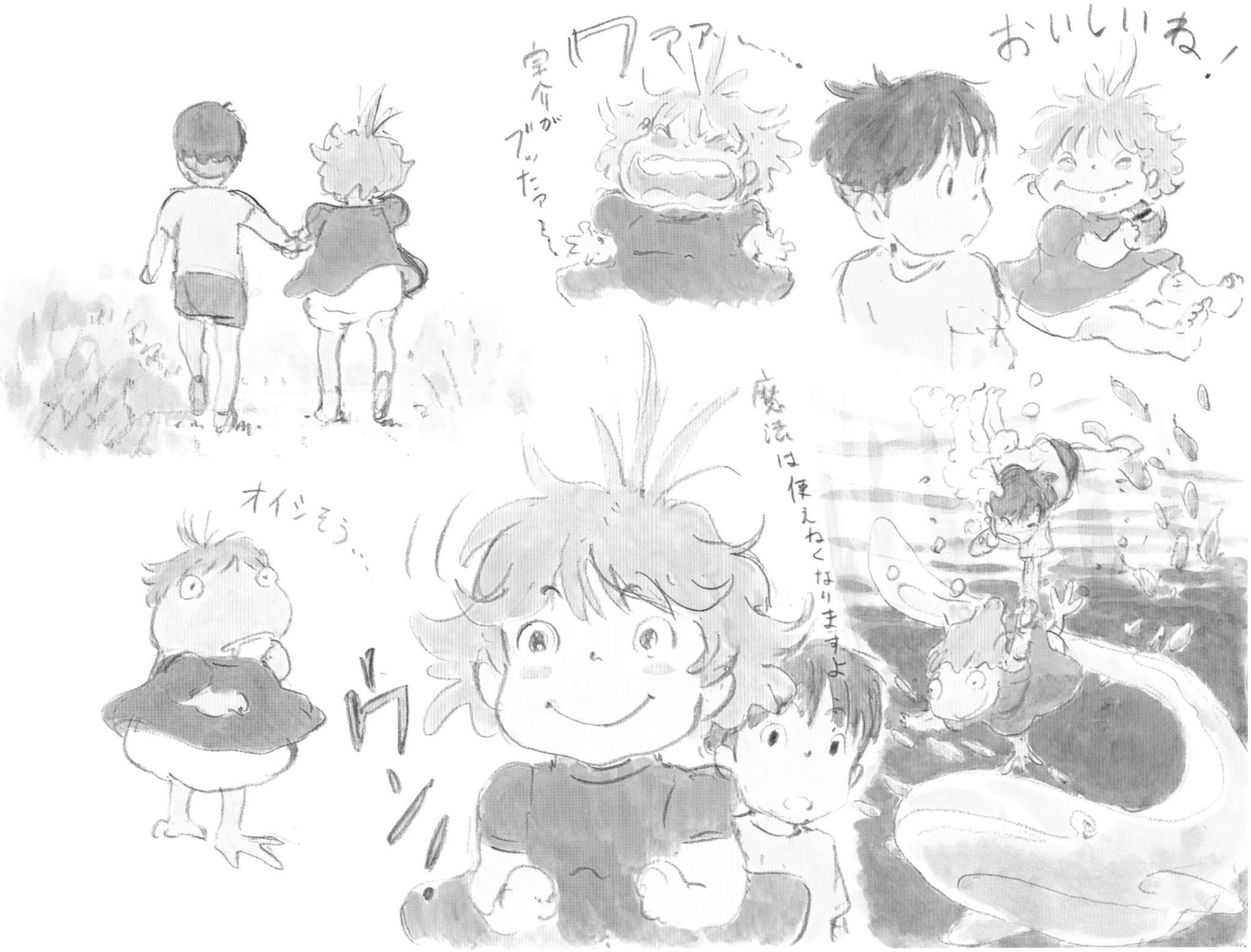
おいしいね！
ワアァ……
宗介がブッたァ
魔法は使えなくなりますよ
オイシそう…

5

1–6 /Character and concept sketches by Katsuya Kondo (Ponyo; Sosuke; Sosuke's mother, Lisa).

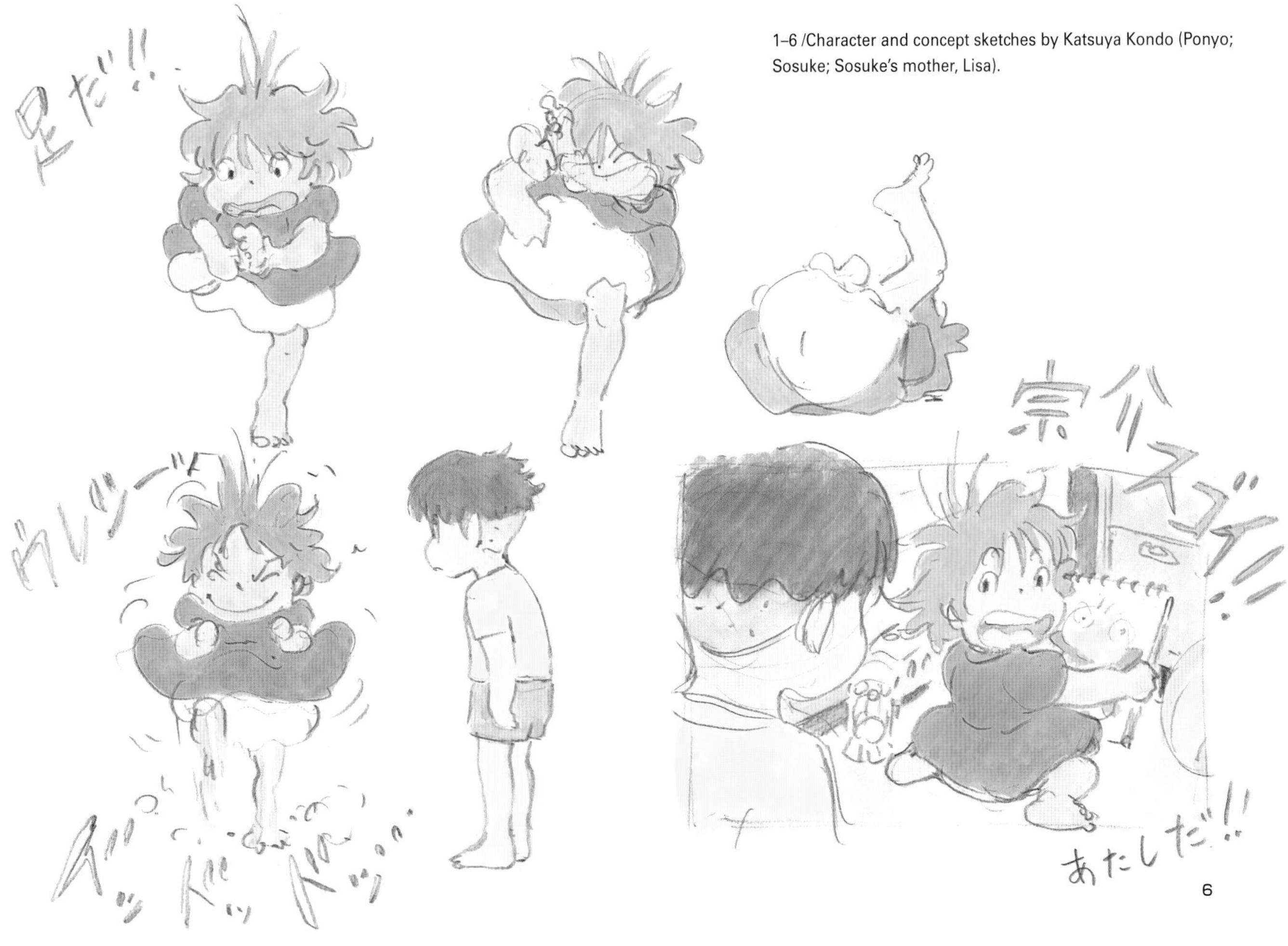
足だ!!
宗介スゴイ!!
あたしだ!!

6

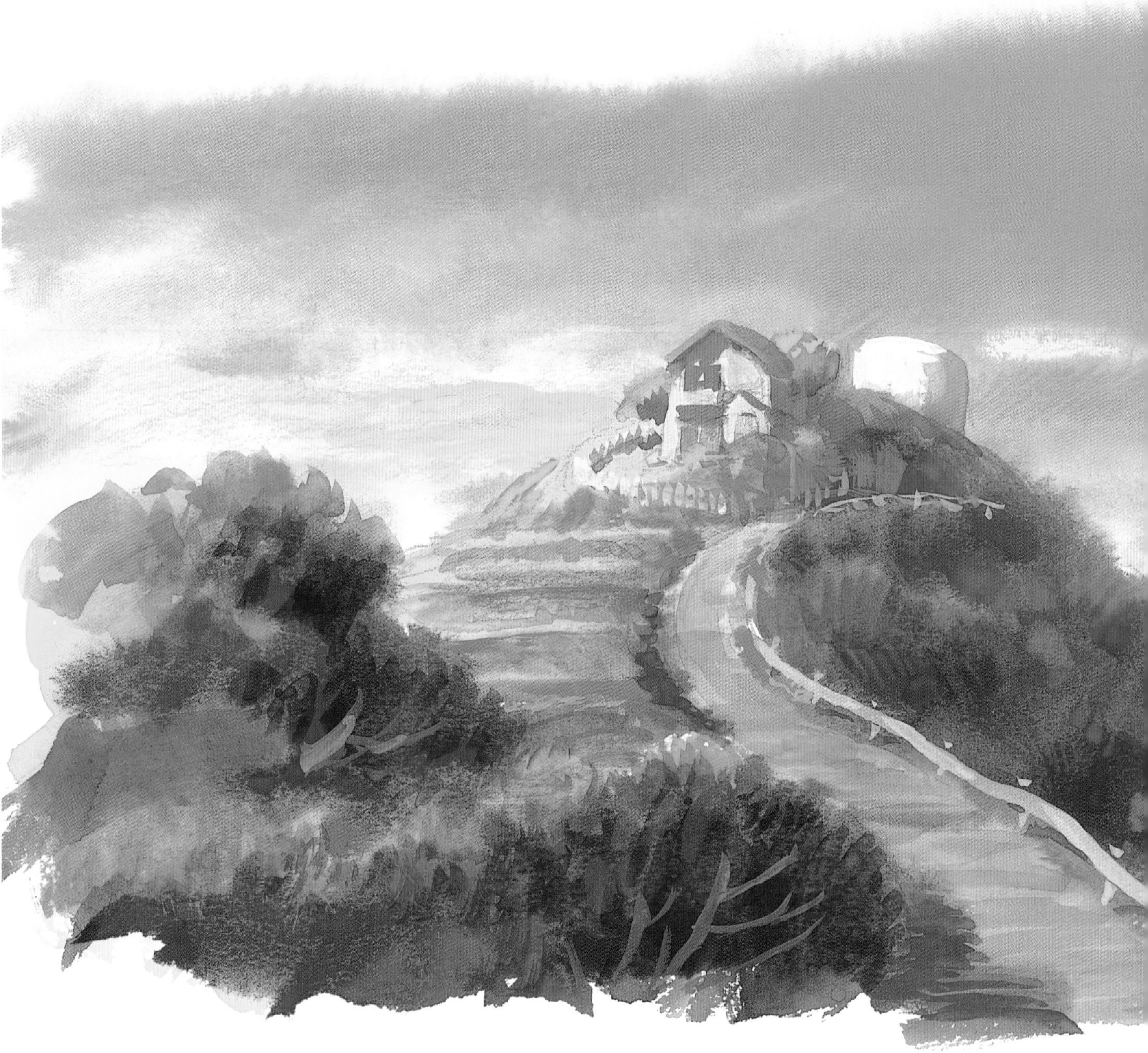

INTERVIEW
NOBORU YOSHIDA
Art Director

1

NOBORU YOSHIDA

Noboru Yoshida was born in 1964 in Shimane Prefecture. After graduating from college, he began his career as a background artist, joining Design Office Mechaman. He later became a freelance artist and took part in the production of Studio Ghibli's *Princess Mononoke* (1997). He worked on *My Neighbors the Yamadas* (1999) and *Spirited Away* (2001) as assistant art director, the Ghibli Art Museum short *Koro's Big Day Out* (2001) and *Ghiblies: Episode 2* (2002) as art director, and shared art directing duties with Yoji Takeshige on *Howl's Moving Castle* (2004).

I had the entire art staff take chances.

—What sort of direction did you receive from Hayao Miyazaki with regard to art on this project?

Yoshida: This was still before he began storyboarding, but he told me that he wanted to move the animation by drawing a lot of frames. Even to move a ship, which would normally be achieved by creating one cel and sliding it, he wanted to draw it entirely by hand. That was the direction he wanted to take with this film. Rather than placing the sea or a ship on top of a background with a predetermined angle and perspective, he wanted to create settings that could be moved freely. So rather than beginning by determining the storyboards or layouts, he started with sketching scenes that had warmth and a little playfulness. It wasn't about making the art more elaborate in the process of creating the key animation and backgrounds, but coming up with a final product while retaining the simplicity and warmth of the concept sketches. Rather than creating a realistic tableau as we have until now, since a large cel of waves, for example, would be laid on top, it was important to create a world of artistic backdrops that could accommodate the spirit of the drawings.

—So the art this time isn't rendered as realistically as in previous Ghibli works?

Yoshida: The initial challenge wasn't about creating elaborate backgrounds but to think about designing a tableau that would match a scene in which something out of the ordinary—Miyazaki called it magic—happens.

—What concept art did you begin drawing first?

Yoshida: The sea was the first thing. I experimented with the sea and waves. Typically, we paint the sea in gradations of blue and add highlights to the key animation, but we couldn't do that this time without considering what the animation would look like. Miyazaki also did a lot of sketches to figure out how the sea ought to look in order to match the style of the film. So, for a while I tried various things like placing cels of waves and ships that either Miyazaki or I drew on top of different backgrounds.

—Did you make a test film?

Yoshida: During this trial and error period, we did a test using concept art (pp.23–24) that included many of the focuses for this film. This image contains a couple key elements. The first is the waves. How do we render the water? The second is the wind. How does the grass look when it's blowing in the wind? Since we were trying to do everything that we would normally do with CG by hand this time, I wanted to see how much we could achieve with 2D animation.

—Then you decided not to use CG from the start?

Yoshida: We did test some digitally processed images, which is different from CG. But we decided they weren't necessary as the tests went on. With a shot of Sosuke running, for example, we would draw a background to show the effect of the wind blowing. As long as the background worked to complement the lines added in key animation, we achieved the overall effect we were after.

—The buildings in the storm scene truly seem to be getting blown by the wind.

Yoshida: The lines of the building are pretty distorted. The perspective isn't very severe in this scene, and we added some digital effects to the movement of the trees here.

—Miyazaki's later sketches were drawn with pastels. Your concept art was drawn to emulate that style.

Yoshida: I started off doing that because you never know what you have until you try it. But once you do, there's no turning back during production, so I just ran with it.

—Is this the first time working in this way?

Yoshida: I had worked with similar materials on the House Foods commercial, *Koro's Big Day Out*, and *Ghiblies: Episode 2*, so I drew from that experience this time. Even if the perspective could be rendered warmly in a particular scene, it has to complement the character that is laid on top, so I had to determine which scenes I needed to hold back on and which I could paint more freely. When it comes to paint, how much is too much varies vastly with the individual. While one person might go all out, another person might see as they go. It's different with every person and with every shot.

—So as an art director, you weren't giving your staff precise instructions.

Yoshida: I was not able to tell staffers how much of a particular paint material to use, or to explain what happens when you color with crayon on top of poster paint and color with poster paint on top of that. Everyone was ad-libbing. As a result, the cautious members of the staff carefully planned out their drawings as they worked, while the daring ones just went for it without knowing what they'd end up with.

—So their personalities come through.

Yoshida: It was interesting to see their personalities come through. But I thought everything would fall into place even if the staff played around and tried different things, so long as we kept to the layout and color palette. So I had the staff take chances with that in mind.

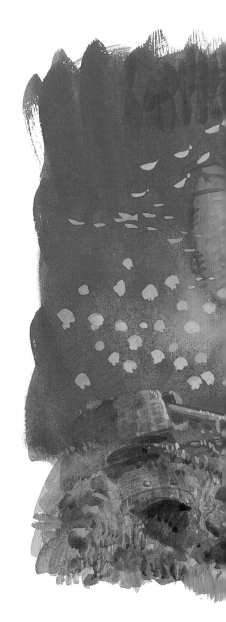

3

1 /Concept art of Sosuke's house (perspective sketch) by Noboru Yoshida. 2–4 /Concept art, drawn by Yoshida from Miyazaki's sketches and storyboards. The concept art in 3 was used in film tests to gauge the light quality rendered in the sunset.

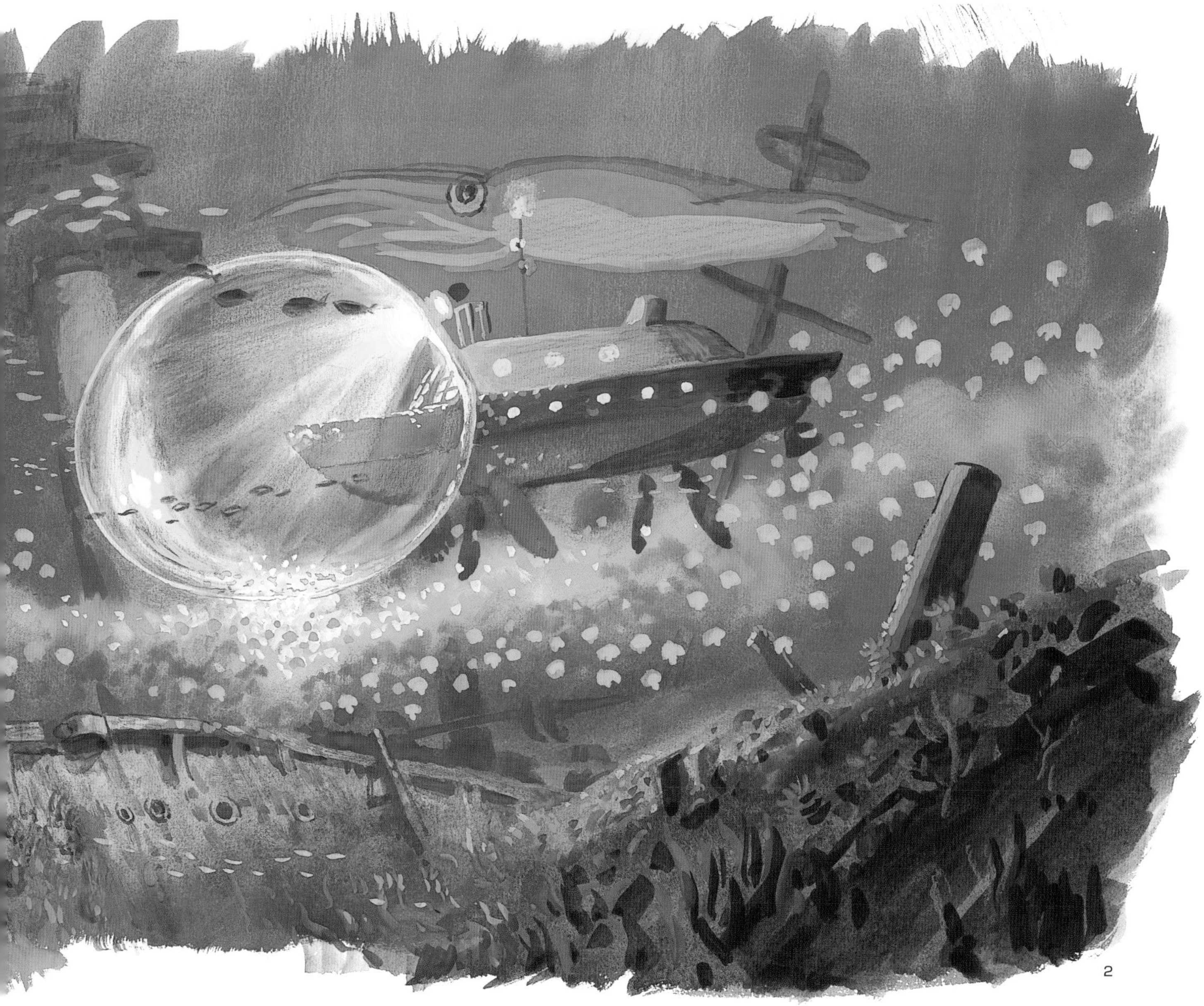
2

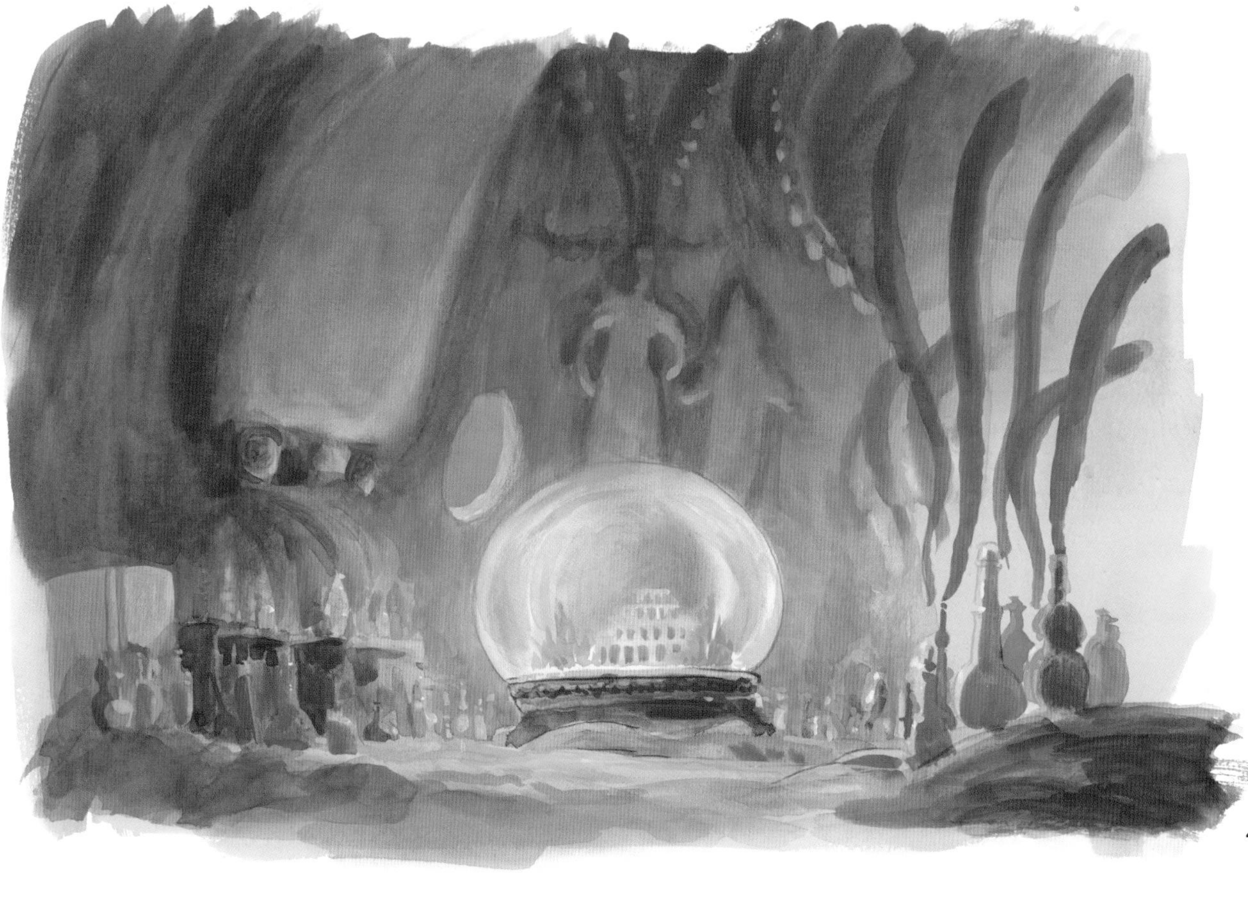
4

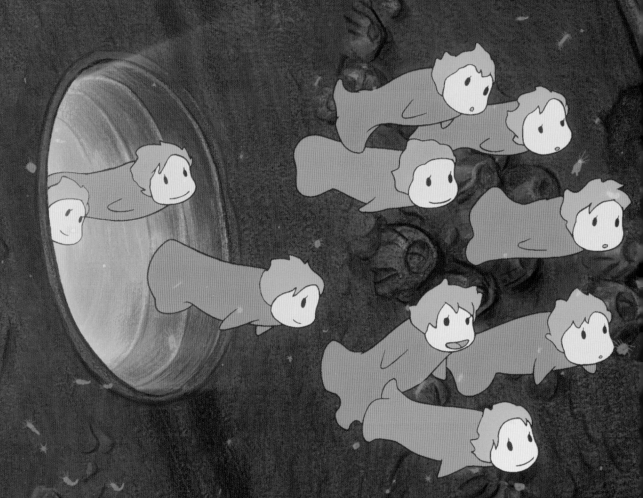

MAKING
THE SCENES-1

This chapter features the raw materials (concept sketches, concept art, background art, character sketches, and character designs) and stills created for the actual film. The story begins with the little fish Ponyo, being sent off by her little sisters and leaving home.

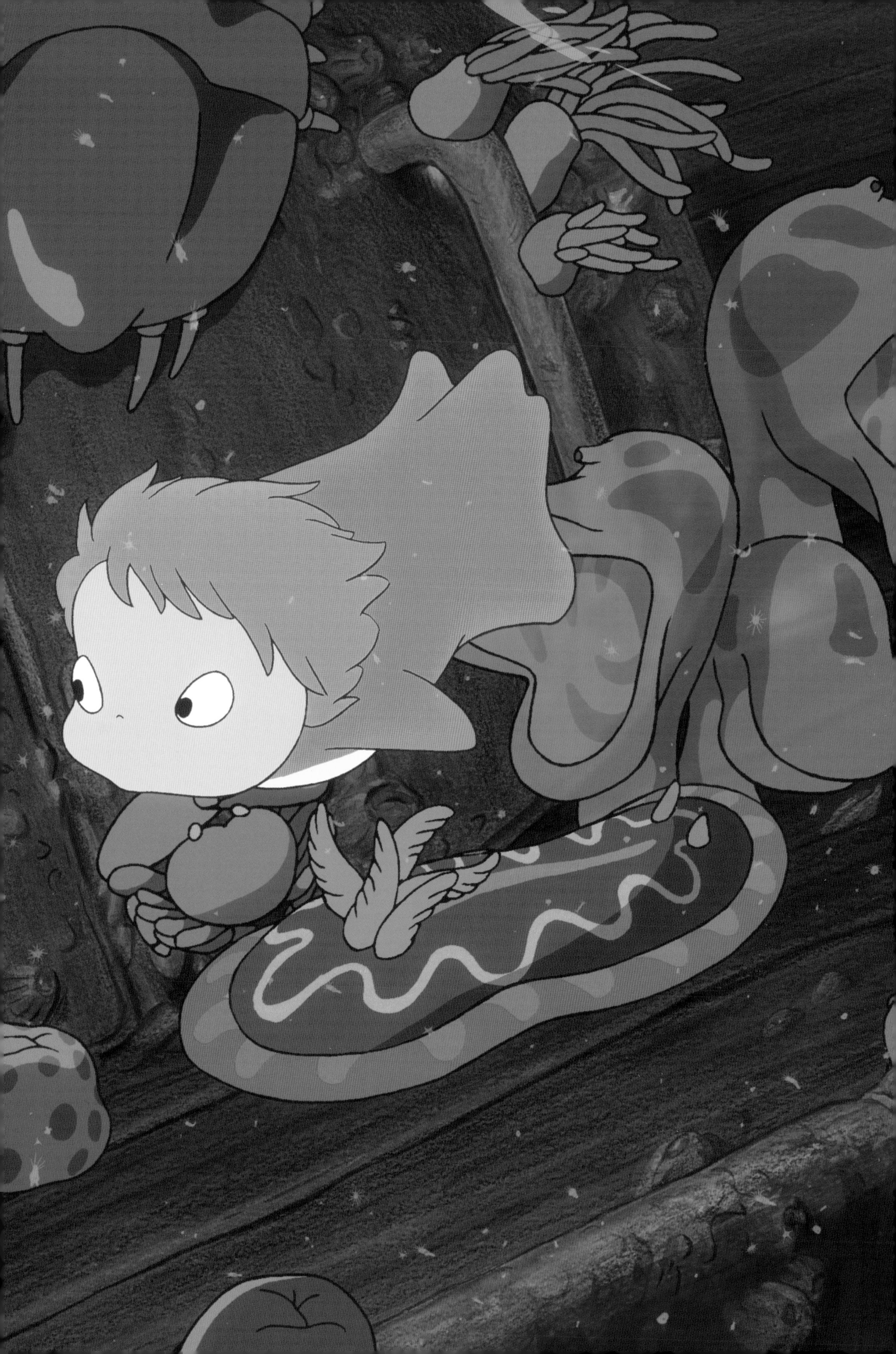

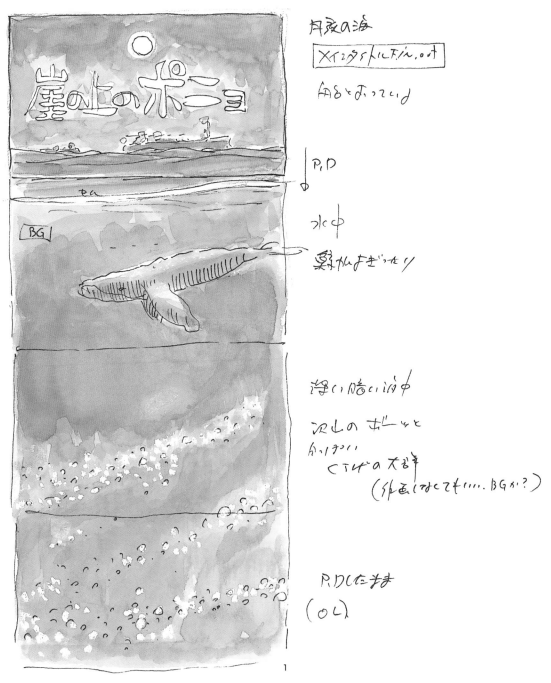

月夜の海

メインタイトルイン・out

何もおっていい

↓P.D

水中

鯨がよぎったり

深い暗い海中

沢山の ボーッと
かけない
くらげの大名
（作画になくても......BGか?）

R.Dしたまま
（OL）

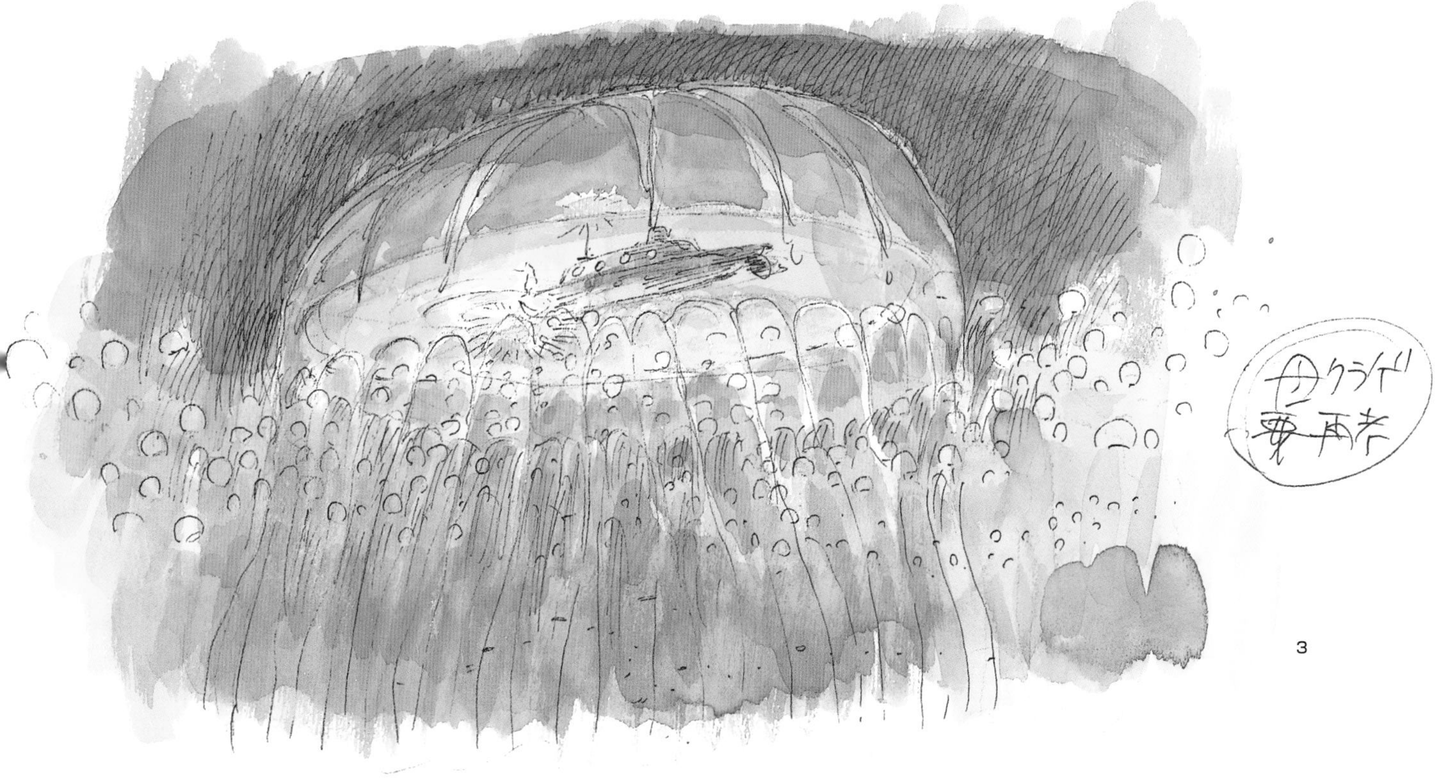

3

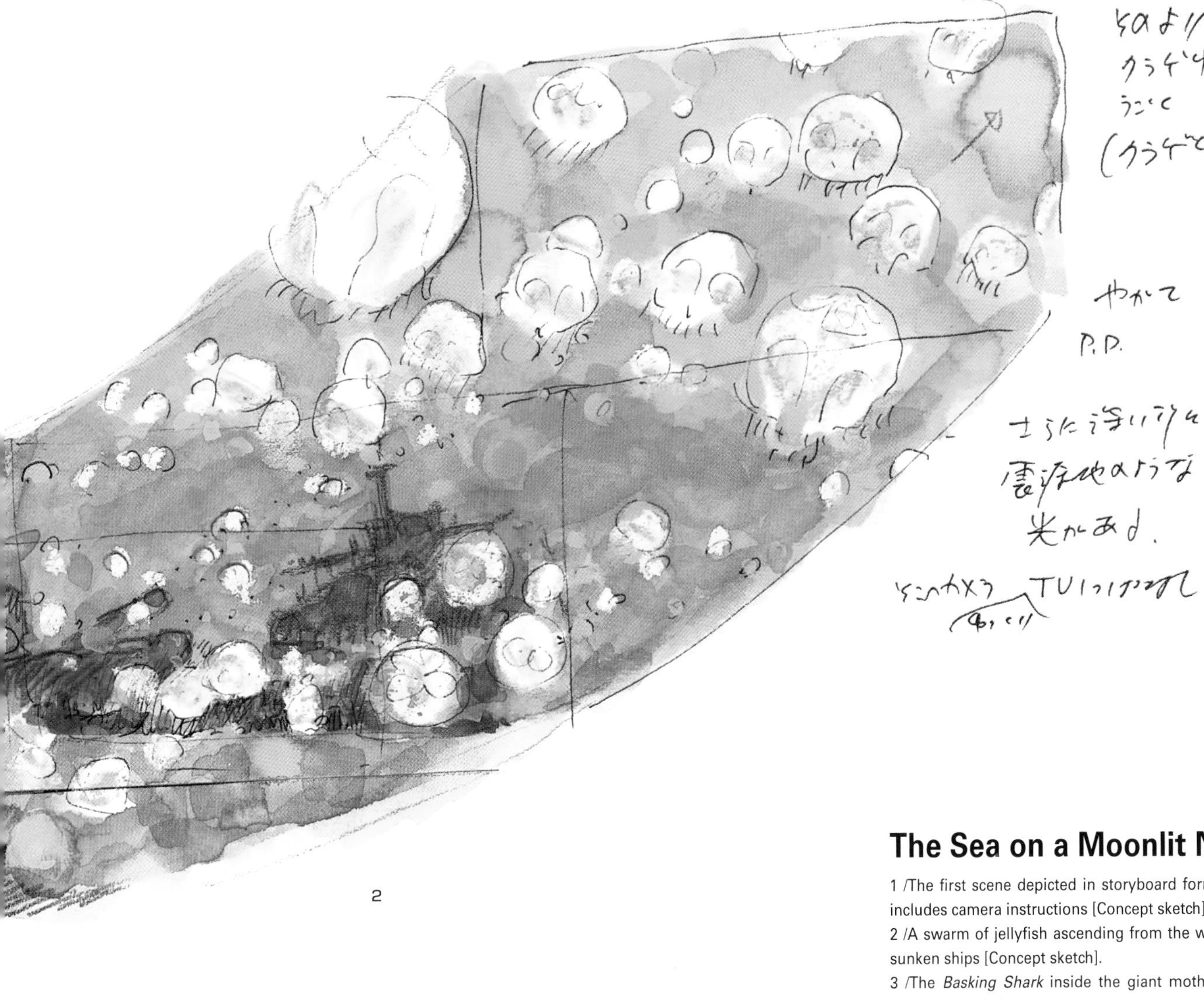
うごく
やがて
P.D.
さらに深い所は
雲海のような
光がある.

2

The Sea on a Moonlit Night

1 /The first scene depicted in storyboard format, which includes camera instructions [Concept sketch].
2 /A swarm of jellyfish ascending from the wreckage of sunken ships [Concept sketch].
3 /The *Basking Shark* inside the giant mother jellyfish [Concept sketch].

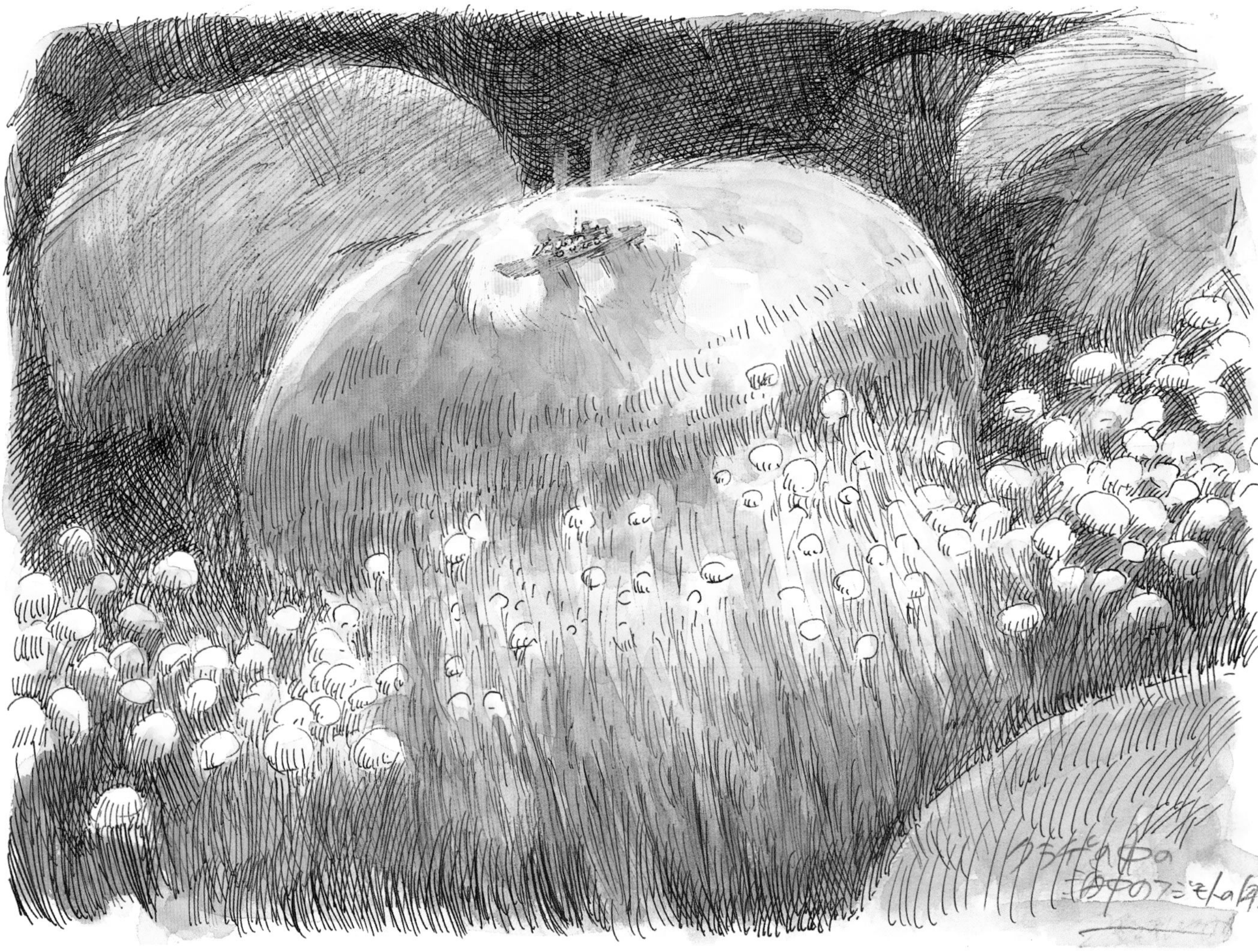
クラゲの中の
海中のフジモトの船

4

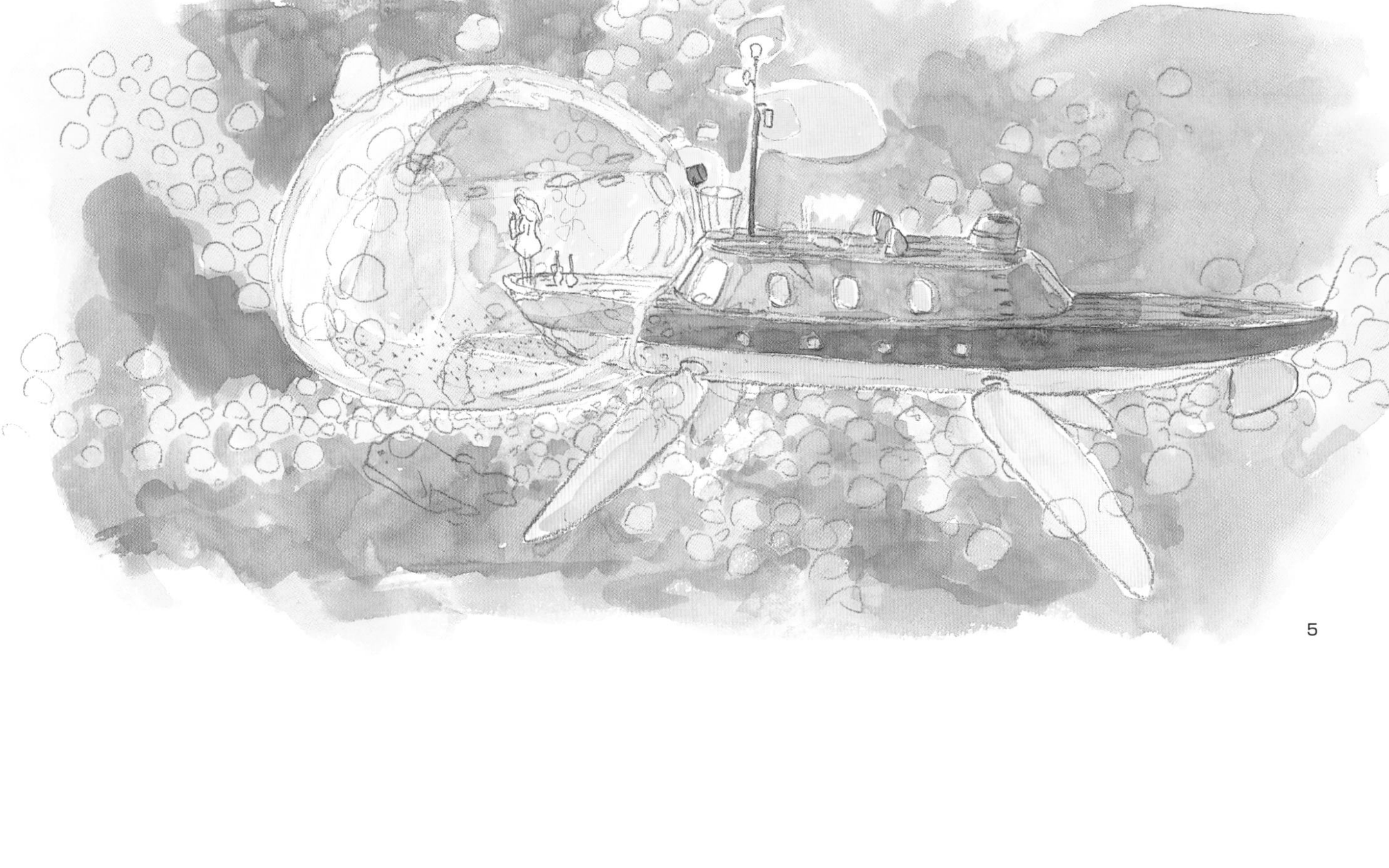

5

4–6 /The *Basking Shark* and the swarm of jellyfish under the sea. This is a scene at the beginning in which Fujimoto, Ponyo's father, stands on the bow, creating jellyfish. It's apparent here that the giant mother jellyfish has changed into an air bubble [Concept sketches].

7 /Part of the opening from a storyboard Miyazaki drew himself. Miyazaki painted many of the shots with watercolors to convey the color scheme to the staff.

8, 9 /Fujimoto pouring the water of life from the *Basking Shark*. Also drawn: the inside of the giant jellyfish, a size comparison of the *Basking Shark* to the surrounding minions, the bottle for the water of life [Concept sketches].

6

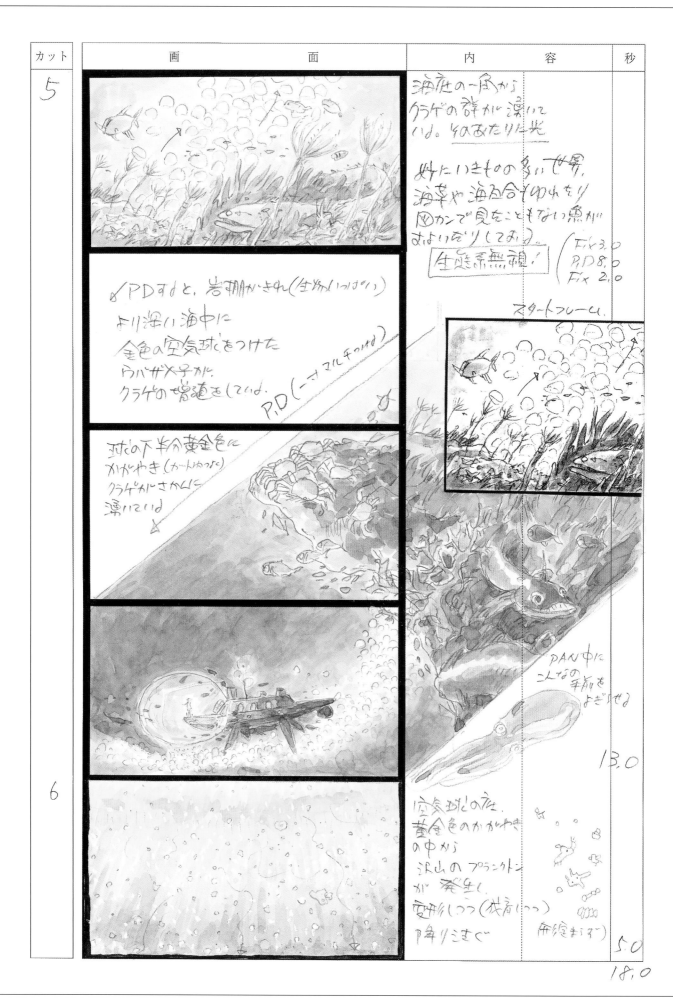

カット	画　　面	内　　容	秒
5		海底の一点から クラゲの群が漂いて いる。そのあたり一光 好たいきもの多い世界、海草や海ろ合やゆれをり 回カンで見をこともない魚が およいぎりしてみる。 生態系無視！ (Fix 3.0 P.D 8.0 Fix 2.0	
	⊘PDすと、岩棚がされ（生物いっぱい） より深い海中に 金色の空気球をつけた ウハザメ子が。 クラゲの嚮道をしている。 P.D (一寸マルチつけ) スタートフレーム.	
	球の下半分黄金色に かがやき (カットかつた) クラゲがさかに 漂いている	PAN中に こんなの手前も よぎりぜる 13.0
6		1空気球との庄. 黄金色のかがやき の中から 沢山のプランクトン が発生し 変形しつつ（成育しつつ） 降りこまで (研究まほう) 5.0
		18.0

フジモト

こんなあへ、なきにいいでしょ

8

9

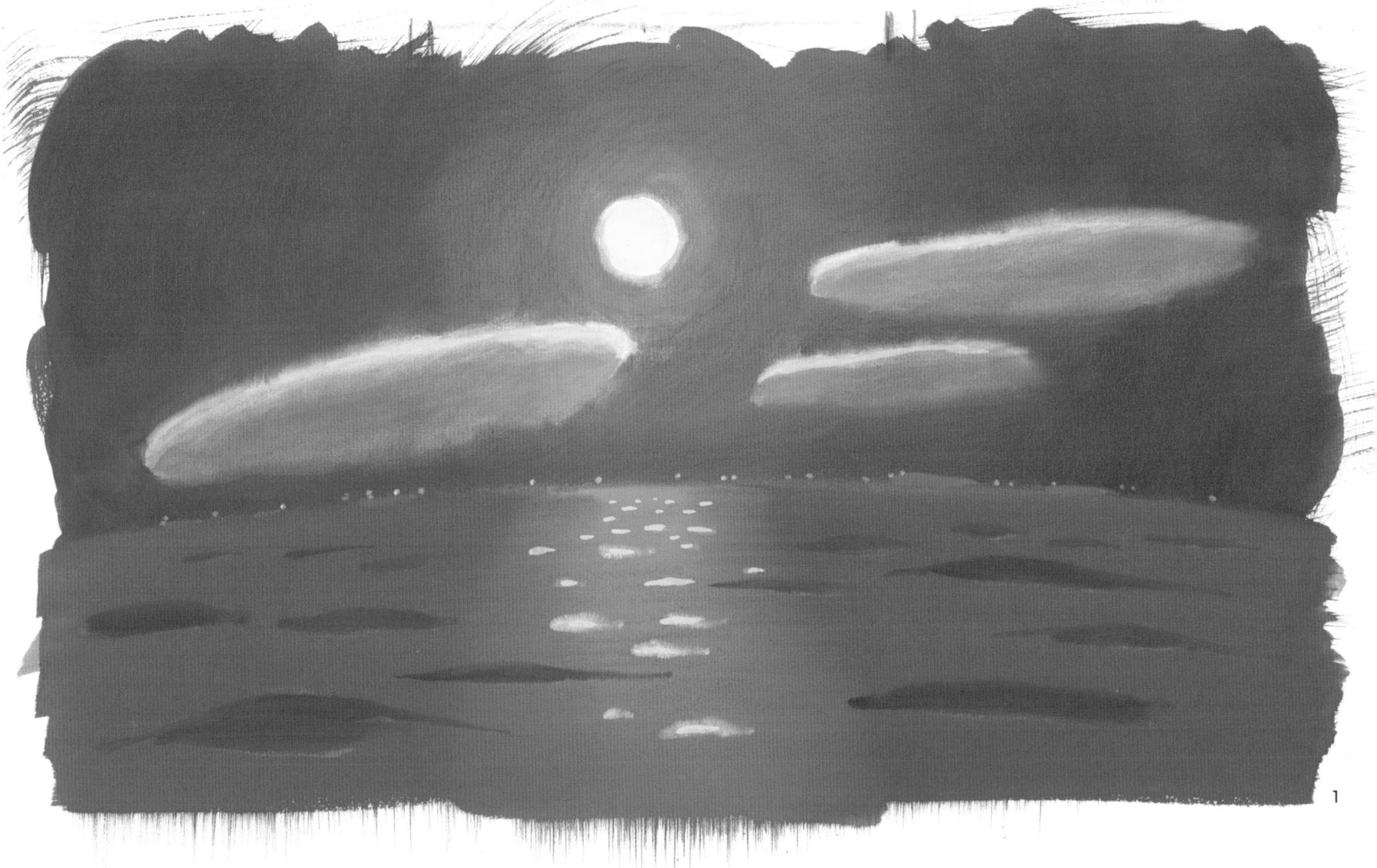

1

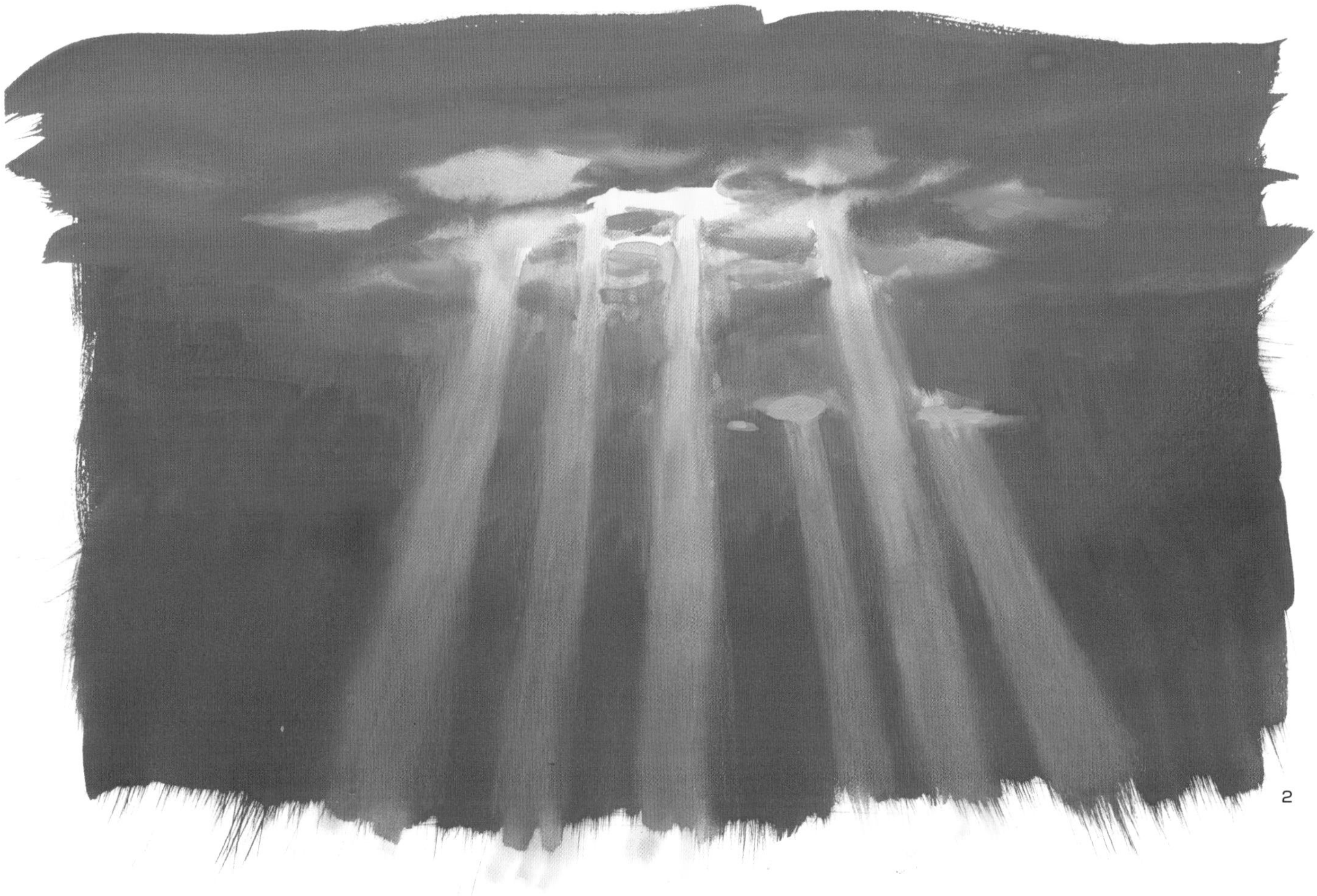

2

1 /The first shot of the sea and full moon [Concept art].
2 /Shafts of moonlight penetrating the water [Concept art].
3 /The *Basking Shark* and swarm of jellyfish beyond the rock covered with marine plants [Concept art].
4 /The *Basking Shark* and jellyfish [Concept art].

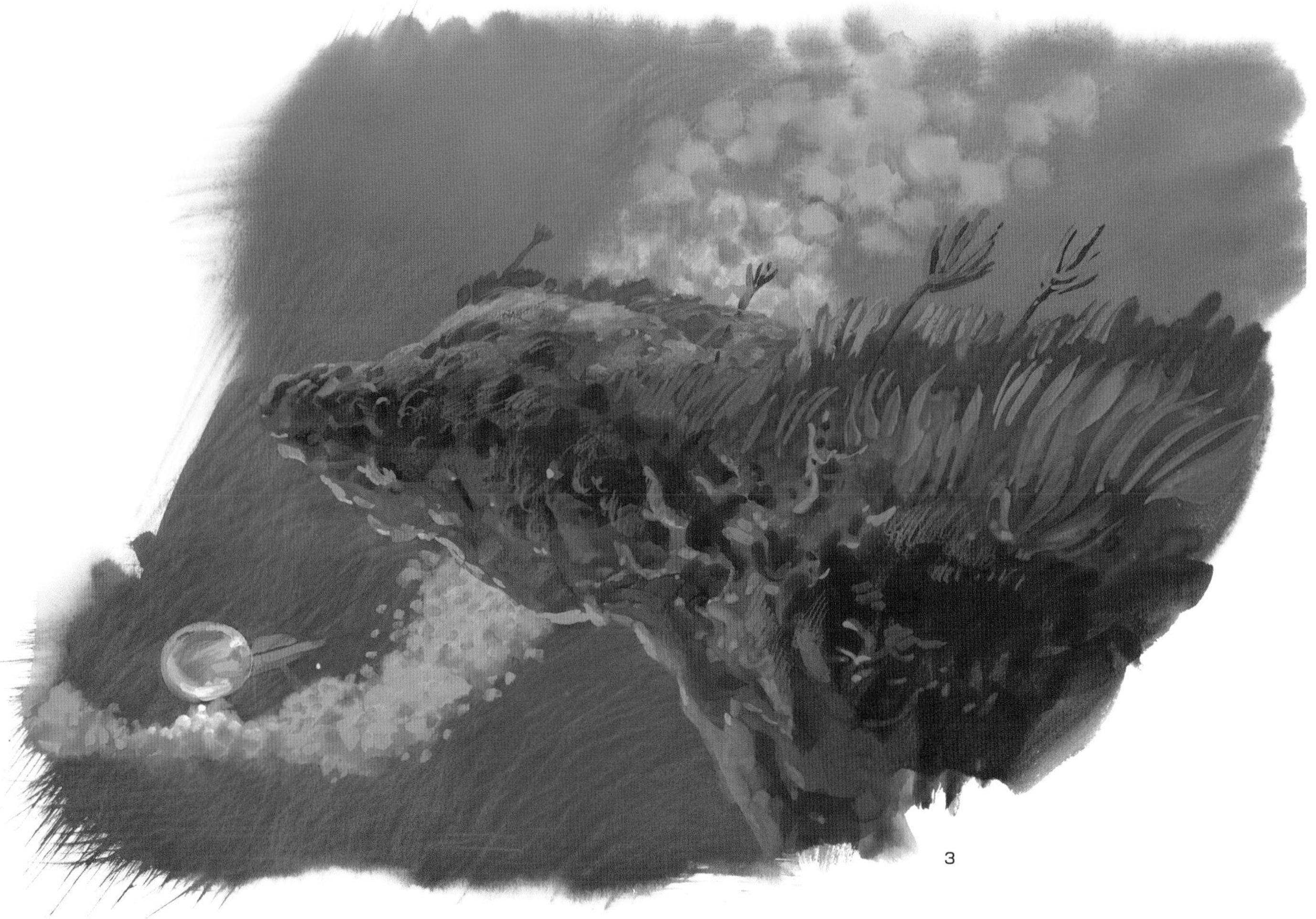

3

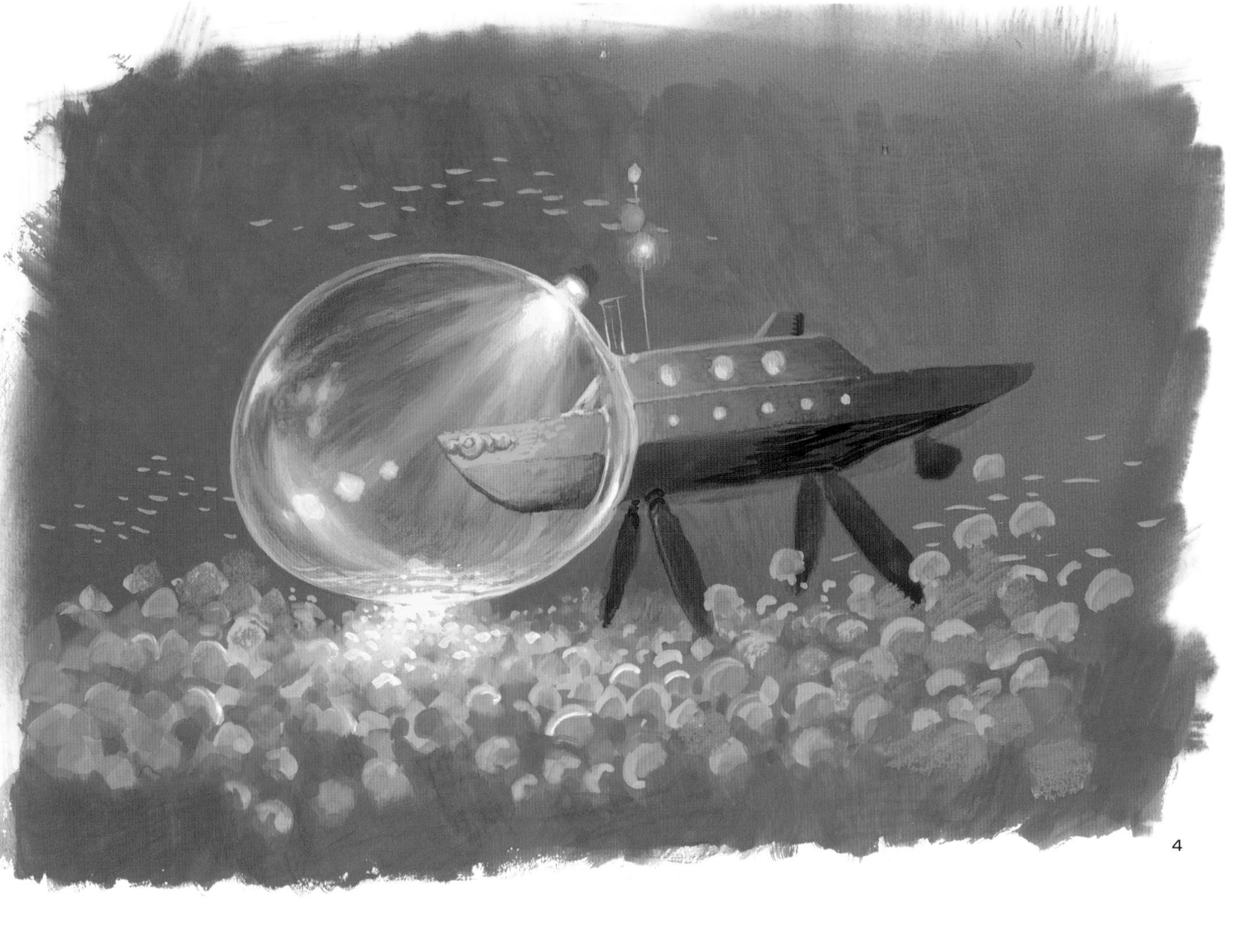

4

ポニョ 金魚姫

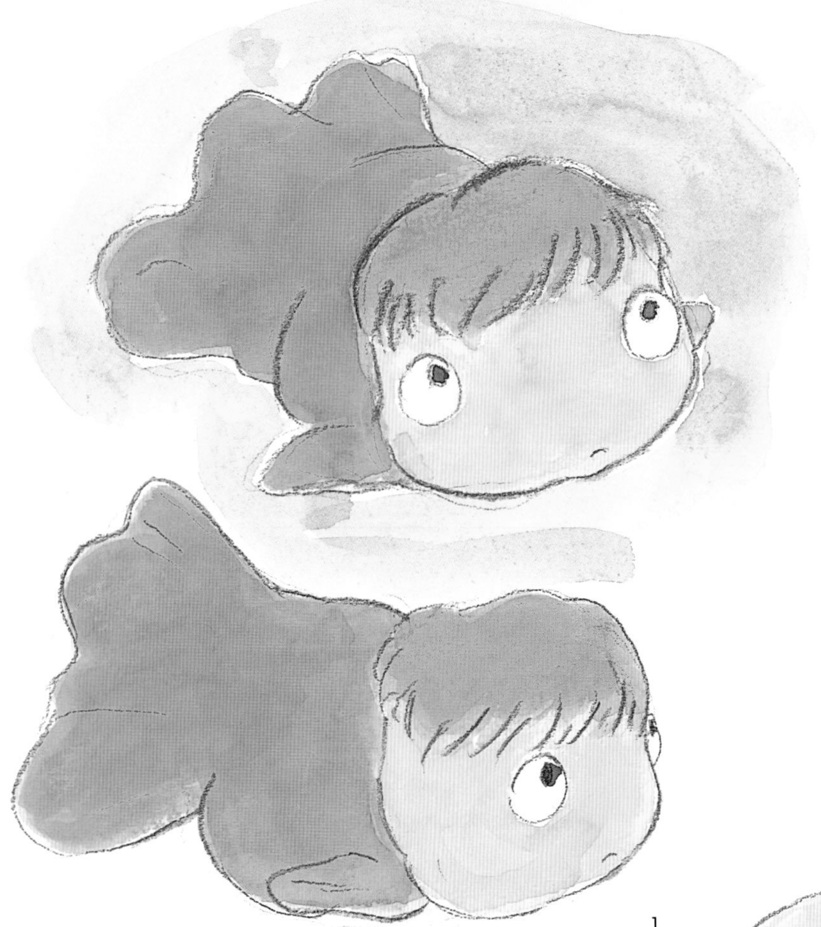

1

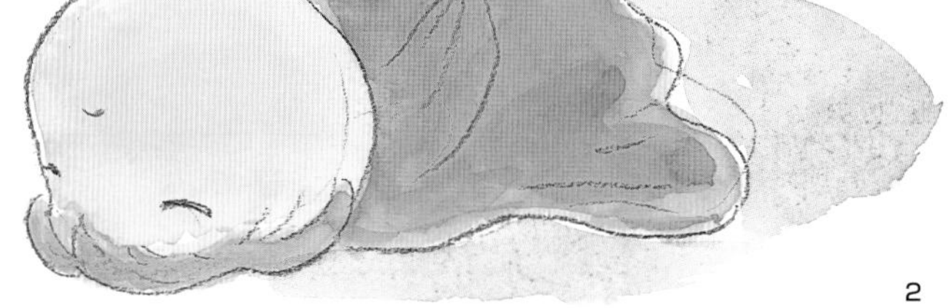

2

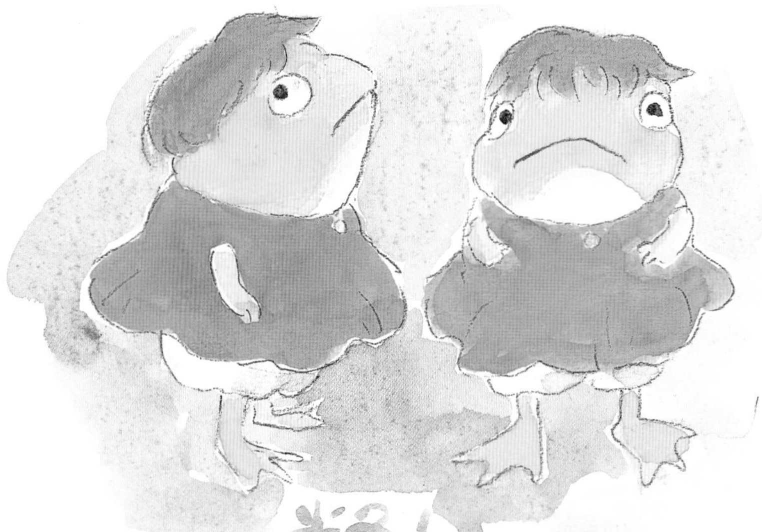
半魚人

3

Ponyo

Daughter of Fujimoto, a sorcerer and former human, and the sea goddess Gran Mamare. Innocent and inquisitive. Leaving home to escape her restrictive father, she meets the human boy Sosuke. She transforms from her goldfish-like appearance into a half-fish, half-human form, and finally into a human girl.

1, 2 /Ponyo, a little fish resembling a goldfish [Concept sketches].

3 /Her magical powers awakened, Ponyo grows arms and legs, becoming half-fish, half-human [Concept sketch].

4 /Escaping from her father, Ponyo ascends to the surface riding atop a jellyfish [Concept sketch].

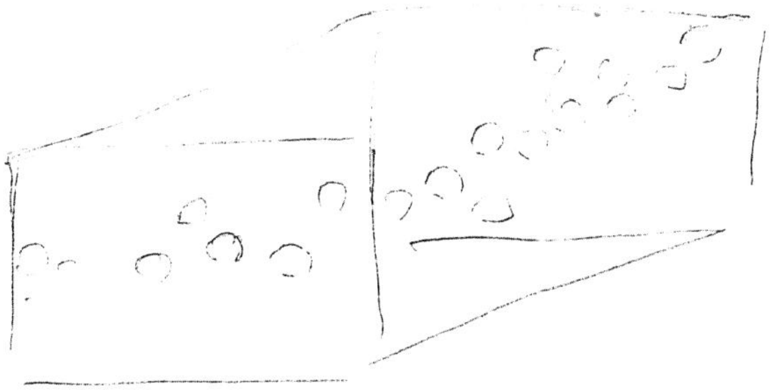

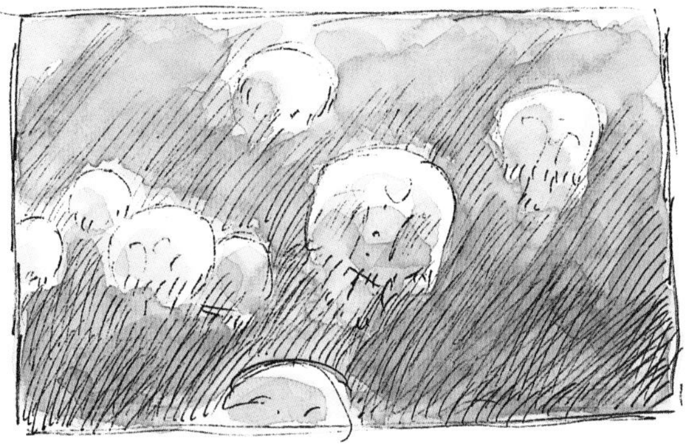

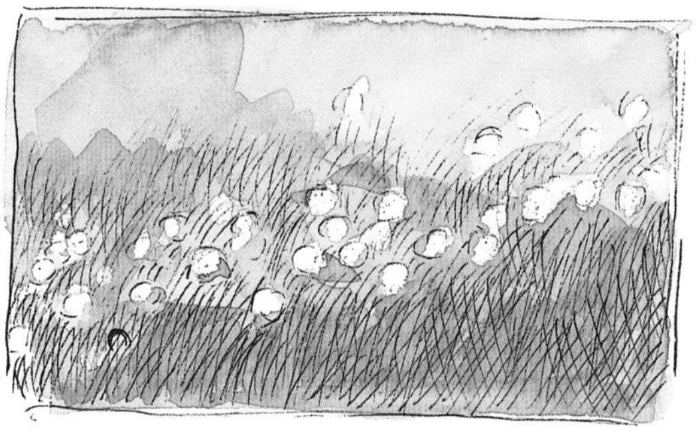

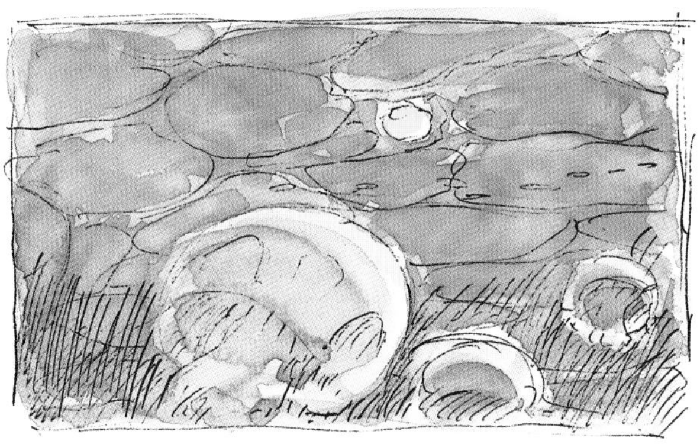

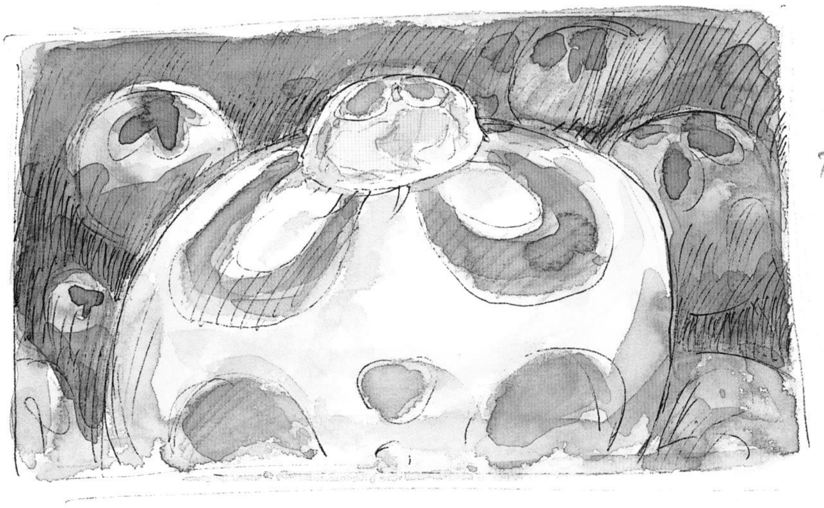

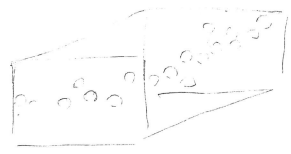

クラゲを
かぶって
クラゲにのって
家出しを
ポニョ

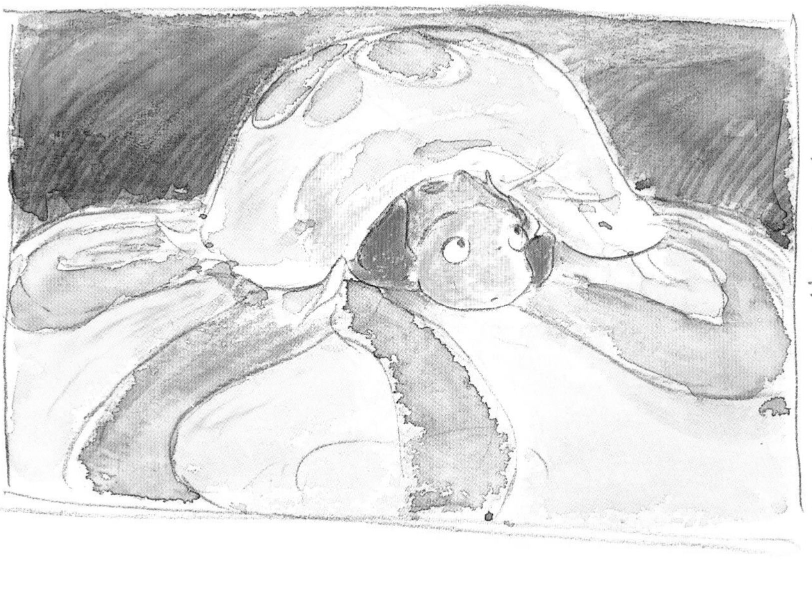

一寸
カオ出し
水面の月を
みたりに

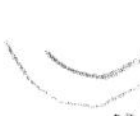

ニッ
脱出成功!!

めでたし。

4

1

2

3

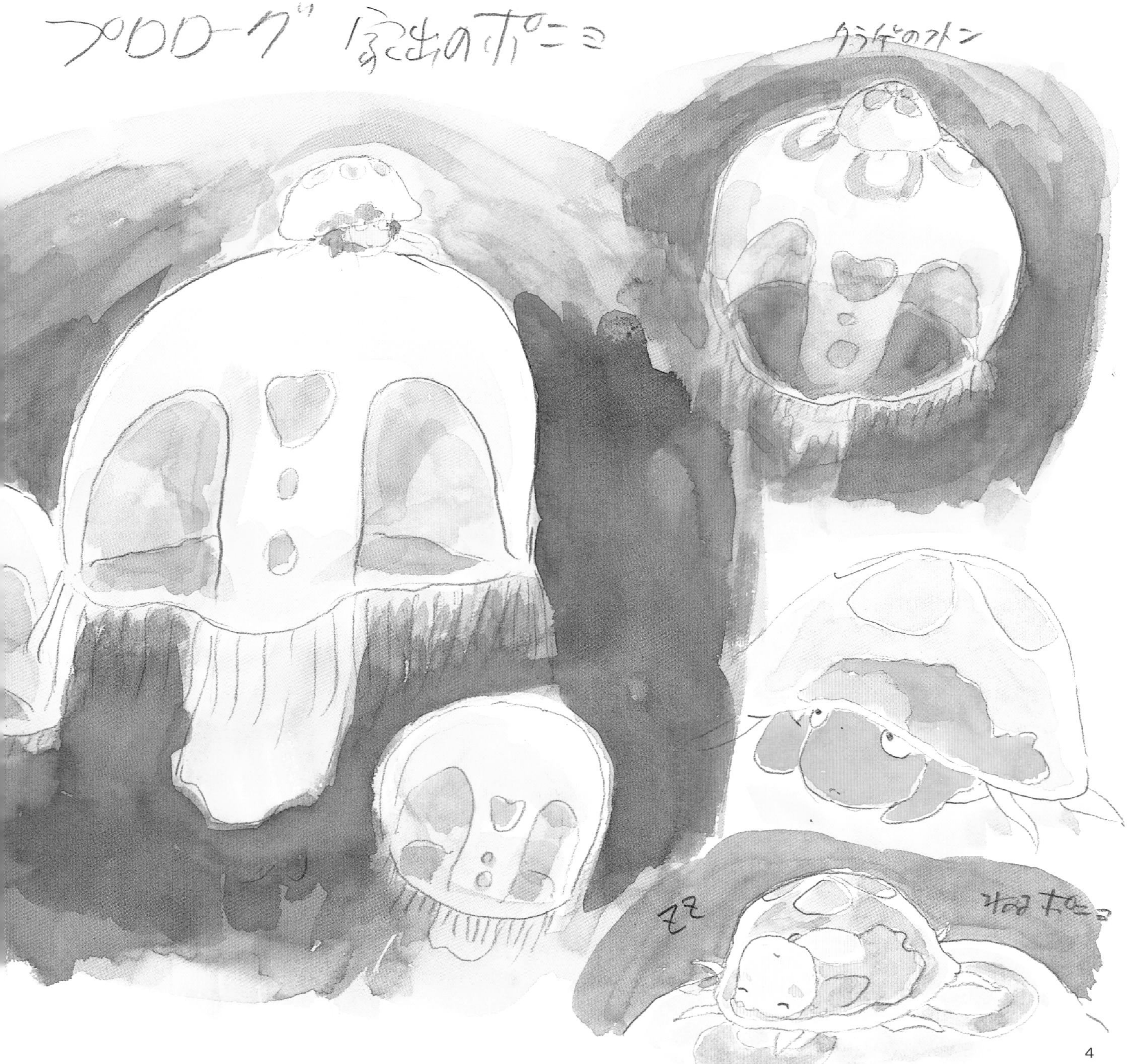
プロローグ 家出のポニョ
クラゲのフトン
ZZ
ねるポニョ

4

Ponyo Leaves Home

1 /Ponyo departing, with her little sisters seeing her off. This scene is flipped in the film [Concept sketch].
2 /Ponyo on top of a jellyfish catching a small jellyfish [Concept sketch].
3 /She wears the jellyfish like a cloak [Concept sketch].
4 /She makes a futon out of the jellyfish and falls asleep [Concept sketch].

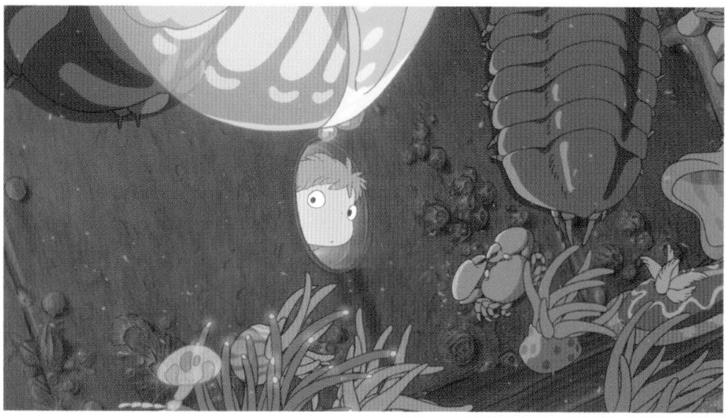
1

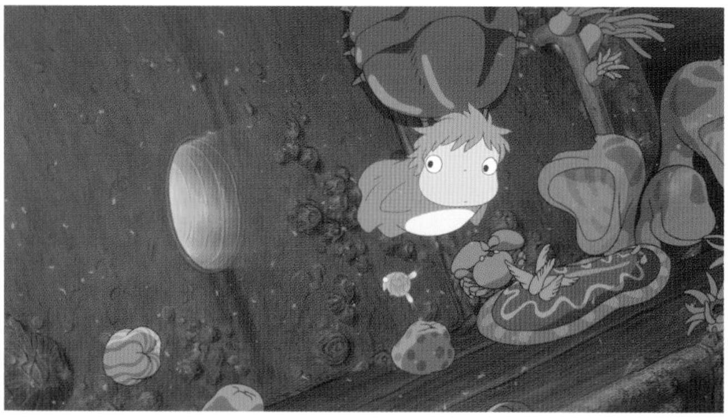
2

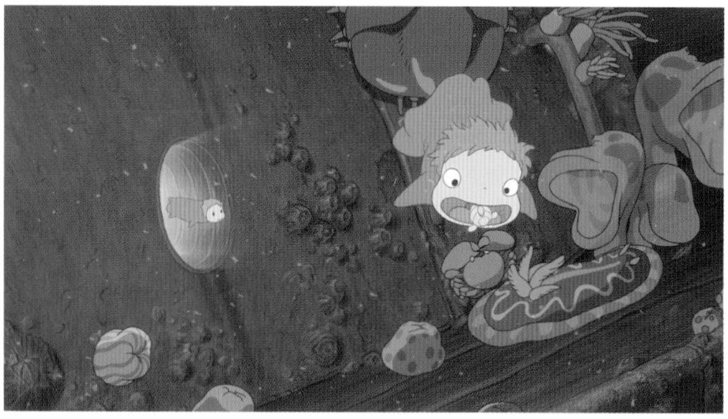
3

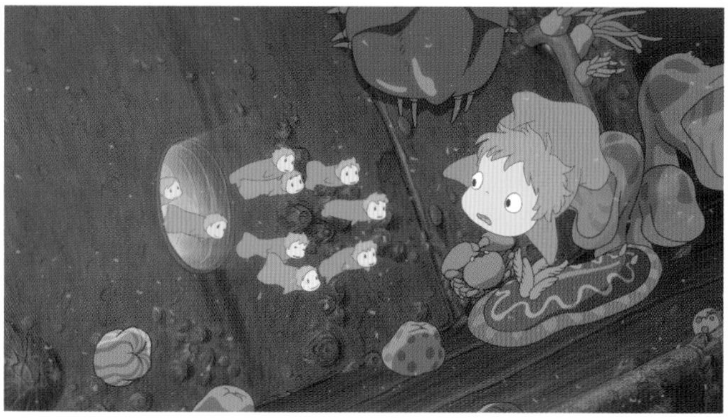
4

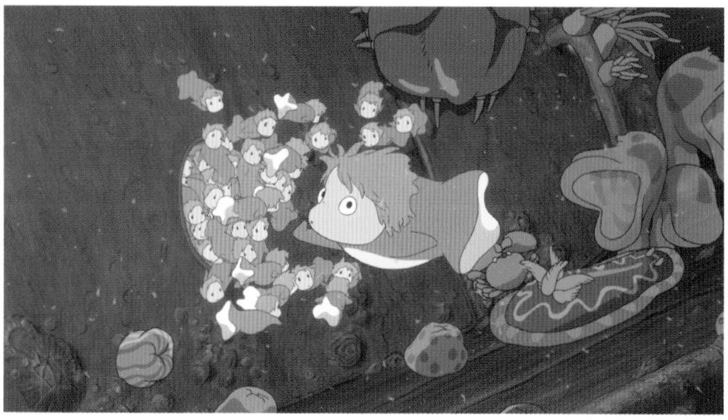
5

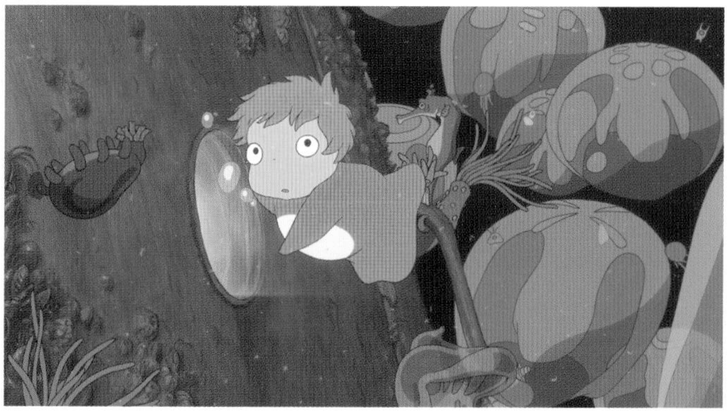
6

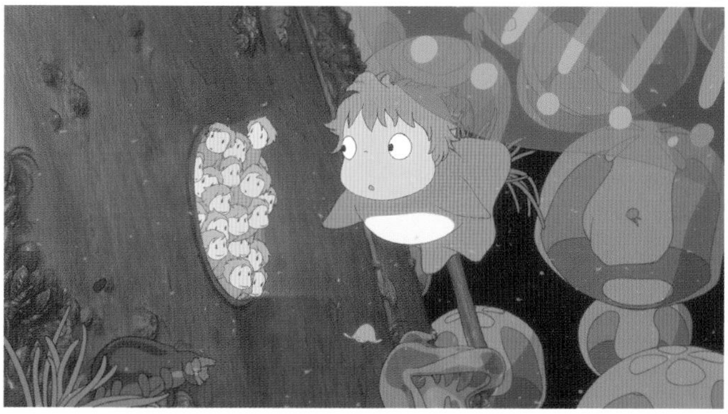
7

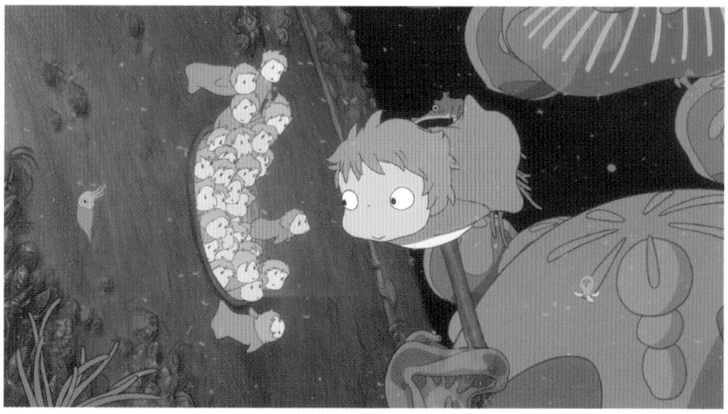
8

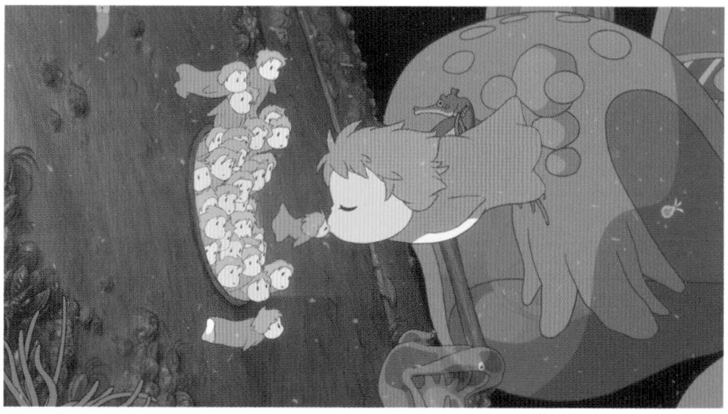
9

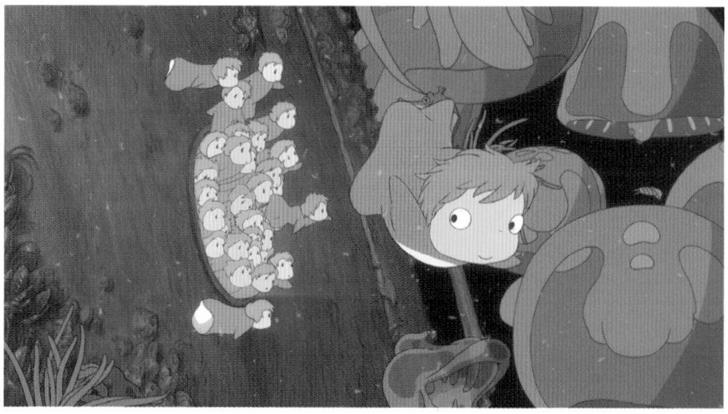
10

11

12

13

14

15

1–10 /Ponyo emerges from the ship's hull, which is caked with trilobites and sea hares. Eluding Fujimoto's eye, she bids her younger sisters farewell and leaves.

11–15 /Moved by the sight of the moon, Ponyo falls asleep inside a jellyfish.

The jellyfish scene at the beginning with all the underwater creatures is, in a way, the scene that encapsulates the entire film. Atsuko Tanaka did all of the drawing here, and as there is a lot of information being conveyed on screen this sequence took a lot of time. And since the scene that follows—in which Ponyo appears out of the *Basking Shark*—is the first time she appears on screen, I paid attention to establishing a proper presence for Ponyo without losing the nuance depicted in the storyboards. Because Ponyo is drawn with simple lines, upon first glance it might appear difficult to make her expressive, but on the contrary it's quite easy from an illustrator's standpoint. Even if the shape is a little off or different, as long as Ponyo's innocent, unrestrained character and her cuteness come through, the rest is fairly adaptable. That's the kind of character she is.

—Supervising Animator: Katsuya Kondo

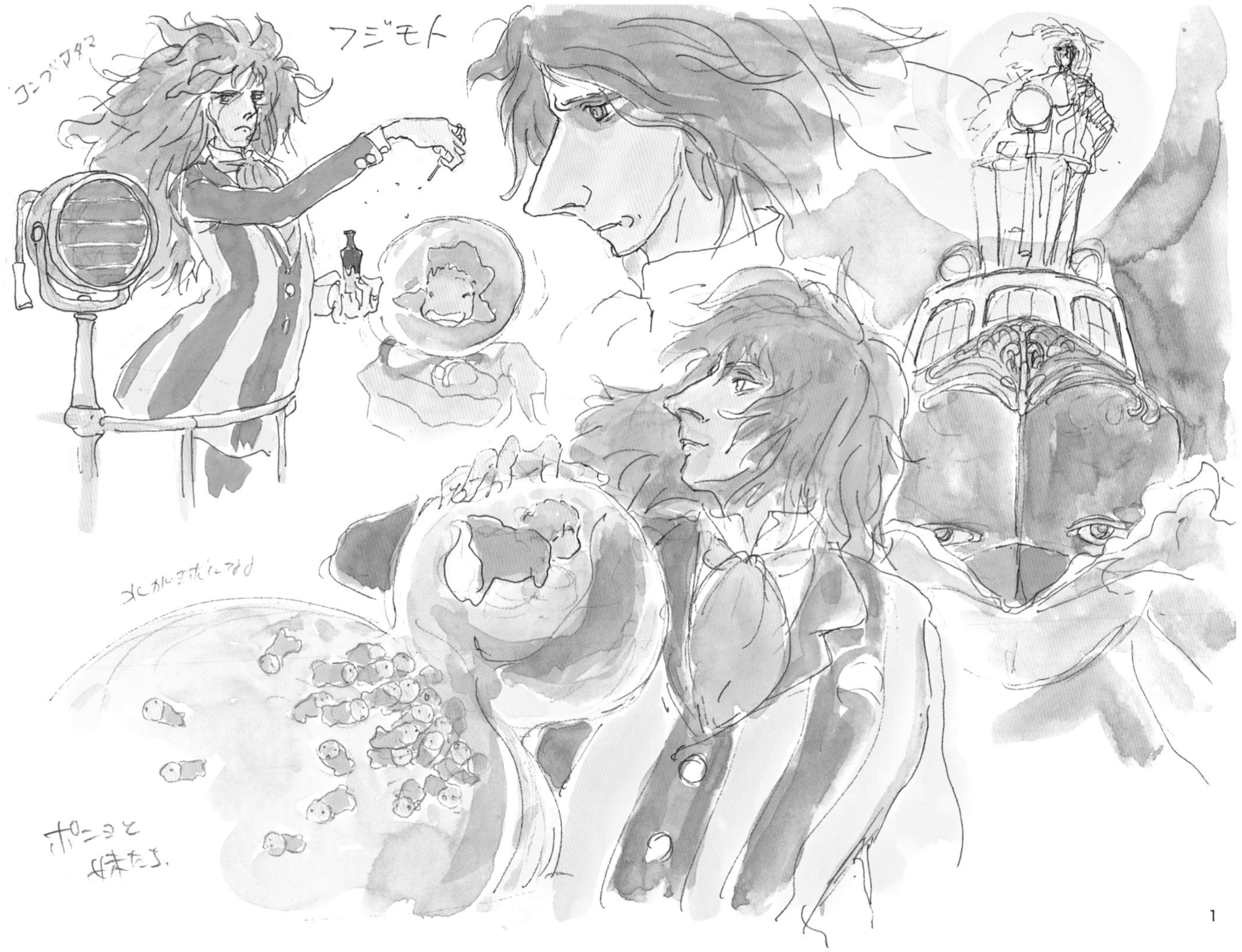
フジモト
ポニョと
妹たち.

1

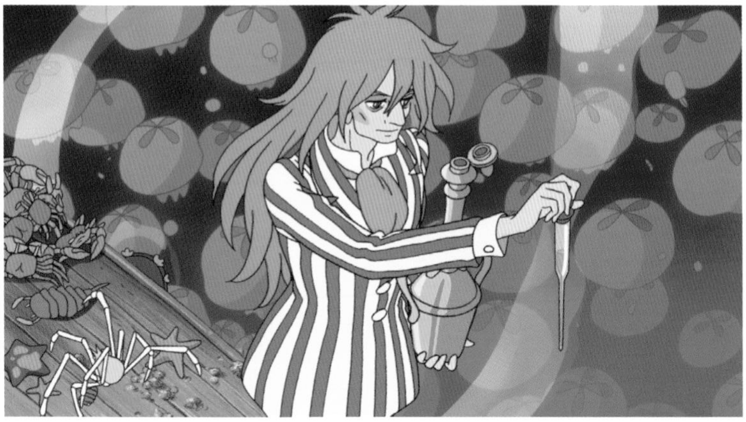

2

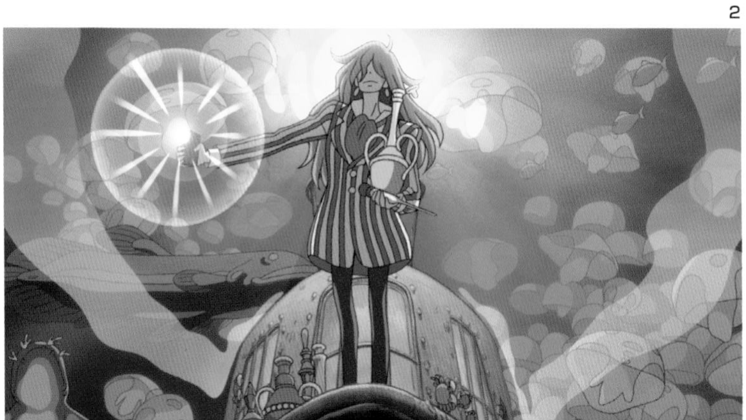

3

Fujimoto

A sorcerer and overprotective father who adores Ponyo. Formerly human, Fujimoto refines vast quantities of the water of life and creates jellyfish and other water creatures to heal the earth of contamination by humans, in order to restore it to its original fertile state.

1 /Fujimoto, Ponyo, and her little sisters [Concept sketch].
2 /Fujimoto creating jellyfish with the water of life.
3 /He emits a signal, touched by the sight of a passing majestic giant squid.
4, 5 /Fujimoto, drawn by Katsuya Kondo from Hayao Miyazaki's concept sketches [Rough character sketches].
6 /Fujimoto turns around, sensing the presence of Ponyo and her little sisters. He does not see Ponyo leaving home, as a Japanese bullhead shark gets in the way.

The character of Fujimoto is, to put it simply, "a restless sort" [*laughs*]. Although basically a handsome man, he looks a little eccentric. I drew him in a slender silhouette to elicit the understanding that he's slightly different from ordinary humans. Takeshi Inamura, who was responsible for the scene in which the minions commanded by Fujimoto first appear, rendered them very faithfully from the storyboards. Miyazaki liked them so much that Inamura became the resident expert amongst the other animators; they all referred to his key animation in order to draw the minions.

—Supervising Animator: Katsuya Kondo

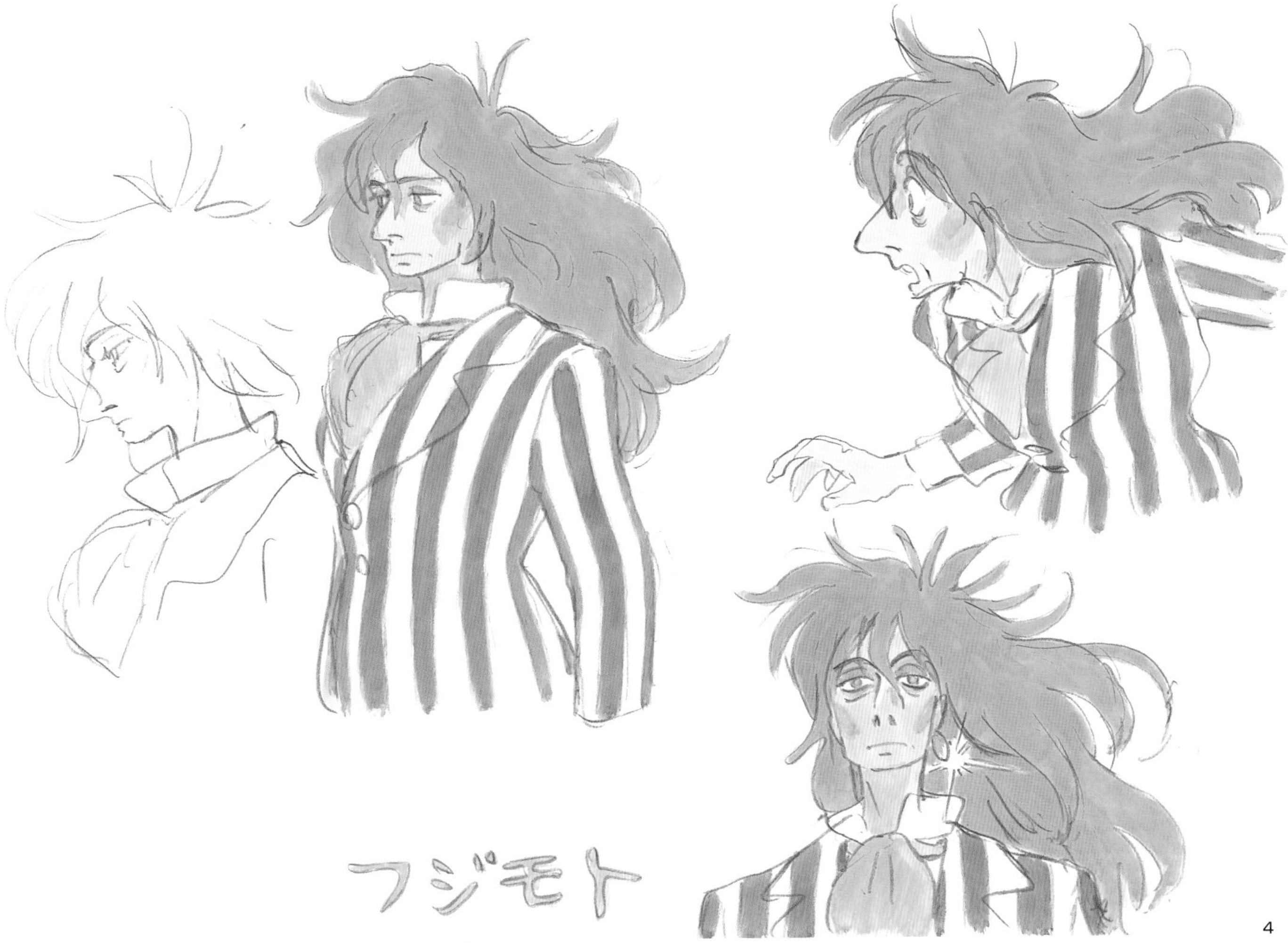
フジモト
4

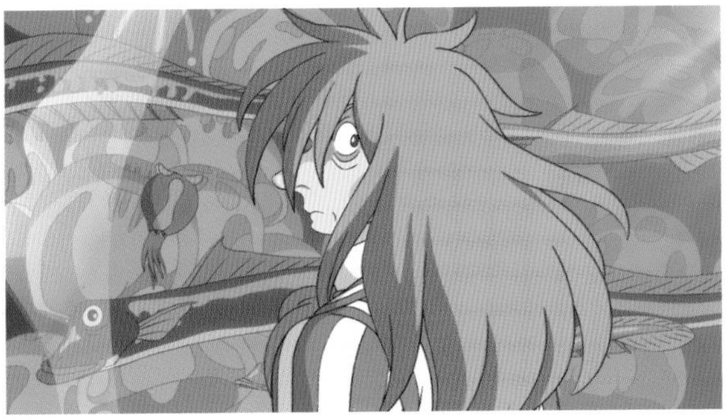
6

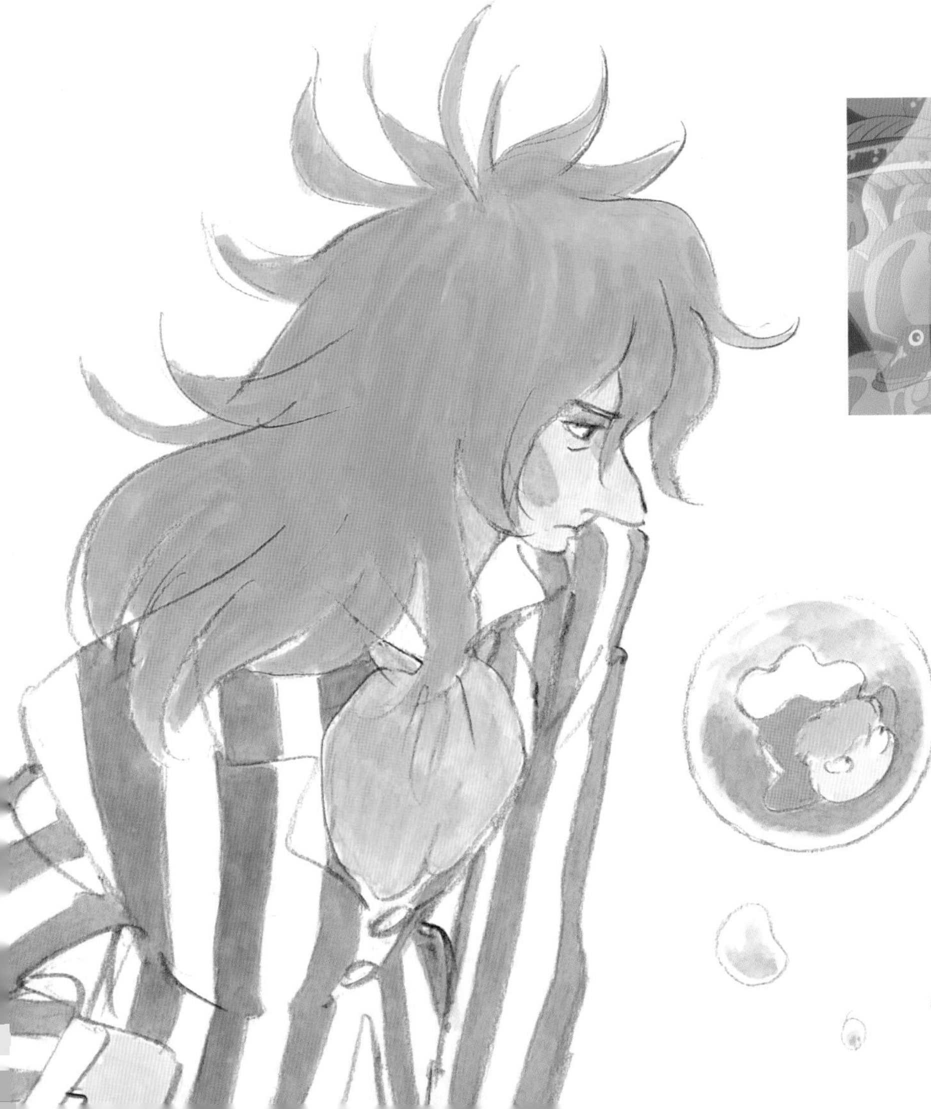
5

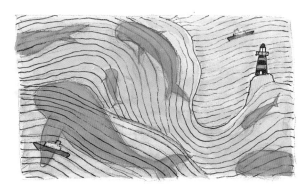

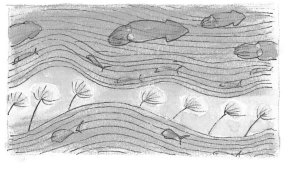

The Opening Title

1 /Concept sketches, drawn by Hayao Miyazaki, of the opening title.
2, 3 /Noboru Yoshida's concept art of the opening title.
4 /The opening stills from the film (uncredited).

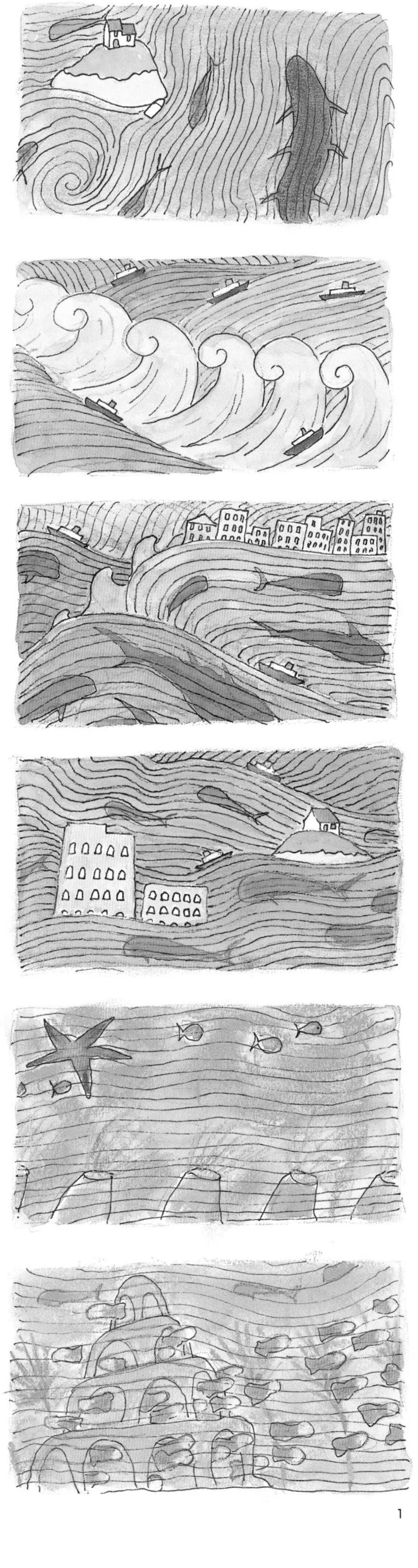

1

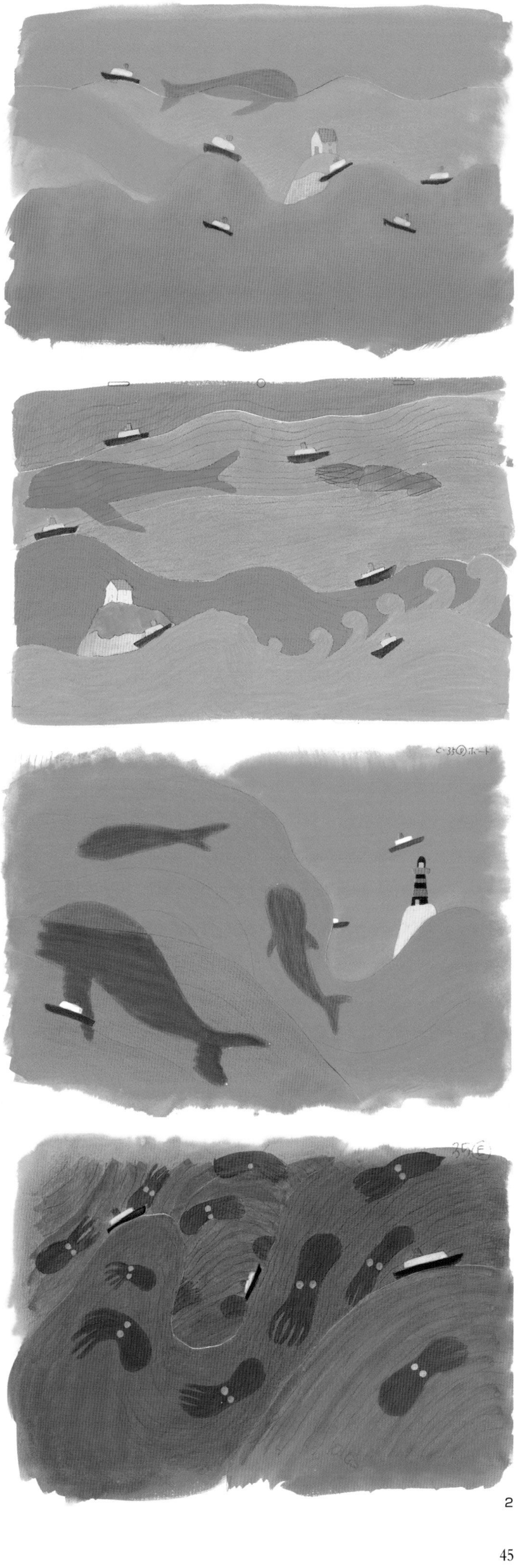

2

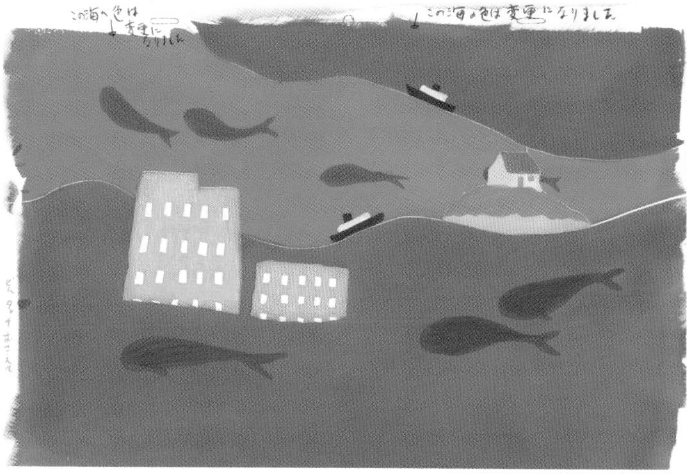

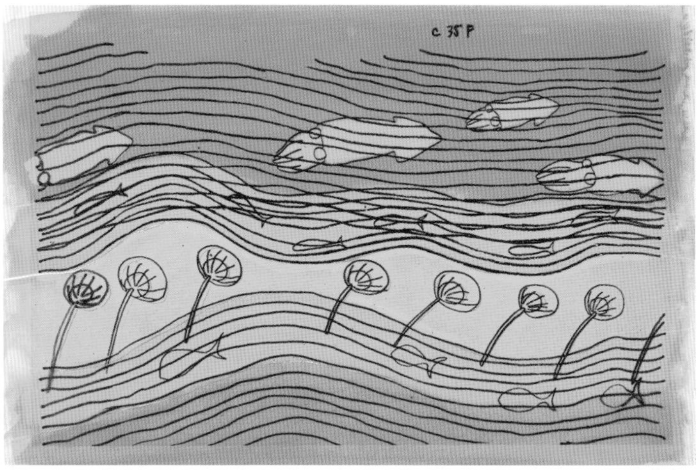
C 35 P

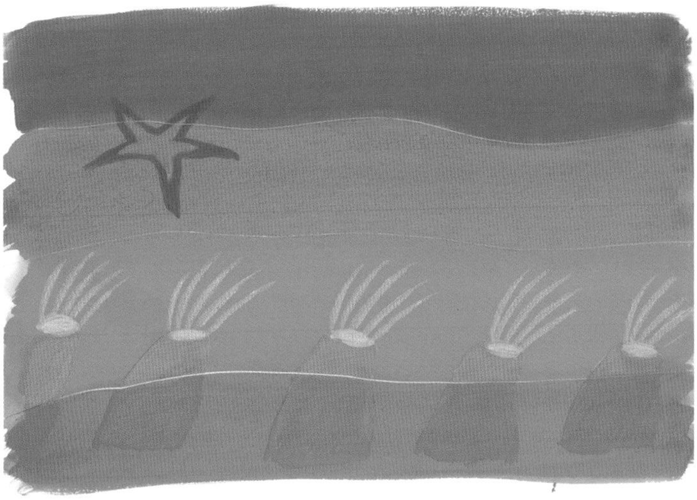

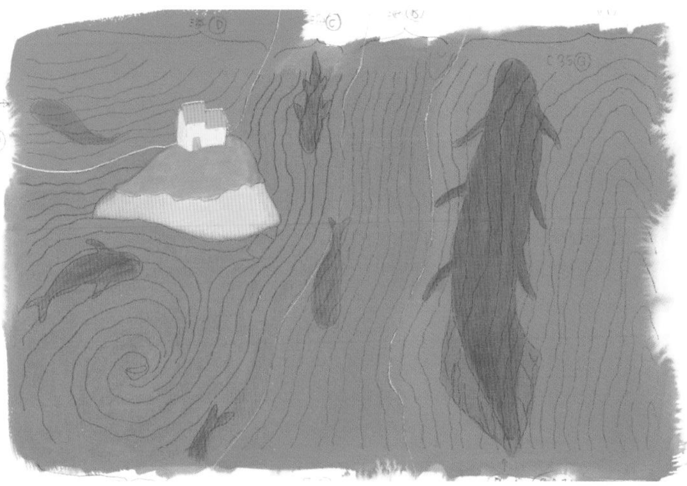

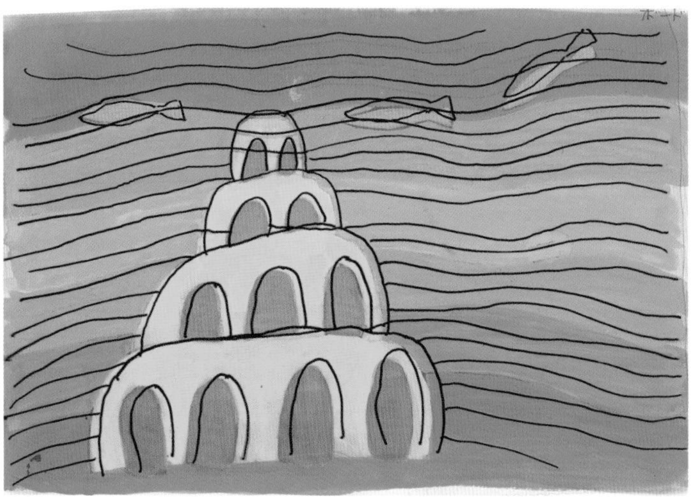

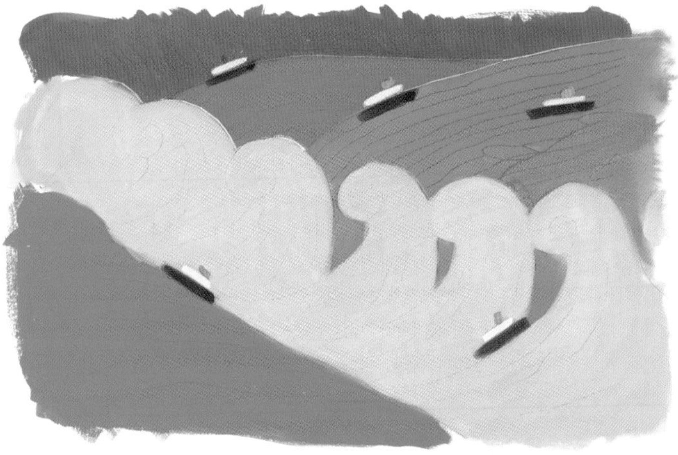

3

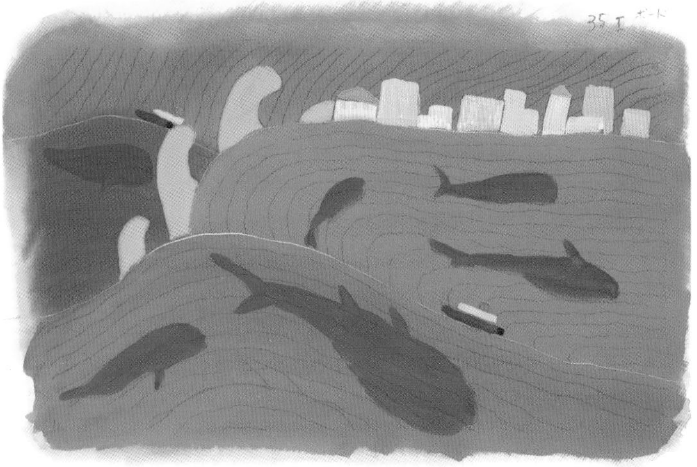

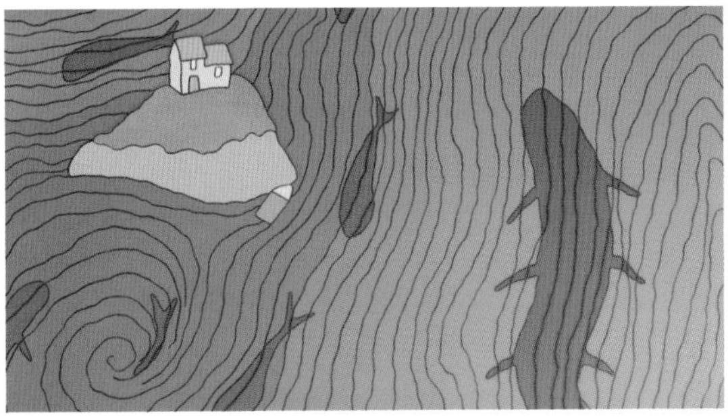
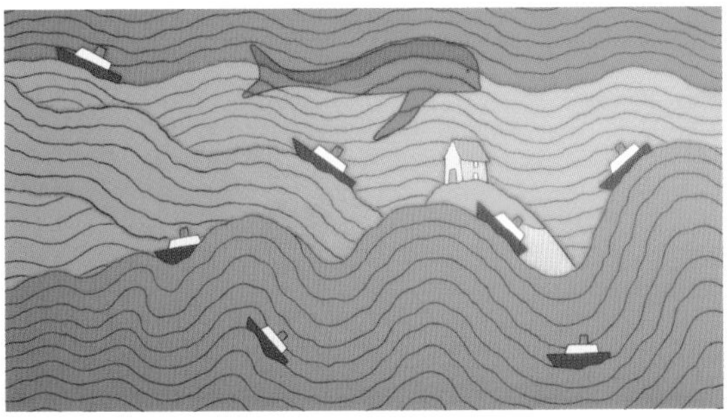
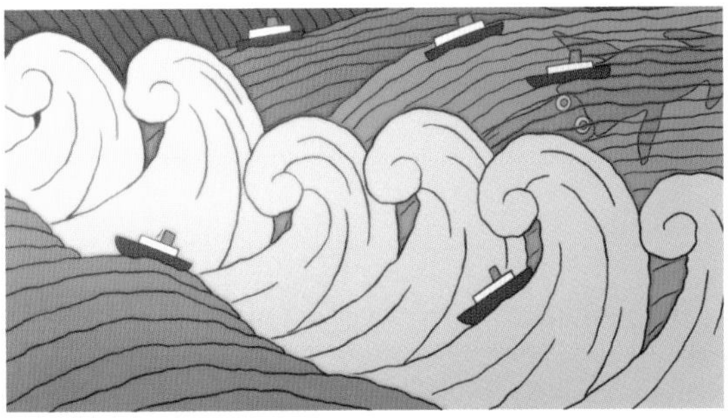
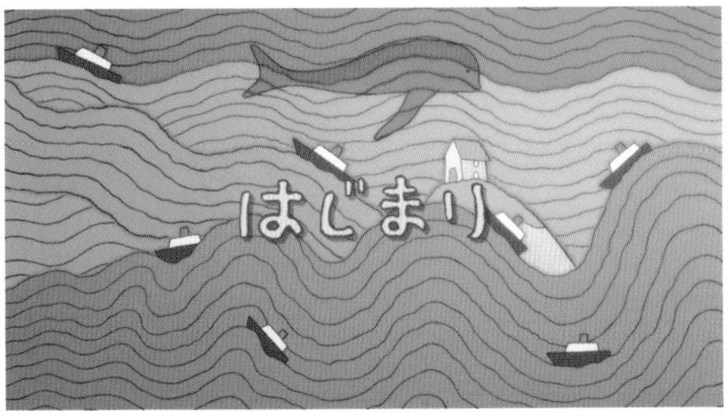
はじまり
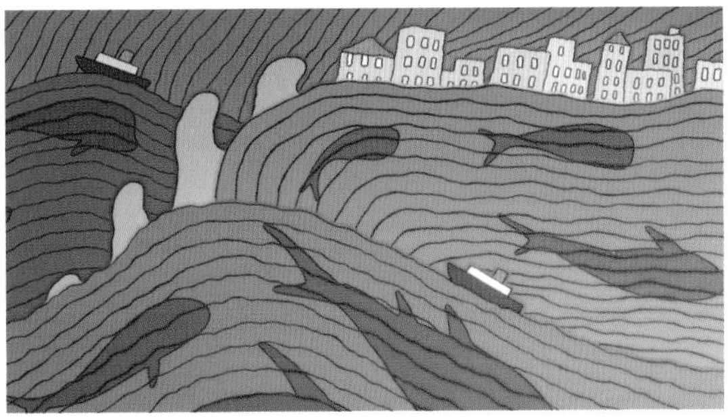
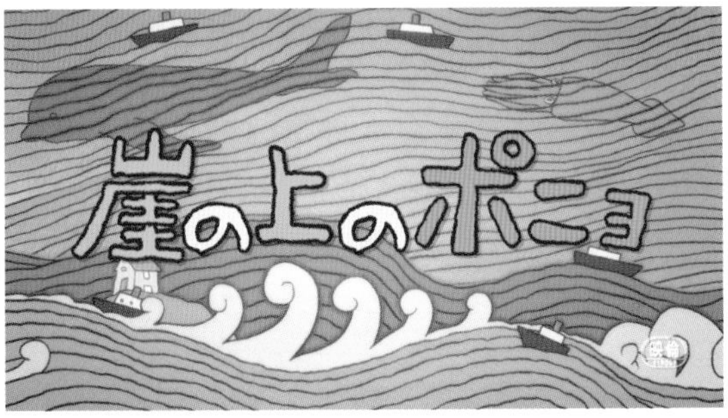
崖の上のポニョ
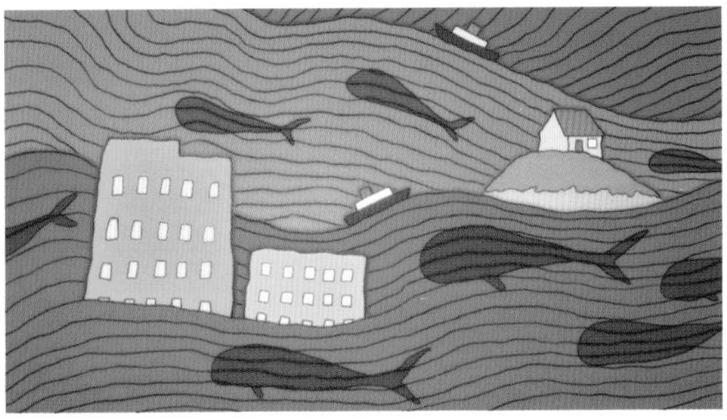
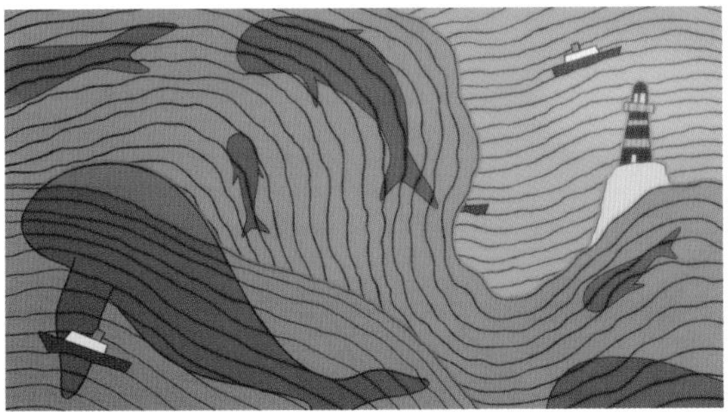
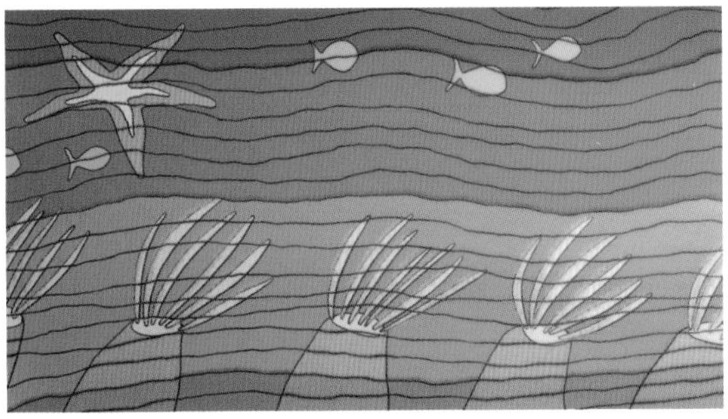
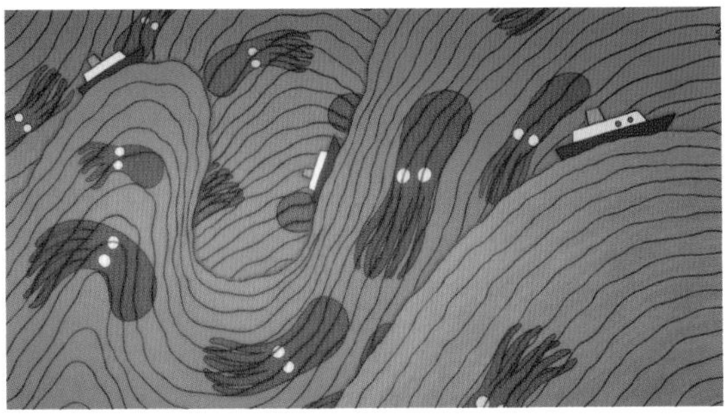
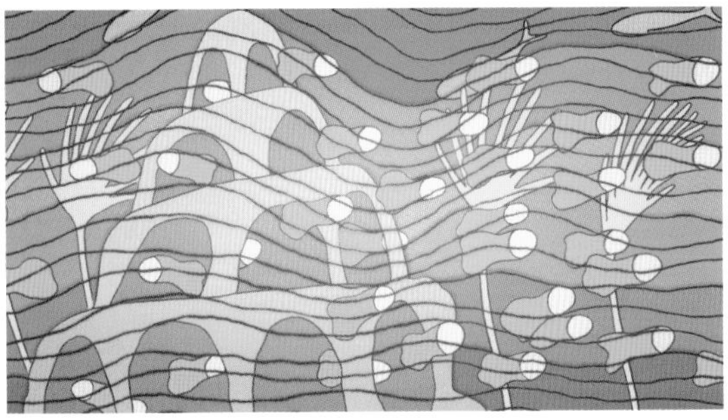
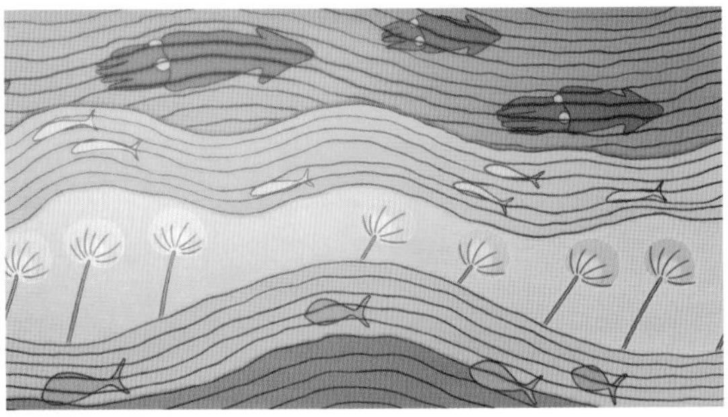

4

朝　陽の出
きらめく海
いきなり船々.

キラキラとし

波,
あるいきから
（船のエンジン音）
ブーンゴブーンゴへ二
コボボーンゴギギシ

海中, さにそそ
ユラユラ
ポニョのの
クラゲ
およぐはくい
（船の音）

ねむっている
ポニョ

さづいて
スクリュー音

さづいて

船尾が
ぐん上を
とびようく

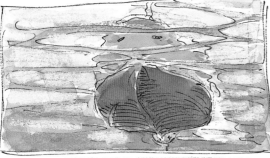

1

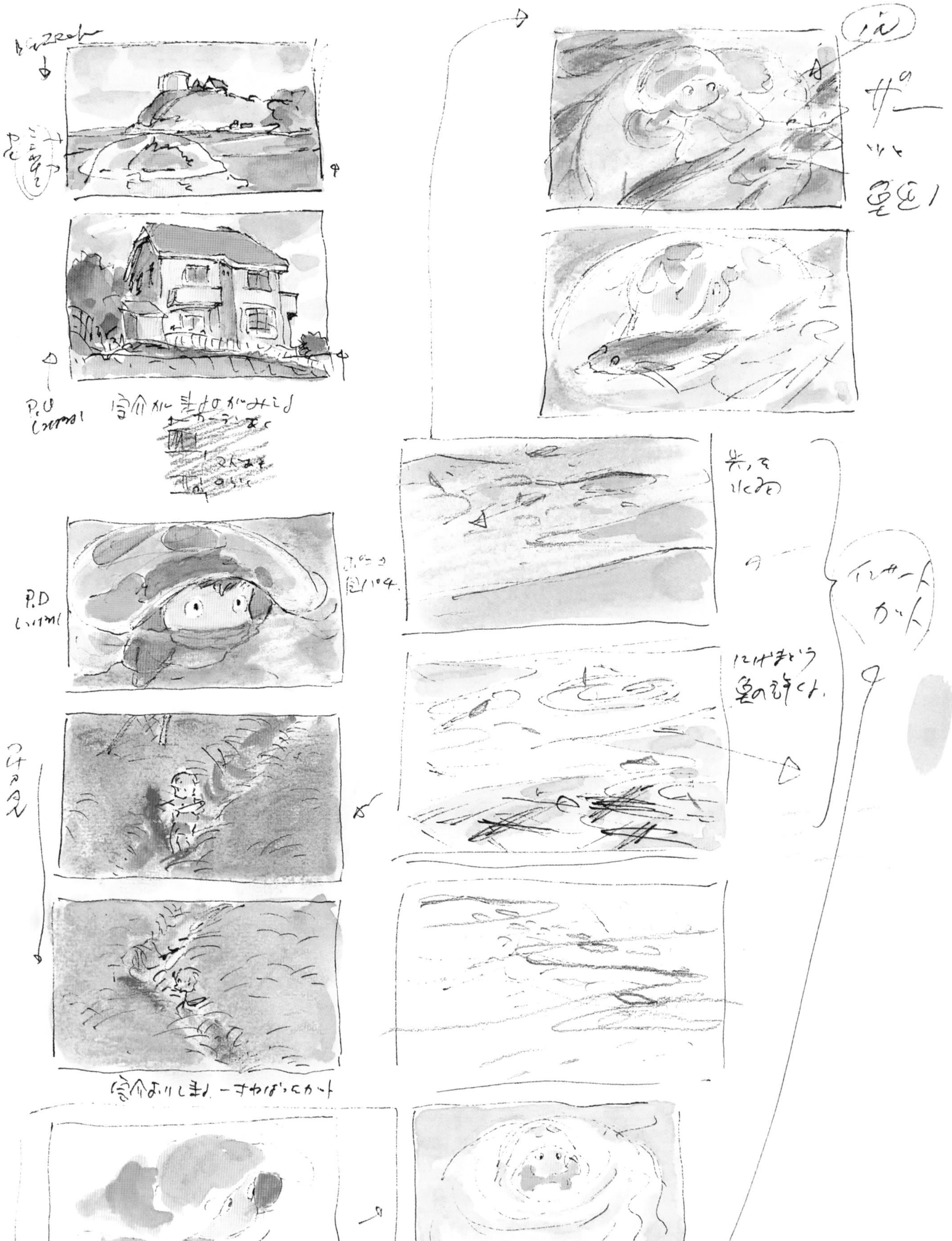

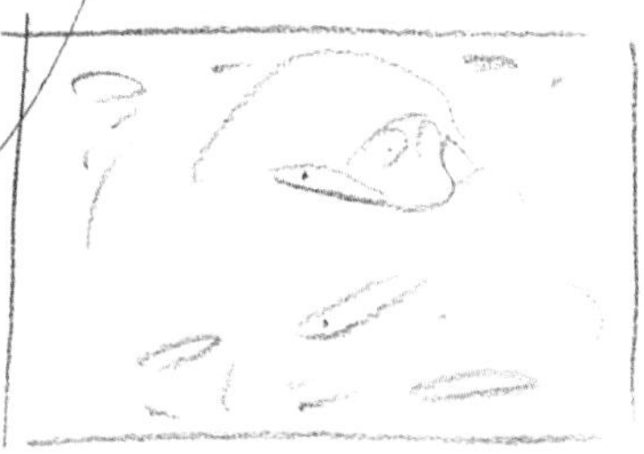

2

1 /The scene, following the opening sequence, in which Ponyo comes to the human world. Drawn in storyboard format, including instructions for sound effects and camera directions [Concept sketches].
2 /The scene in which Ponyo spots Sosuke, also drawn in storyboard format [Concept sketches].

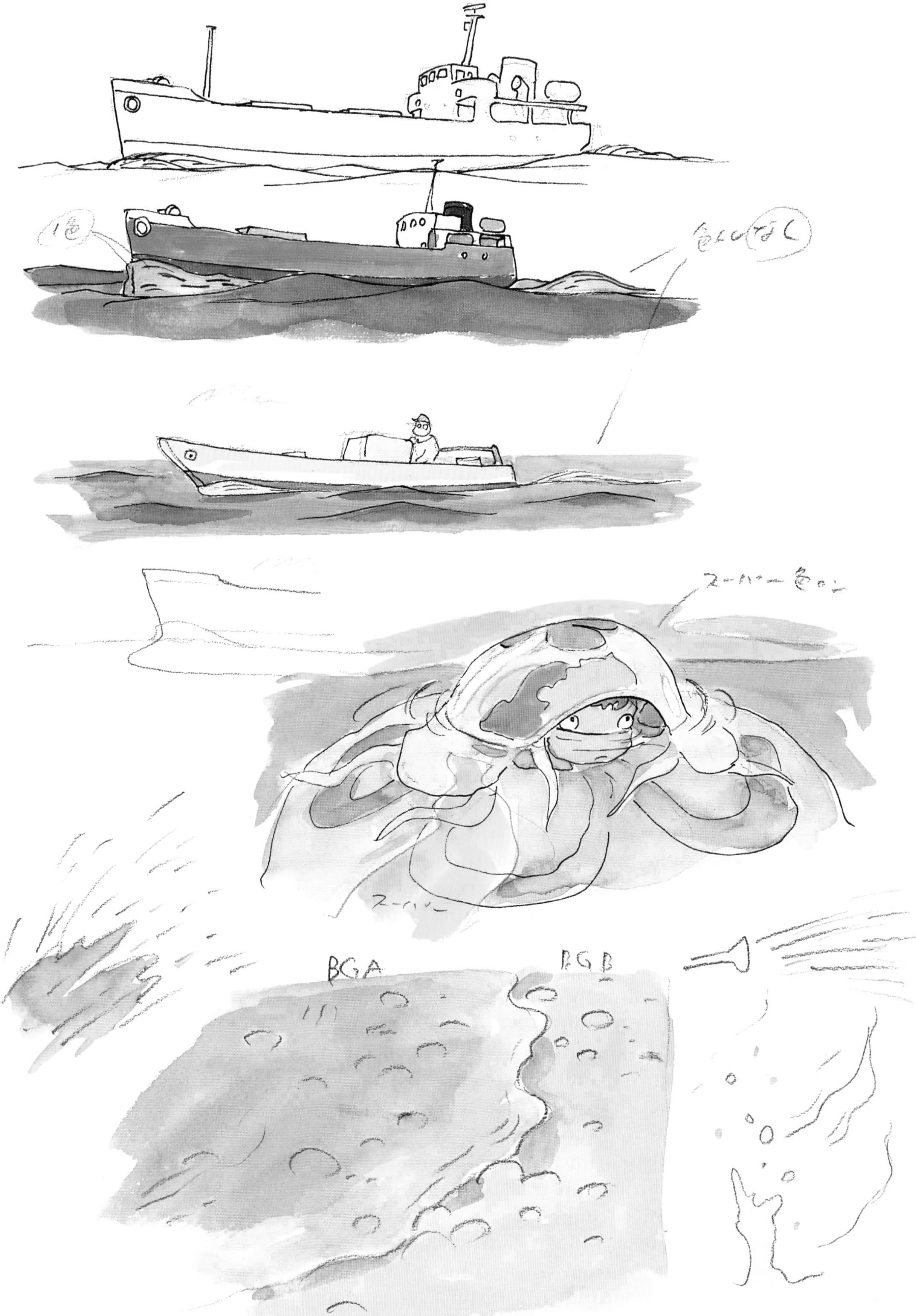
スーパー
BG A
BG B

1

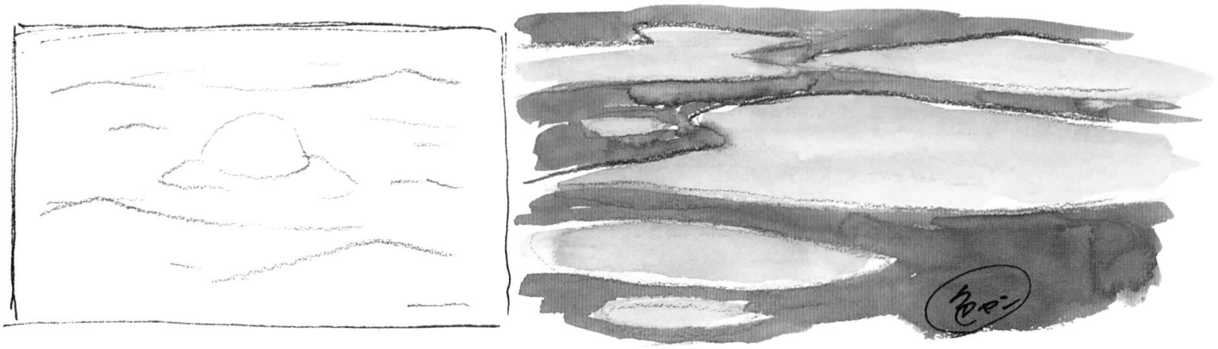
色セン

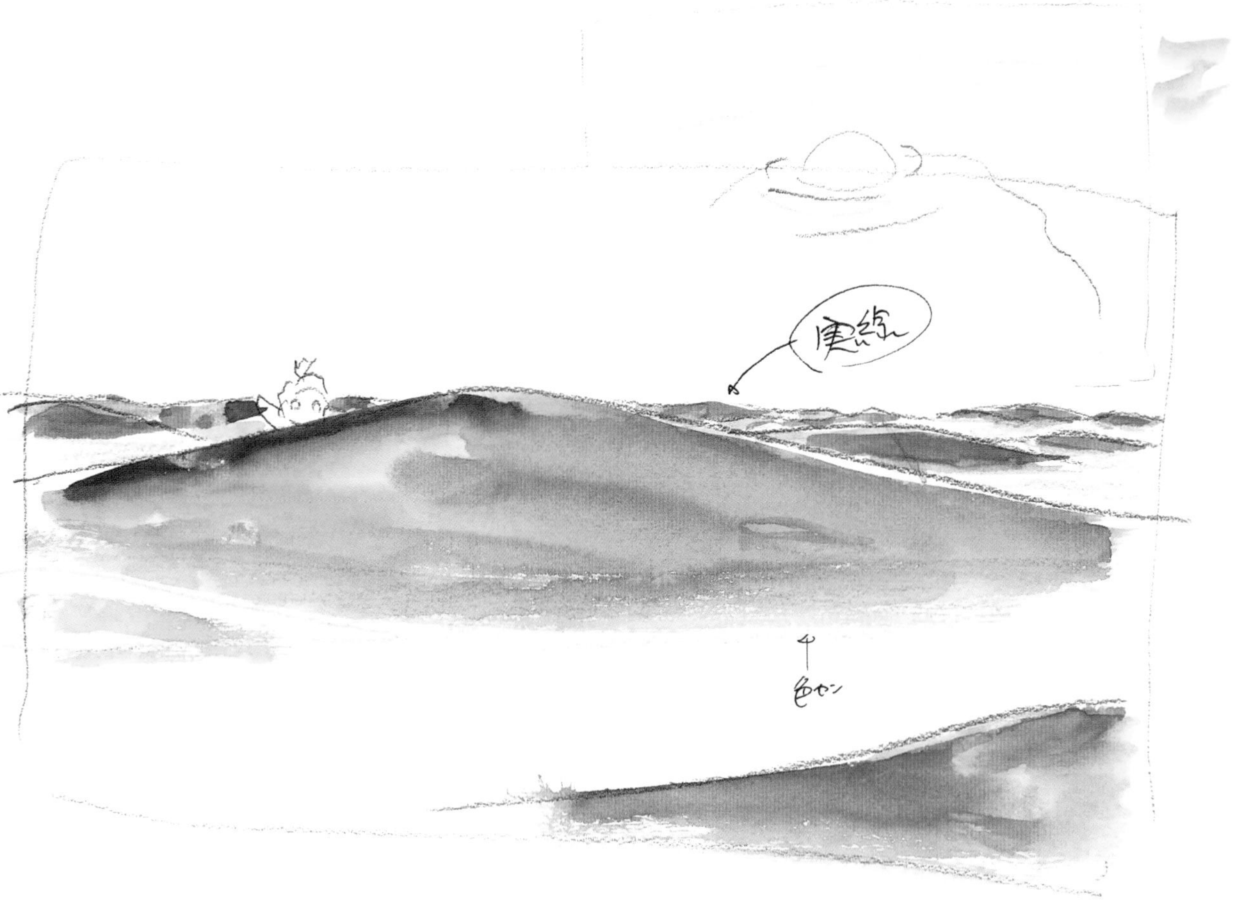
実線
色セン

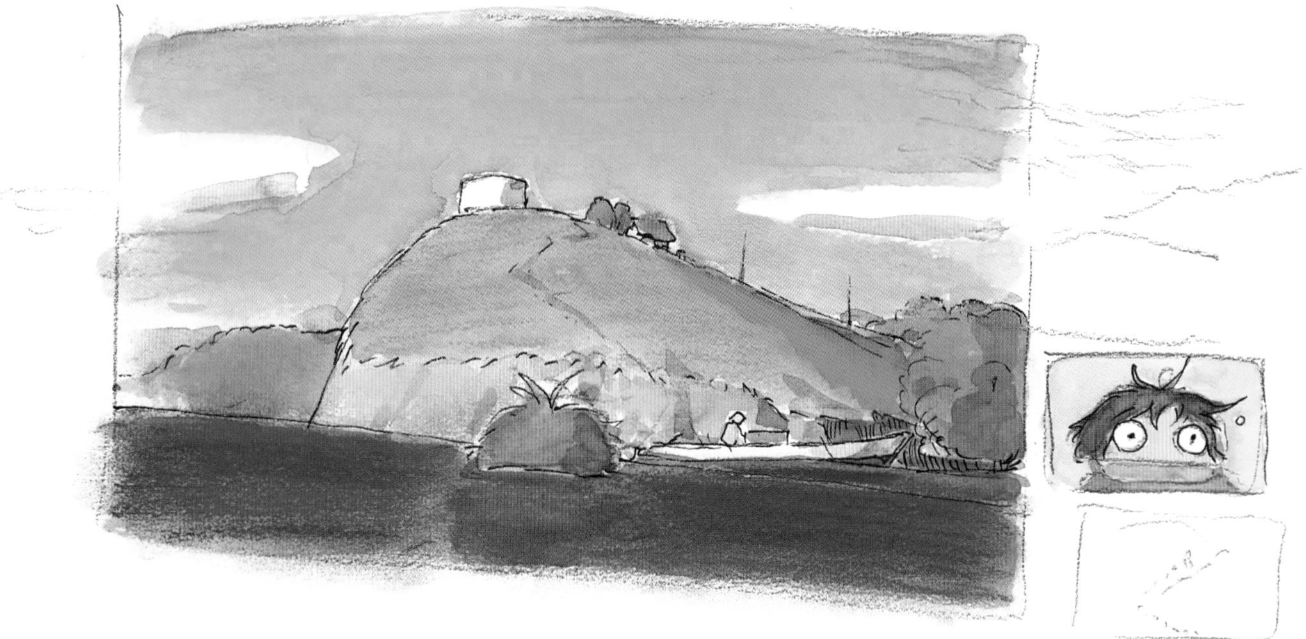

2

1, 2 /Sketches of Ponyo, a passing boat, and waves. The policy of using solid lines and color lines separately is demonstrated here [Concept sketches].

1–3 /Ponyo looks at Sosuke until running into a fishing boat [Concept sketches].
4 /She awakens near the sea's surface and gets caught in the trawl net of a passing fishing boat [Concept sketches].

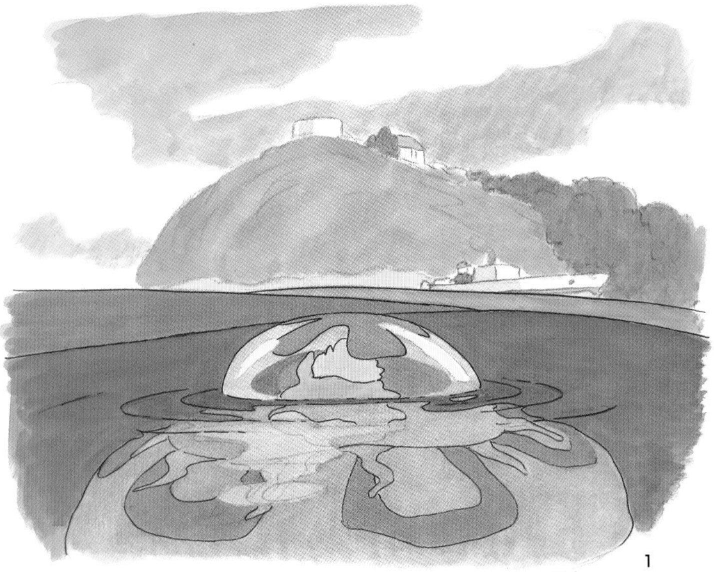

1

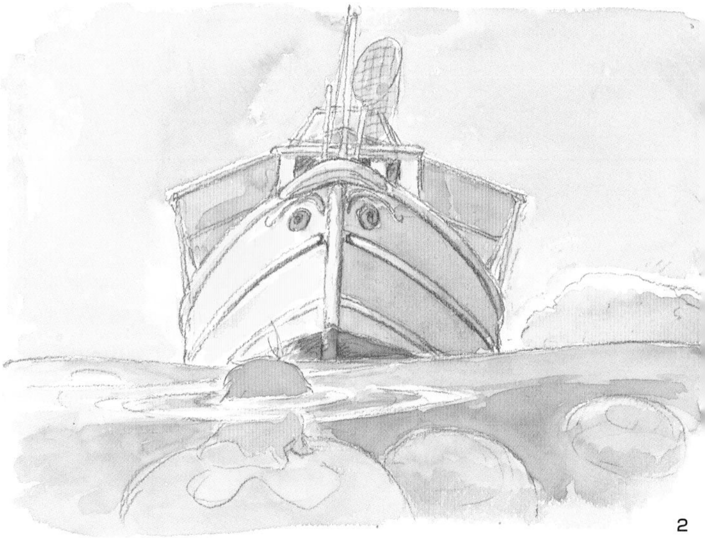

2

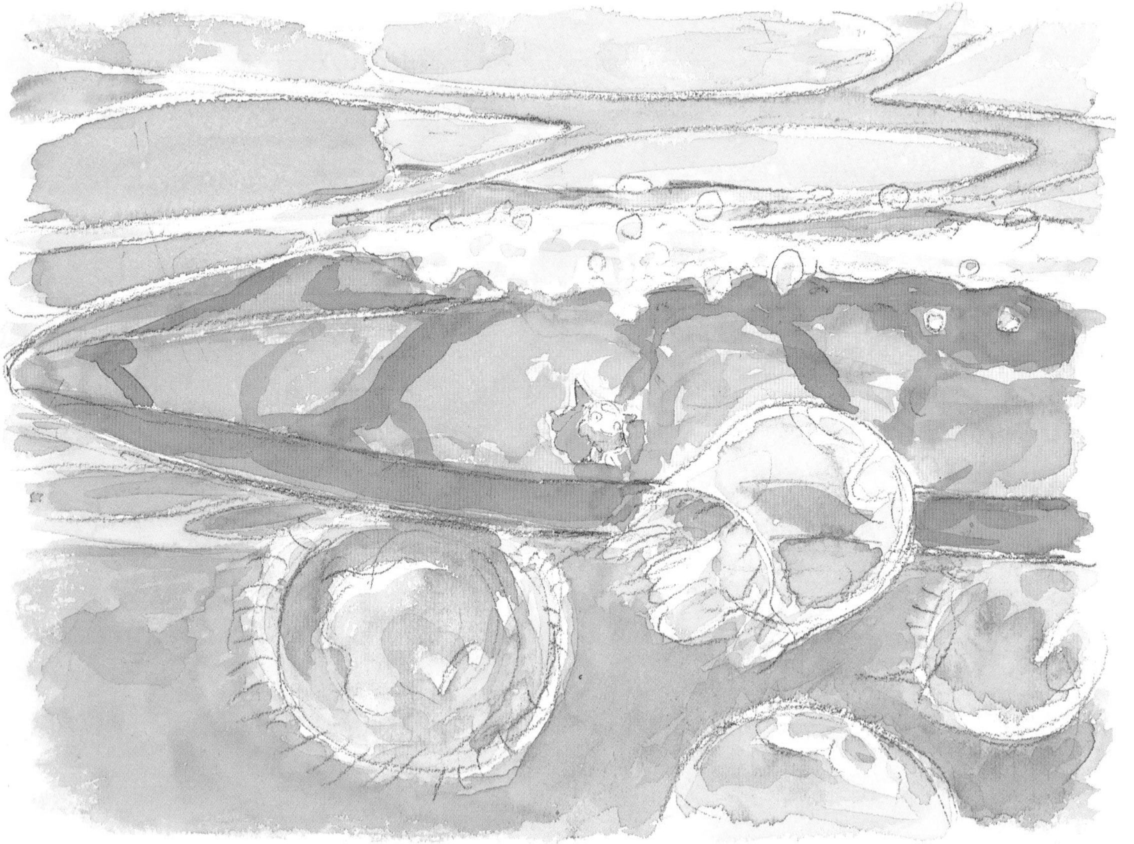

3

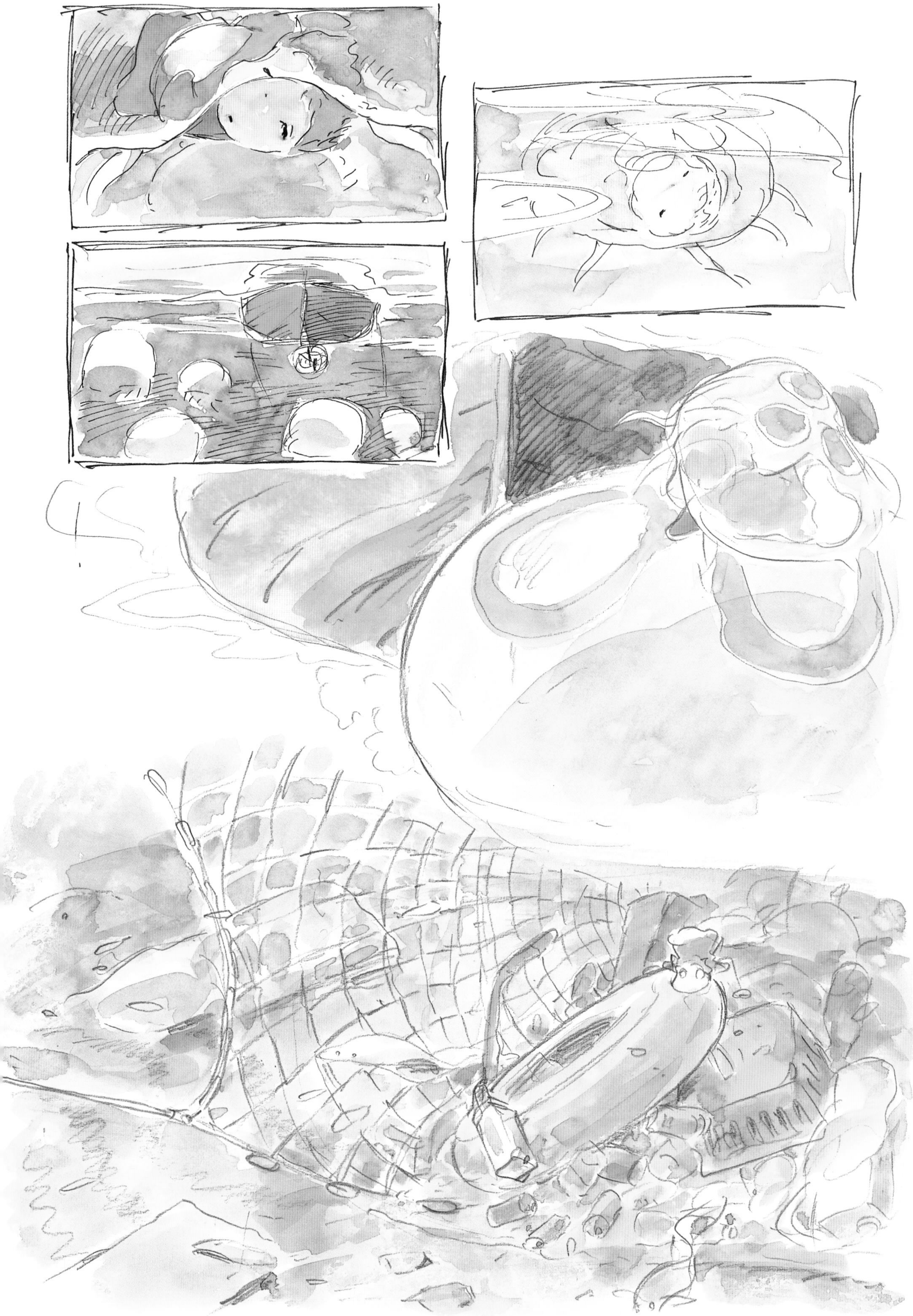

4

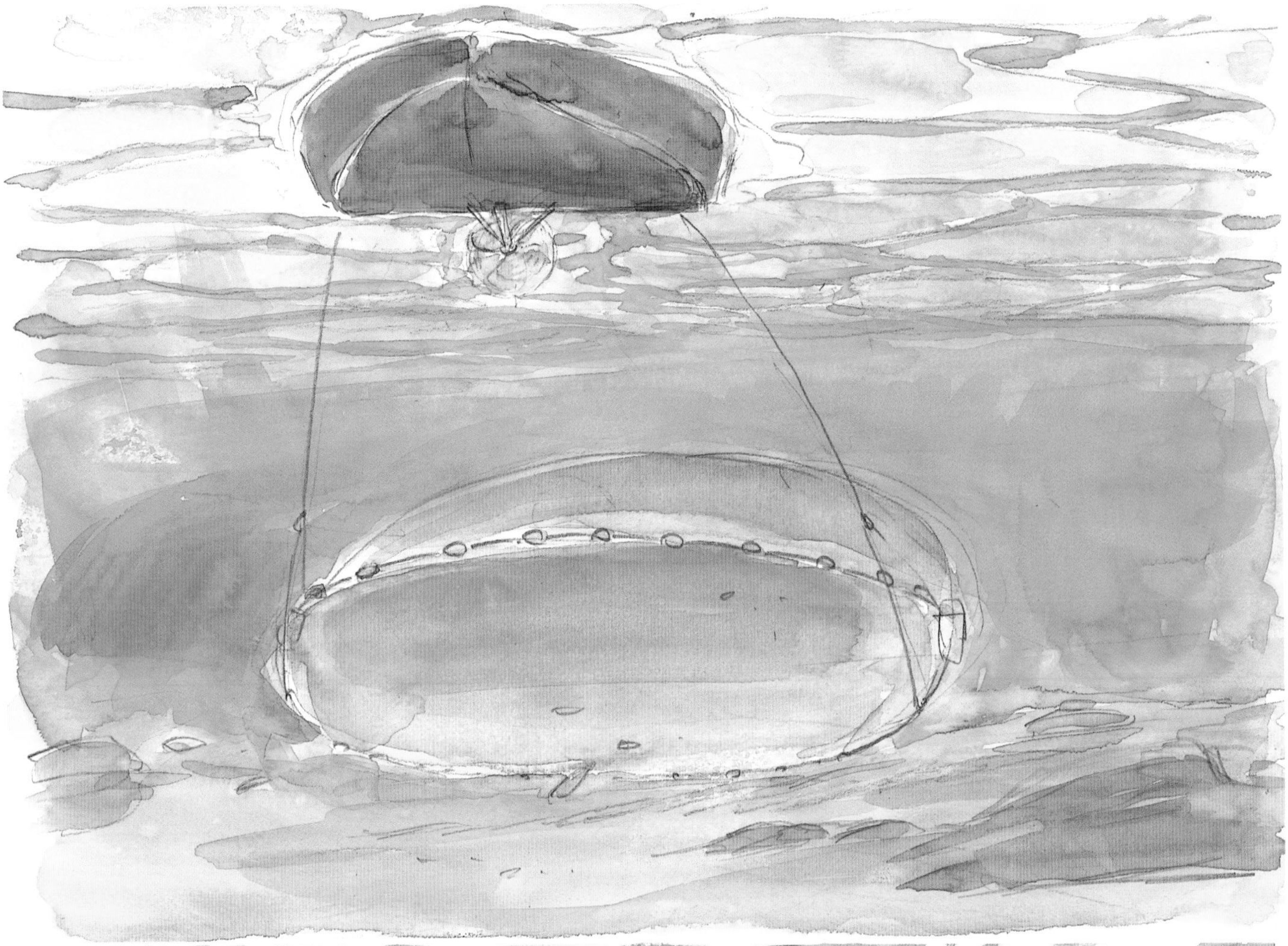

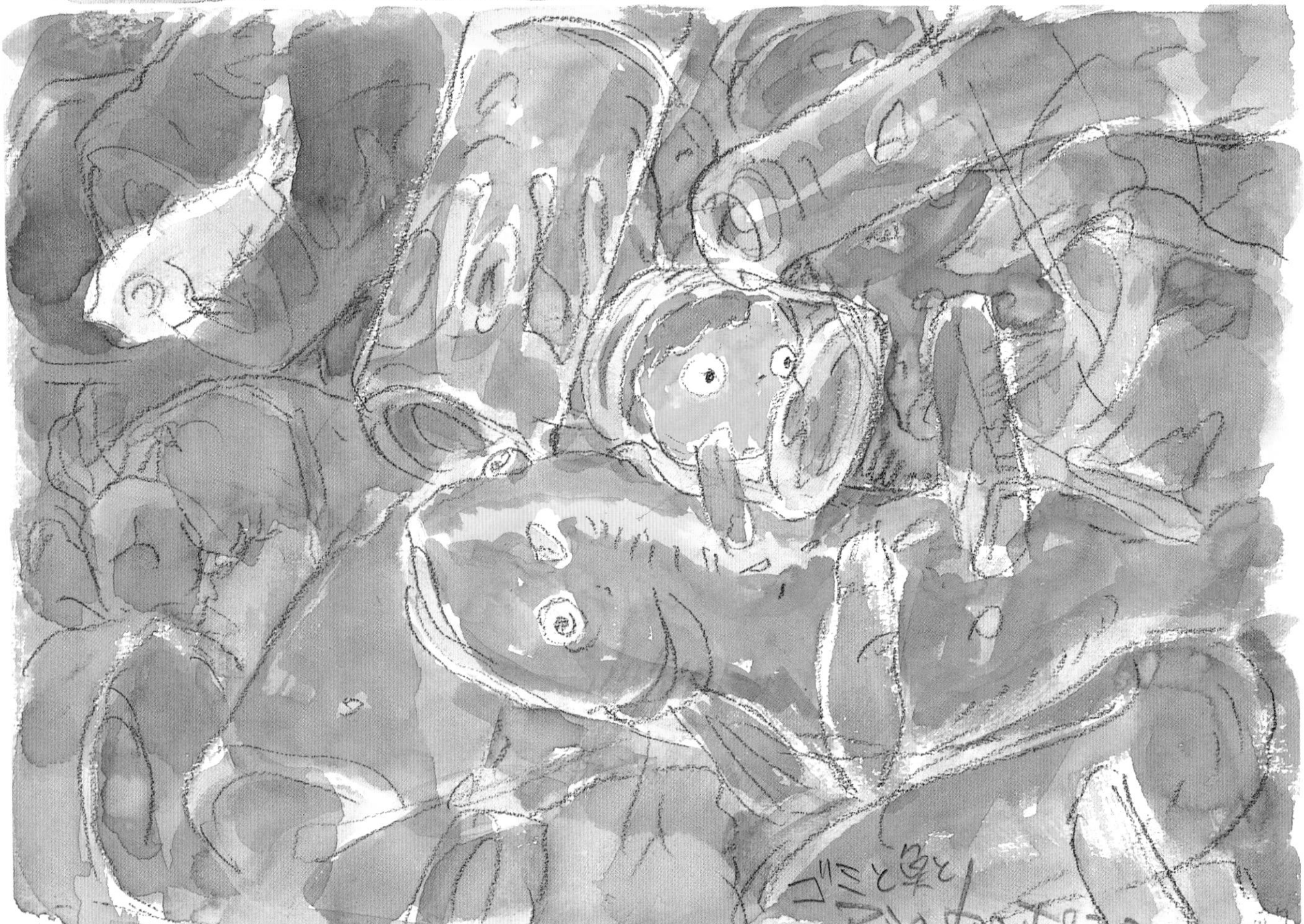
ゴミと魚と

1

To the Human World

1 /The small fishing boat and trawl net seen from Ponyo's point of view. The sea floor is littered with garbage, which was dumped by humans. The net sweeps up the garbage along with the fish from the sea floor [Concept sketch].
2–10 /Swallowed up by the net along with the garbage, Ponyo gets stuck in a jelly jar and cannot get out.

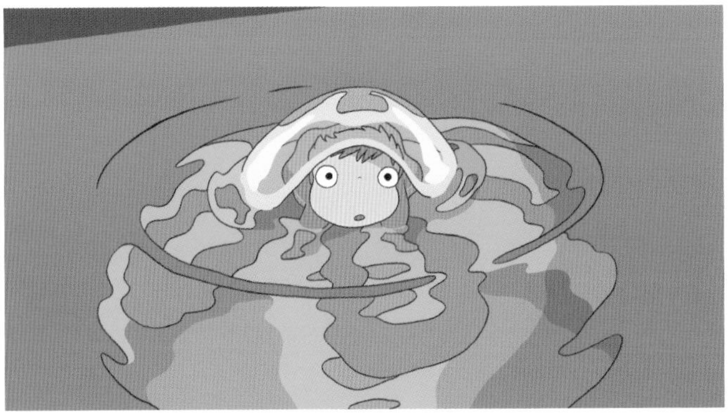

2

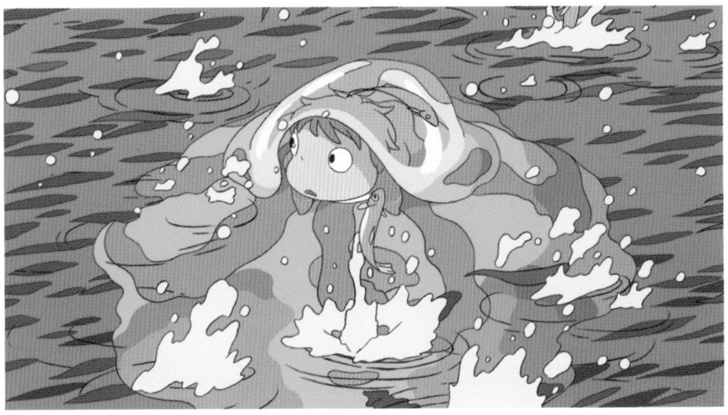

3

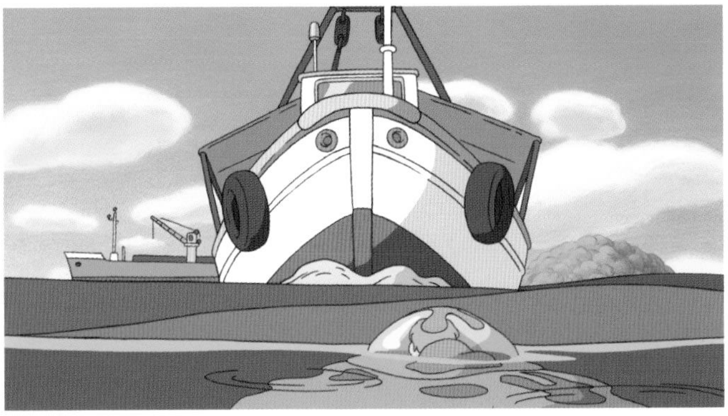

4

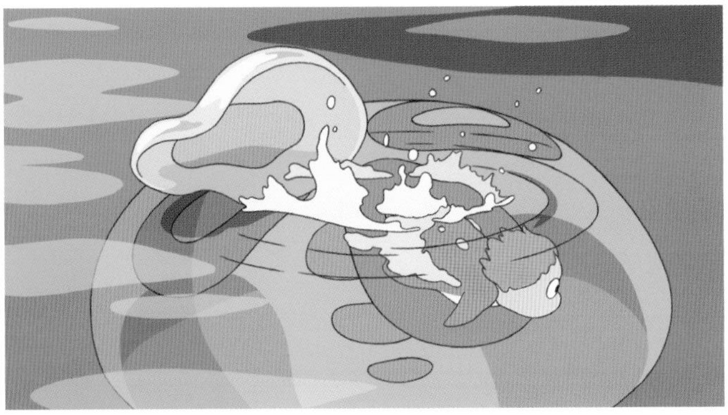

5

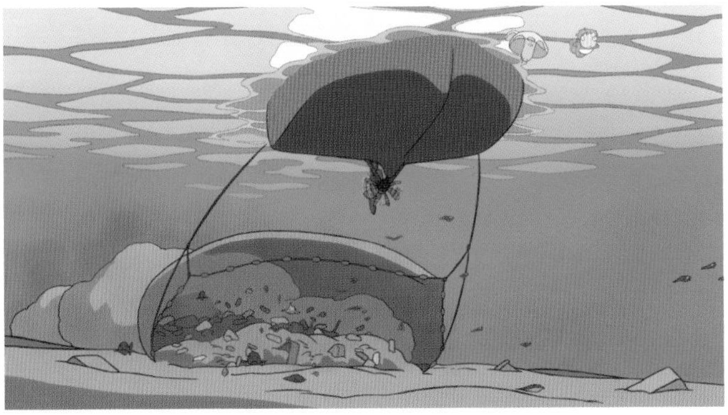

6

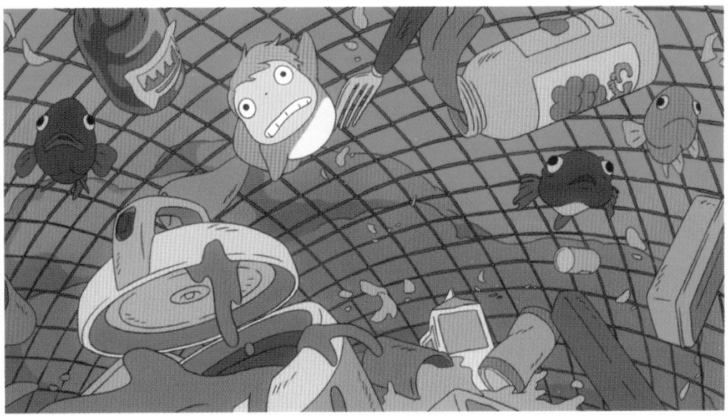

7

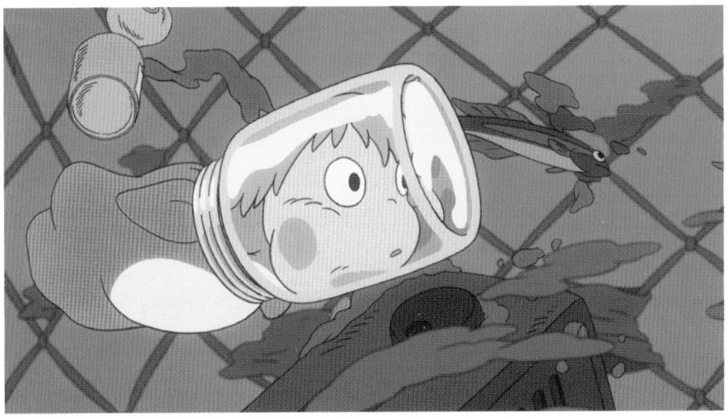

8

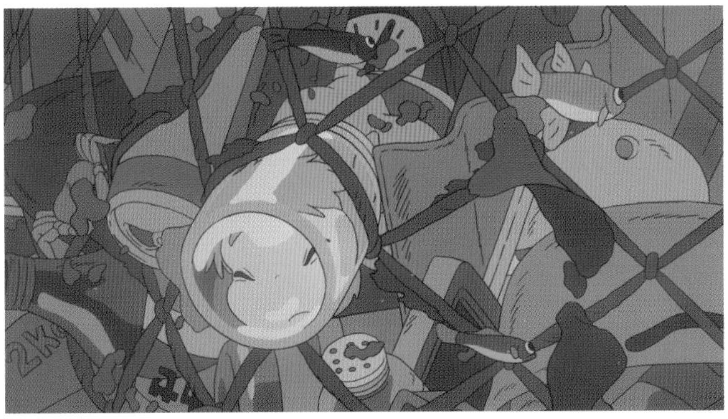

9

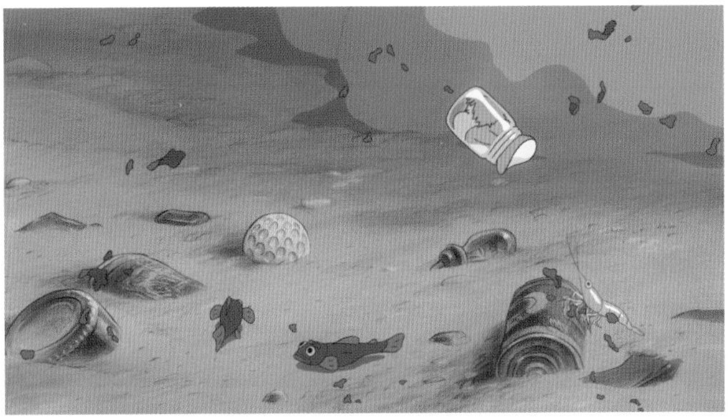

10

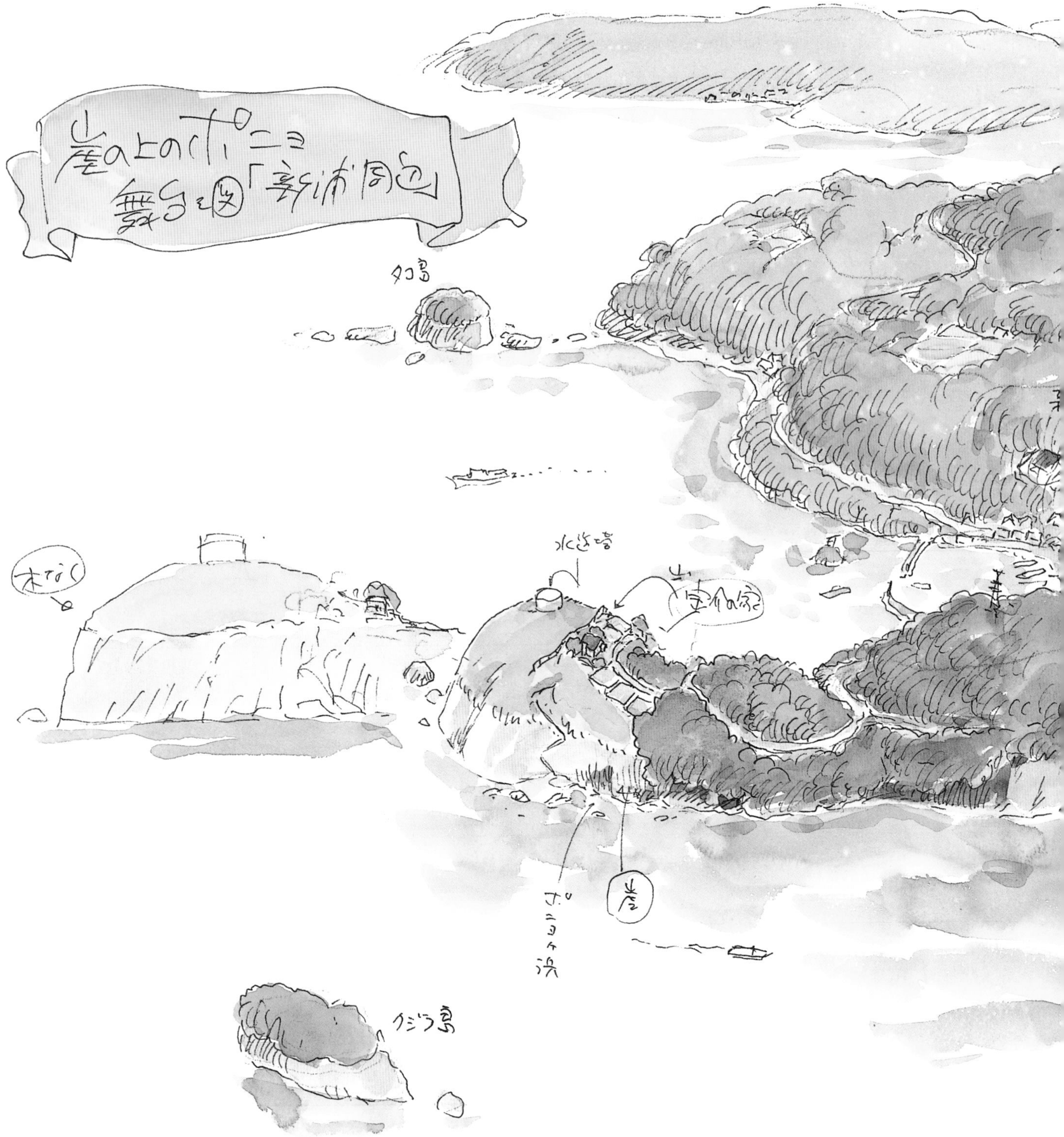
崖の上のポニョ
タコ島
木なし
宗介の家
崖
クジラ島

1 /The port town and its environs, where the story is set [Concept sketch].
2 /Bird's-eye view of the area surrounding Sosuke's house. The structure resembling a fish eye is a water tank [Concept sketch].

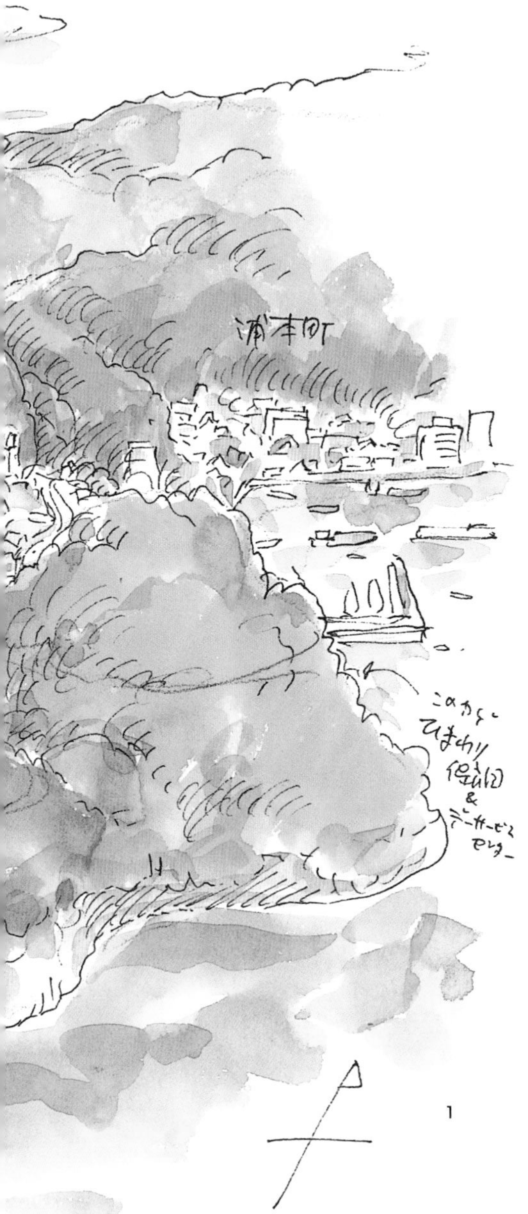
浦本町
このあたり
ひまわり
保育園
&
デイサービス
センター

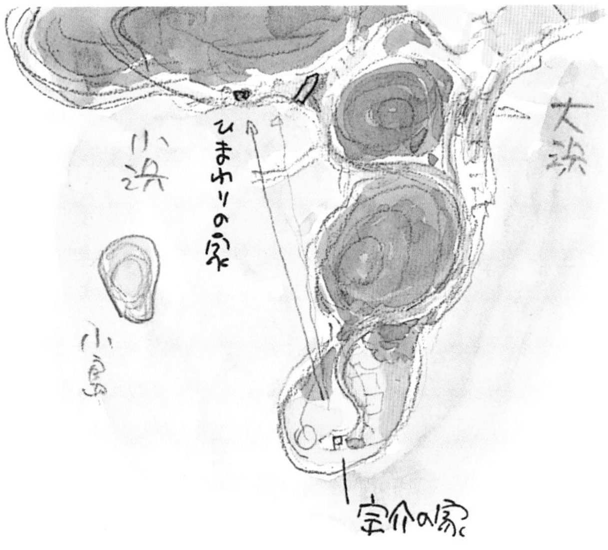
ひまわりの家
小浜
大浜
小島
宗介の家

1

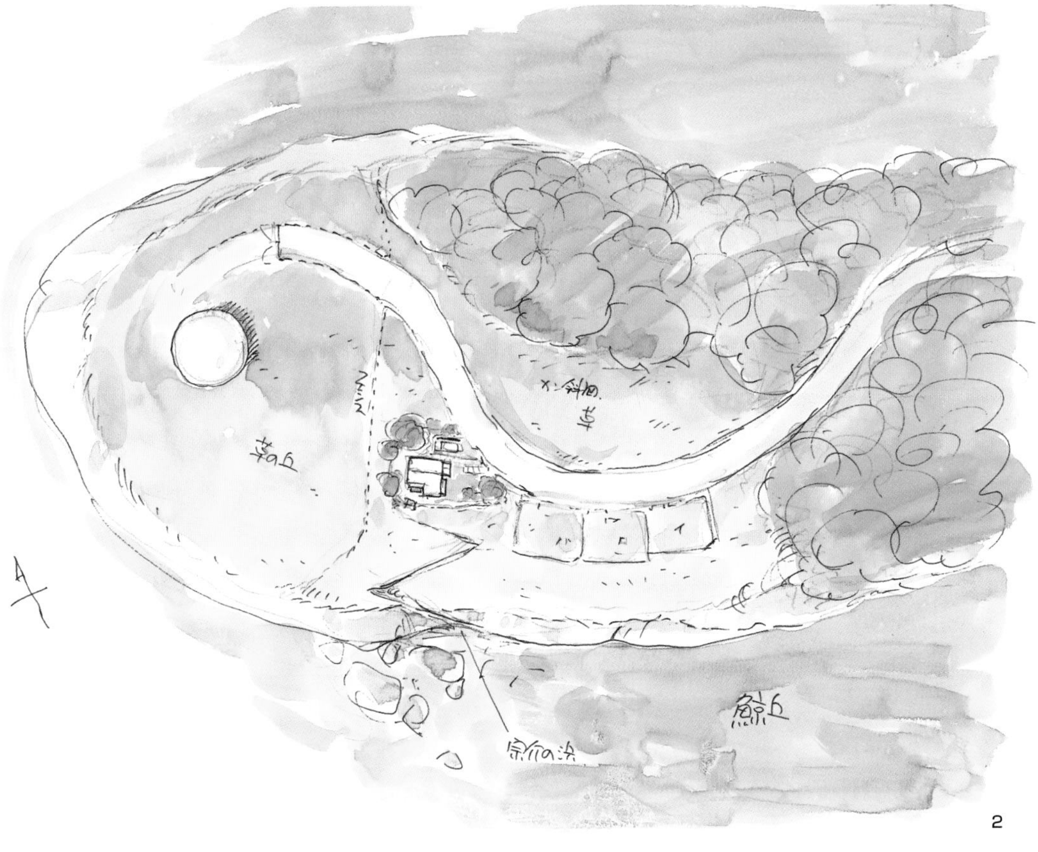
草の丘
ゆるい斜面
草
イ
ロ
ハ
宗介の浜
鯨丘

2

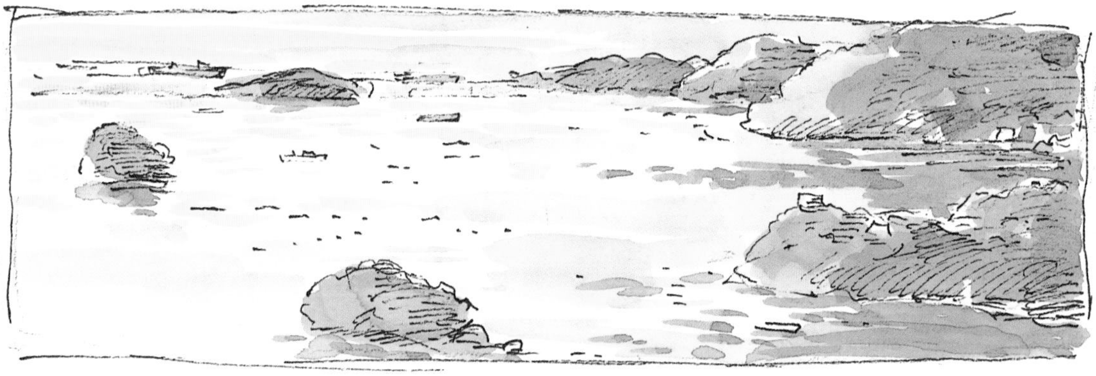

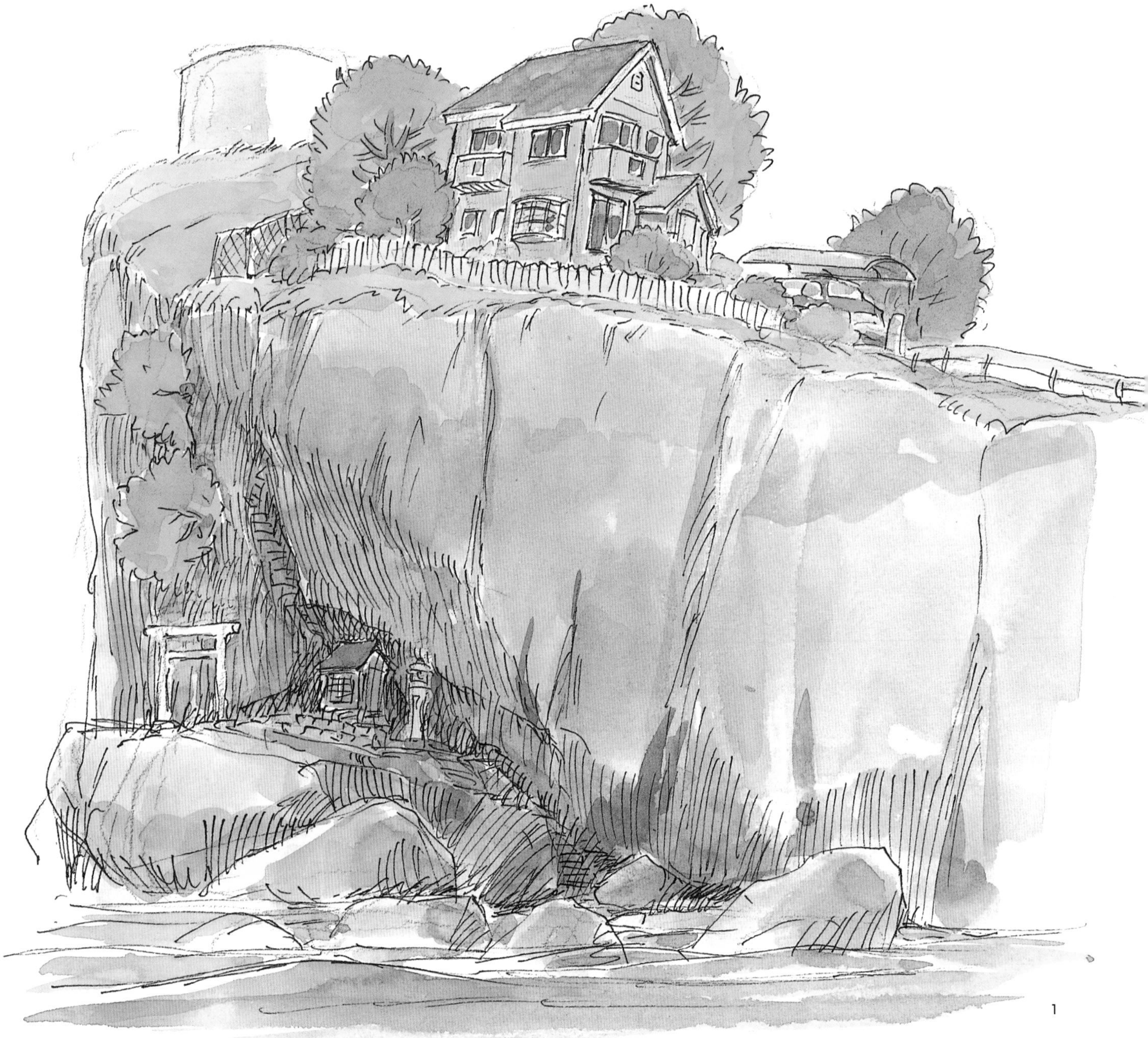

1

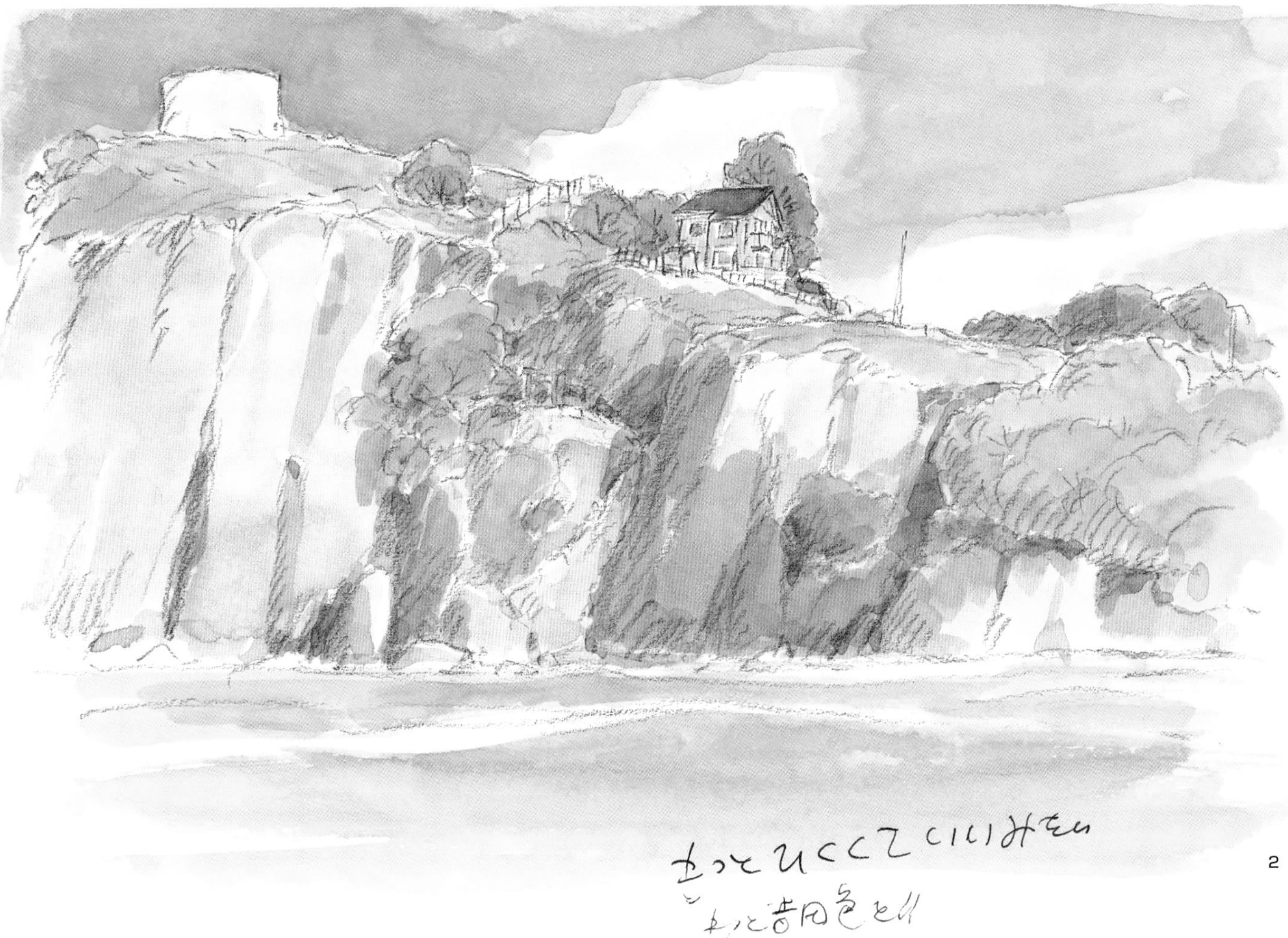
もっとひくくていいみたい

2

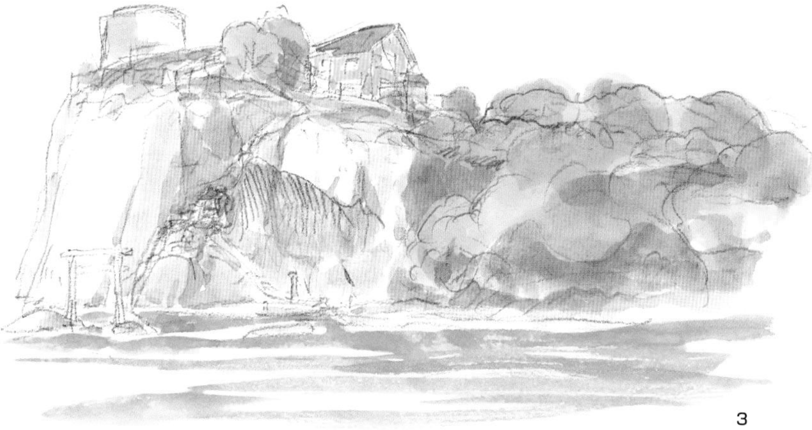

3

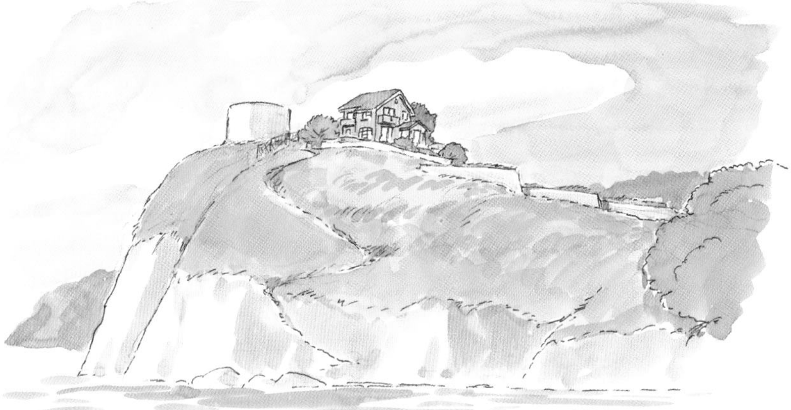

4

The House on the Cliff

1–4 /Perspective sketches of Sosuke's house. Originally, there was a small shrine on the rocky outcropping. Suggestions regarding the height of the cliff and the position of the water tank (white structure) to the house were being considered [Concept sketches].

1 /A view of the bay bathed in the morning light [Concept art].
2 /Perspective art of Sosuke's house as seen from the sea [Concept art].

The setting of the port town was based on a small town along the Seto Inland Sea, which we actually visited as research. There was the bay, docks, and the town sloping up into the mountains. I drew sketches while trying to recall the color of the sea close to where I was born and how the waves looked there. But the way we rendered the color of the not-so-blue sea, and the way the waves surge like huge shadows, were the results of our research trip.

Since the world of Ponyo has an overall soft, storybook quality, the characters lack shading. We elected not to use very sharp colors. We also drew simple, round clouds rather than realistic-looking ones. The roof of Sosuke's house was originally black. Although many roofs actually are black, it lacked visual impact. So I tried red, and Miyazaki said, "That looks better." He's always liked red triangular roofs and also used them in *My Neighbor Totoro*. A house on a cliff with an ocean view. While Sosuke's house may be an inconvenient place to live [*laughs*], in a way, it may be an ideal landscape for Miyazaki.
— Art Director: Noboru Yoshida

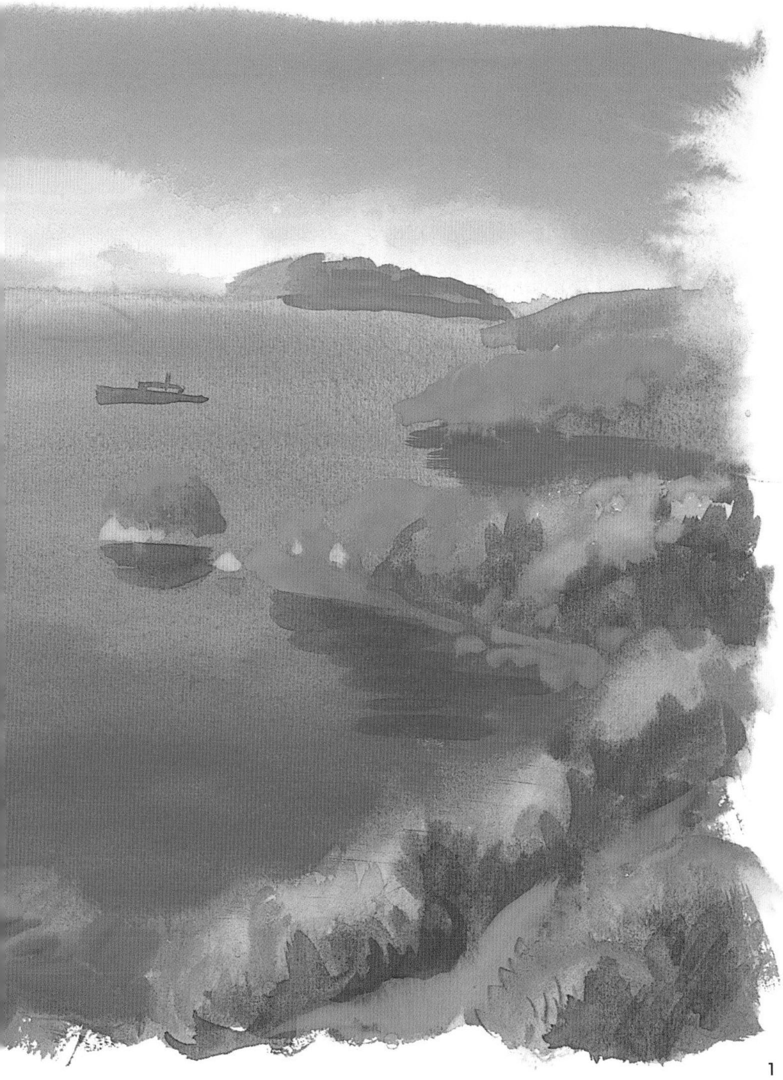

1

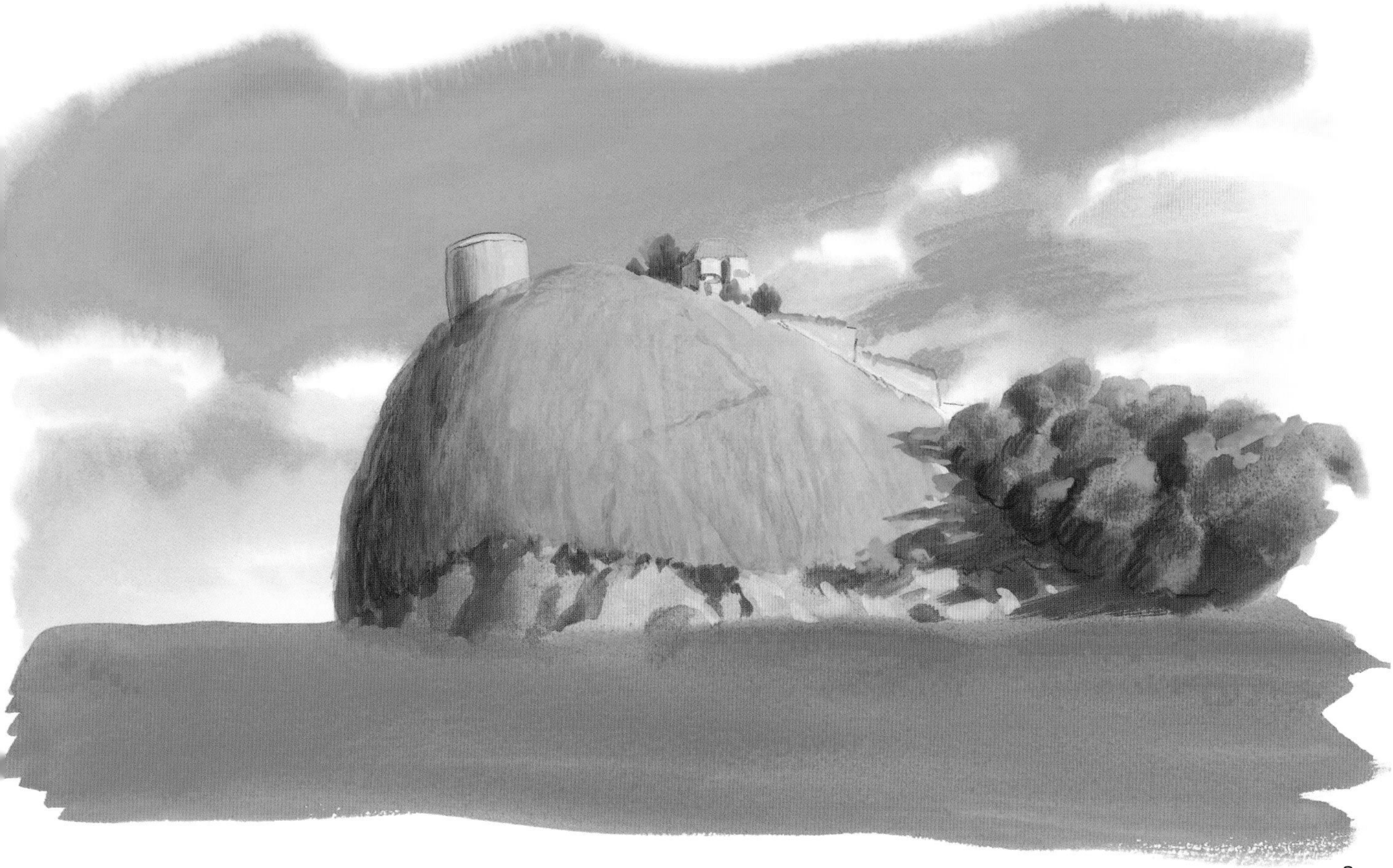

2

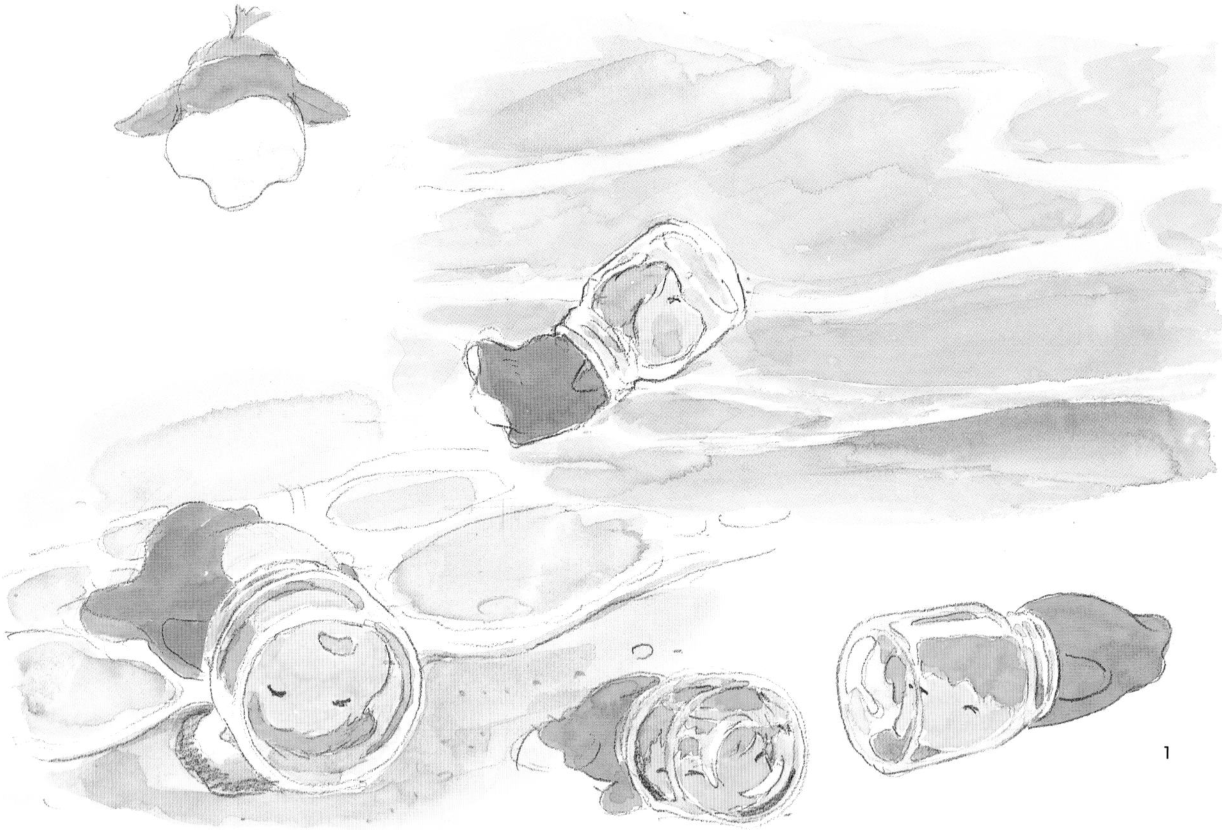

1

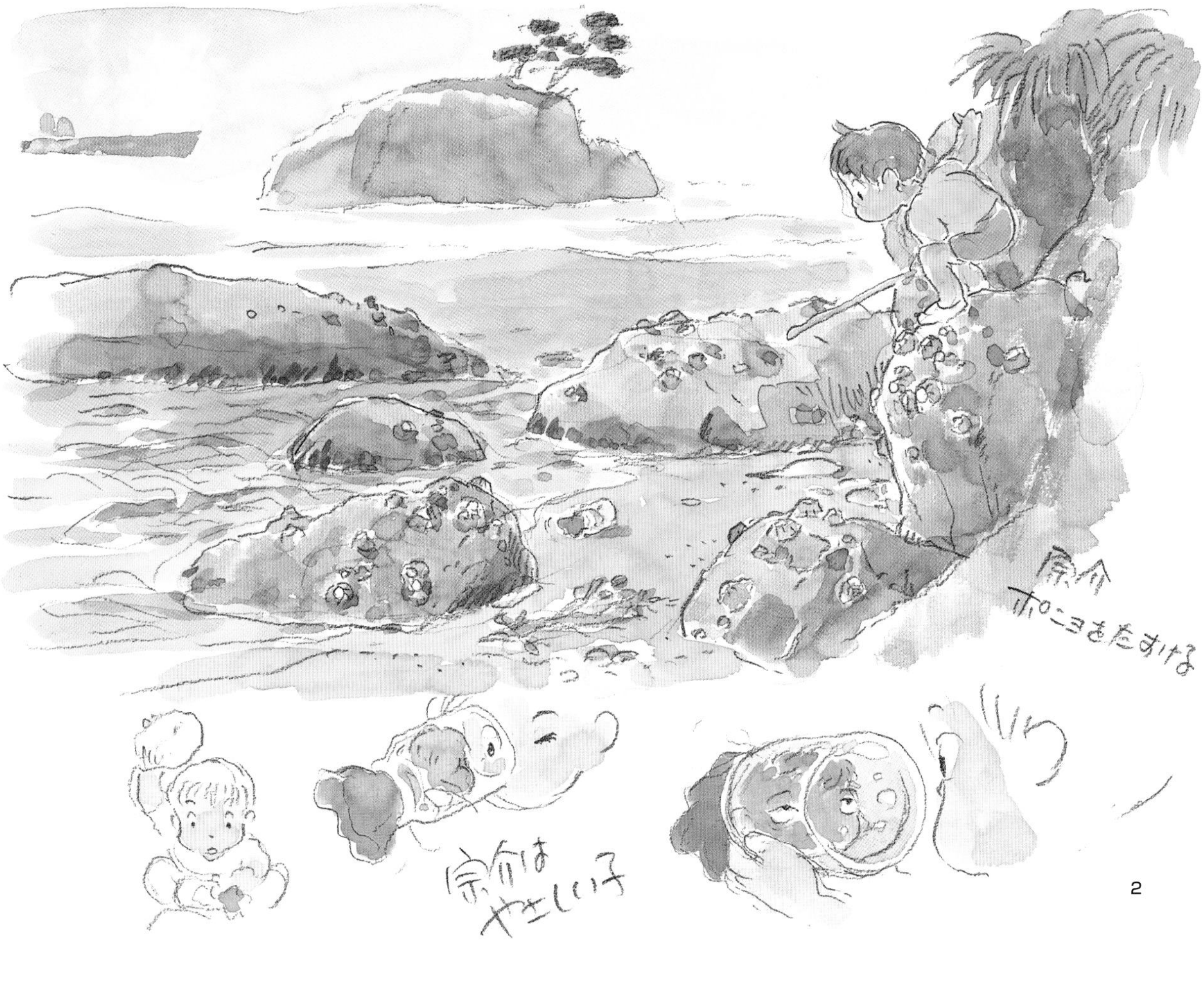
宗介
ポニョをたすける
宗介は
やさしい子

2

1 /Ponyo remains stuck in the jar as she washes ashore [Concept sketch].
2 /Sosuke finds Ponyo [Concept sketch].
3 /Sosuke breaks the jar to rescue Ponyo and takes her home. The moment Ponyo licks the blood from Sosuke's wounded finger, her magical powers are awakened [Concept sketch].

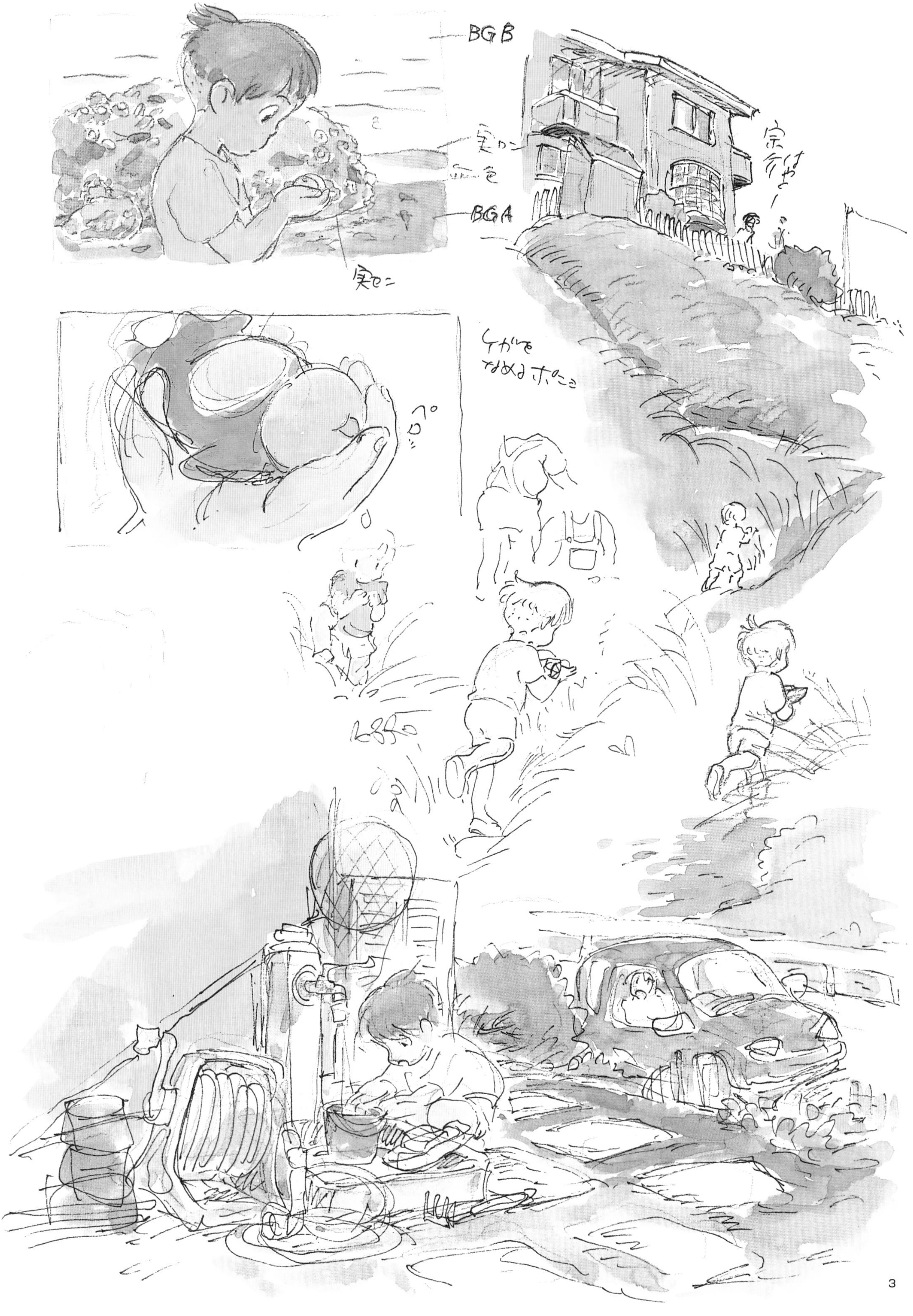
BG B
実カン
血色
BG A
実セニ
宗介はやく!
ケガをなめるポニョ
ペロ

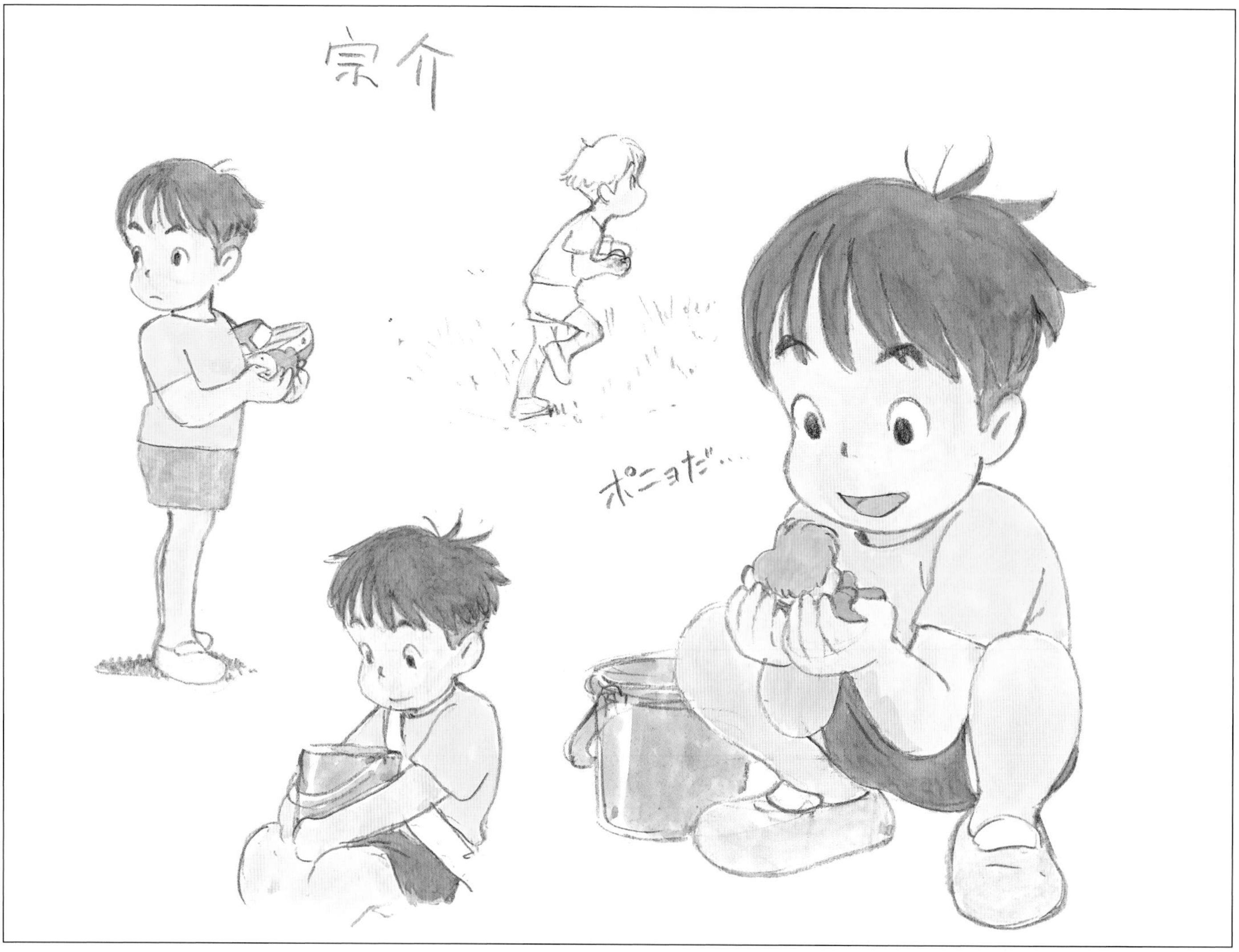
宗介
ポニョだ…

1

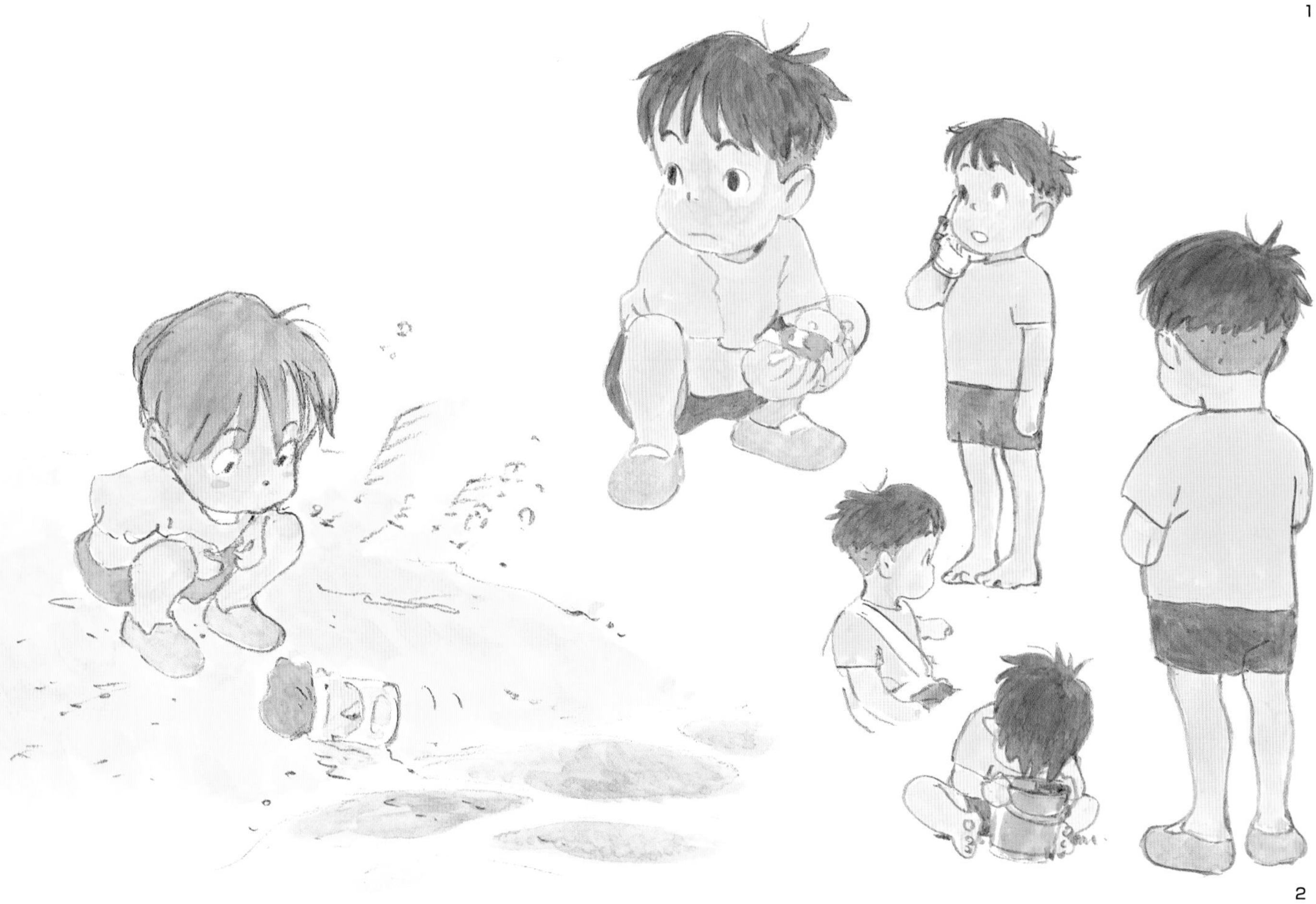

2

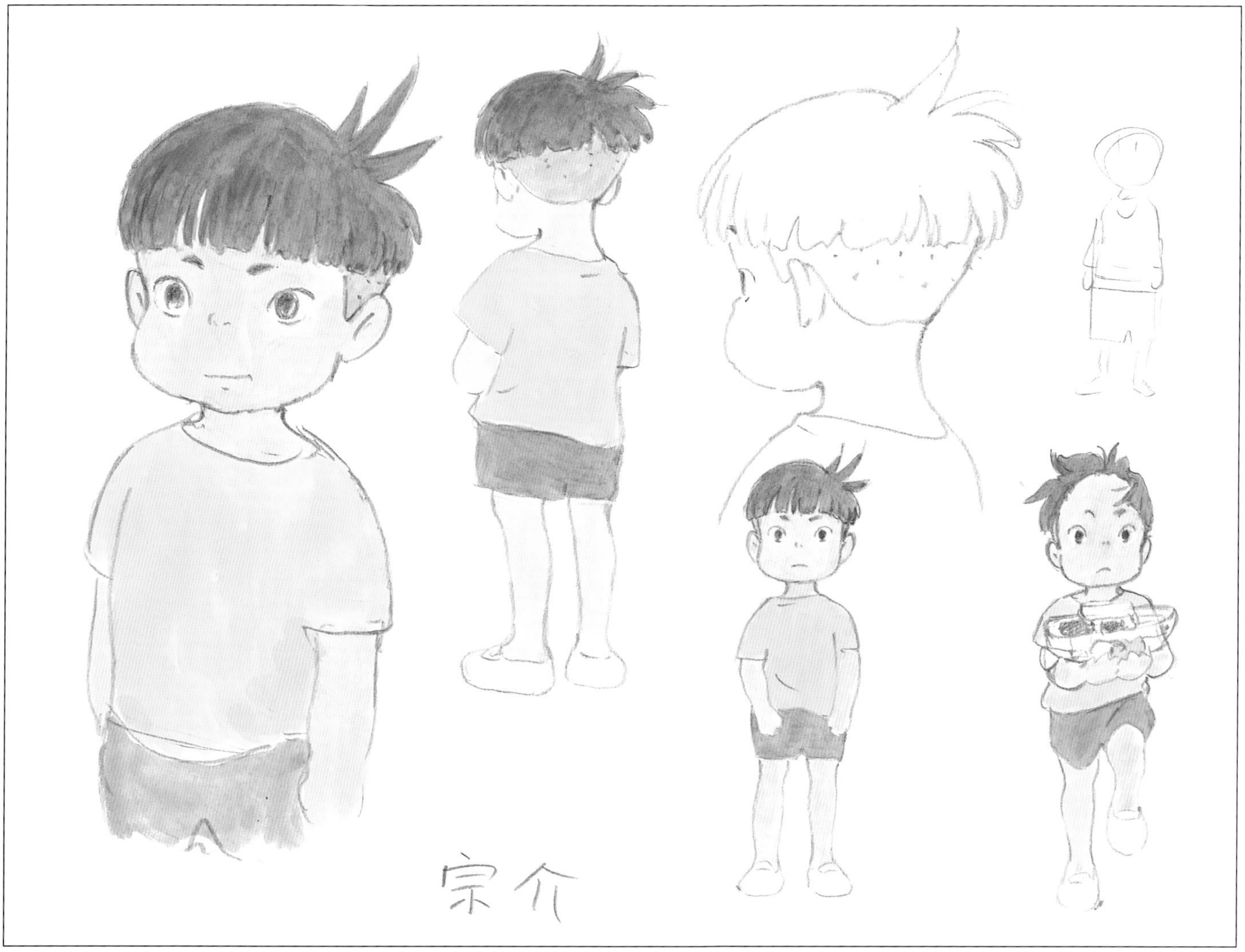
宗介

3

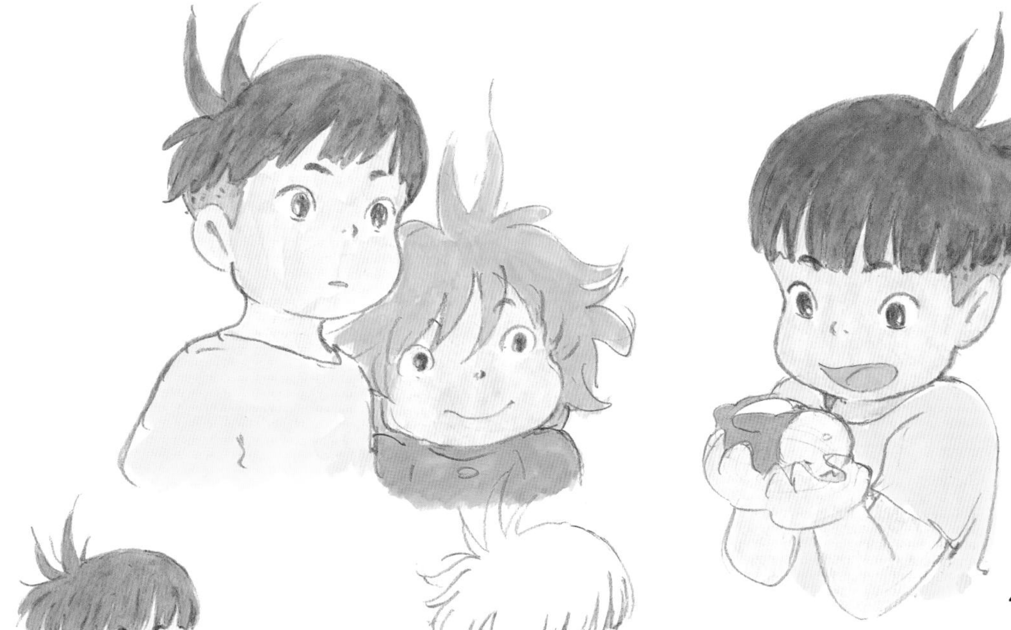

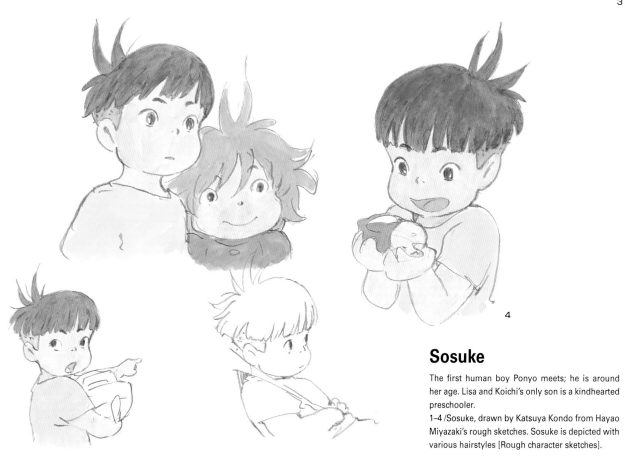

4

Sosuke

The first human boy Ponyo meets; he is around her age. Lisa and Koichi's only son is a kindhearted preschooler.

1–4 /Sosuke, drawn by Katsuya Kondo from Hayao Miyazaki's rough sketches. Sosuke is depicted with various hairstyles [Rough character sketches].

The Encounter with Ponyo

1–6 /Sosuke, who goes to the shore to play with his toy steamboat in the moments before going to school. There, he finds a goldfish-like creature trapped inside a glass jar and rescues it, cutting his finger. This is Sosuke's fateful encounter with Ponyo.

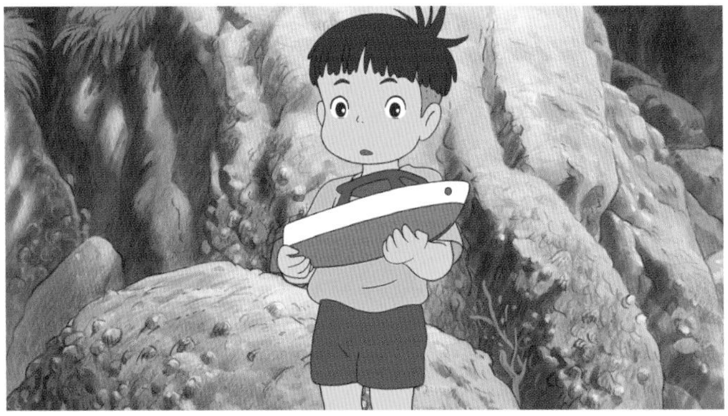

1

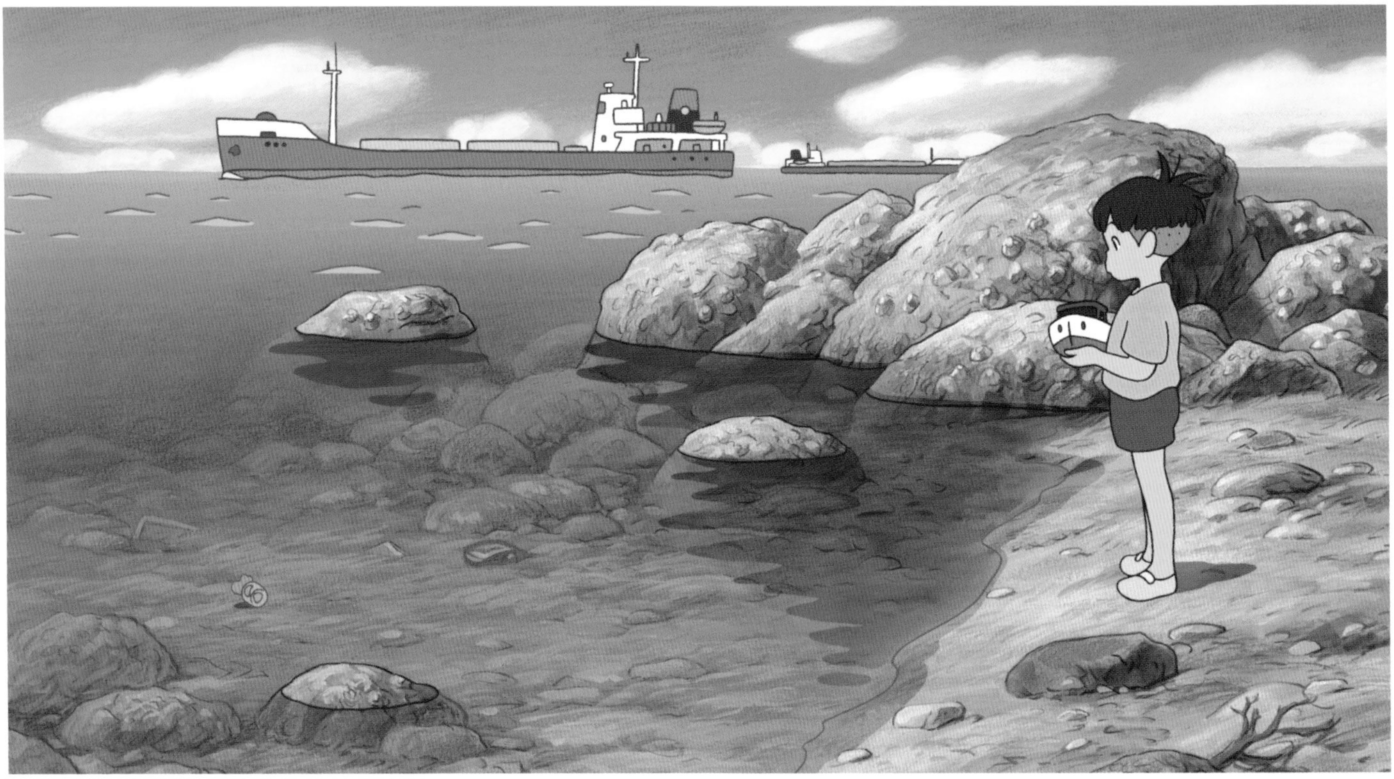

2

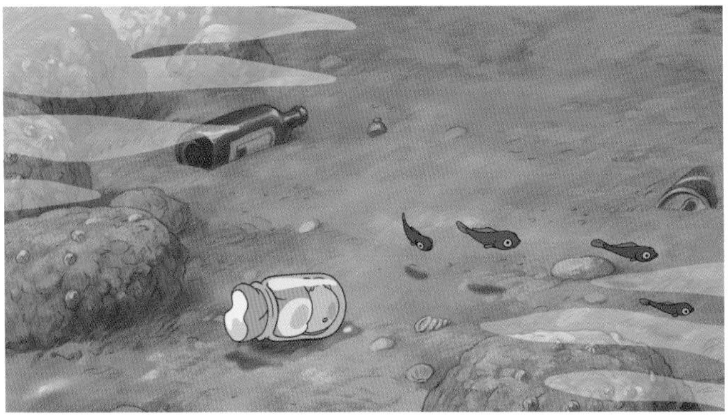

3

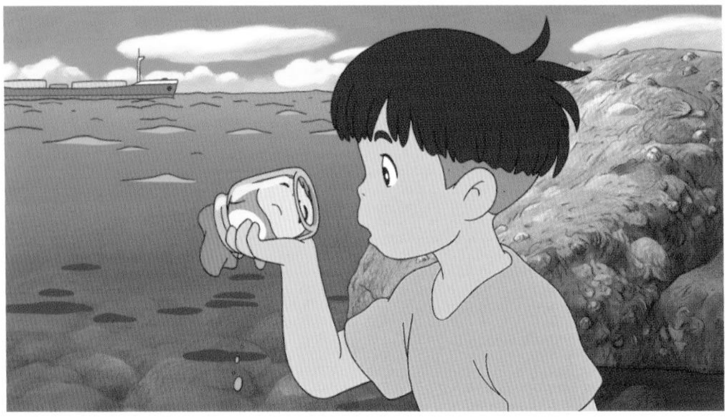

4

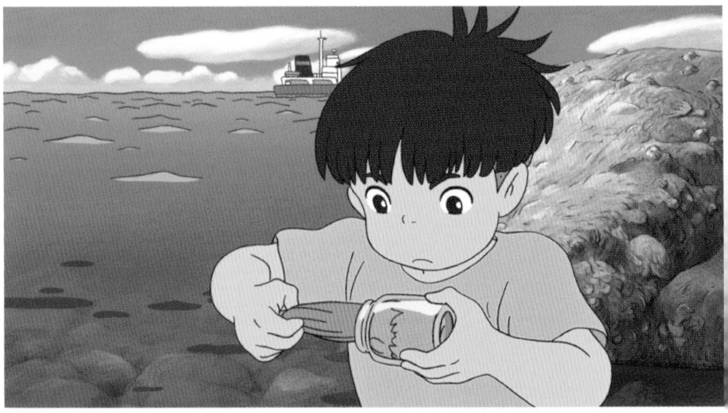

5

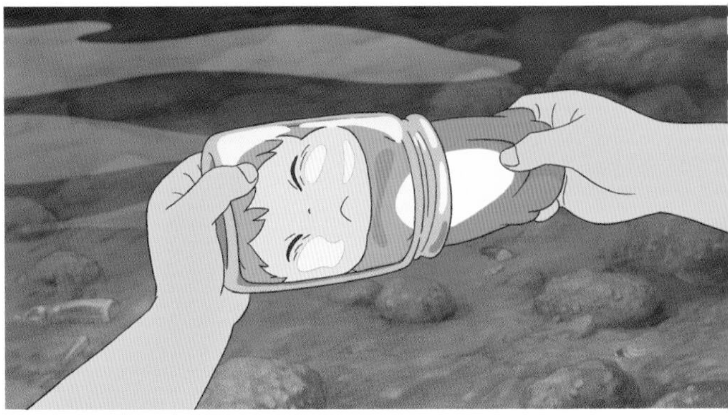

6

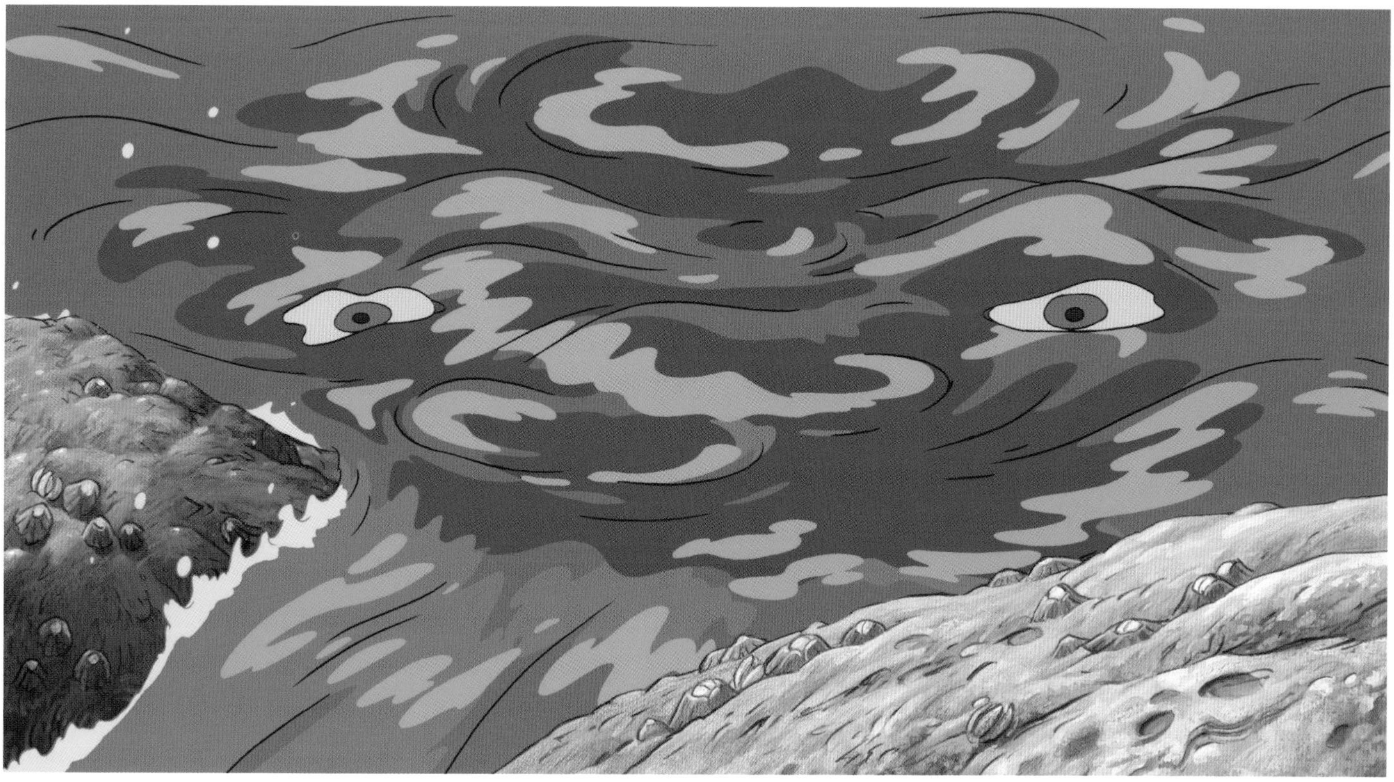

7

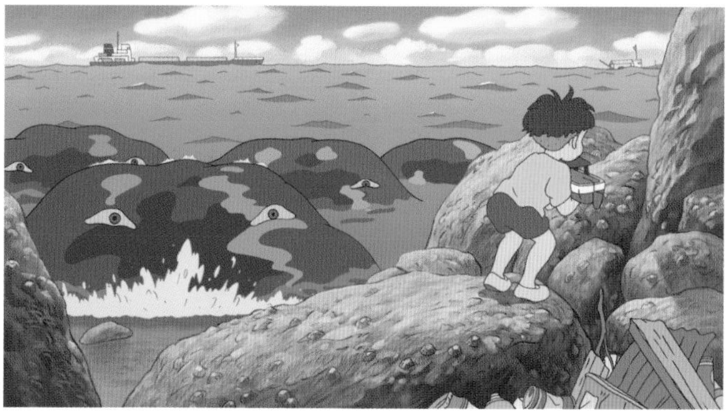

8

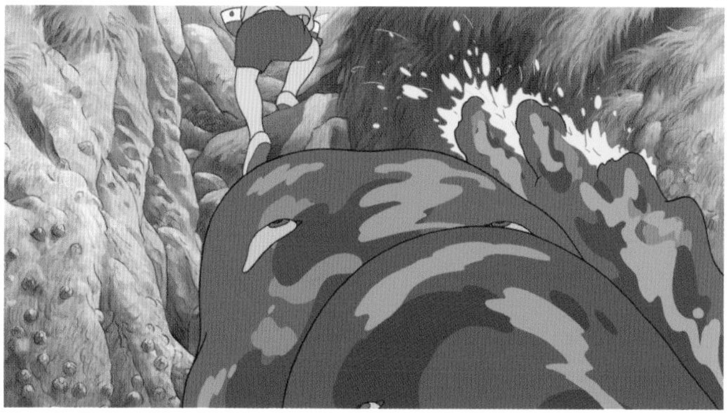

9

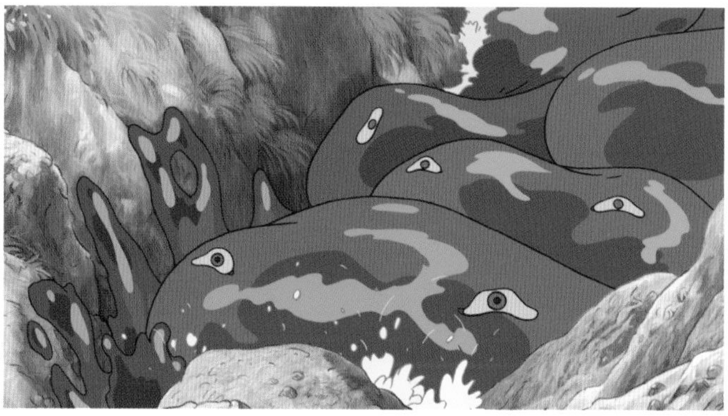

10

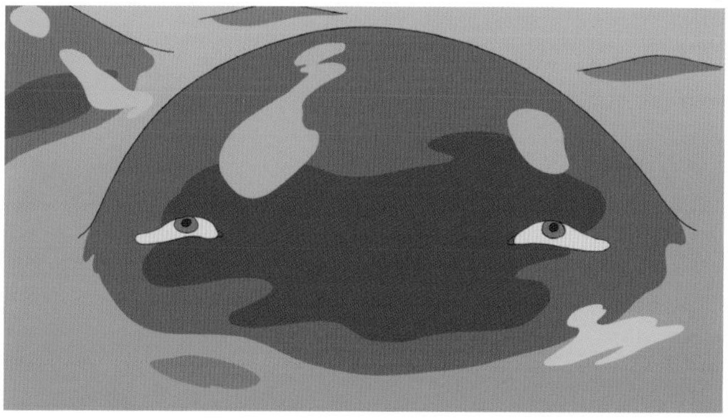

11

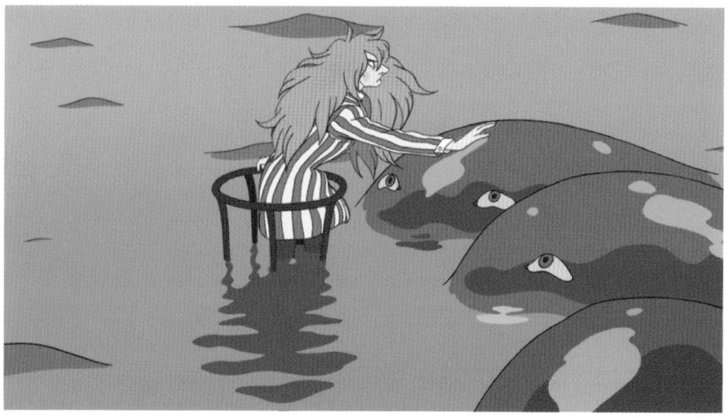

12

Minions

Aquatic creatures loyal to Fujimoto. They are made of water and take on the form of sea monsters when brought to life by Fujimoto's magic.
7–12 /Fujimoto dispatches the minions to retrieve Ponyo, but Sosuke takes Ponyo without noticing the monsters, who appear to him as waves.

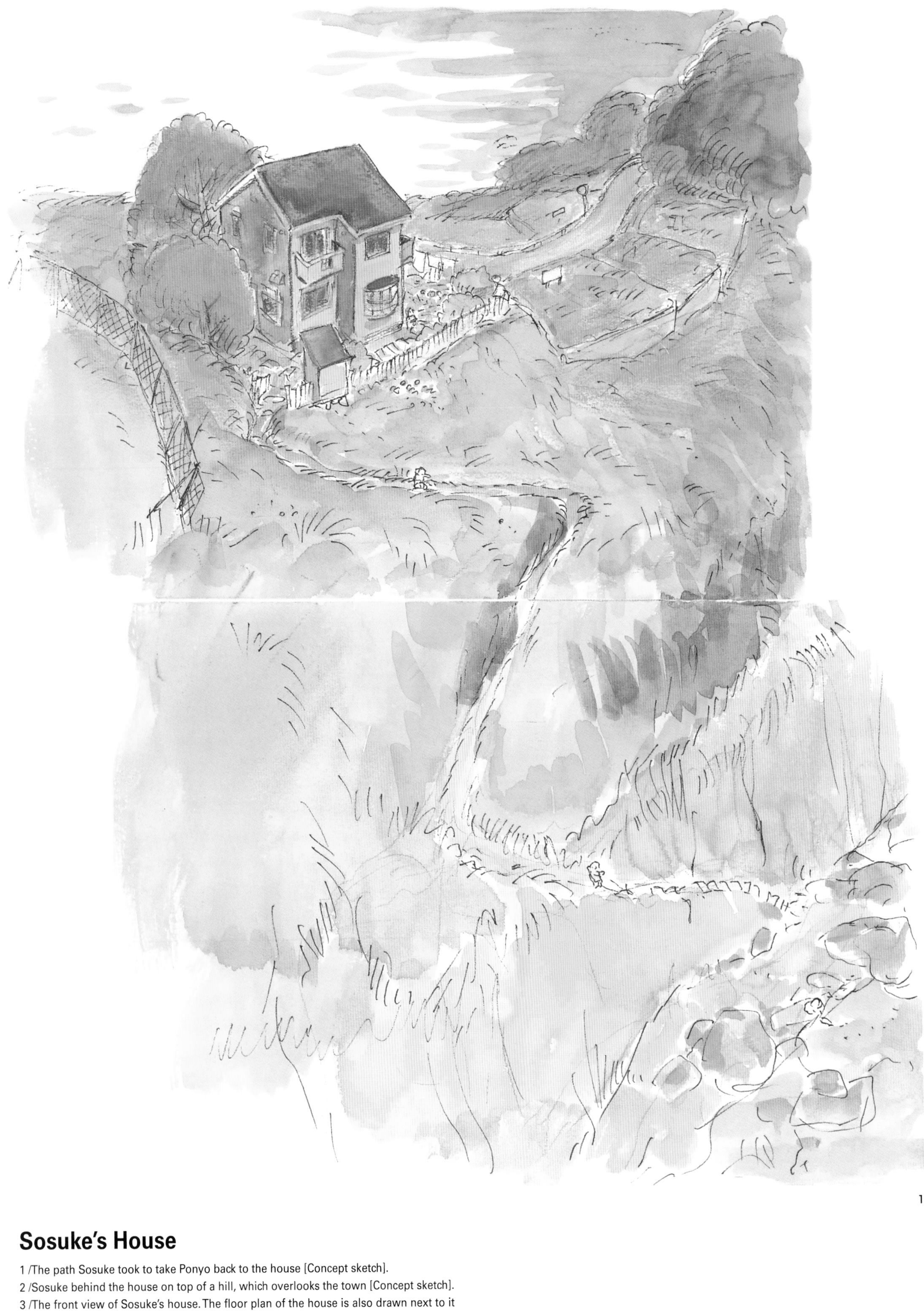

1

Sosuke's House

1 /The path Sosuke took to take Ponyo back to the house [Concept sketch].
2 /Sosuke behind the house on top of a hill, which overlooks the town [Concept sketch].
3 /The front view of Sosuke's house. The floor plan of the house is also drawn next to it [Concept sketch].

宗介より
沖の上を
何とこの。

1F
3LDK.

69

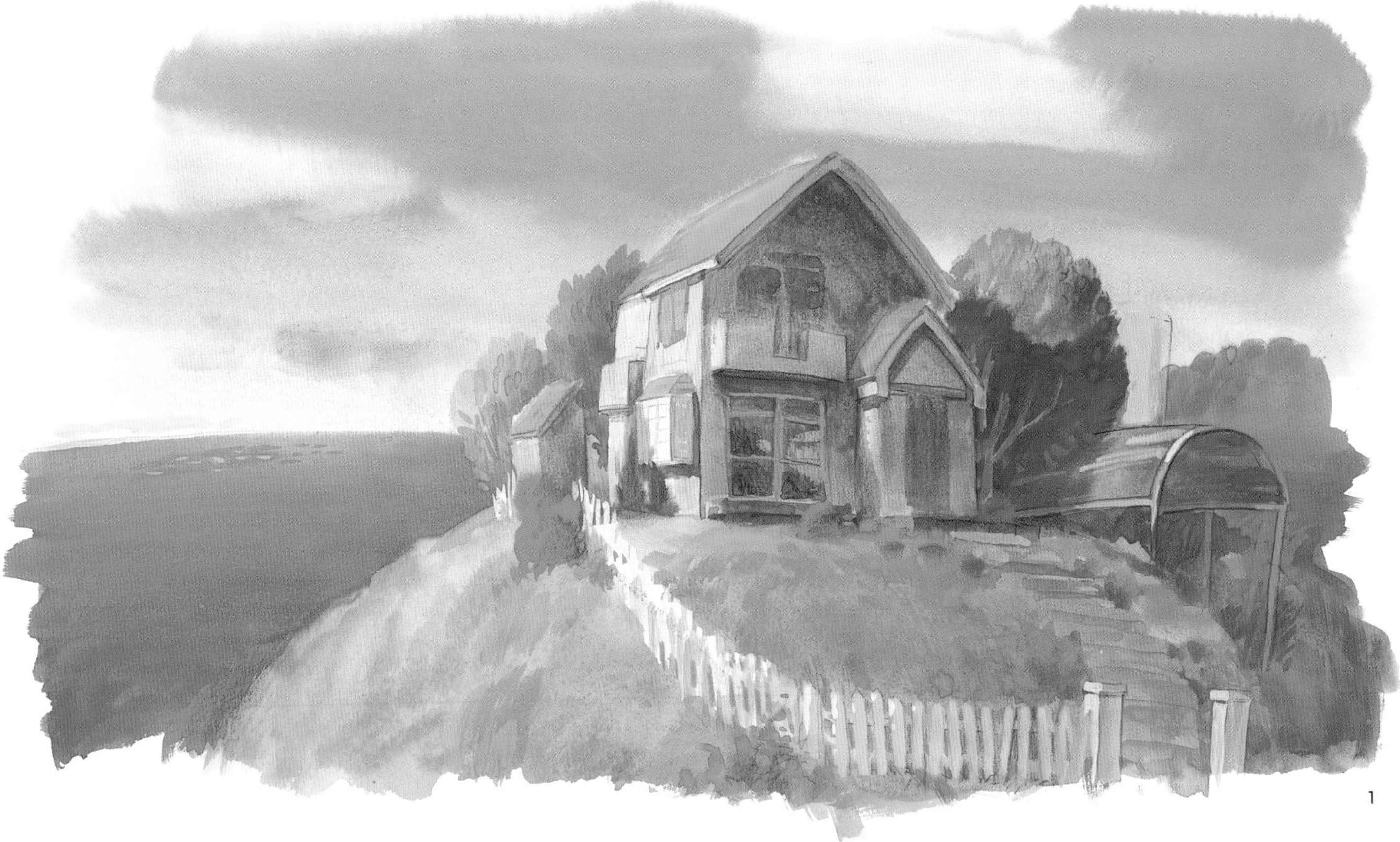

1

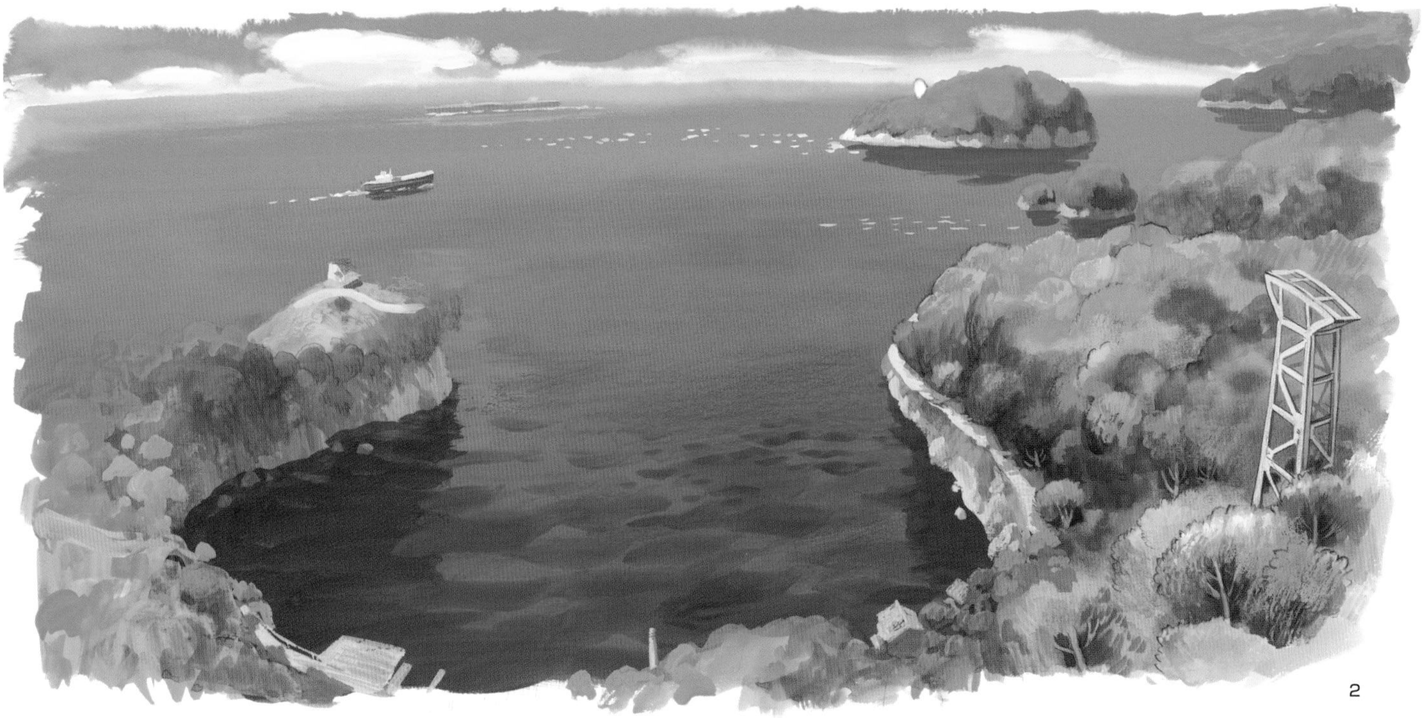

2

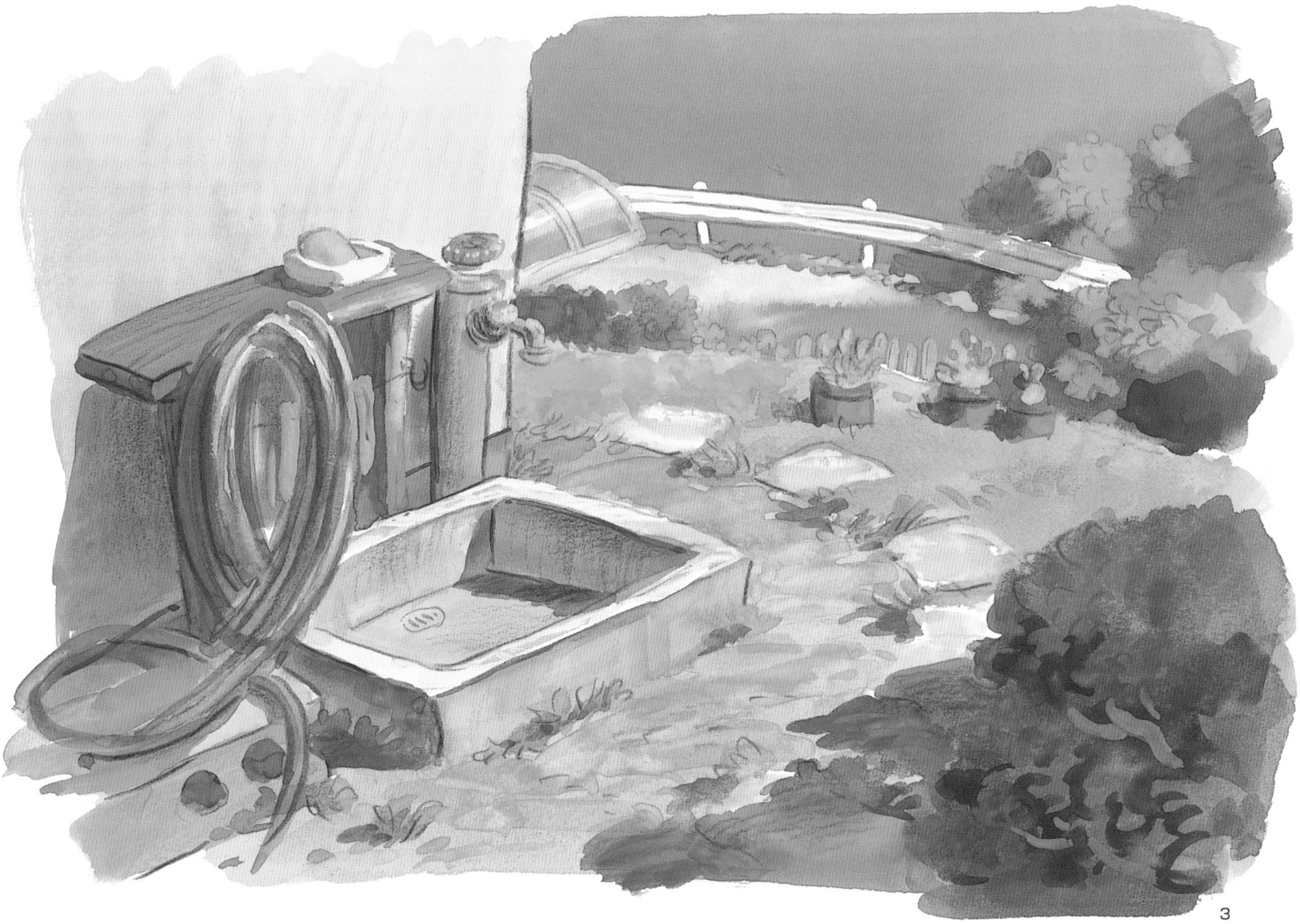

3

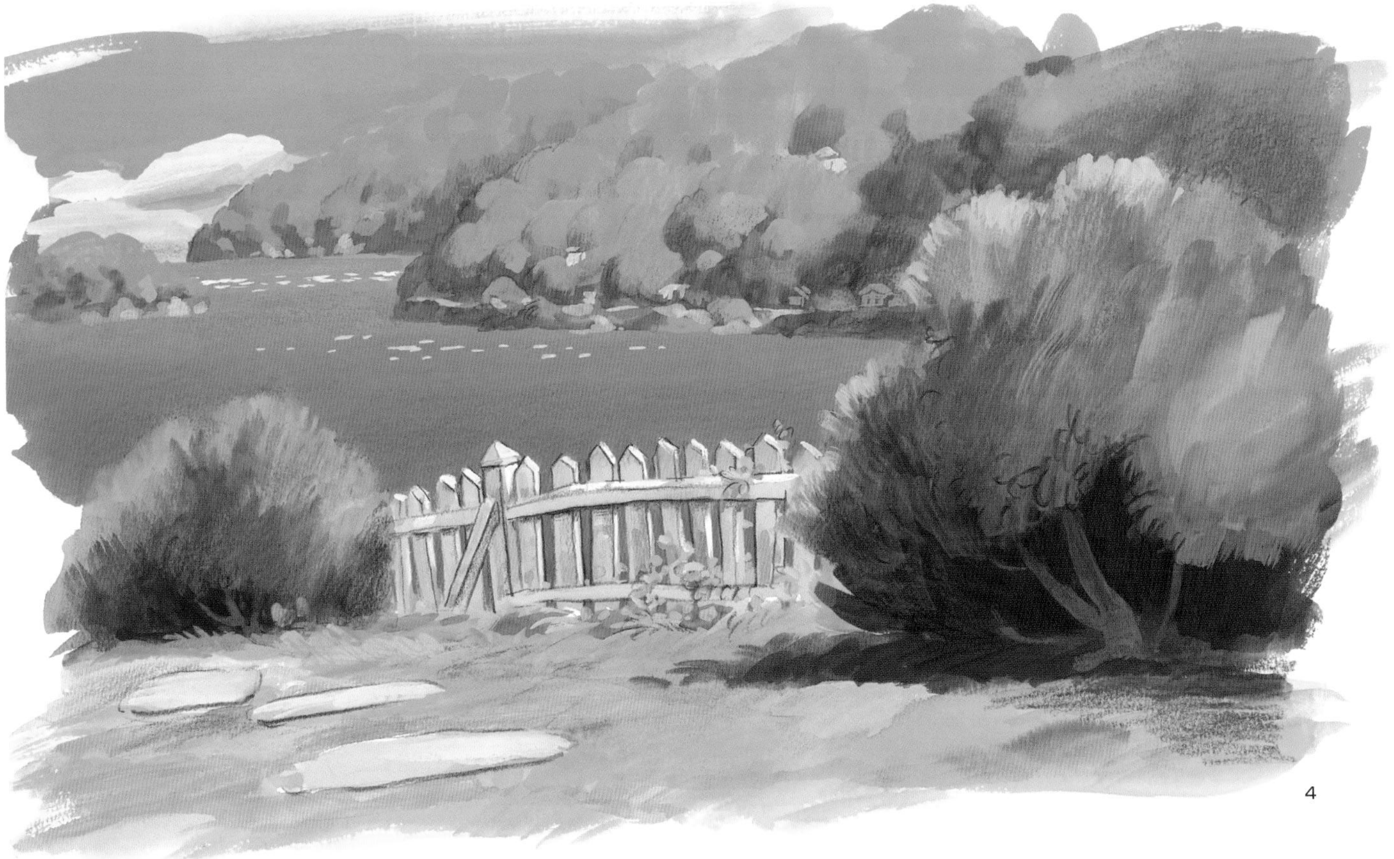

4

1 /The exterior of Sosuke's house with the sea in the background [Concept art].
2 / A bird's-eye view of the bay. Sosuke's house is on top of a hill on a promontory on the left [Concept art].
3 /The wash area behind Sosuke's house [Concept art].
4 /The yard of Sosuke's house facing the sea [Concept art].

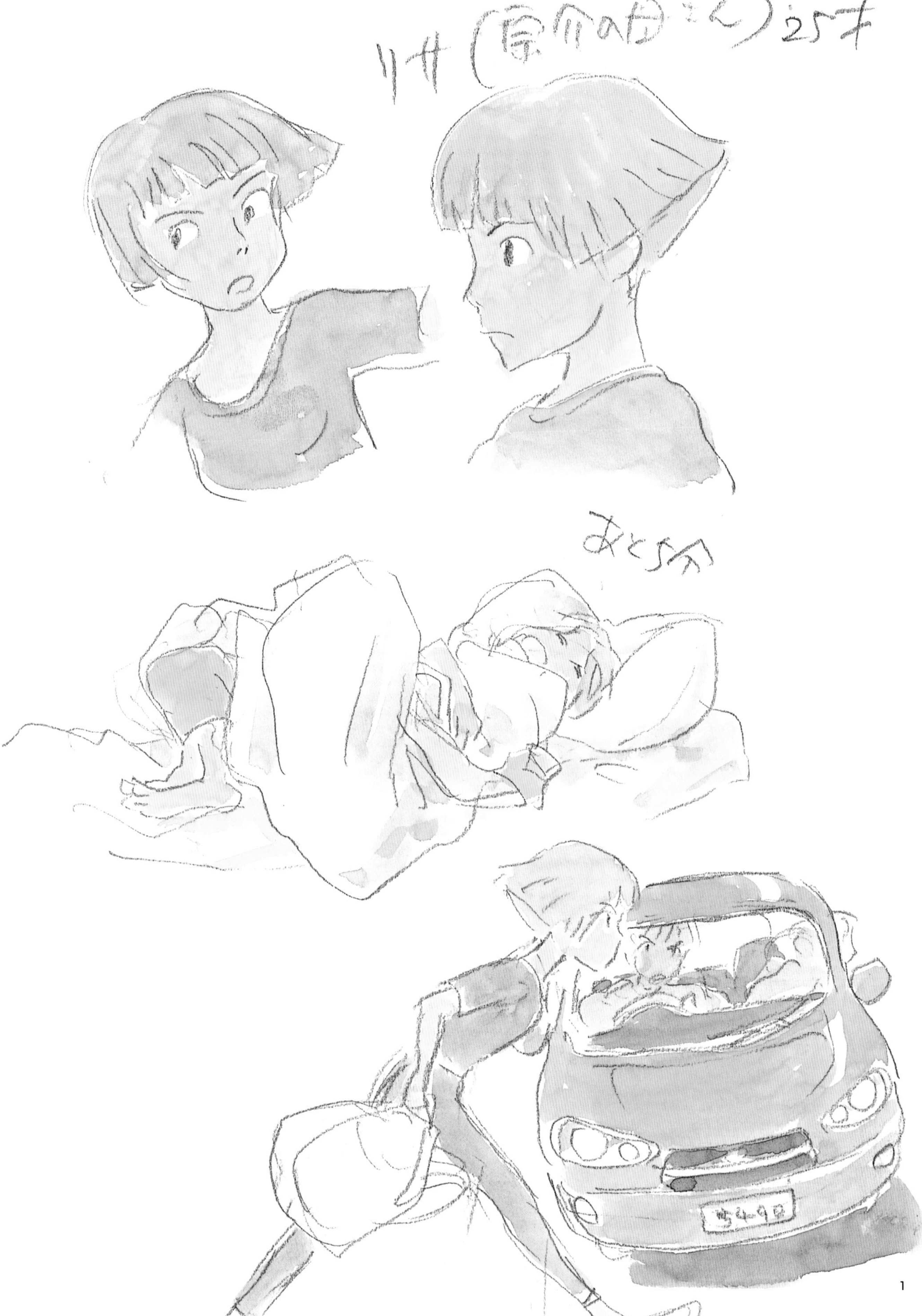
リサ（宗介の母さん）25才
あと5分
1

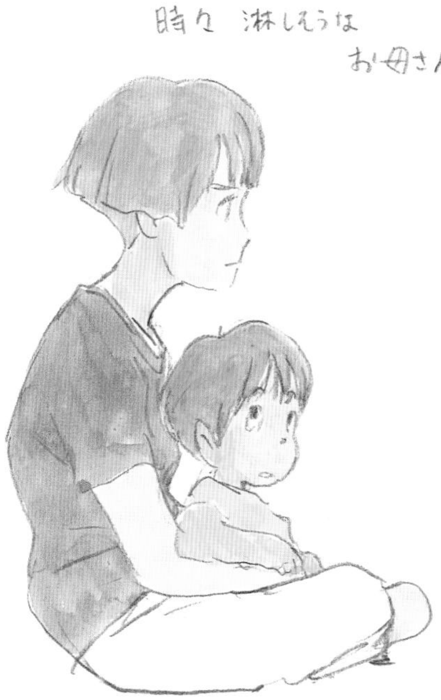
時々 淋しそうな
お母さん。

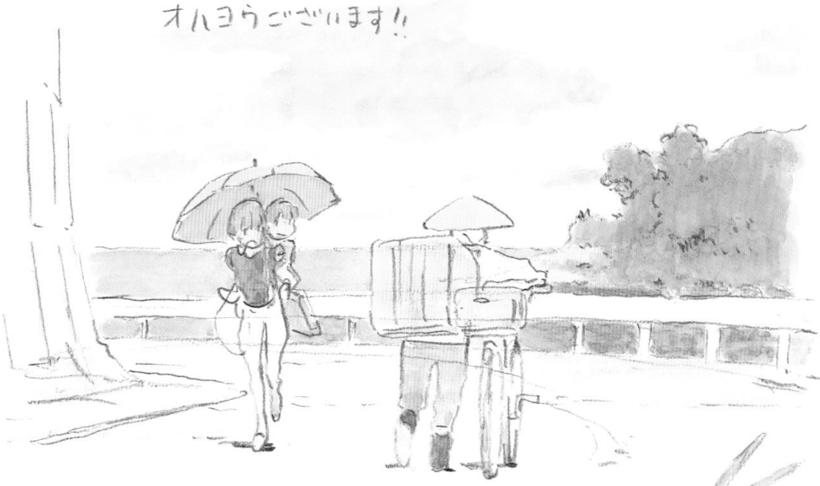
オハヨウございます!!

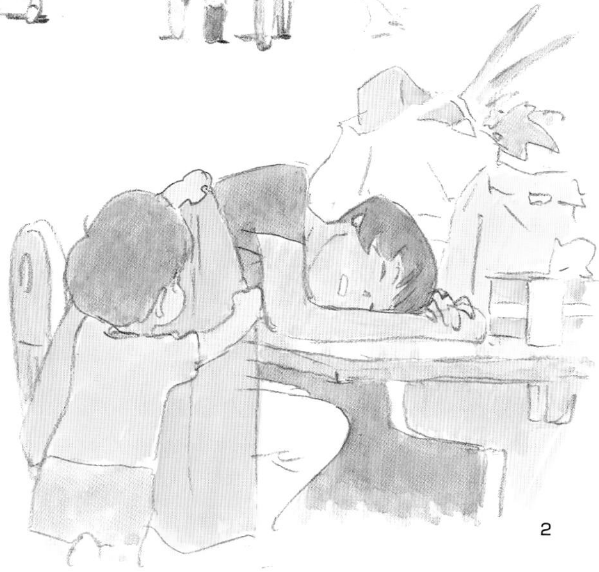
2

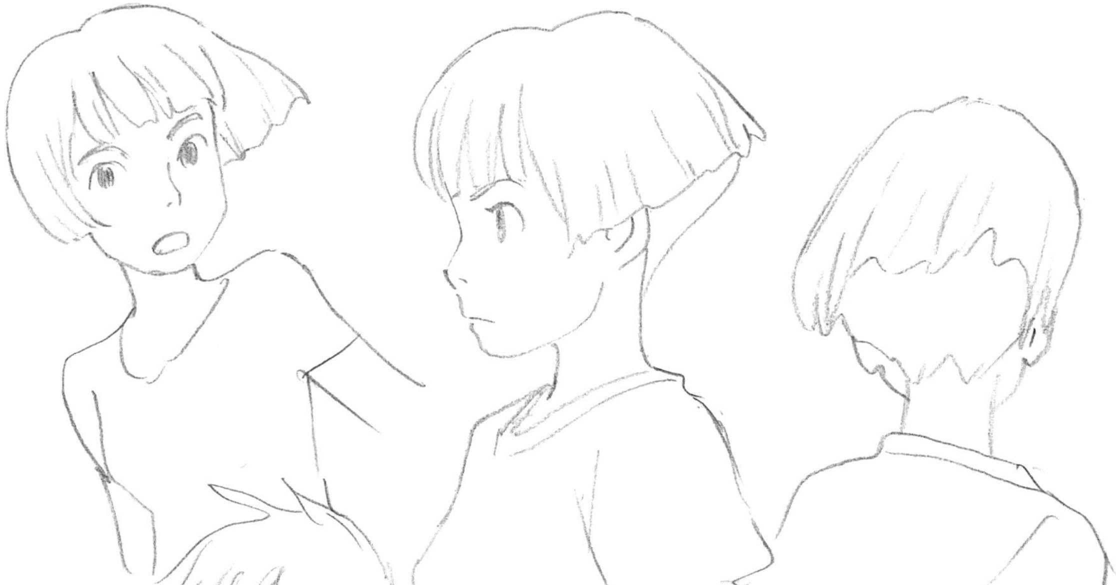
3

Lisa

Sosuke's mother. An energetic housewife who also works at a daycare service center for the elderly. In one storyboard, Miyazaki wrote, "She is a heroine out of a world with swords and magic!"
1 /Sketches of Lisa by Hayao Miyazaki [Concept sketch].
2, 3 /Lisa, drawn by Katsuya Kondo from Miyazaki's rough sketches [Rough character sketches].

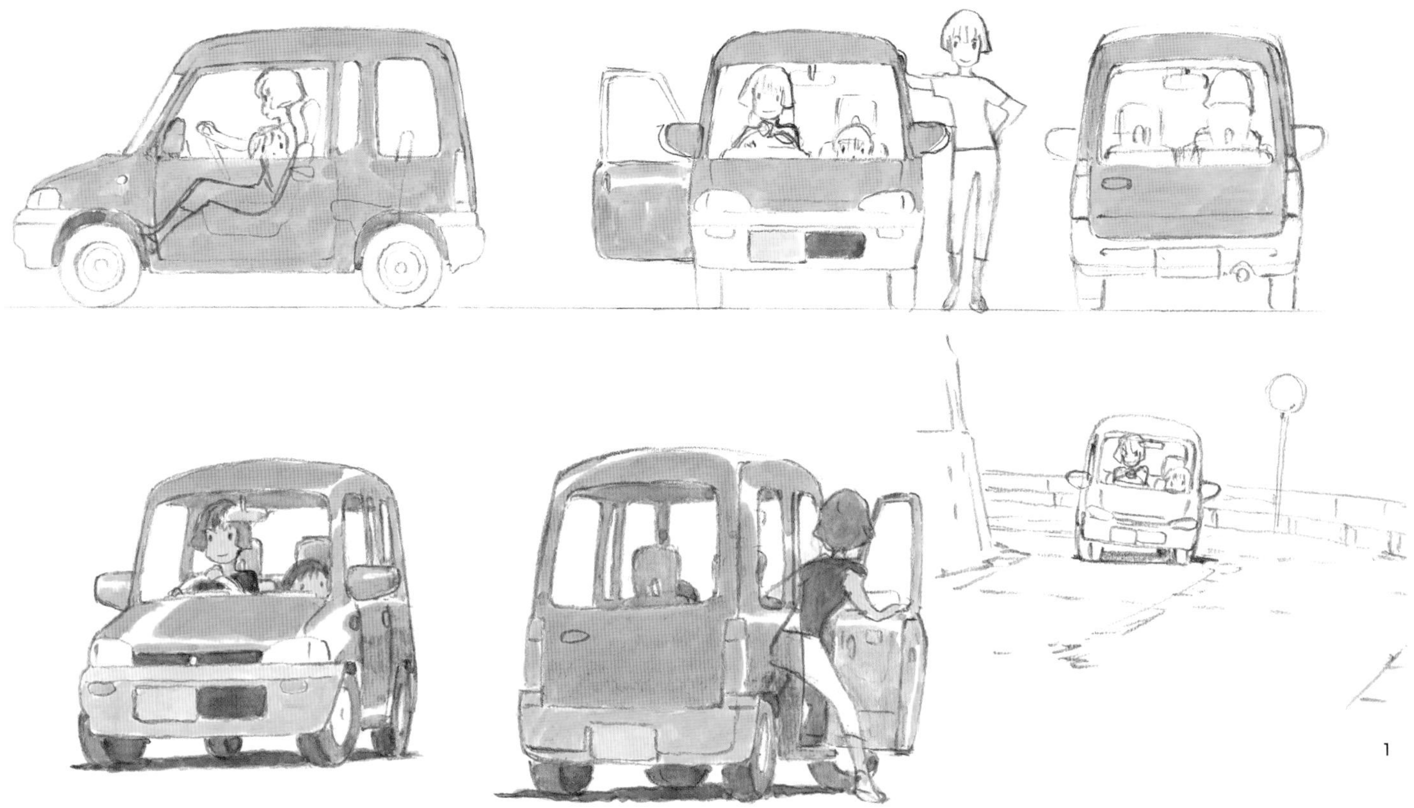

1

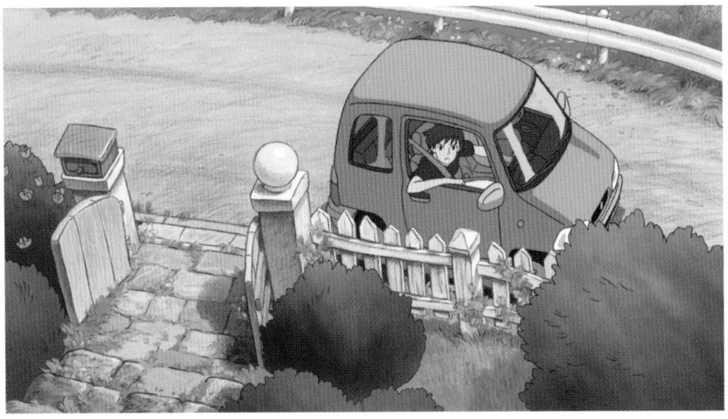

2

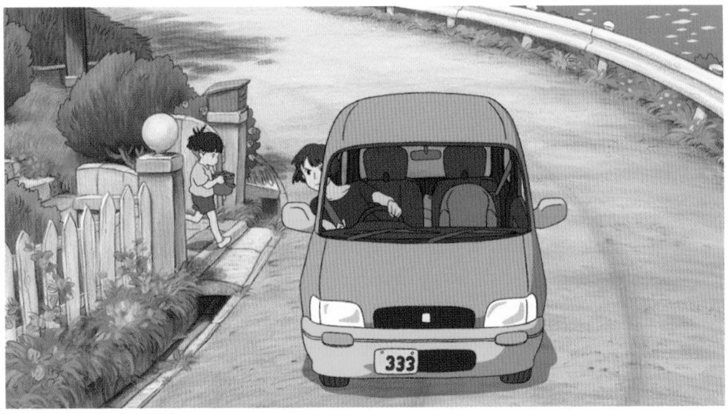
333

3

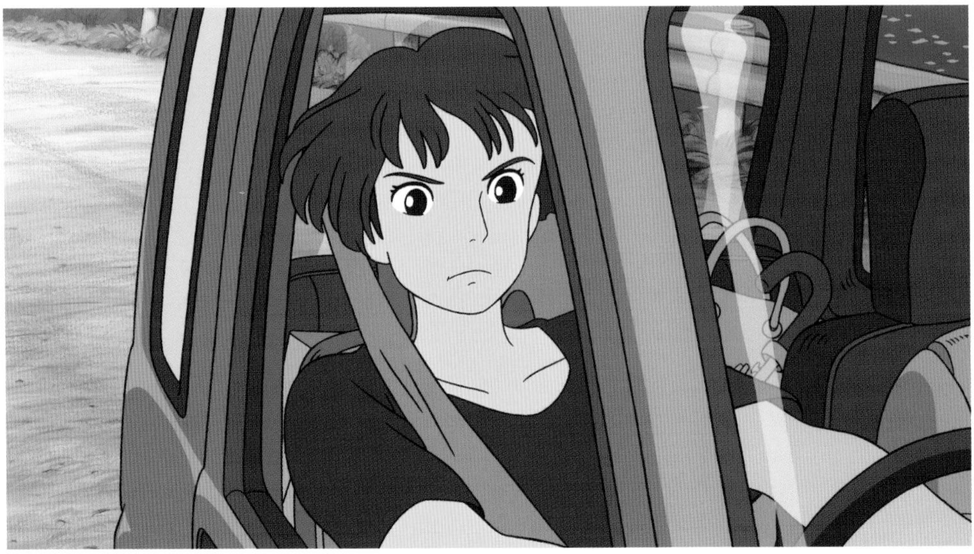

4

The Lisa-Mobile

1 /Sketches of Lisa's beloved car by Katsuya Kondo. A somewhat truncated compact car. The back seat is always cluttered with bags [Rough character sketches].
2–4 /Lisa's daily routine is to commute to the daycare service center and drop Sosuke off at the preschool next door.

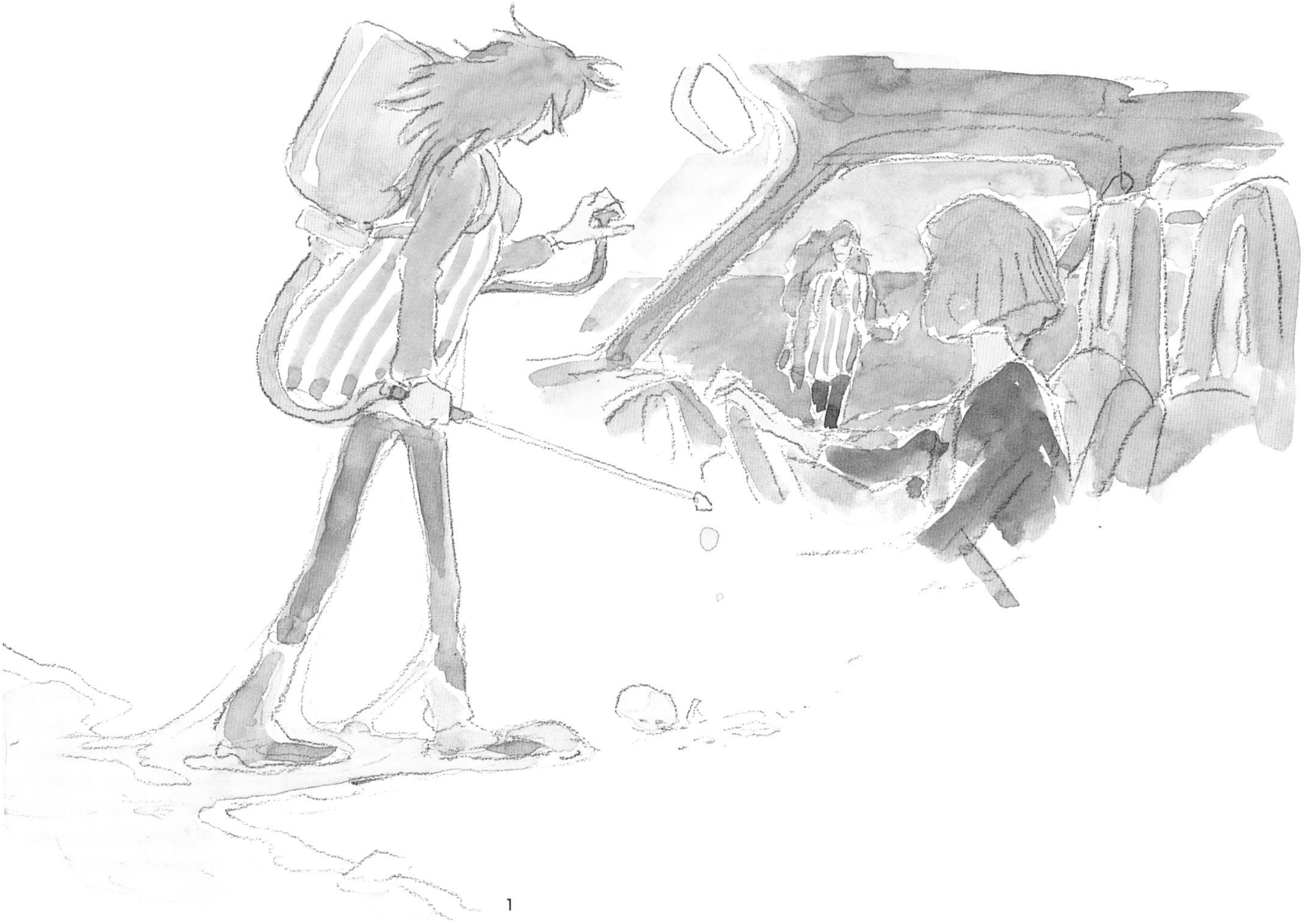

1

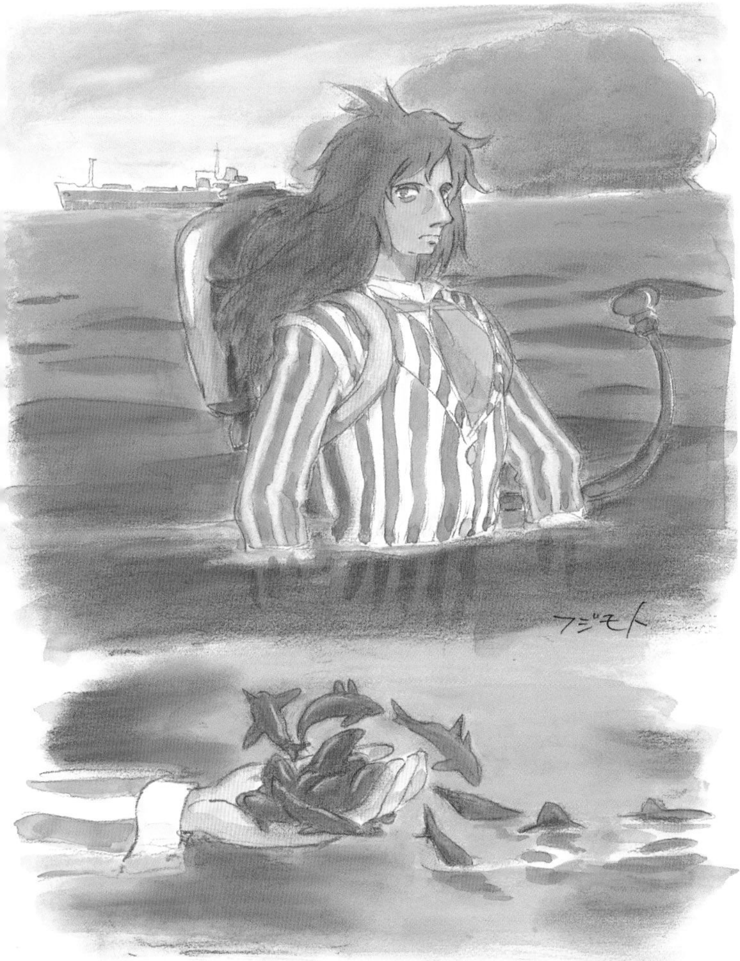
フジモト
水魚を放つ

2

Fujimoto Comes Ashore

1, 2 /Fujimoto comes ashore in search of Ponyo. He sprays deep-sea water to stay hydrated but is scolded by Lisa, who thinks he is spraying weed killer. [Concept sketches]

MICHIYO YASUDA

Michiyo Yasuda was born in Tokyo. She began her career as one of the first employees at Toei Doga (now Toei Animation) in 1958. She became acquainted with both Takahata and Miyazaki through her union activities and took part as clean-up animator on *Little Norse Prince*. *Future Boy Conan* (1978) was the first film for which she was responsible for the entire color design. Since Studio Ghibli's founding she supported various directors as chief color designer. She has been responsible for the color design on almost all of Ghibli's films from *Nausicaä of the Valley of the Wind* (1984), *Spirited Away* (2001), and *Tales from Earthsea* (2006), to *Ponyo* (2008).

COMPLEMENTARY COLORS

The backgrounds were mainly green and blue. Sosuke's shirt was yellow. Ponyo was red and the pail green. I had a difficult time assigning color values because Ponyo was surrounded by many complementary colors. I kept Ponyo red and opted not use too many gentle colors. Even so, the color wasn't pure red or exactly to the point of being very sharp, but it wasn't all that pale either. I stopped short of making Ponyo as intense as the backgrounds and was careful not to assign an equally saturated color to background images. Sosuke was always surrounded by a variety of colors even underwater, but I enjoyed the challenge of working with complementary colors.

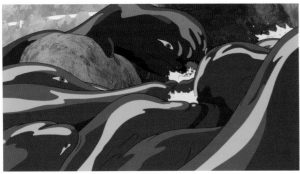

MINIONS

When I saw the concept sketch of Ponyo standing on top of the minions and the sketch of the minions pouring down from the sky, I had initially planned to make the creatures more ink-colored or gray. But then the water would lack color, so after some trial and error, the minions became the color they are now. The sea creatures were rendered to look like both fish and blue waves. Since the scene shots were completed in random order, I was always thinking about the overall balance as I assigned colors values for each shot.

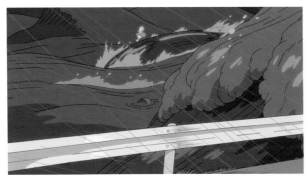

PONYO'S STORM

The storm that Ponyo causes comes from her desire to see Sosuke. While the background has turned only a little dark due to the storm, the sea looks even darker because it is also affected by the presence of the minions. For this reason, I considered how the spray of the waves might be better kept dark, as opposed to making them white, and then I came up with various reasons for why the spray would be dark. Working on *Ponyo*, I often felt like I was coming up with my own rationalizations for certain color choices.

INTERVIEW
MICHIYO YASUDA
Chief Color Designer

I attempted to skate a fine line between two conflicting color intensities.

I believe I heard about *Ponyo* from Miyazaki rather early on. He shared with me fragments of what he was envisioning a little at a time, explaining that it was a "story about a little goldfish based on 'The Little Mermaid.'" He told me he wanted to move the animation by hand-drawn frames rather than by digitally created 3D animation. He also wanted to know what would happen if we focused on the sea, which has always existed below our line of sight, and pulled it right up to our eye level. He wanted to render the sea as a living and breathing entity. This was the image he wanted to attempt to capture with *Ponyo*.

After some time had passed, he showed me the concept sketches of Ponyo for the first time. I was surprised. Although the sketches were of Ponyo not yet human, it wasn't about the design or the color—the character itself was appealing even as a goldfish. That was my first impression of Ponyo.

Miyazaki and I never talked about the color design in very specific terms. He mentioned wanting to outline the sea with solid black lines instead of with color lines—we did discuss that. But Miyazaki already had a set color scheme such as yellow for Sosuke's clothes and red for Ponyo, as she's a goldfish.

It was also extremely helpful that his storyboards were colored this time. I was able to see how he wanted the water surface to look dark here and even darker there by referring to the storyboards, even in cases where the colors ended up being changed. Although I encounter the same concerns about color design on every film, the clues are always in the storyboards. But as I had planned to go with a daring color design on *Ponyo* from the beginning, it was very helpful to have colored storyboards conveying Miyazaki's intentions as a reference.

The color saturation of the art was unusually high this time. The colors were intense rather than pale. So, I had to design a color scheme while thinking about color saturation in the same way. Colors tend to look dirty if I tone them down too much, and if I raise the color intensity to that of the background art the colors tend to look gaudy on a cel frame. I tried to skate that fine line. A reflection in the water, or anything else for that matter, looks different when one changes the color saturation. Although I had initially believed that I could do the job by relying on prior

A sample image, created as a reference for colors assigned to the main characters.

knowledge and methods, I later realized, "It's different with Ponyo." Miyazaki also said, "Ponyo is different, after all" on numerous occasions.

The biggest challenge was the treatment of the water. The most obvious departure this time was that I hardly used any of the same colors that I used in previous films. Also, just because scenes took place underwater didn't mean that I needed only to add a few blue tints. My understanding of colors, which worked in the past, wasn't enough. If I were to tint Ponyo with a blue hue because she is underwater, for example, she would no longer be Ponyo. Which was why, when Ponyo is in the pail, the parts of her body in the water are almost the same color as the parts emerging from the surface of the water.

Since I had to add some color to render images reflected on the water's surface, I added those colors with a subtler touch than usual. Plus, the color intensity and hues were different with every shot, from the look of the water spray to the underwater shots—everything. The water was made to look abstract at times and extremely realistic at others.

I was reminded how amazing Miyazaki is in that he always has a clear point of view. For example, in a shot where parts of Ponyo's and Sosuke's bodies are submerged in the water, I used a lower color intensity for the parts that were in the water. But when their bodies are submerged entirely in the next shot, Miyazaki asked me to use a gentle palette, instead of underwater colors, so the two characters would look cheerful and adorable. That's why I think the audience is affected by the beauty of Miyazaki's films.

I've cultivated many skills during my time working with Miyazaki. I now have a foundation from which I can determine what I would normally do and how I might handle an unusual situation. On *Ponyo*, many times, I felt like I was

able to reconfirm which techniques and methods worked for a given situation. For example, once the colors for the dark part of the storm looked right, then both the color of the sea and the subsequent shots naturally followed suit. I was able to employ this method for detailed work as well.

I was allowed to do a wide variety of things on *Ponyo*. I was able to try new techniques that I might not have been able to do elsewhere. I had a wonderful experience.

THE COLOR OF CROWD SCENES

In cases where people appear deep in the frame, I typically do not use too many colors to differentiate one person from the next, even if there were a mob of people. It was acceptable to merely convey that there were a lot of people onboard the boats without using too many colors. But in the case of Ponyo, I didn't get the sense that there were many people aboard until I colored in the people in the background too. That aspect of using color to convey numbers was different from my previous work. I worked on the crowd scenes with Miyazaki's help.

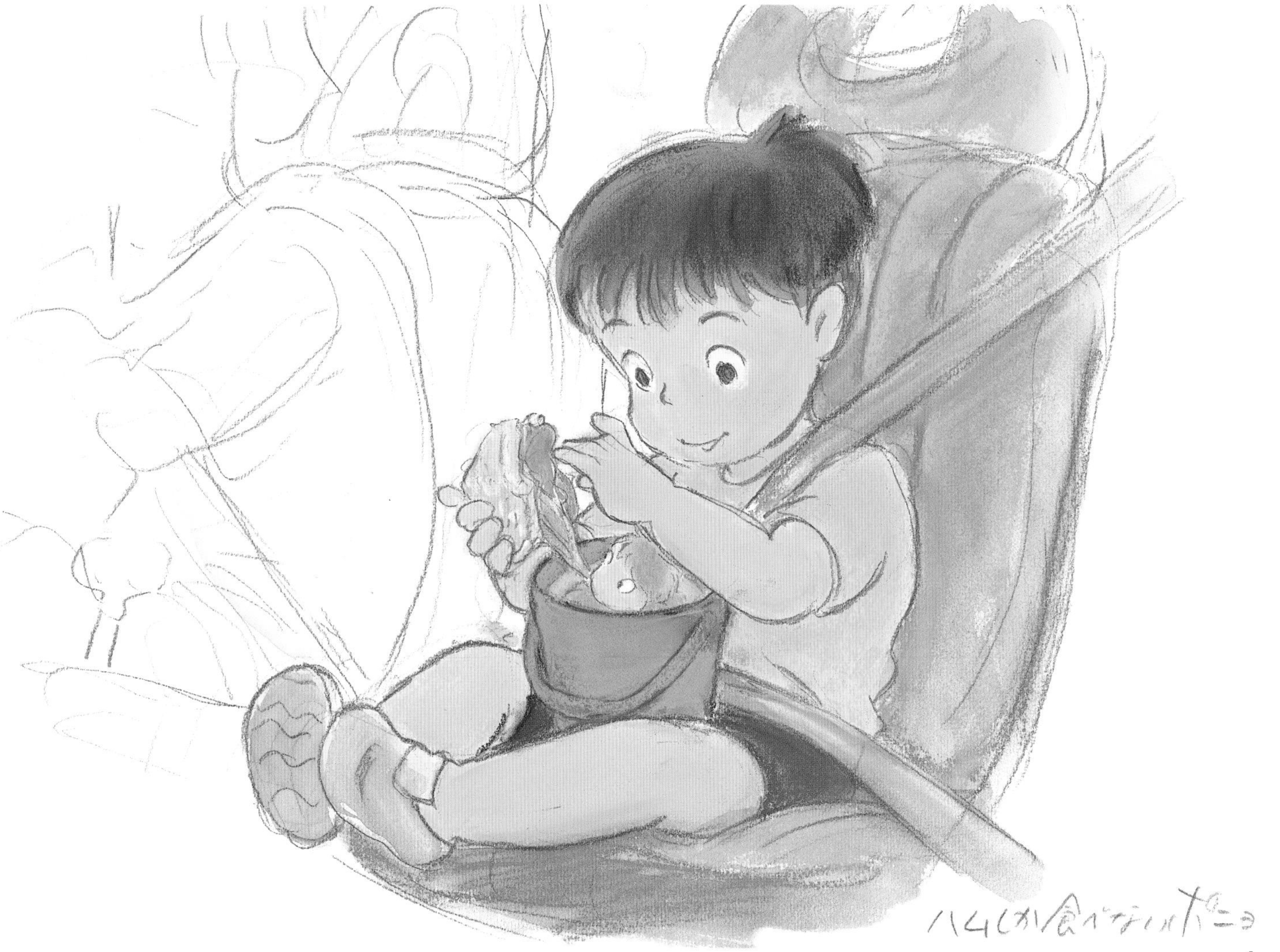
ハムしか食べないポニョ

1

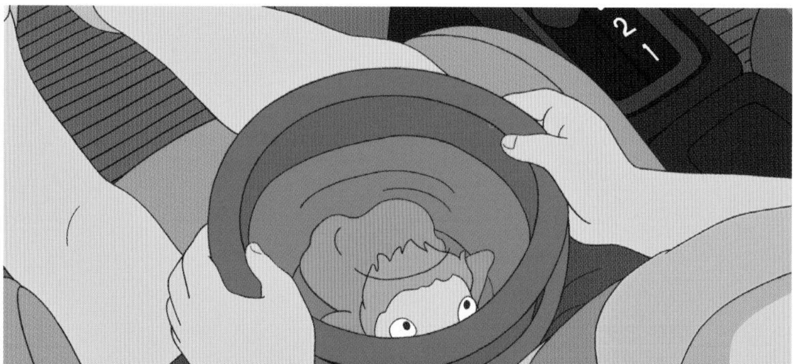

2

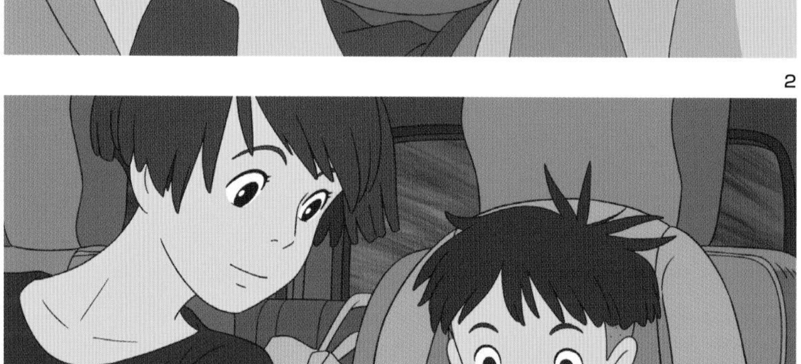

3

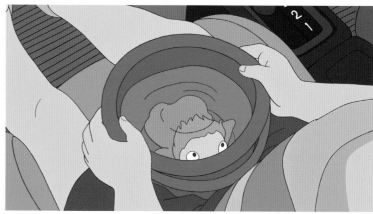

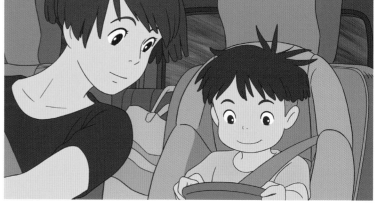

Ponyo Eats Ham

1 /Sosuke taking Ponyo to preschool in a pail [Concept sketch].
2 /A wary Ponyo. Sosuke gently tells her, "Don't worry, I'll take good care of you." The cut on his finger is completely healed.
3 /Lisa peers in and says, "She sure is pretty."
4–9 /When Sosuke shares his sandwich with Ponyo, she devours the ham with a ferocity that would put a piranha to shame.
10 /"Her name is Ponyo. She likes to eat ham...She might do magic. That's the secret."

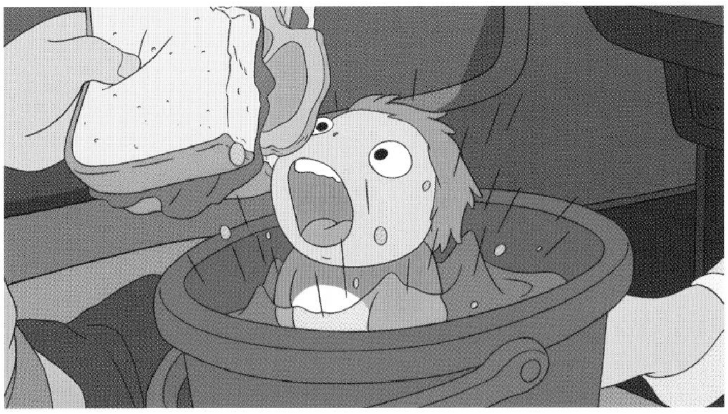

4

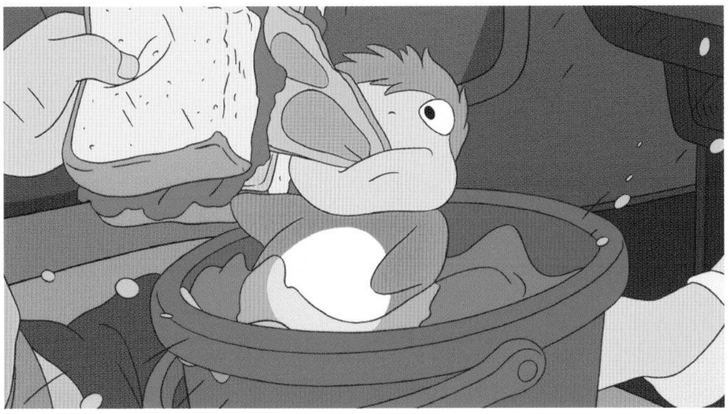

5

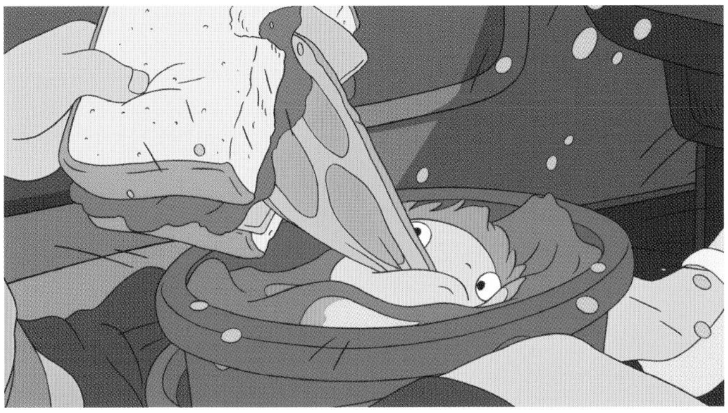

6

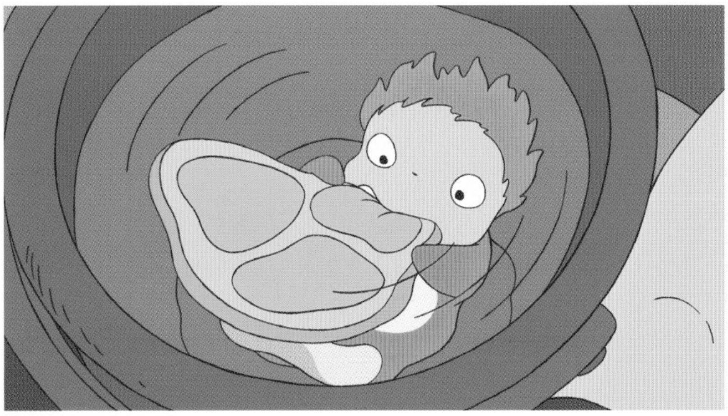

7

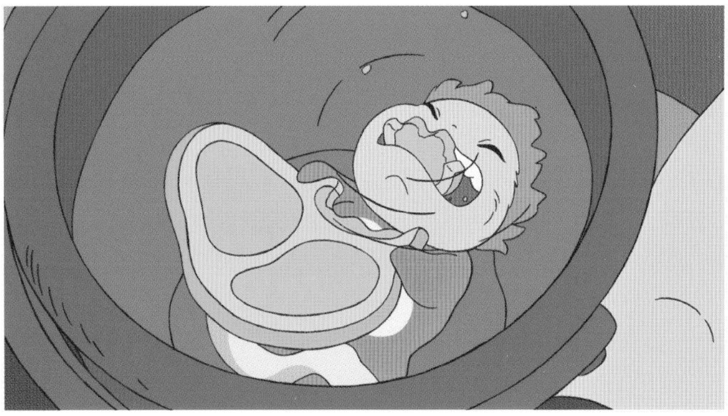

8

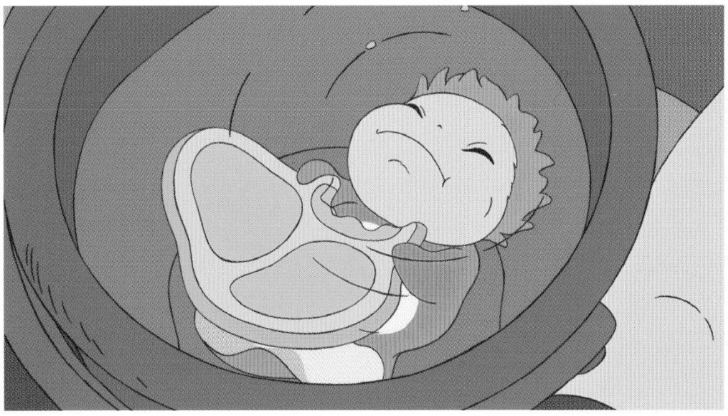

9

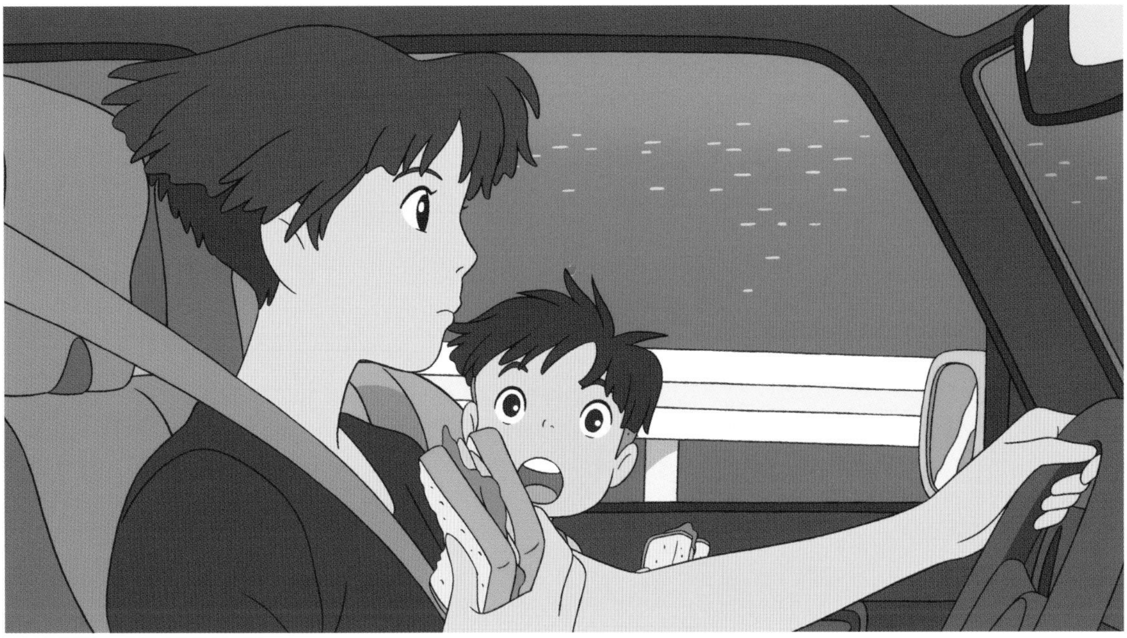

10

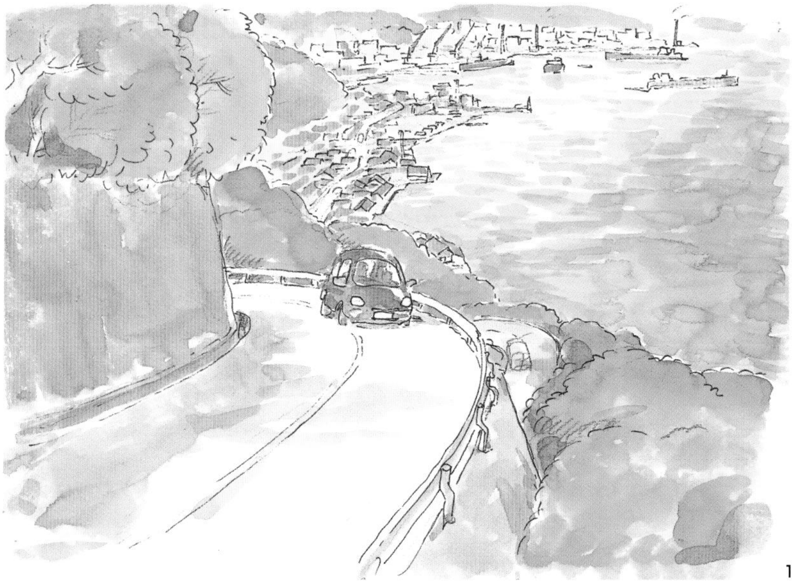

1

To Town

1 /Lisa's car heading up the pass toward the Sunflower House [Concept sketch].
2 /Bird's-eye view of the town seen from the port side [Concept sketch].
3 /Lisa's car waiting for a domestic cargo ship to go into dry dock. Since the road passes through the docks, an attendant oversees traffic [Concept sketch].
4 /Lisa's car crossing the drawbridge after the cargo ship goes into dry dock. The drawbridge was changed to a steel structure in the film [Concept sketch].

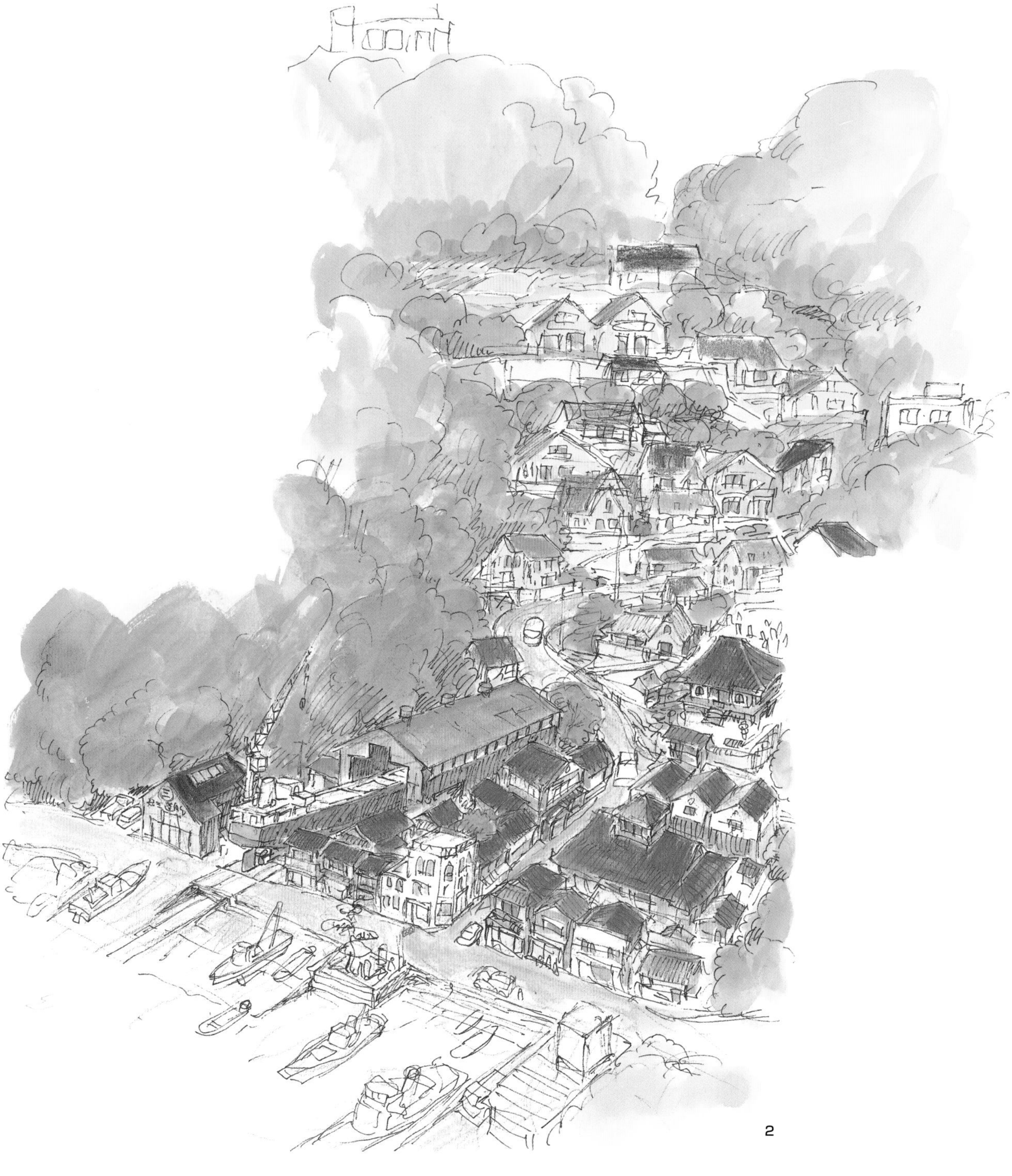

2

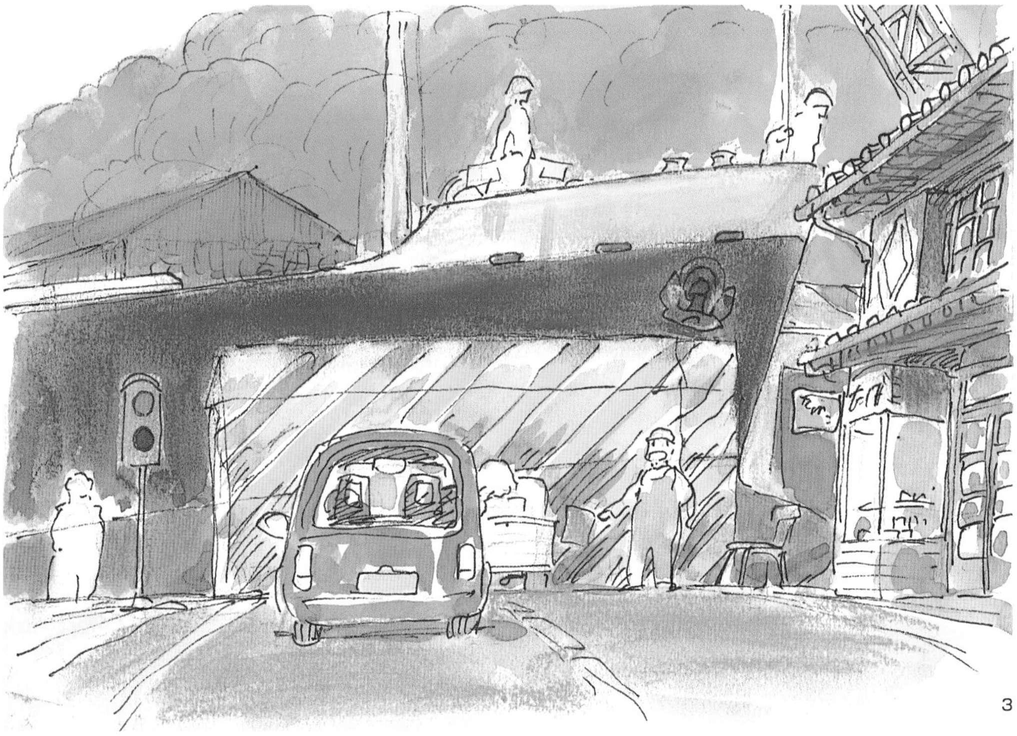

3

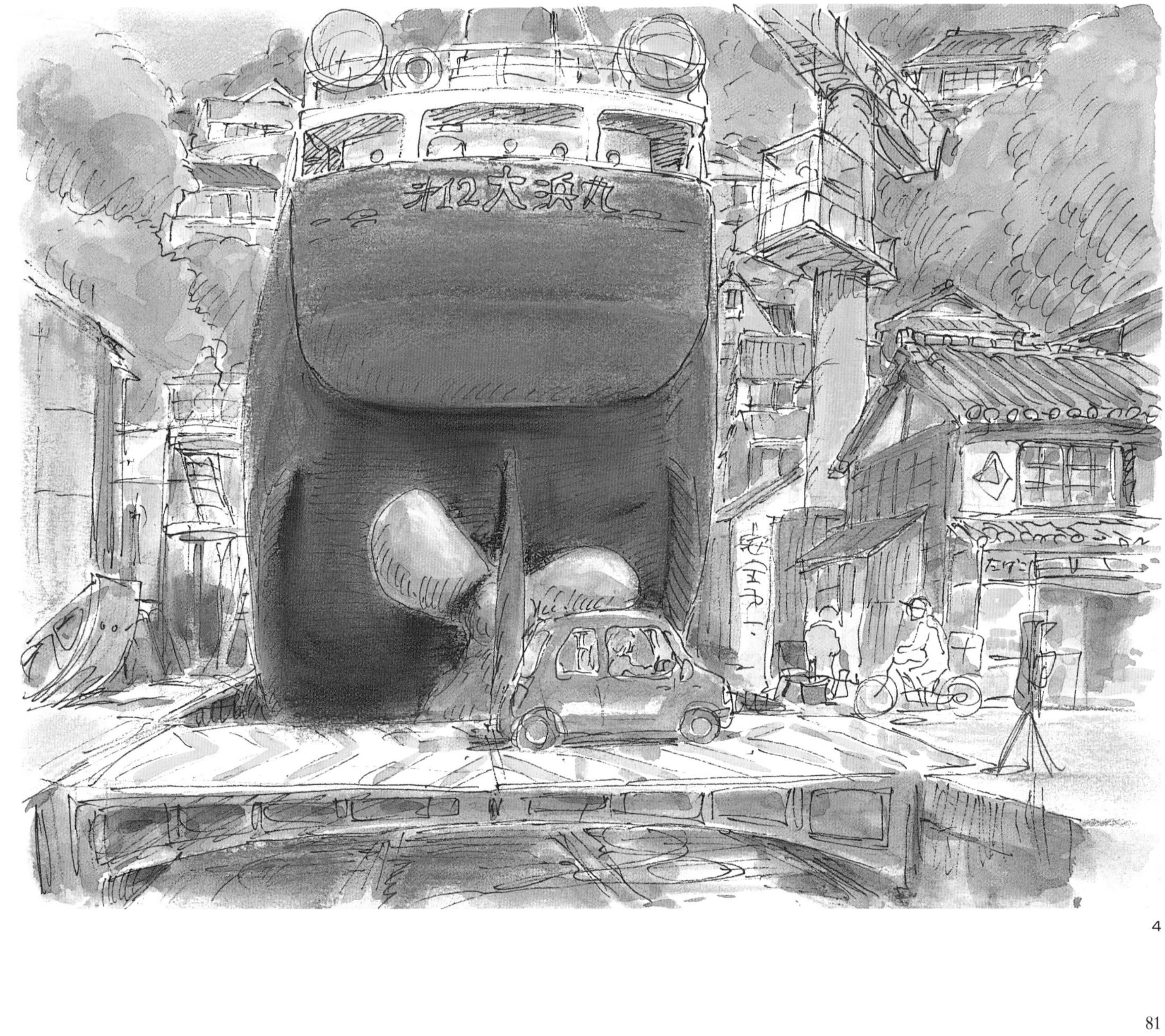
第12大浜丸

4

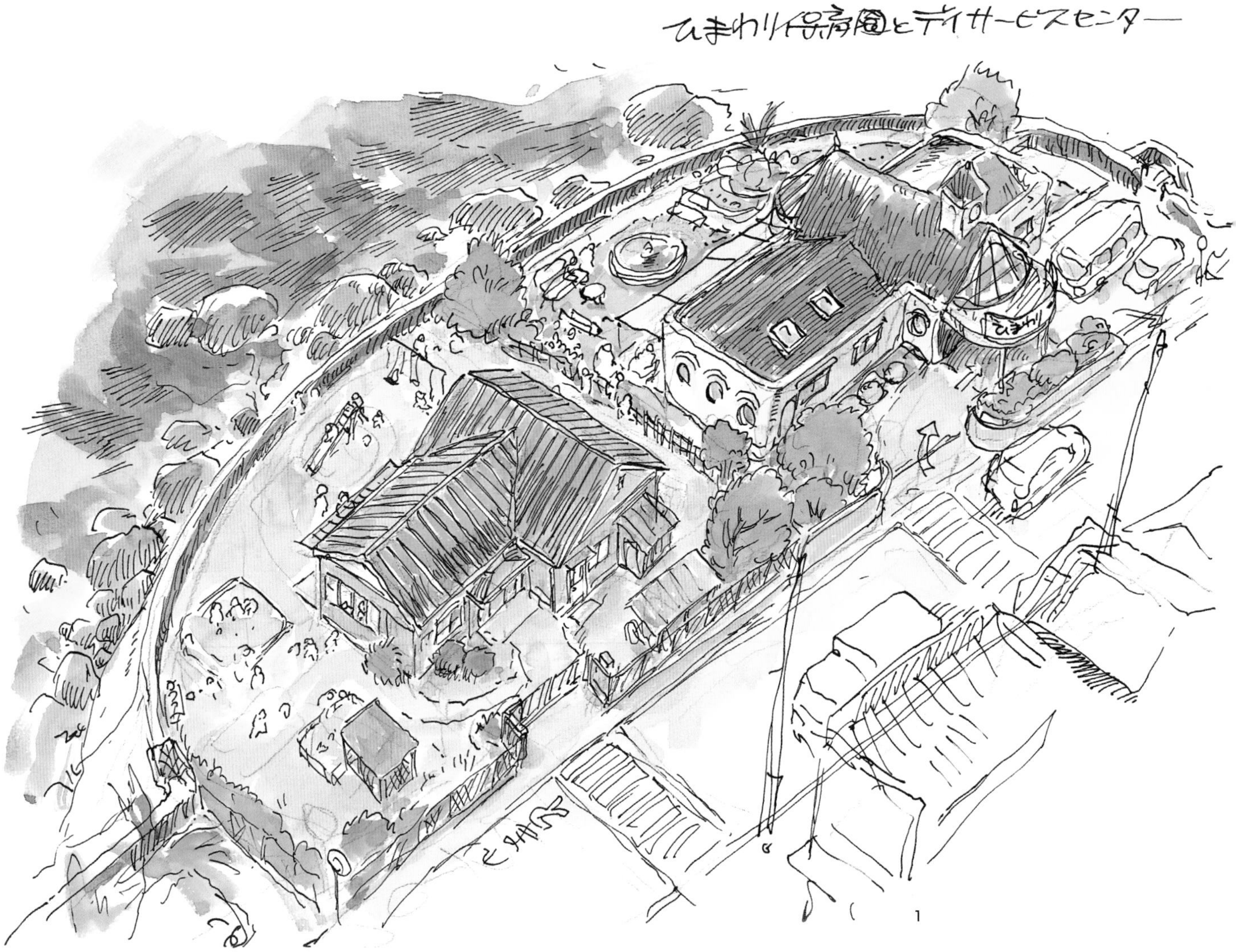
ひまわり保育園とデイサービスセンター

1

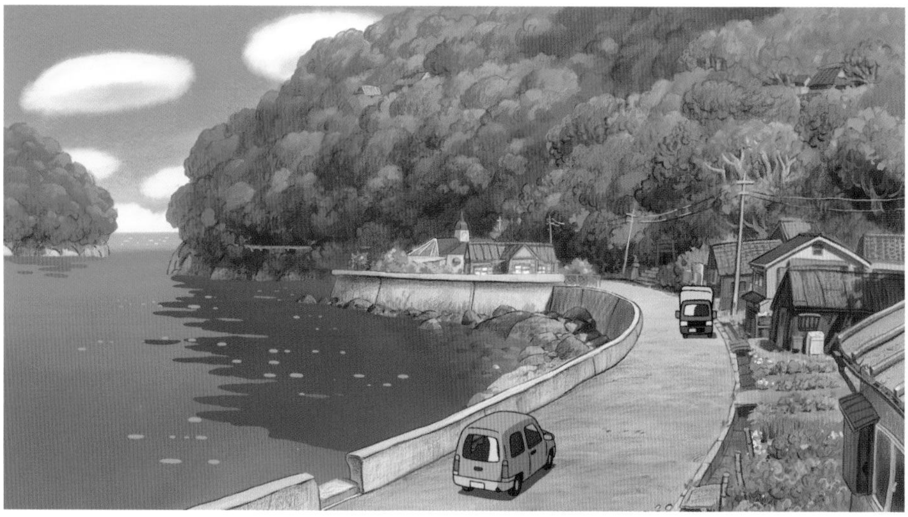

2

The Sunflower House

1 /Bird's-eye view of the Sunflower House, a daycare service center for the elderly, and the Sunflower Preschool, which Sosuke attends [Concept sketch].
2 /Perspective art of the Sunflower House and Sunflower Preschool, located along the embankment.
3 /Exterior view of the Sunflower House [Concept art].
4 /Exterior view of the preschool [Concept art].

Miyazaki wanted the Sunflower House to look colorful. Even though it is a center for the elderly, I used bright colors, so it wouldn't look too much like a hospital. The area is blooming with flowers. The image is that of a summer paradise where it's warm regardless of the season and elderly women can bask in the sun. So I used red for the roof as I did with Sosuke's house, and later Miyazaki told me, "Your artwork is always so colorful" [*laughs*].

—Art Director: Noboru Yoshida

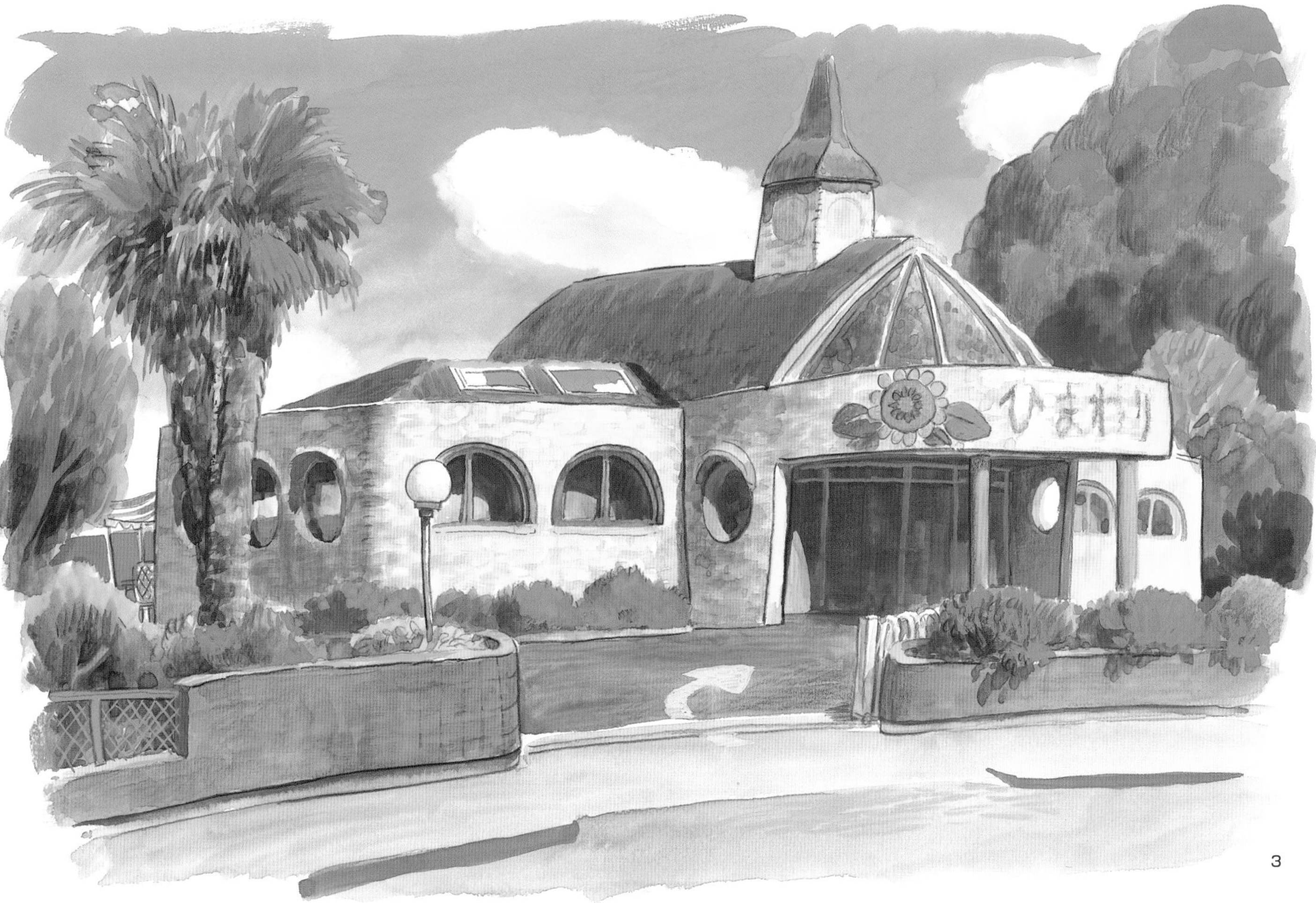
ひまわり

3

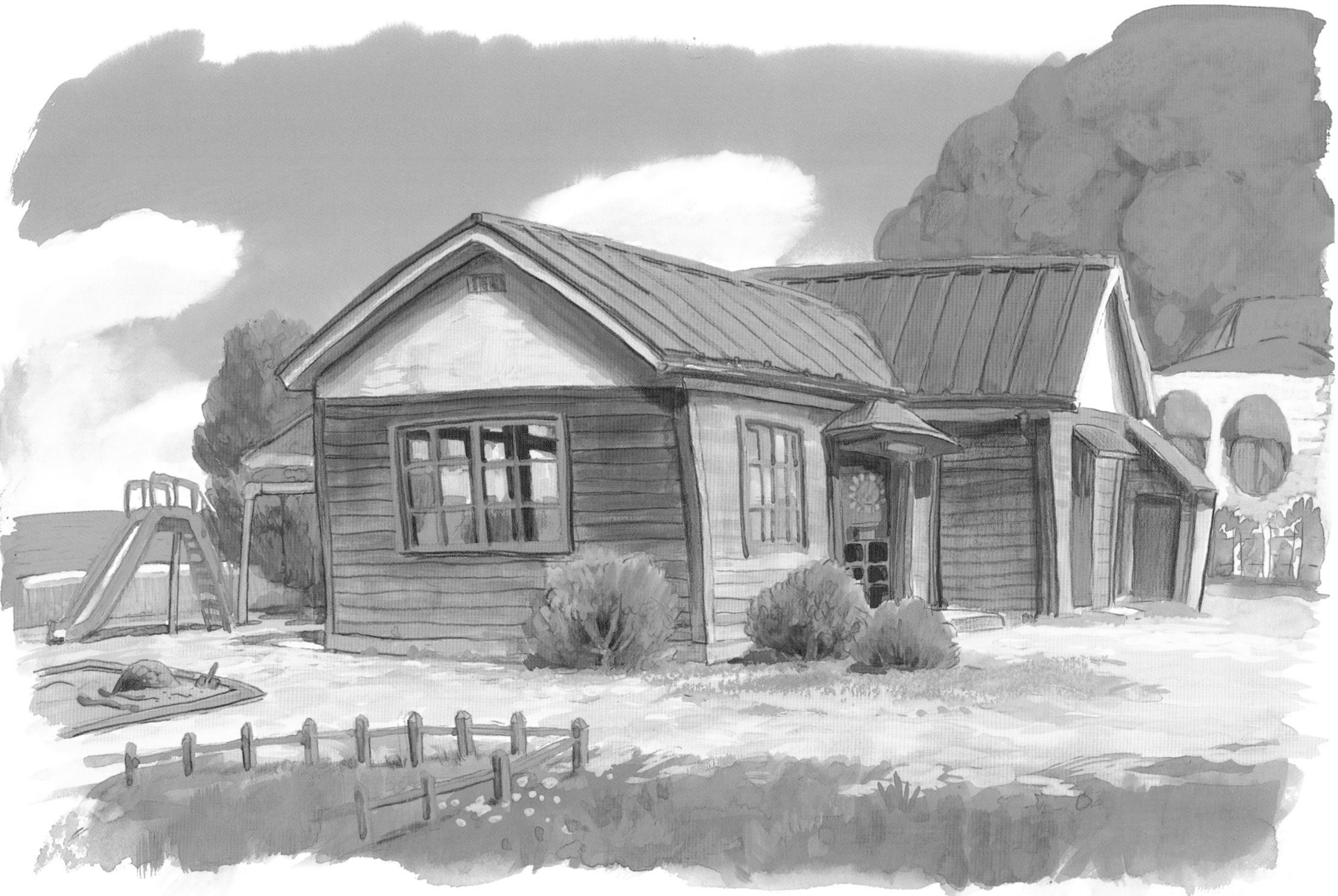

4

The Staff at the Sunflower House

1 /Sosuke arriving at the Sunflower House. He is so absorbed with carrying Ponyo in the pail that he forgets to say hello to Yoshie and Toki.
2 /Sosuke arriving at preschool.
3 /The people working at the Sunflower House. Saito also drives the courtesy minibus, also called the Sunflower [Rough character sketches].

The character designs for minor characters such as the staff and the elderly ladies at the Sunflower House and Kumiko were based on Miyazaki's concept sketches and rough sketches. Since Miyazaki seemed to be going for a kind of modern look, I integrated that thinking into the characters and fashions. Although Kumiko might wear a frilly dress and a big ribbon like out of a '60s girls' magazine, for example, she might also wear some leggings underneath because she is a modern girl. I added my own details while preserving the outline Miyazaki had envisioned. I also used characters drawn by key animators, such as the preschool teacher drawn by Ai Kagawa, making only a few modifications of my own.

—Supervising Animator: Katsuya Kondo

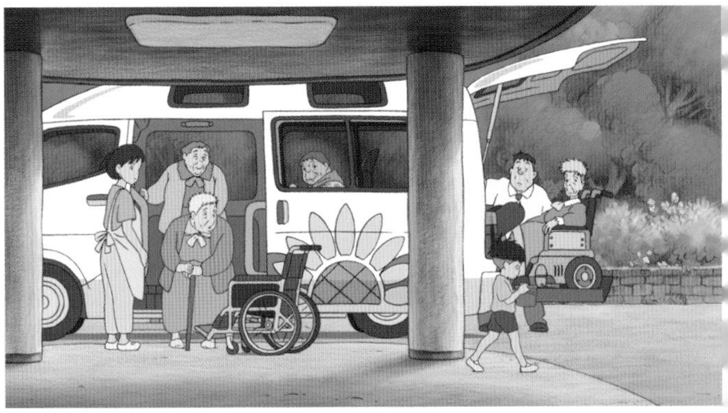

1

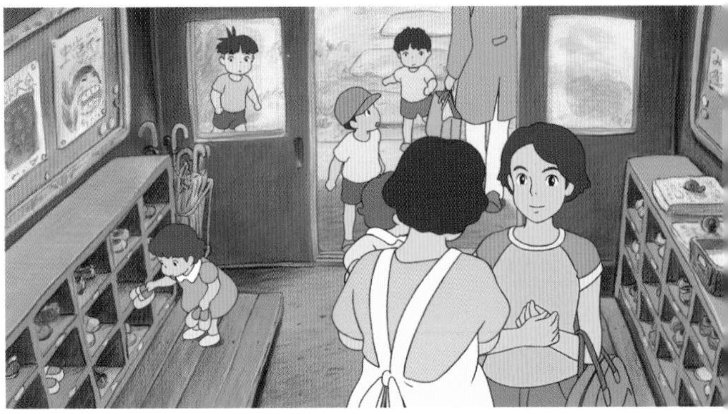

2

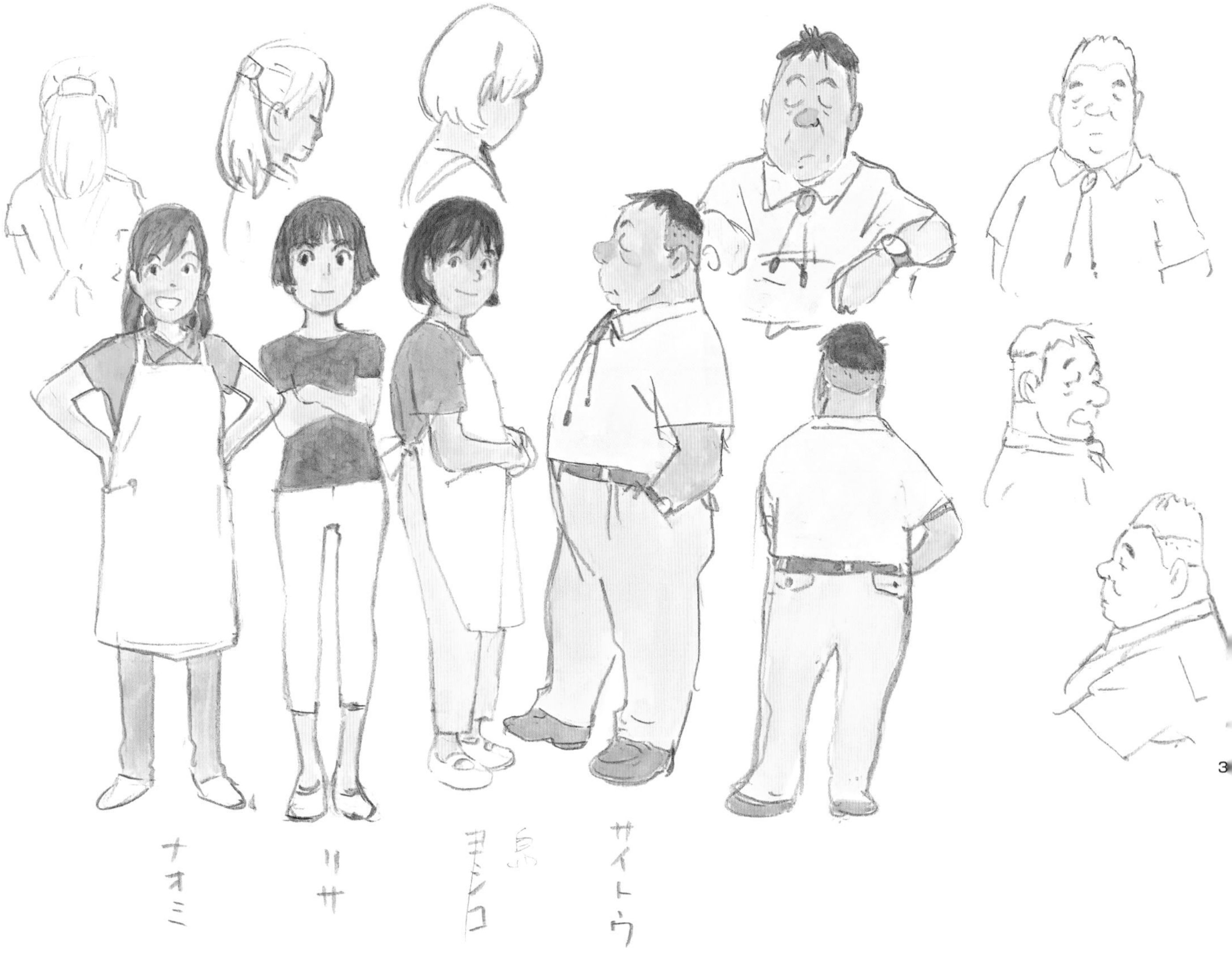
ナオミ
リサ
ヨシコ
サイトウ

3

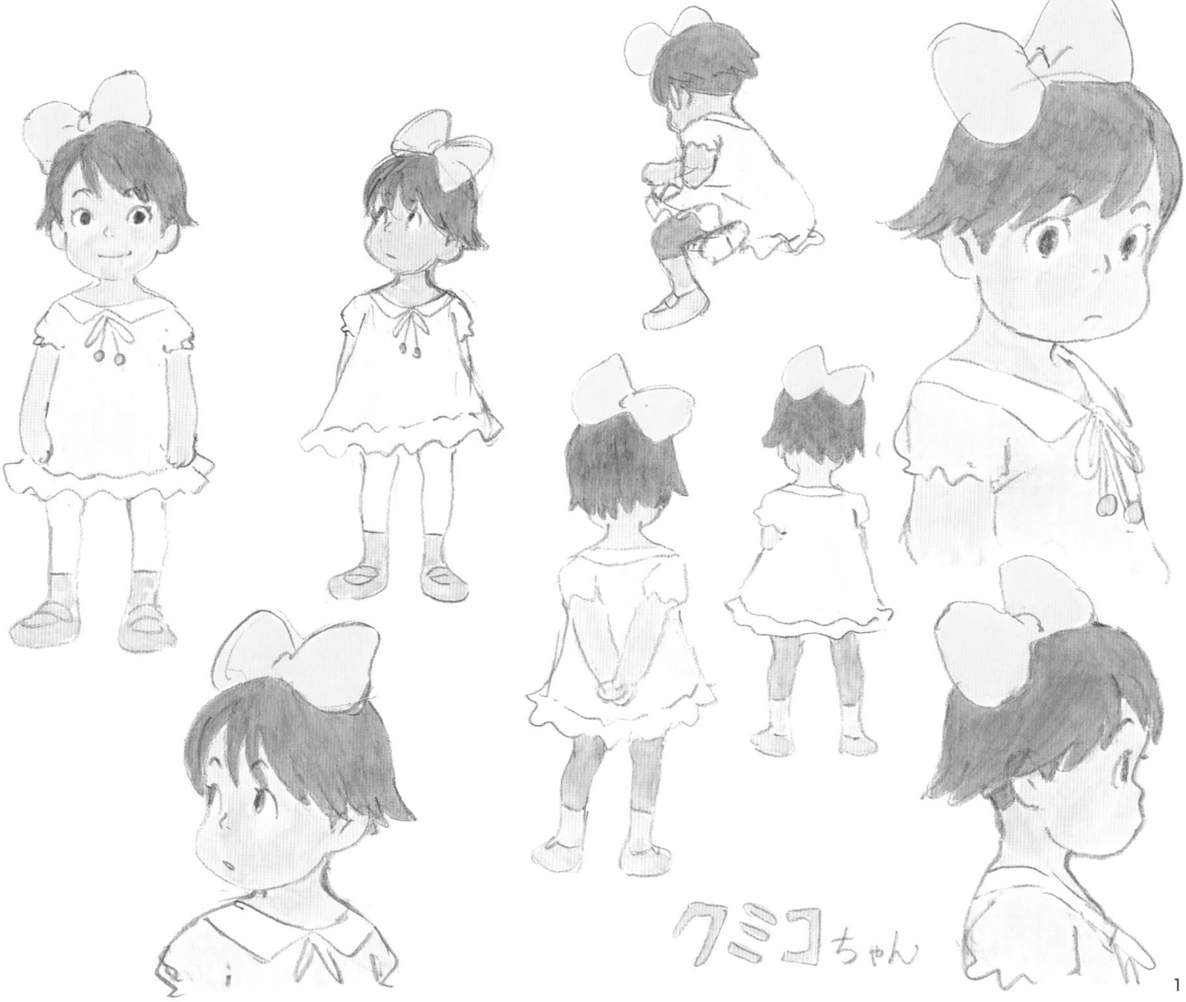
クミコちゃん
1

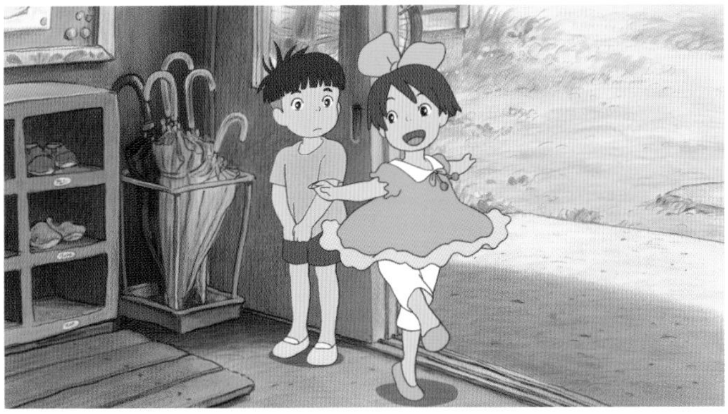
2

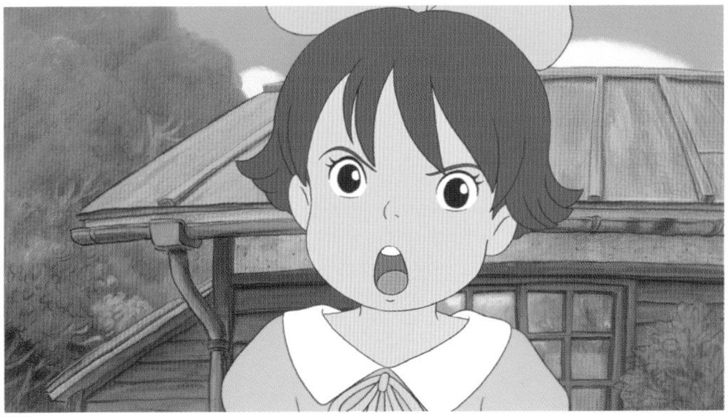
4

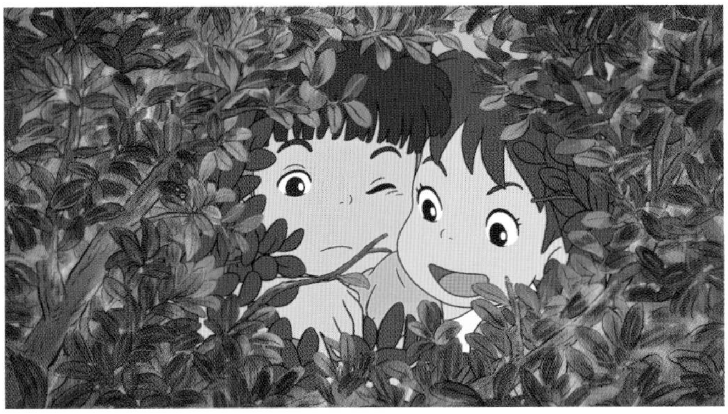
3

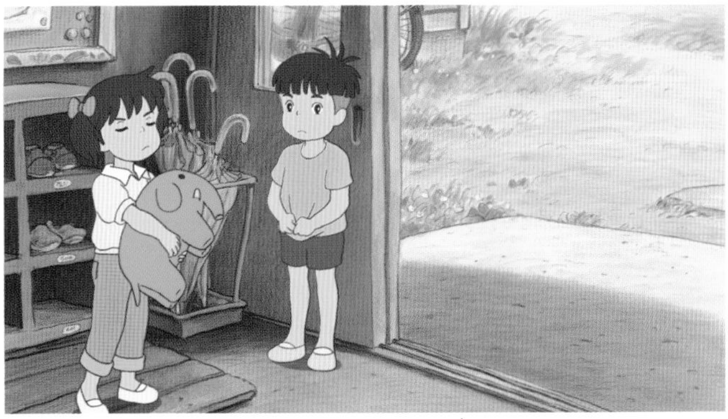
5

Kumiko

1 /Sosuke's friend. A precocious girl who is learning ballet [Rough character sketch].
2 /Kumiko showing off her new dress to Sosuke.
3, 4 /She finds Ponyo hidden in the azalea bushes. She insults Ponyo, and Ponyo squirts her with water.
5 /Sosuke is brusque with Karen, who wants to play with him.

1 /Sosuke, who can't help but be preoccupied with Ponyo inside the pail.
2, 3 /Ponyo squirting Sosuke with water. Unlike with Kumiko, she does so as an expression of affection.
4 /The yard at the Sunflower House. The yard is planted with lots of flowers such as gladiolus and rose moss [Concept art].

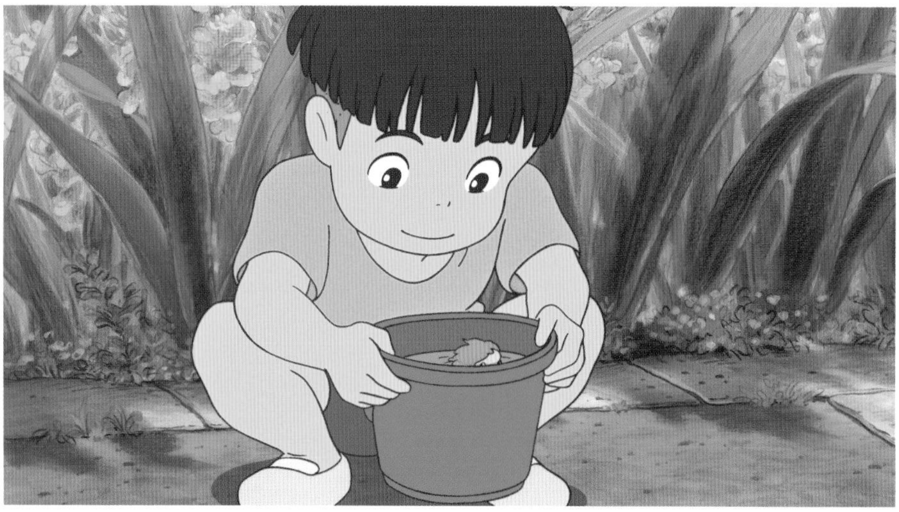

1

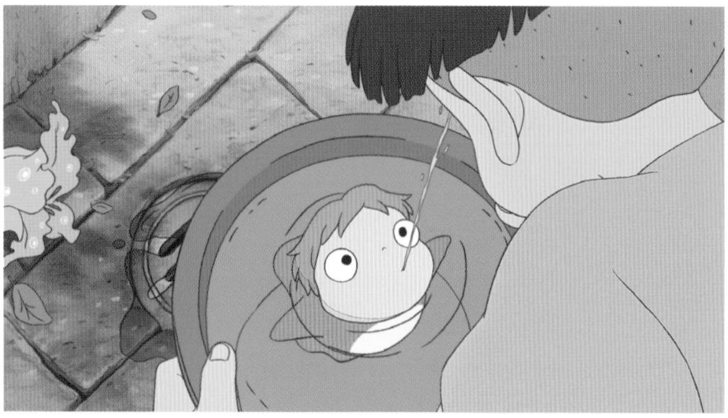

2

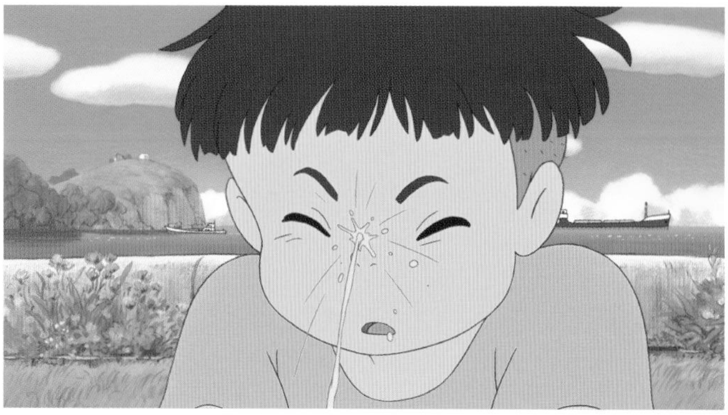

3

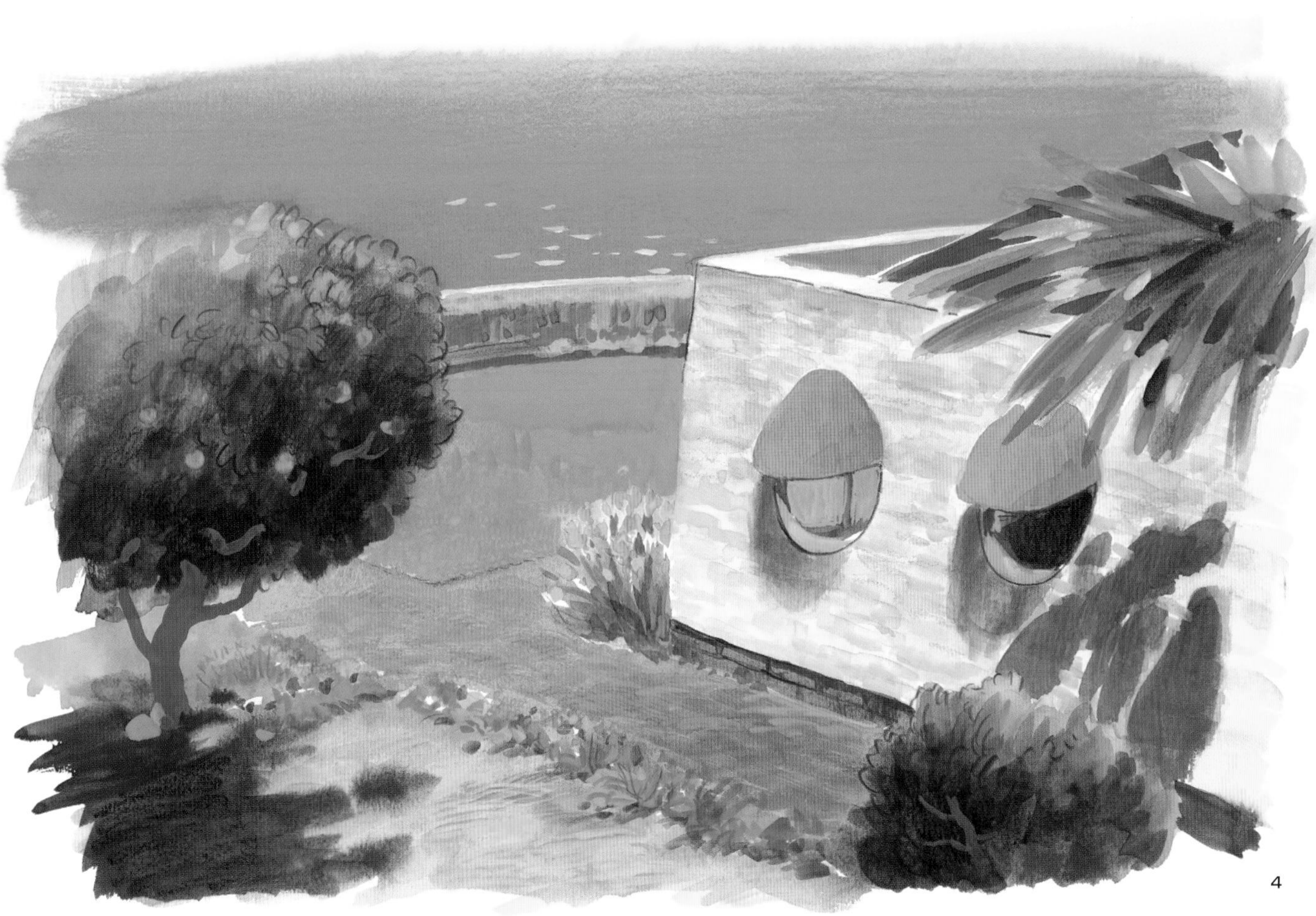

4

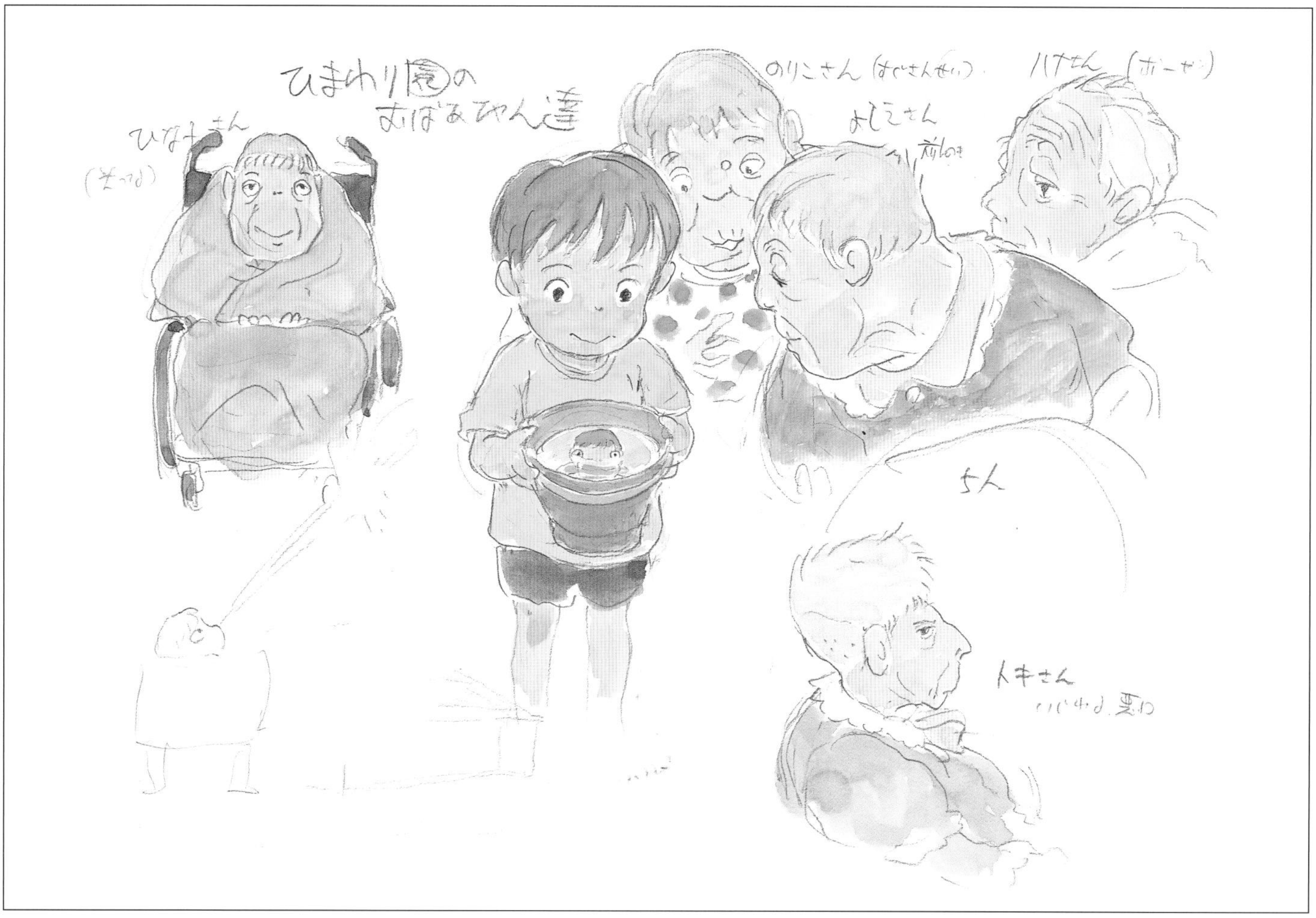
ひまわり園の
おばあちゃん達
のりこさん
ハナさん
よしえさん
トキさん

1

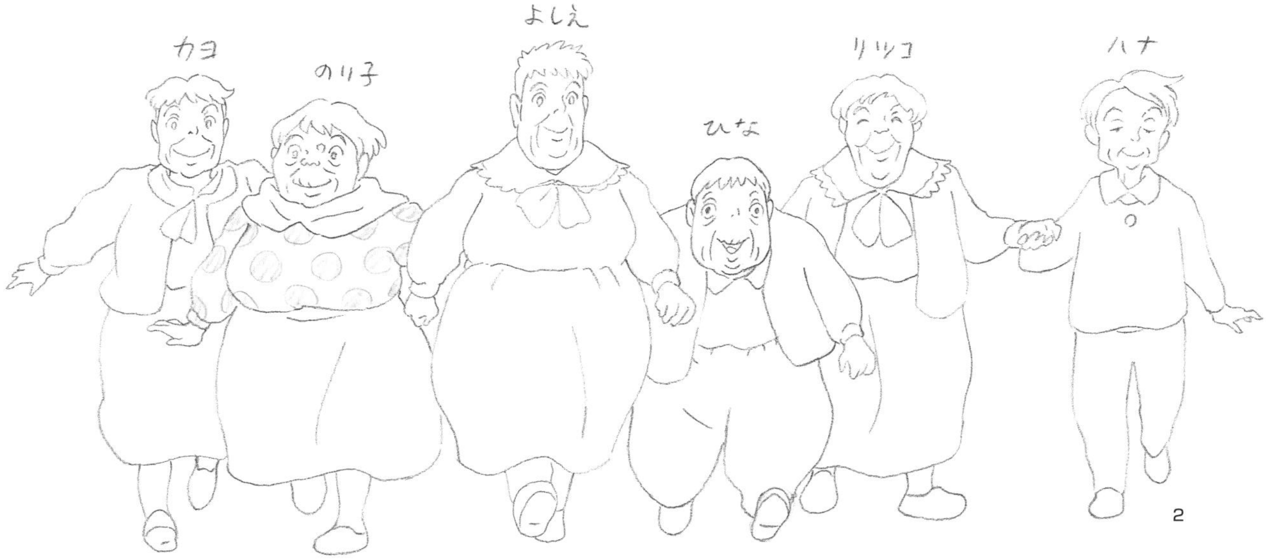
カヨ
のり子
よしえ
ひな
リツコ
ハナ

2

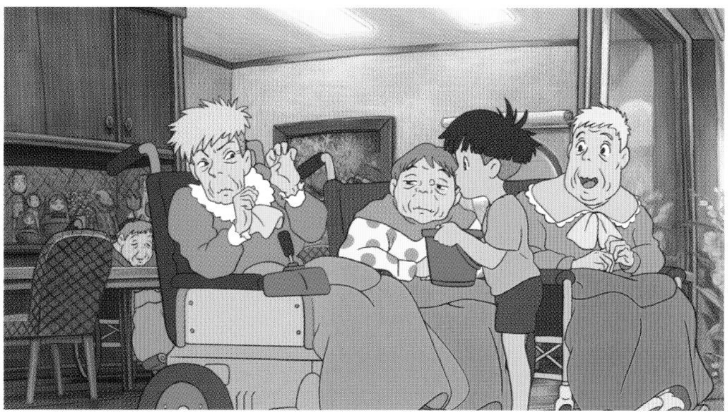

3

The Elderly Ladies

1 /The elderly women at the daycare service center. They are accustomed to seeing Sosuke [Concept sketch].
2 /A height comparison of the elderly ladies, who recover their health in a later scene [Character design].
3 /Toki, who looks at Ponyo and makes a fuss, saying that she has "a real face." Legend has it that a tsunami follows when a human-faced fish washes ashore.

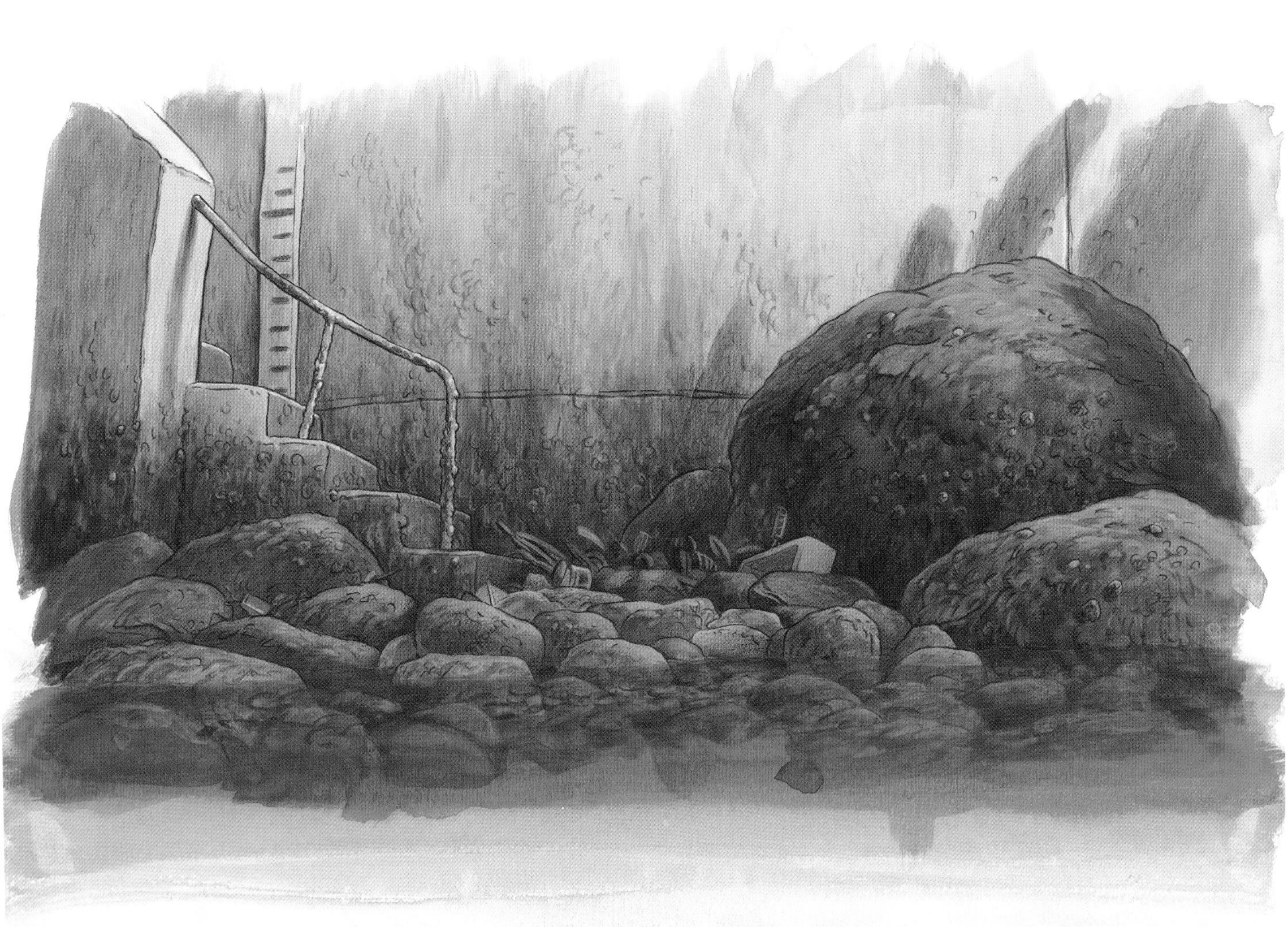

1

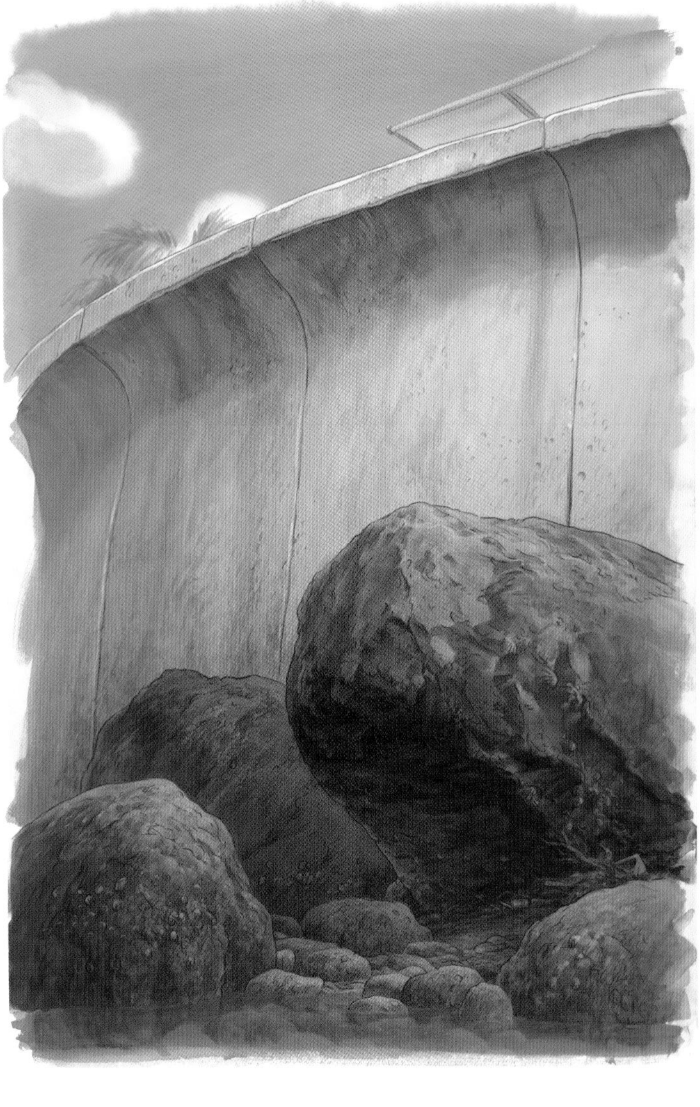

2

Usually I use poster paint to create the backgrounds; then I color the base in a pale color, adding subtle hues and shading on top of it. This time, with *Ponyo*, I added things like tints or detailed expressions with colored pencil on top of what I drew with poster paint. The problem was you could always keep drawing details if you wanted to, so it was difficult to decide when to stop.

The art staff and I all basically drew freehand, almost never using a ruler. Even with one line, it might start out thick and finish up thin in the end. By employing that kind of touch with the brush, we attempted to draw expressive lines rather than monotonously uniform lines. We actually didn't use black colored pencil either. What look like black outlines upon first glance are actually dark brown or brown-grey lines, which are either thicker or thinner depending on the touches we put on the brushes. In thinking about how the background would match the characters, the chief color designer, Michiyo Yasuda, also made very subtle color palette assignments with every shot, which contributed to a softer impression overall.

—Art Director: Noboru Yoshida

"So-su-ke"

1 /The rocky area under the embankment where Sosuke brings Ponyo. Garbage has washed up here as well [Background].
2 /The embankment to which Lisa comes looking for Sosuke and the rocky area below—apparently Sosuke's secret hideaway [Background].
3–10 /Ponyo, speaking a human language for the first time, pronounces Sosuke's name. A touched Sosuke says his name, and they share their fondness for each other.

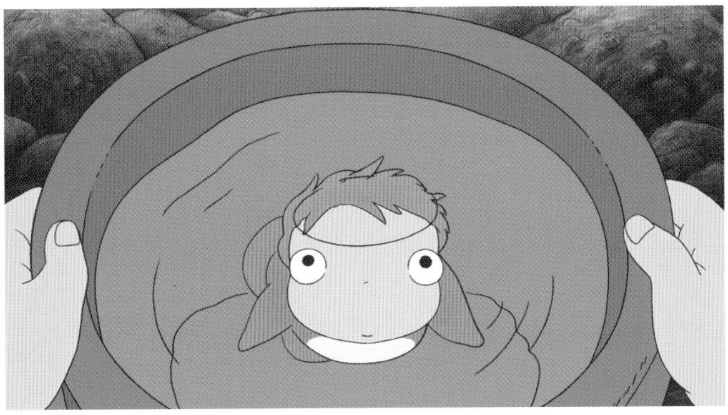
3

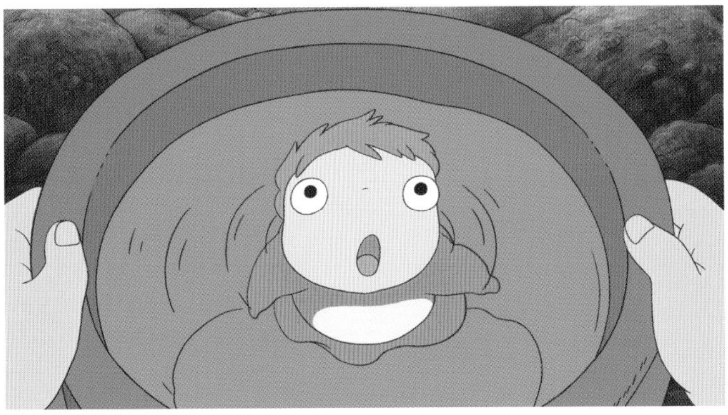
4

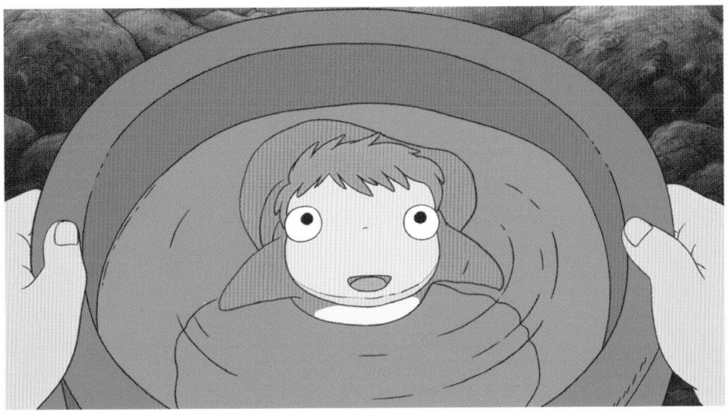
5

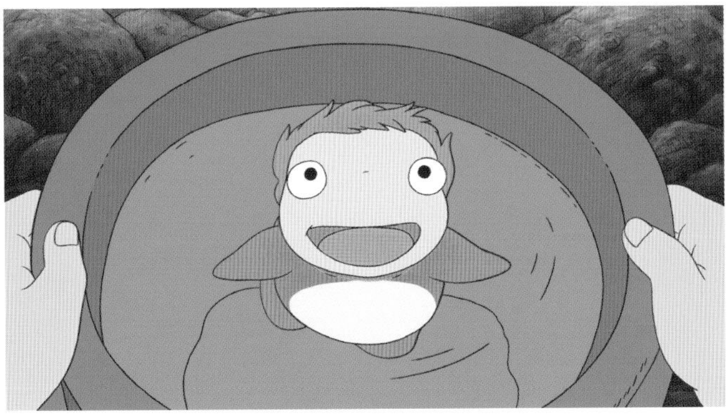
6

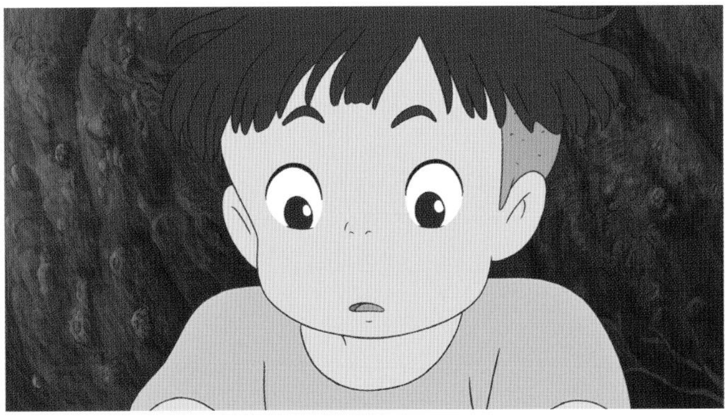
7

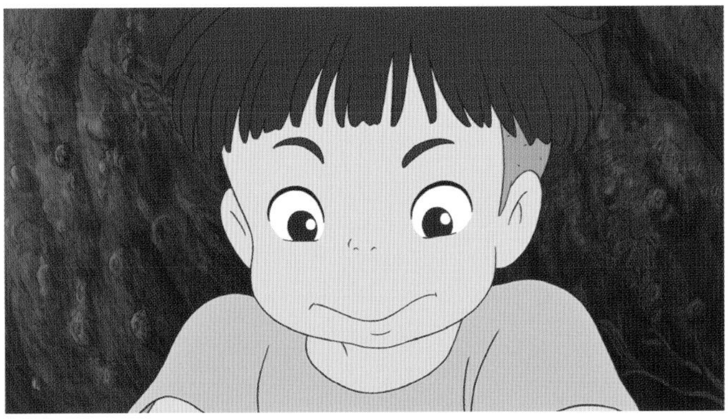
8

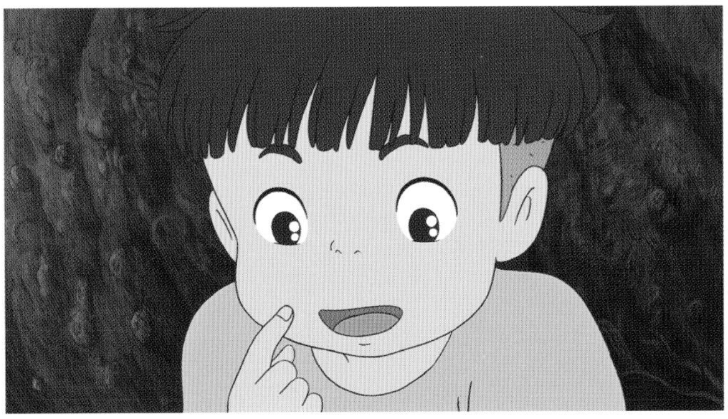
9

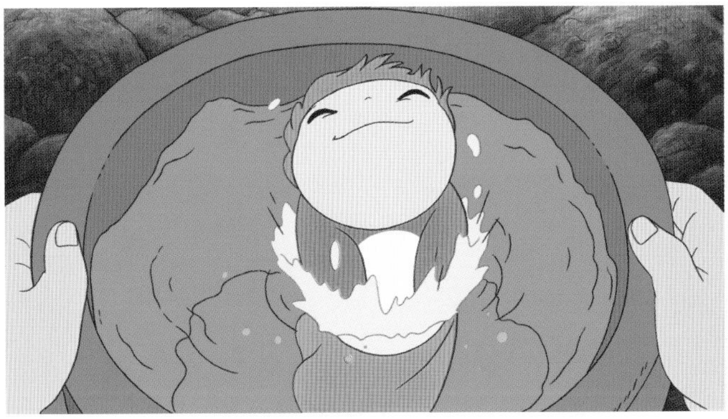
10

1–5 /Fujimoto, who comes chasing after Lisa's car. When he scoops the seawater in his hand, it transforms into little minions. They make a beeline for Sosuke and Ponyo.
6 /A scene drawn by Katsuya Kondo in which Sosuke and Ponyo are engulfed by the minions and become separated [Concept sketches].

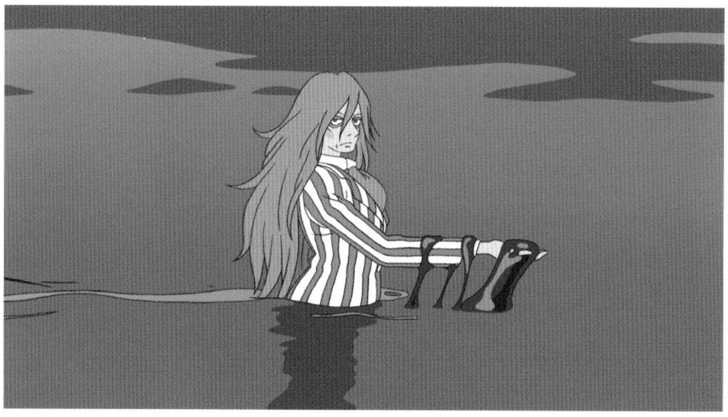
1

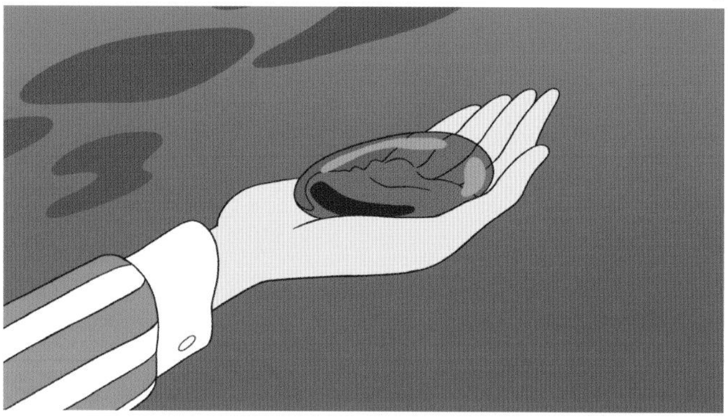
2

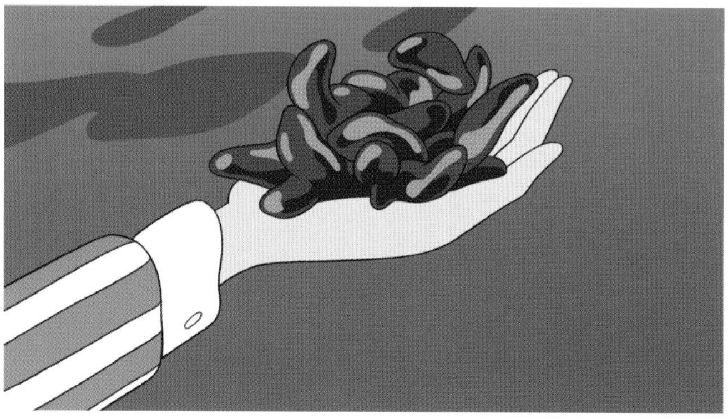
3

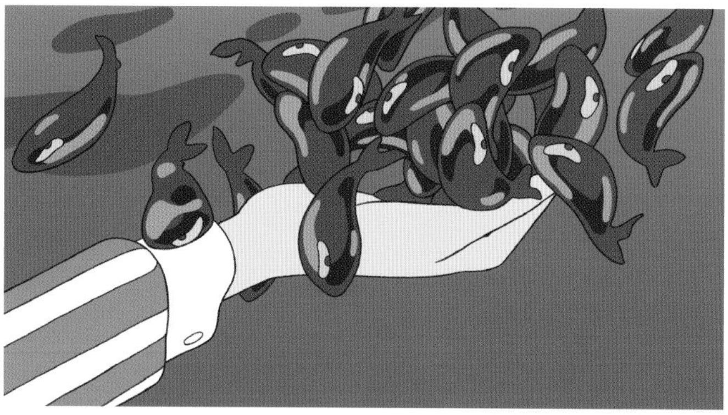
4

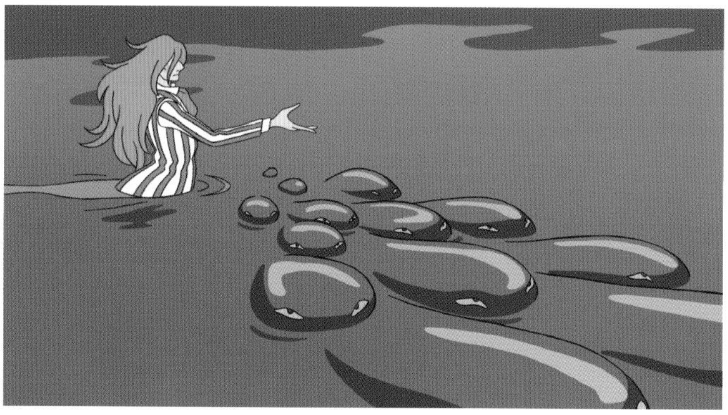
5

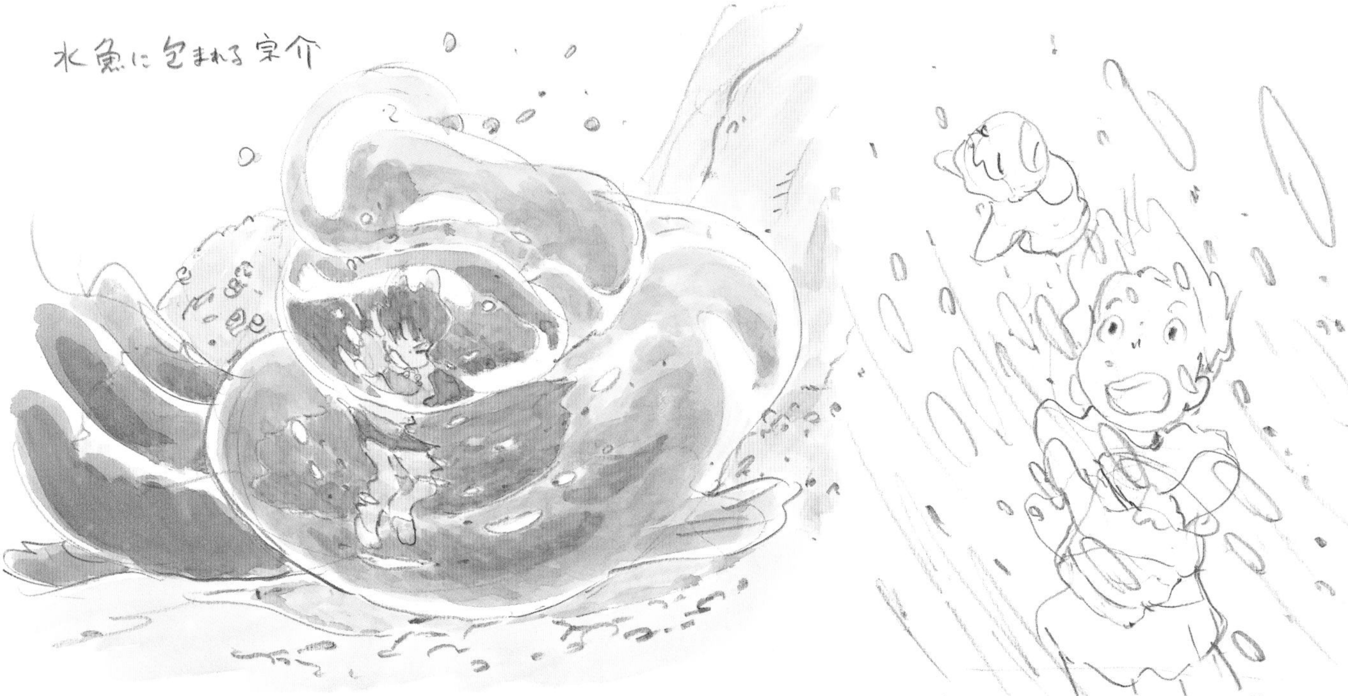
水魚に包まれる宗介
6

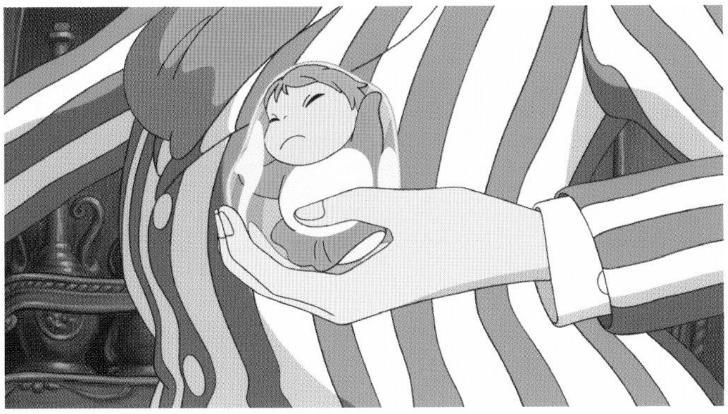

1

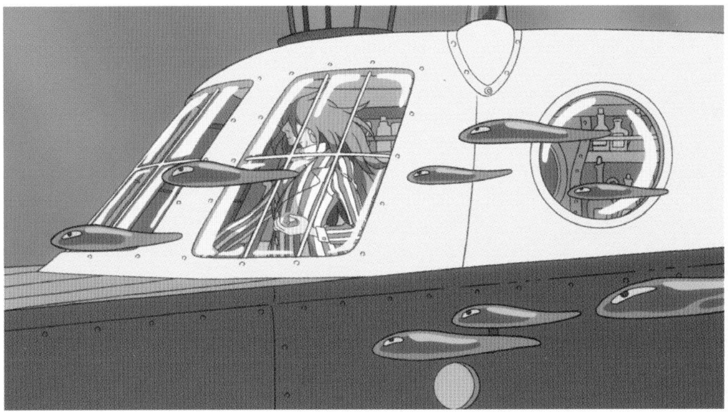

2

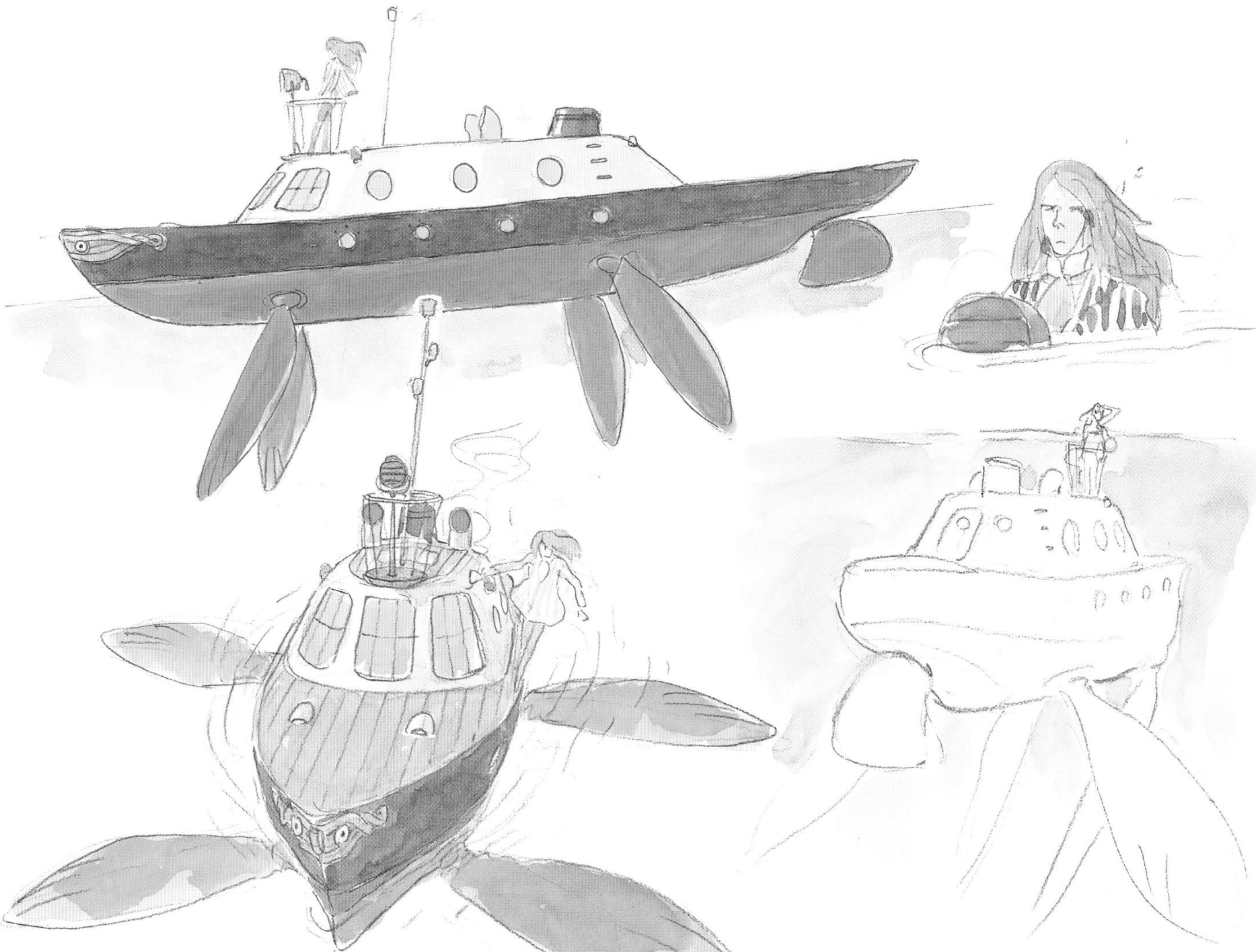

3

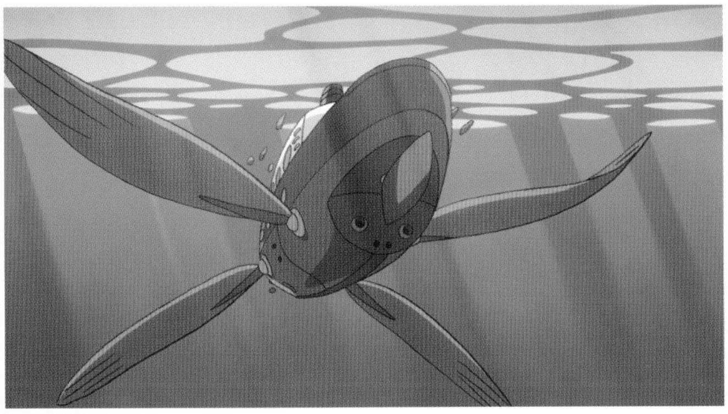

4

The *Basking Shark*

1 /Ponyo, who has been confined inside a water sphere by Fujimoto's magic.
2 /Fujimoto, inside the cabin of the *Basking Shark*. The minions follow alongside him.
3 /Fujimoto's submarine, the *Basking Shark* [Concept sketches].
4 /The *Basking Shark*, transporting Ponyo back to the deep sea.

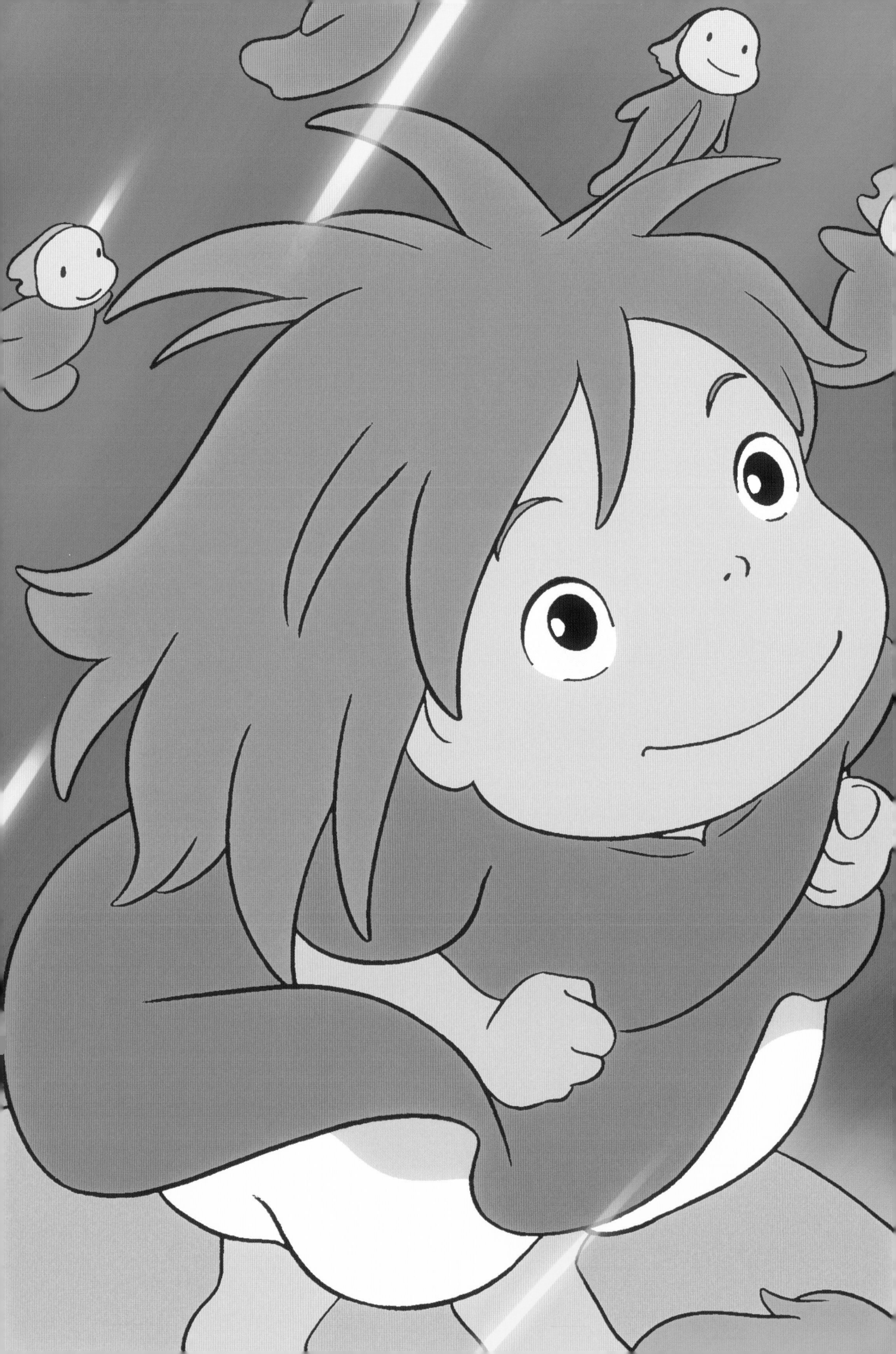

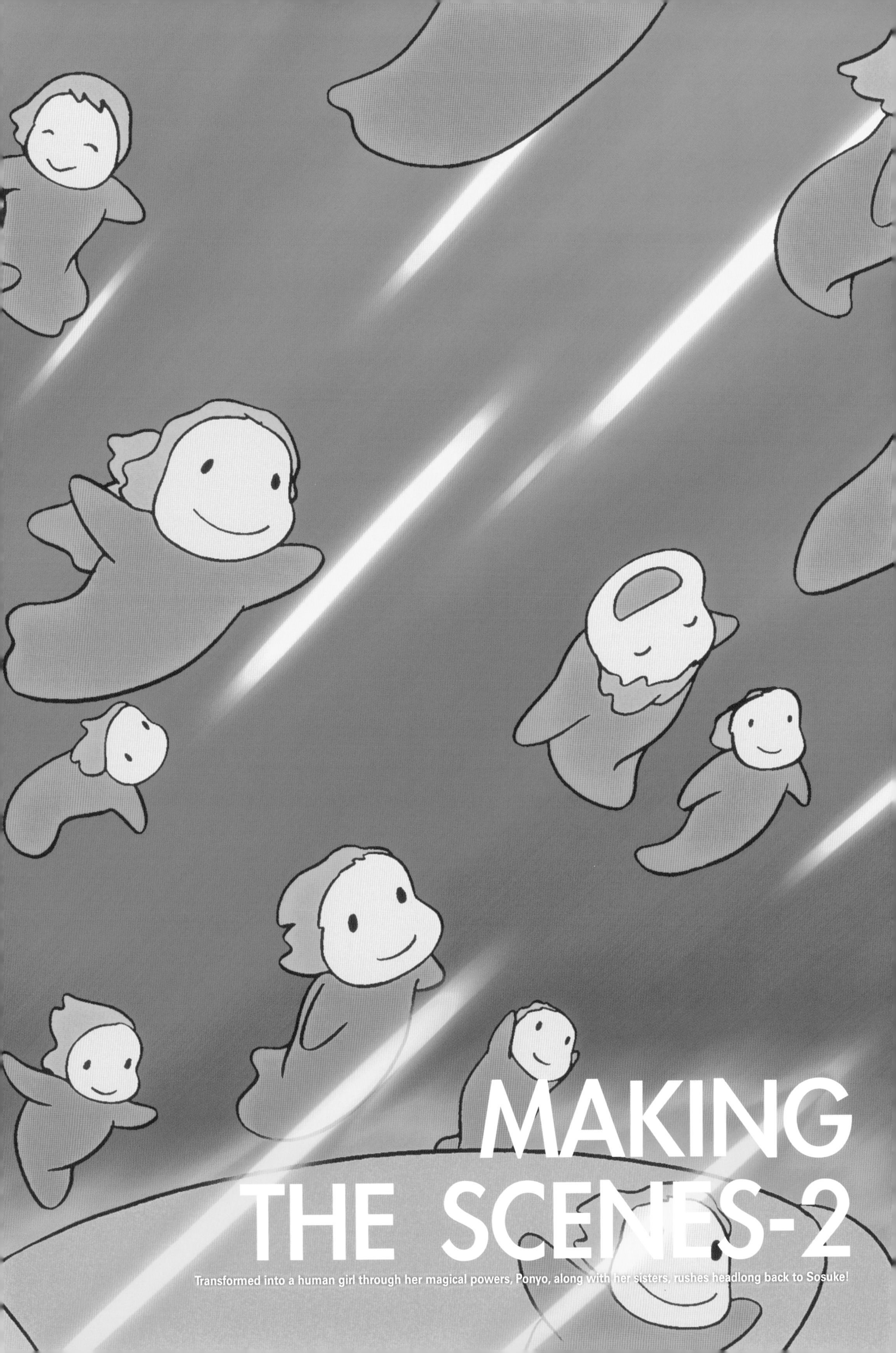

MAKING THE SCENES-2

Transformed into a human girl through her magical powers, Ponyo, along with her sisters, rushes headlong back to Sosuke!

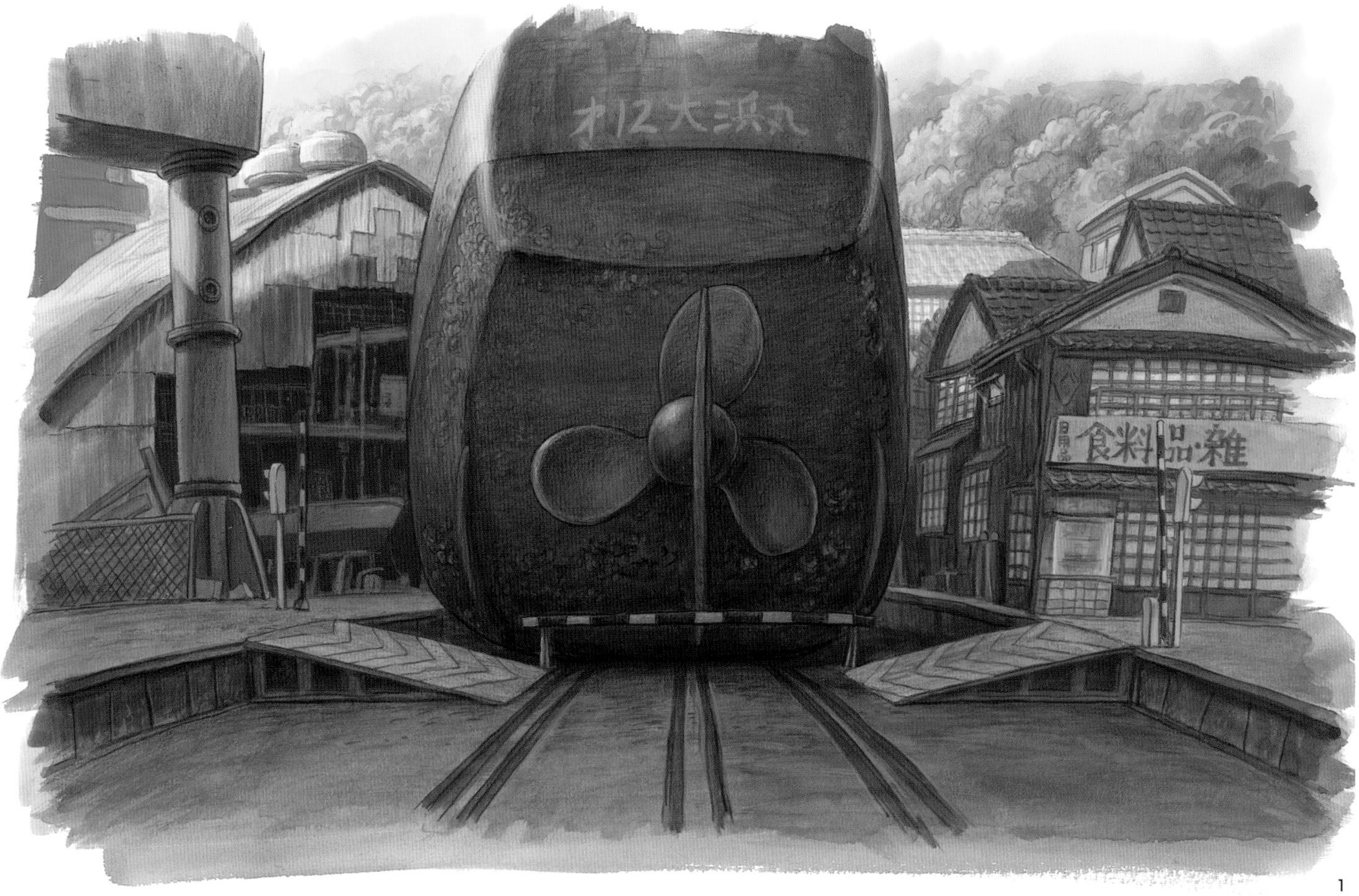
オ12大浜丸
食料品雑

1

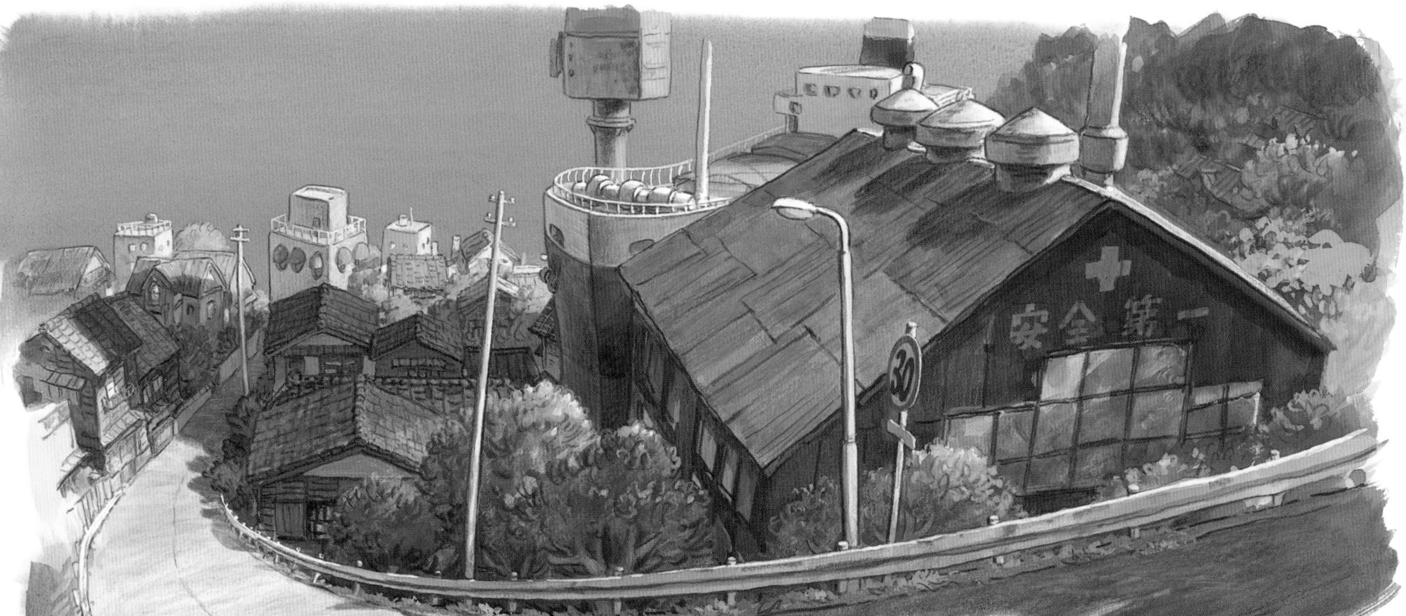
安全第一
30

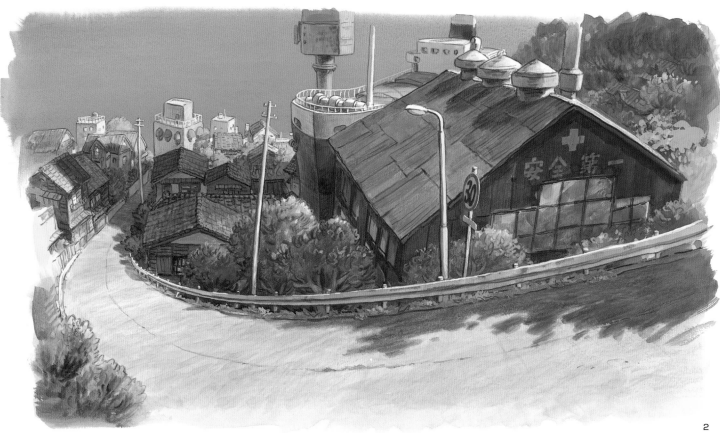

2

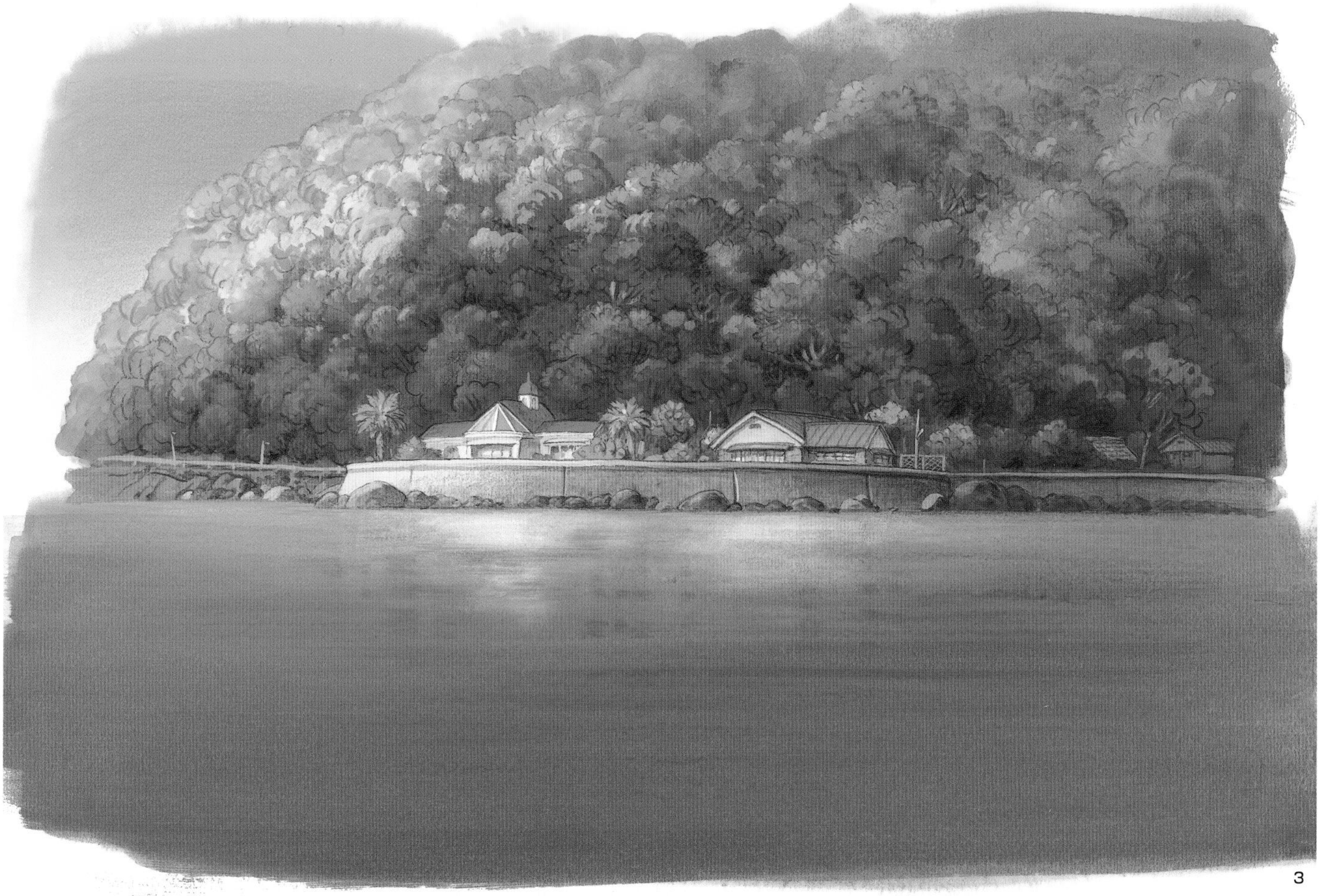

3

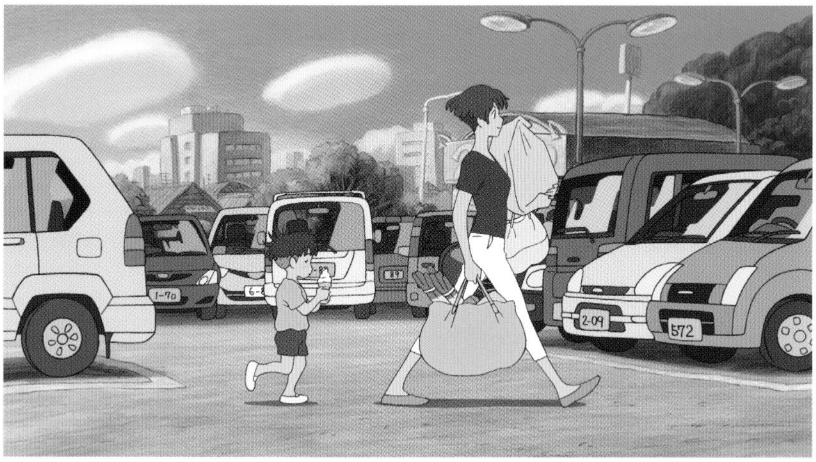
2-09
572

4

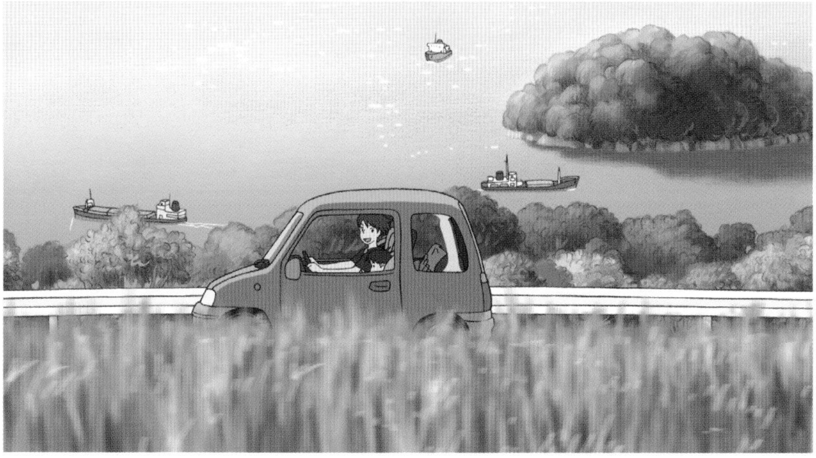

5

After Shopping

1 /The docks through which Lisa's car passes [Background].
2 /The hill road behind the docks, which leads back to Sosuke's house [Background].
3 /The Sunflower House and Sunflower Preschool as seen from the sea. It's late afternoon with the sun beginning to set [Background].
4 /Lisa and Sosuke heading home after shopping at the supermarket in the next town. Heartbroken after Ponyo is taken from him, Sosuke is still in shock even though Lisa has bought him an ice cream cone.
5 /Lisa's car speeding back home. Happy that Koichi is coming home on this day, Lisa tries to console Sosuke, saying "She wasn't meant to live in a bucket. The ocean is home to her."

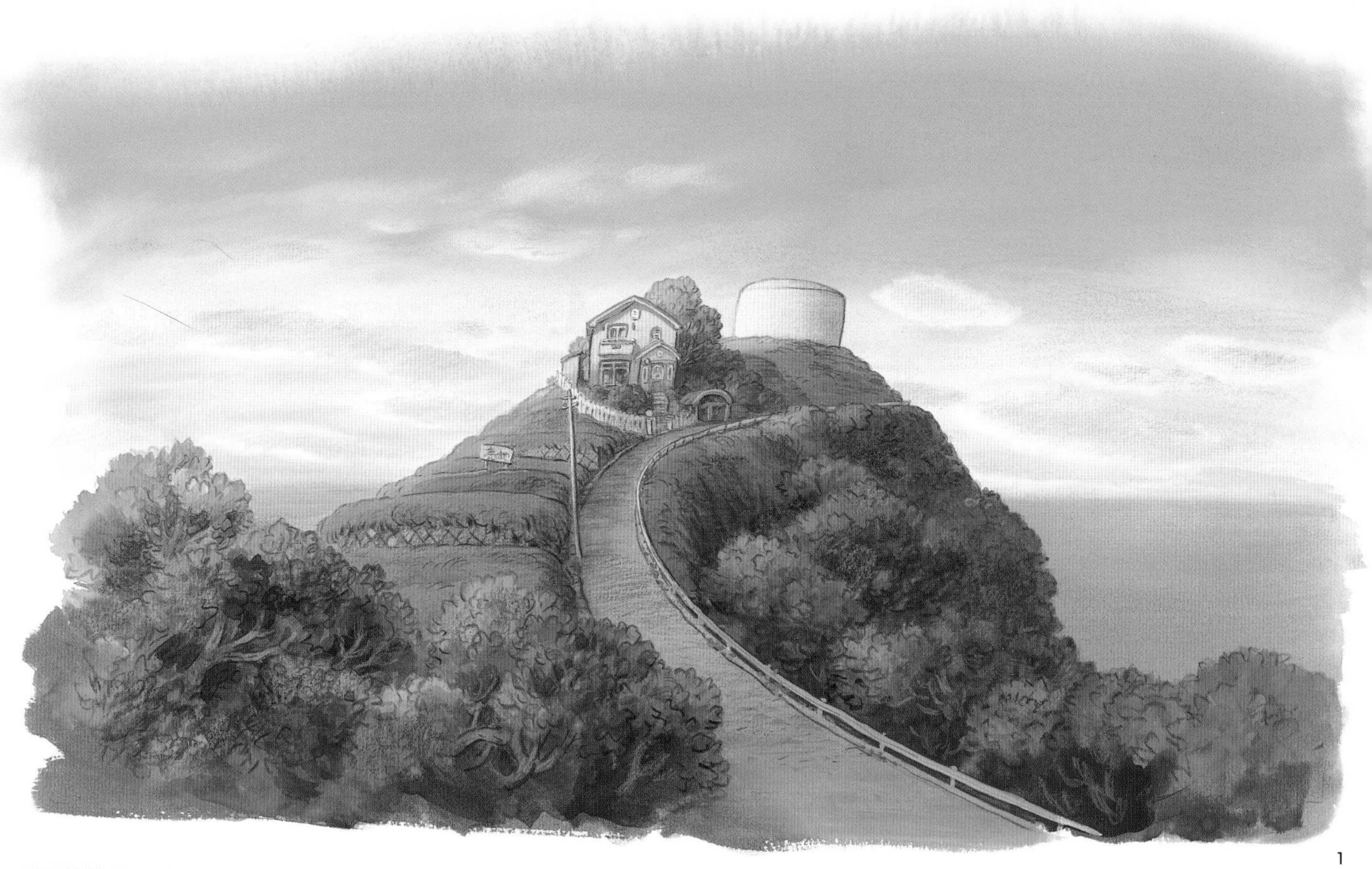

1

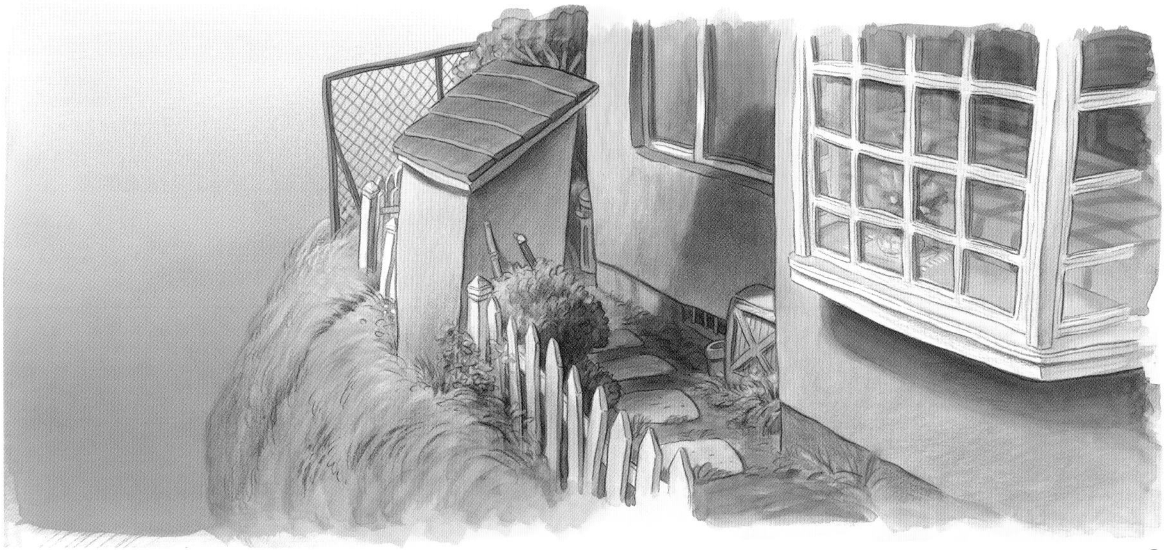

2

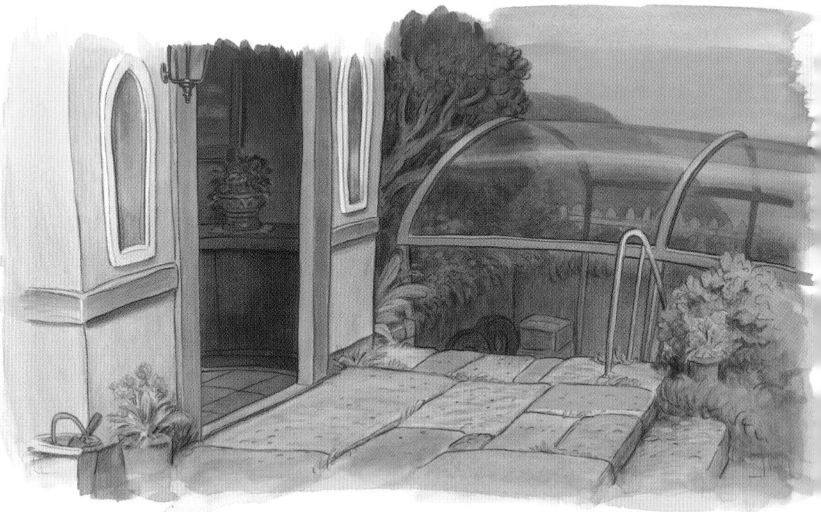

3

Before Dusk

1 /Sosuke's house on the promontory, as seen from a distance [Background].
2 /The side of the house. A gate leads to the path that goes down to the rocky shore [Background].
3 /The entrance. The stairs connect the entrance to the garage [Background].
4 /Sosuke's house bathed in the faint evening light [Background].

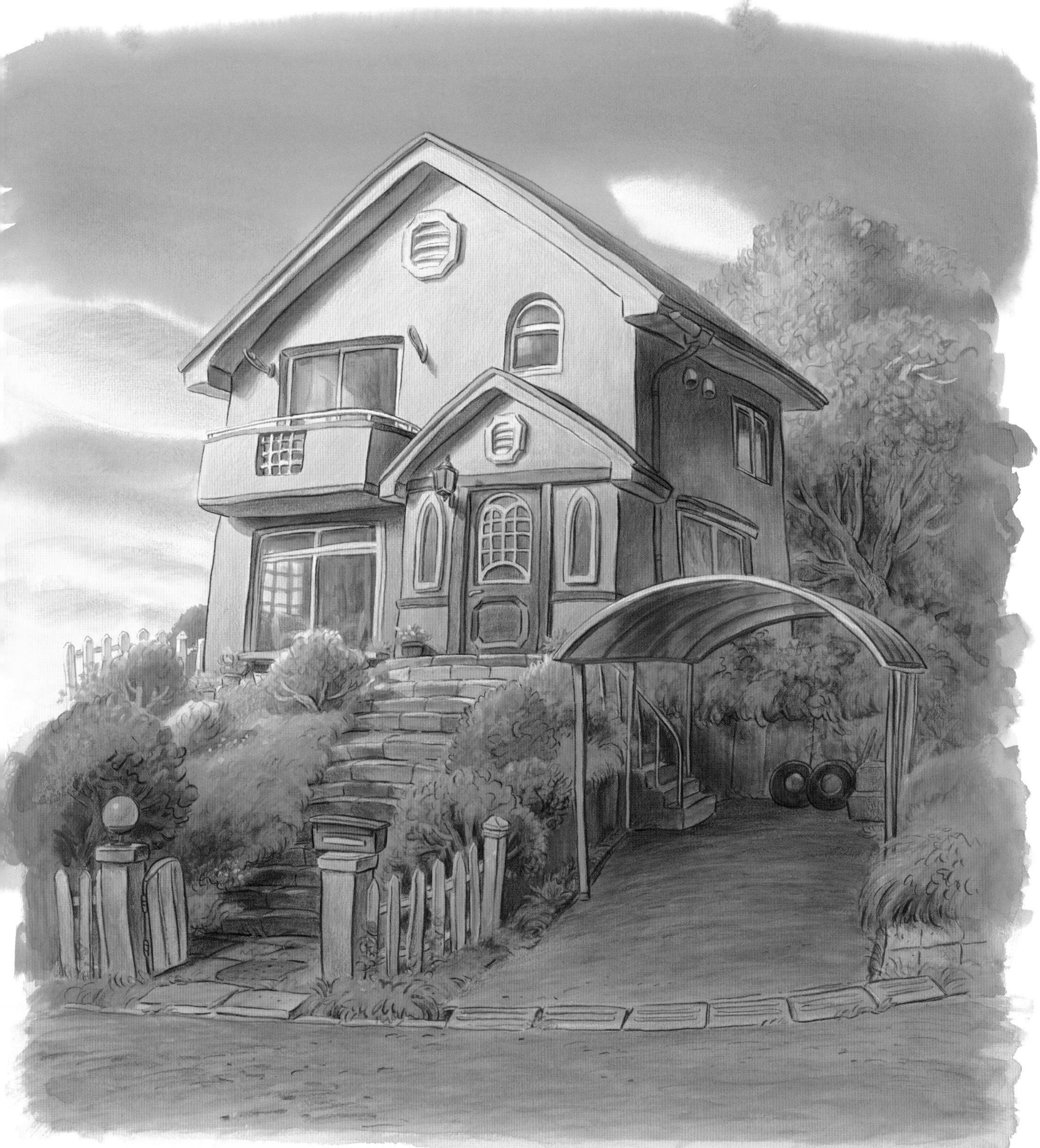

4

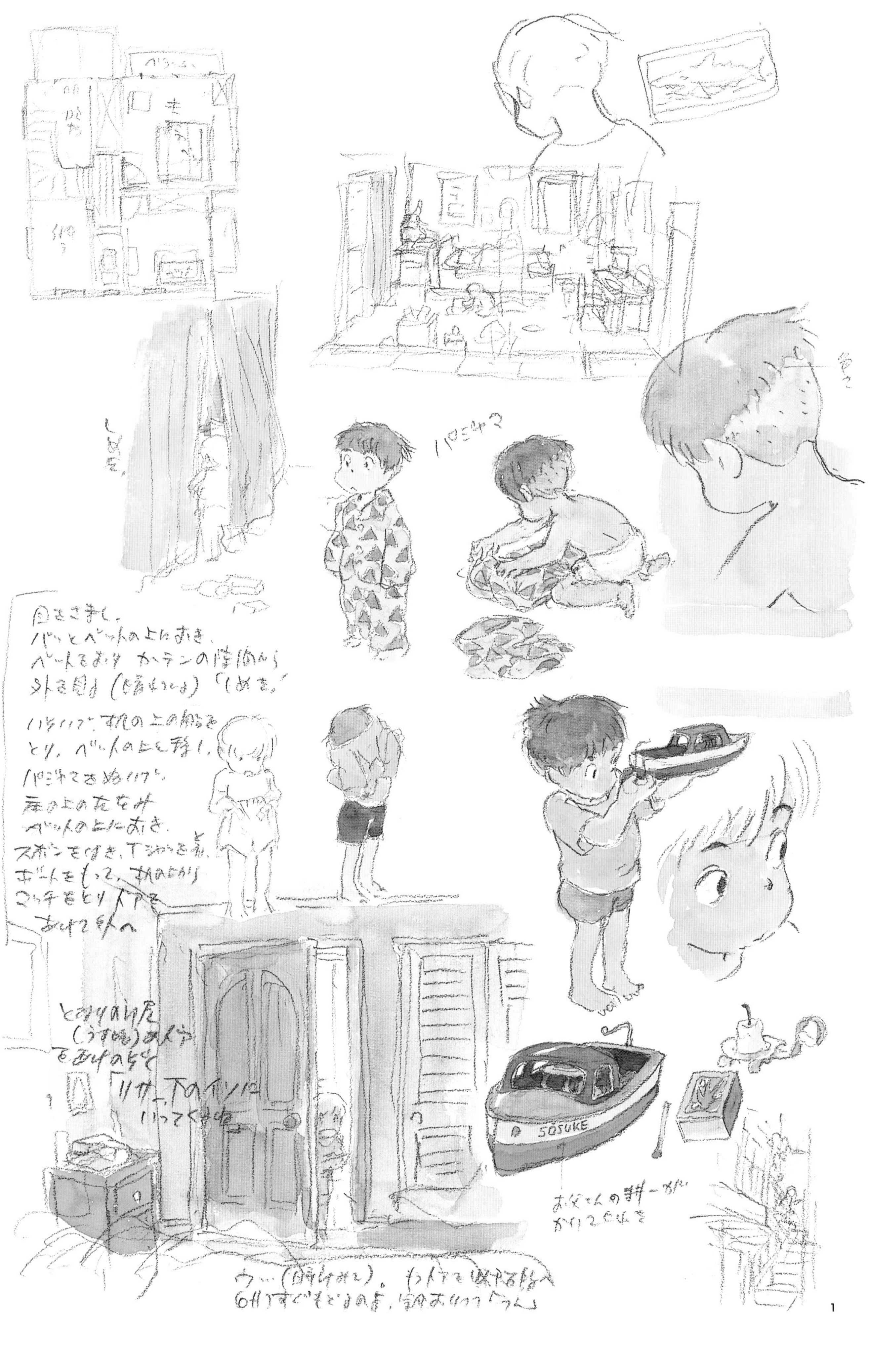
パジャマ
目をさまし、
ベッドをおり カーテンの陰から
外を見る（晴れている）「しめた。」
パジャマをぬいで、
ズボンをはき、Tシャツを着、
ボートをもって、
あけて外へ。
となりの部屋
（うす暗い）
SŌSUKE

1

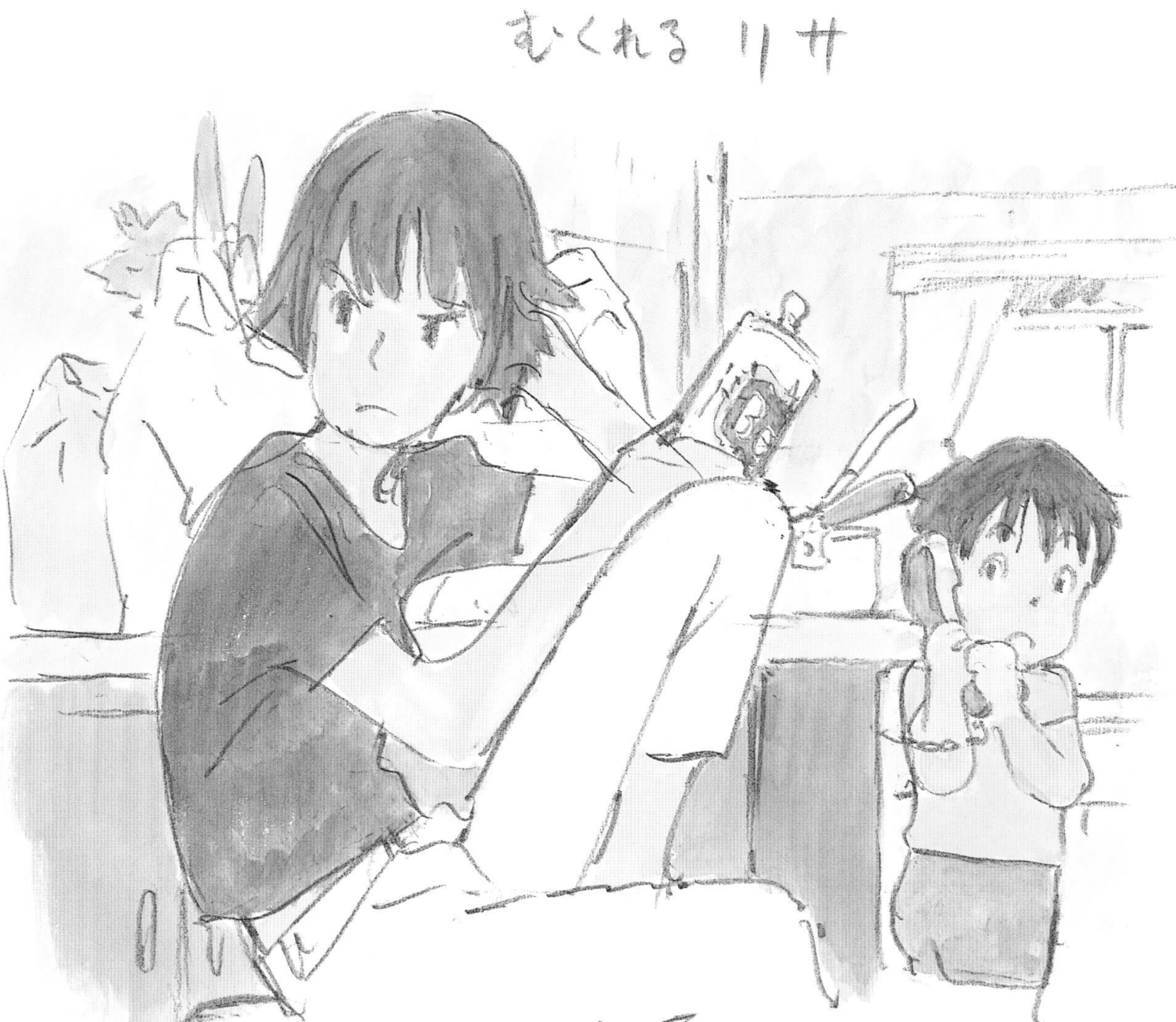
むくれる リサ

2

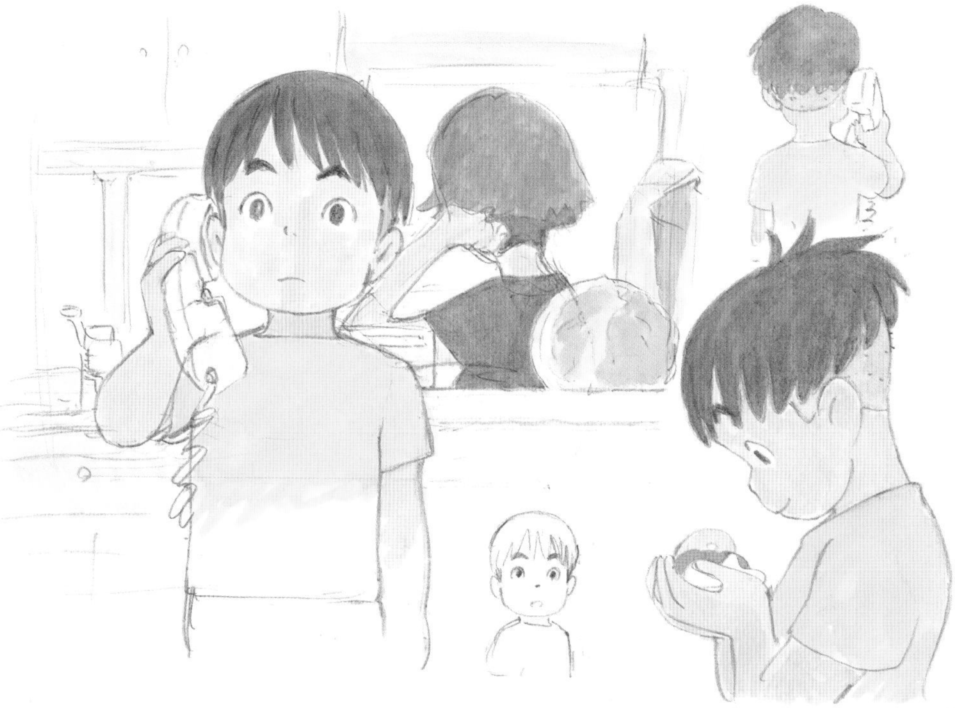

3

1 /A scene, drawn by Miyazaki, of Sosuke's morning before he finds Ponyo. This scene does not appear in the film [Concept sketches].
2, 3 /Sosuke and Lisa, drawn by Katsuya Kondo [Concept sketches].

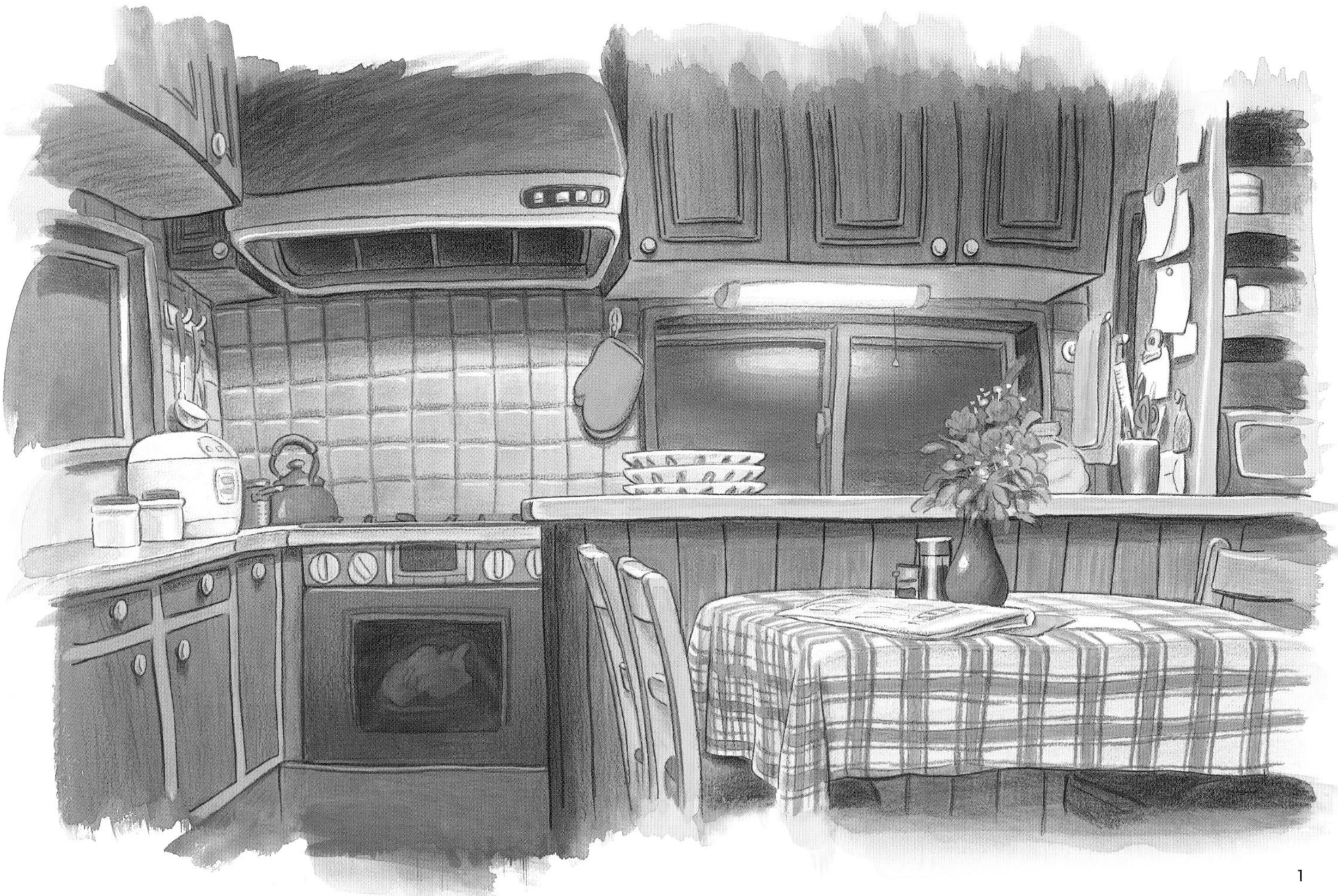

1

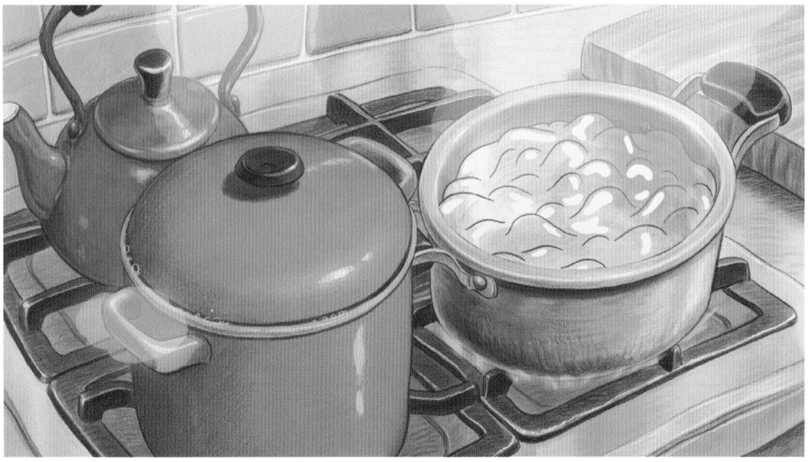

2

The Kitchen and Living Room

1 /Lisa's kitchen—still sparkling new [Background].
2 /A steaming pot of stew. A pot of water is boiling next to it in order to cook spinach for Koichi, who doesn't get enough vegetables.
3 /A small workplace in the corner of the living room. Koichi's desk is here [Background].
4 /The living room with a low sofa set and table [Background].

Although Lisa's kitchen looks simple, I consciously used brighter tones because it would give off a lonely impression if I went with a palette that was either too chic or too subdued. I used a lot of red here too, so Miyazaki called my work colorful [*laughs*]. I also distorted the inside of the kitchen a little by using curved lines. I thought the room would look too tidy if rendered with straight lines; the disparity between the character and background would be accentuated by distorting the lines.

—Art Director: Noboru Yoshida

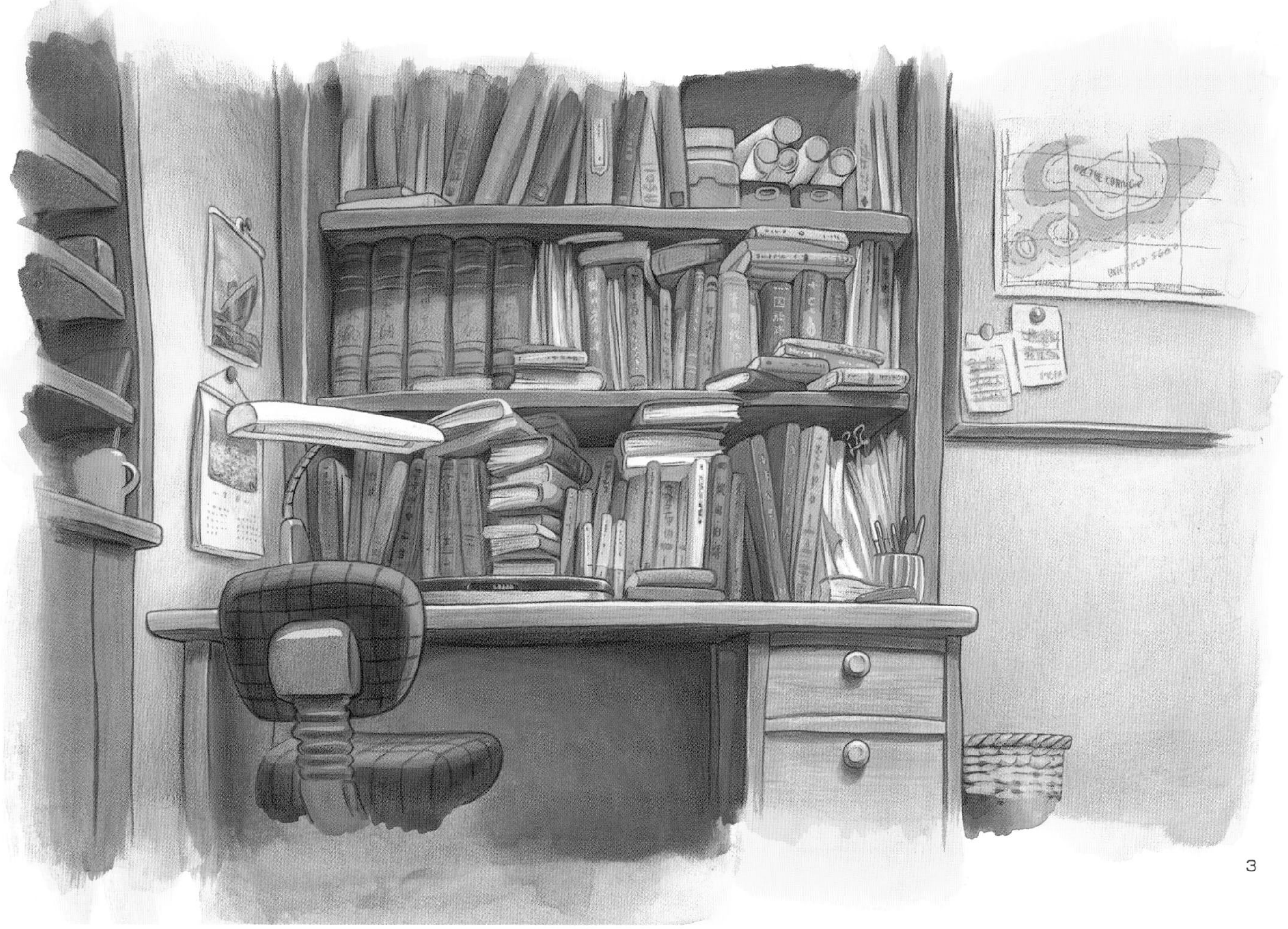

3

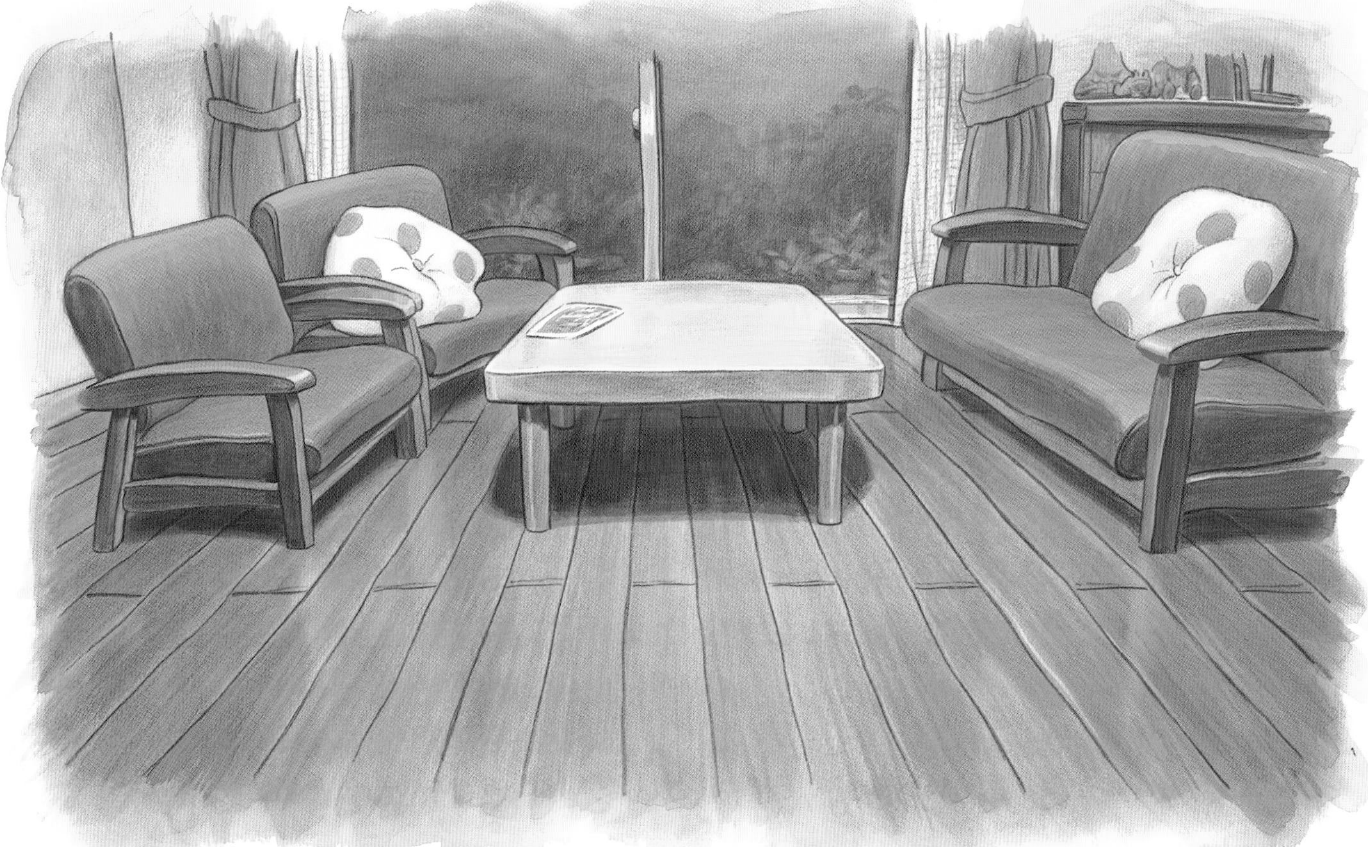

4

1

2

3

1 /Sosuke's house, now dark. Only the light in Sosuke's room upstairs is on, as Sosuke and Lisa wait to communicate with Koichi [Concept art].
2 /Same [Background].
3 /The entire house is lit up, as if to reflect Lisa's brightened mood after being consoled by Sosuke [Background].

The Family

1 /Sosuke and Lisa, reading the signal from the passing *Koganei Maru* [Concept sketch].
2, 3 /Koichi sends a message via the signal device—"Dad says he loves you"—to which Lisa indignantly returns a message in response.
4 /A collection of expressions and poses for Koichi, Sosuke's father and captain of the *Koganei Maru* [Character design].
5 /Sosuke turning on the light next to Lisa, who sulks on the bed.
6 /Lisa, recovering her good mood after Sosuke consoles her, "Don't cry, Mom."
7 /"Don't you worry, Sosuke. You did your best. Ponyo will be fine."

For the message sent from the *Koganei Maru*, we accurately depicted the timing of how the message would be sent in Morse code. However, there is such a thing as rhythm, and since the way in which Lisa sends her message also conveys her anger, we did change the rhythm of her message a bit so that her emotions were easier to animate.

—Supervising Animator: Katsuya Kondo

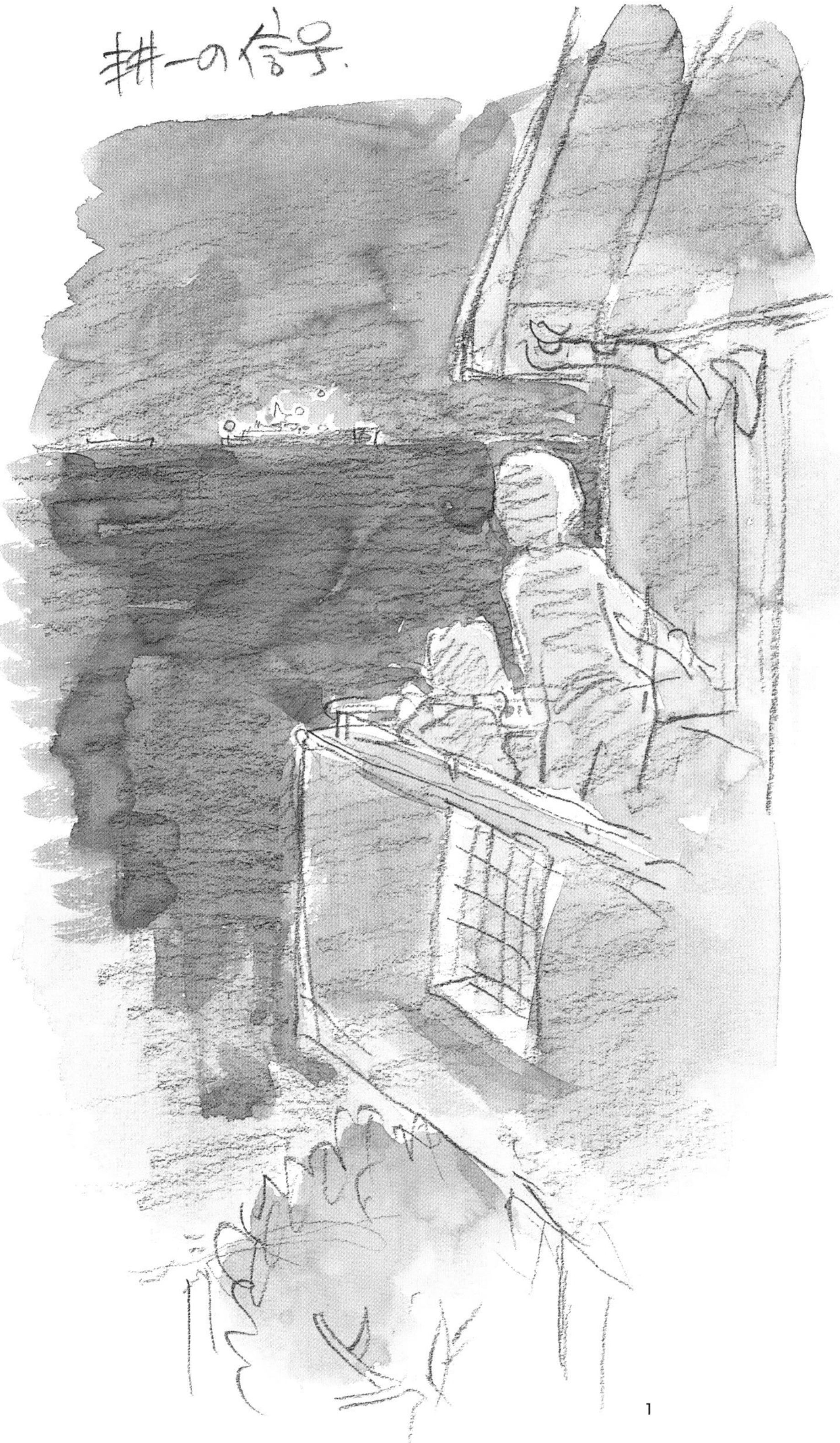
耕一の信号.

1

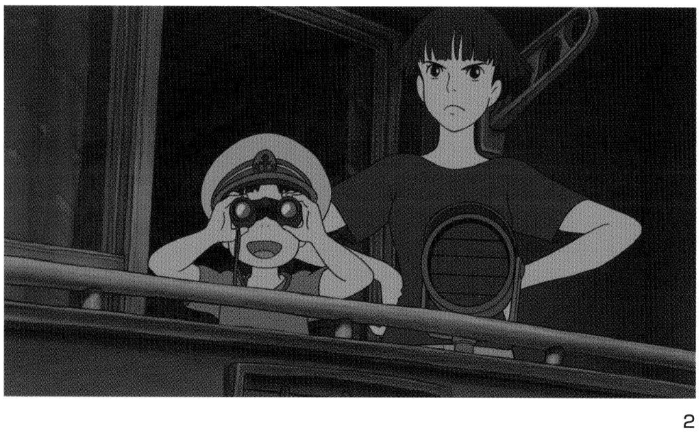

2

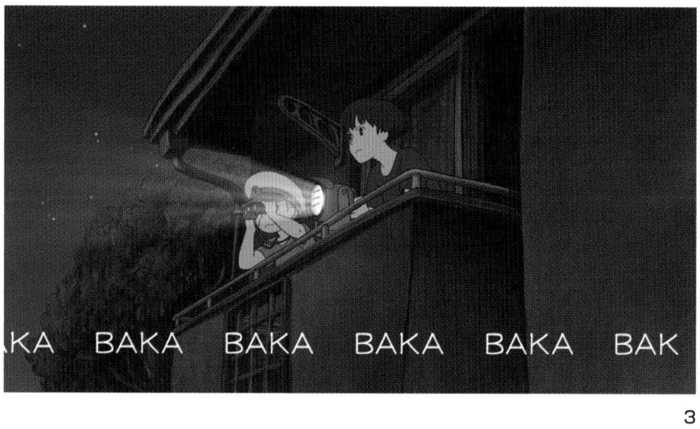
KA BAKA BAKA BAKA BAKA BAK

3

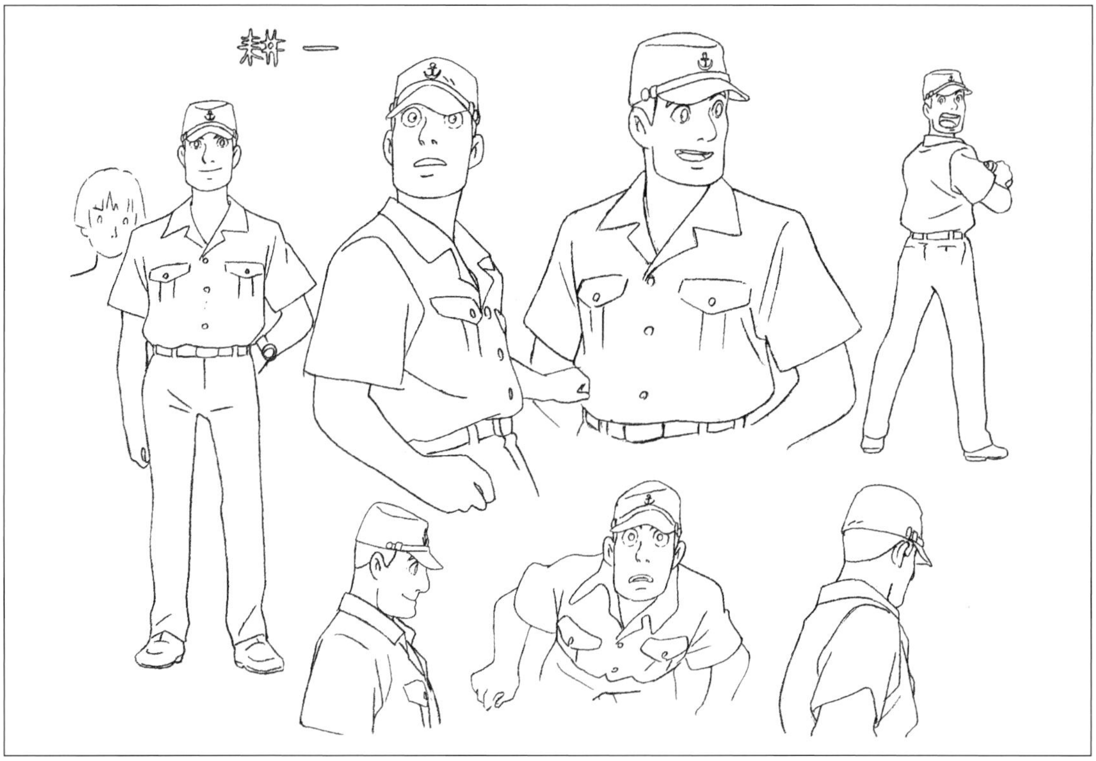
耕一

4

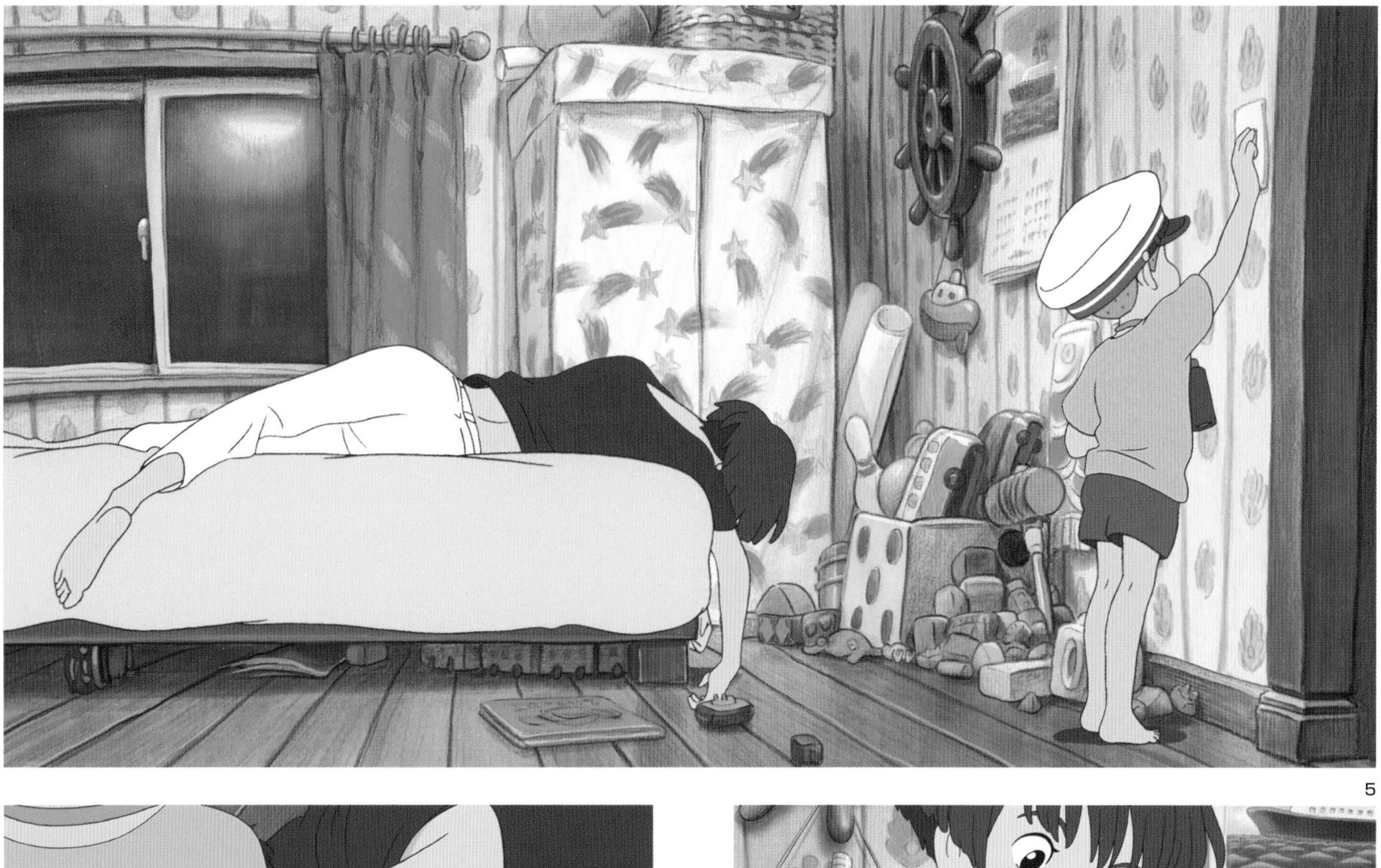

5

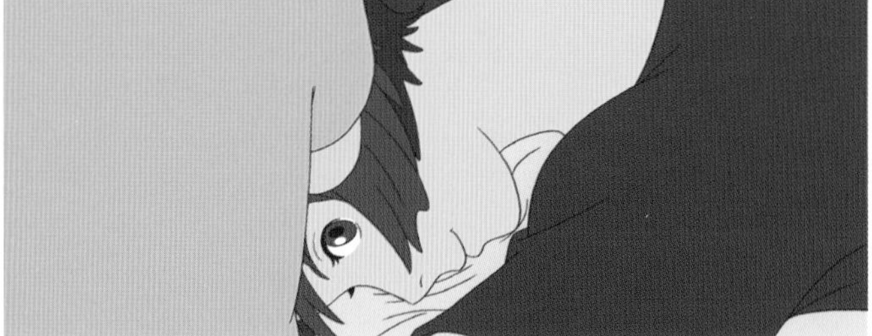

6

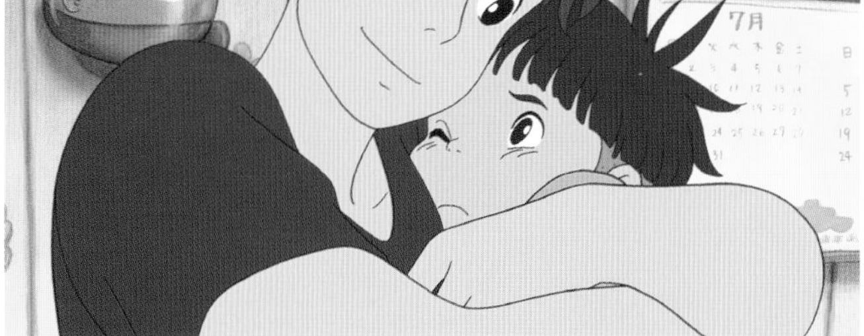
7月

7

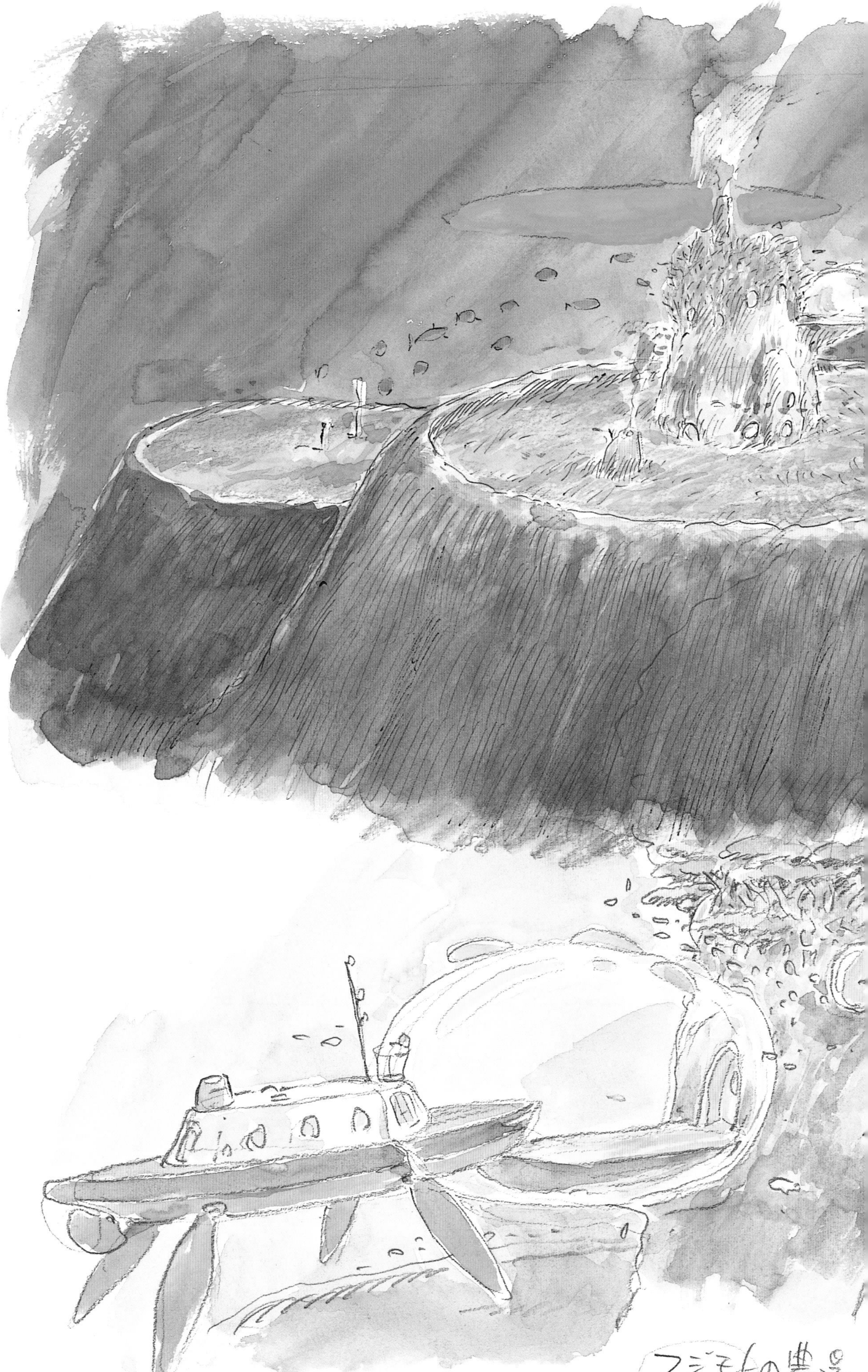
フジモトの農場

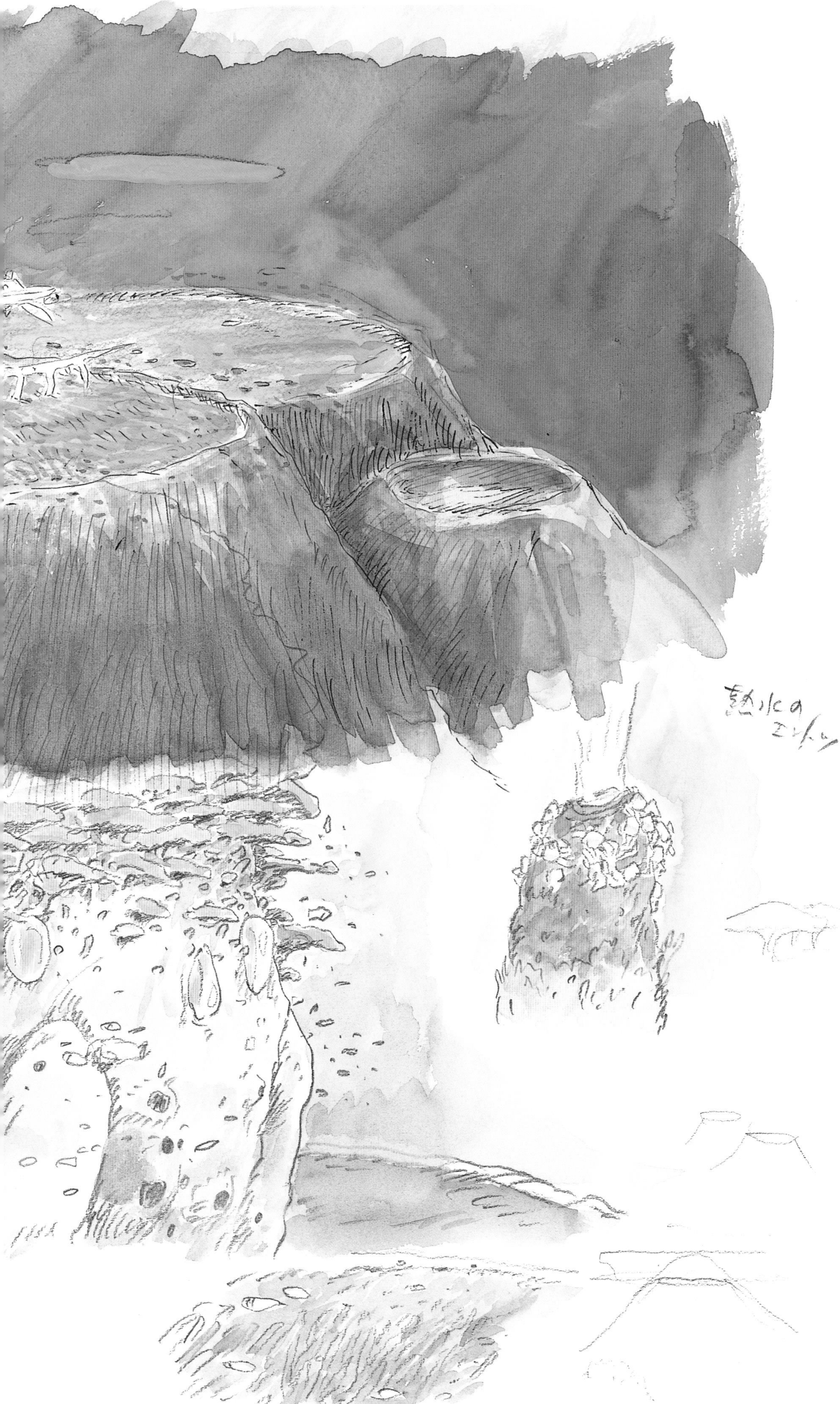
熱水のエントツ

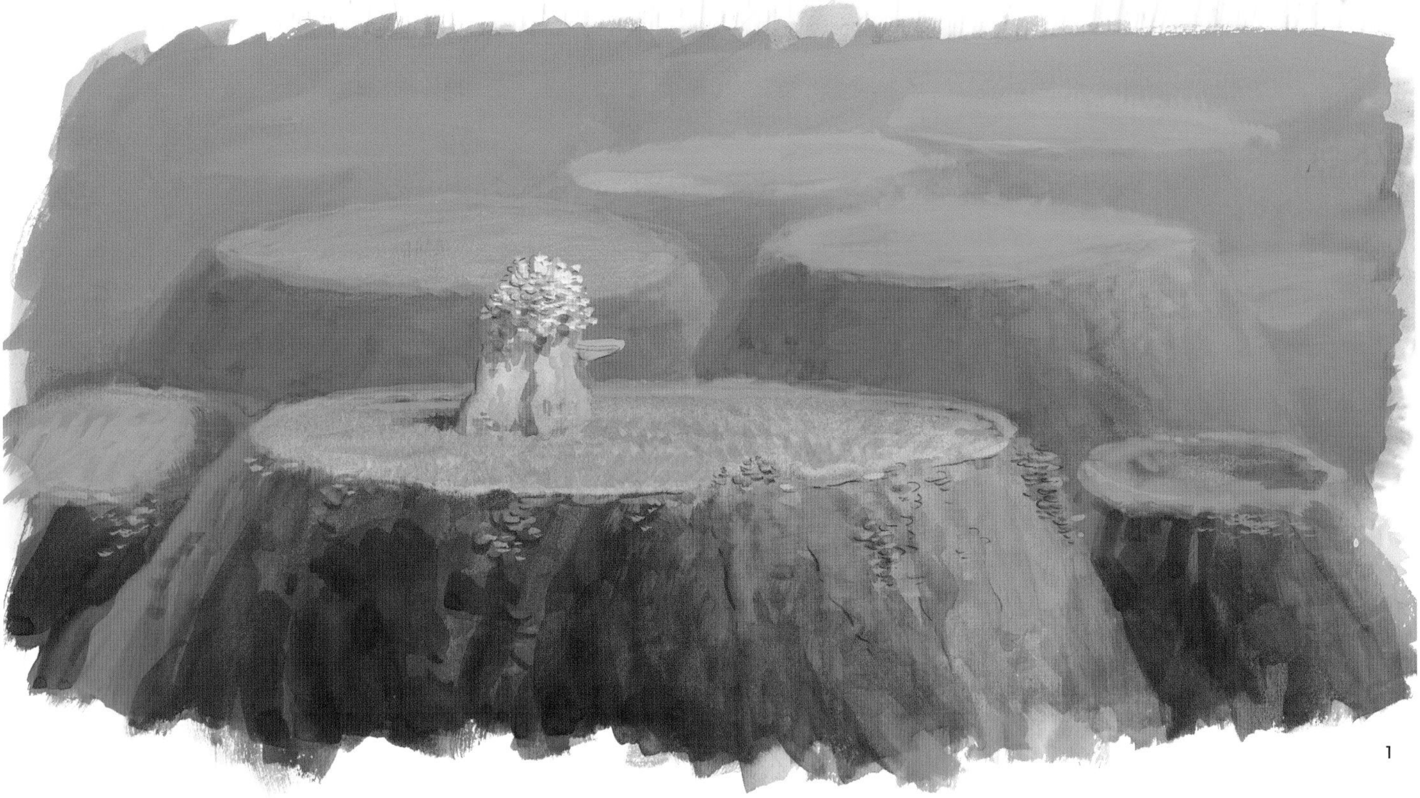

1

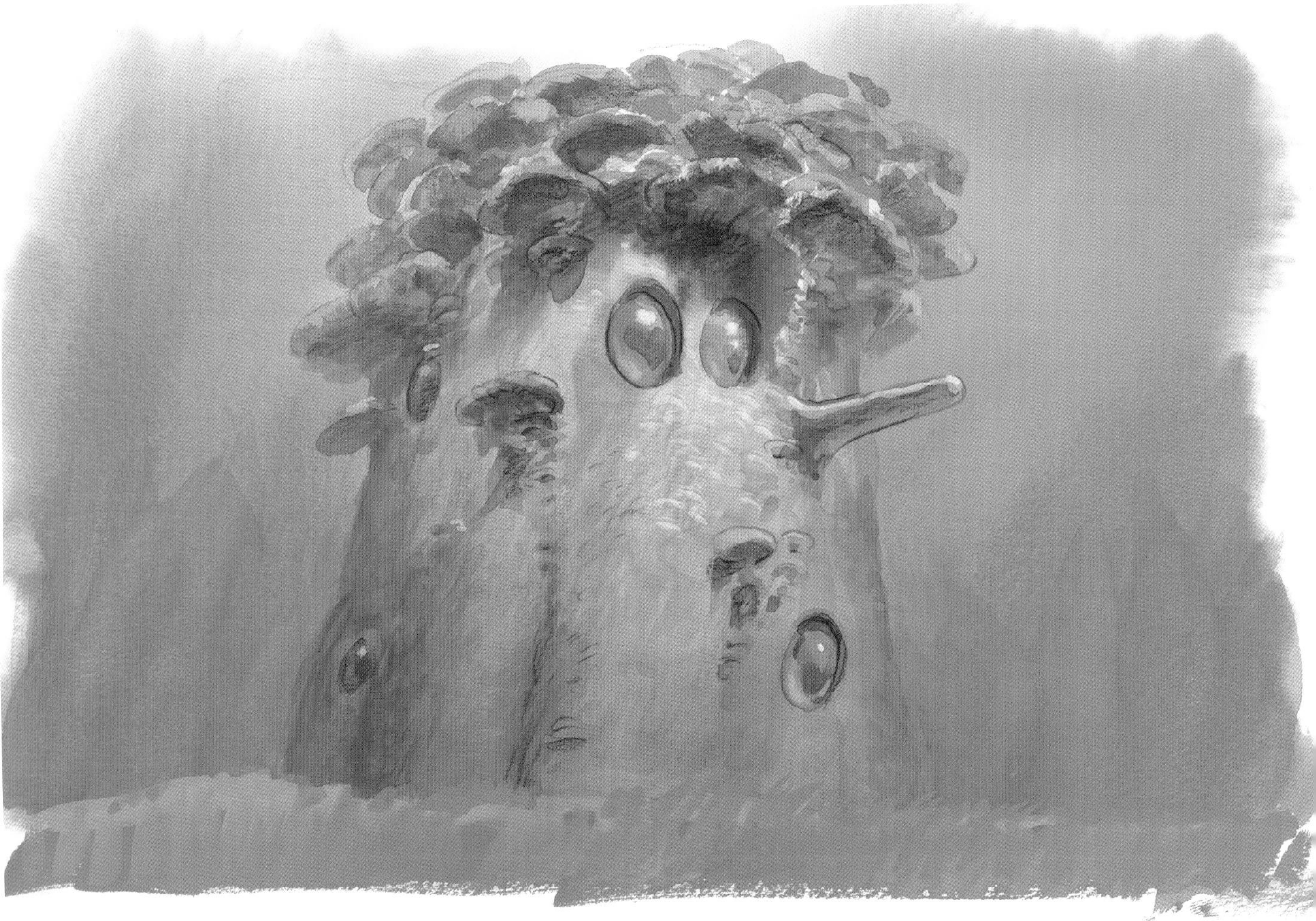

2

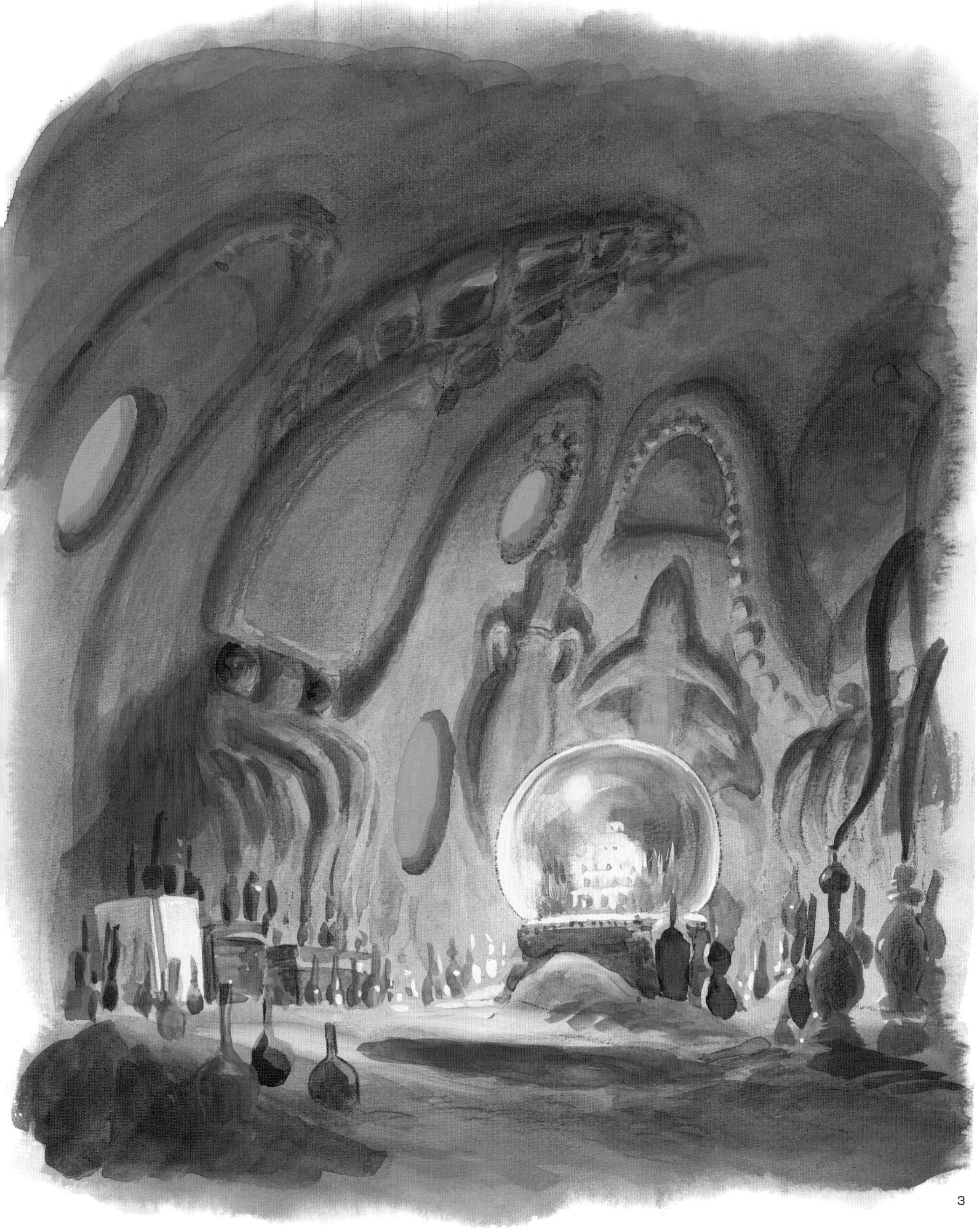

3

The Farm Under the Sea

P.106–107 /Panoramic views of the underwater farm where Fujimoto has his laboratory [Concept sketches].
1 /Same [Concept art].
2 /The Coral Tower, the control tower of the dwelling [Concept art].
3 /The center of the tower, where the water of life is refined [Concept art].

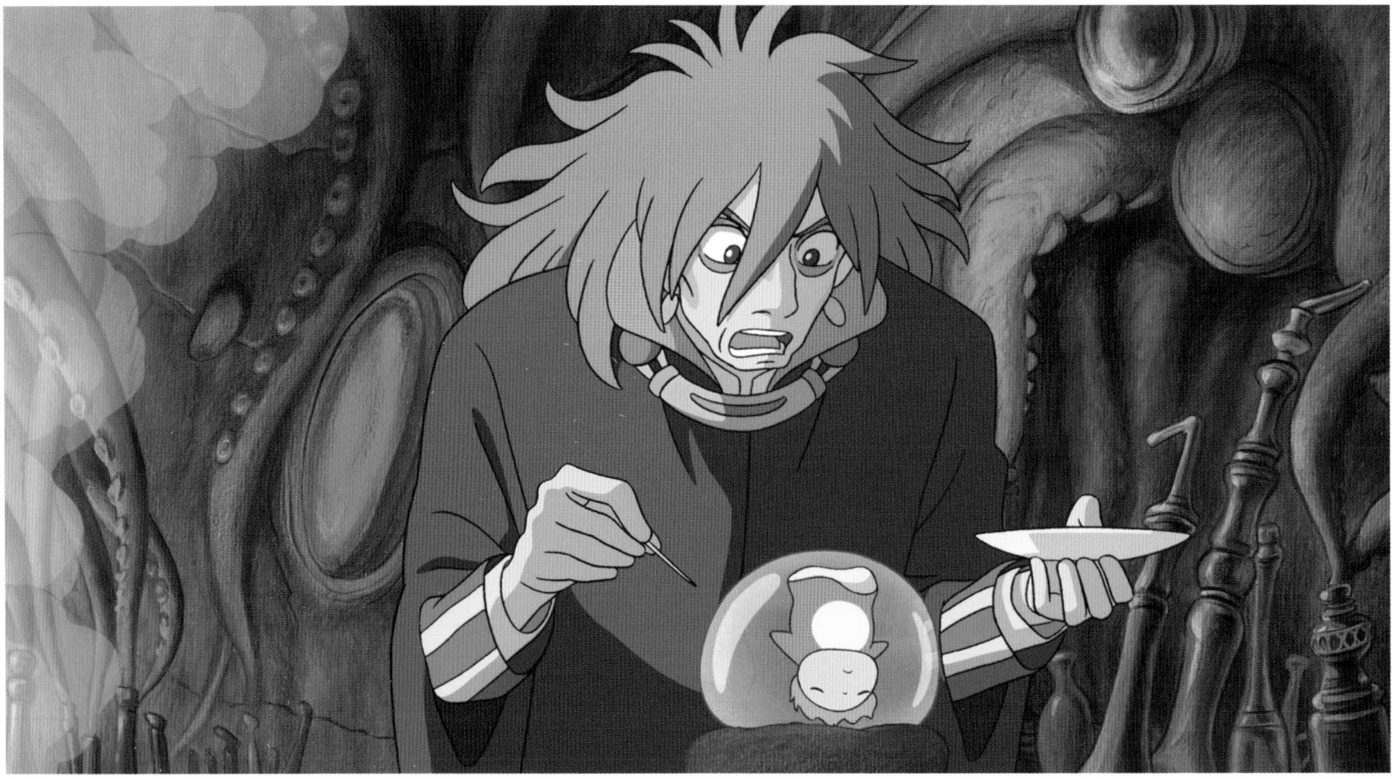

1

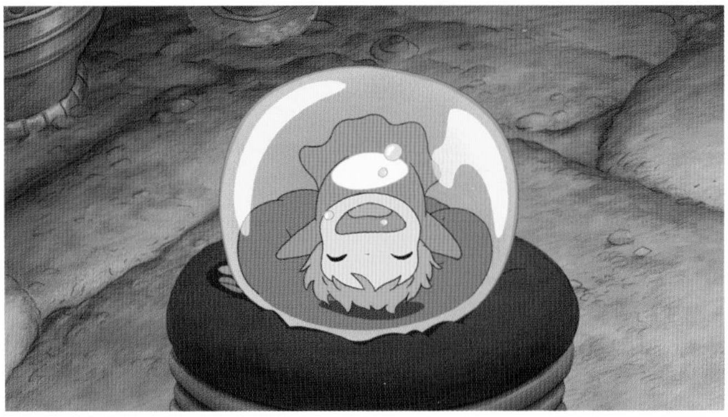

2

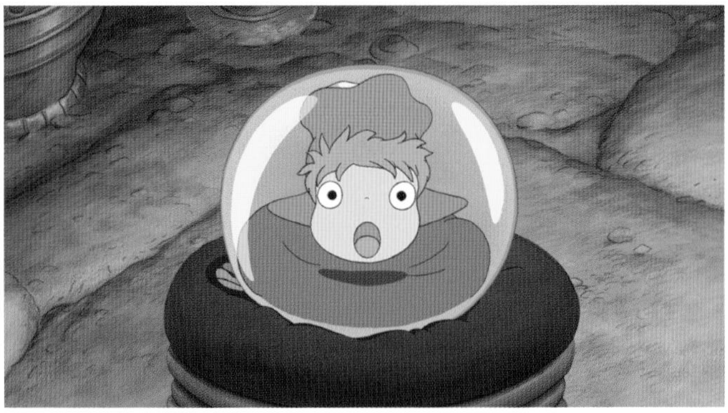

3

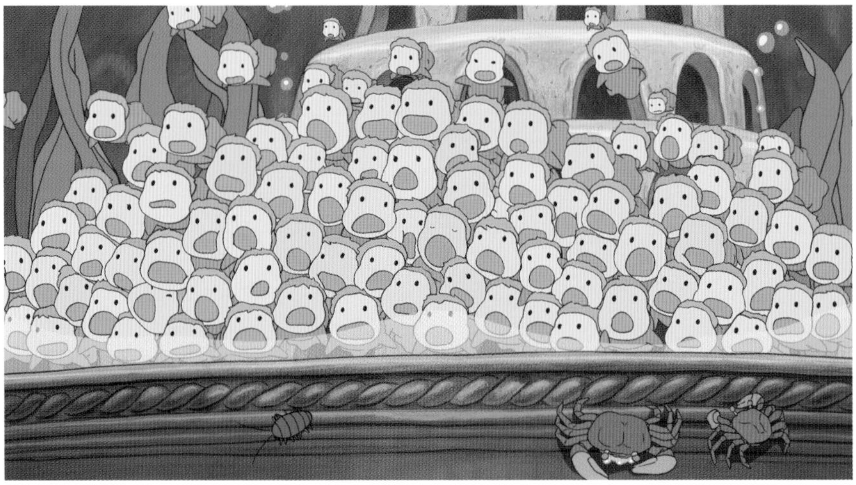

4

Ponyo's Big Transformation

1 /Ponyo, spitefully saying, "I want ham!" to Fujimoto, who tries to feed her something resembling a seaweed ball.
2, 3 /Resisting the given name "Brunhilde," she says defiantly, "It's Ponyo," and declares, "Ponyo loves Sosuke! I will be a human too."
4 /Ponyo's little sisters, looking on in awe as Ponyo holds her own against Fujimoto.
5–10 /Ponyo, transforming into a half-fish, half-human, as she shouts, "I don't want these flippers anymore!"
11 /"What? Oh, no! Don't tell me you've tasted human blood!" The astonished Fujimoto magically suppresses Ponyo's powers and puts her back to sleep.

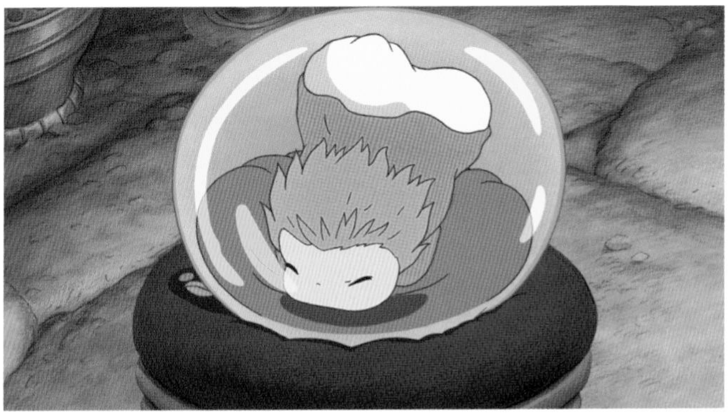
5

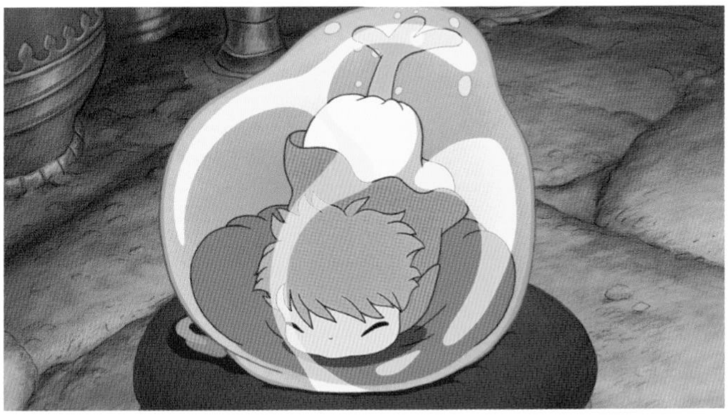
6

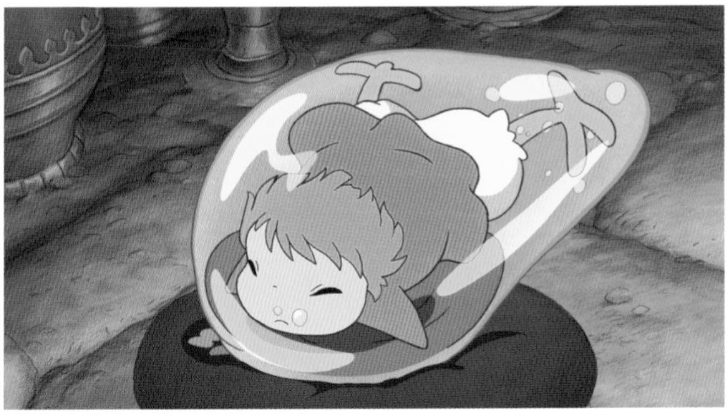
7

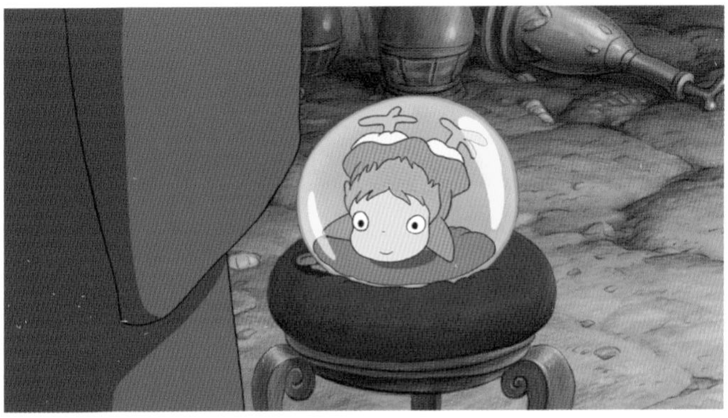
8

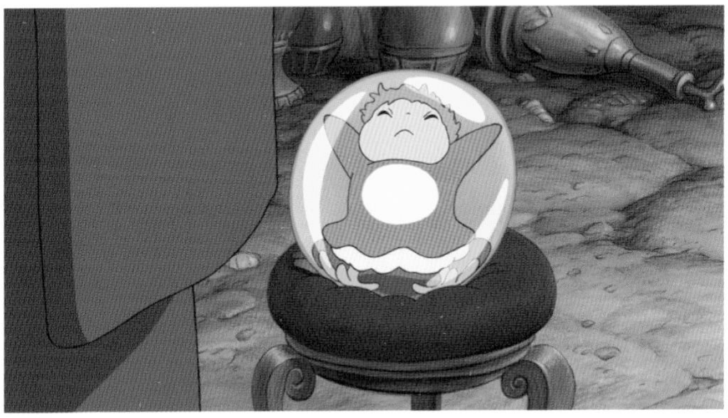
9

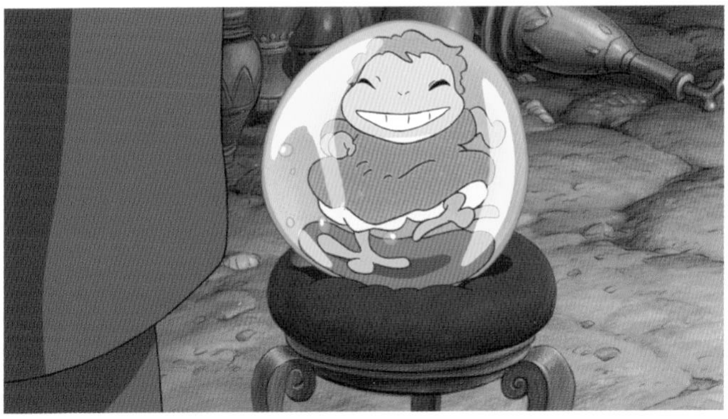
10

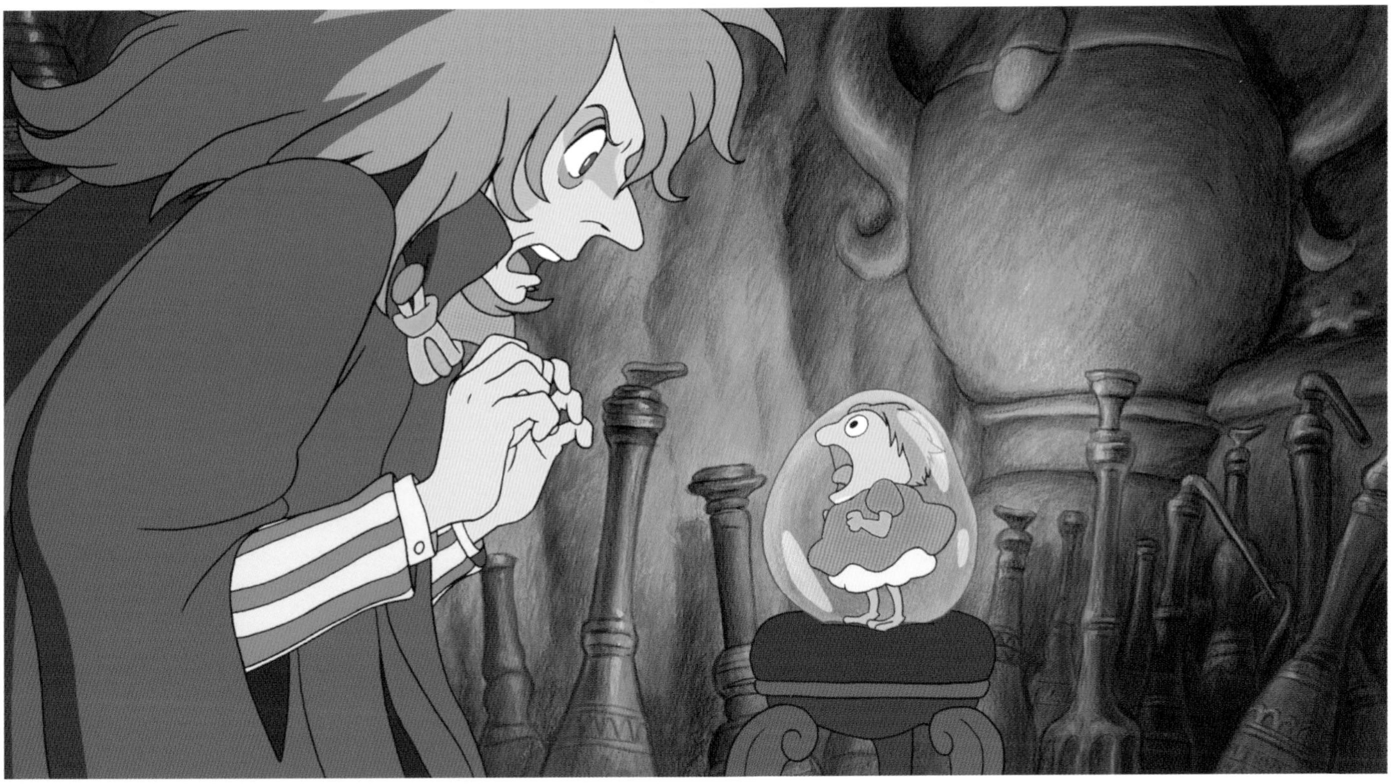
11

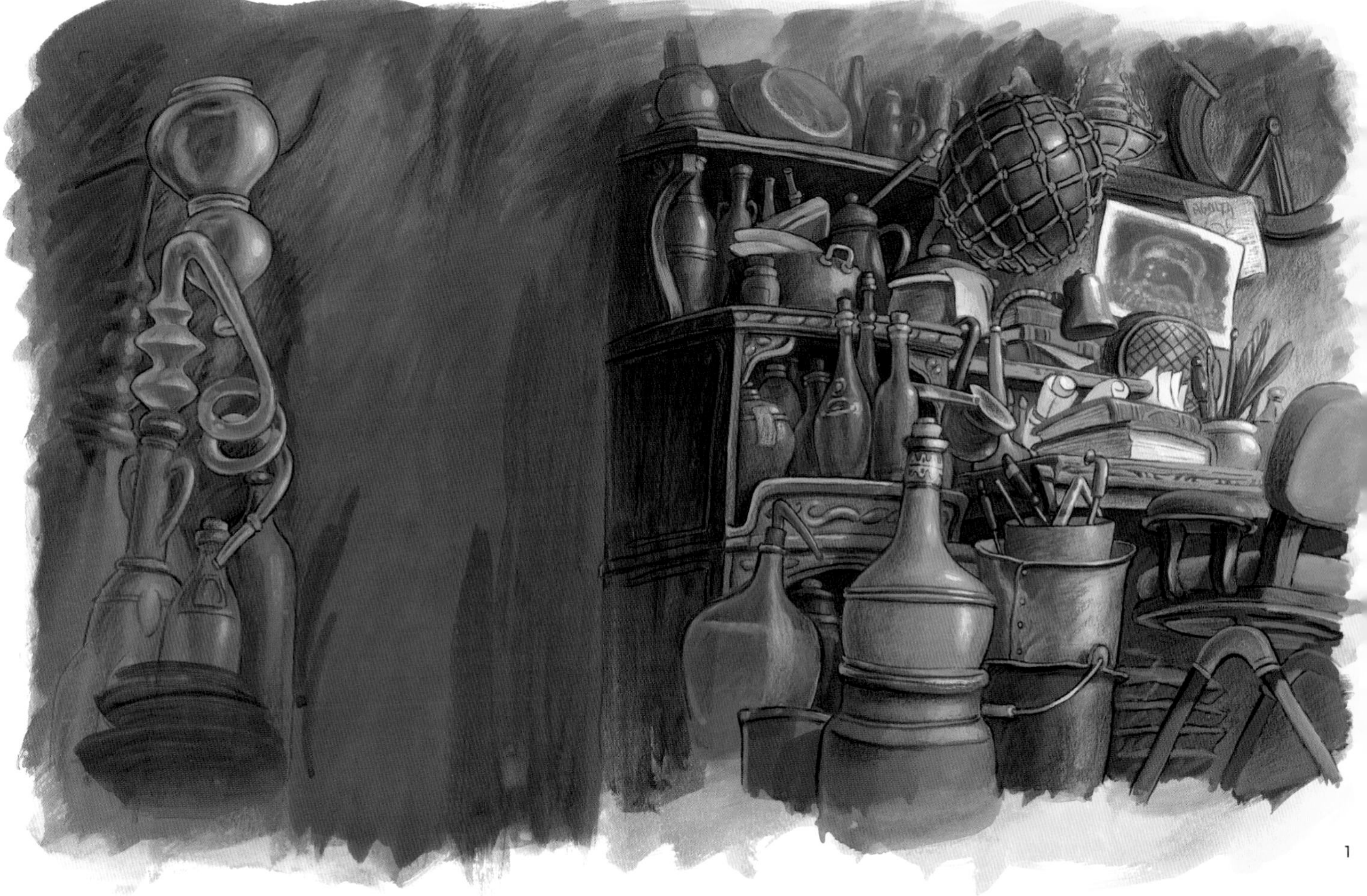

1

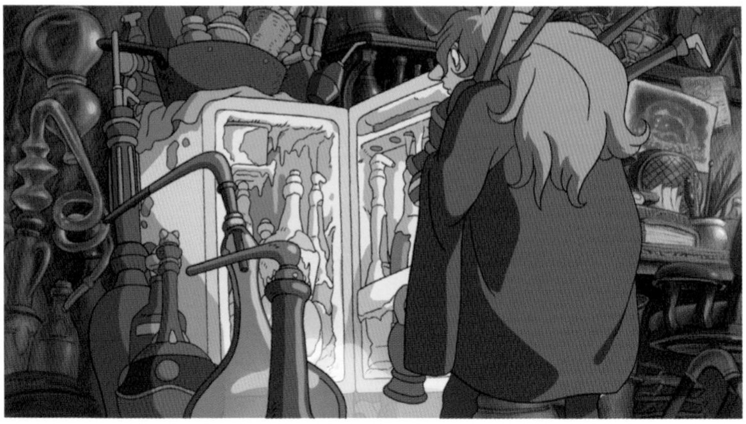

2

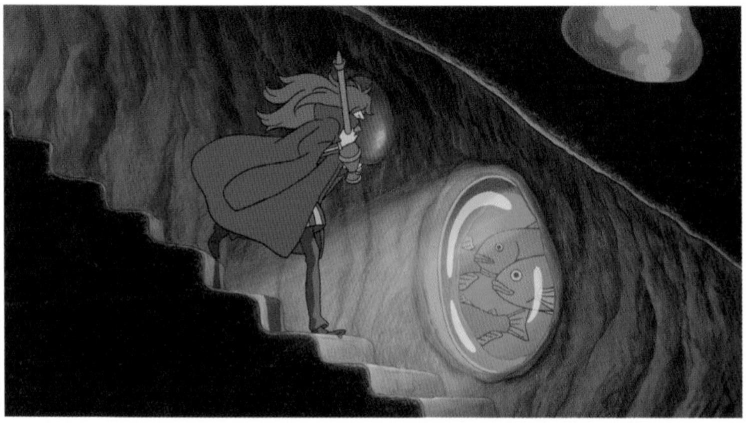

3

Inside the Laboratory

1 /A corner of Fujimoto's laboratory. The refrigerator is not shown here because it was part of a cel which was laid on top [Background].
2 /Fujimoto, putting bottles of the water of life into the refrigerator.
3 /Fujimoto takes a refined bottle downstairs.
4 /The entrance to the stairs leading down to the basement [Background].
5 /The staircase corridor leading down to the basement [Concept art].

According to Miyazaki's story, Fujimoto was apparently a pupil of Captain Nemo from *20,000 Leagues Under the Sea*. And so, he's lived for over a hundred years and diligently converted the Coral Tower into a laboratory by himself. The water spheres, in which Ponyo and her little sisters are confined, were of vital importance, along with the sea, in terms of how we rendered the water for this film. These spheres are not made of glass but water. Therefore, we drew backgrounds in soft colors and lines, while giving thought to how images might look inside the water sphere, how a water sphere might look from inside a water sphere, and how to delineate between the air and water. The camera supervisor, Atsushi Okui, also ended up adding some effects, such as making the surface of the sphere look curved or as though it's quivering.

—Art Director: Noboru Yoshida

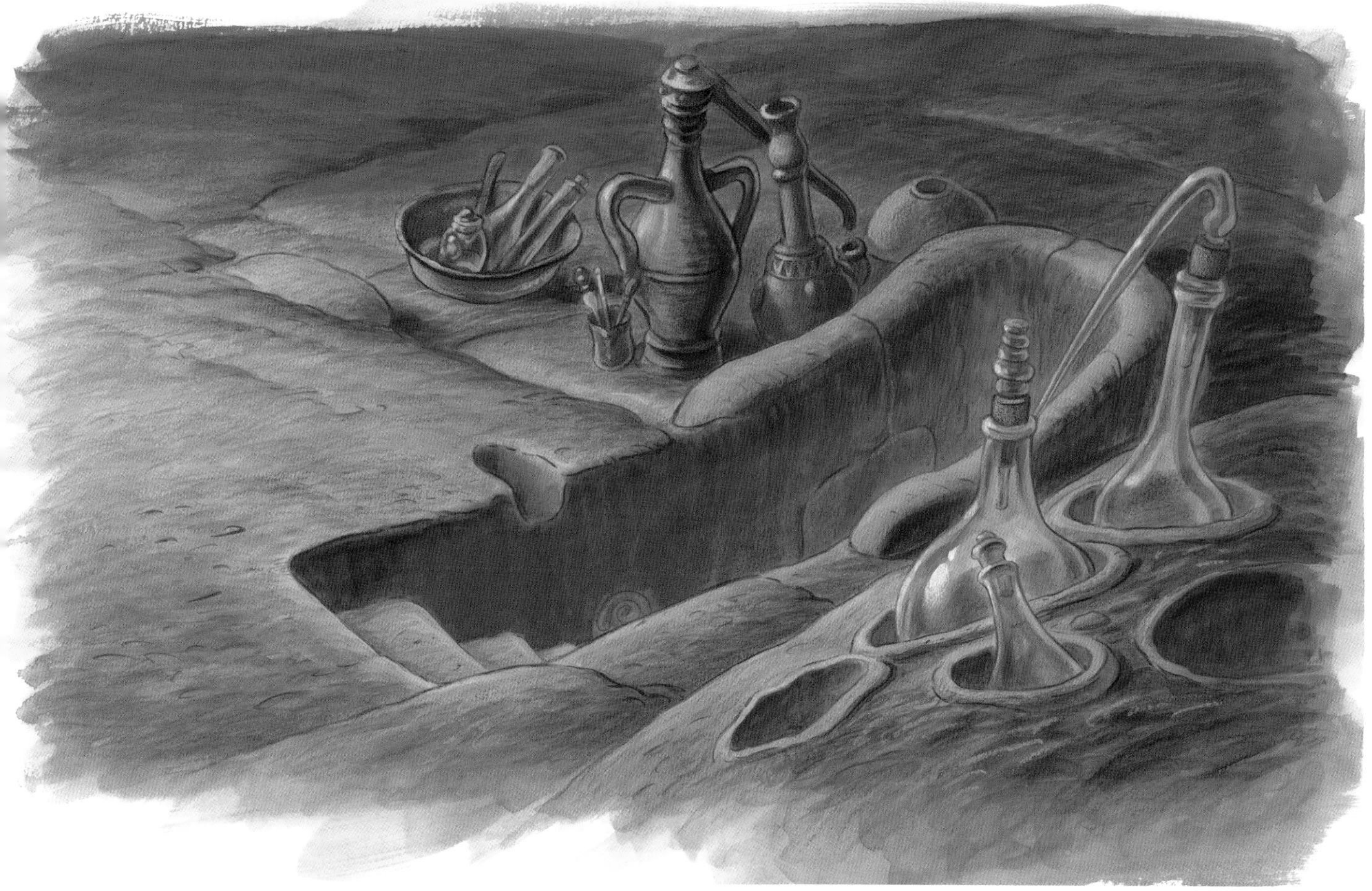
4

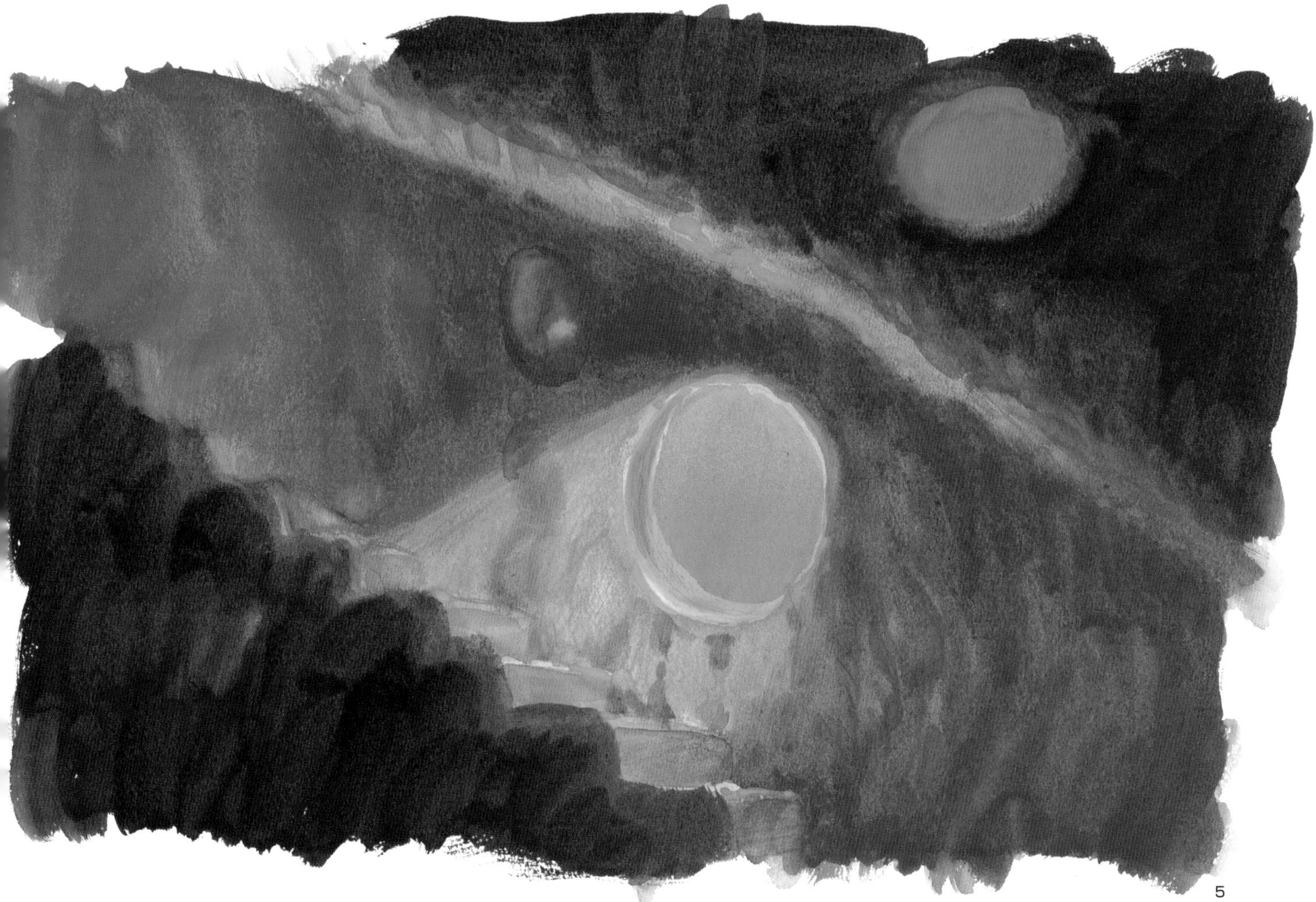
5

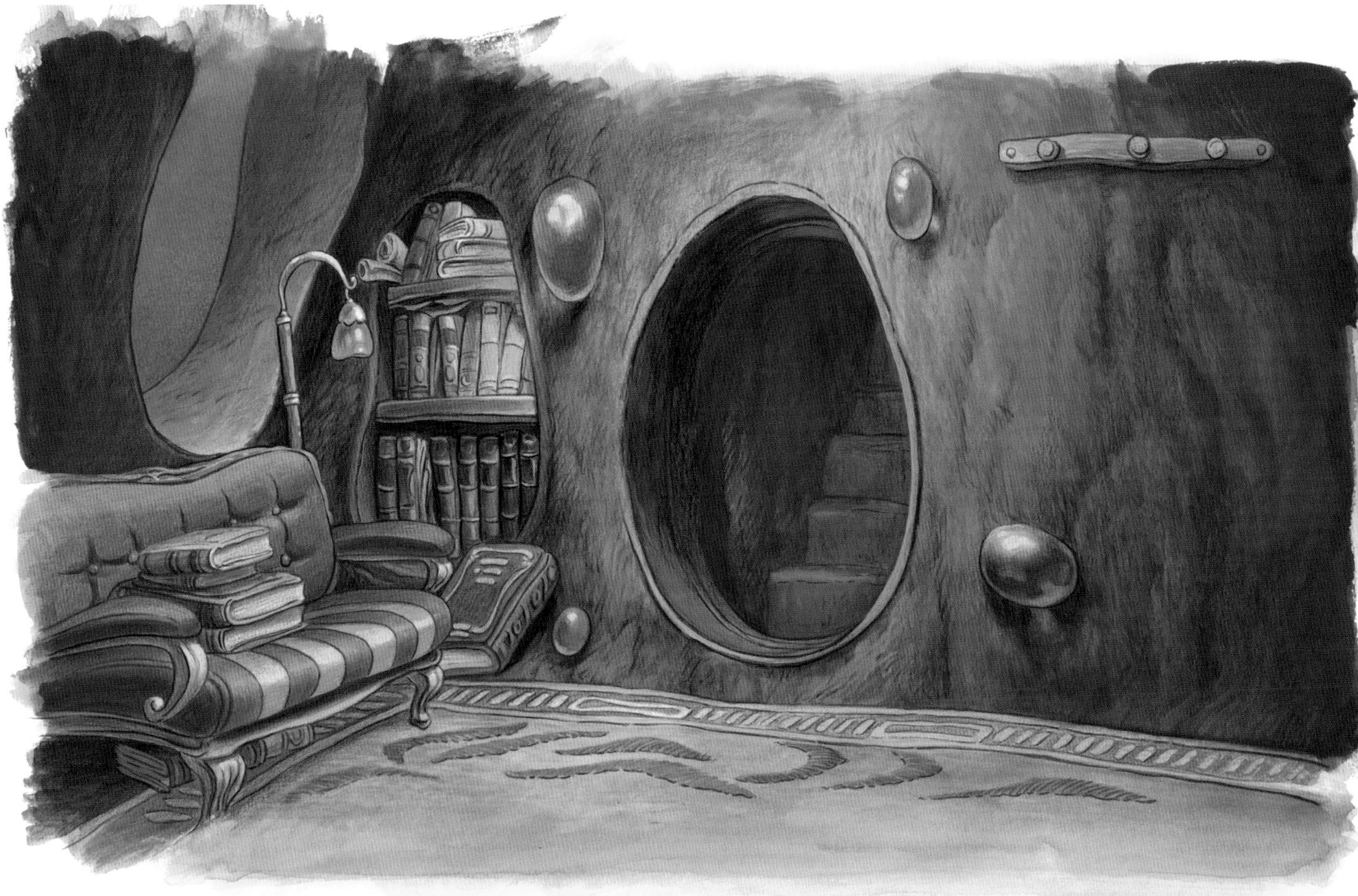
1

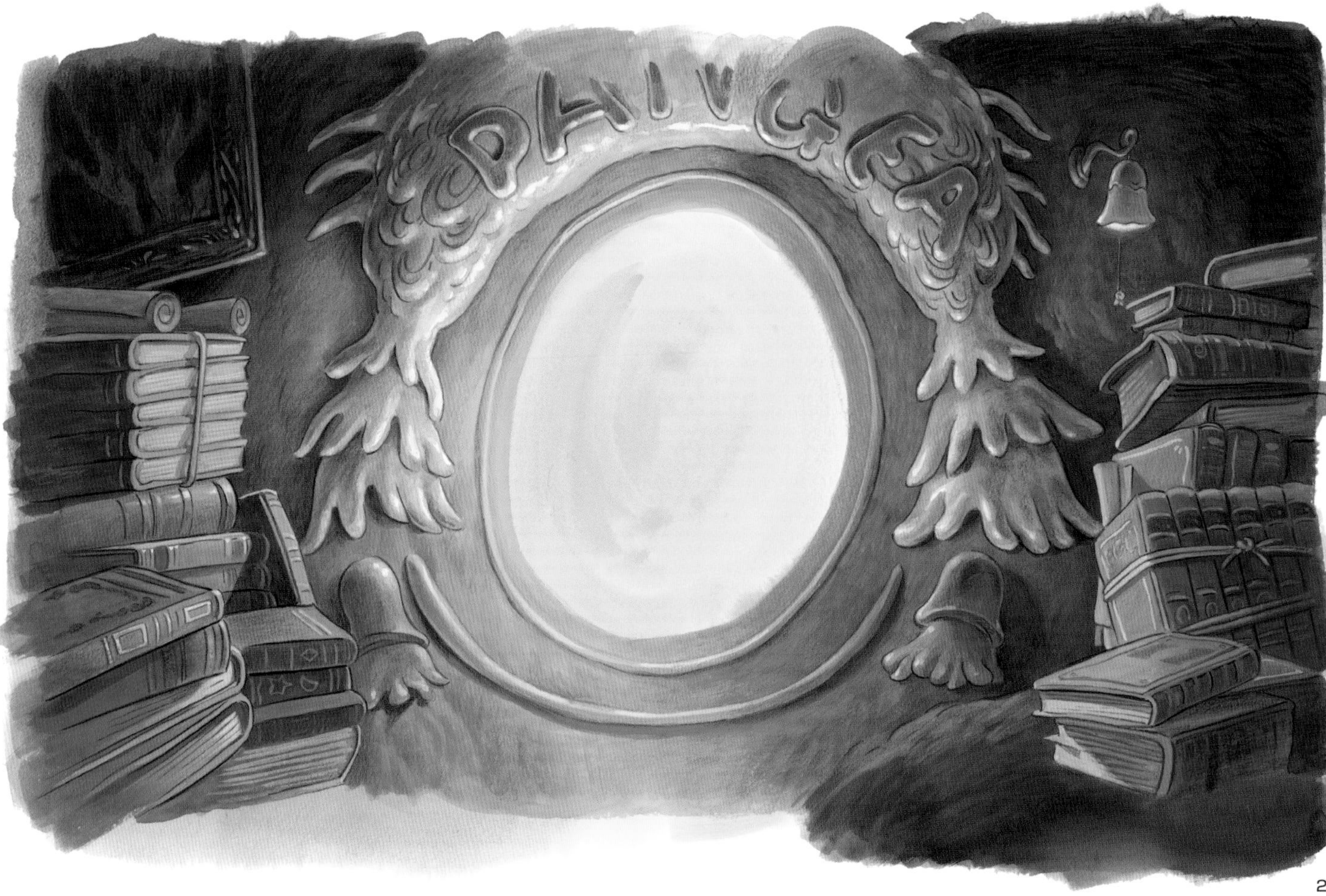
2

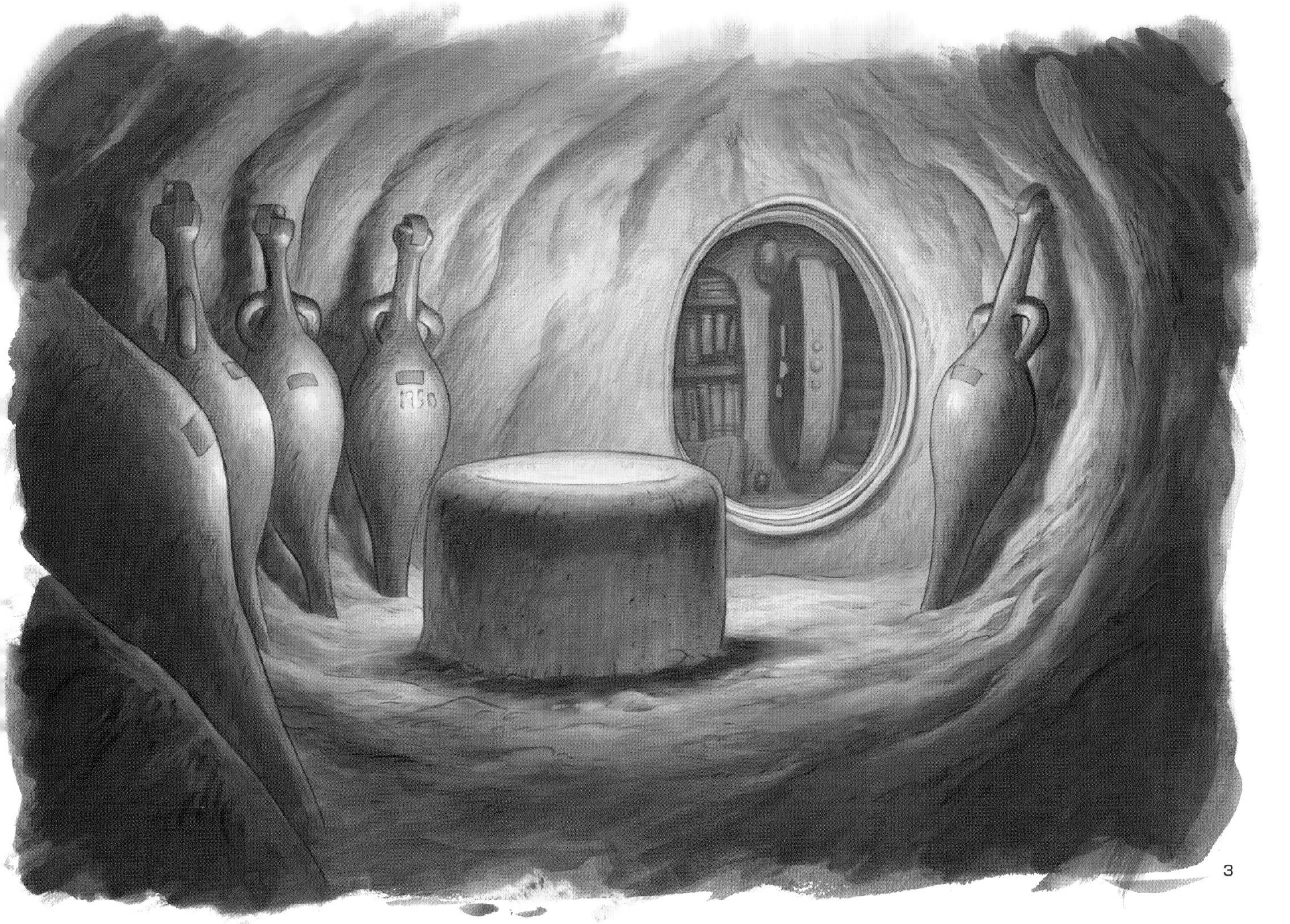

3

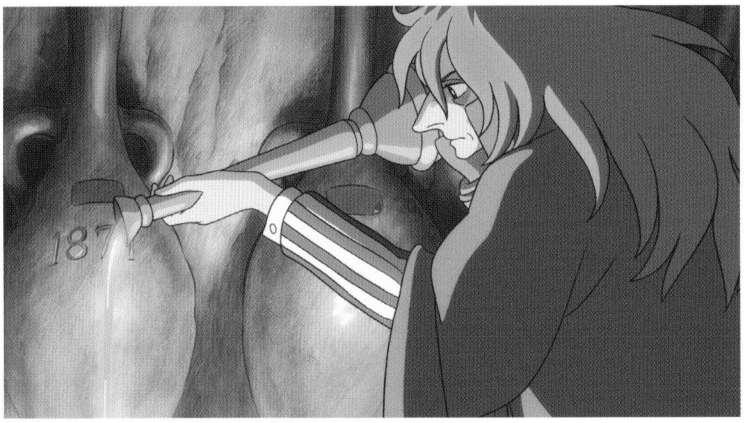

4

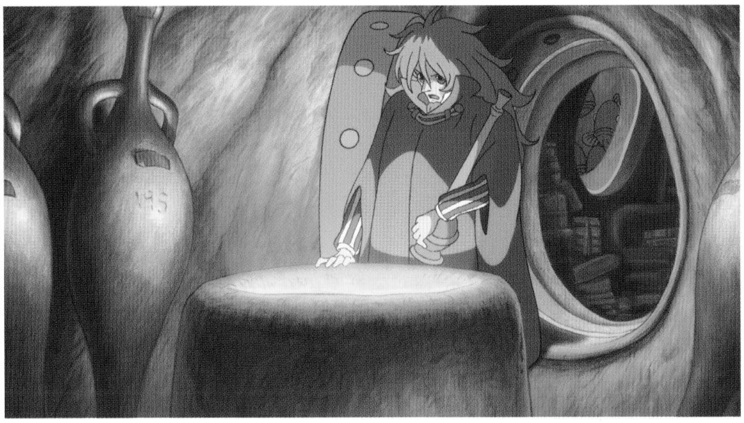

5

The Water of Life

1 /Fujimoto's room and laboratory. The door to the opening in the middle of the room is added later via cels, as it must be animated to open and close [Background].
2 /The entrance leading to the storage room of the water of life. Again, the door is added later with cels [Background].
3 /The inside of the storage room, housing a well [Background].
4, 5 /Fujimoto, pouring the water of life into the well. "When this well is full, the Age of the Ocean will begin again. An explosion of life to match the Cambrian Age. An end to the era of those abominable humans."

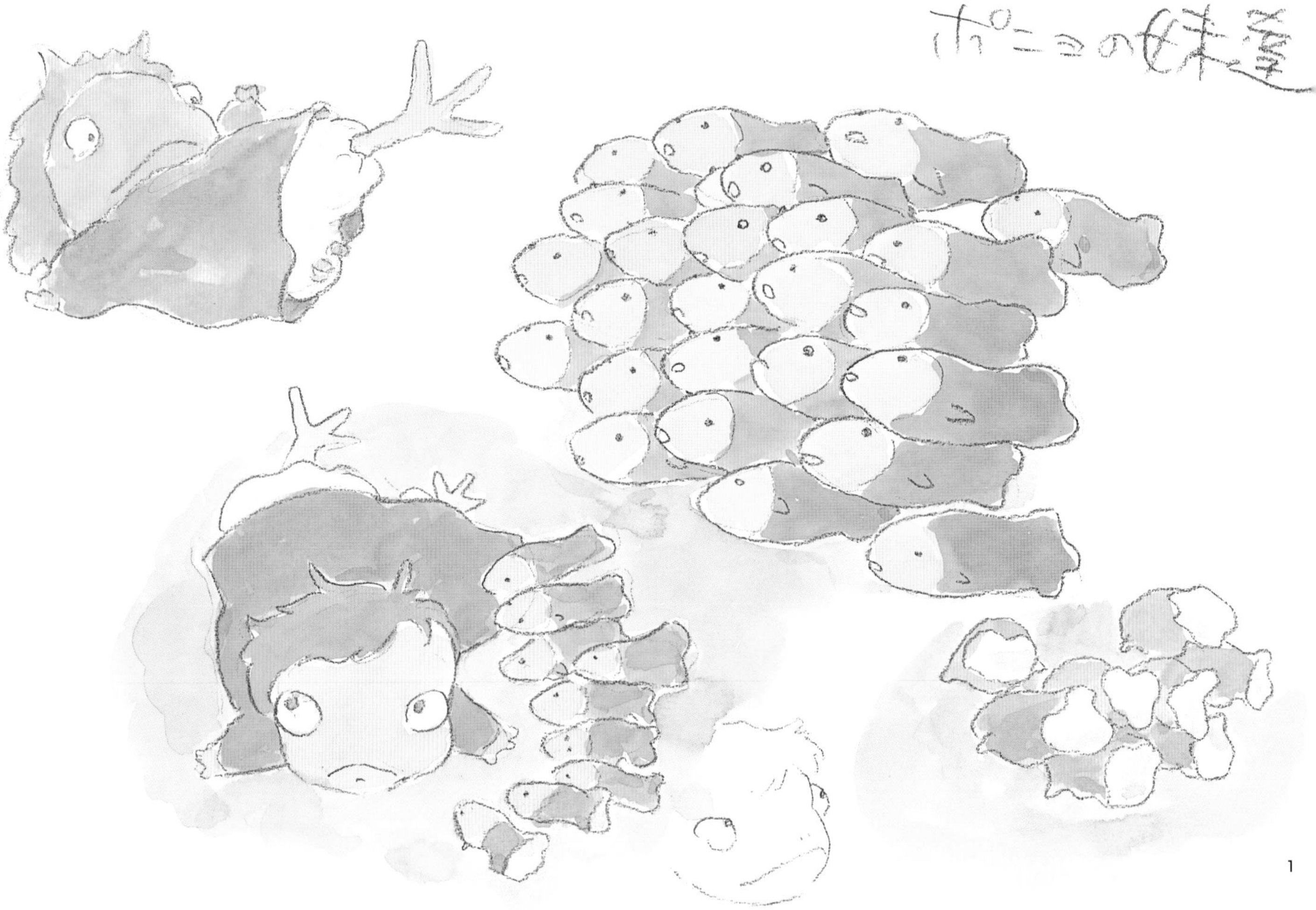
ポニョの妹達

1

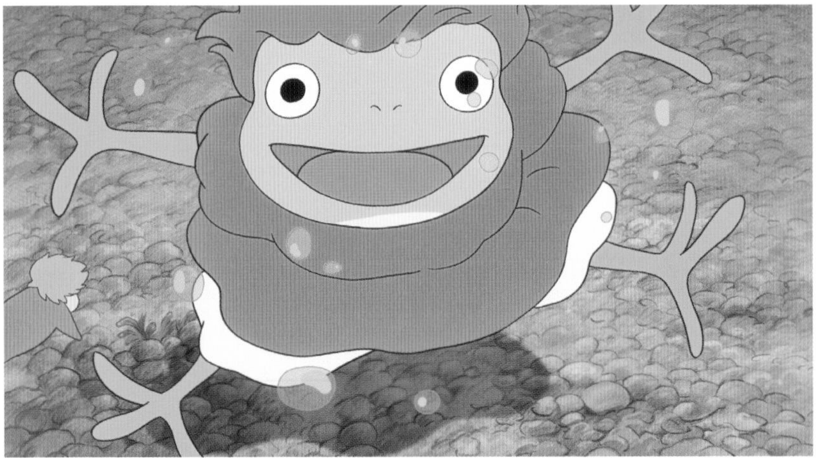

2

Ponyo's Little Sisters

1 /The little sisters coming to Ponyo's aid [Concept sketches].
2 /Ponyo, restored with the help of her little sisters.
P.117 /Ponyo, freed thanks to her little sisters, who gnawed on the skin of the water sphere and broke through. They are surprised and excited at the sight of Ponyo with not only arms and legs but teeth.

The animation for scenes in which Ponyo's little sisters appear was divided up among the staff with each shot. Each team was composed of a lead animator and several assistant animators. Once the lead animator drew a layout with the overall movements determined, the assistants drew the sisters accordingly, and I made any necessary modifications in the end—that was the process. However, it wasn't enough just to have a lot of sisters onscreen. Each sister needed to move as an individual character. The scene in which the sisters rescue the half-fish, half-human Ponyo was divided into three stages—beginning, middle, and end—and the assistant animators drew each sister carefully. We didn't use any copies or CG, of course, because everything was drawn by hand this time. While the work was painstaking, it was easier to create the movements of an ensemble by hand than by CG, and we took on this task because we wanted to render those movements to our hearts' content.

—Supervising Animator: Katsuya Kondo

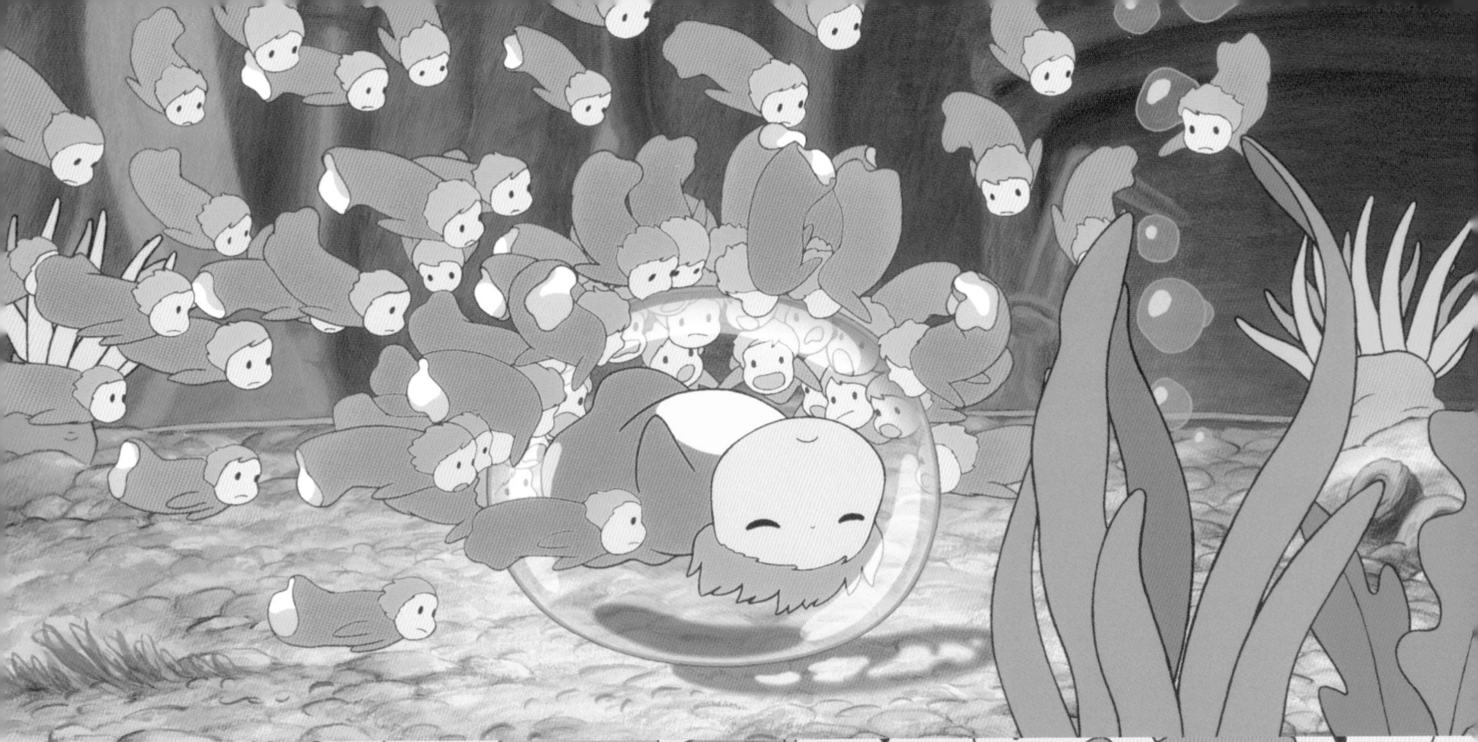
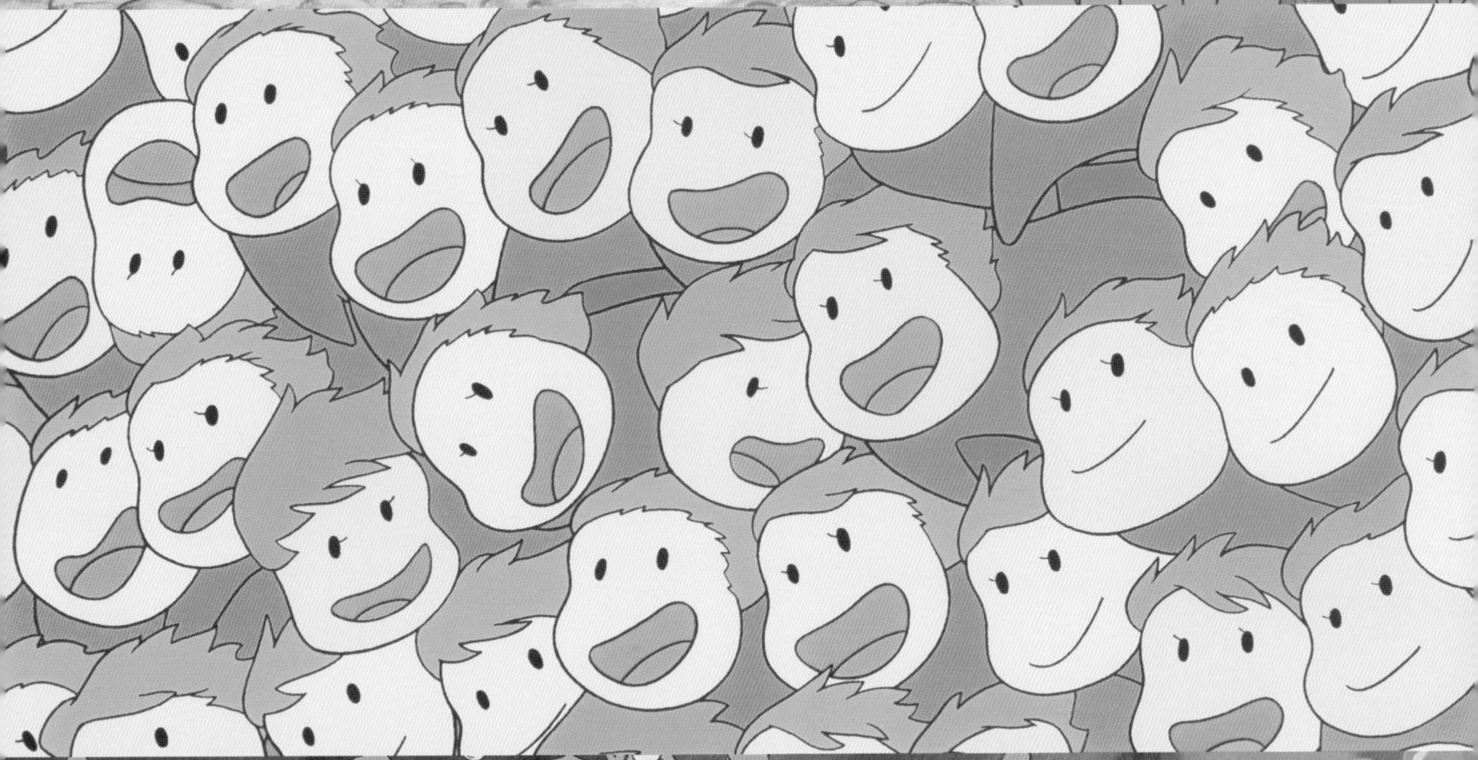
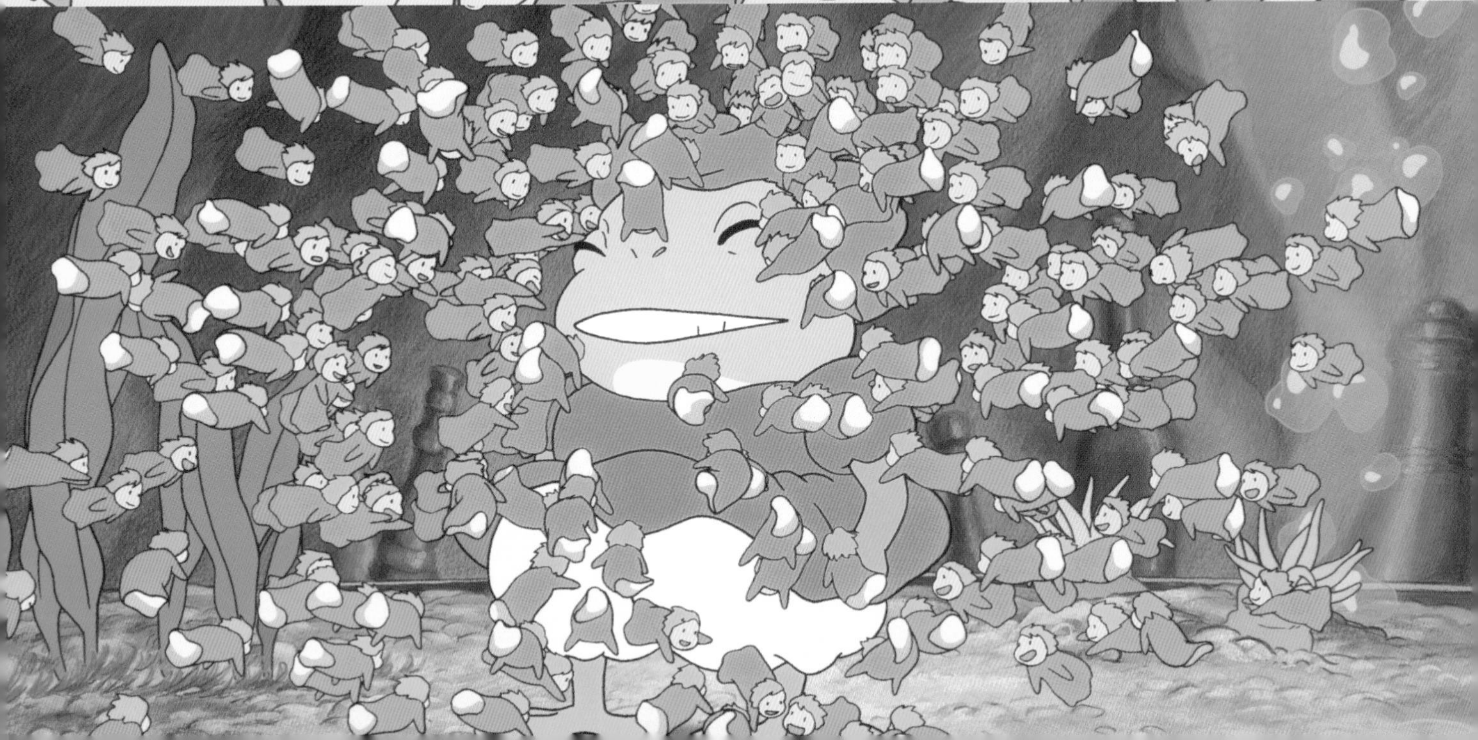

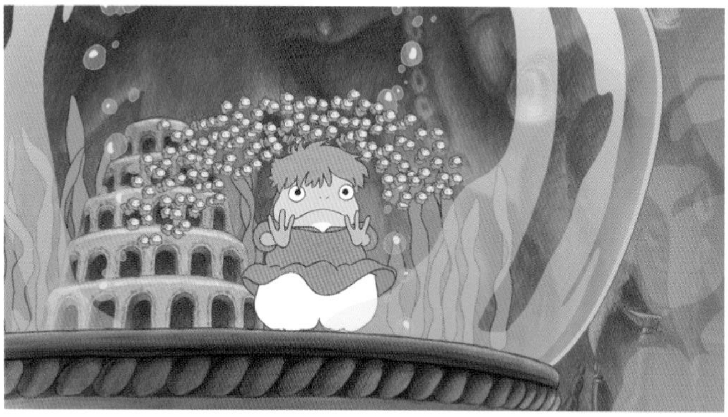
1

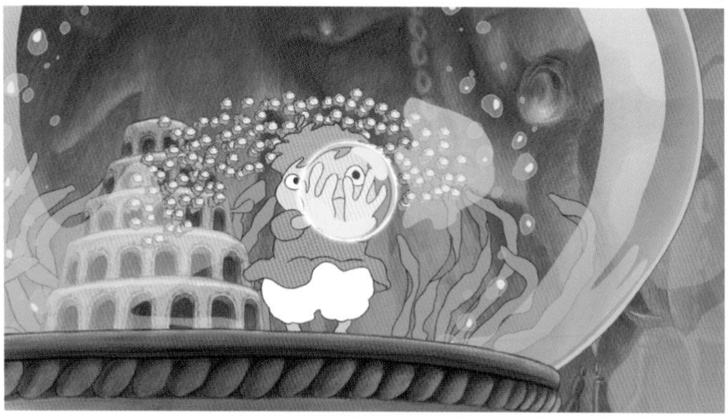
2

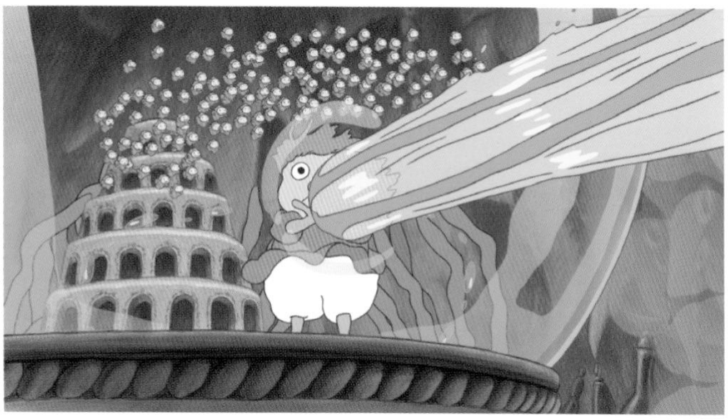
3

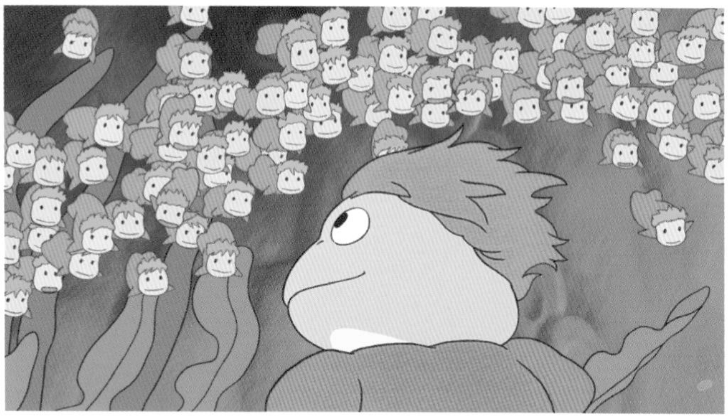
4

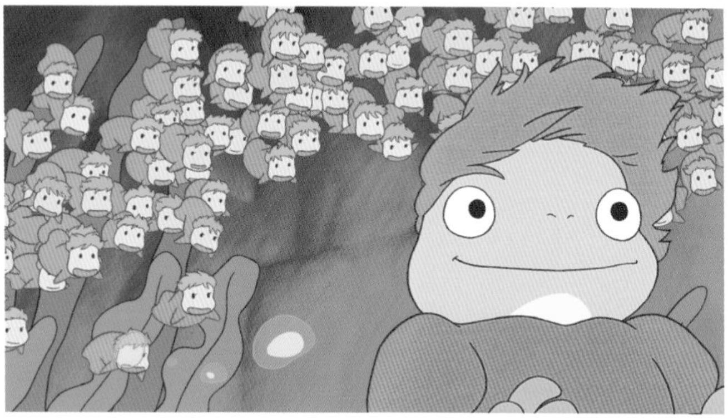
5

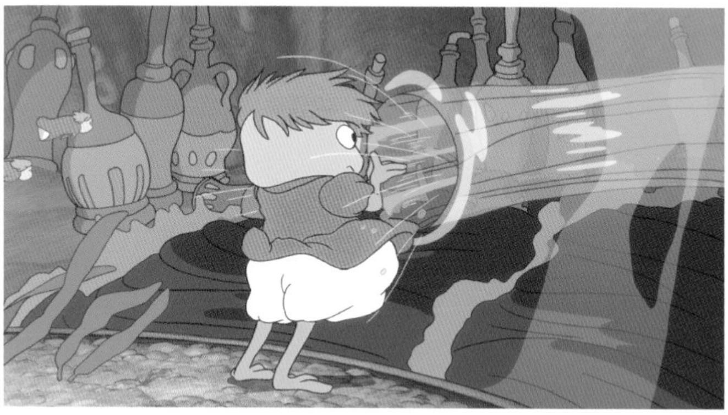
6

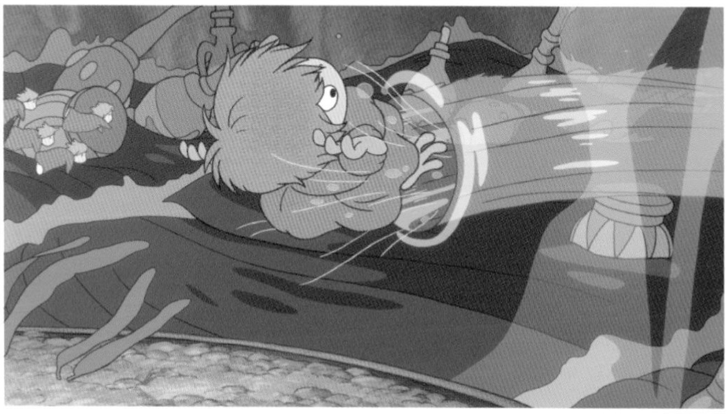
7

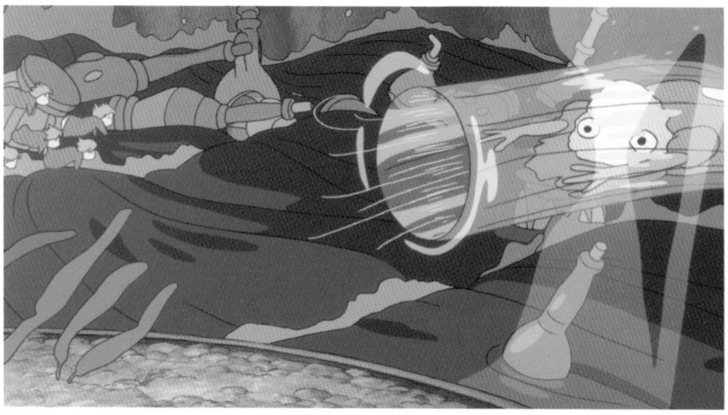
8

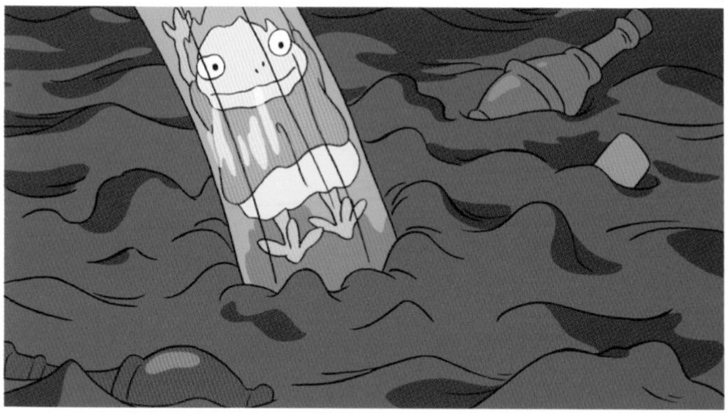
9

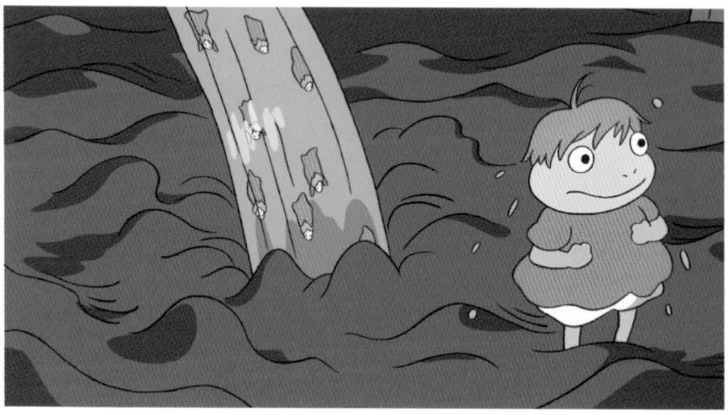
10

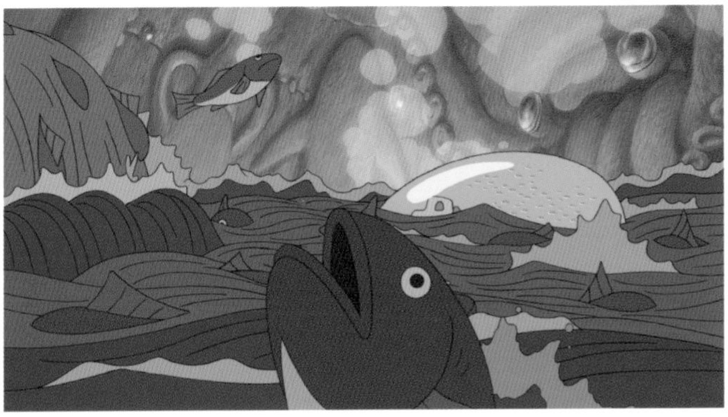

11

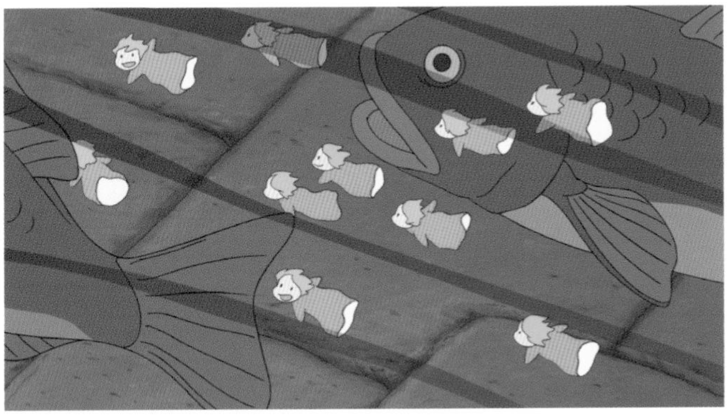

12

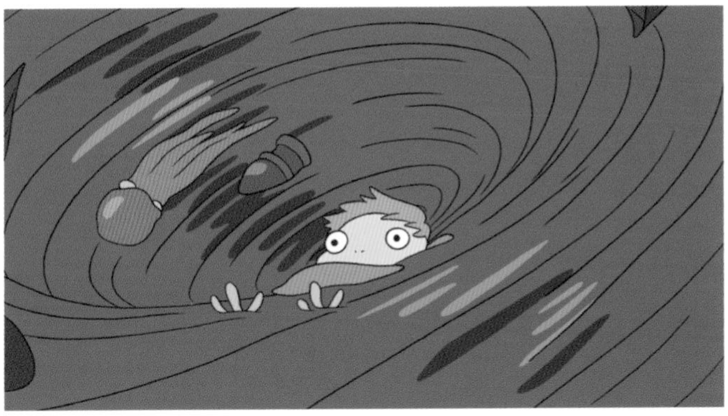

13

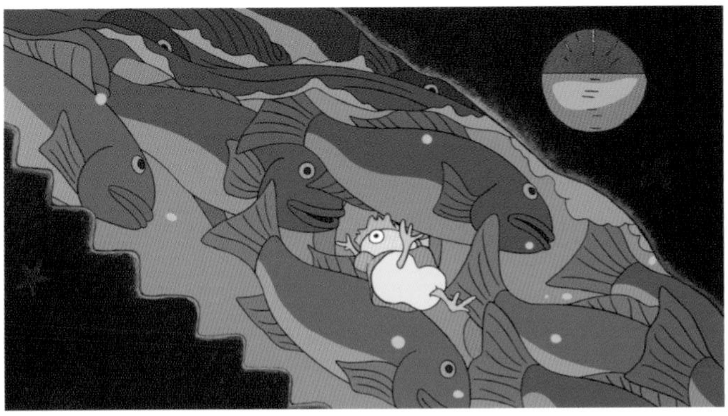

14

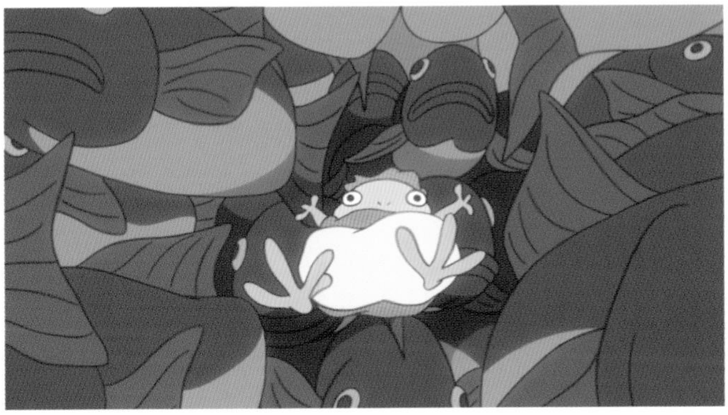

15

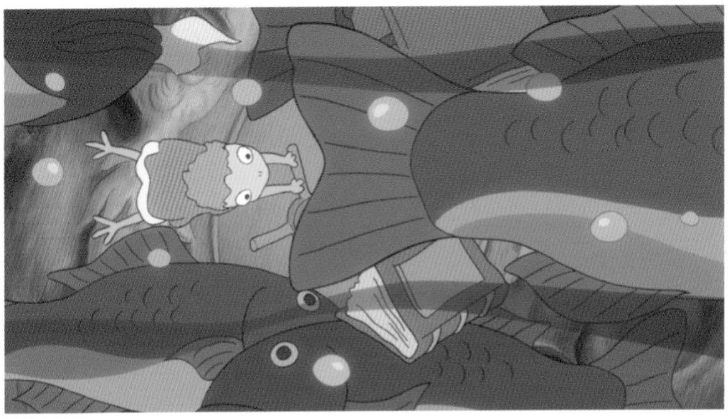

16

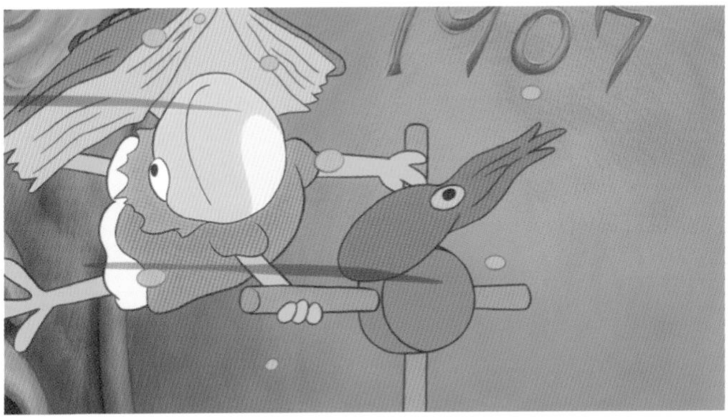
1907

17

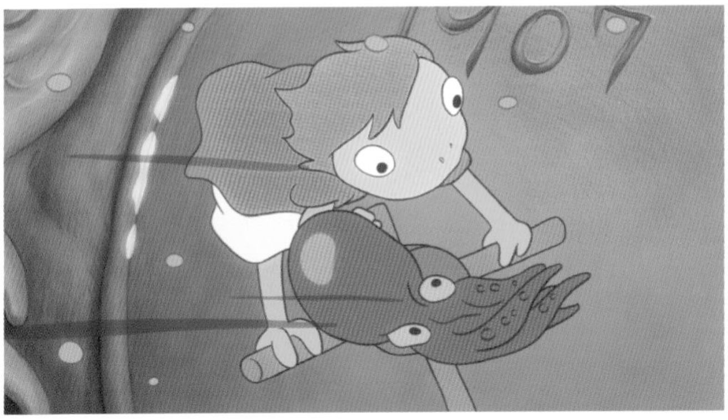
1907

18

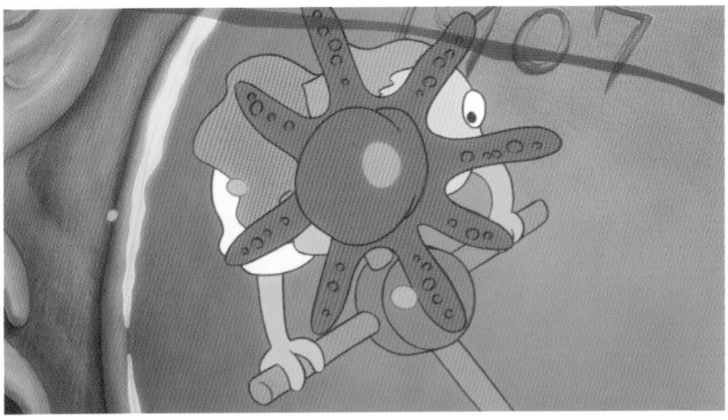

19

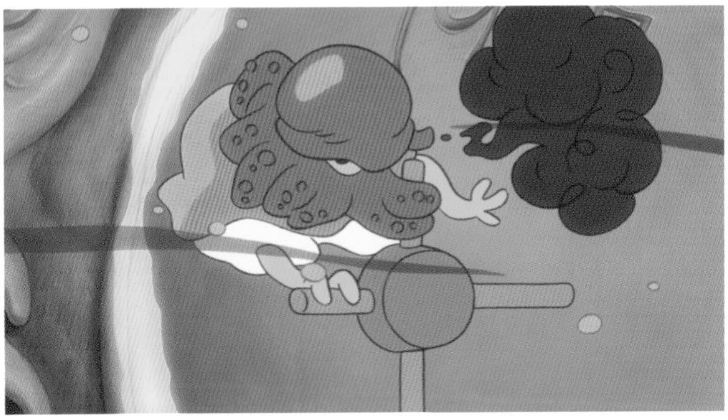

20

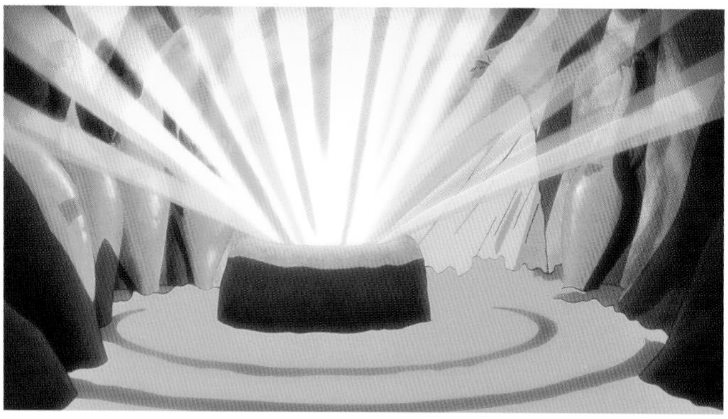
21

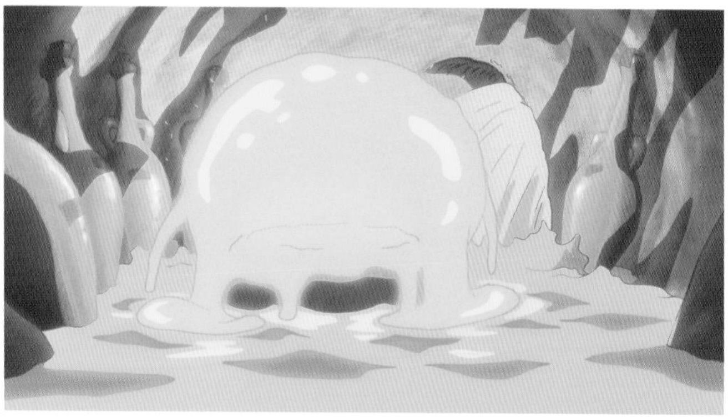
22

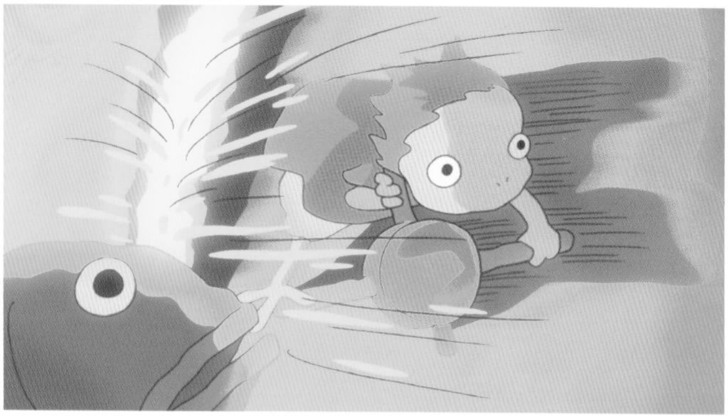
23

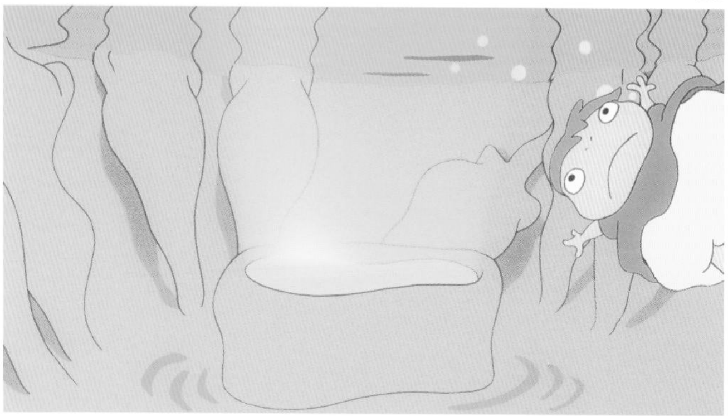
24

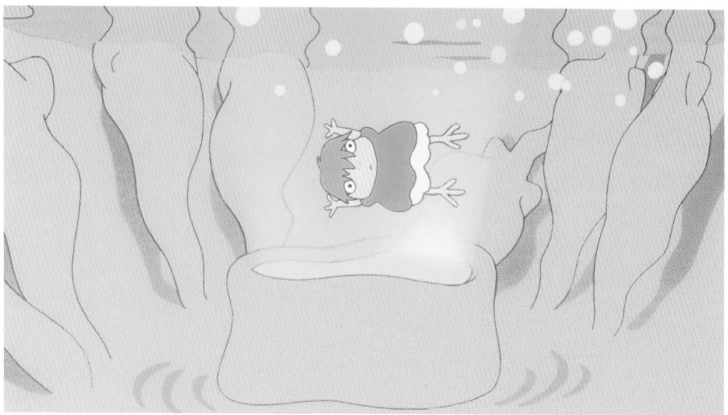
25

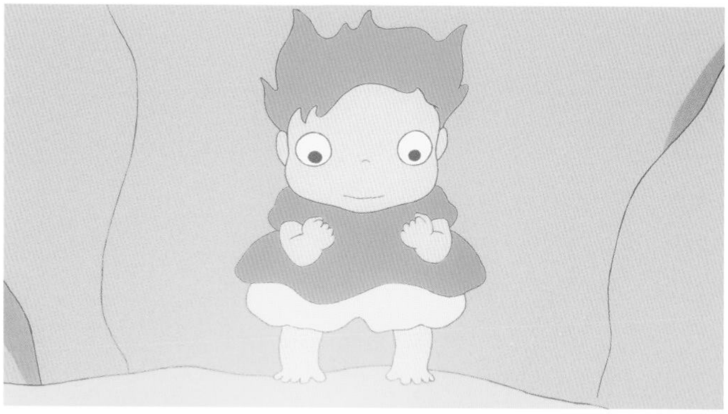
26

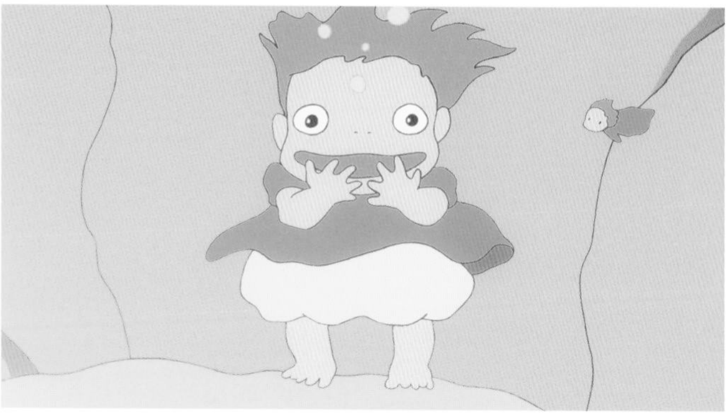
27

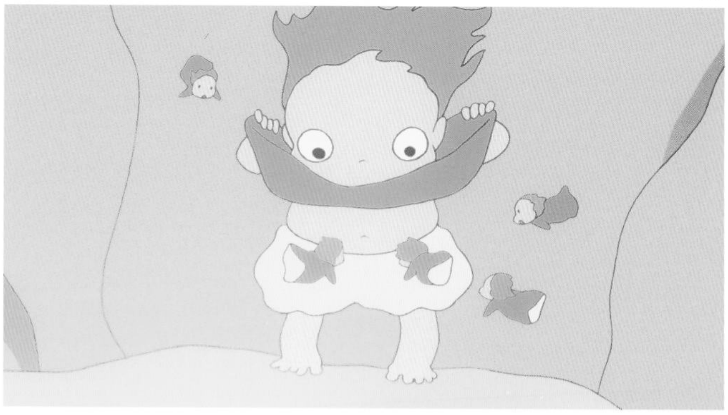
28

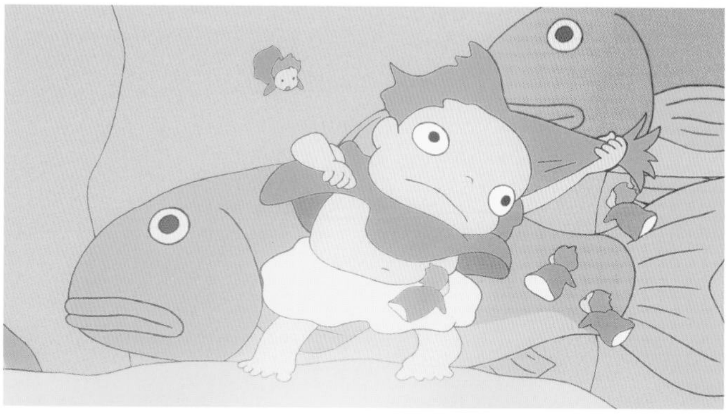
29

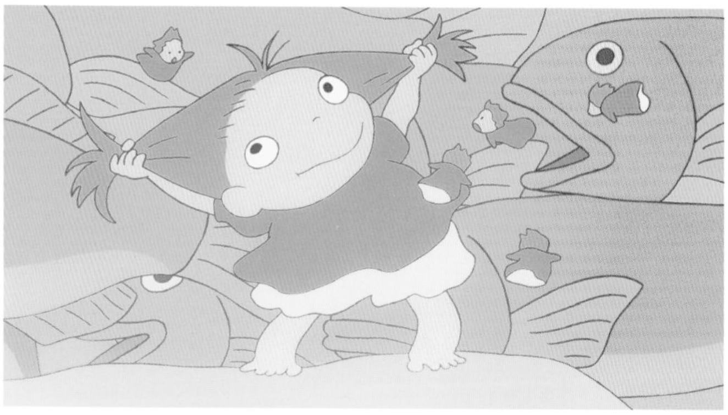
30

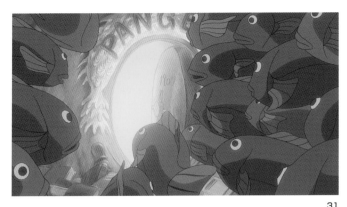

31

32

33

34

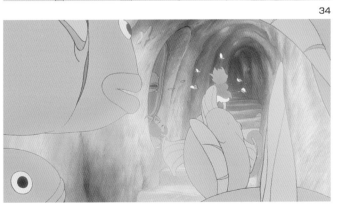

35

Ponyo's Rebellion

1–5 /Ponyo, opening a hole in the large water sphere enveloping the Nursery Tower. She proudly looks back at her little sisters before walking out.

6–10 /Ponyo, carried out by the current. Her little sisters follow.

11–15 /Fujimoto's laboratory is also swept away, as Ponyo opens a hole in the window, letting sea water gush in.

16–20 /Ponyo, fighting the torrent, latching onto the door handle and turning it.

21–25 /The well, containing the water of life, overflows and a magical combination of liquid and light spills forth.

26–30 /Ponyo, transforming from half-fish, half-human into a human girl. She has a belly button, and her hair is longer!

31–35 /Ponyo, going up the stairs of the Coral Tower with her little sisters and some gawking fish.

Shinji Otsuka created the drawings for the scene in which Ponyo escapes the water sphere and gets swept out along with the minions, and for the scene of her metamorphosis inside the water of life. He was the animator who most faithfully and fundamentally embodied Miyazaki's theme to "make a well-rounded film using a few simple lines." For myself, even while I adhered to Miyazaki's thinking, I found my direction wavering when I worried about whether to draw more detail or stop. But Otsuka drew not only the original drawings but key animation, and was able to achieve Miyazaki's theme so completely that it wasn't necessary for me to make any changes [laughs]. Although I might make a few timing changes, Miyazaki said that making any changes to Otsuka's drawings would take some guts, even for him. Which is to say that Otsuka's drawings were so powerful that I felt tested as a supervisor and couldn't help but feel like I had to give it my all.

—Supervising Animator: Katsuya Kondo

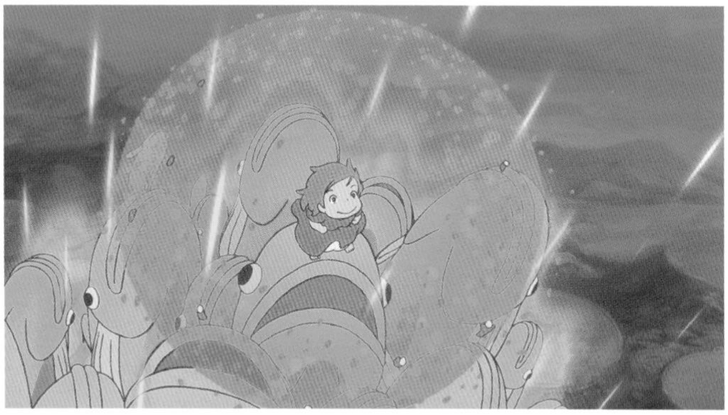

1

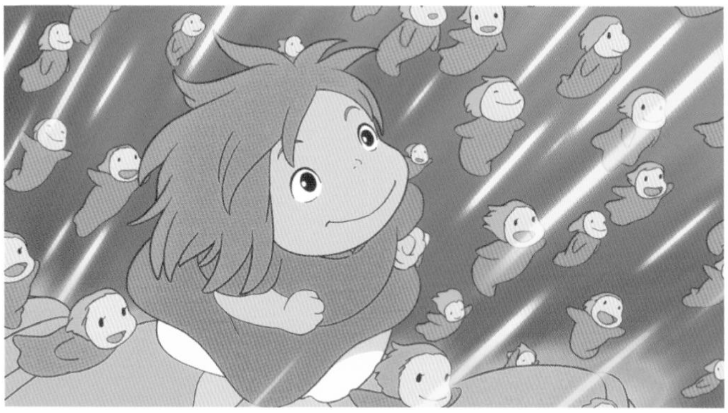

2

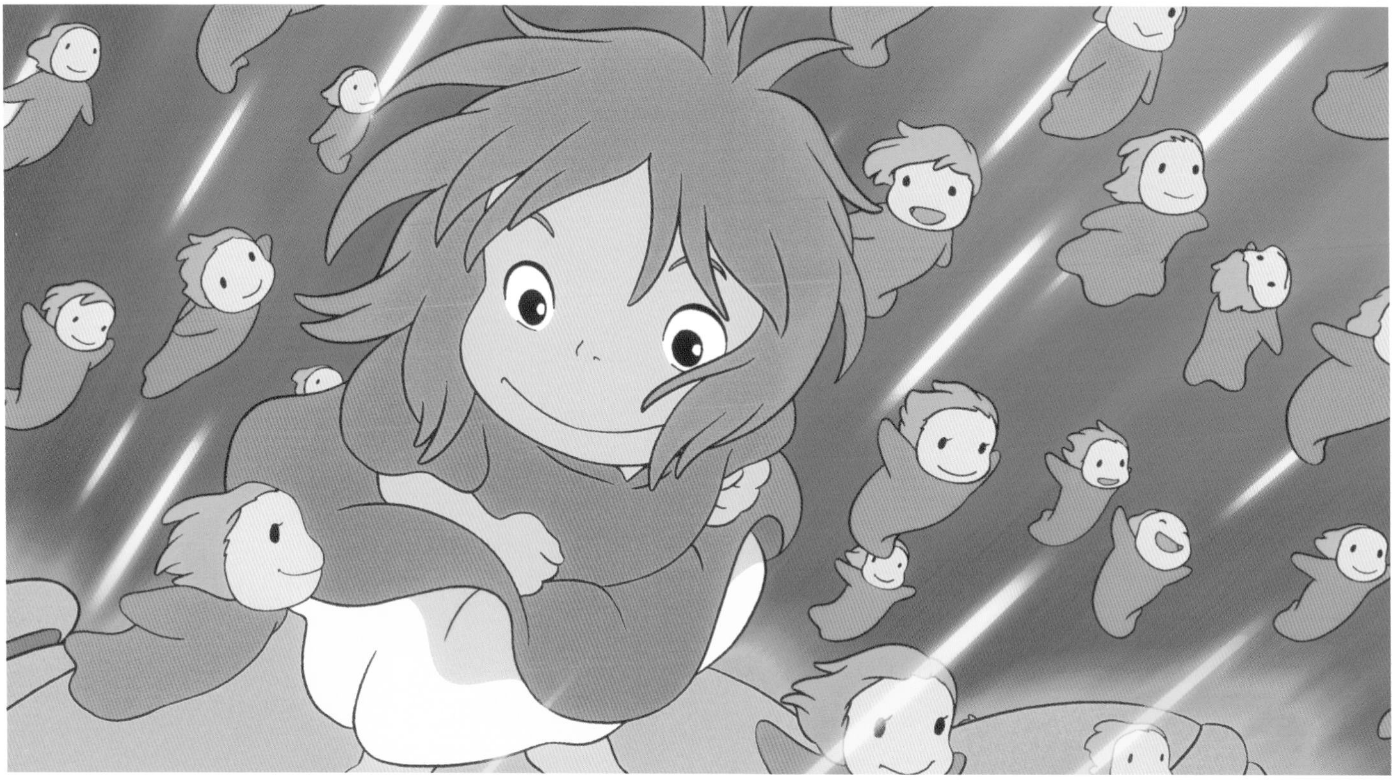

3

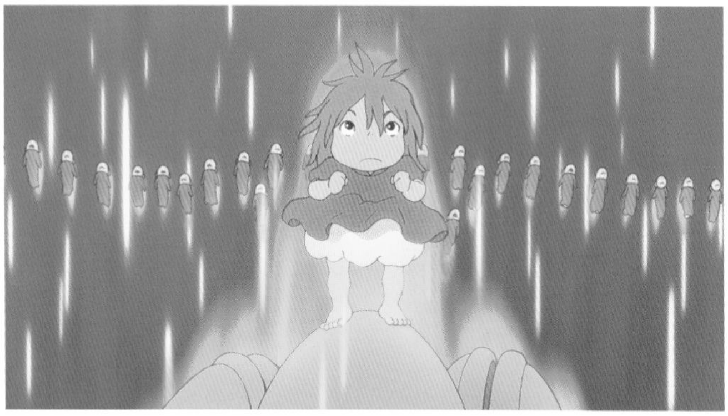

4

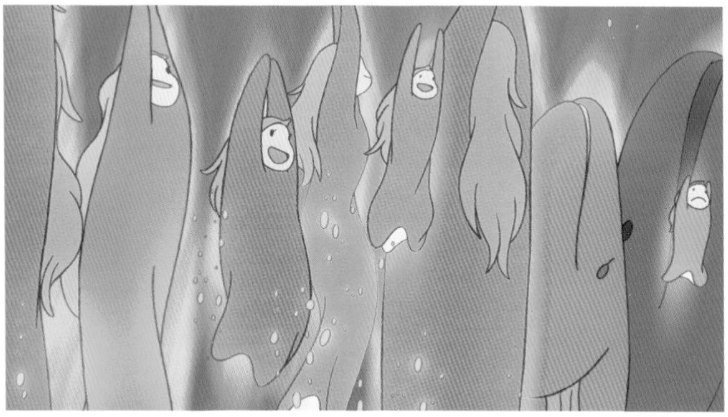

5

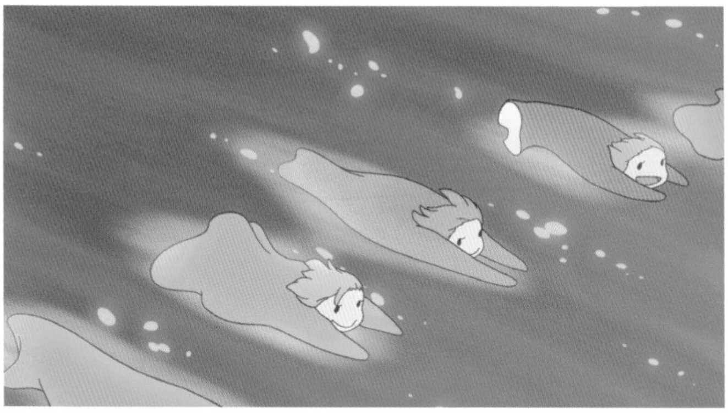

6

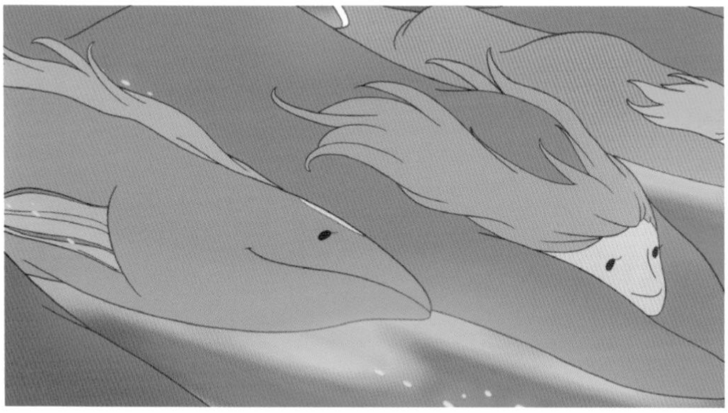

7

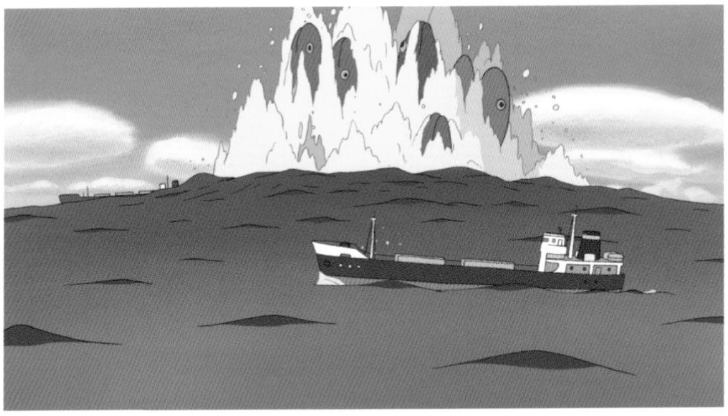

8

Ponyo's Great Escape

1–7 /Ponyo and her sisters, escaping the Coral Tower along with a school of giant, gold-colored fish. One after another, the cheerful sisters metamorphose into minions and fly in formation.
8 /The giant minions, shooting high above the surface.
9, 10 /The minions come back down around the *Koganei Maru* and surge forward like a tsunami.
11 /The human Ponyo running atop the minions.
12 /A dumbfounded Koichi watching her go.

Hiromasa Yonebayashi was responsible for drawing the swarm of minions, which were transformed into gigantic fish. Even Miyazaki said of him, "He's skilled at drawing monster-like creatures that no one's seen before," and Yonebayashi was truly impressive in the way he was able to render his creation without hesitation.

—Supervising Animator: Katsuya Kondo

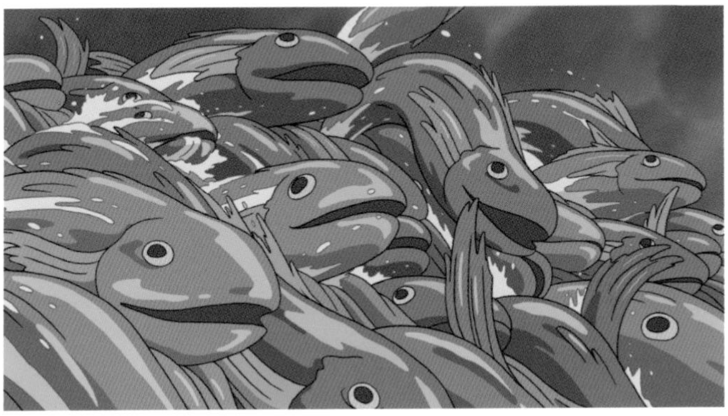

9

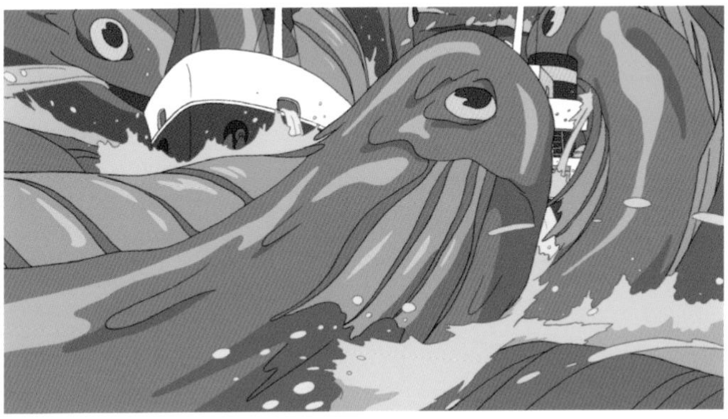

10

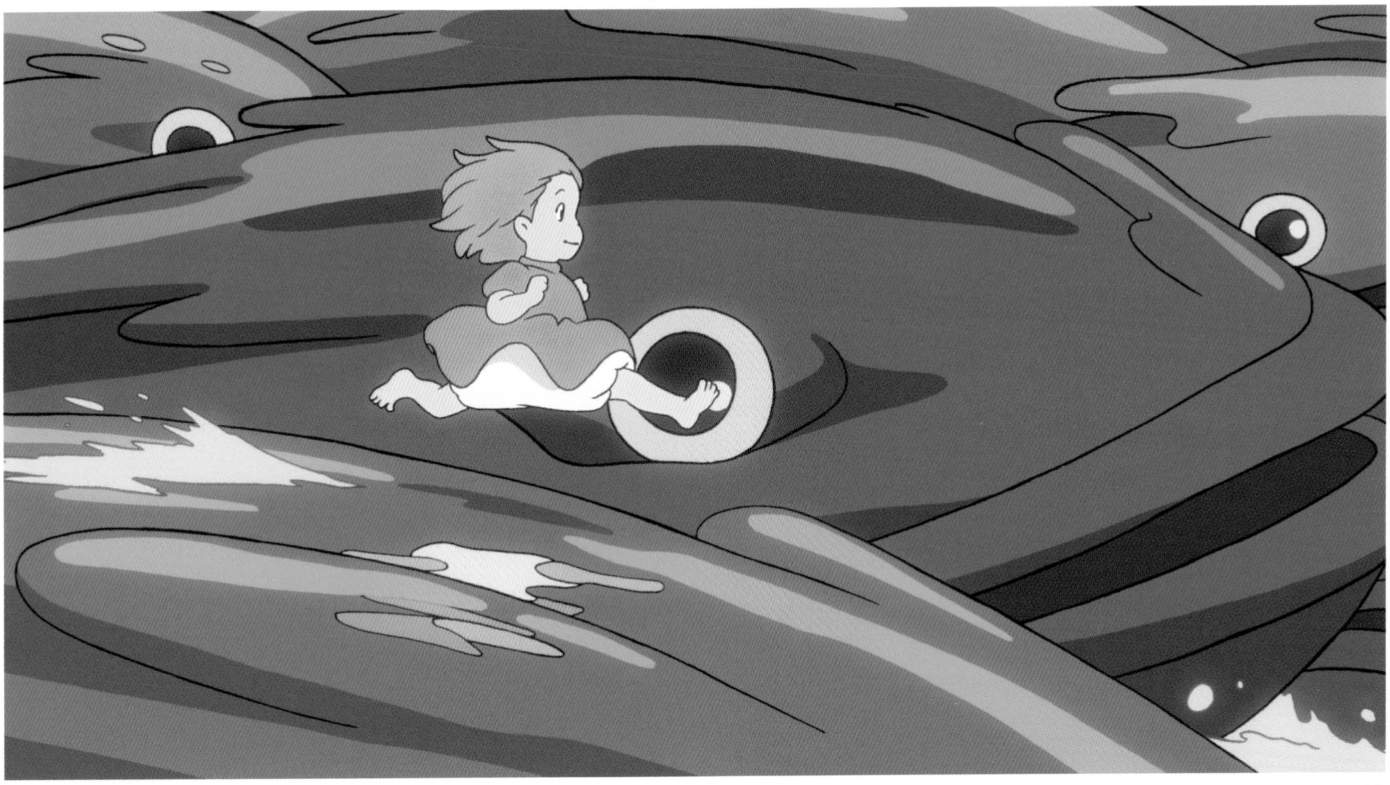

11

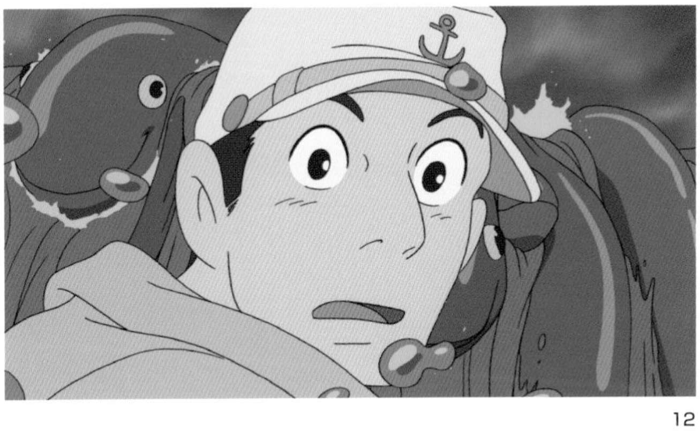

12

ATSUSHI OKUI

Atsushi Okui was born in 1963 in Shimane Prefecture. He began his career in 1981 at Asahi Productions as a cinematographer. He earned his first cinematographer credit with *Dirty Pair* (1987). He later served as cinematographer on *Mobile Suit Gundam: Char's Counterattack* (1988) and on such Ghibli productions as *Porco Rosso* (1992), *Umi ga Kikoeru* (1993), *Pom Poko* (1994), *Whisper of the Heart* (1995), *Princess Mononoke* (1997), and *My Neighbors the Yamadas* (1999). He was also camera supervisor on *Spirited Away* (2001), *Ghiblies: Episode 2* (2002), *Howl's Moving Castle* (2004), and *Tales of Earthsea* (2006).

INTERVIEW
ATSUSHI OKUI
Director of Digital Imaging

I felt better realizing that I only needed to do what I would normally do.

My title in the opening credits is quite simply "photography," as the look of this film is simple, but the job itself wasn't all that different from what I have done in the past. We scanned the backgrounds, combining them with the colored key animation, and then adding camera and special effects to create the final picture.

Since Miyazaki decided to go back to the basics and draw everything by hand, there was no need for 3DCG on *Ponyo*. So, I had the staff who would normally work on 3DCG assist with creating special effects while also helping out with photography. The special effects staff, aside from the usual duties, were also involved with processing the backgrounds and working with the photography staff on various areas as the production warranted.

Miyazaki was particularly exacting about how to render the water on this film [1]. Since the sea was one of the main characters this time around, the movements of the waves and water were rendered as hand-drawn creations through a process of trial and error. While the surface of the water and caps of the waves were drawn in key animation, everything else was matched with the backgrounds as a foundation.

Since the water's edge was obviously moved by animation, we created a mask layer to insert the background seamlessly with the action. We mainly focused our efforts on this type of mask work [2].

Although it's certainly possible to render the water more realistically using digital effects, effects are sometimes incompatible with hand-drawn animation, so we limited their use to only certain areas such as to reinforce the rippling effect of the water. While adding such atmospheric effects during photography seems to be a growing trend in recent animation, at Ghibli we don't create the backgrounds or color design with the expectation that anything will be added digitally. Since the atmospheric effects are incorporated into the backgrounds and are certainly considered during the color design stage, we rarely have to add such effects when the animation and backgrounds are assembled during photography.

While this doesn't have to do with atmospheric effects, in the analog days we used to photograph the composites of cels placed on top of backgrounds. Although the cels are transparent, that transparency degrades as more and more

1

2

3

4

cels are layered on top, affecting the look of the backgrounds. But since that is no longer the case in digital, the backgrounds tend to look completely unfiltered. However, compensating for this isn't as easy as digitally adding a filtering effect reminiscent of the look created by cels being laid on top of one another. Despite technological advances, in the end, these kinds of adjustments must be made by people and differ depending on the colors being used.

Even so, one good thing about going digital is that we no longer have to worry about removing the spots and dust from the cels. That was the most time-consuming part of the analog process. With that step no longer needed, we're now able to give greater care to other areas. *Ponyo* was an enormous undertaking for the key animators and ink and paint staff, as there were roughly 170,000 frames drawn for this film.

When Miyazaki initially announced his intention to "move the animation by using distinct, solid lines and drawing entirely by hand" and to "depict the backgrounds with a pastel touch," I struggled with the visual composition. At first, I began with the mask work on the waves and tested shots of a tree in a yard blowing in the wind, but for the elements that we would add during photography—such as the expressions of light—I struggled with determining how much was enough to enhance the film.

In fact, there were shots that had to be reshot, and in the beginning, I refrained from adding too much digitally. But if you hold back too much, some parts do not mesh well with the rest. At a certain point, I made up my mind that I needed to add some digital effects to areas that required it. What prompted this decision was a shot in the middle part of the film of the lights coming on when the generator is turned on in Lisa's house [3]. I was given two separate backgrounds, one for before and one for after the light is turned on, with the filament drawn in and the glowing effect meant to be rendered by shining a light from under the frame. We tried photographing it as intended in the beginning, but everyone said that something didn't look right. So we created another version where we digitally enhanced the glow of the light, which looked better, and that's when my uncertainty was dispelled.

For the scene in which Lisa sets up the antenna, art director Noboru Yoshida also drew a background accentuating the stars, which looked great as a picture, but didn't translate as a photographed image. So we enhanced the stars to look not so much like they're twinkling, but instead gleaming, and tried to create an air of fantasy.

But since the look of the world would be ruined if the added effects were too intrusive, we were especially careful about bringing out the realism and presence of the world of *Ponyo*. Of course, the effect of showing reflections on a wet road or on top of a minion is a convention of animation, and we carefully handled those just as we always have. With regard to the candle in the steamboat scenes, Miyazaki wrote, "like Calcifer," in the storyboards, so we used the same method as we did with Calcifer on *Howl's Moving Castle*.

In that sense, I think we were able to work as we always have in the end. While I might have had regrets had I continued to worry as I had in the beginning, it was fortunate that I was able to right myself and come to the conclusion that I should do just what I would normally do.

5

6

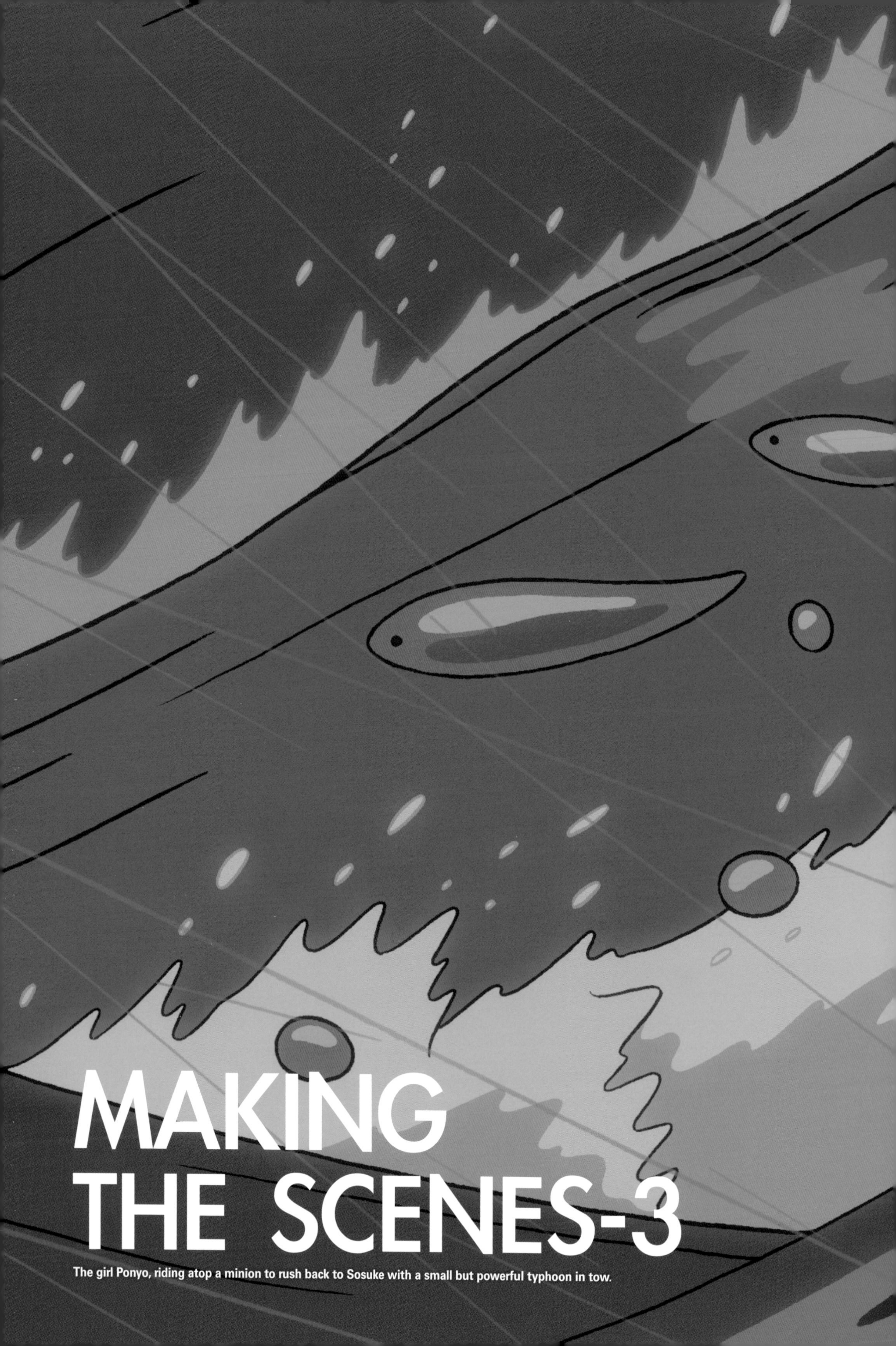

MAKING THE SCENES-3

The girl Ponyo, riding atop a minion to rush back to Sosuke with a small but powerful typhoon in tow.

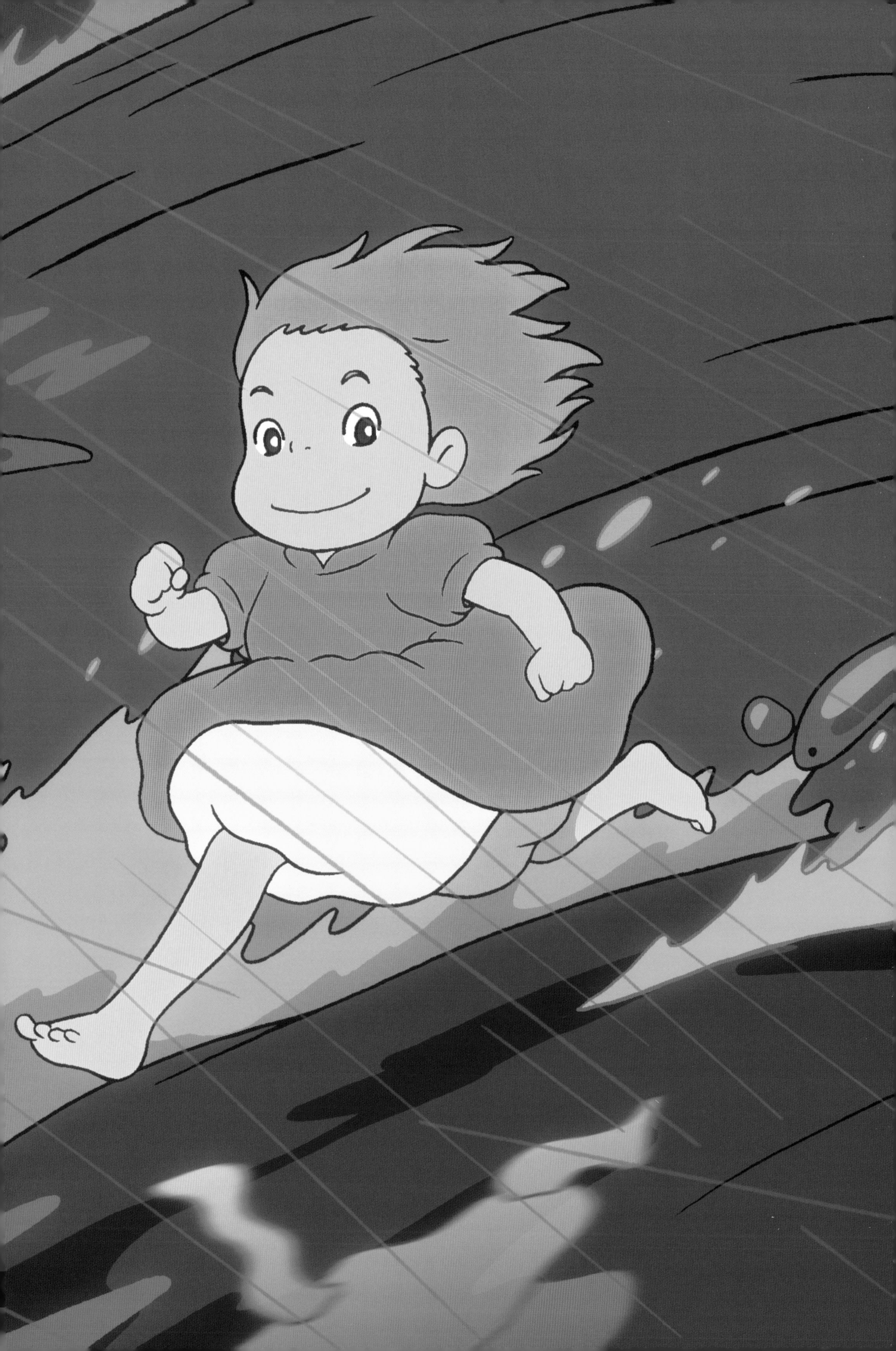

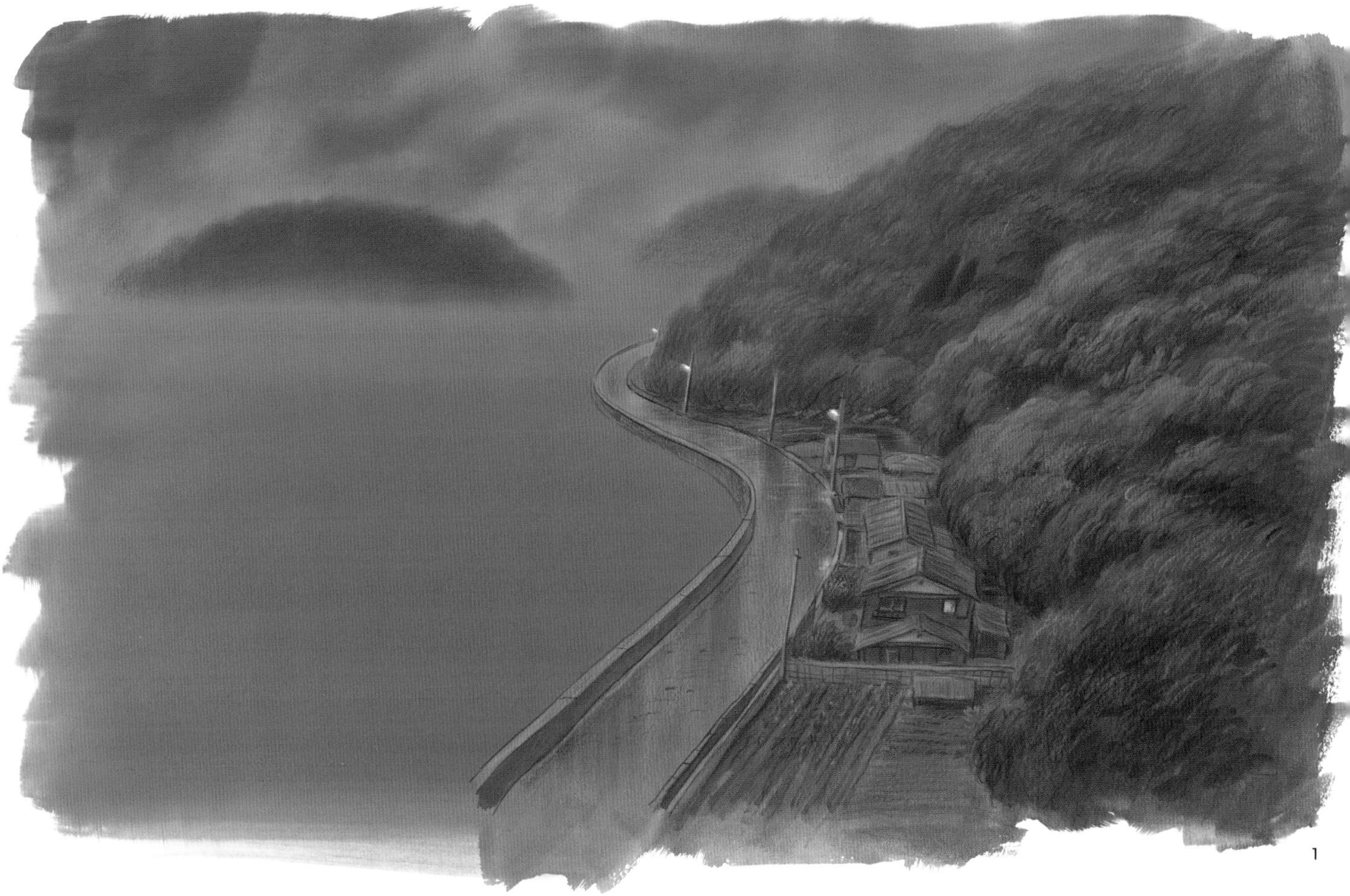

1

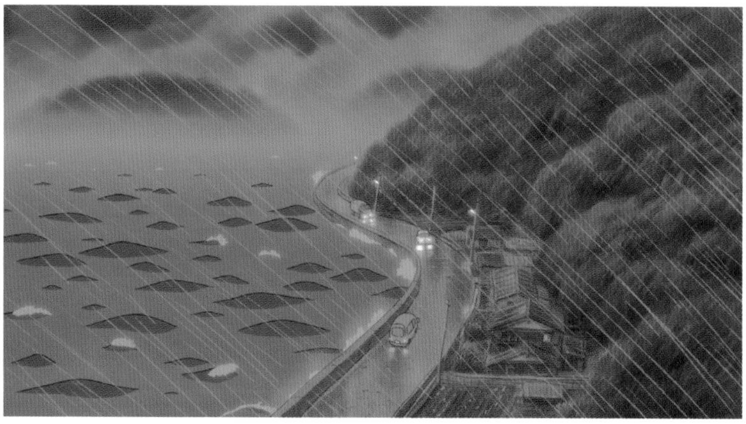

2

The Typhoon Strikes

1 /The road to the Sunflower House, misty from the wind and rain [Background].
2 /The preschool lets out early due to the approaching typhoon.
3 /The preschool in the rain. Parents are in cars picking up their children in the actual shot [Background].
4 /The entrance of the daycare service center. The scene in which Sosuke, wearing a raincoat, comes looking for Lisa [Background].

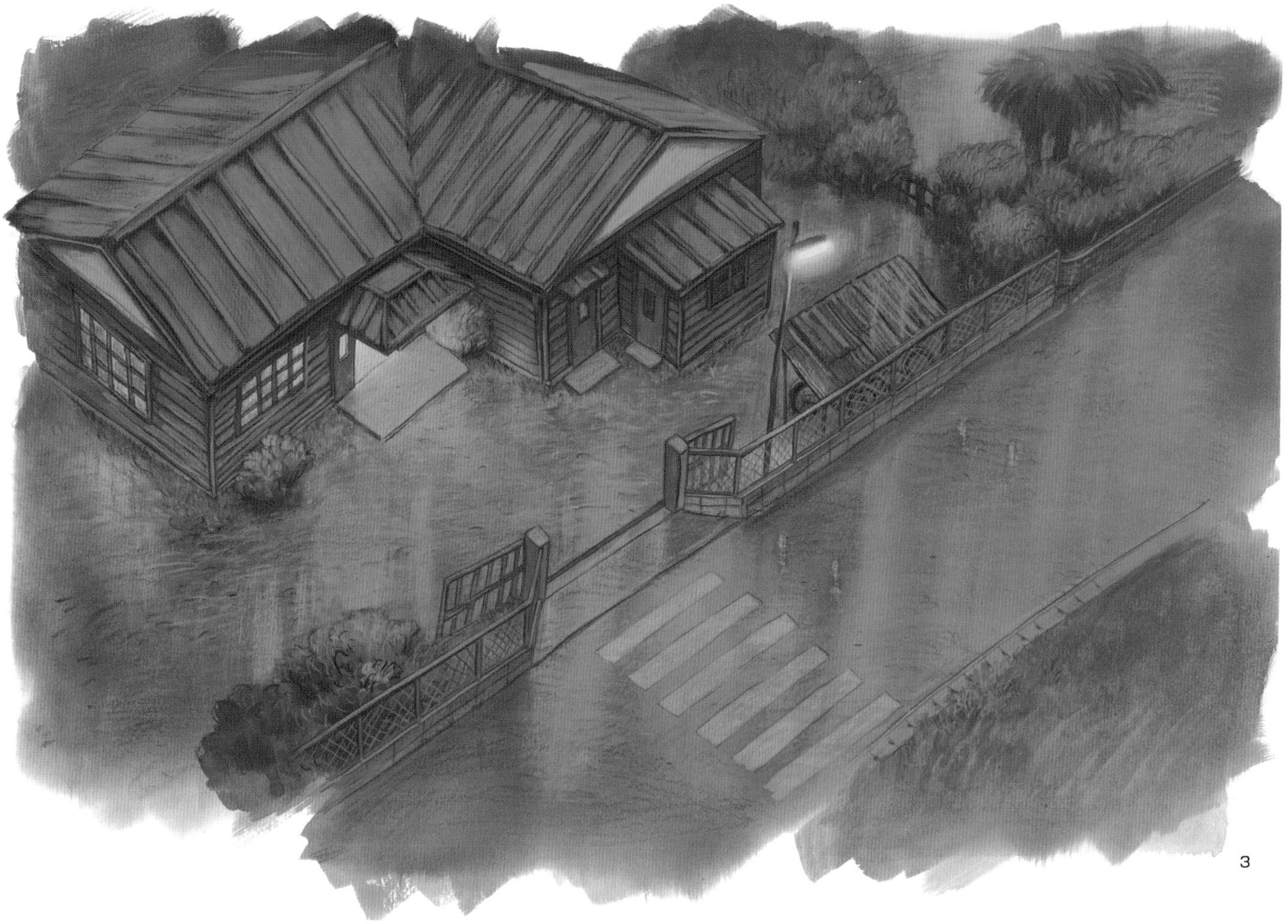

3

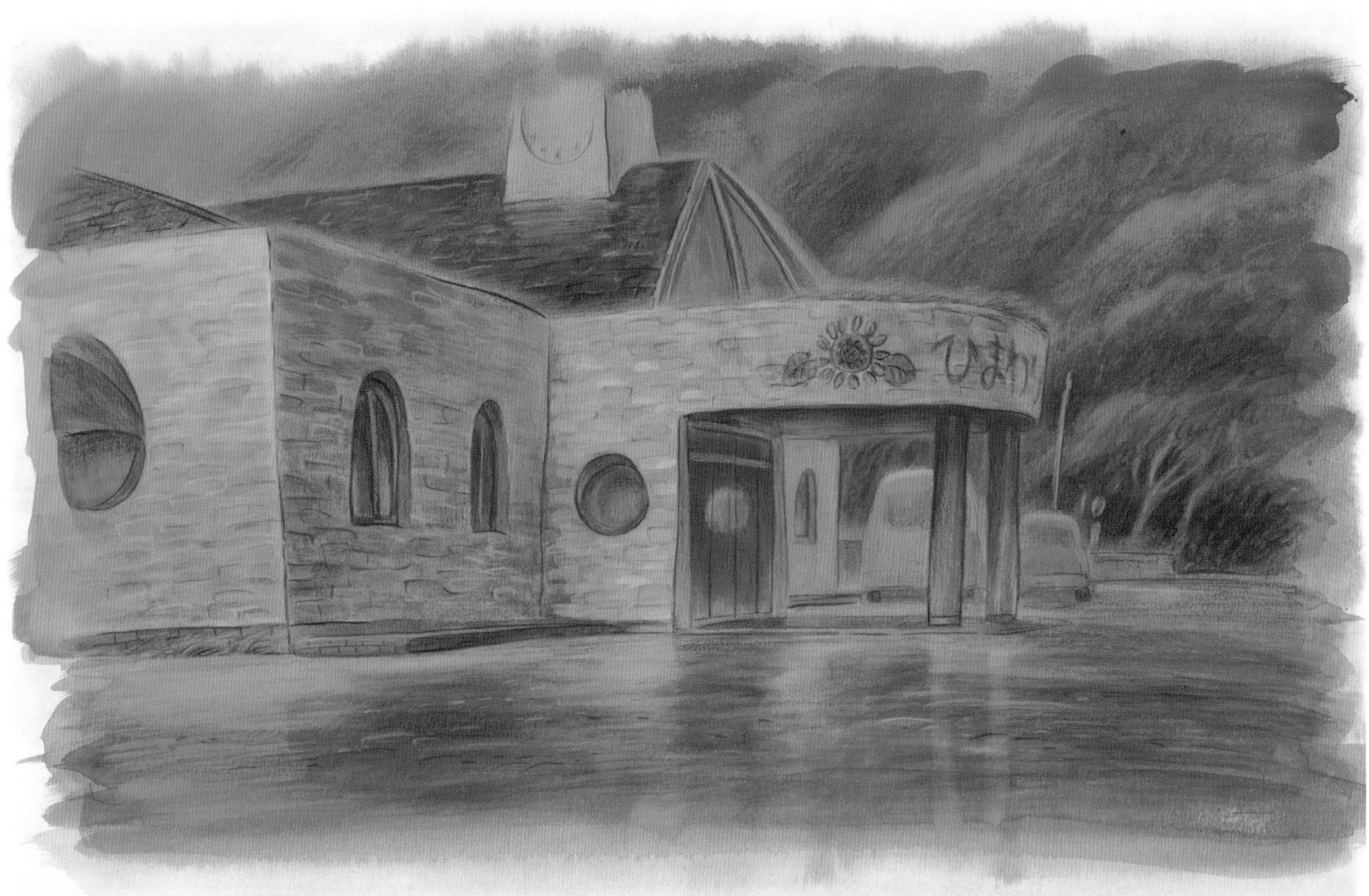
ひま

4

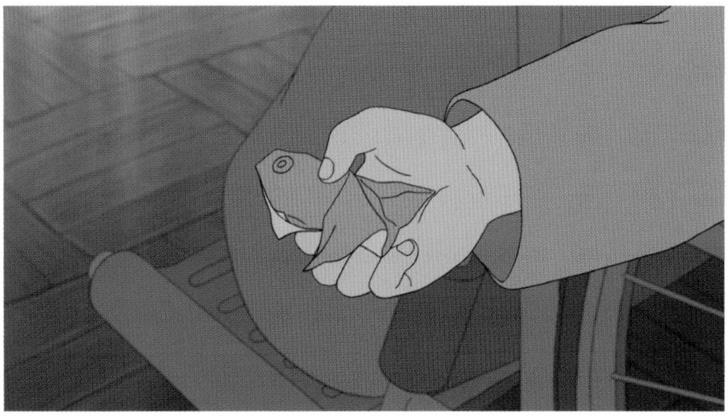

1

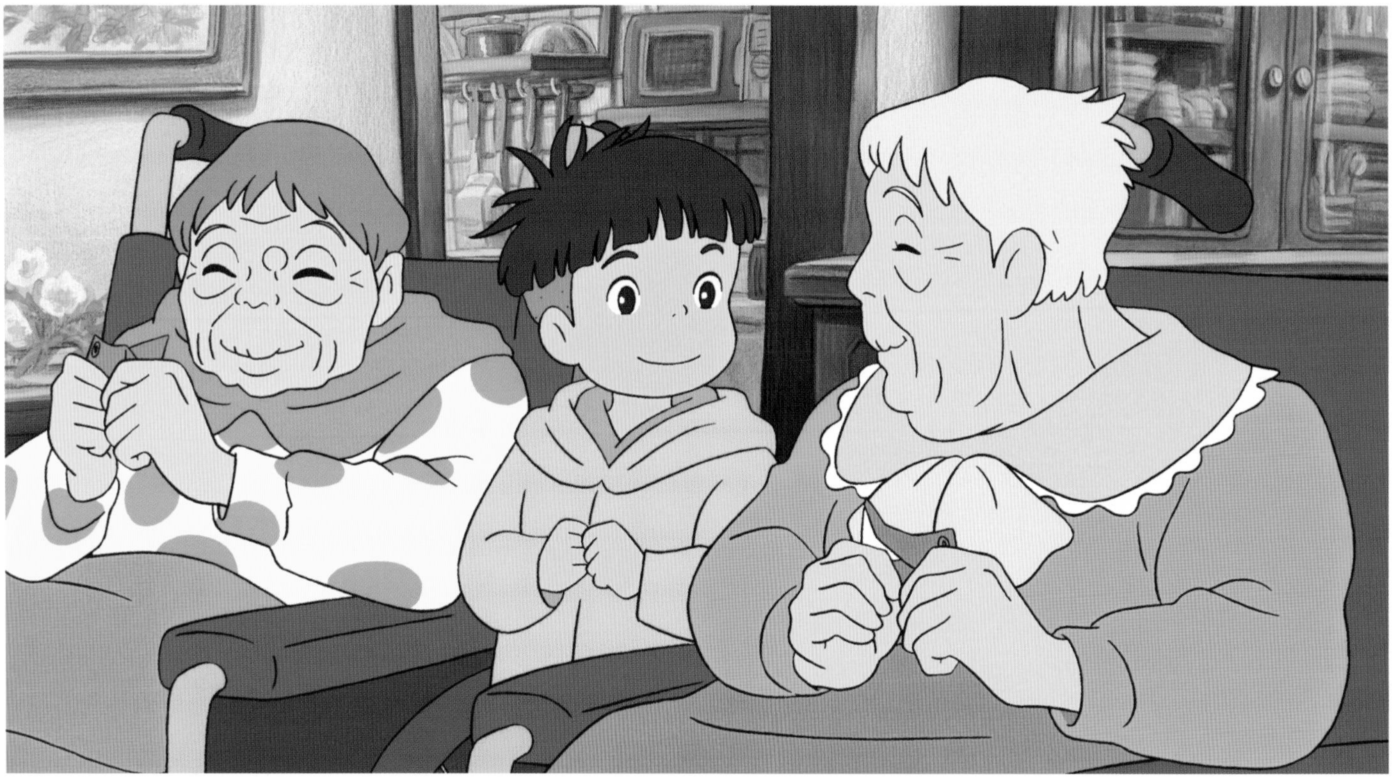

2

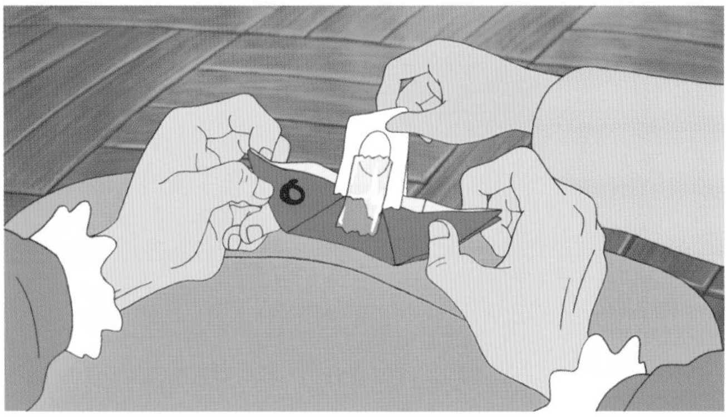

3

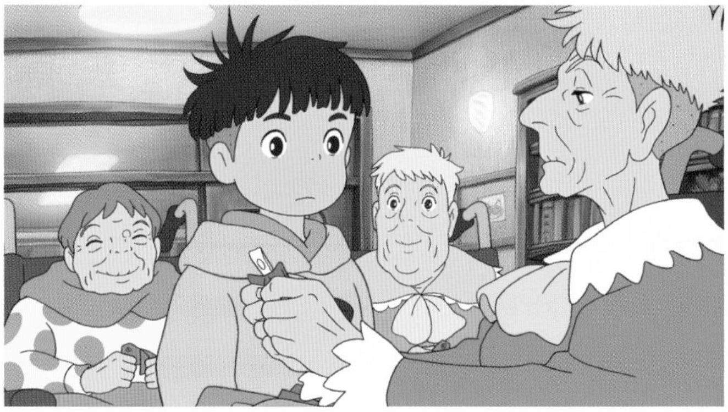

4

Lucky Goldfish

1 /With the lights out, Sosuke gives the nervous elderly ladies goldfish made of origami.
2 /Yoshie and Noriko, happy to have the lights back on. "We've got our lucky goldfish to keep us company, so I'm sure we'll be just fine."
3 /Sosuke gives an origami *Koganei Maru* to Toki but...
4 /She rudely says, "It's...a grasshopper," in her usual way.

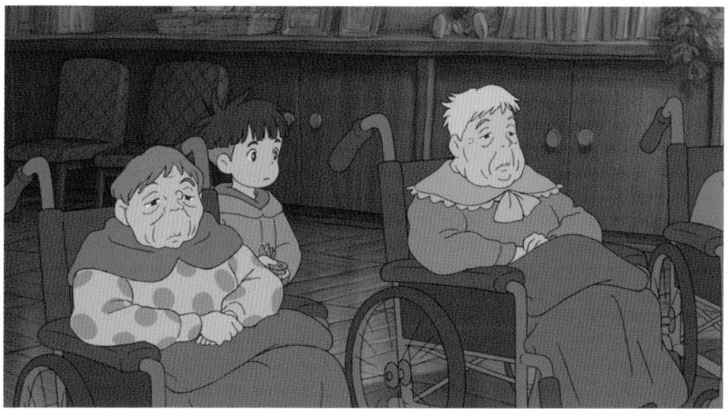

5

5 /The elderly women, who appear a little nervous in the dark.
6 /Yoshie's wheelchair and Toki's electric wheelchair [Character design].
7 /Naomi busily working even during the blackout. She urges Lisa to go home.
8 /Shima taking the meals to the elderly women staying the night. Lisa comes for Sosuke.

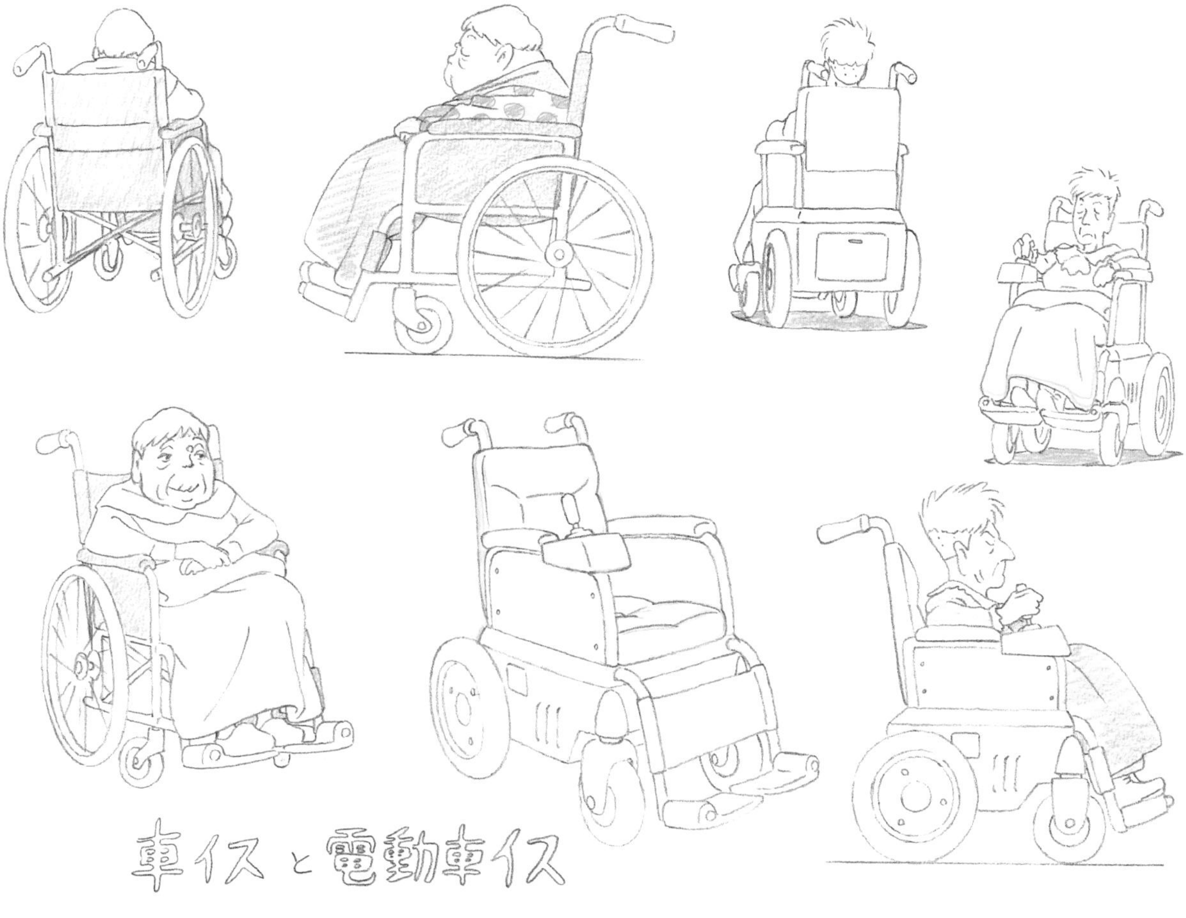
車イスと電動車イス

6

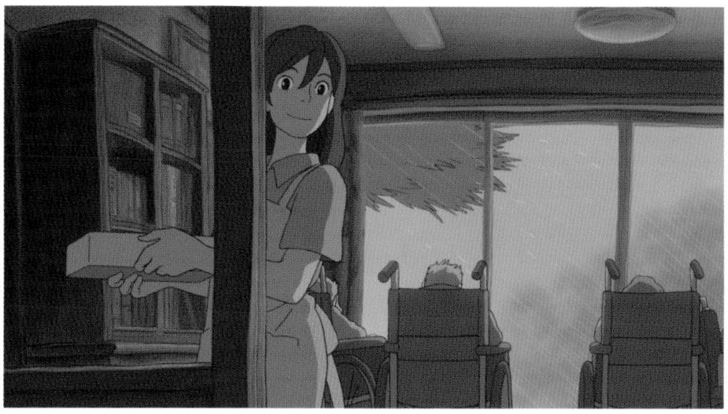

7

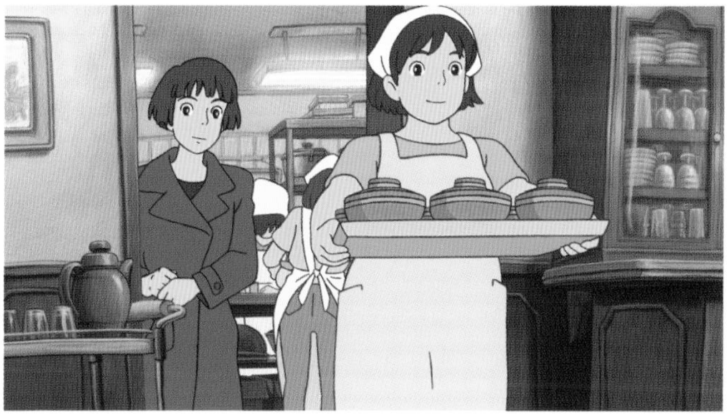

8

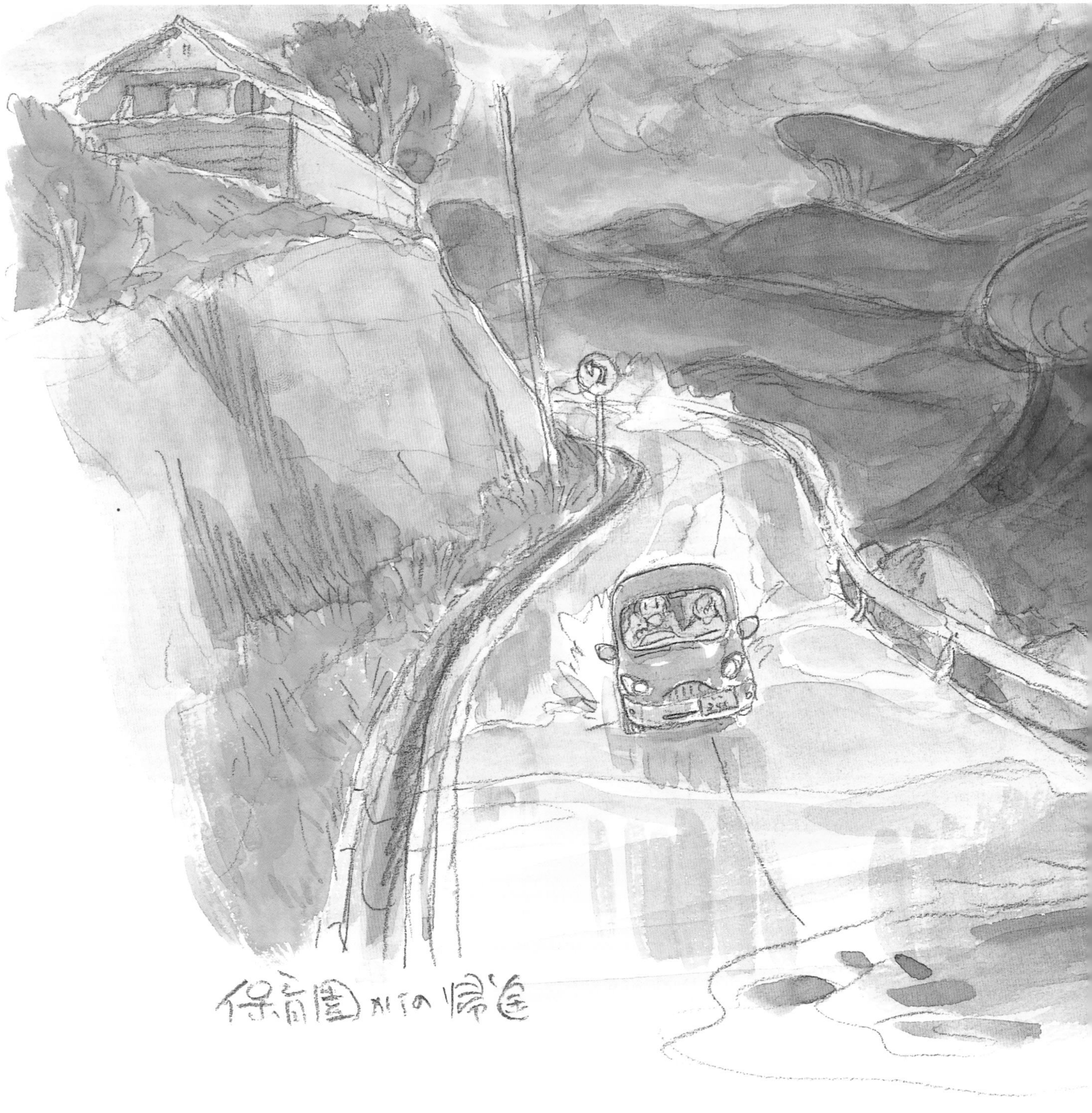
保育園からの帰途

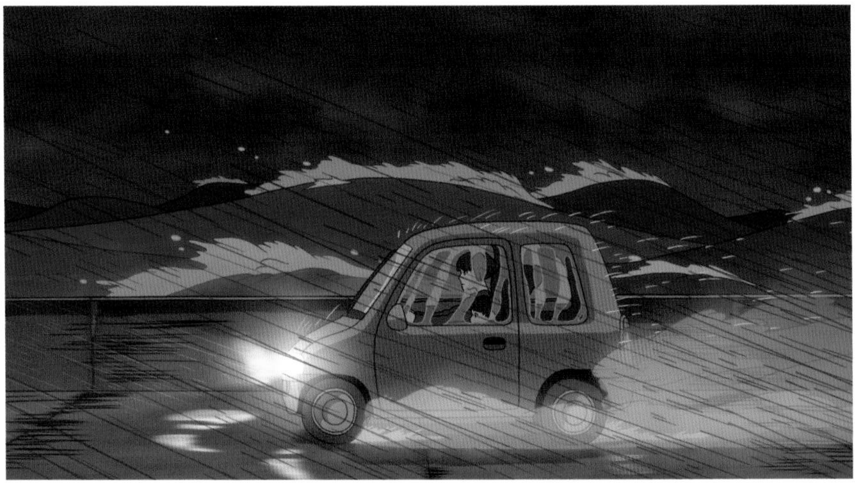

2

The Road Back from the Preschool

1 /Lisa's car speeding home in the torrential rain. A large wave surges from behind [Concept sketch].
2 /Lisa's car traveling along the embankment.
3, 4 /The huge wave pursuing Lisa's car [Concept sketches].

1

3

宝くじのみ!!

4

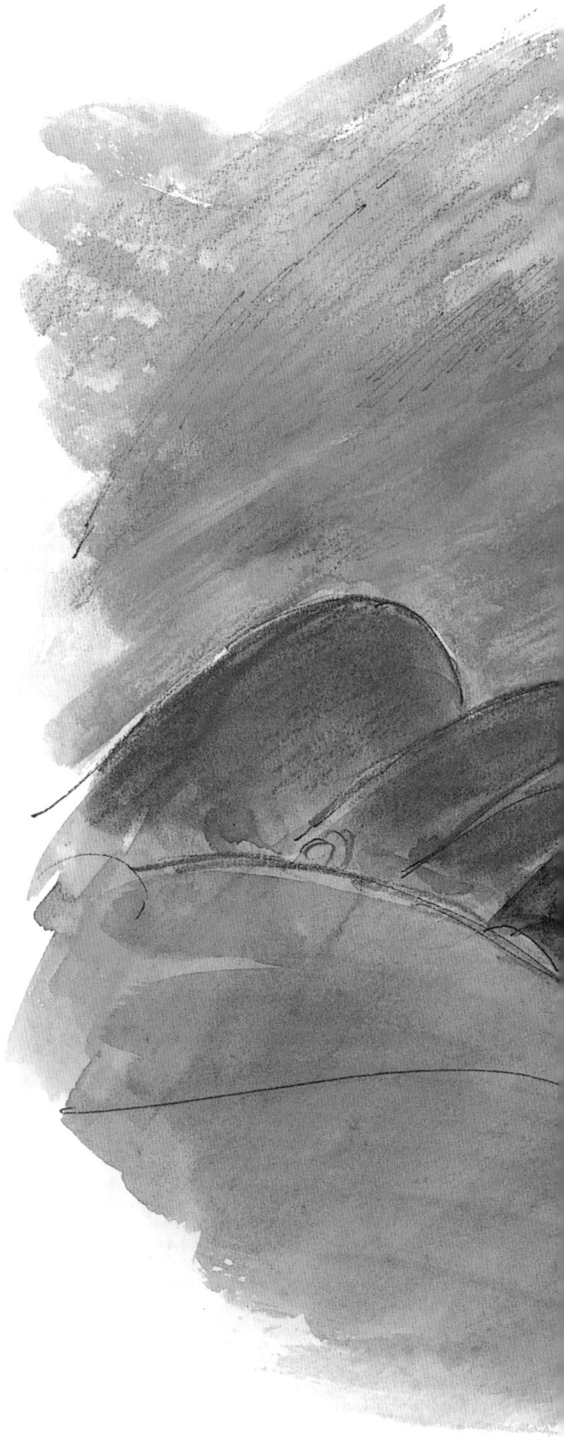

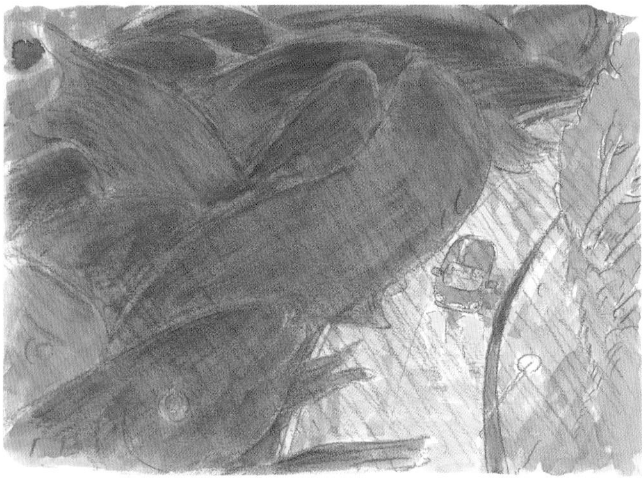

1

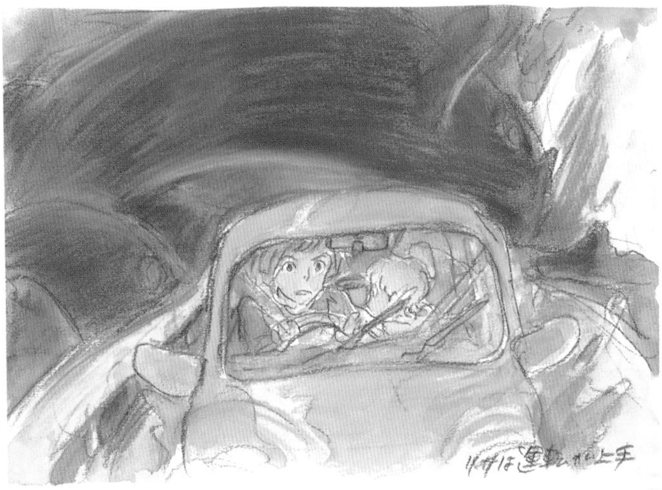
リサは運転が上手

2

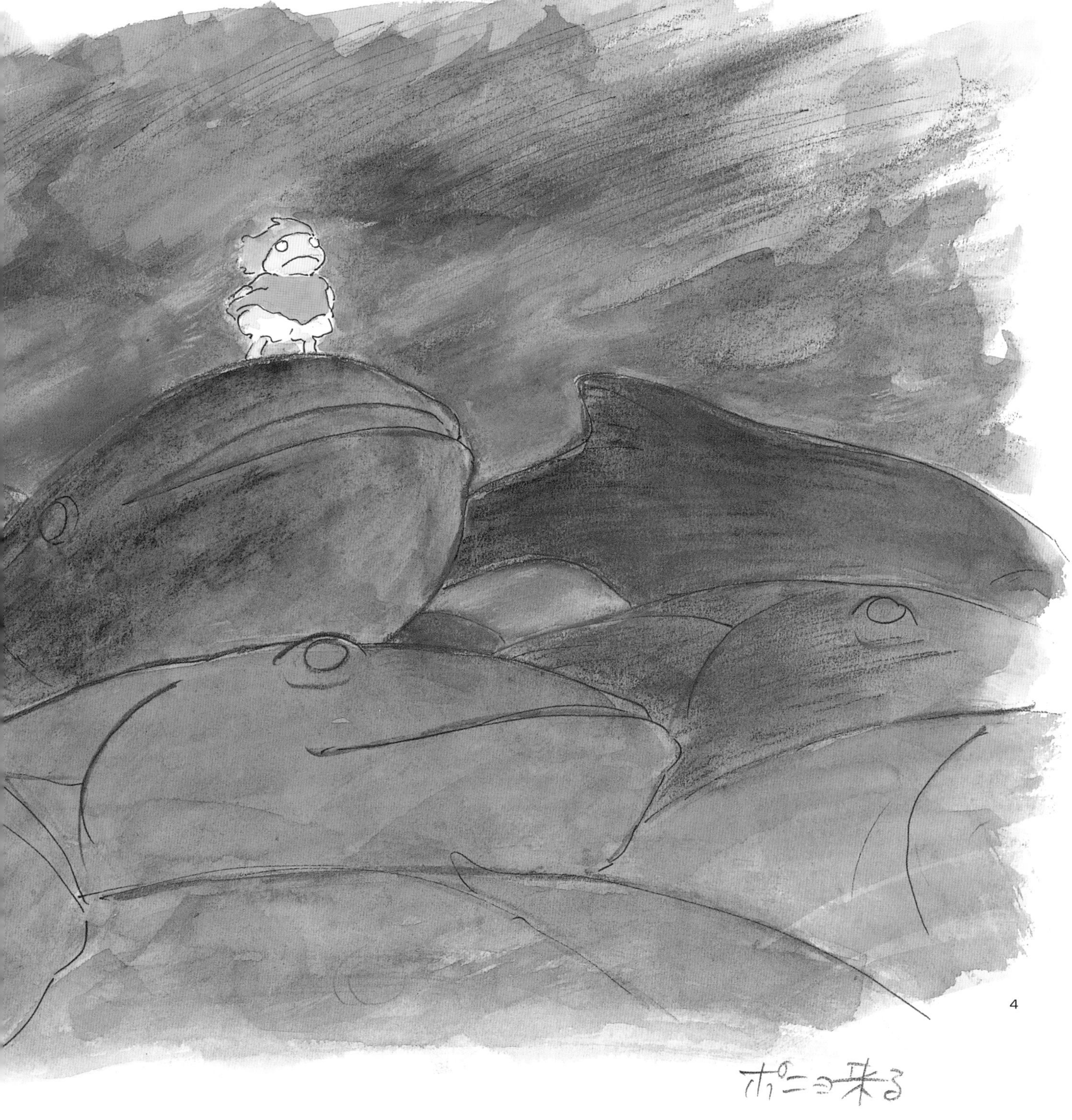
ポニョ来る

4

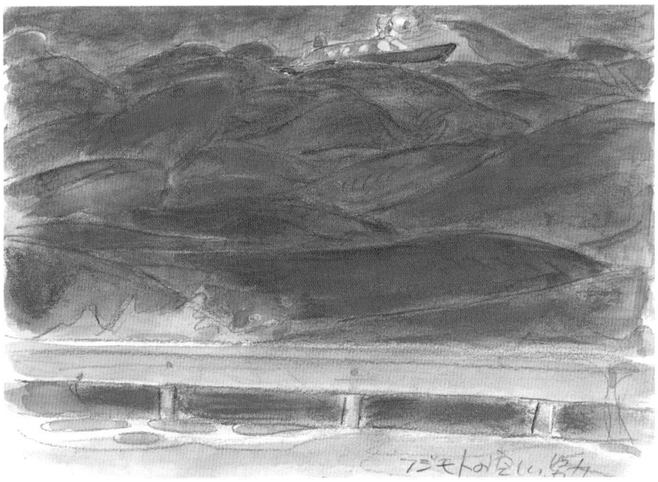
フジモトの追い込み

3

1 /Lisa's car racing. The surging wave of minions [Concept sketch].
2 /Just then, only Sosuke sees... [Concept sketch].
3 /Fujimoto and the *Basking Shark*, chasing after Ponyo. A scene not in the film [Concept sketch].
4 /Ponyo riding atop a minion [Concept sketch].

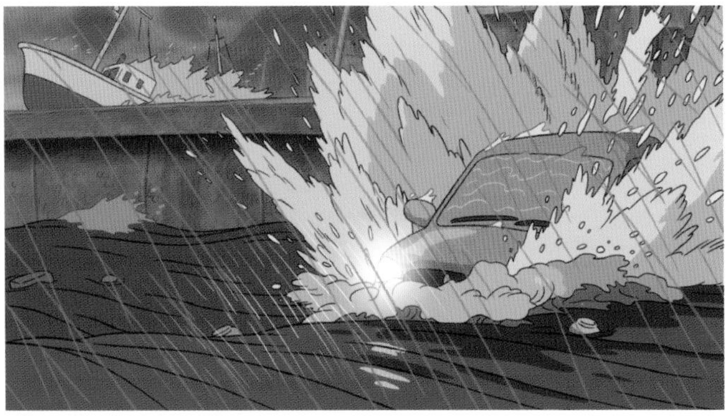

1

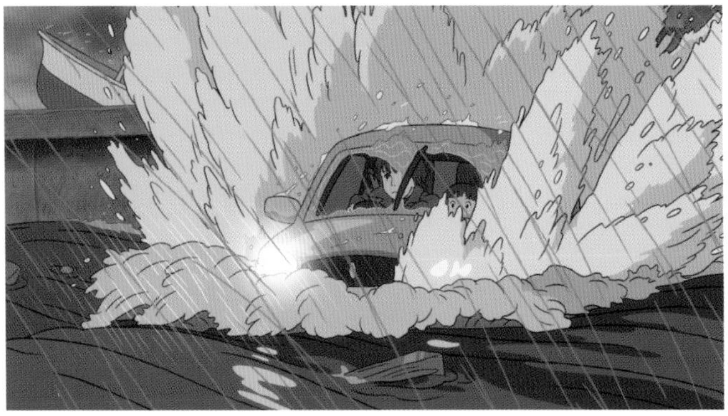

2

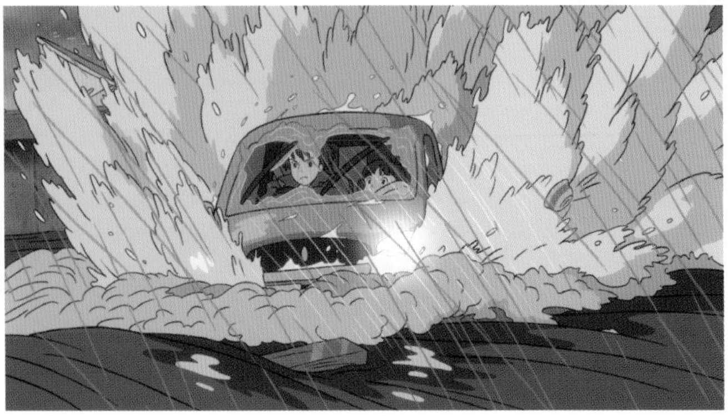

3

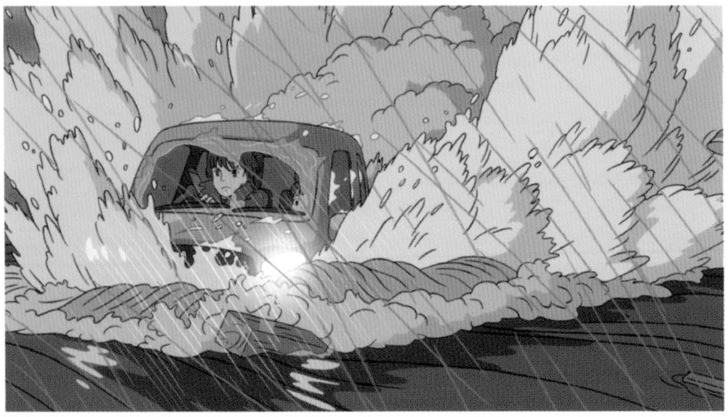

4

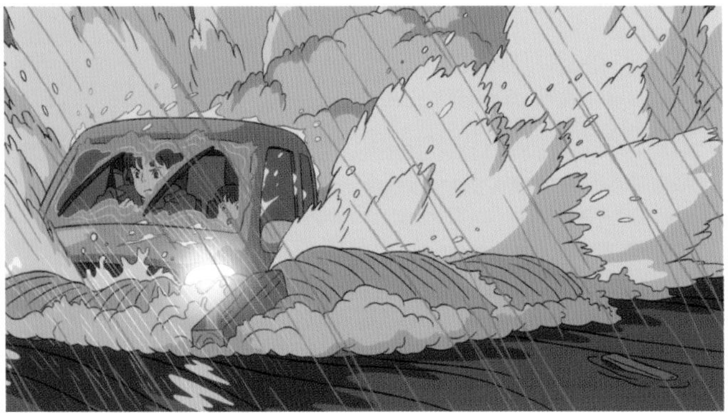

5

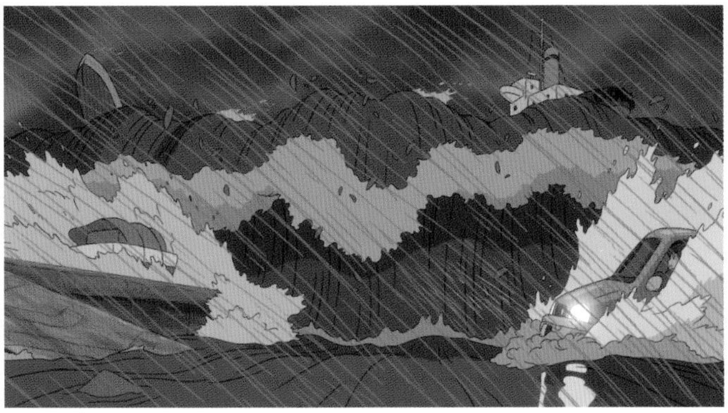

6

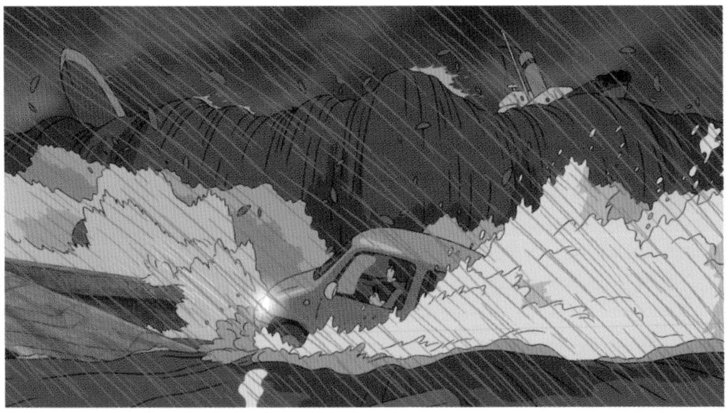

7

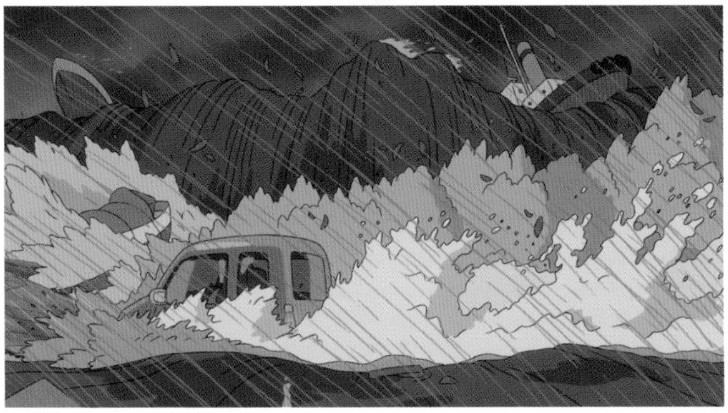

8

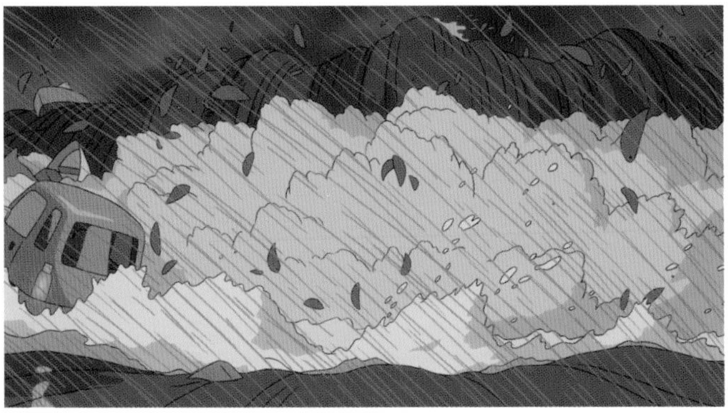

9

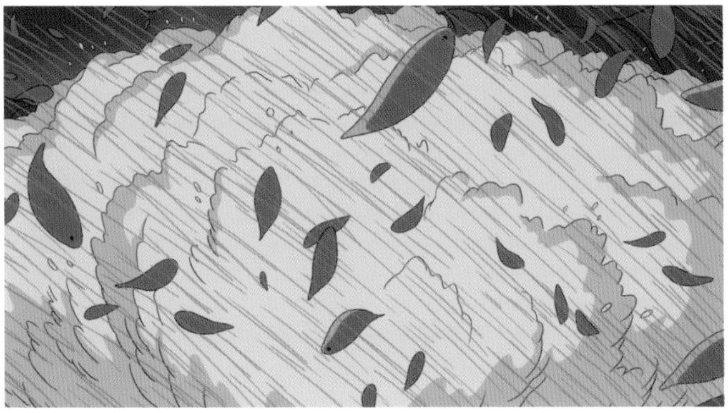

10

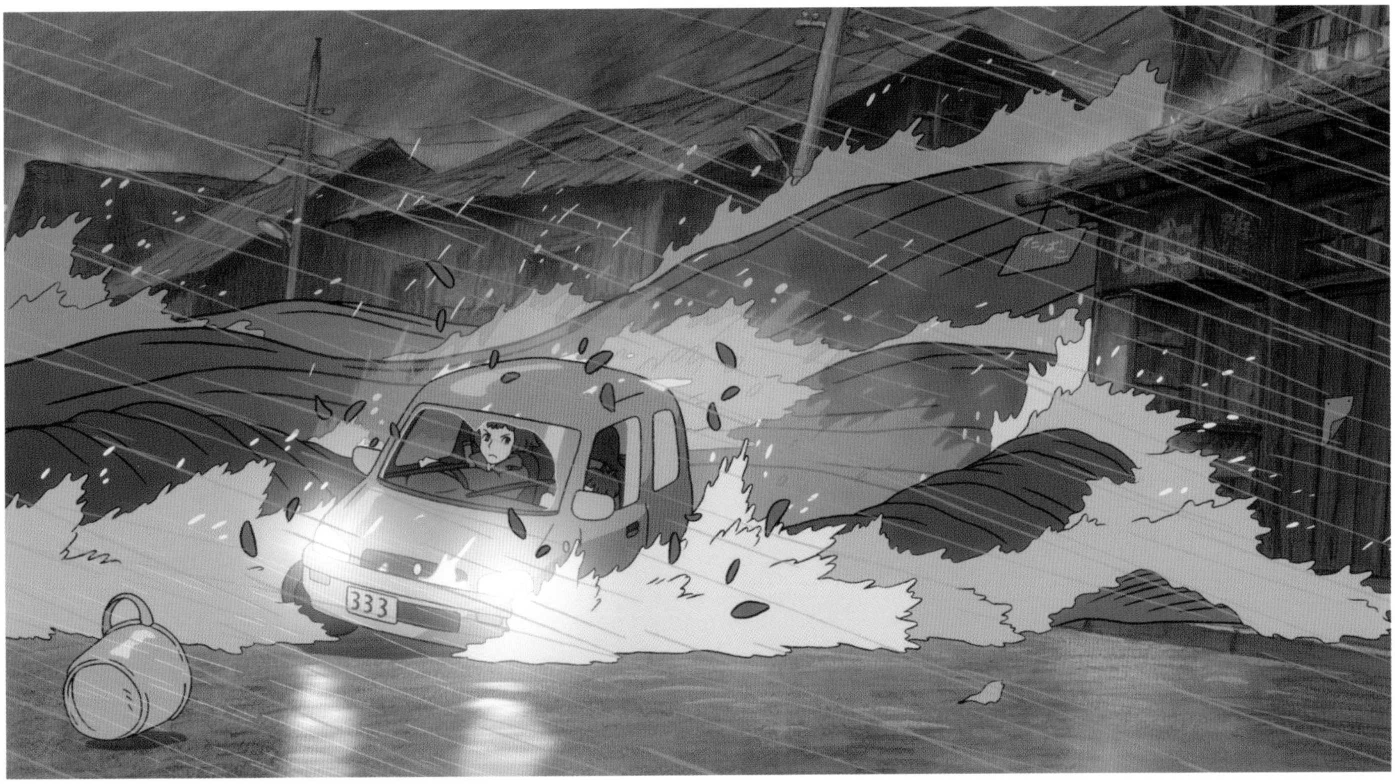
333

11

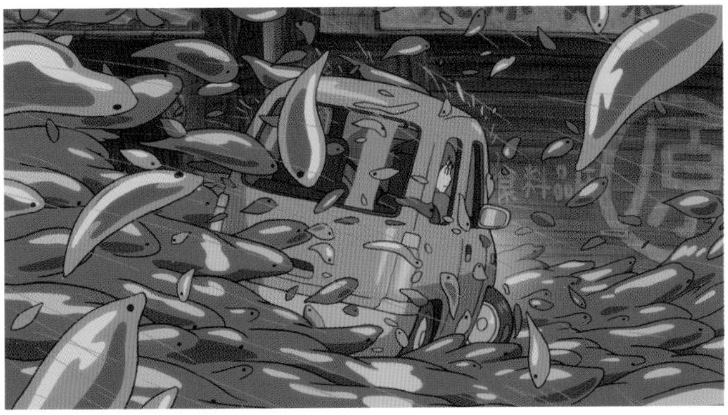

12

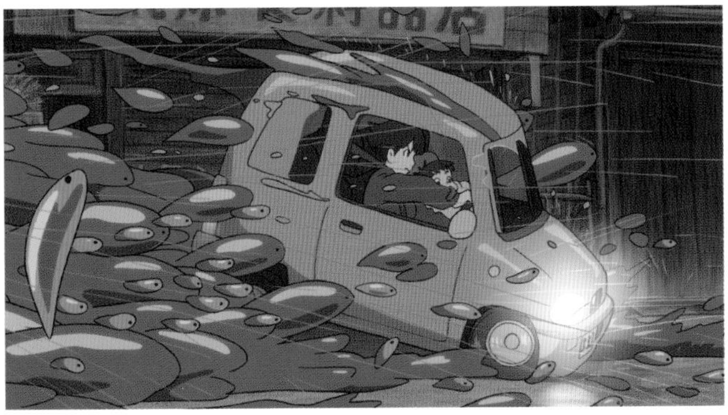

13

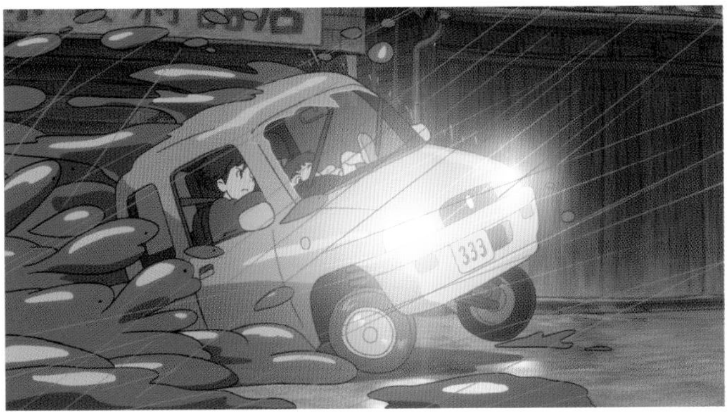
333

14

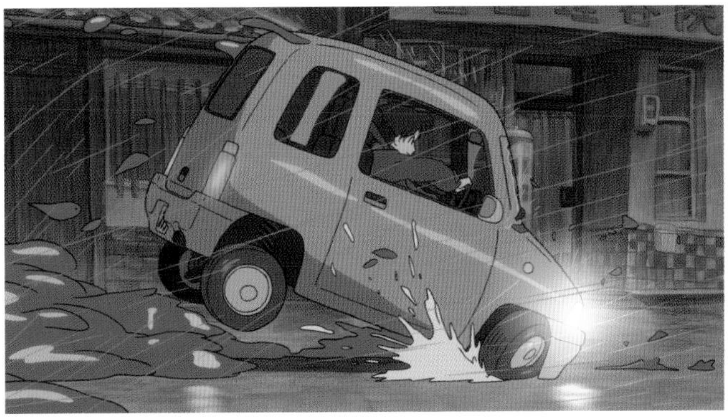

15

In the Storm

1–10 /In the raging storm, Lisa seizes the right moment to cross the docks even as they're almost swallowed by the waves.
11–15 /Lisa's car racing and spinning past storefronts, along with the water—actually minions—flooding the docks.

The action sequence of Lisa's car racing through the storm was key animator Akihiko Yamashita's place to shine. He created so many of the drawings with such speed that I thought he might have torn through about a fourth of the drawings himself. I was amazed by how he was able to produce the drawings so effortlessly with a cool face, whatever the scene. He enjoyed the work so much that he told me, "It's like I became an animator to work on this film." Yamashita was also responsible for the scene of the fishing boat trawling the garbage at the beginning of the film. Even though many different elements were included in each shot, he was able to draw them while thinking about the overall balance across the scene. When it came to rendering the actions of Lisa's car, I left everything up to him.

—Supervising Animator: Katsuya Kondo

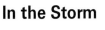

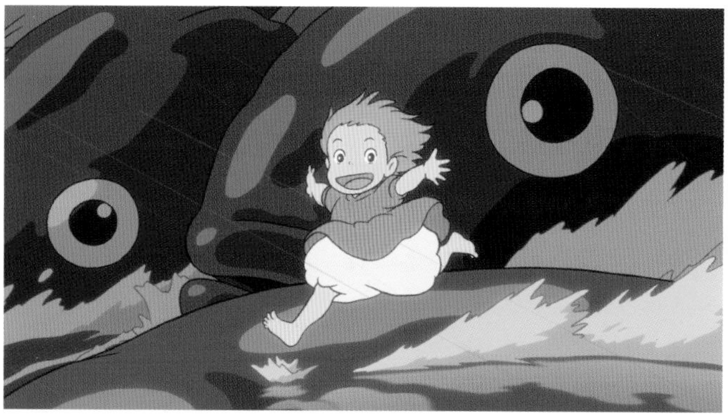

1

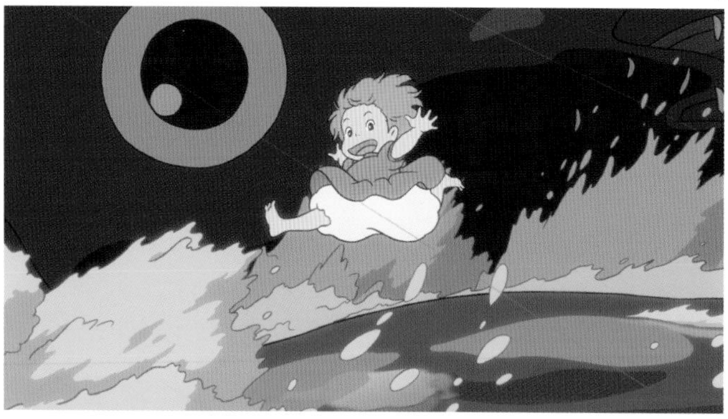

2

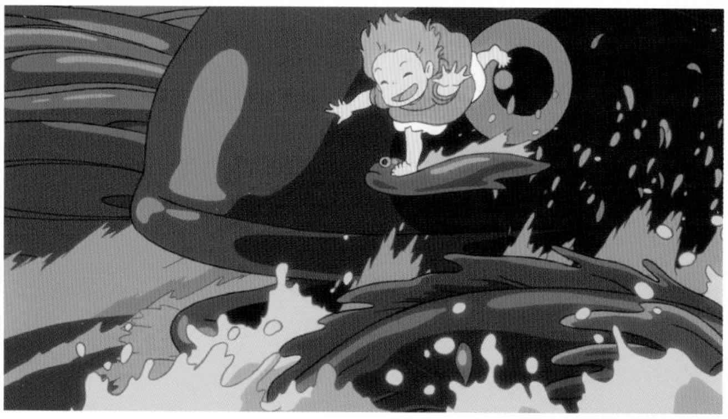

3

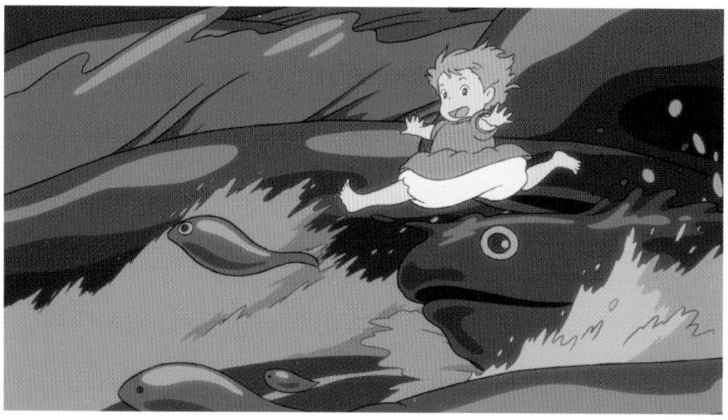

4

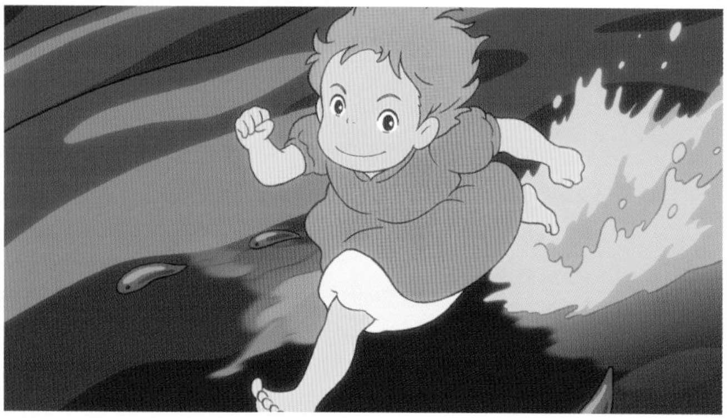

5

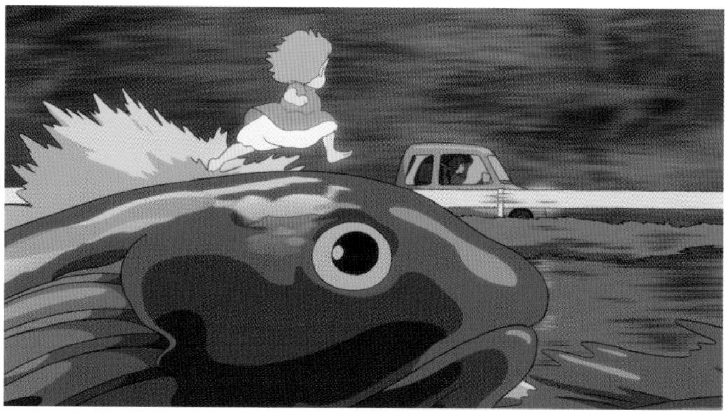

6

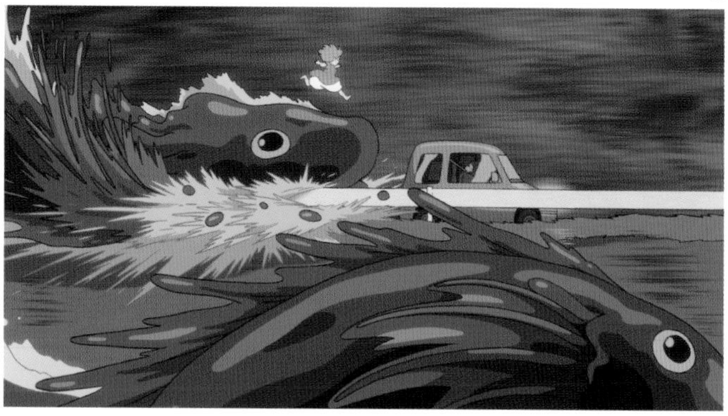

7

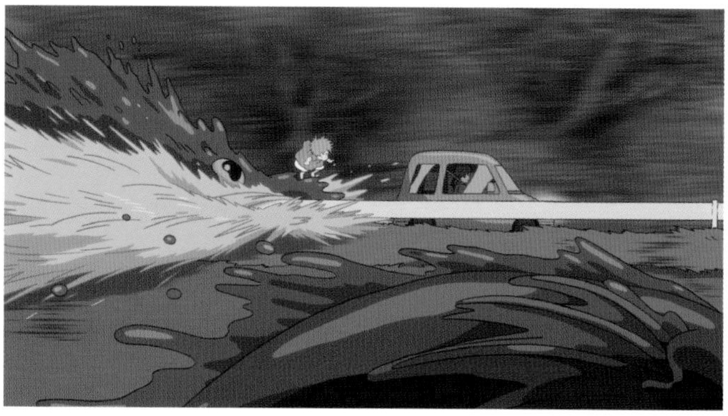

8

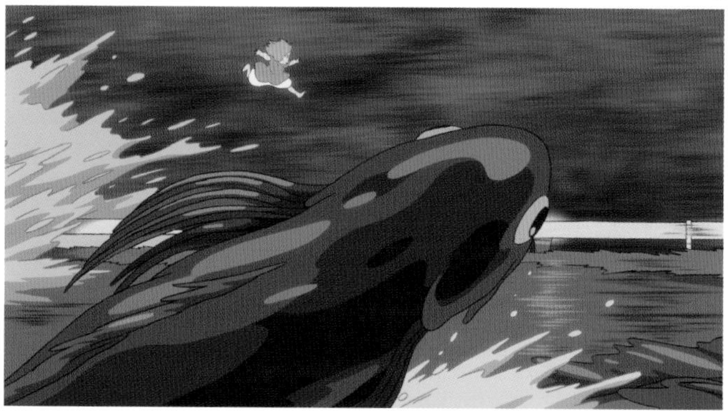

9

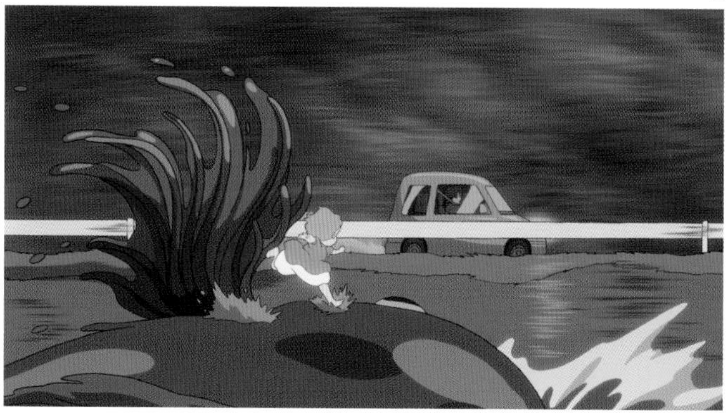

10

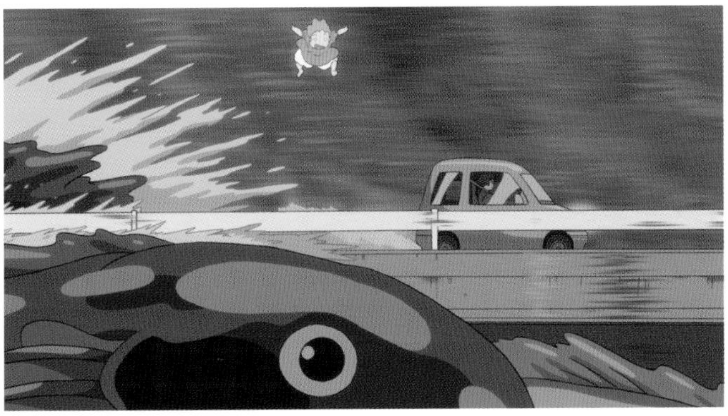
11

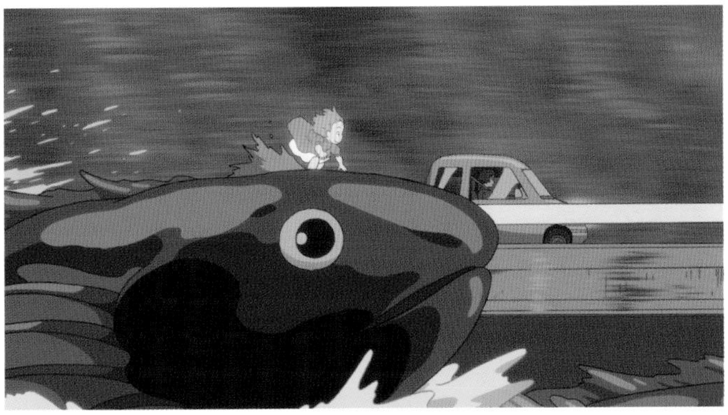
12

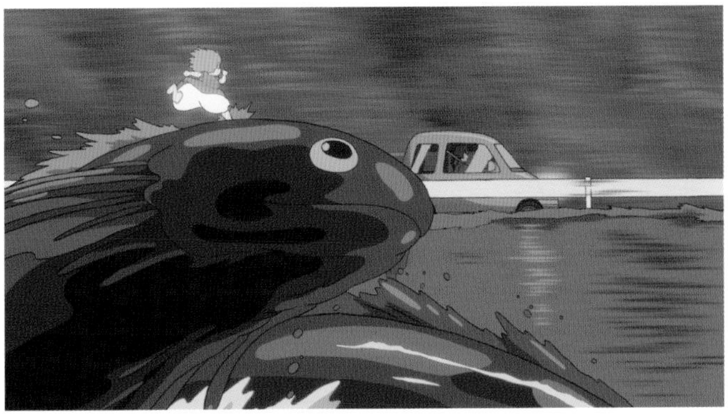
13

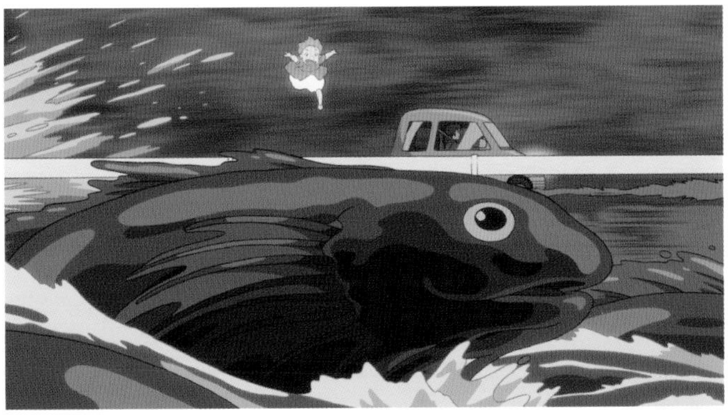
14

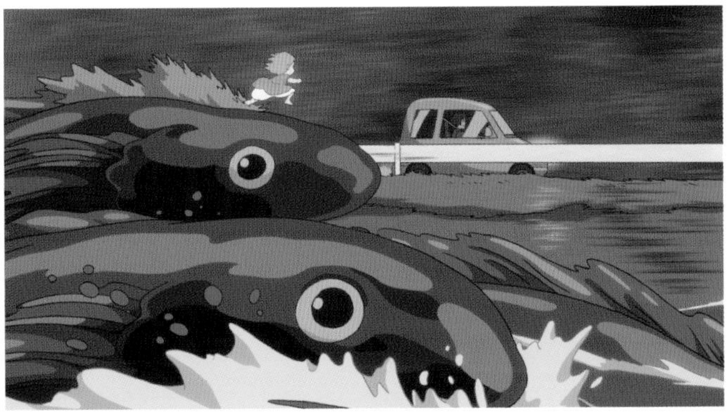
15

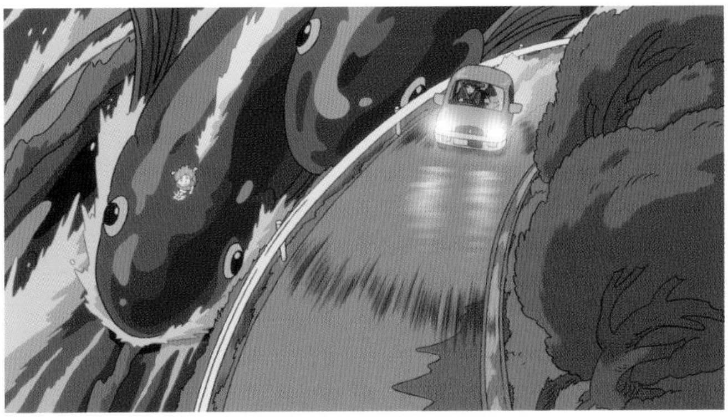
16

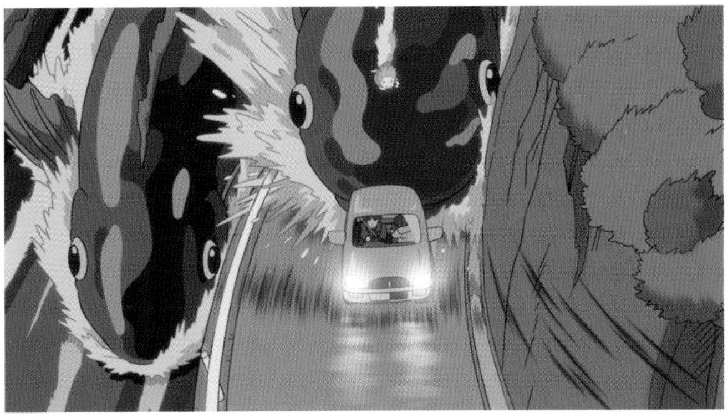
17

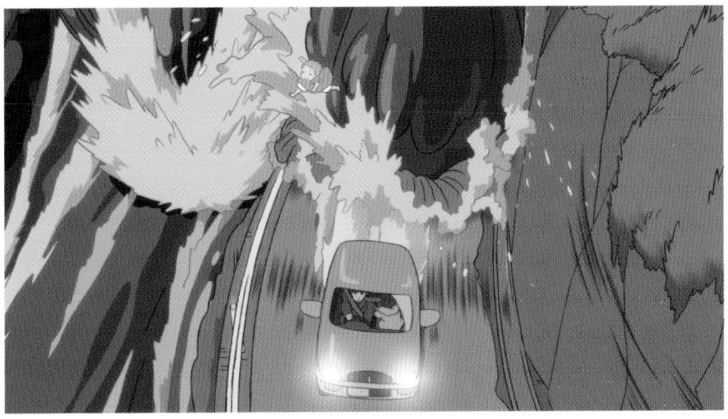
18

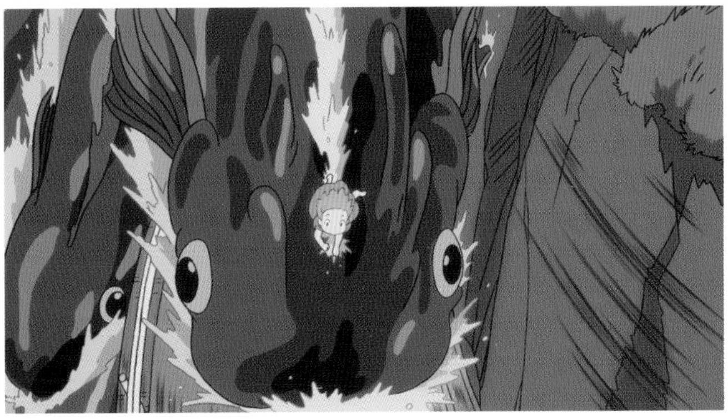
19

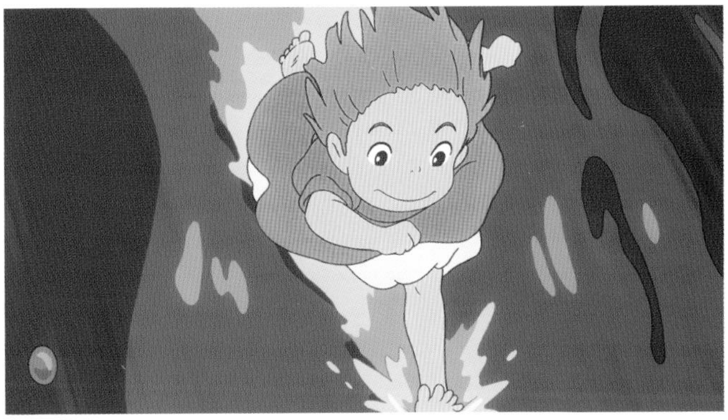
20

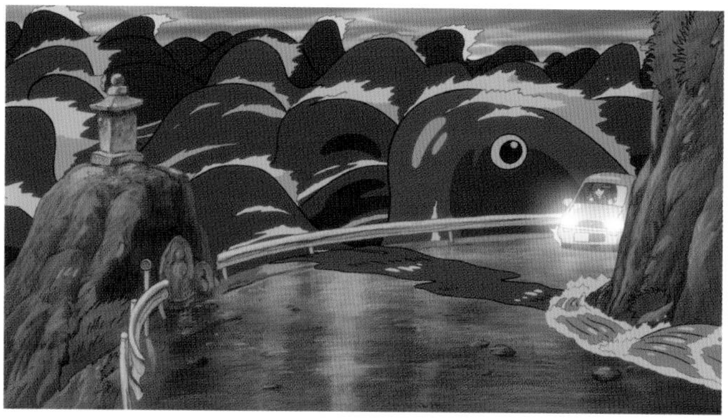

21

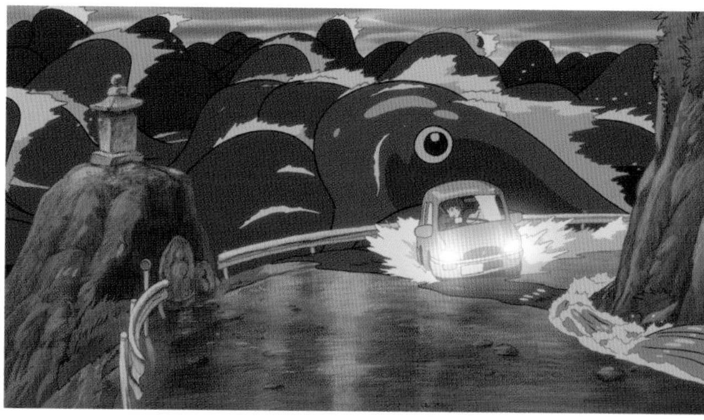

22

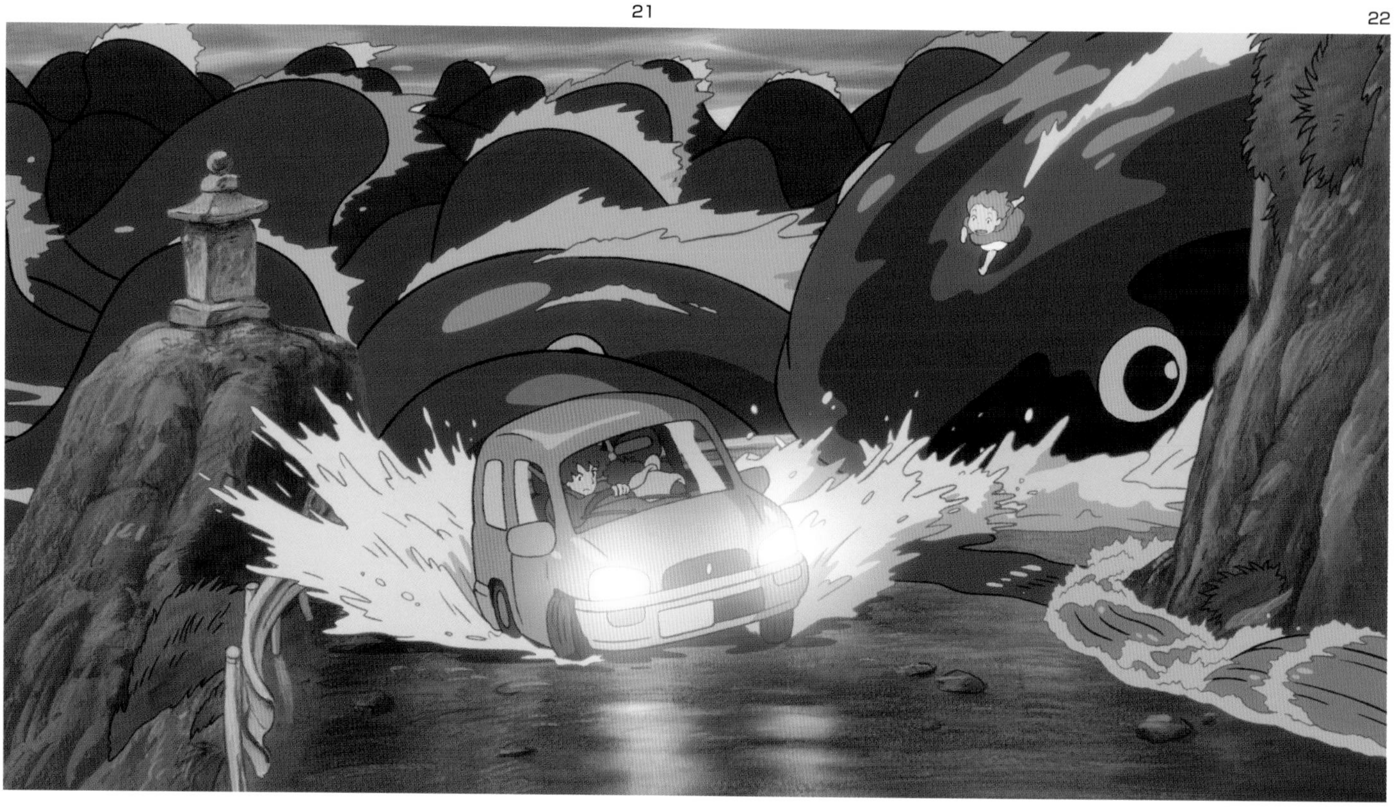

23

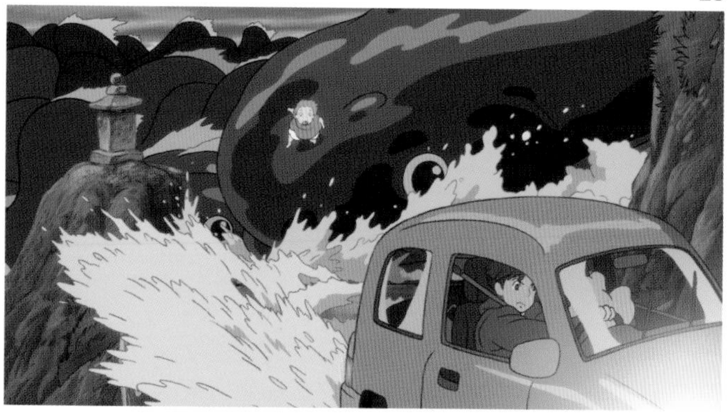

24

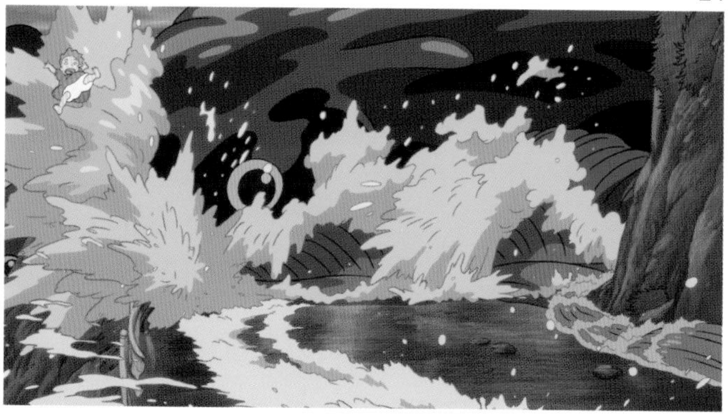

25

1–20 /Ponyo, atop the minions, chasing after Lisa's car. Overjoyed to find Sosuke, she bounds across the backs of the minions, but Lisa outmaneuvers the waves.
21–25 /Ponyo flying off the minion as it fails to navigate the turn and crashes against a rock.

The scene of Ponyo running on top of the water creatures to chase after Lisa's car was very time-consuming to render. Makiko Niki was responsible for this scene, which was rather long and required drawing many frames due to all the action. Ponyo is a carefree child who means no harm, and her cuteness really comes through in this scene as she jumps around.

—Supervising Animator: Katsuya Kondo

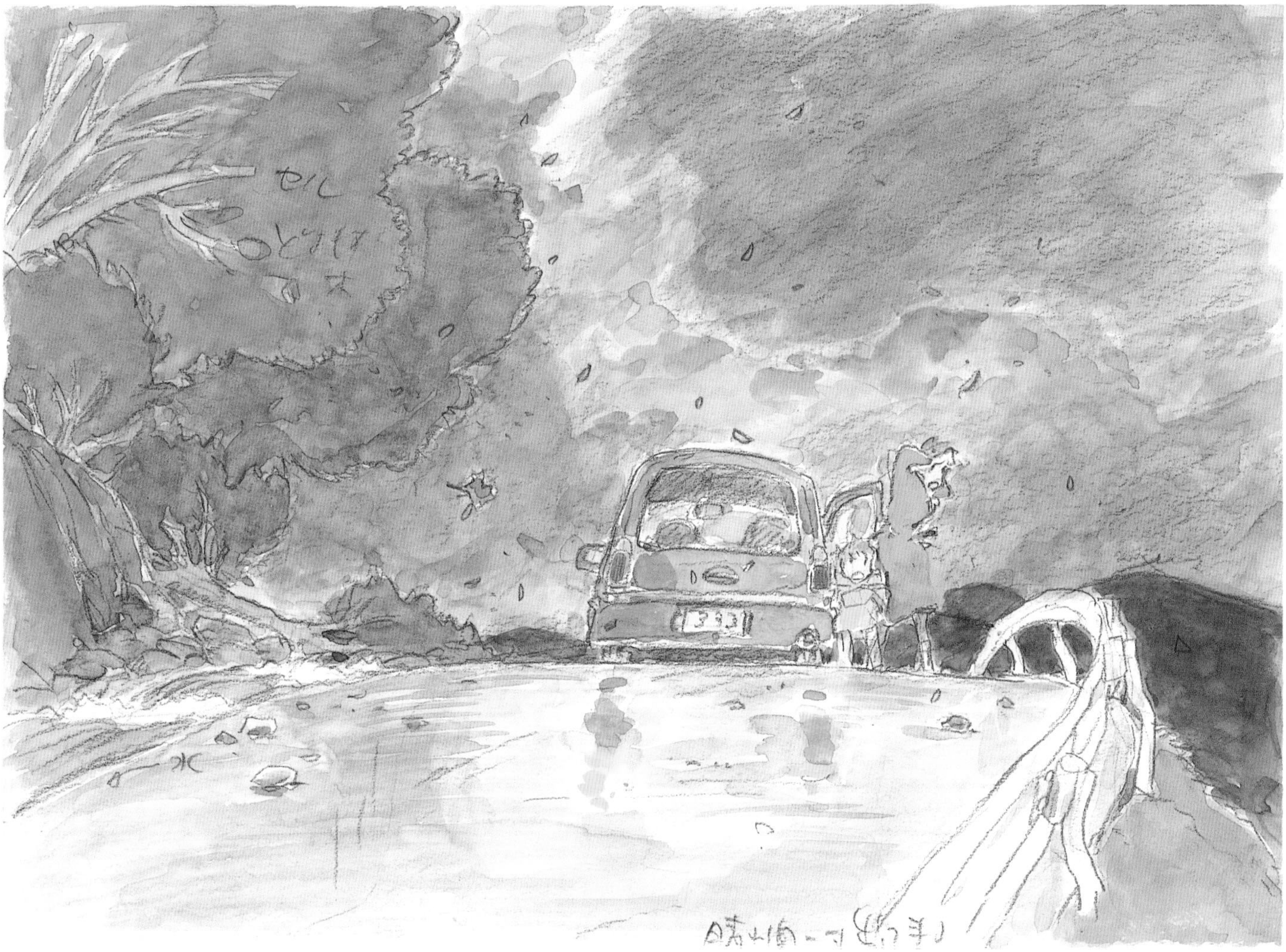

1

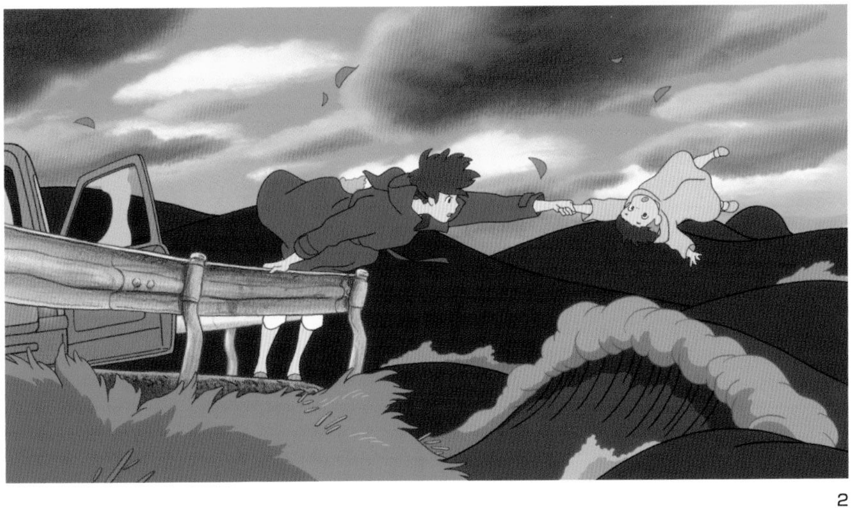

2

1 /"Mom, the little girl just fell in!" shouts Sosuke. Lisa stops the car to look around but... [Concept sketch].
2 /Lisa grabbing hold of Sosuke to keep him from being swept away by a gust of wind.

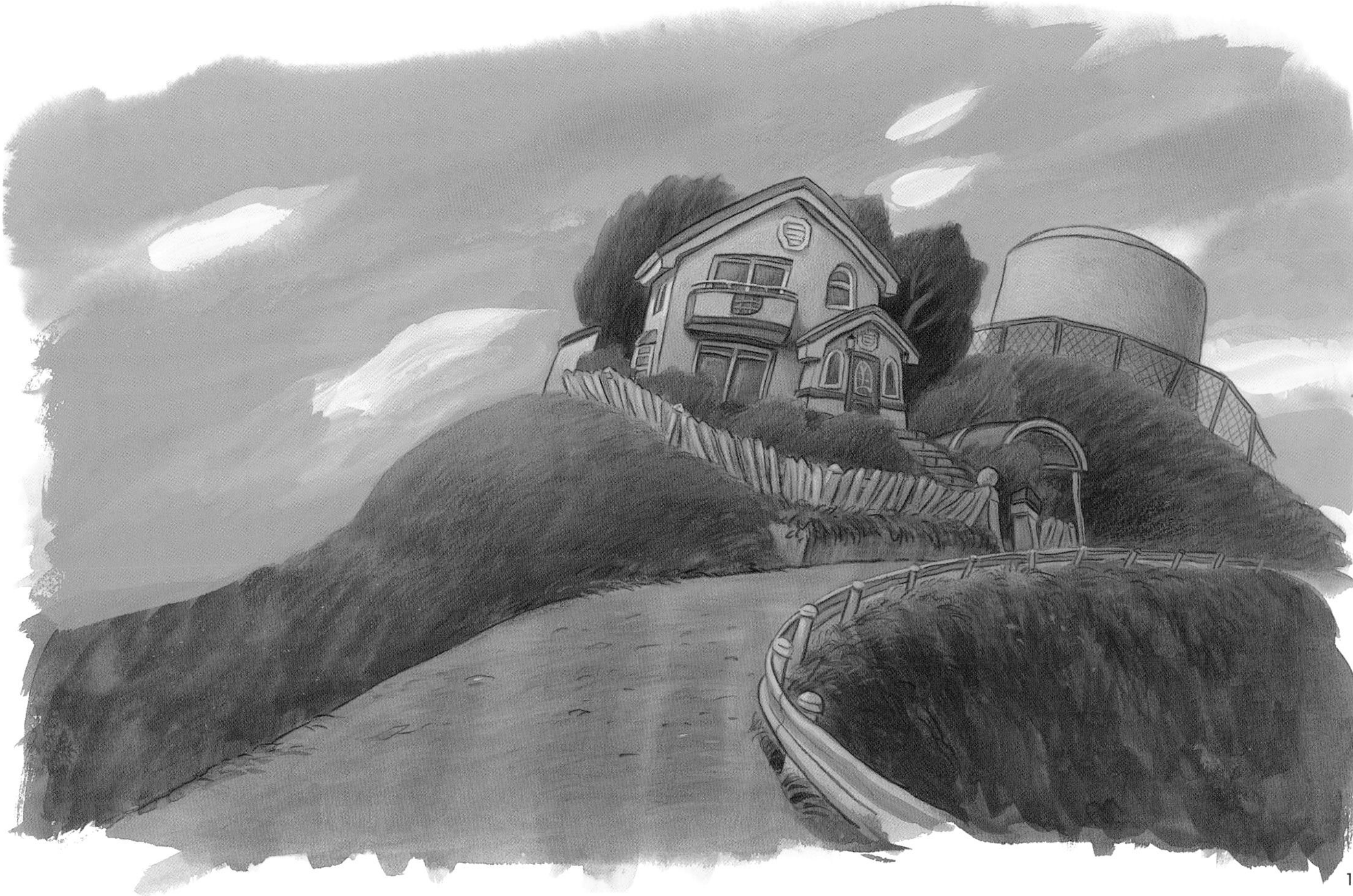

1

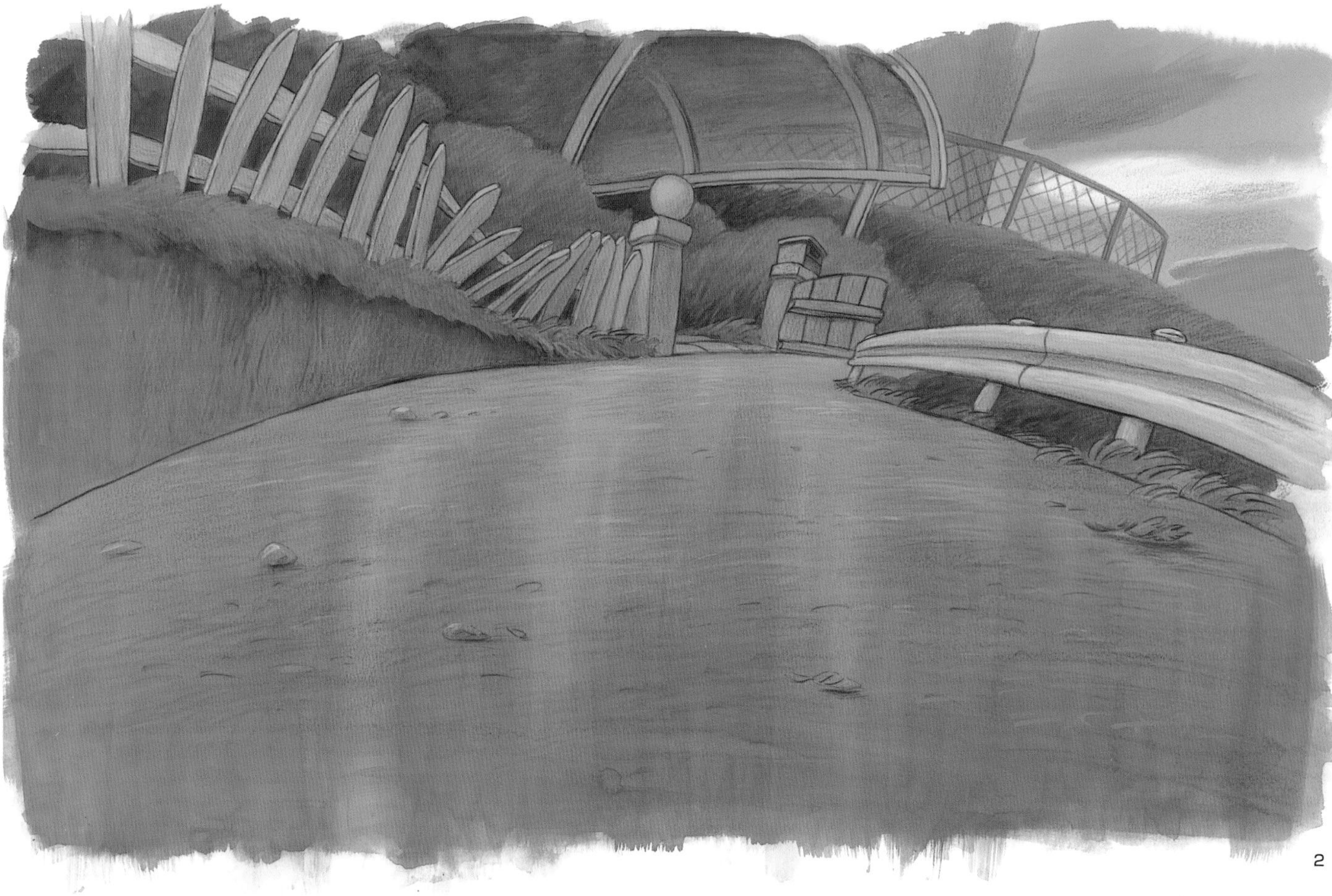

2

3

1 /The house, to which Lisa's car is headed, is distorted and crumpled by the storm [Background].

2 /The road in front of the house. In the completed shot, the pail that Sosuke left out as a marker for Ponyo is blown away by the wind [Background].

3 /Sosuke's house, rendered to look as if it is leaning from the force of the violent wind [Concept sketch].

Shinji Otsuka oversaw the scene of Sosuke's house buckling from the force of the typhoon. Since Miyazaki had drawn the house to look distorted in the storyboarding stage, Otsuka created the layouts to show the house as if it might fall over in the direction of the wind. Miyazaki seemed to worry, saying, "Maybe it should look more normal." But once the scene was completed according to the layouts, it wasn't strange at all. By combining the images of rattling windows and clouds being swept along by the wind, the scene just worked as part of the world of *Ponyo*. Artistically, I think we were able to achieve an interesting effect with this scene.

For this storm scene, we drew the grass and trees being blown in the direction of the wind and created the rest of the movement with animation. It was a scene made possible by the method of combining background art and cel art to create a single image and by the process of rendering the waves we'd initially developed via trial and error.

—Art Director: Noboru Yoshida

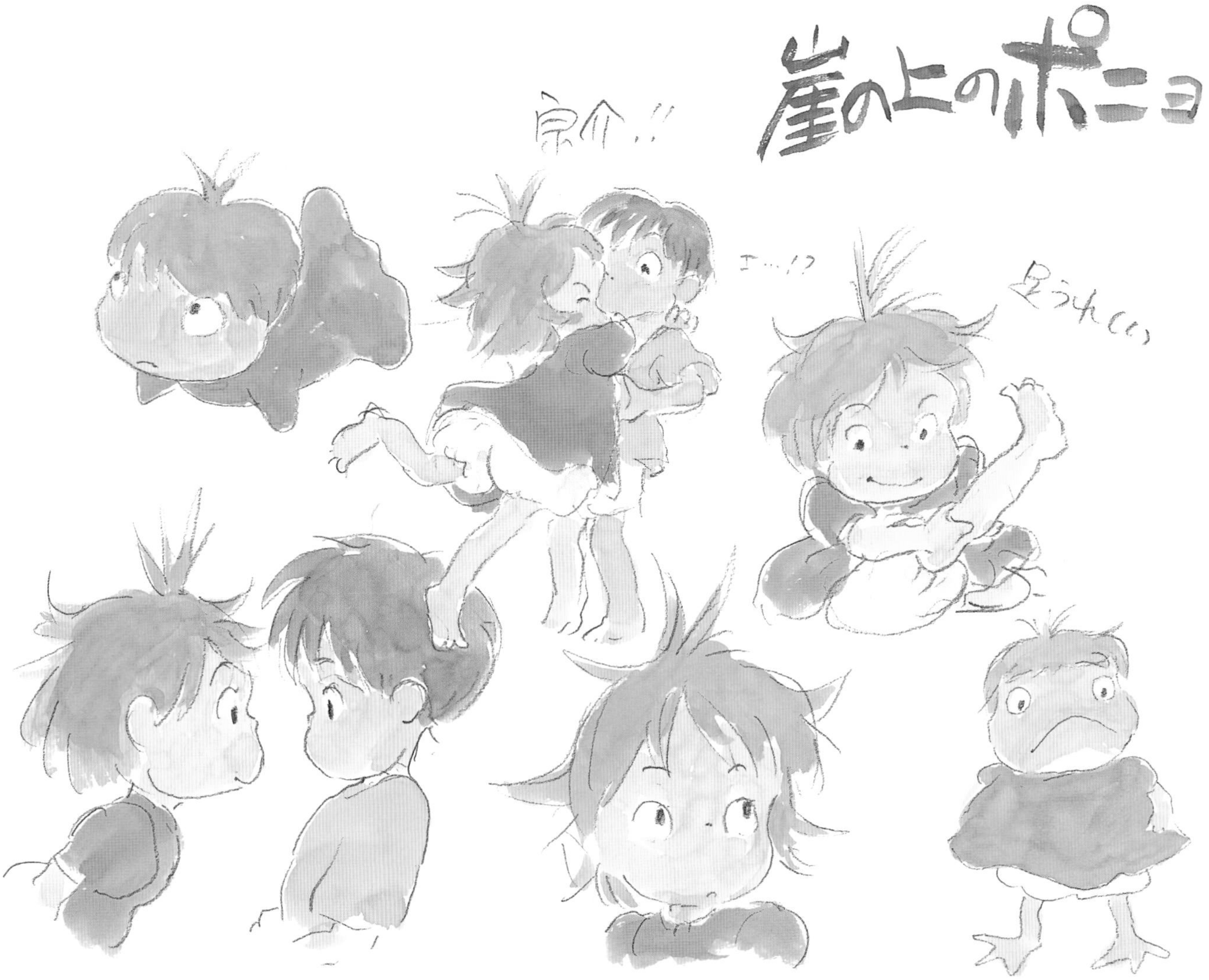
崖の上のポニョ
宗介!!
エ…!?

1

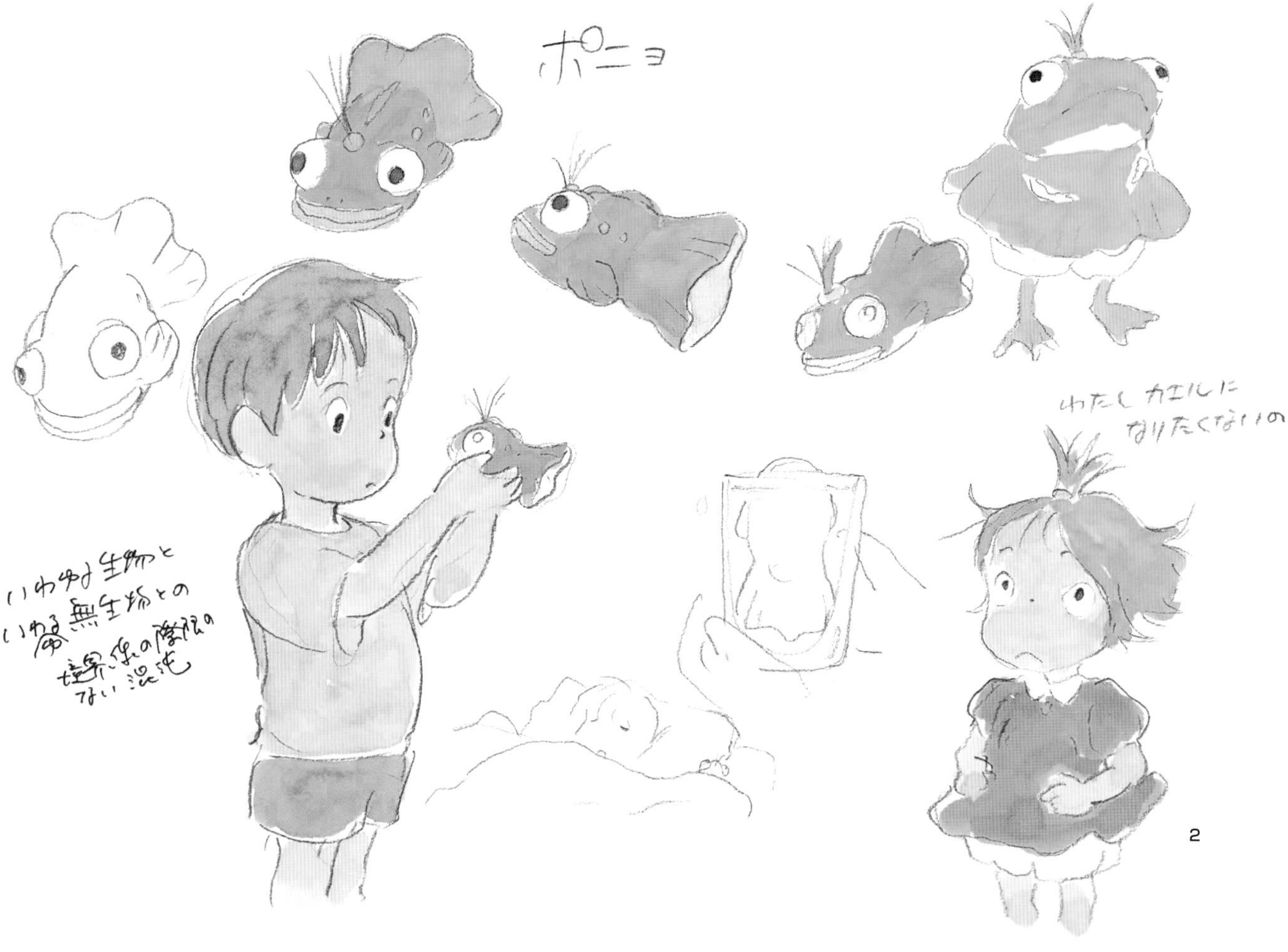
ポニョ
わたしカエルに
なりたくないの
いわゆる生物と
いわゆる無生物との

2

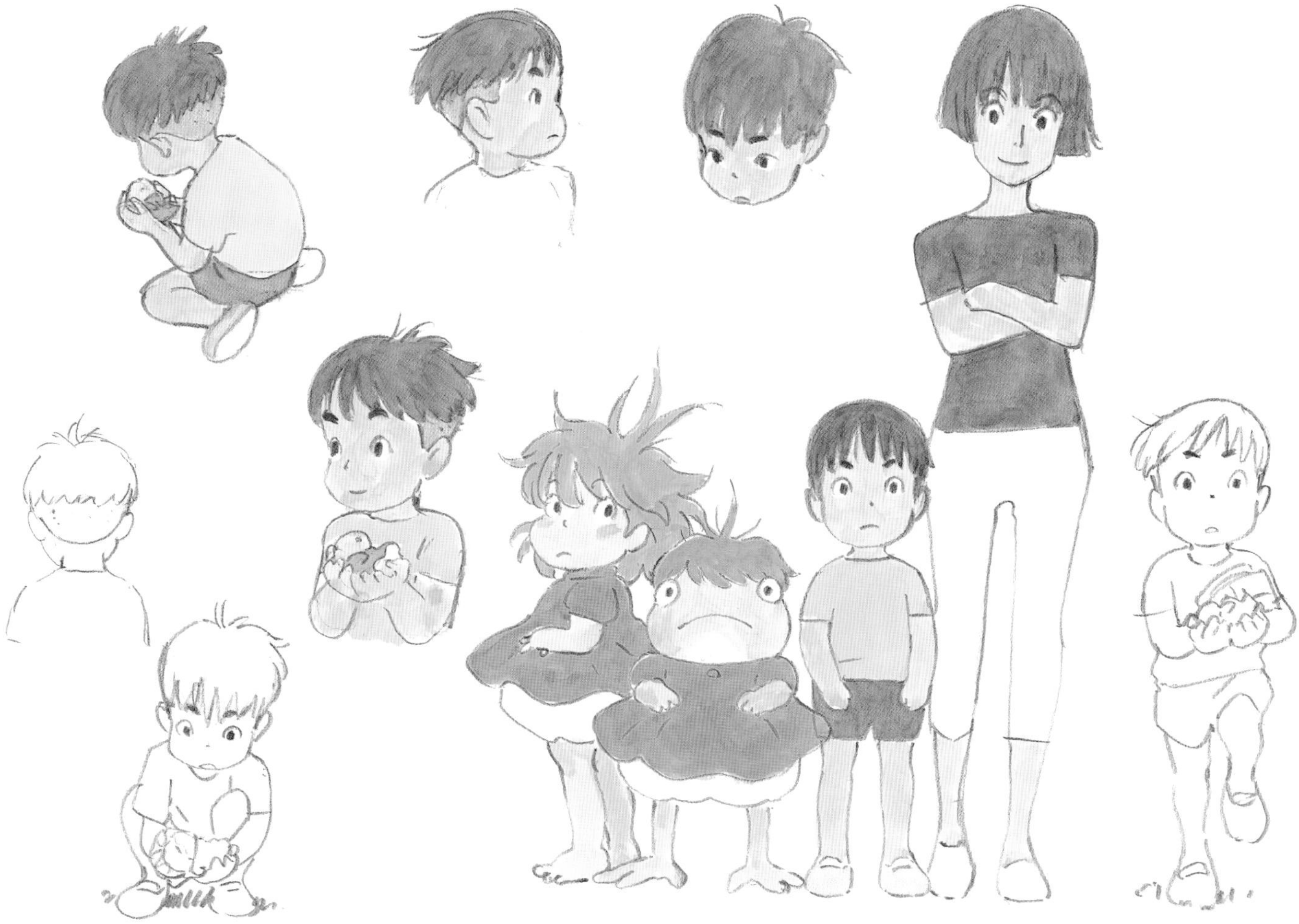

3

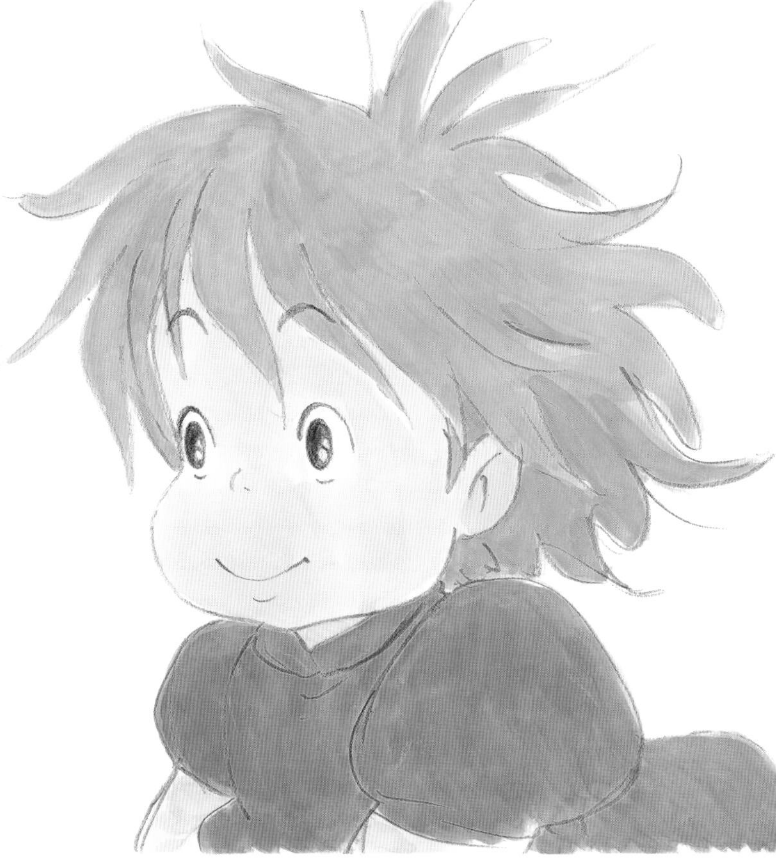

4

The Girl Ponyo

1, 2 /Ponyo as a fish, as half-fish, half-human, and as a girl, drawn by Hayao Miyazaki [Concept sketches].
3, 4 /The girl Ponyo and Sosuke, sketched by Katsuya Kondo [Rough character sketches].
5–8 /A collection of the girl Ponyo's expressions and poses by Katsuya Kondo [Rough character sketches].

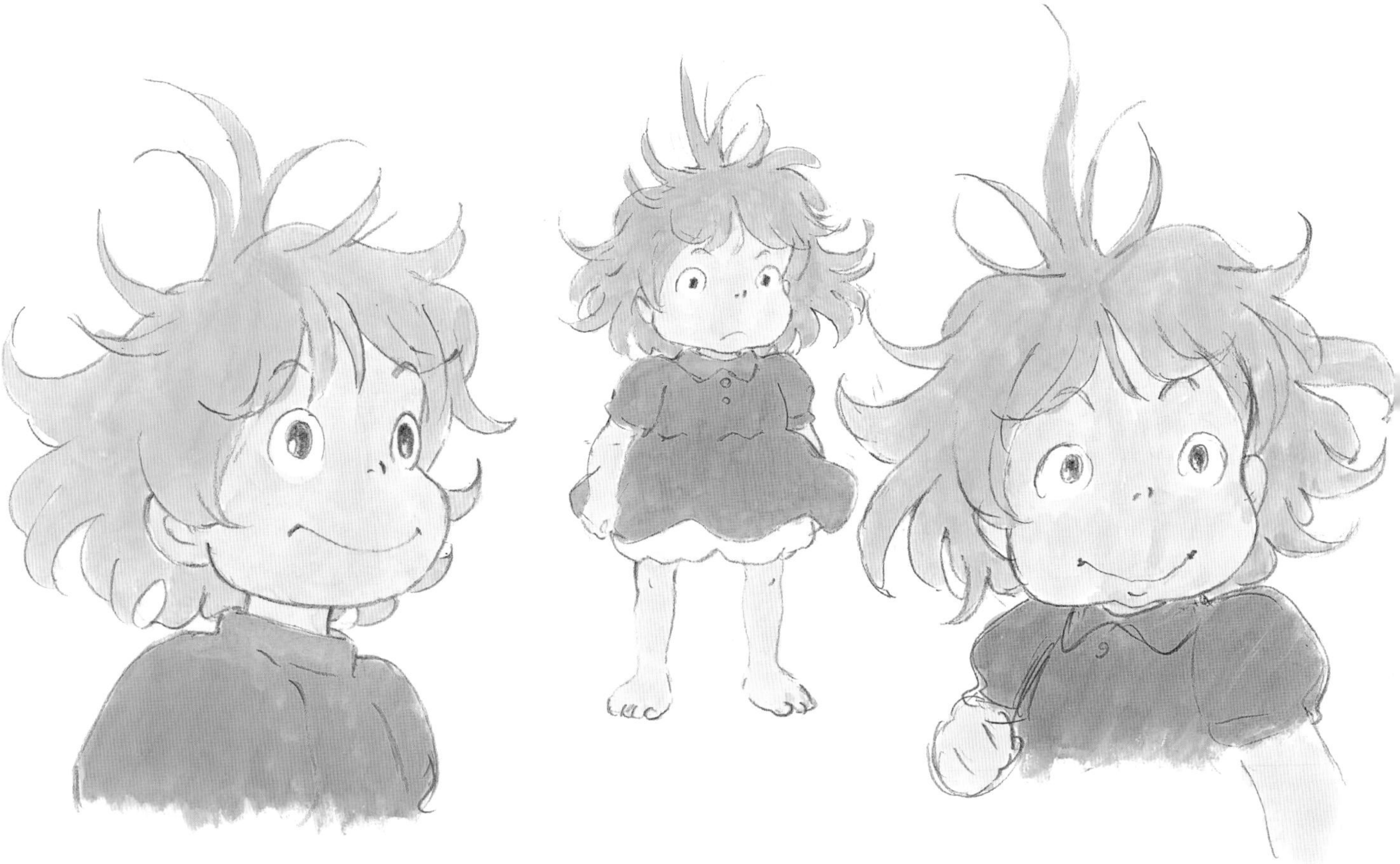

5

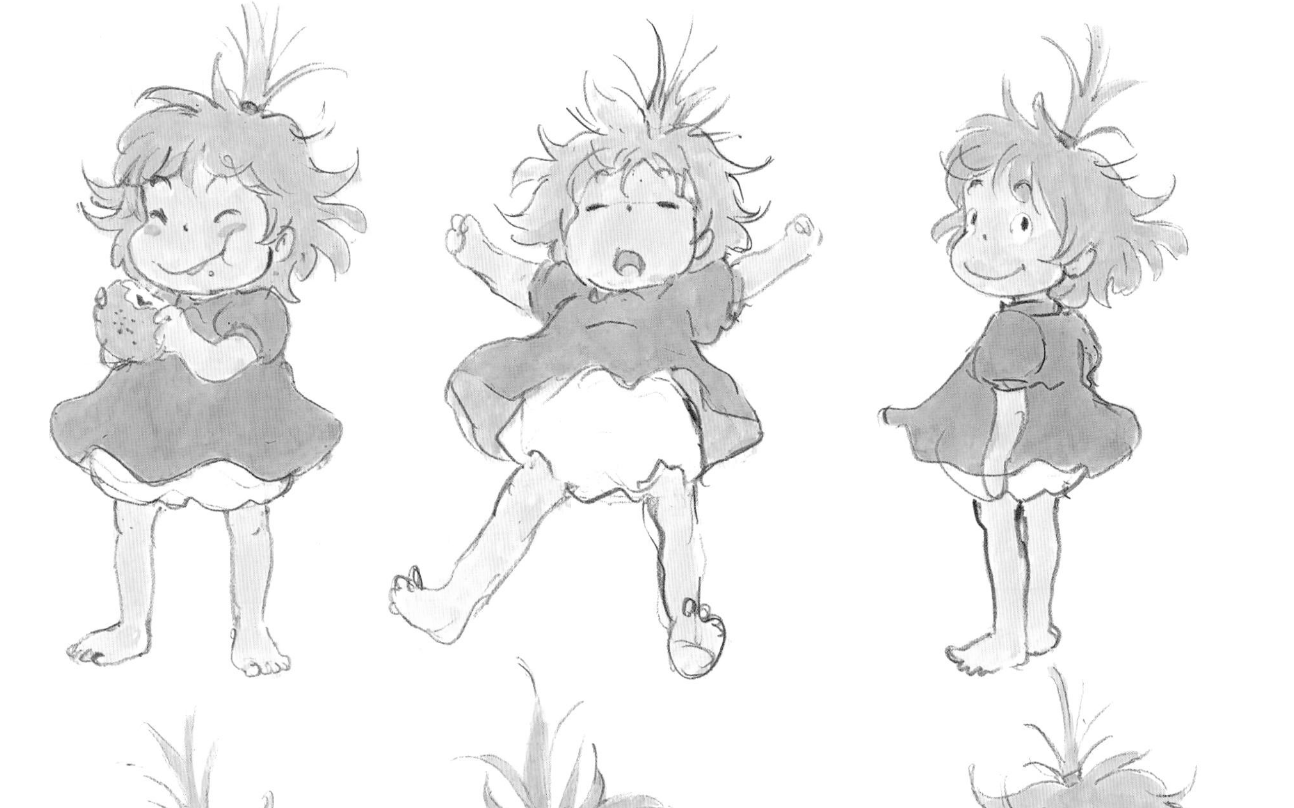

6

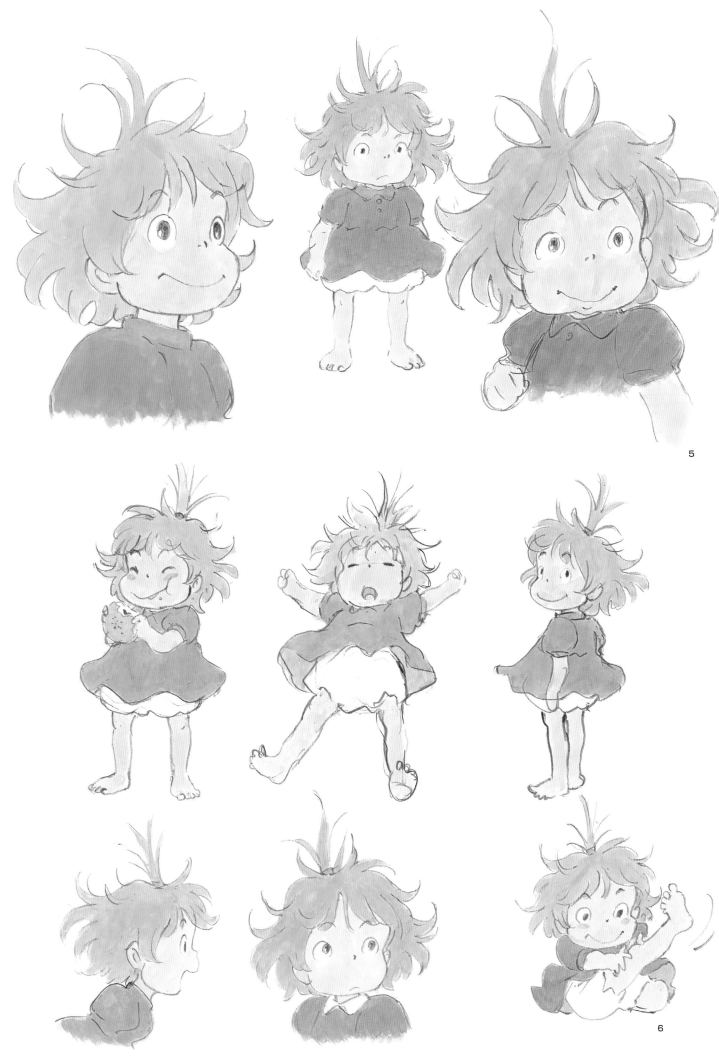

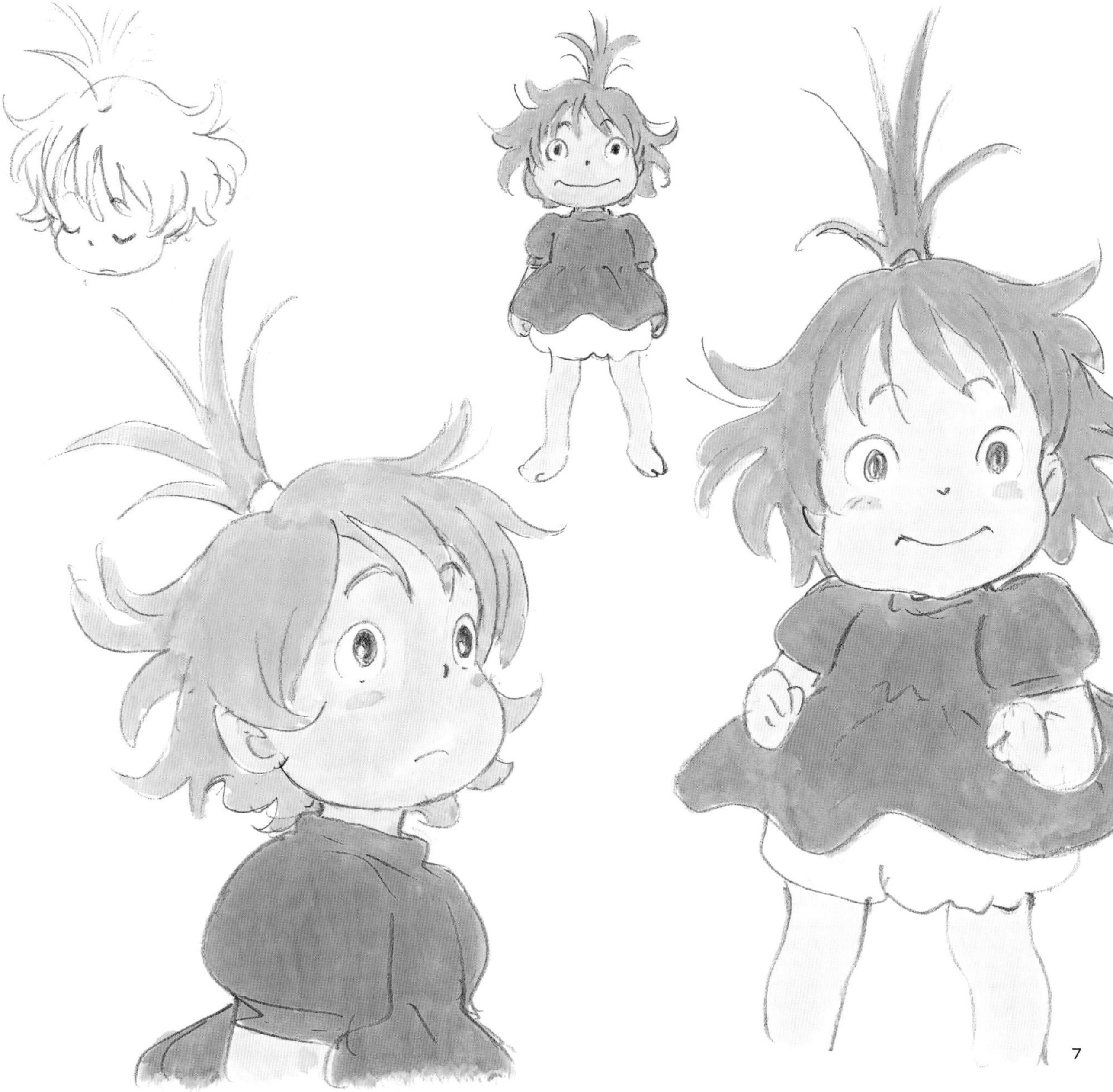

7

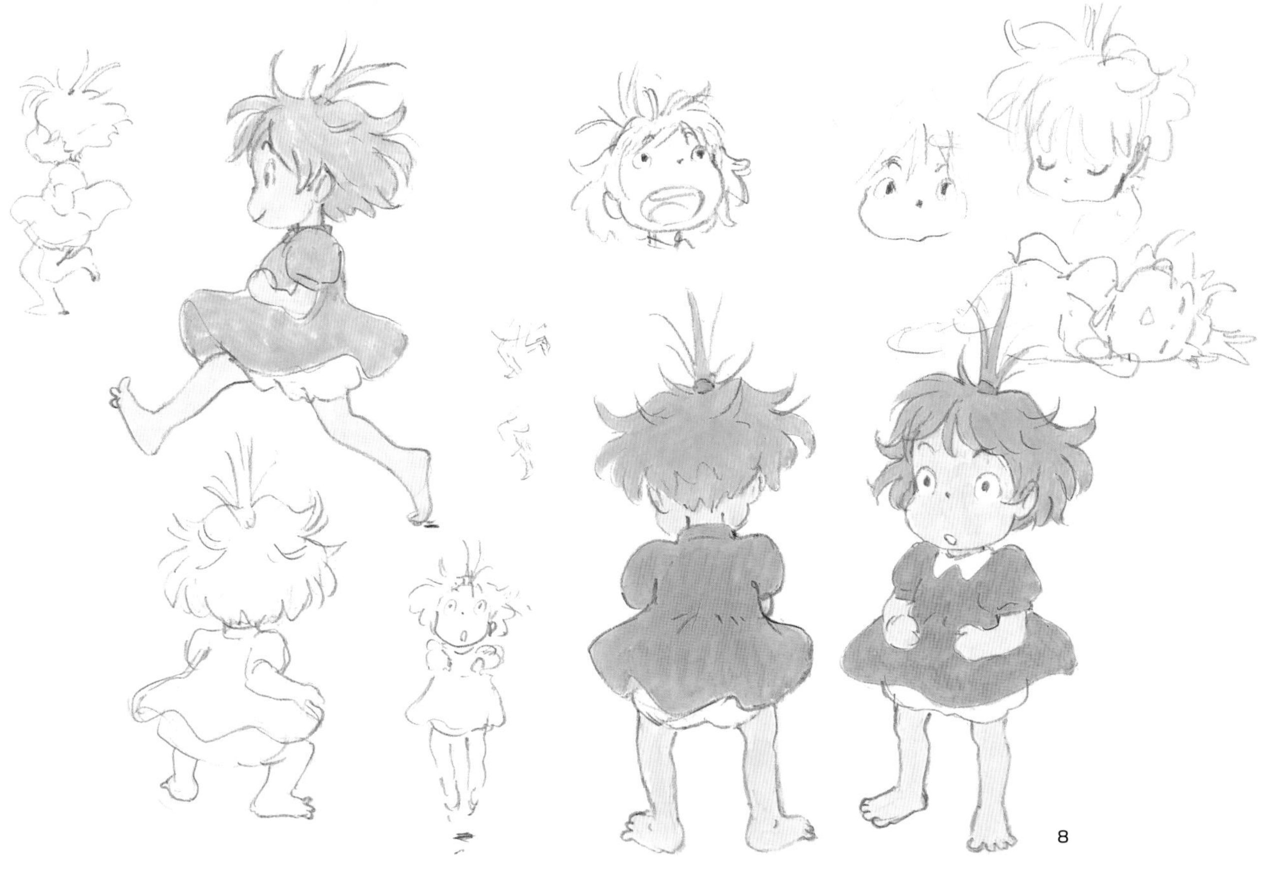

8

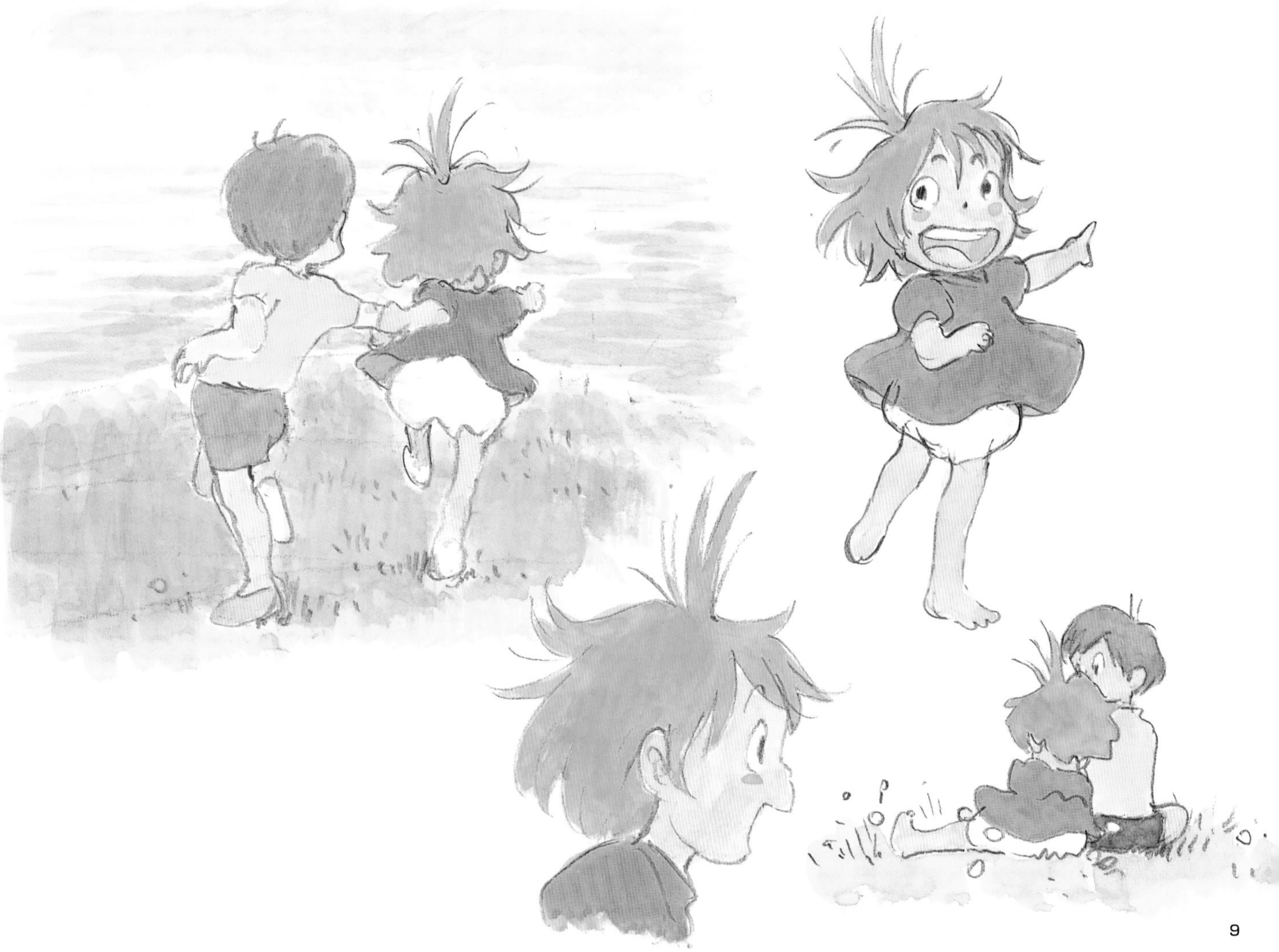

9

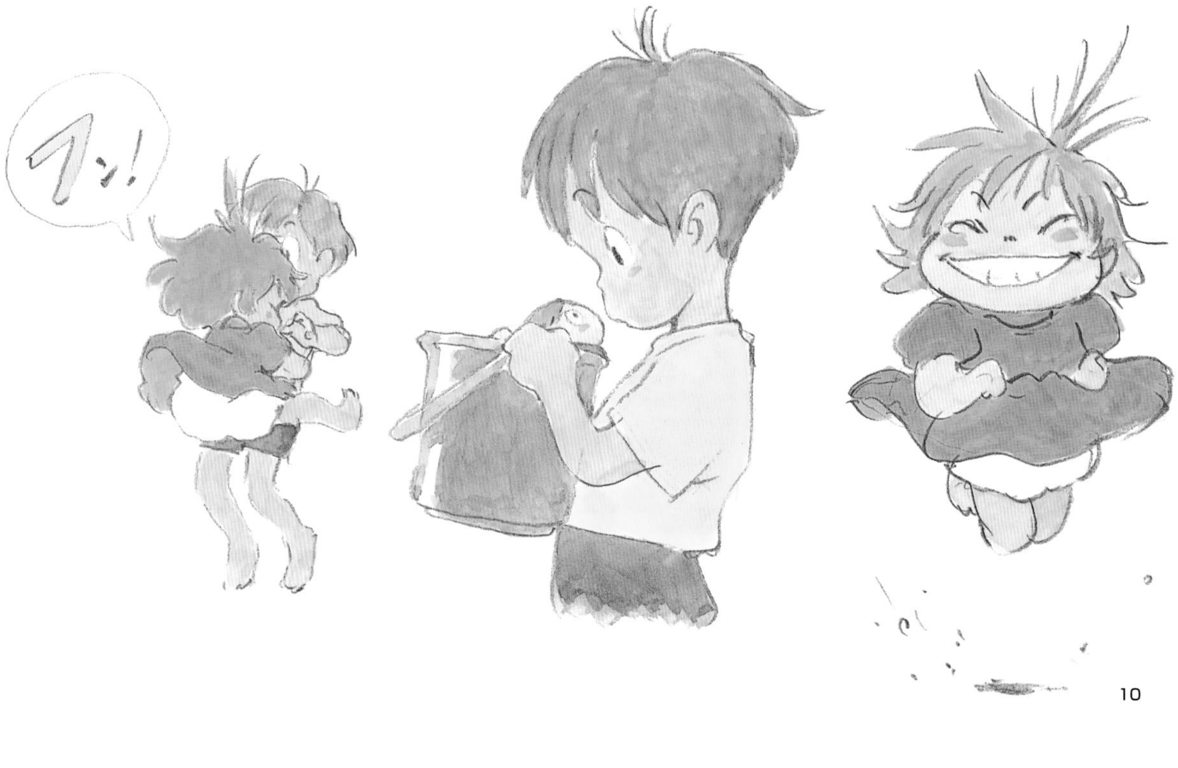
フン!

10

9–13 /The girl Ponyo with Sosuke, drawn by Katsuya Kondo [Rough character sketches].

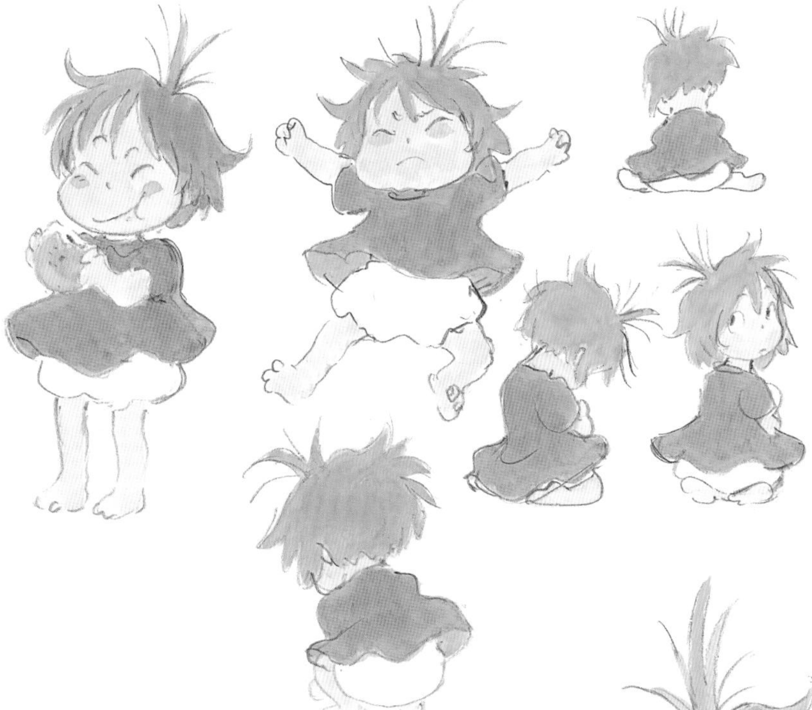

11

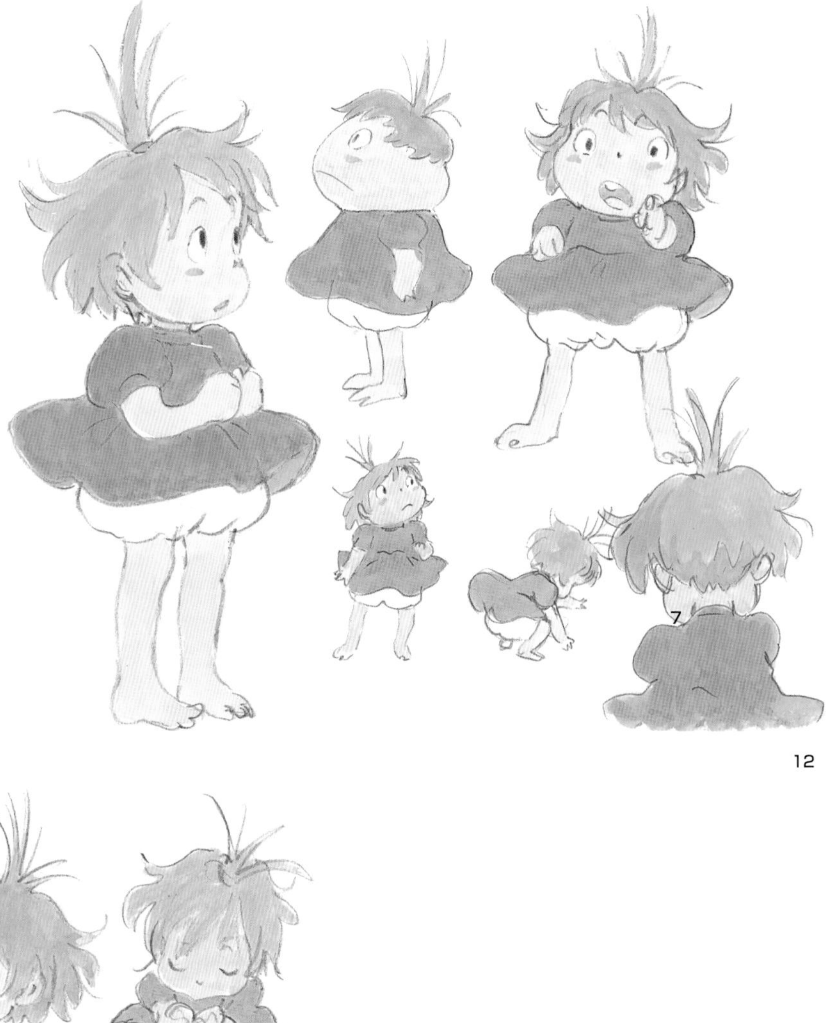
7

12

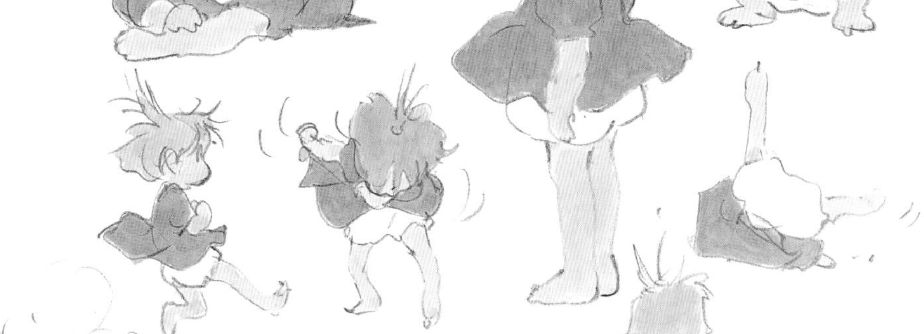

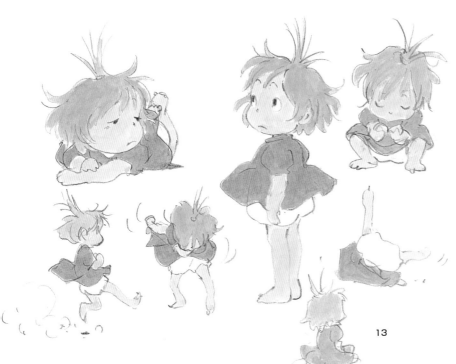

13

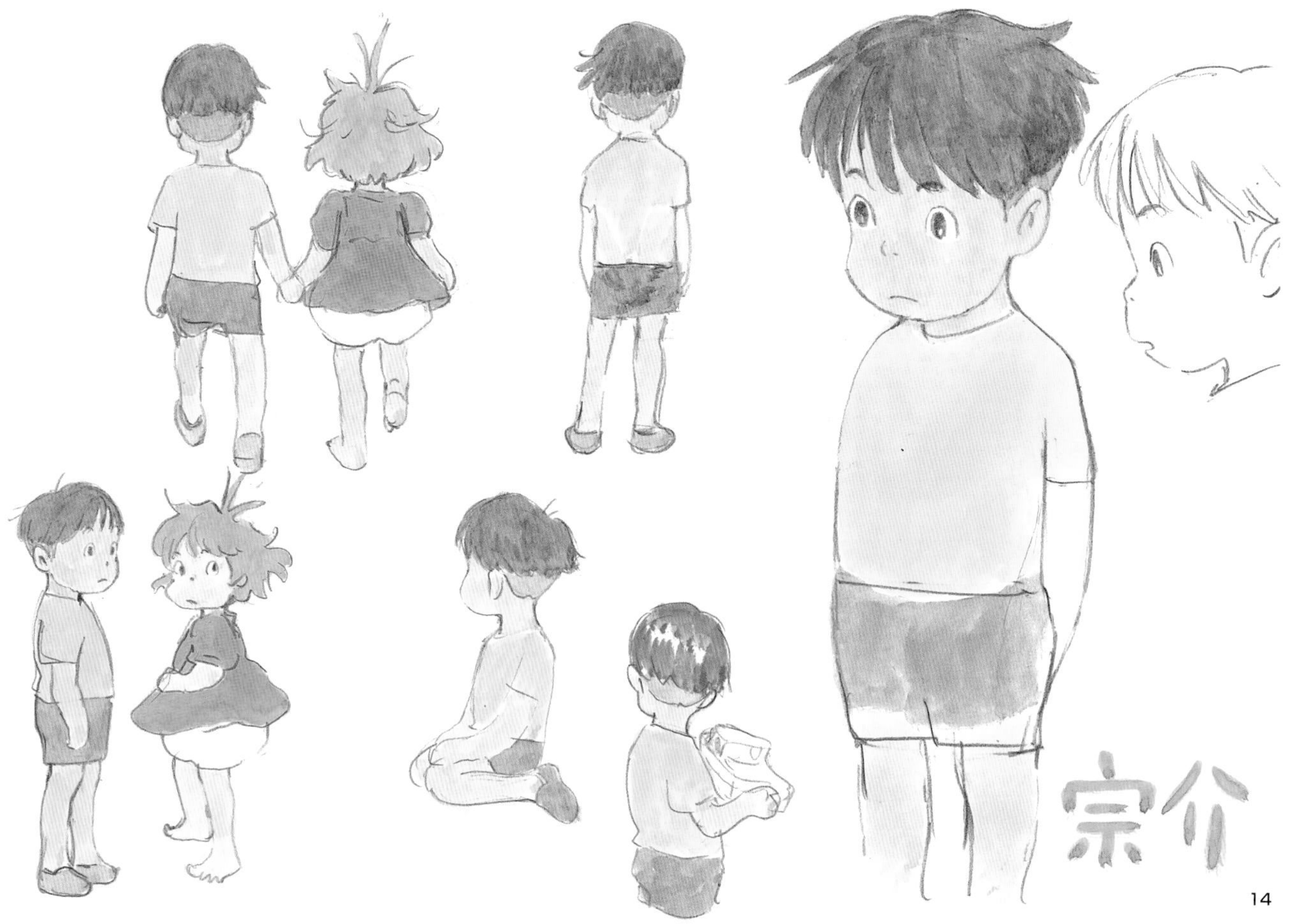
宗介

14

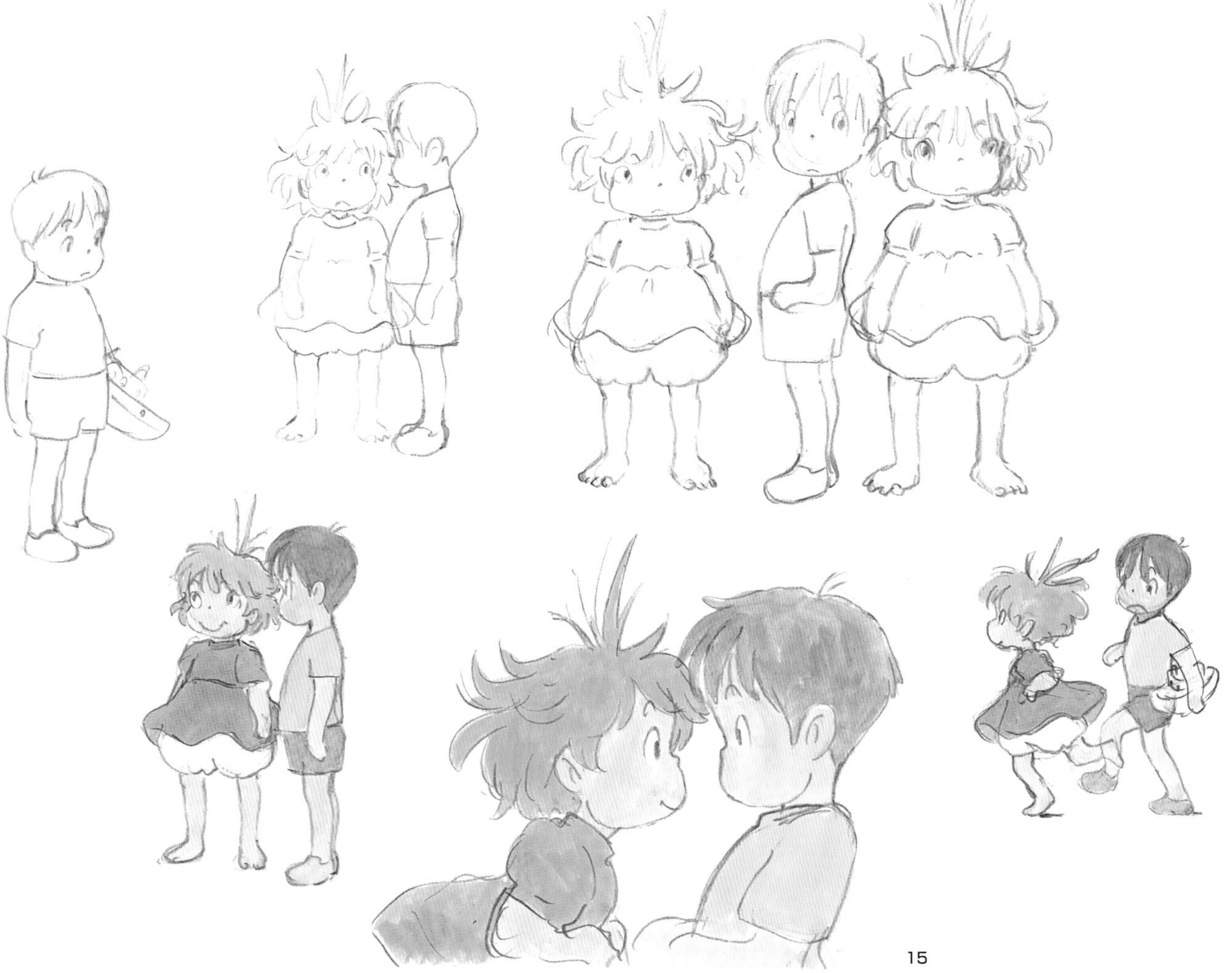

15

14–19 /Sosuke and Ponyo, sketched by Katsuya Kondo [Rough character sketches].
20 /The image of Ponyo's transformation [Rough character sketch].

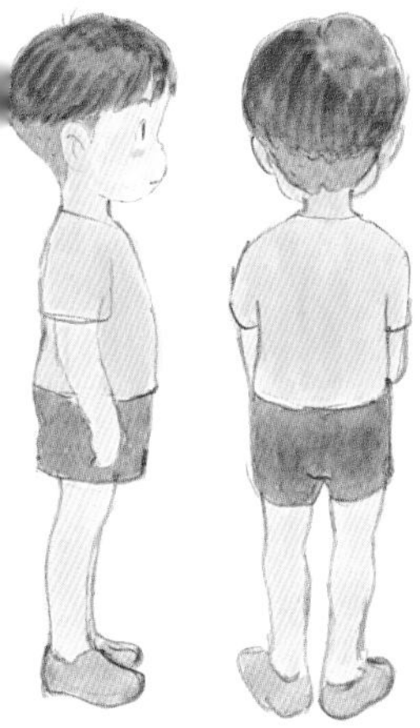

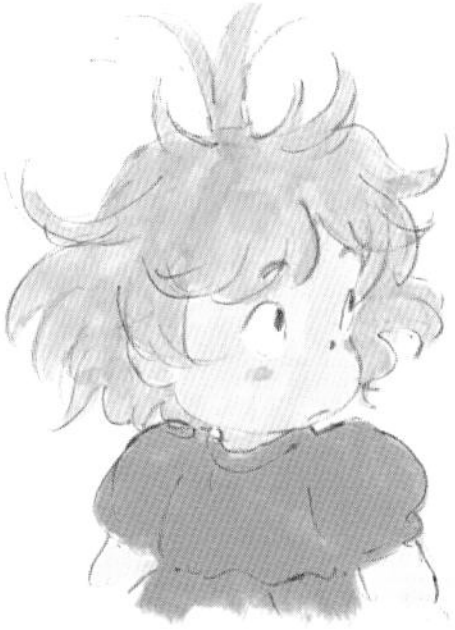

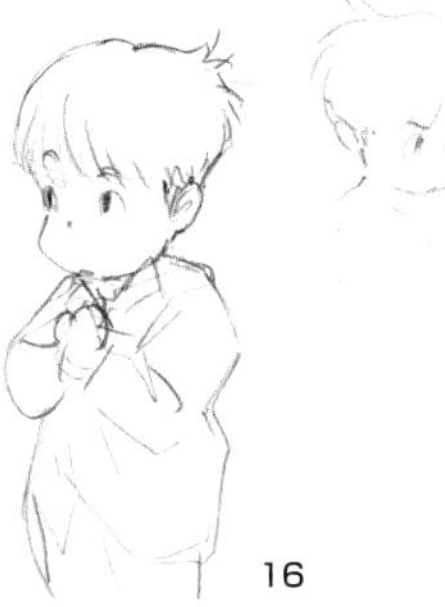

16

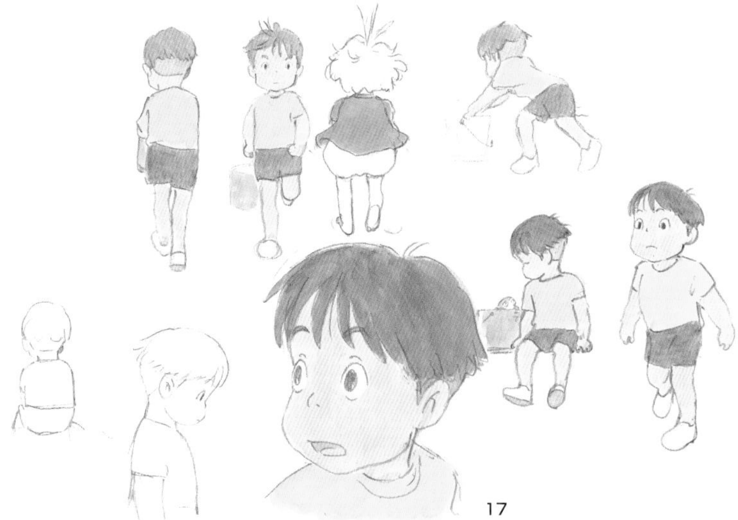

17

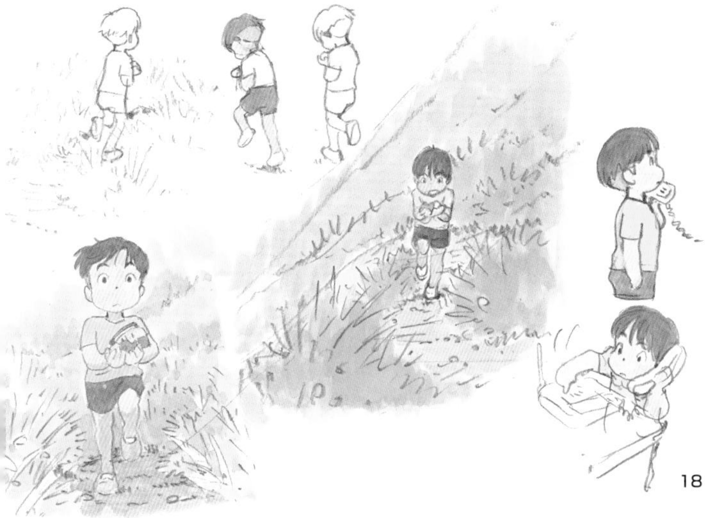

18

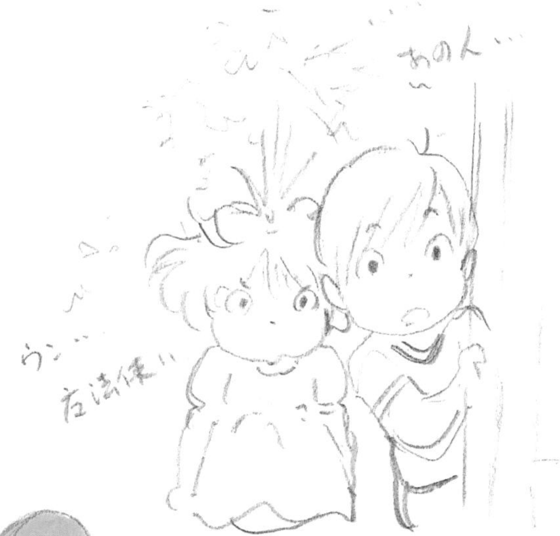

19

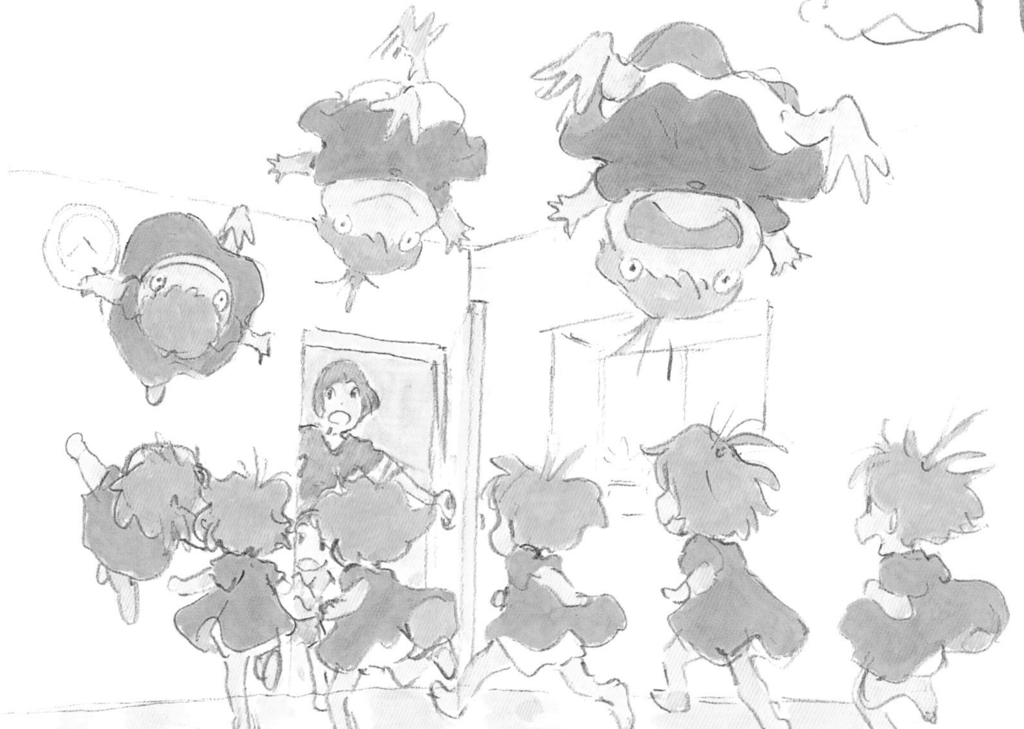

20

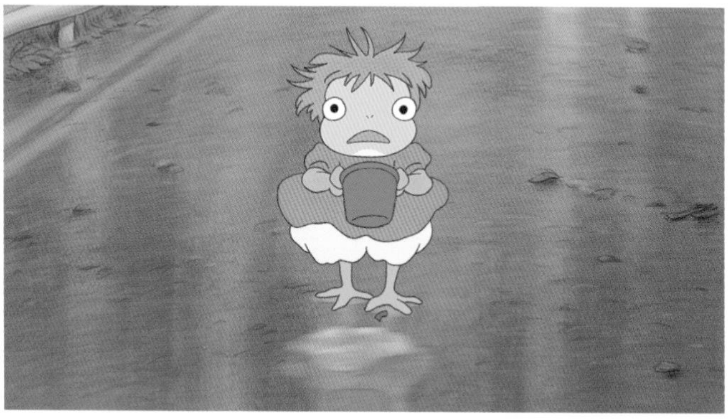
1

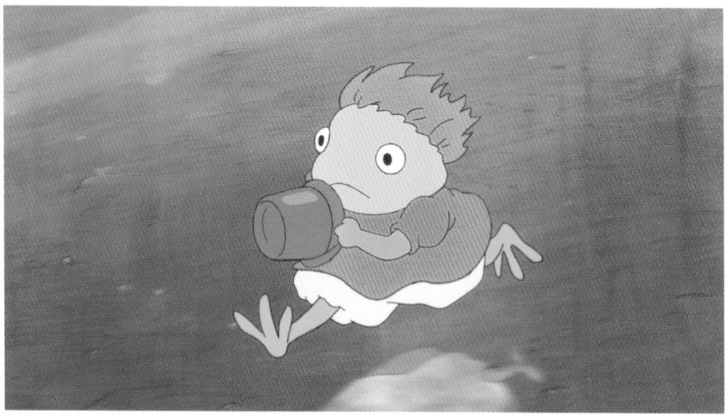
2

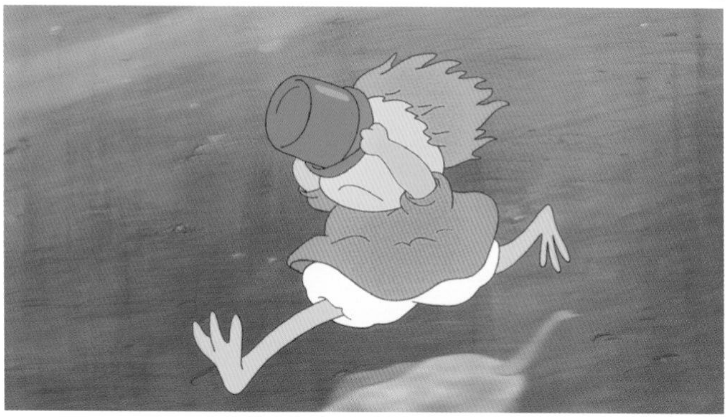
3

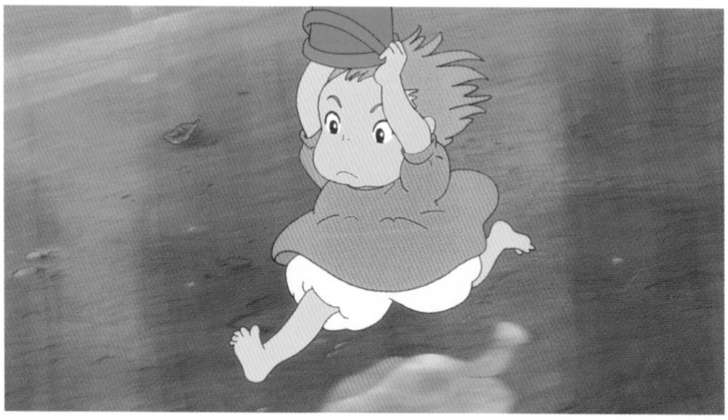
4

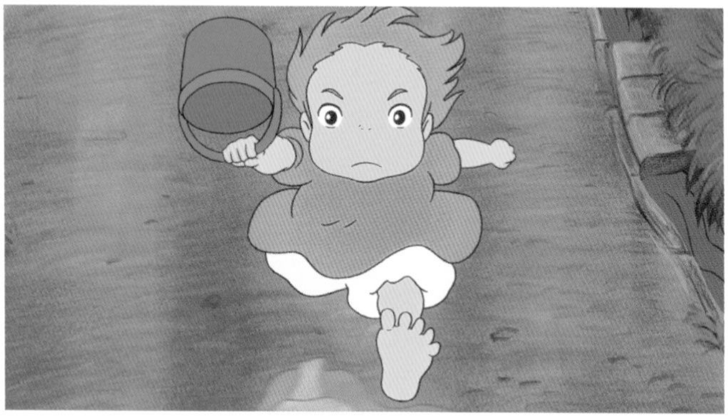
5

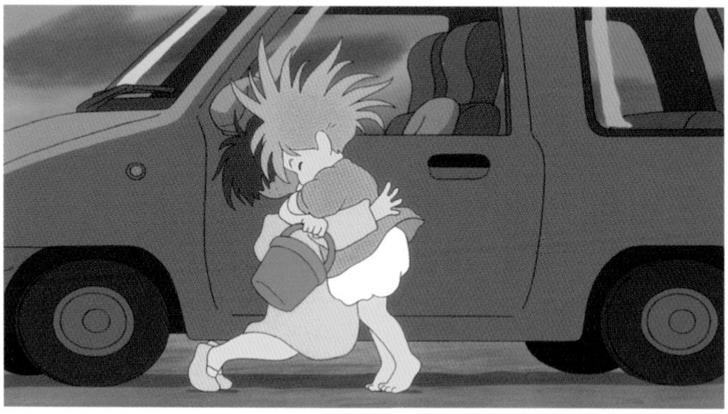
6

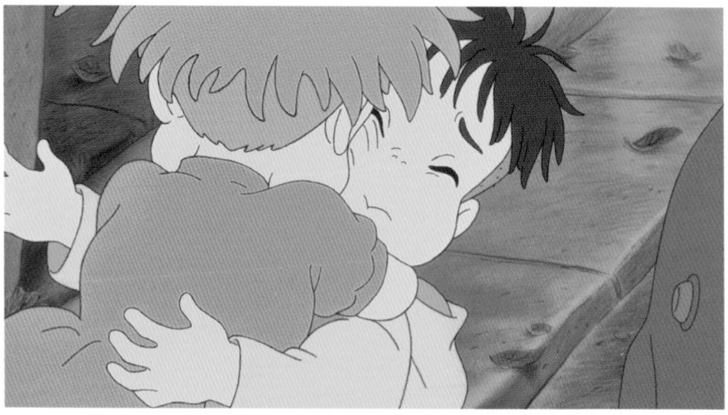
7

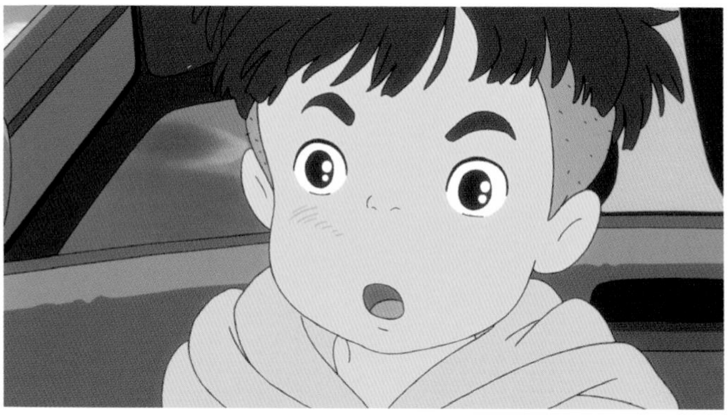
8

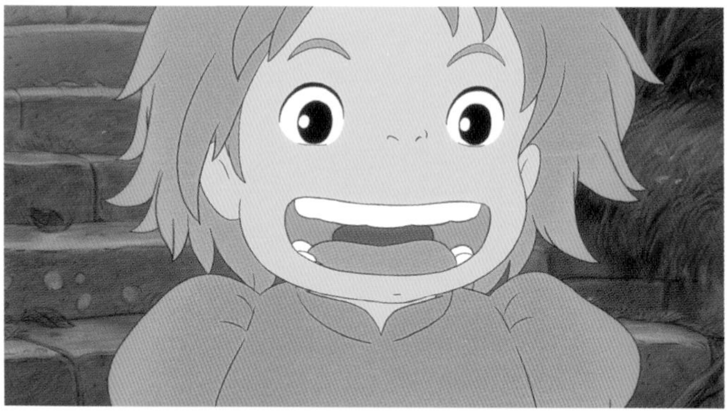
9

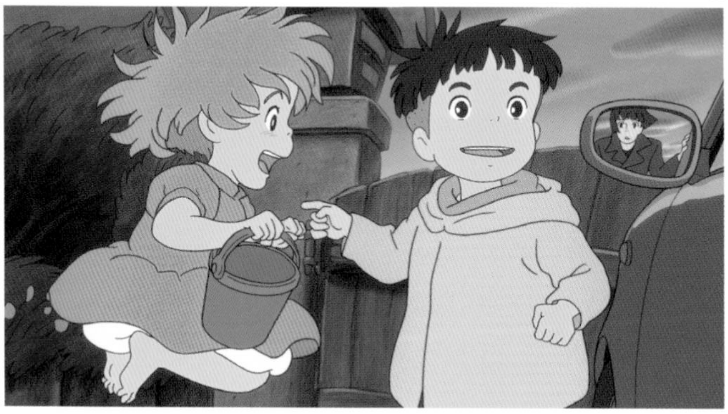
10

Ponyo Returns

1–5 /Ponyo picking up the memorable pail after emerging from the waves. She finds Sosuke and dashes headlong toward him!
6–10 /Ponyo joyfully throwing herself into Sosuke's arms. Sosuke recognizes her. "It *is* you!"
11–15 /Ponyo's little sisters leap into the air in peals of joy as if to celebrate their reunion.
16 /Ponyo proclaiming to her little sisters, "I found Sosuke!"

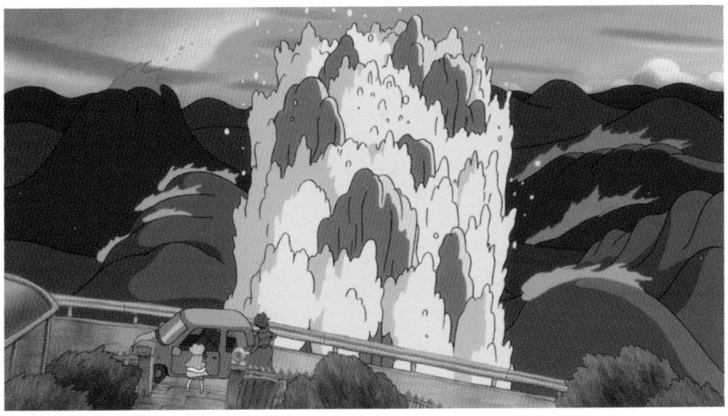

11

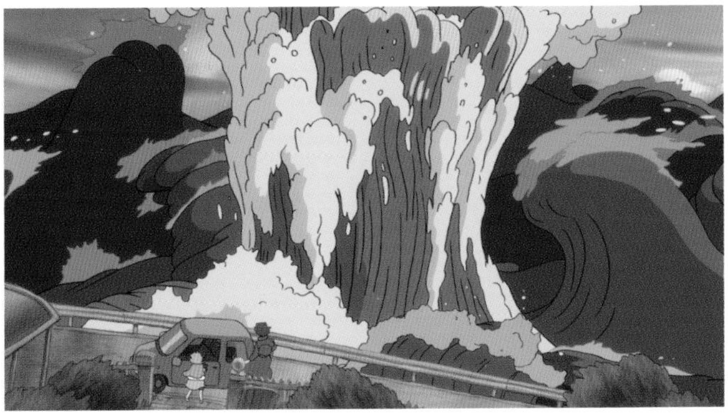

12

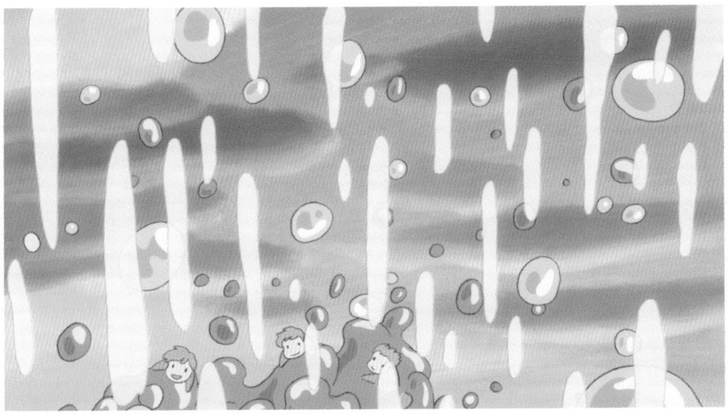

13

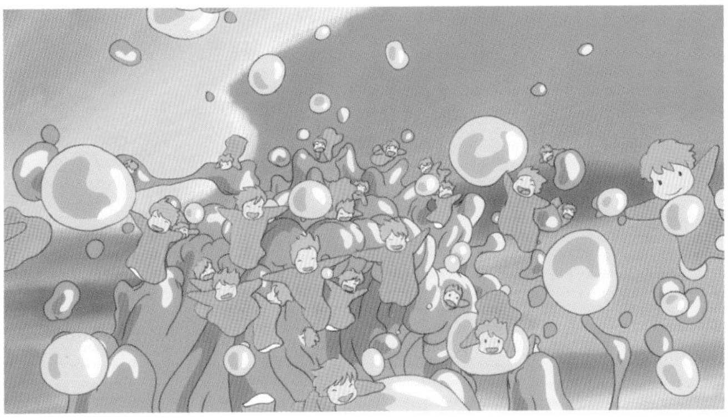

14

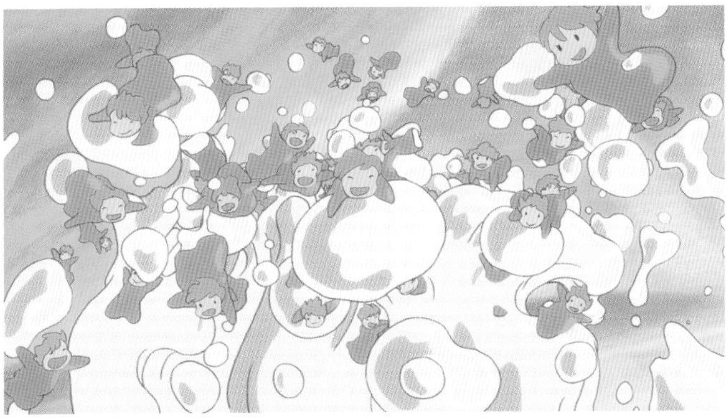

15

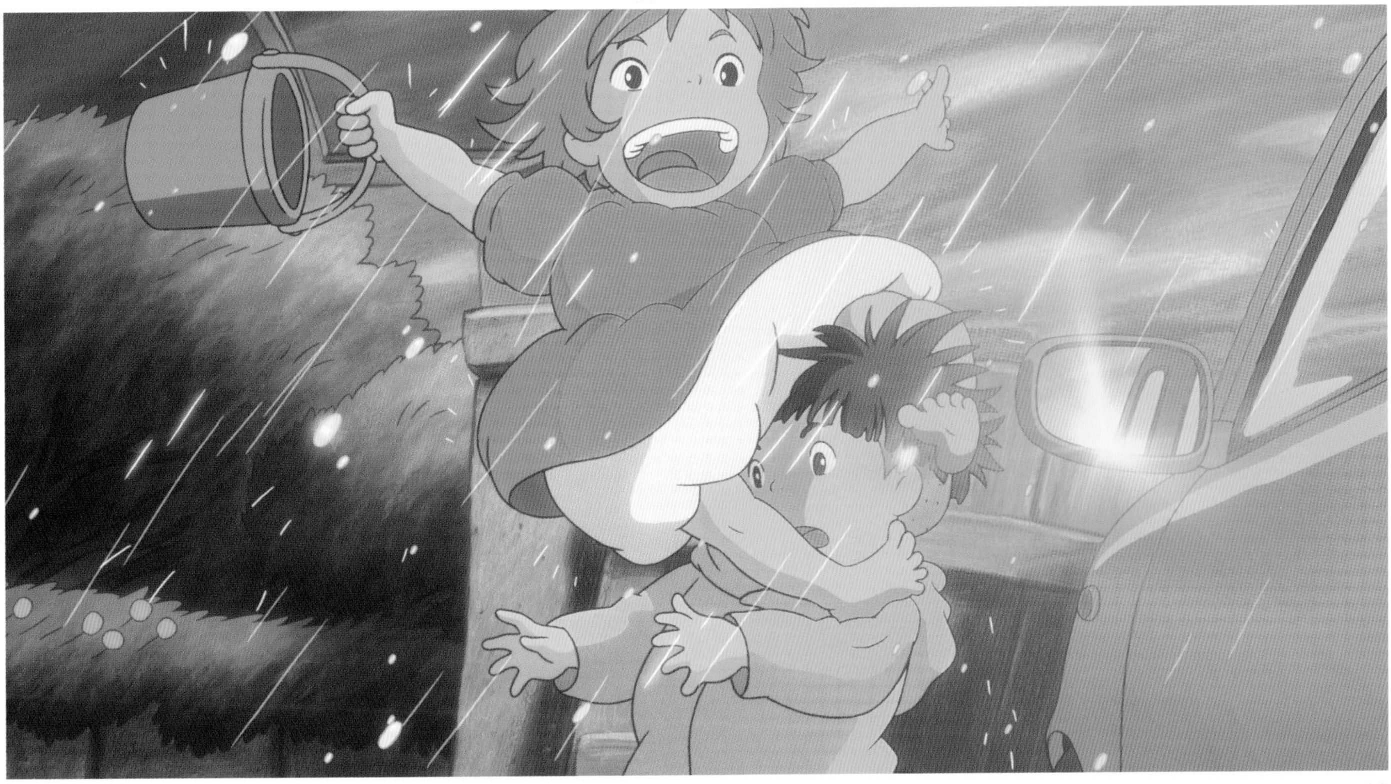

16

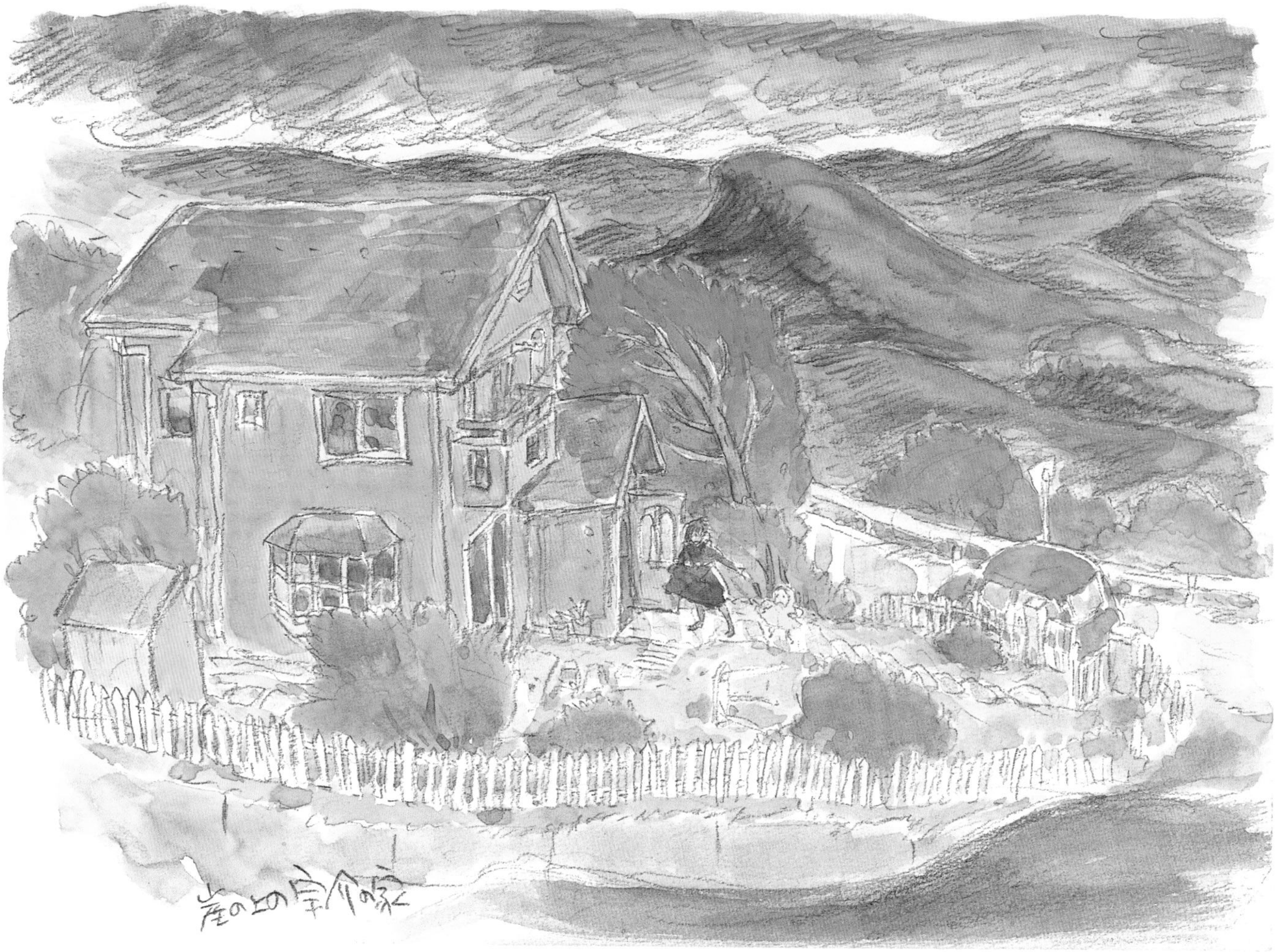
崖の上の宗介の家

1

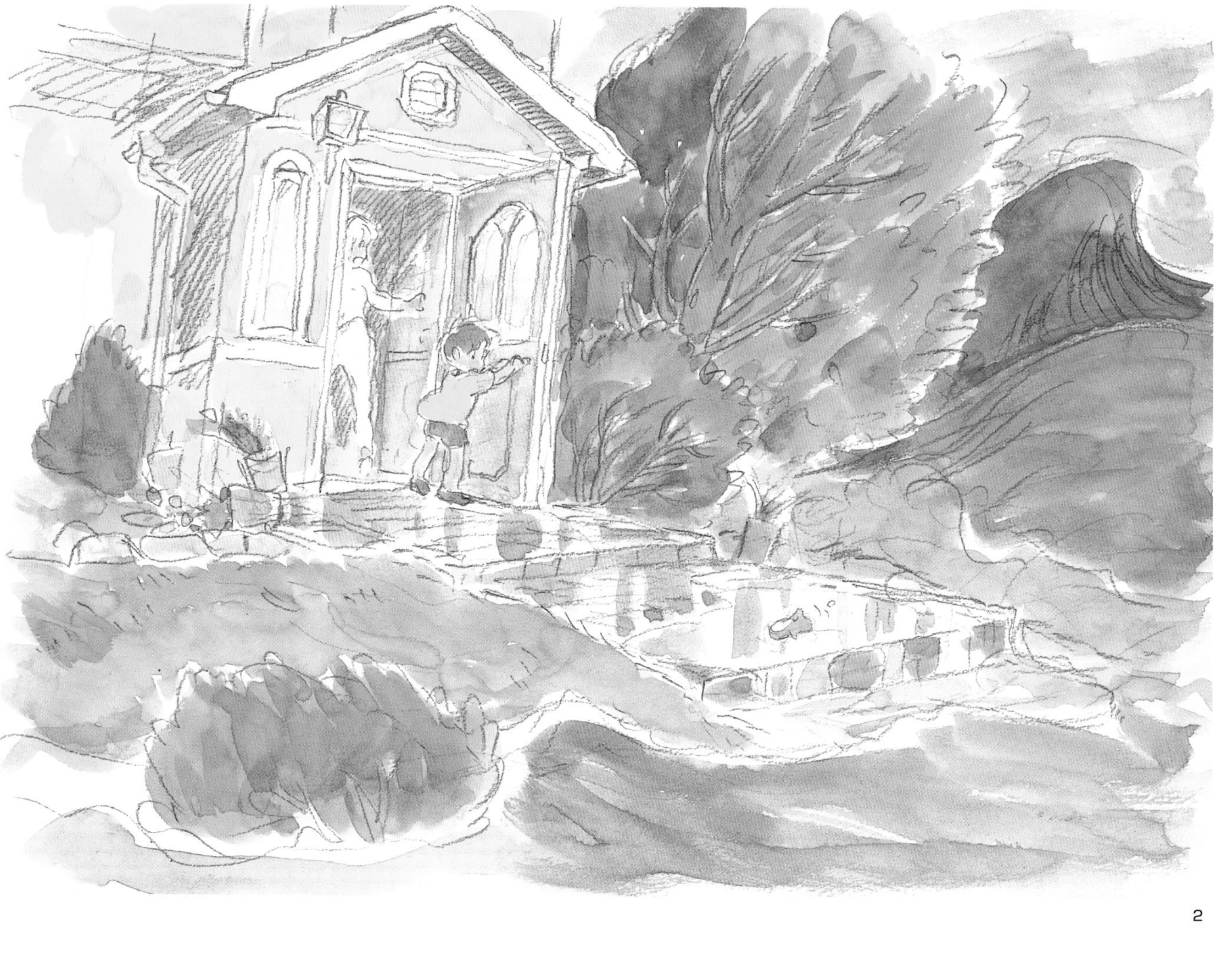

2

宗介

ポニョ

リサ

3

1 /Sosuke and Lisa, making it home to escape the storm [Concept sketch].
2 /The little fish Ponyo, washed up in front of the house. A different reunion scene from the actual film [Concept sketch].
3 /A scene of Ponyo showing up at the front door as a girl was also considered [Concept sketch].

やさしい色になりました。

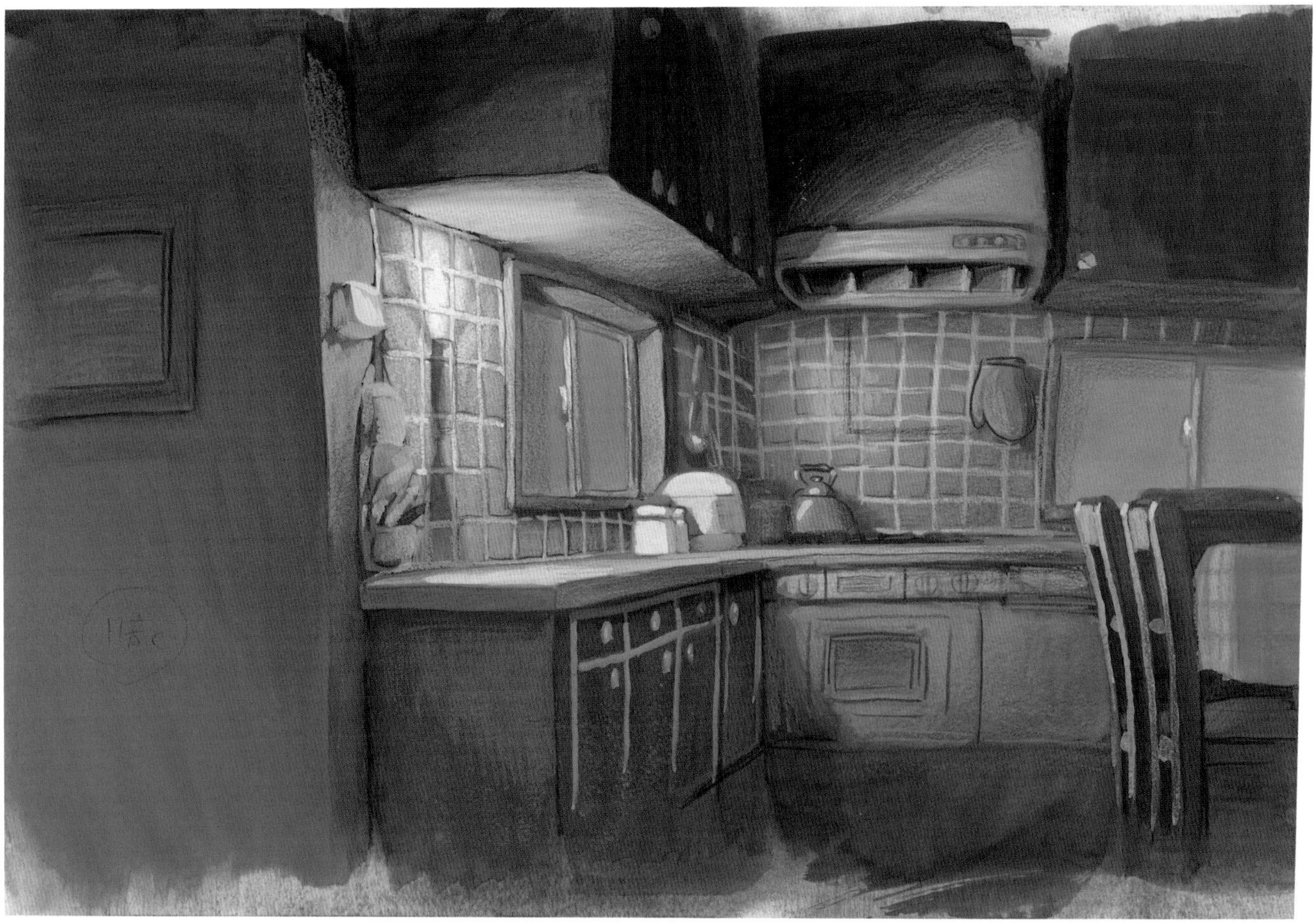

1

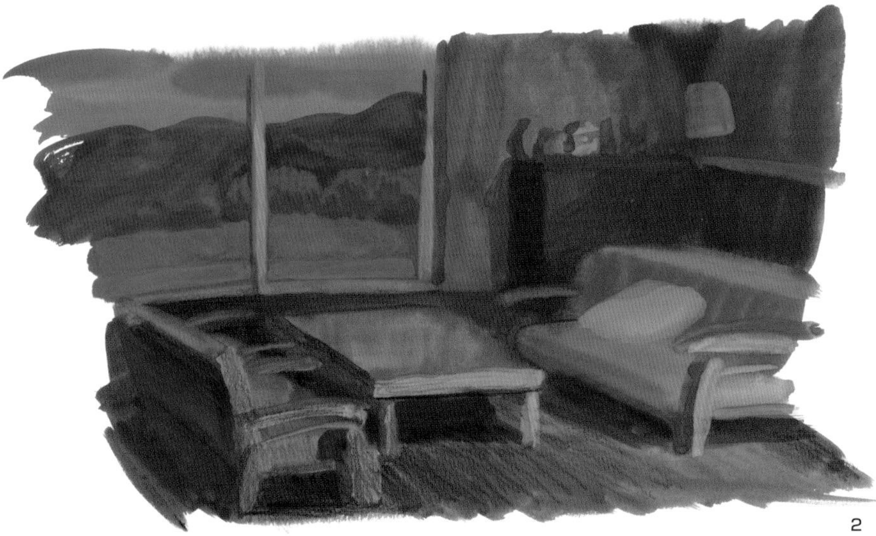

2

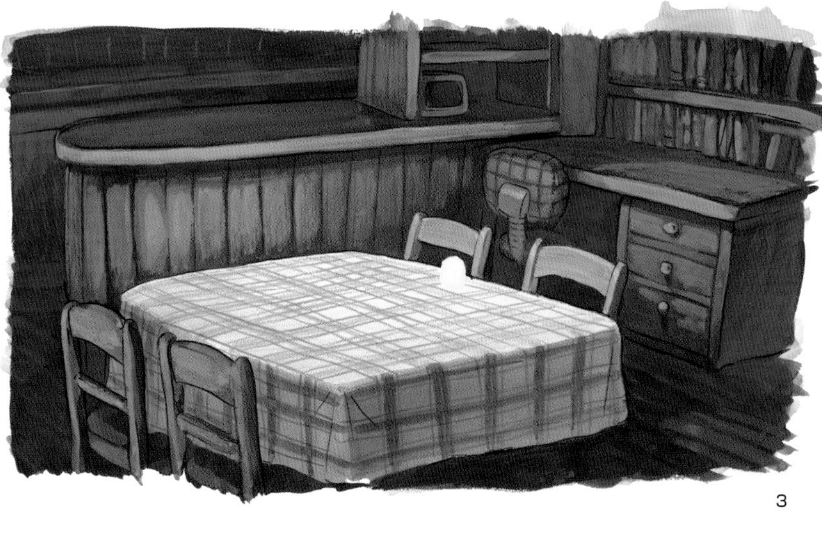

3

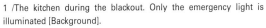

1 /The kitchen during the blackout. Only the emergency light is illuminated [Background].
2 /The living room during the blackout [Concept art].
3 /The kitchen table, also during the blackout [Concept art].
4 /Ponyo admiring the small lantern that Lisa hands her.
5, 6 /Lisa wraps an excited Ponyo in a towel, which Ponyo is enamored with: "I really like this thing!"
7, 8 /"Okay, who assumes the water is working?" "I do!" "I do!"
9 /Sosuke and Ponyo playing with their toes, while Lisa prepares tea.

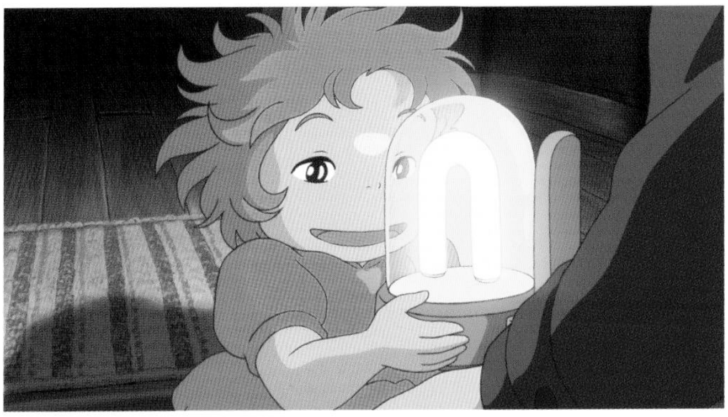

4

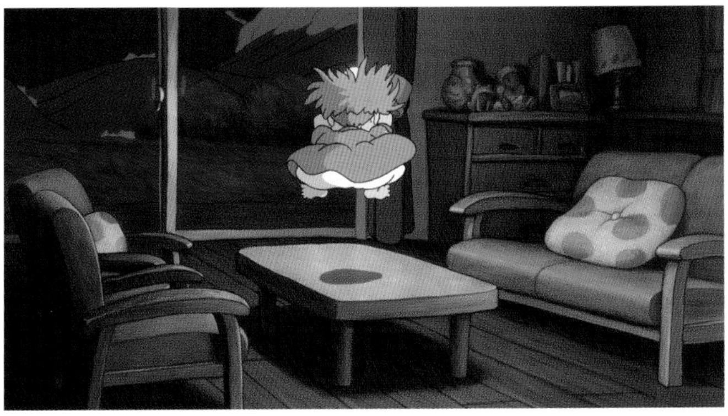

5

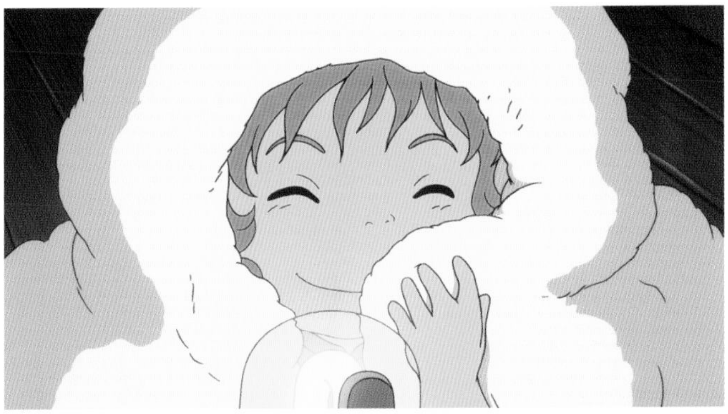

6

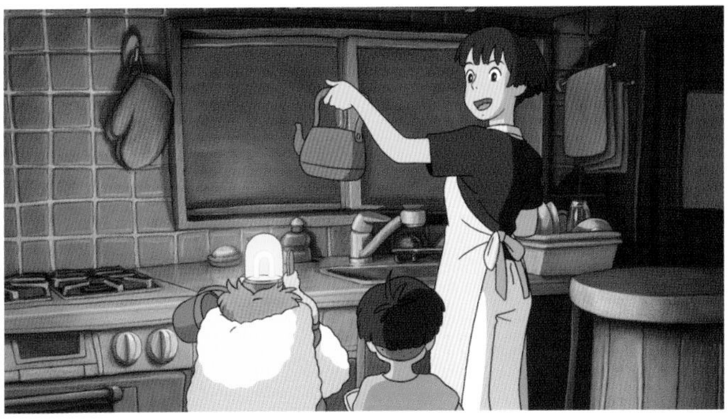

7

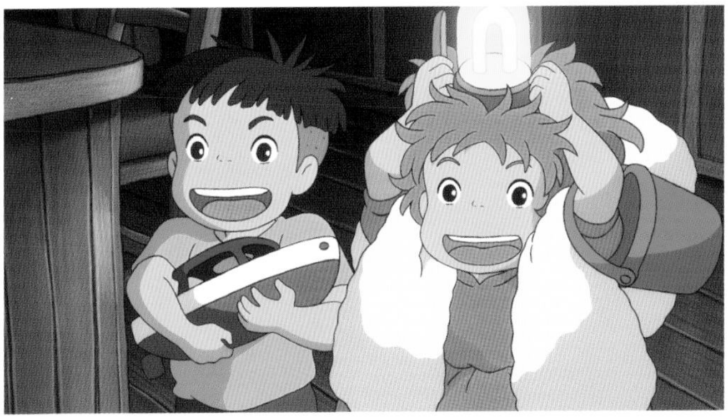

8

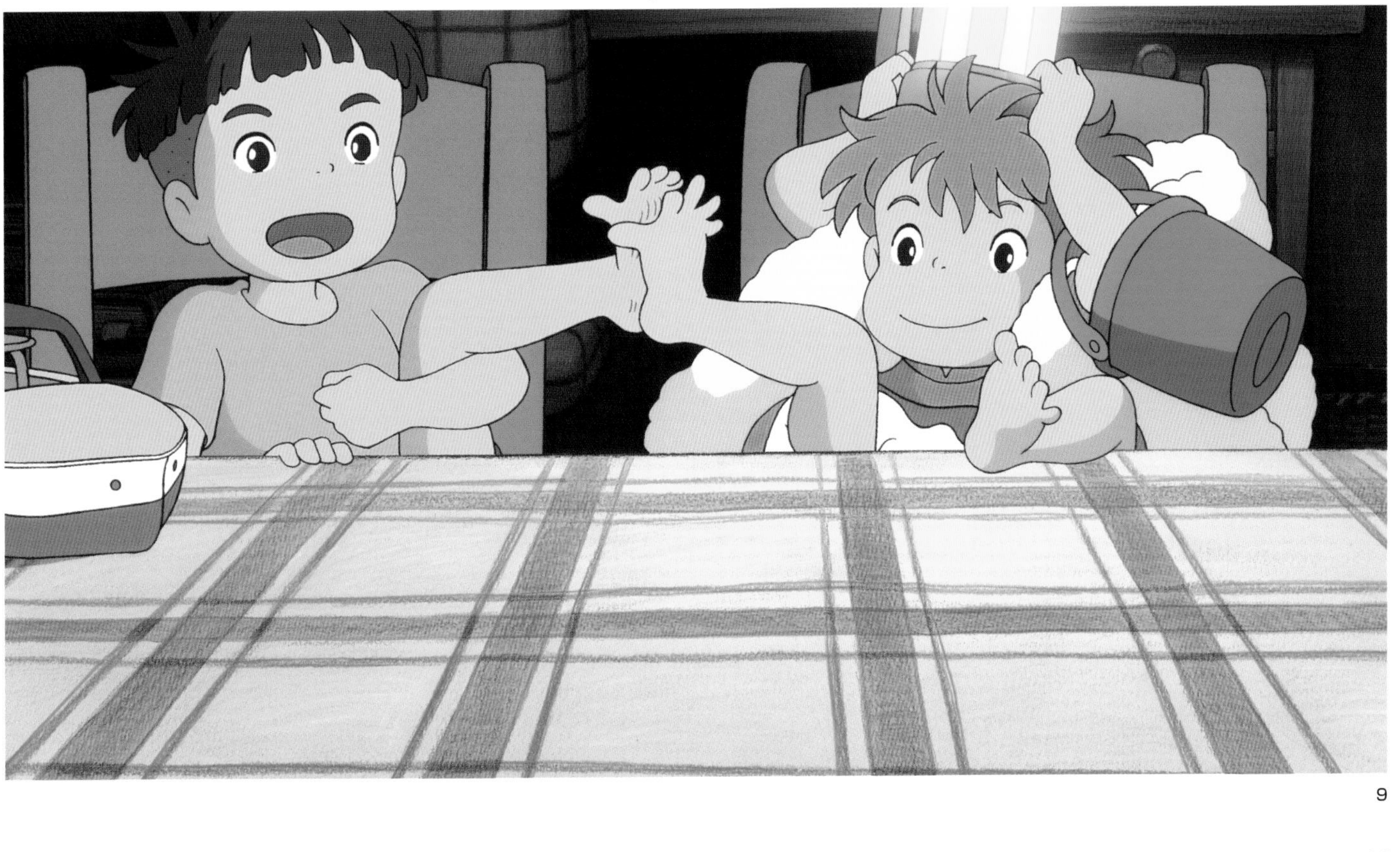

9

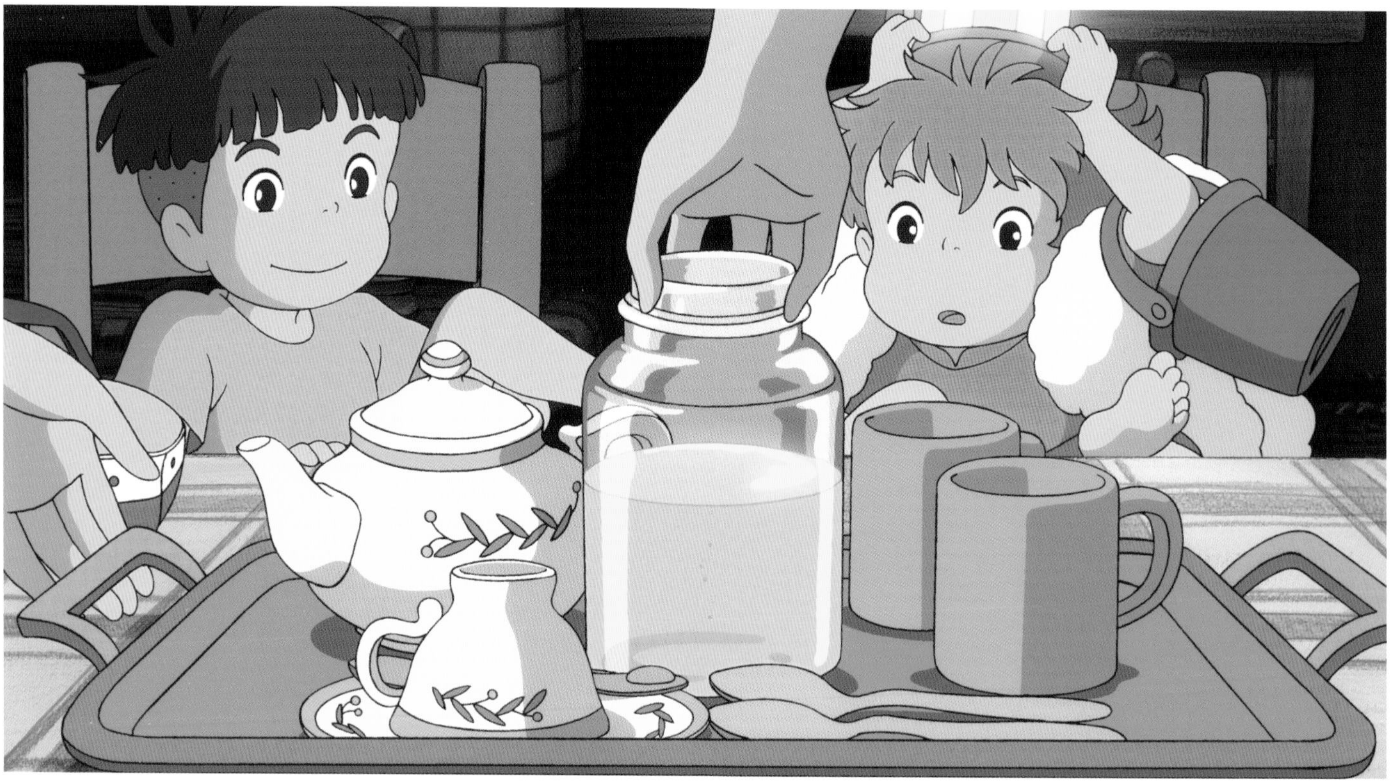

1

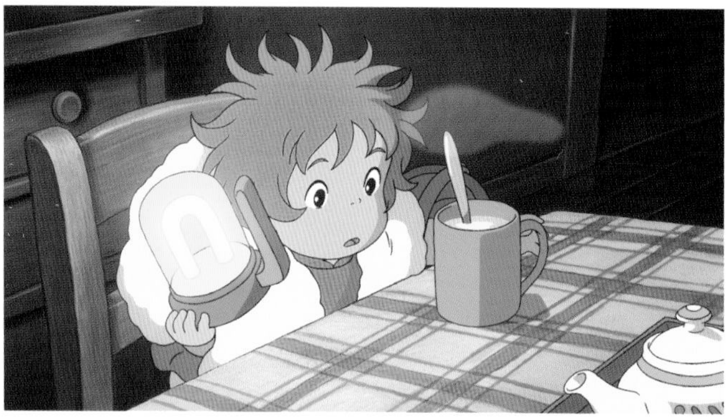

2

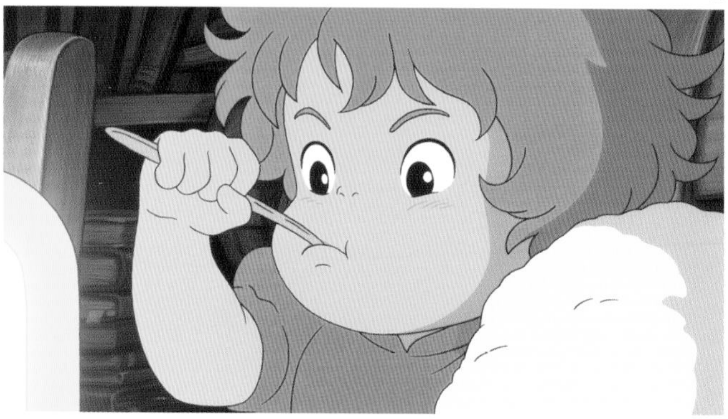

3

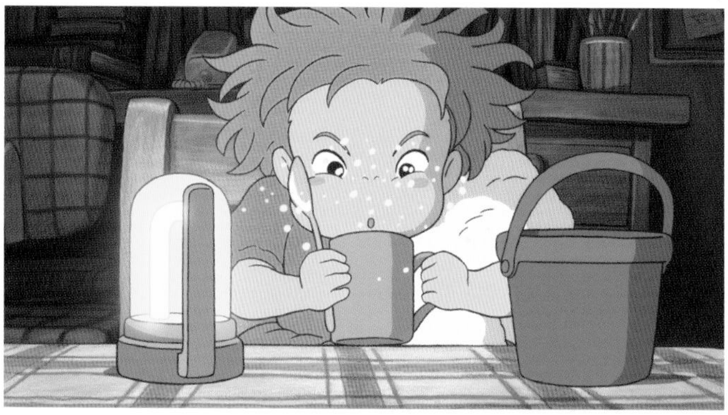

4

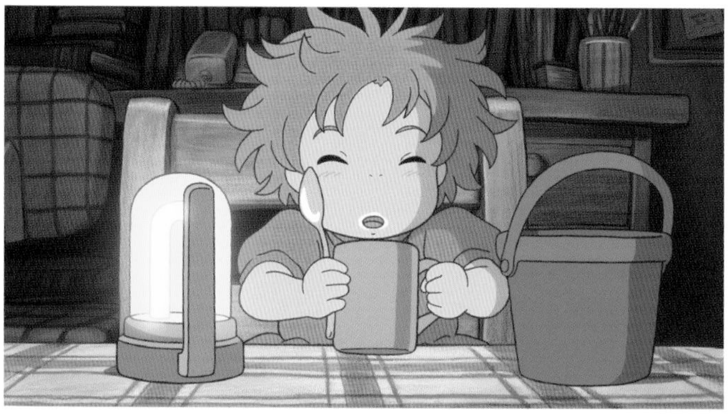

5

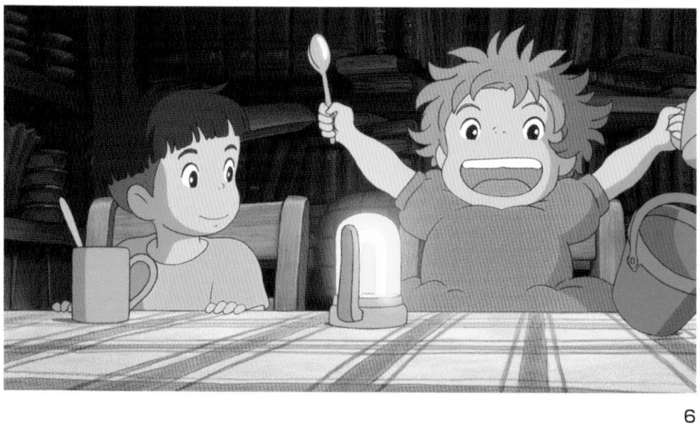

6

Hot Milk with Honey

1 /A tray placed on the table. The tea is for Lisa and hot milk with honey for the children.
2–5 /Ponyo setting down the lantern to drink the milk. She rejoices over her first taste of honey.
6 /"So, what would the two of you like to do now?" "Ponyo wants ham!"

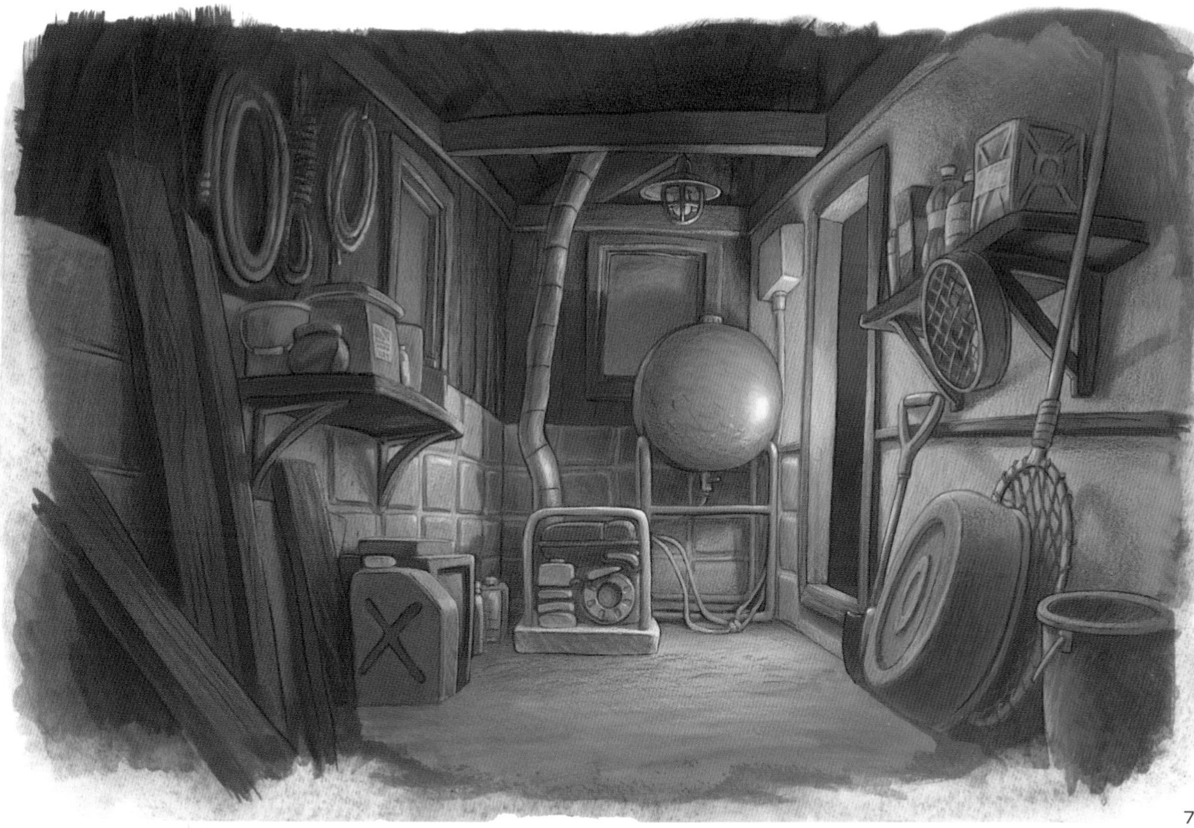

7

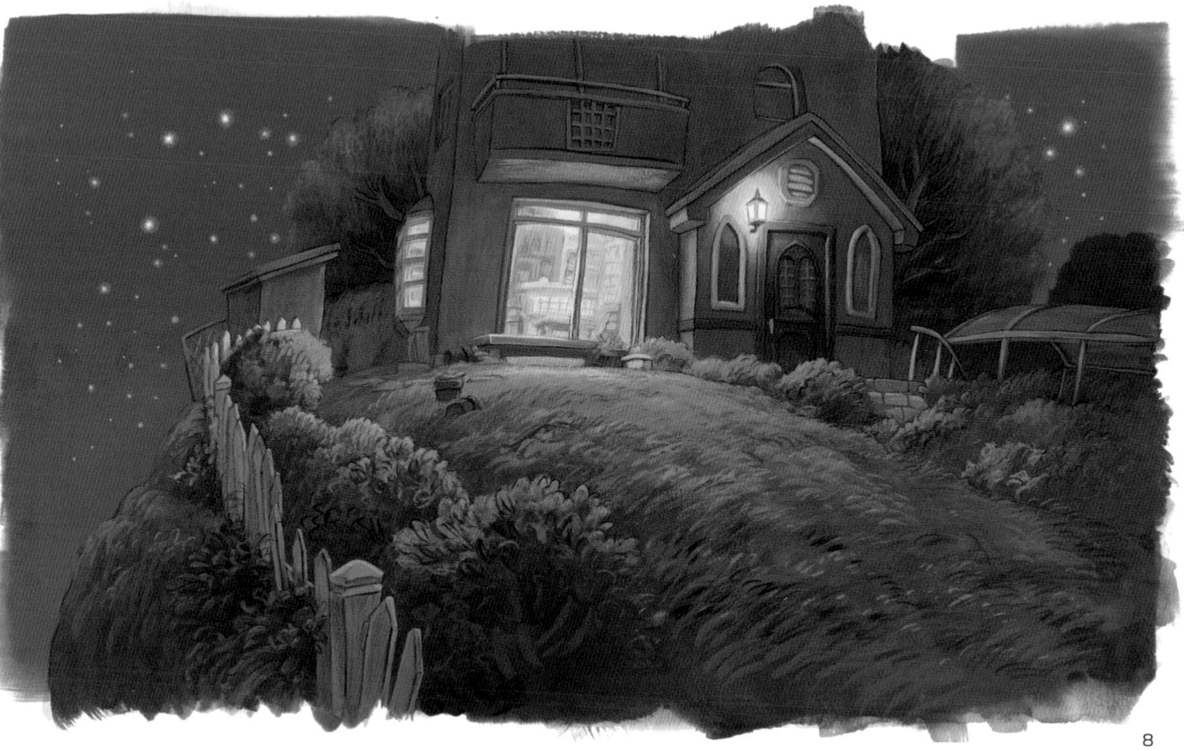

8

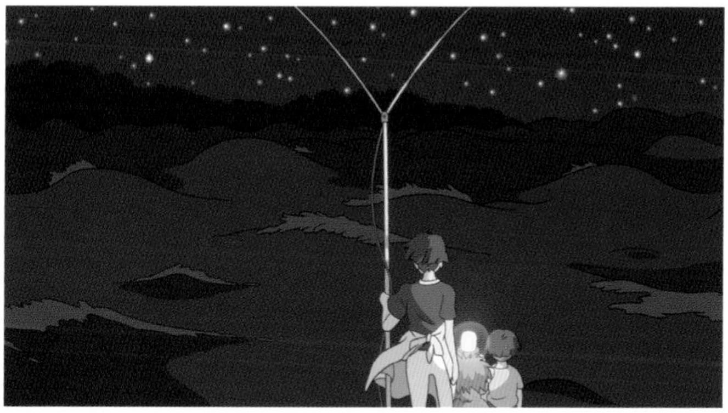

9

7 /The shed with a generator, gasoline container, and exhaust duct. Lisa decides to run the generator in order to contact Koichi over the radio [Background].
8 /The lights are on at Sosuke's house; the generator is running with the help of Ponyo's magic [Background].
9 /Lisa and the children raising the antenna under the stars. But there's too much static to make contact.

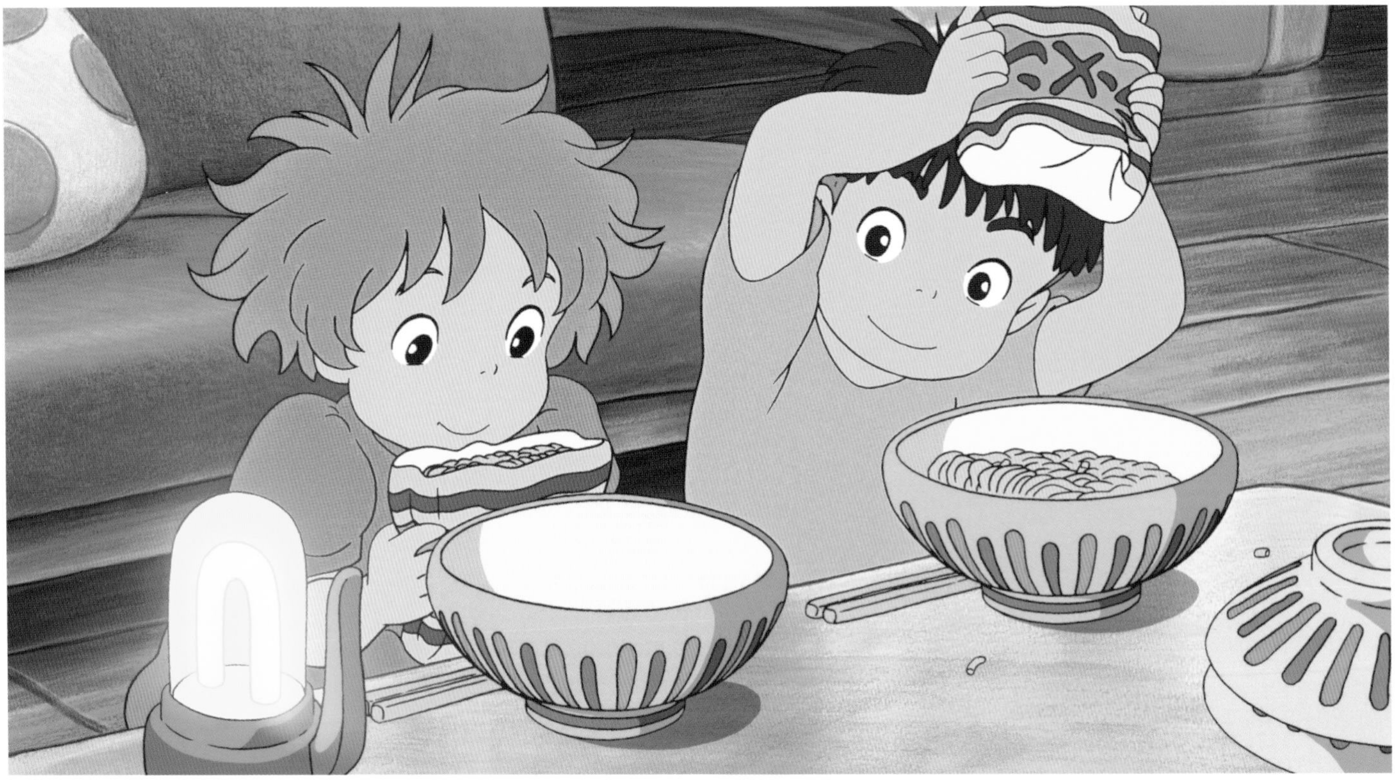

1

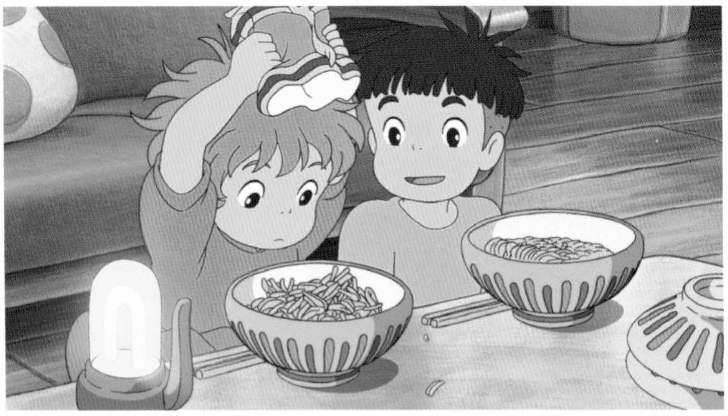

2

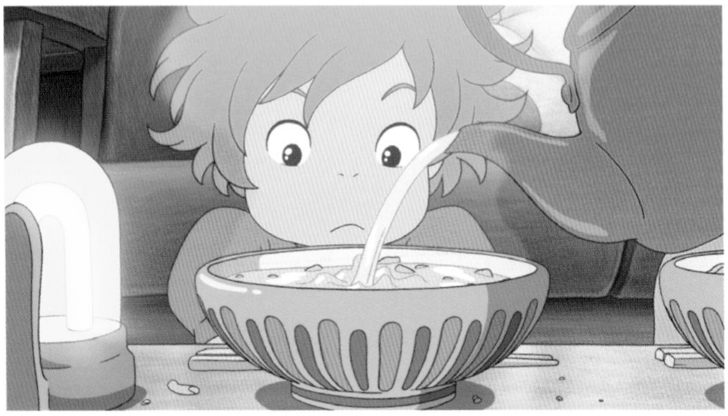

3

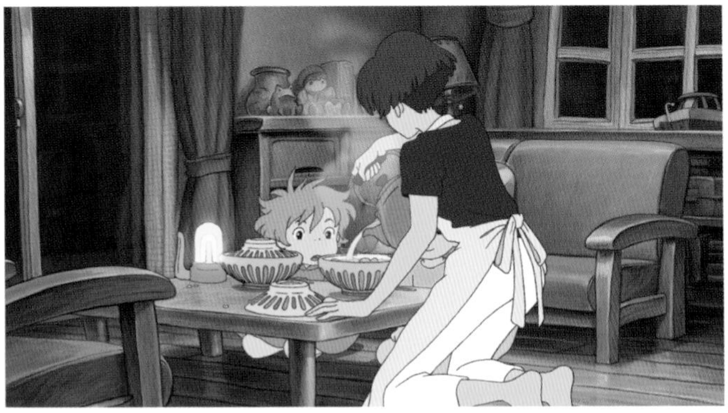

4

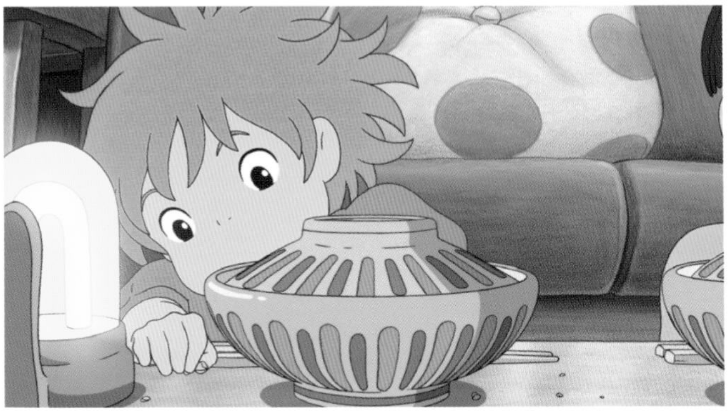

5

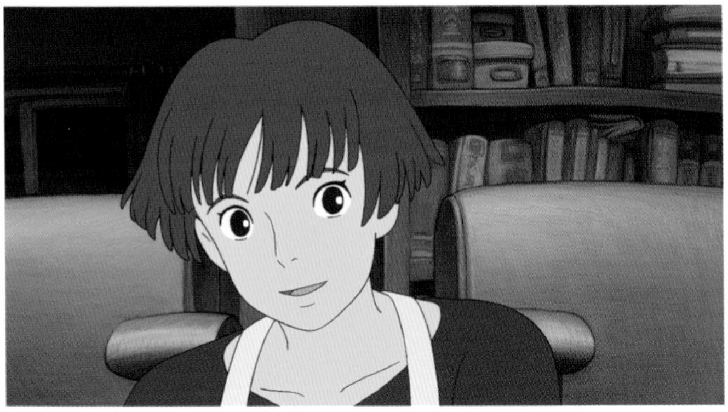

6

Ponyo and Ramen

1, 2 /Ponyo, fascinated by her first experience with ramen. She looks as if she's watching a new kind of magic.
3, 4 /Lisa pouring the hot water: "Be careful, it's really hot."
5 /Ponyo eating a piece off the table.
6, 7 /Lisa says, "Close your eyes," as she slips something into their bowls.
8, 9 /"Get ready to look now." "Abracada...bra!" A delicious bowl of ramen with egg and ham is ready to eat.
10, 11 /Ponyo, reaching out and eating the ham.
12, 13 /Ponyo, suddenly becoming very tired as she eats the ramen, falls asleep.

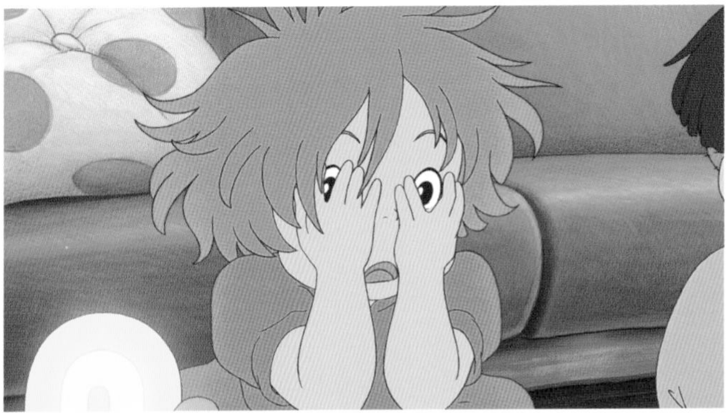

7

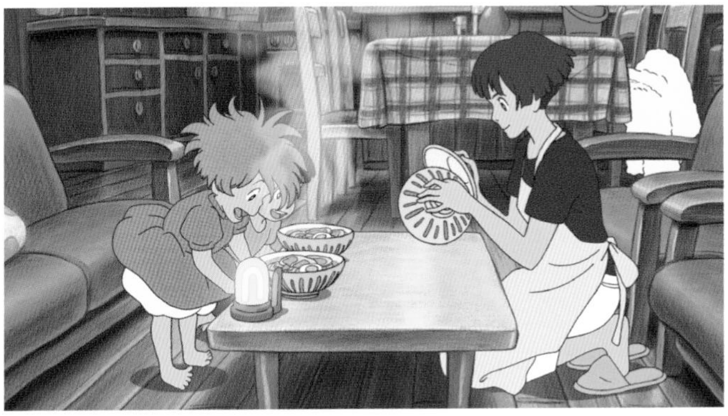

8

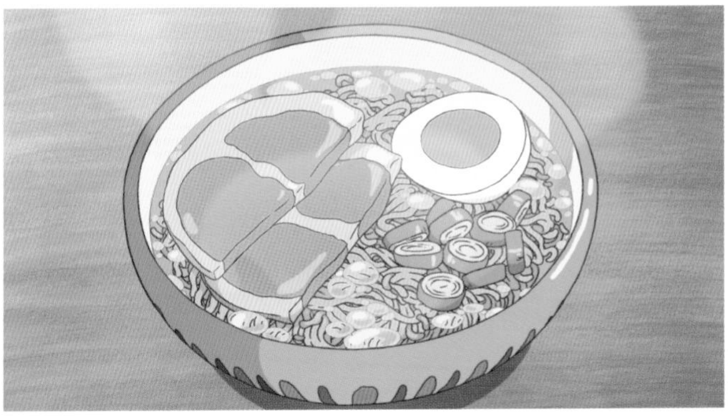

9

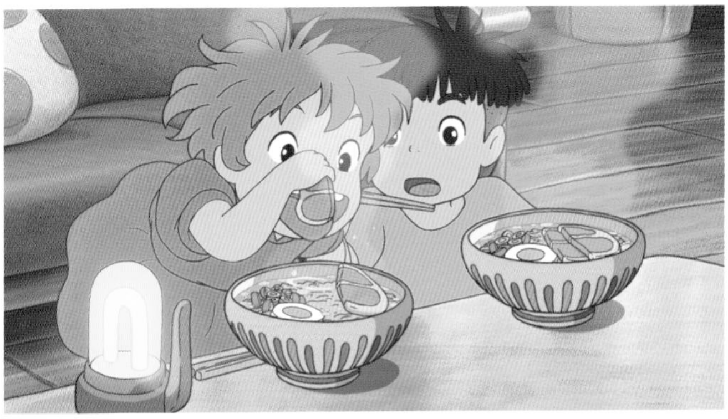

10

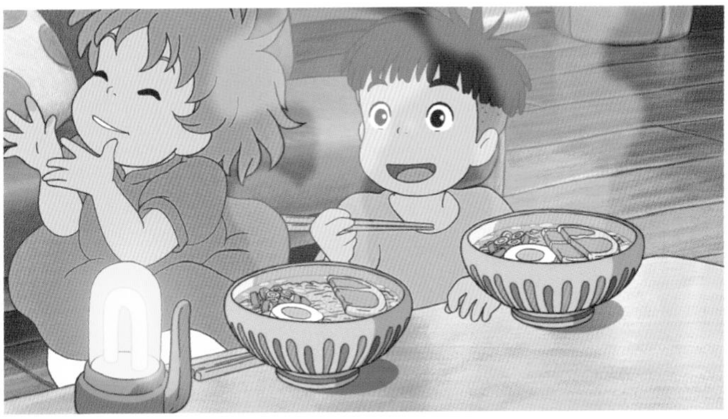

11

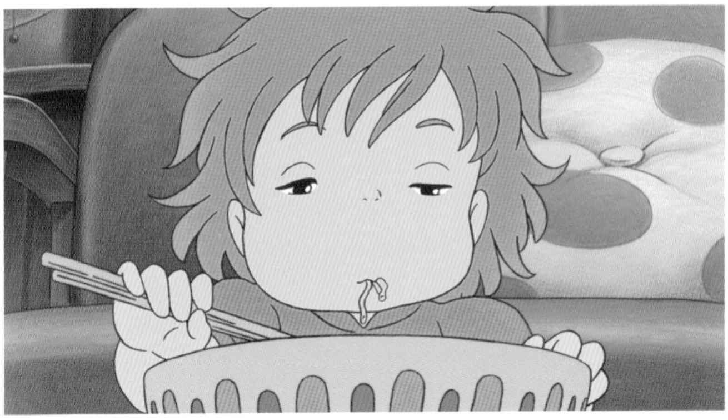

12

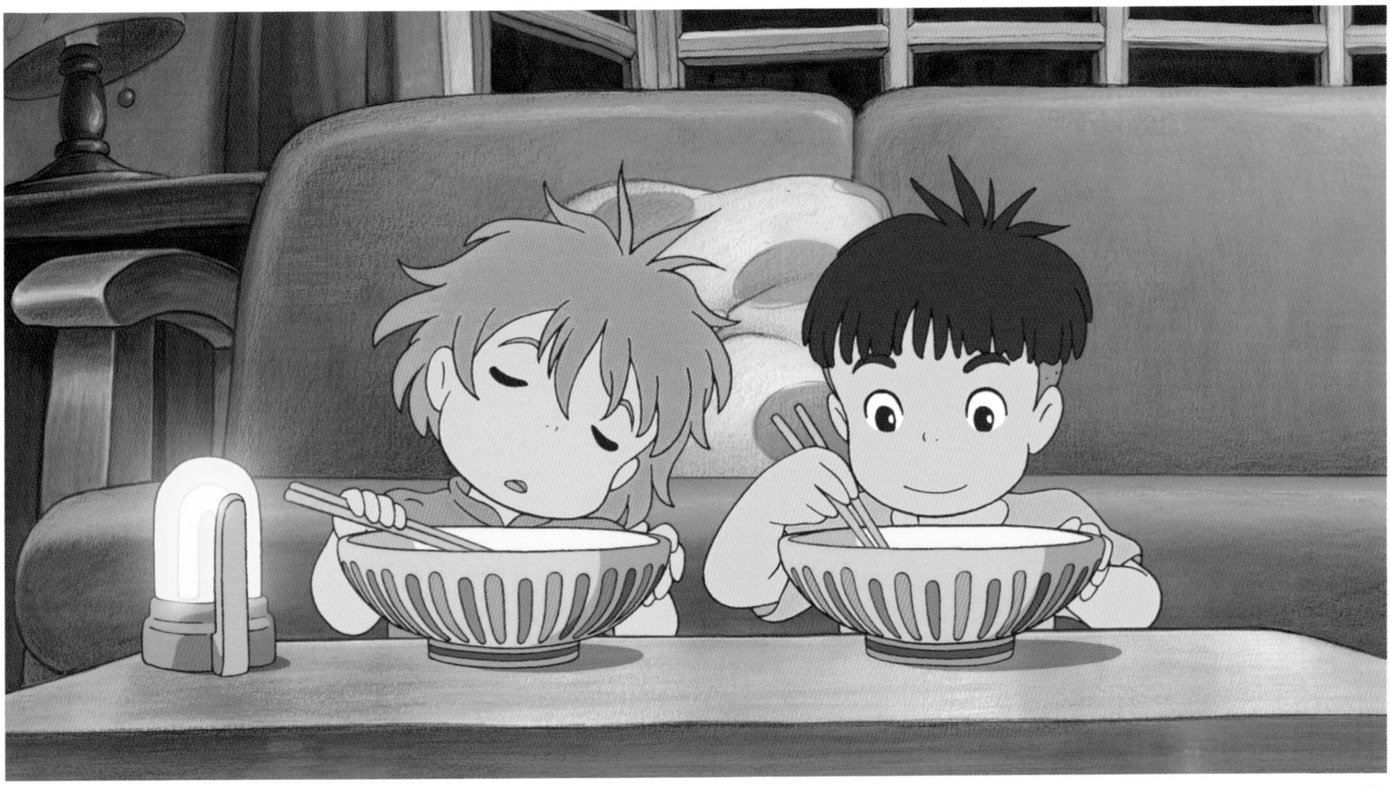

13

Sosuke and Lisa

1 /Lisa laying Ponyo on the couch and putting a blanket over her.
2 /It's quiet outside, and they can see lights moving at the top of the mountain.
3 /Lisa, deciding to check on the Sunflower House, asks Sosuke to watch over the house.
4 /"You have to be the man of the house, tonight. Let Ponyo sleep, wait for me ...You can do it, I'll be back."
5, 6 /Sosuke, sending off Lisa, who leaves stocked with emergency supplies.
7 /Lisa's car goes off in the dark.
8 /Sosuke, wearing a captain's hat, sits by Ponyo's side as if to protect her.

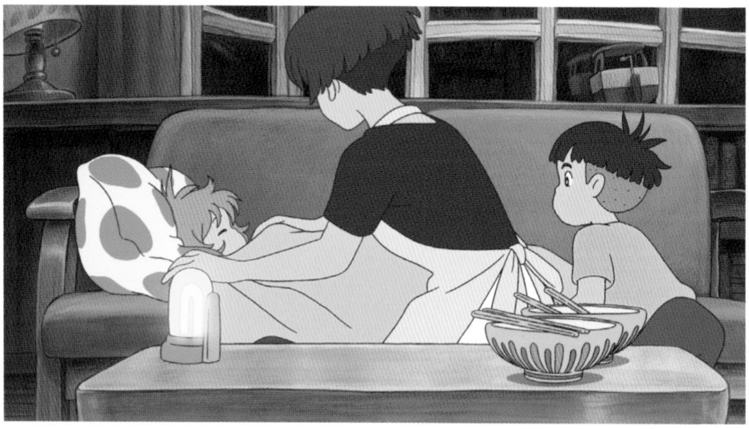

1

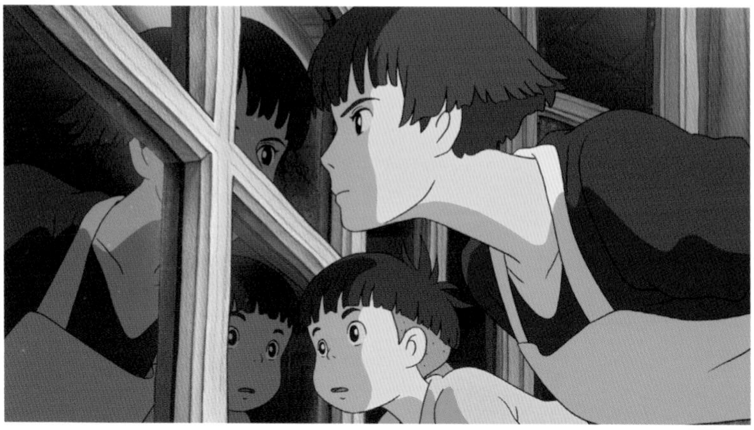

2

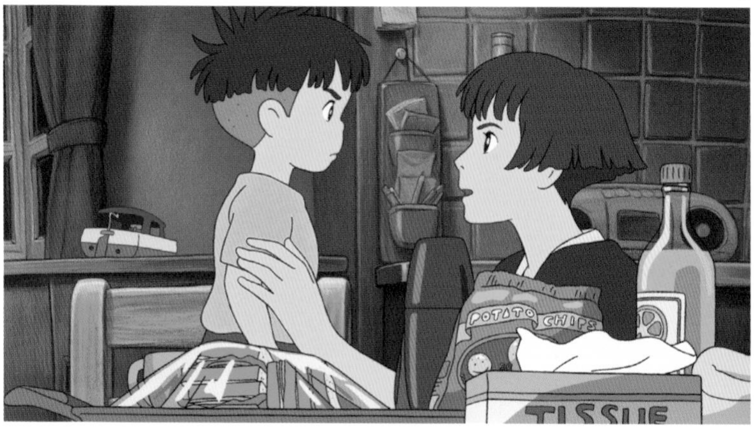
POTATO CHIPS
TISSUE

3

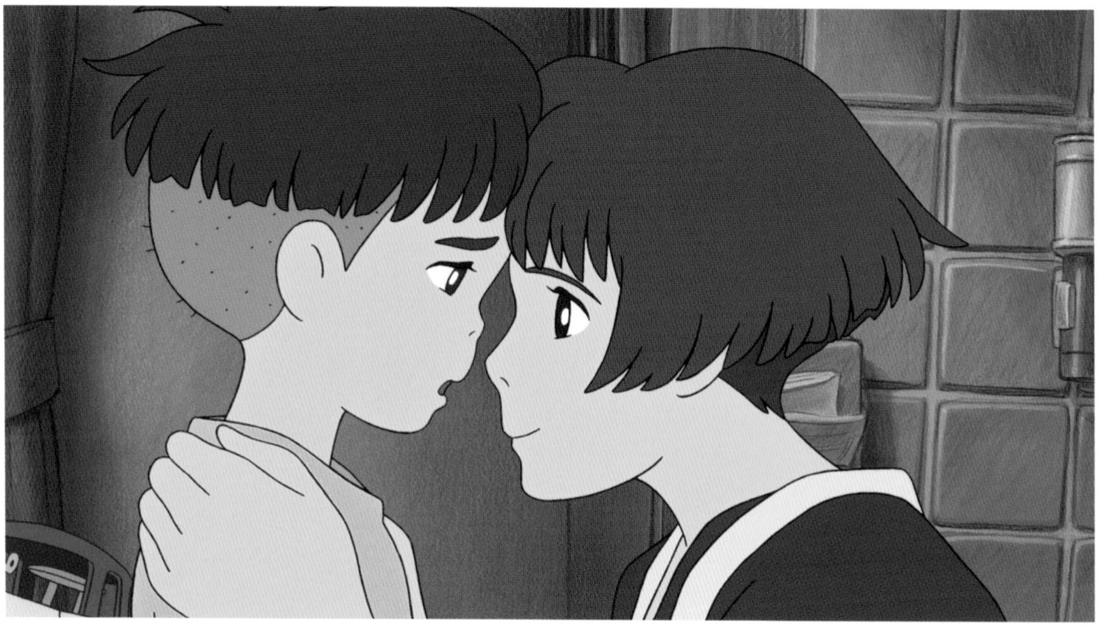

4

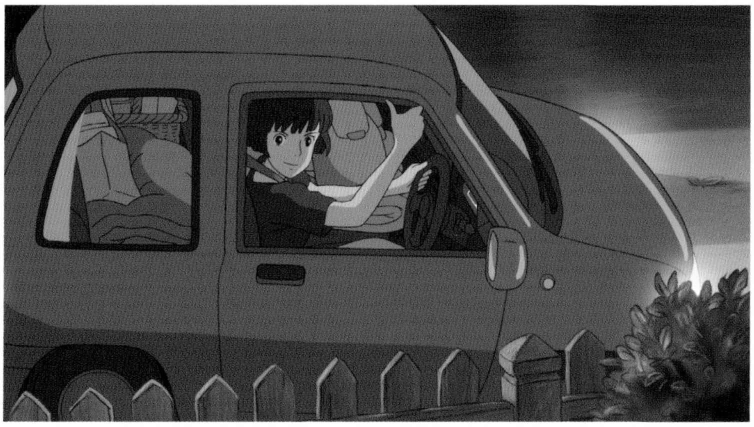
5
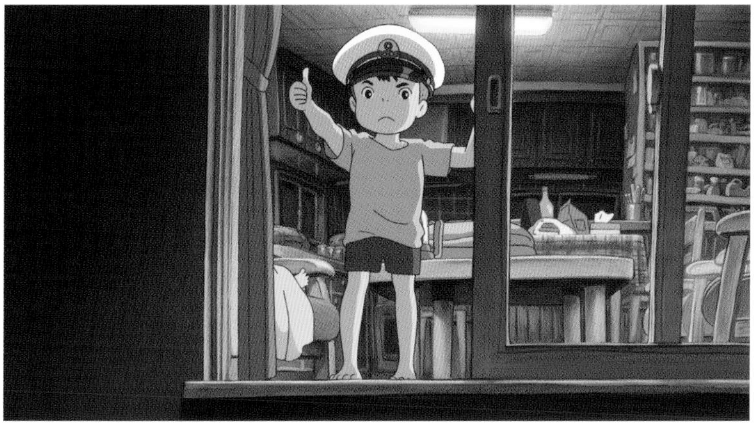
6
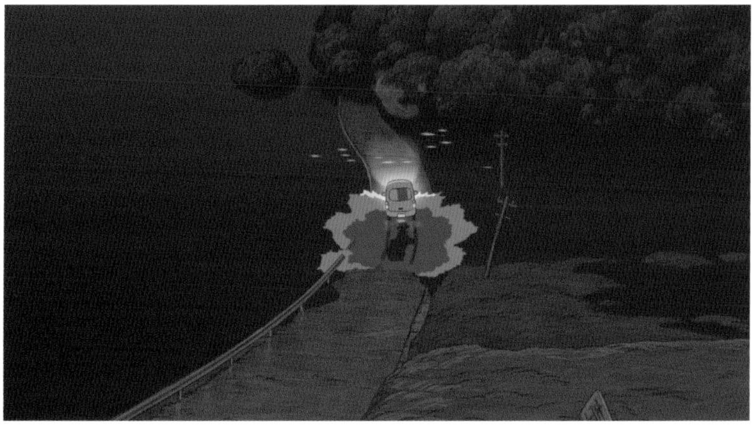
7
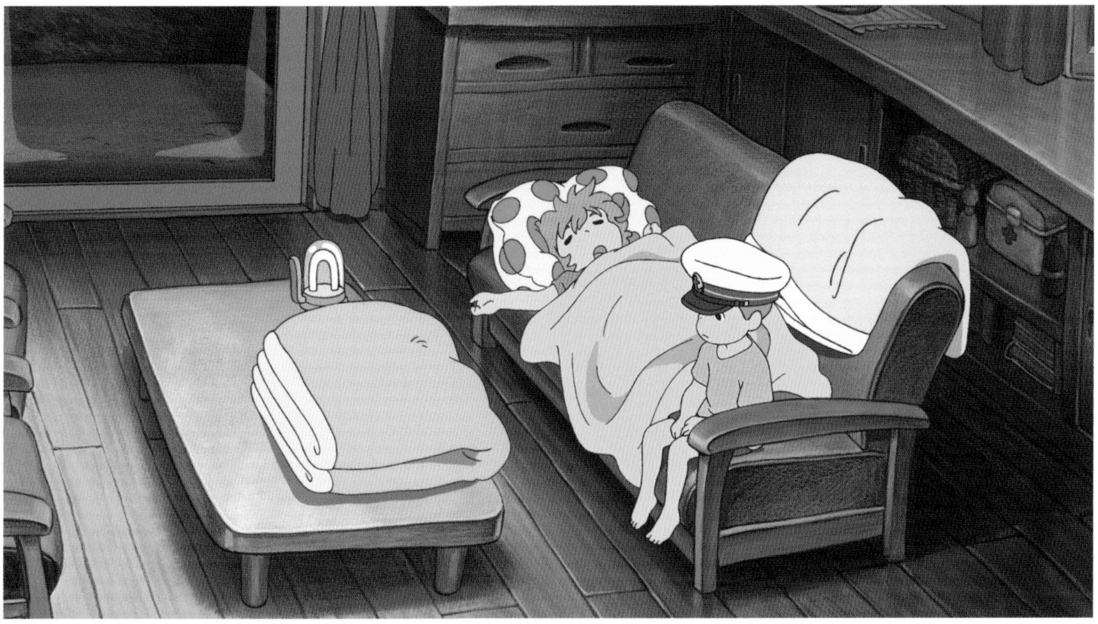
8

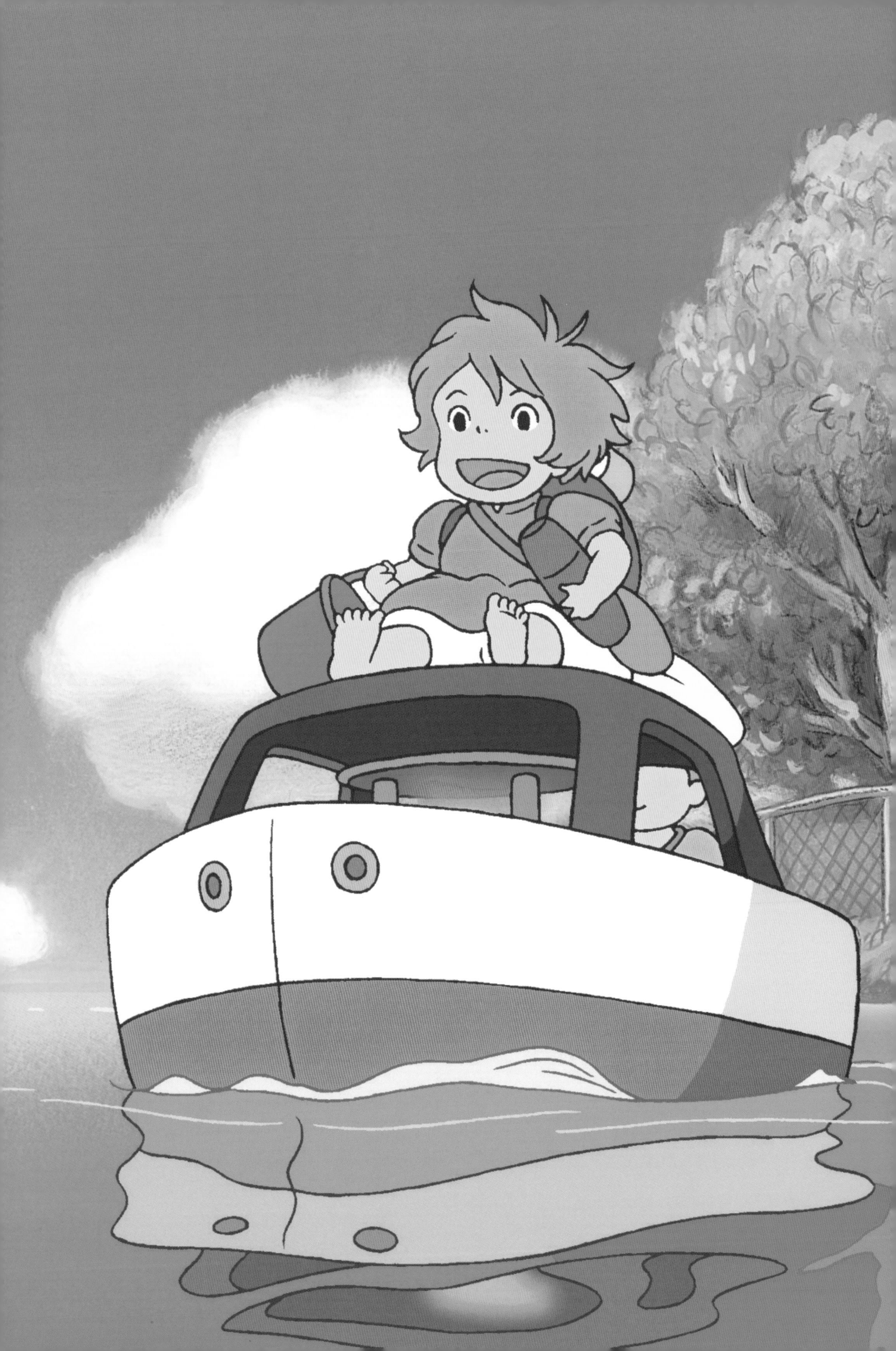

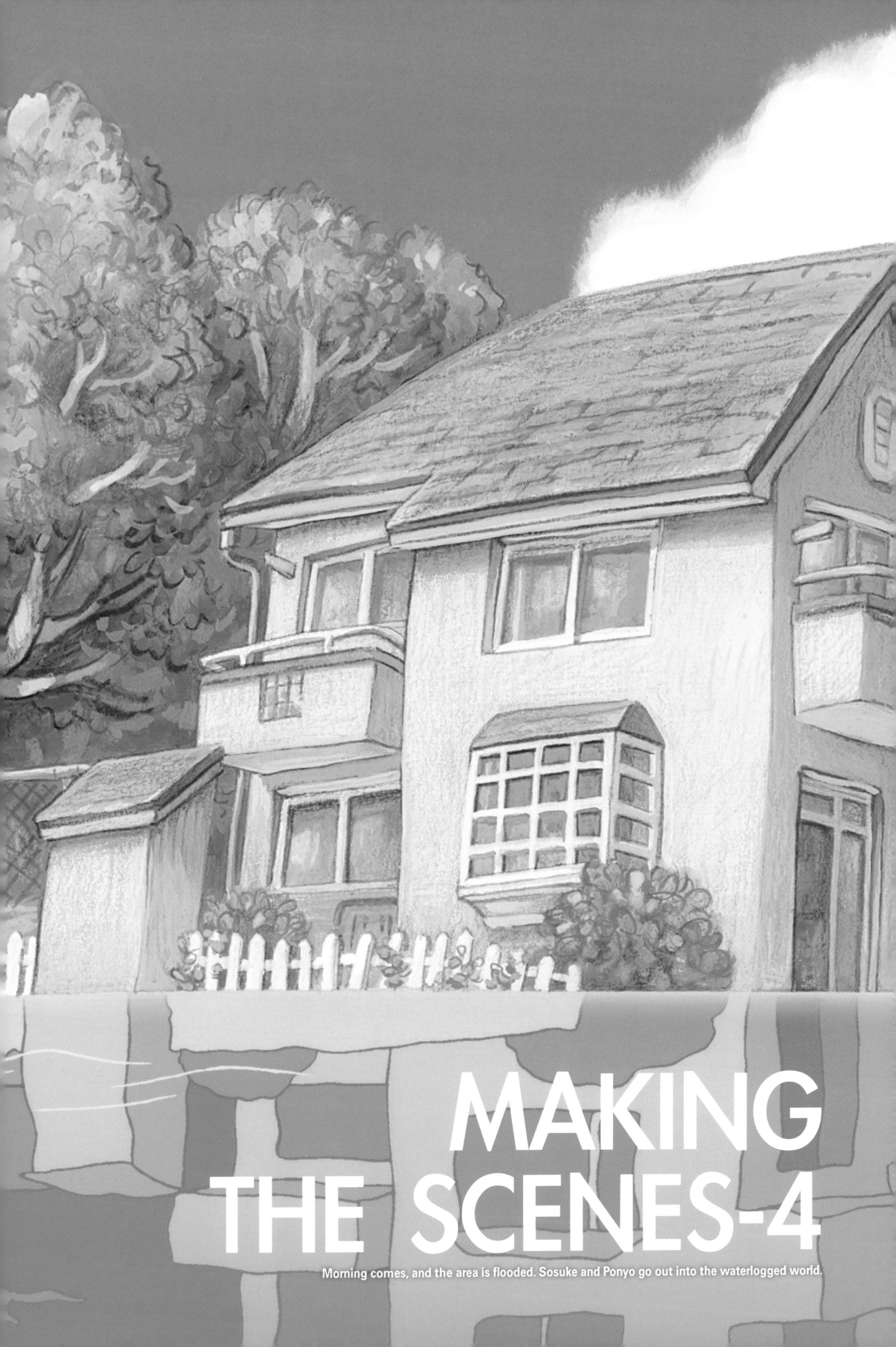

MAKING THE SCENES-4

Morning comes, and the area is flooded. Sosuke and Ponyo go out into the waterlogged world.

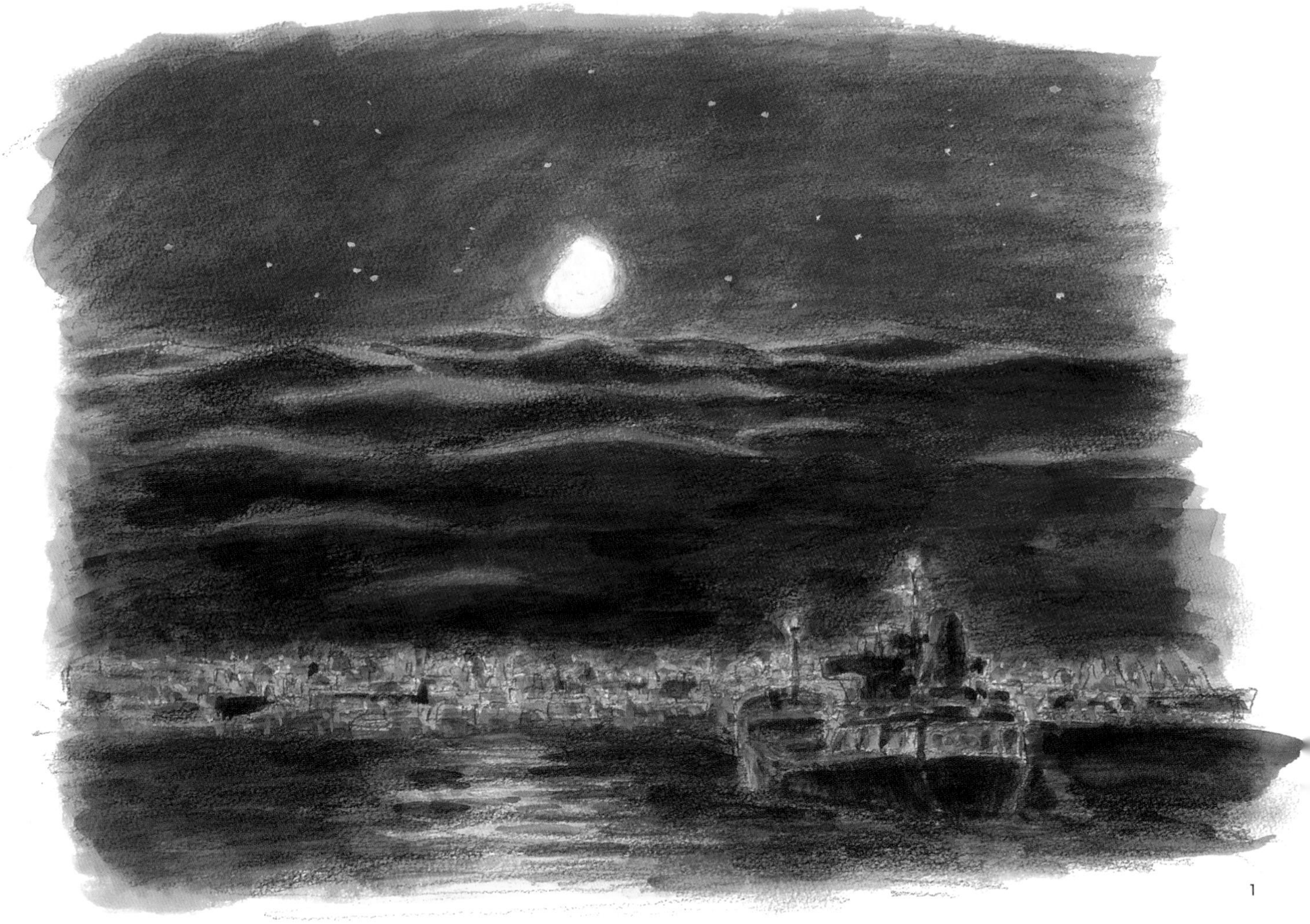

1

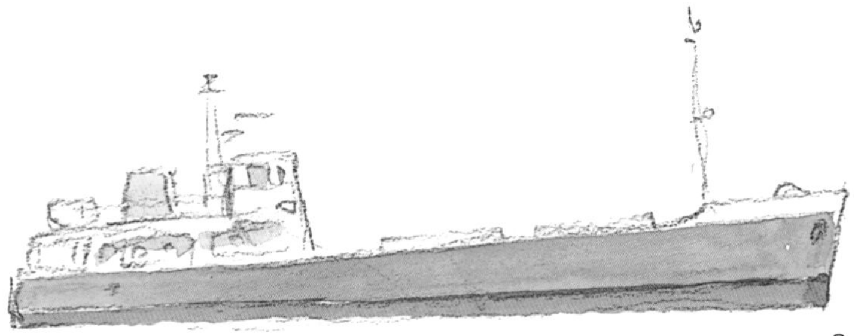

2

The *Koganei Maru* Adrift

1 /A stalled and radioless *Koganei Maru* comes upon what looks like a graveyard of ships [Concept sketch].
2 /A sketch of the *Koganei Maru* [Concept sketch].
3 /The strange sight on the horizon before the *Koganei Maru*. The sea is swelled up like a mountain.
4 /What appears to be city lights are countless stranded ships, unable to move in any direction.
5 /Koichi and the helmsman Arai, dumbfounded by this strange occurrence.

The night scenes in general were darker than usual, which proves to be especially trying for the background artists. And that's because the lines drawn with colored pencil stand out in darker scenes. So I had the staff look for other materials that could create the same look and experiment with whether they could replicate the touch of the pencil-colored daytime backgrounds with poster paint. In that sense, the night scenes might have leaned toward a relatively realistic look rather than a storybook style.

Miyazaki was also very particular about the scene where the gathering of ships at night was made to look like city lights. He changed the color palette a number of times, and Atsushi Okui, the camera supervisor, also made the size of the lights smaller to accentuate the scale of this scene.

—Art Director: Noboru Yoshida

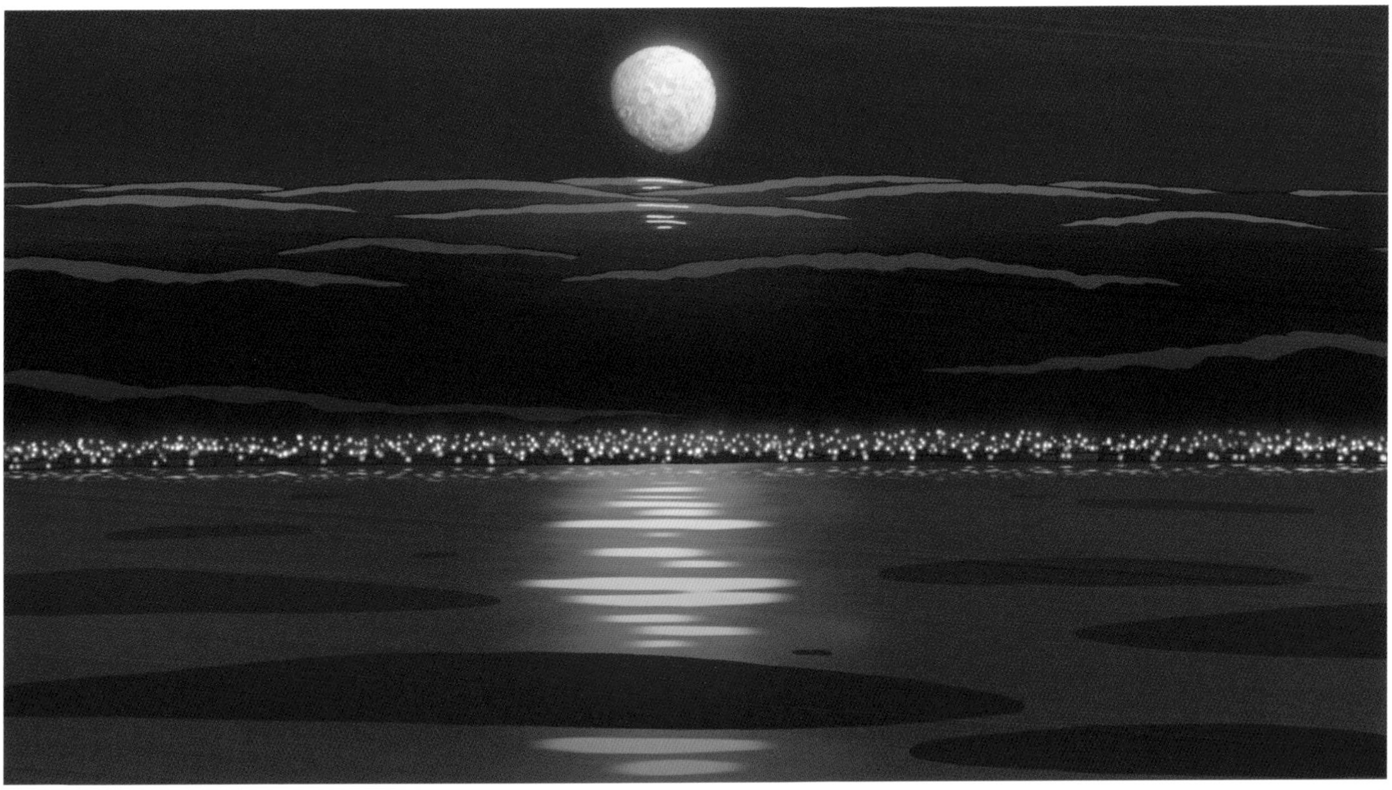

3

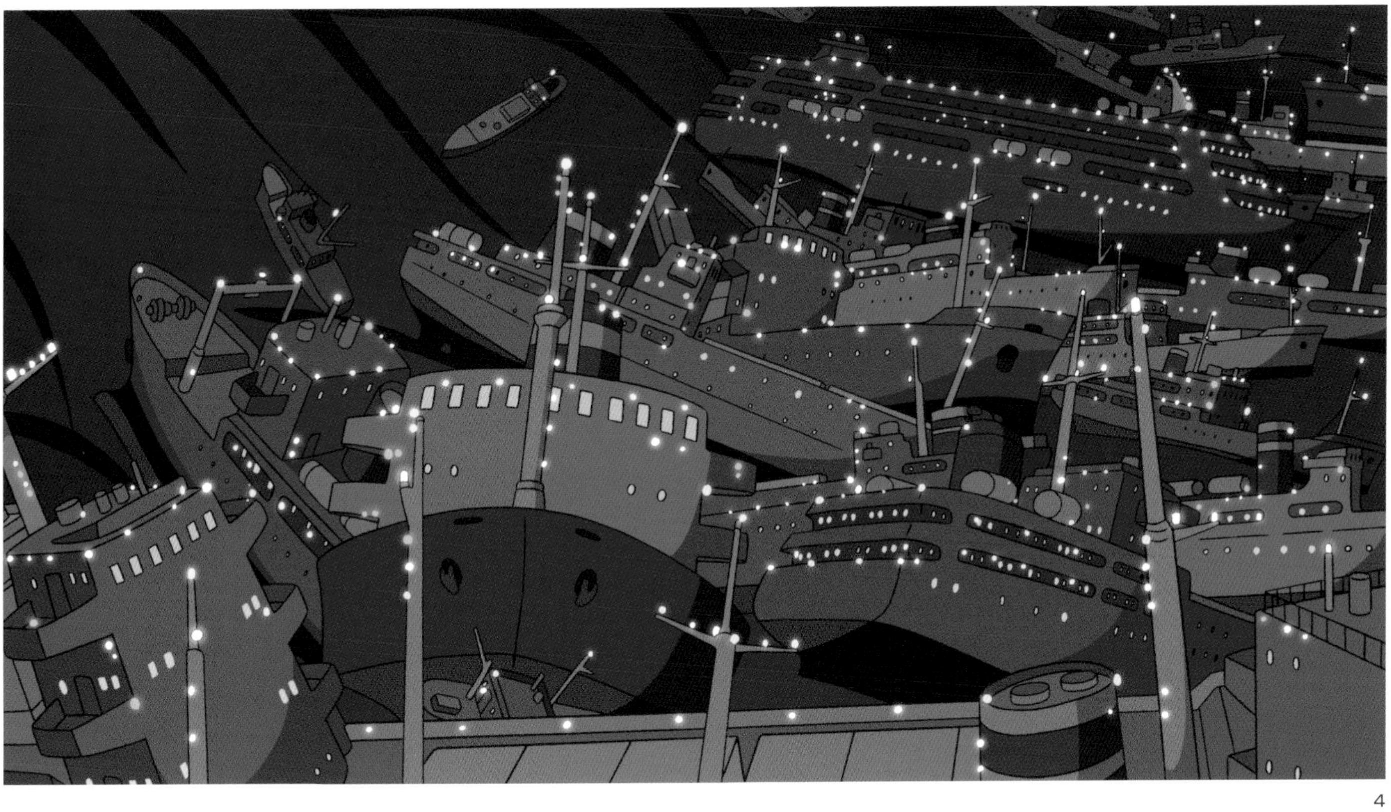

4

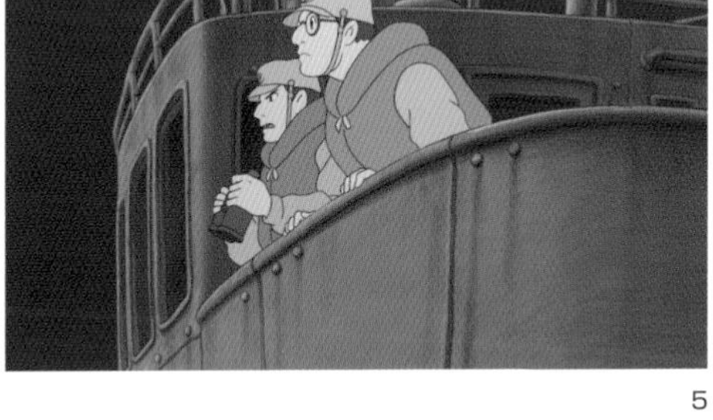

5

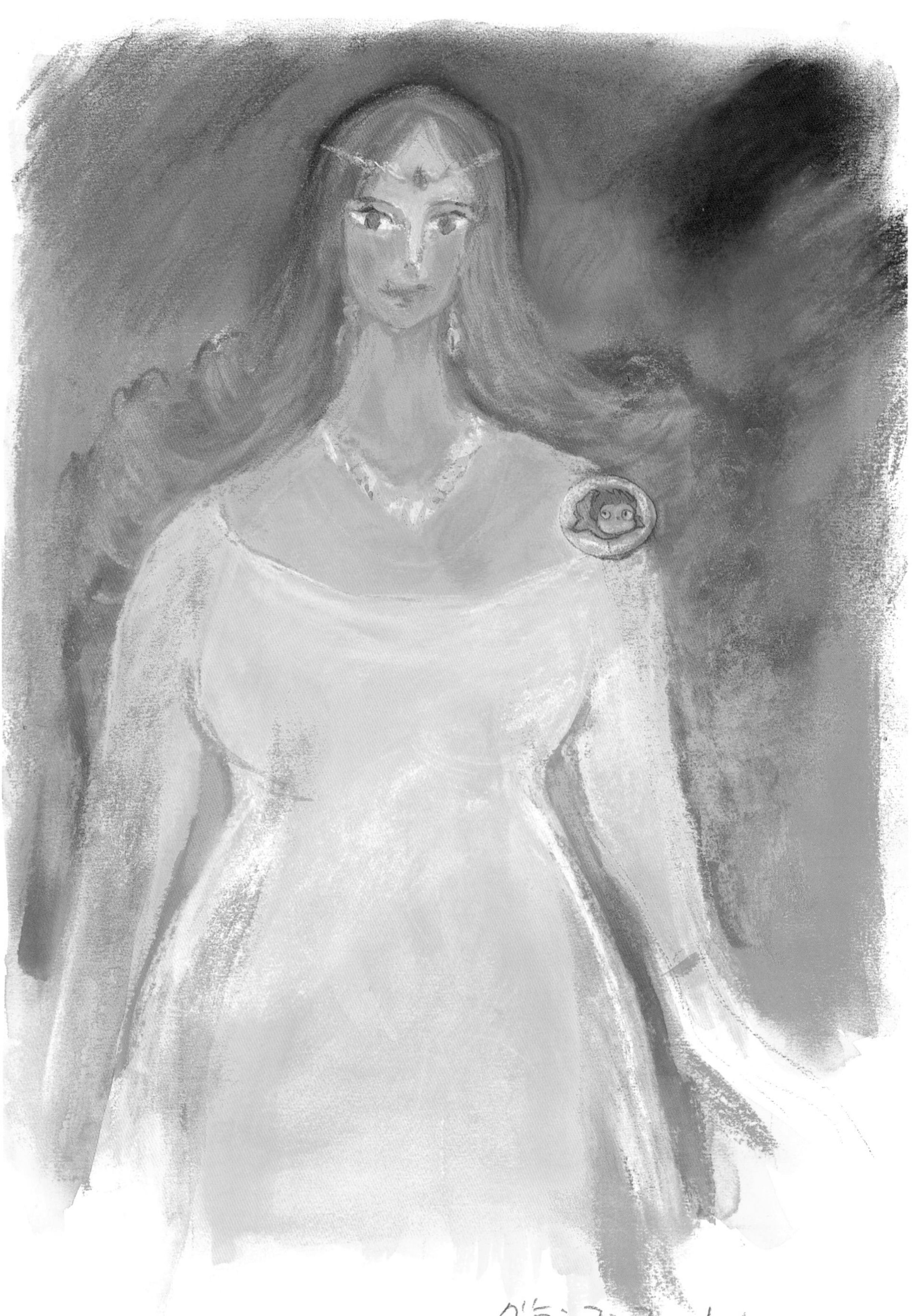
グランマンマーレ

1

Gran Mamare

1 /Ponyo's mother Gran Mamare, with Ponyo inside the water sphere [Concept sketch].
2–5 /The engine starts running when Gran Mamare overtakes the *Koganei Maru* from behind. "I just saw the Goddess of Mercy!" – the crew put their hands together in prayer.

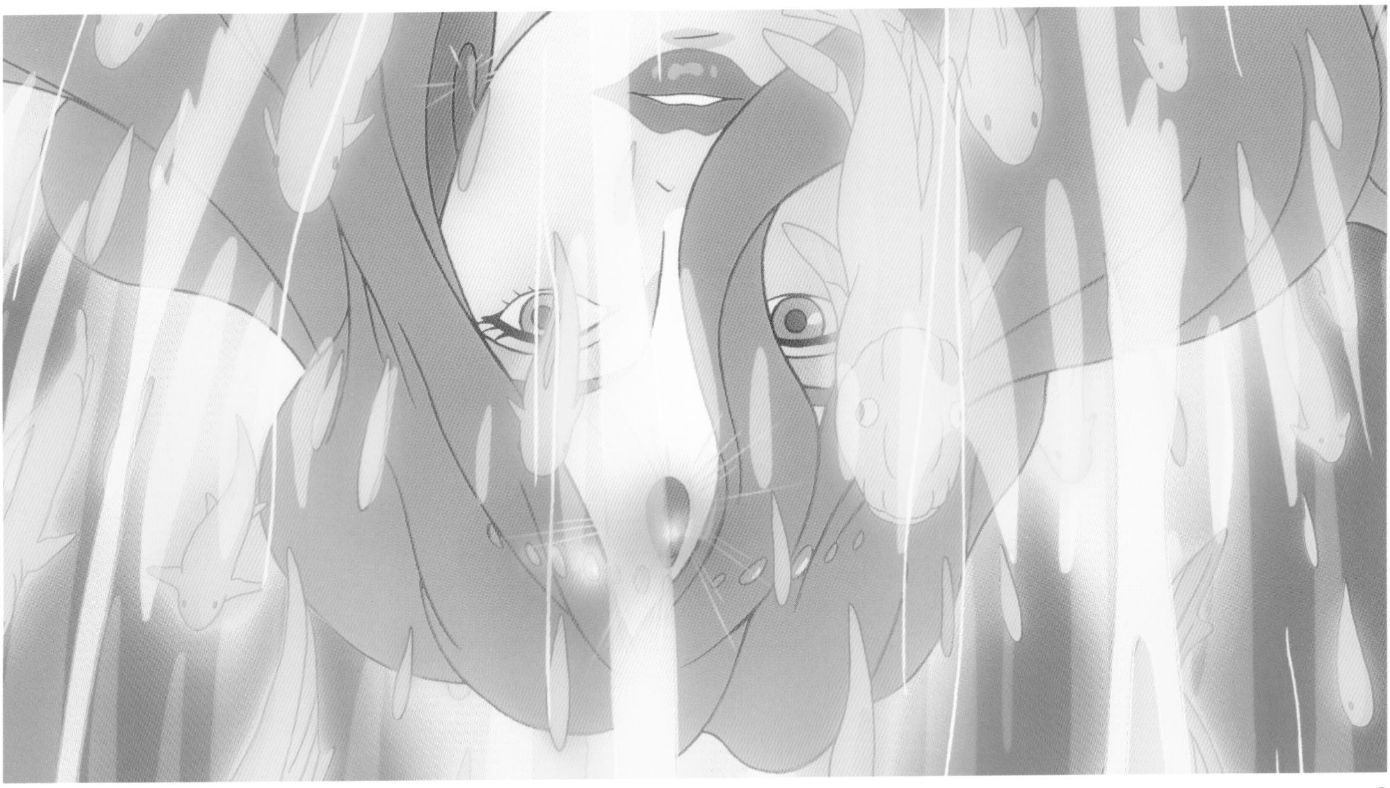

2

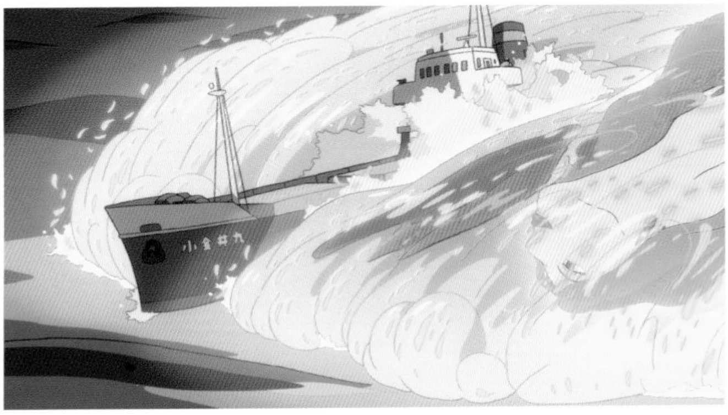

3

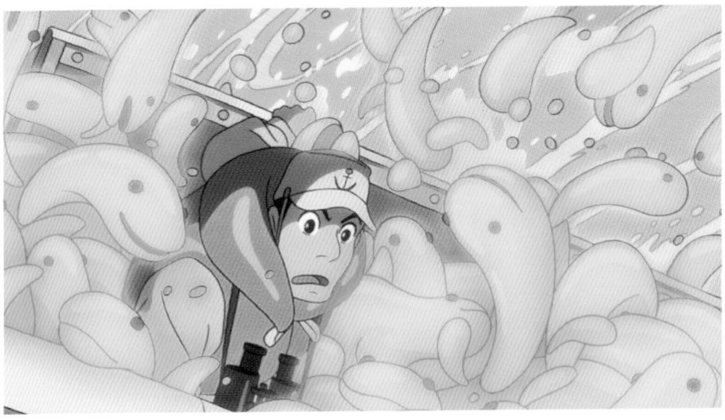

4

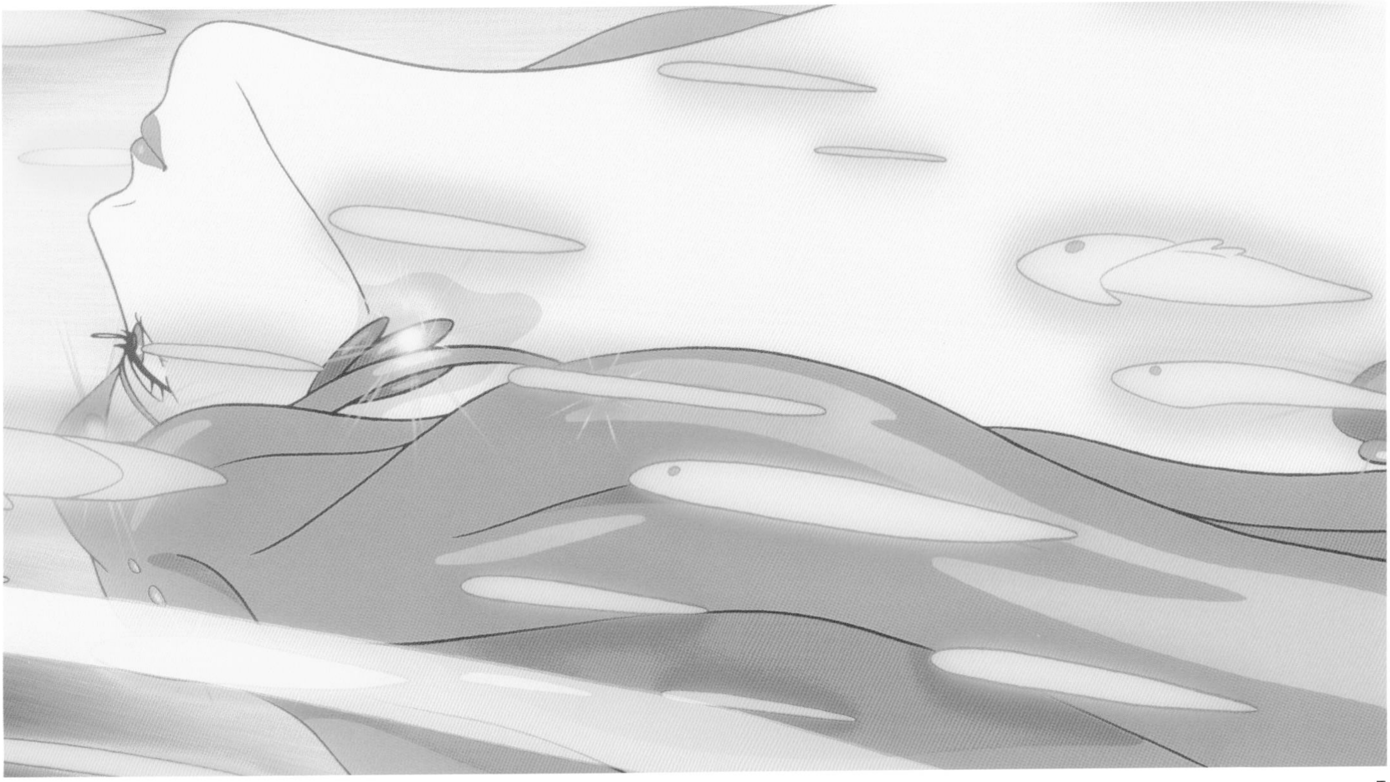

5

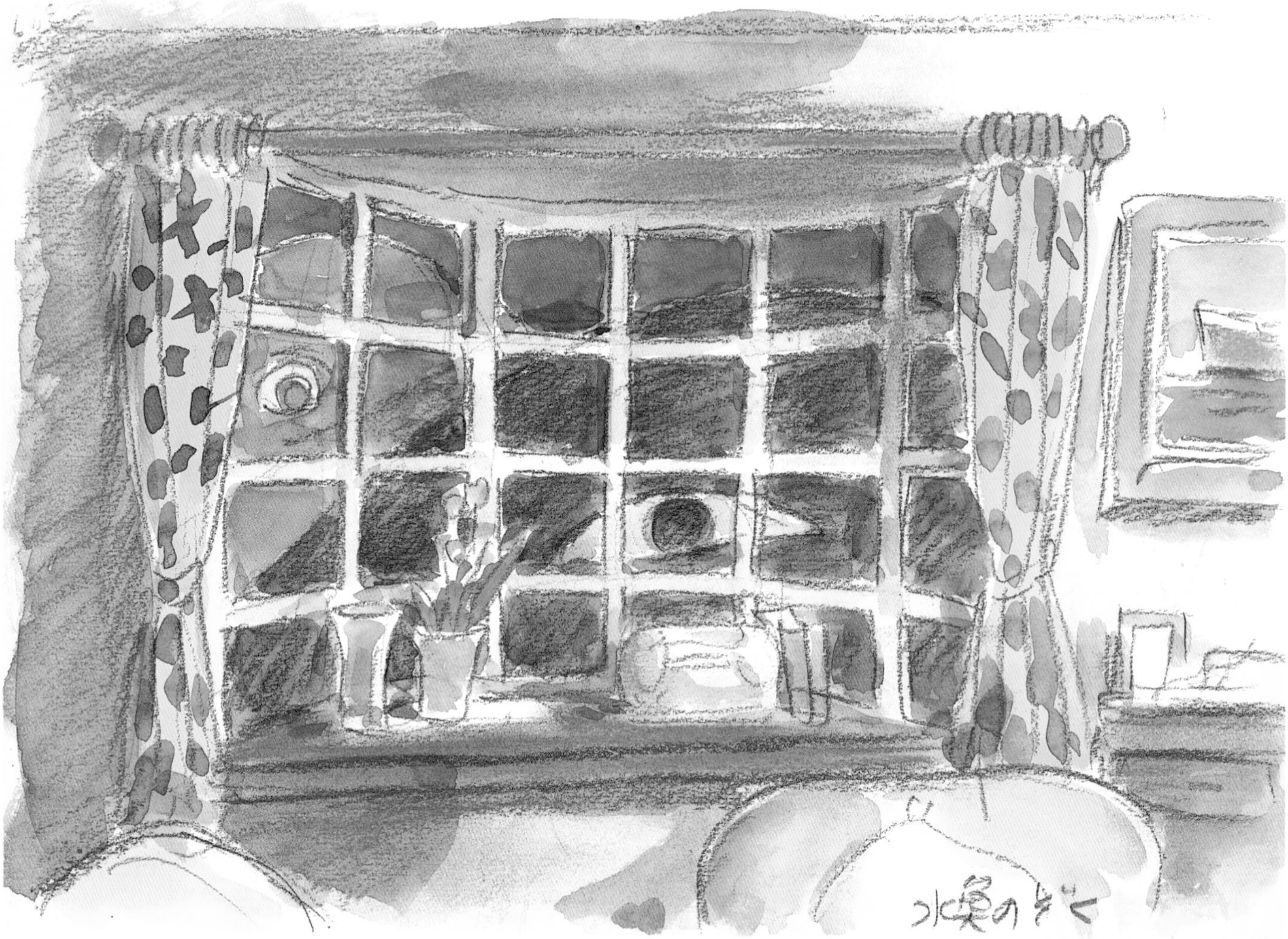

1

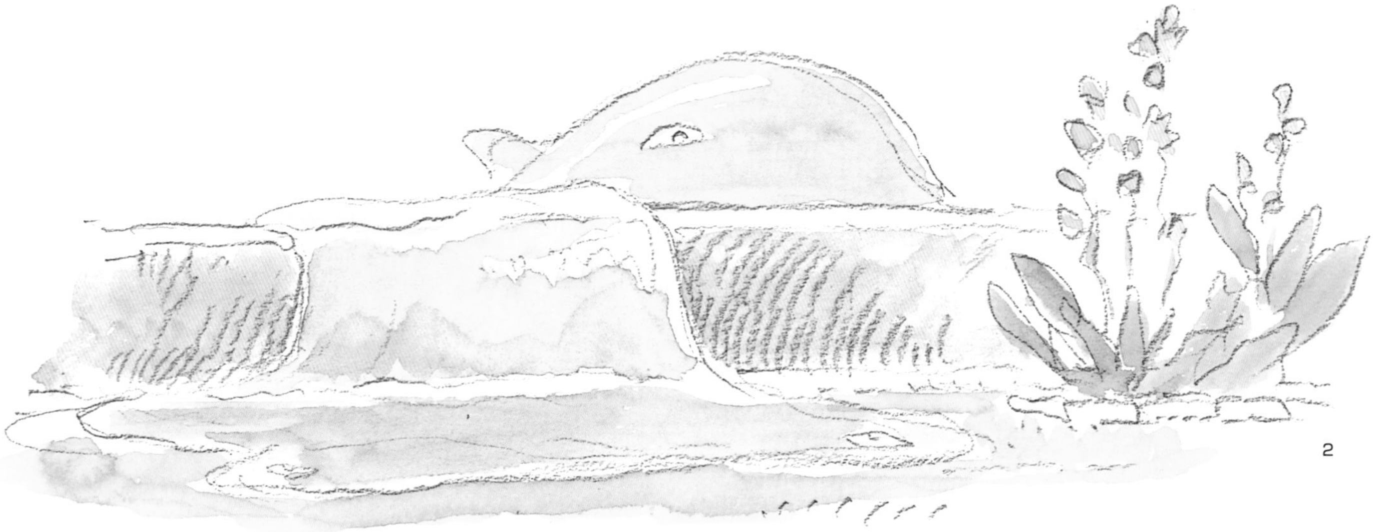

2

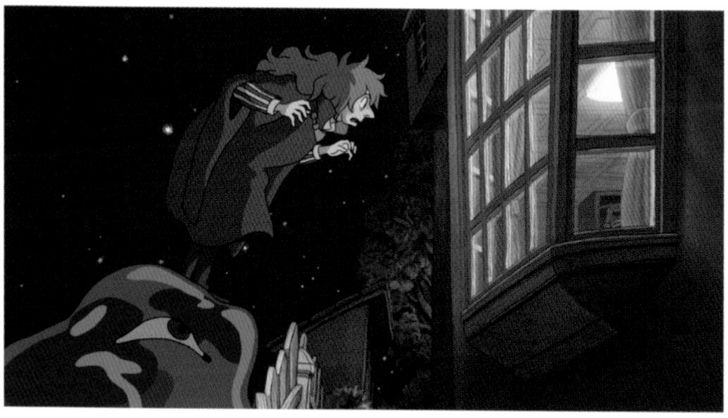

3

A Father's Shock

1, 2 /The minions coming to Sosuke's house in search of Ponyo [Concept sketches].
3 /Fujimoto, on a minion, coming to check on Ponyo. He is astonished not only by the barrier around the house but at the sight of Ponyo as a human.
4 /Katsuya Kondo's image of Gran Mamare [Rough character sketches].

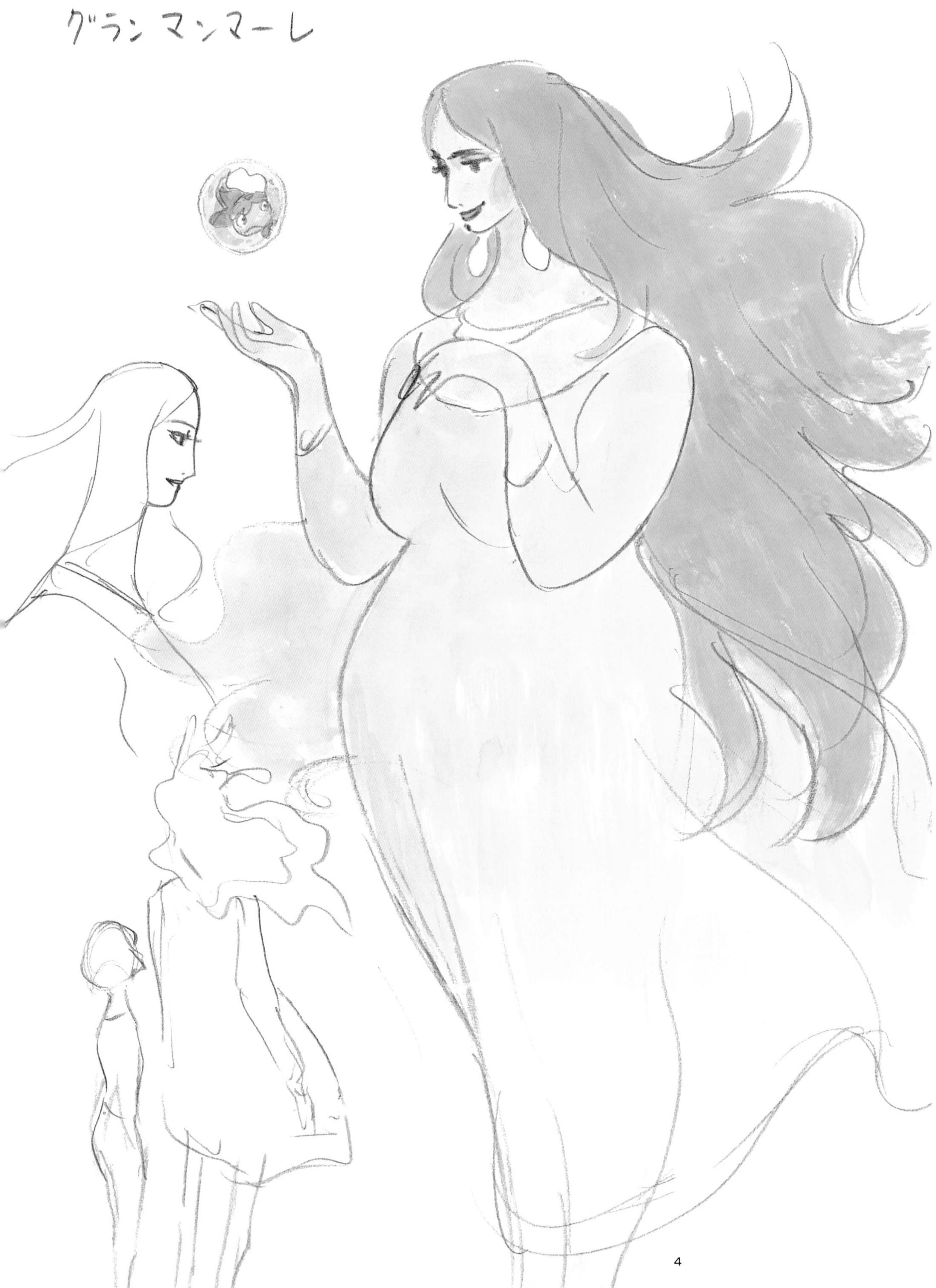
グラン マンマーレ
4

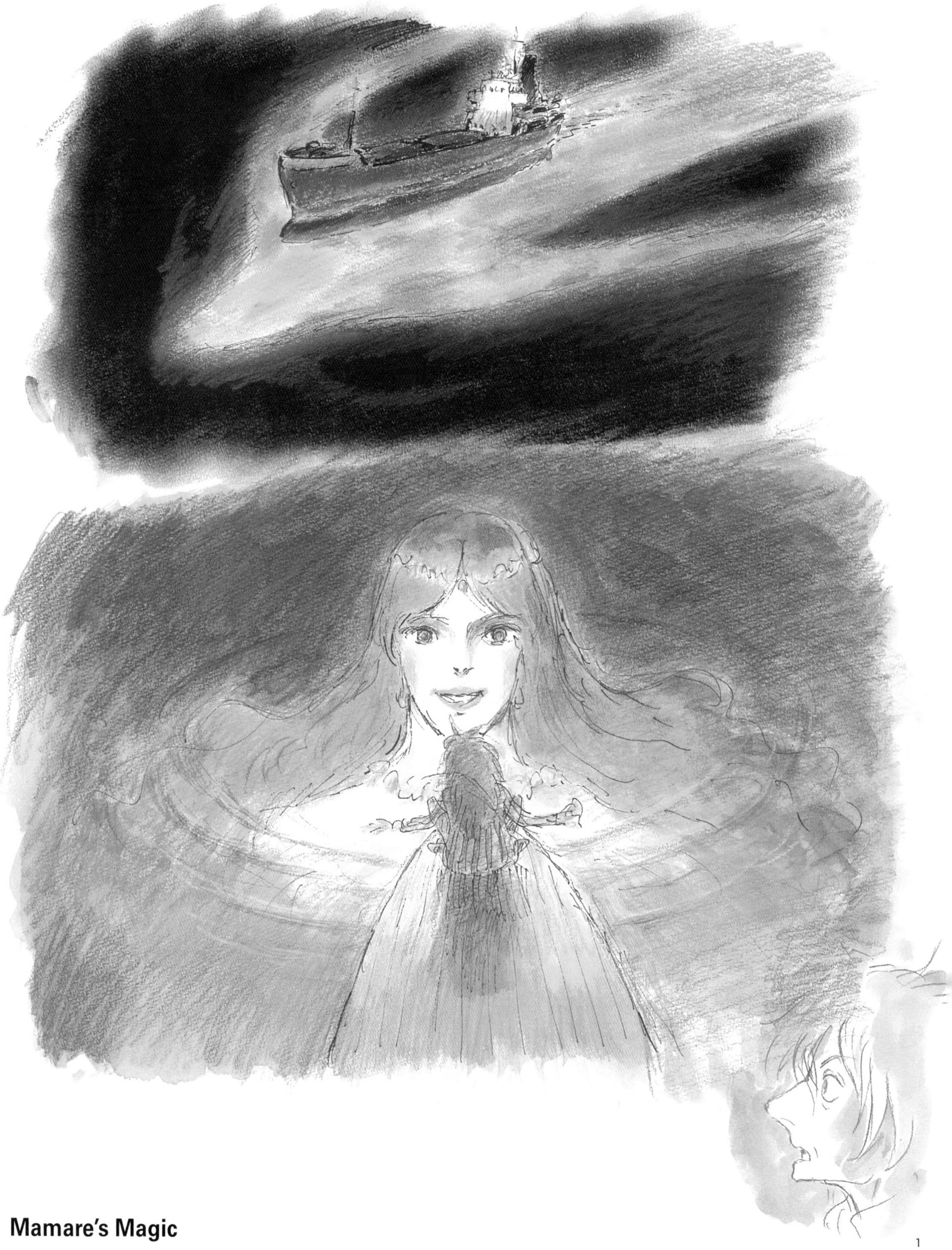

1

Mamare's Magic

1 /Gran Mamare passing beneath the drifting *Koganei Maru* and appearing before Fujimoto [Concept sketches].
2–8 /Fujimoto tells her that Ponyo's magic has torn a hole in the world threatening the planet with destruction. "Listen, my darling. Why don't we let Ponyo become human for good," Mamare answers, deciding to put Sosuke through a test.

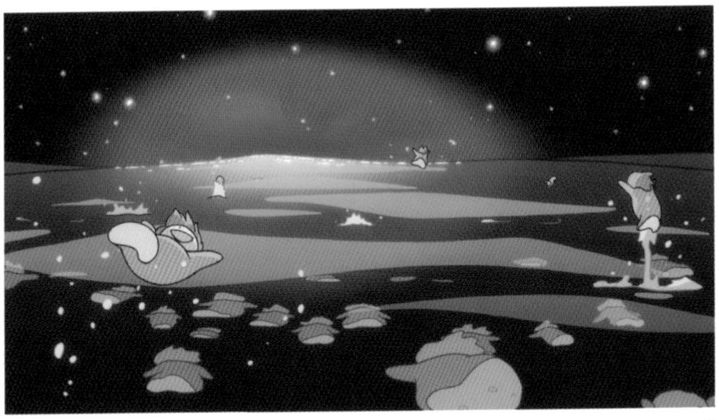
2

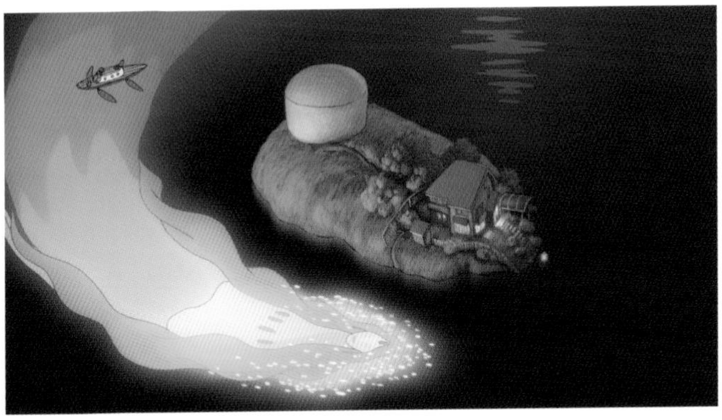
3

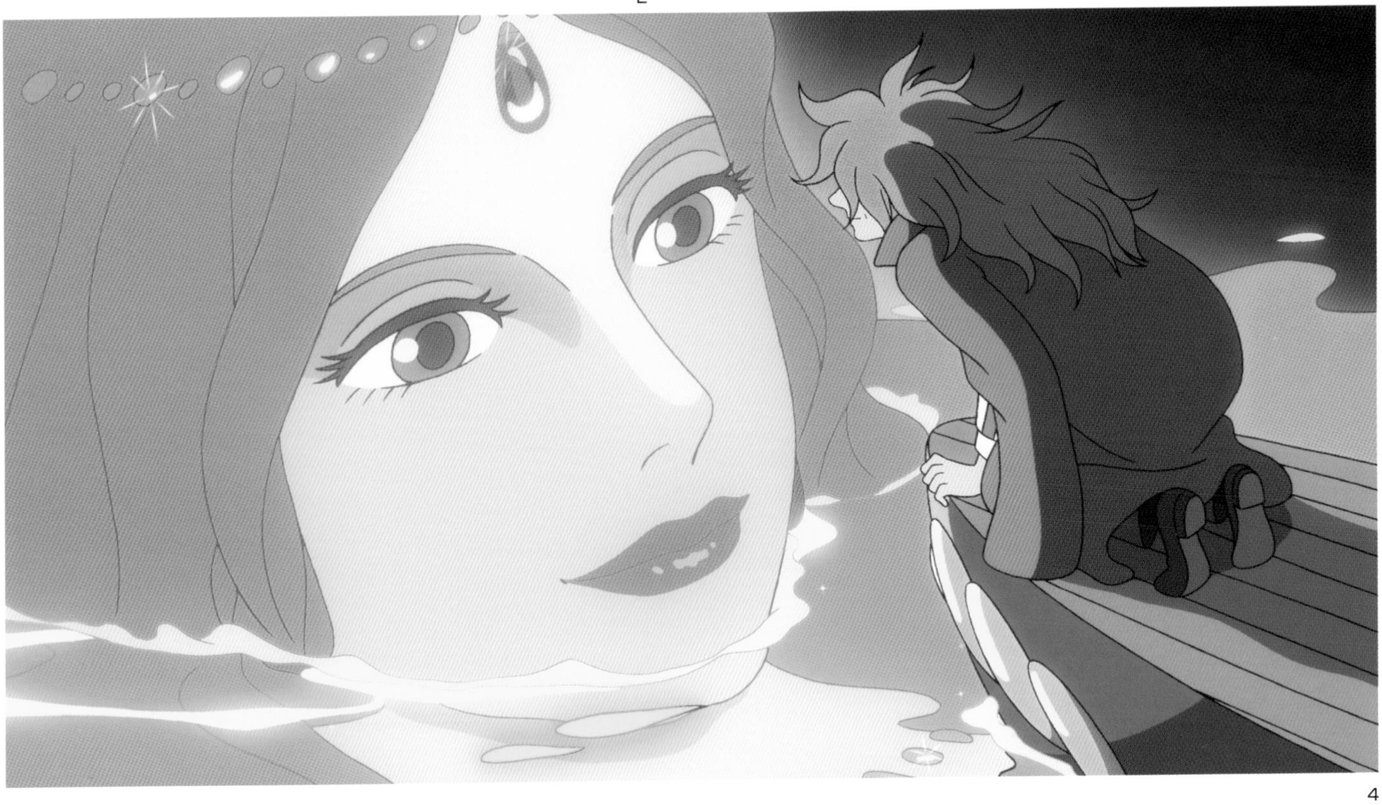
4

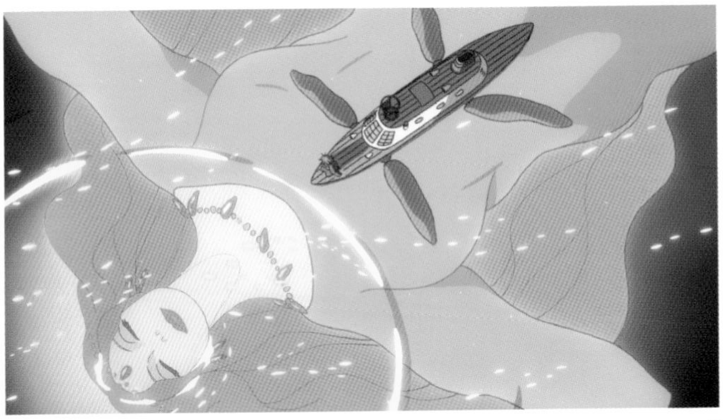
5

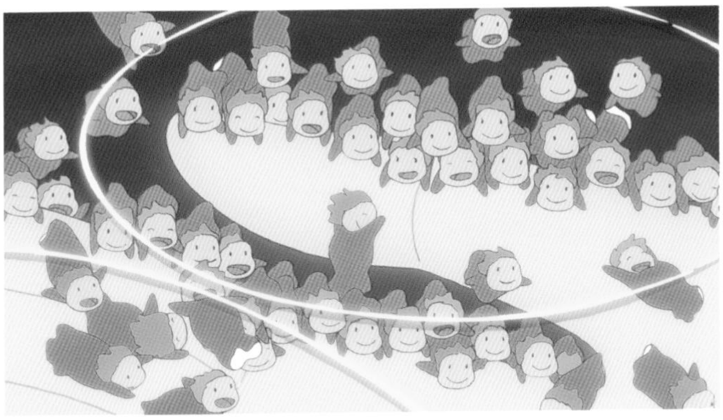
6

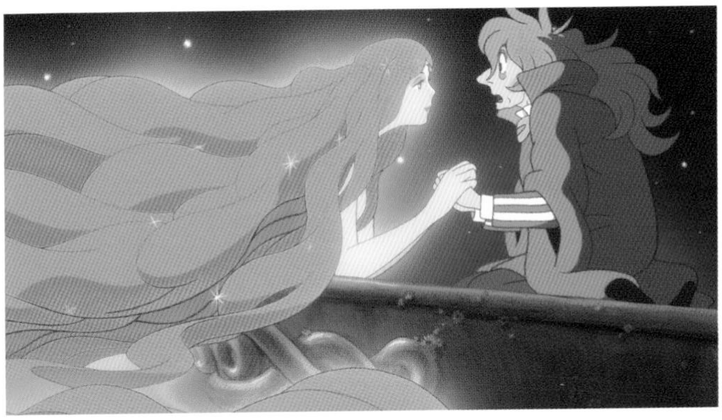
7

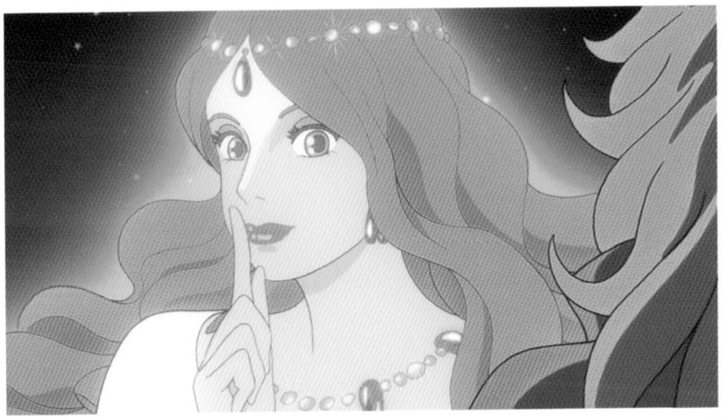
8

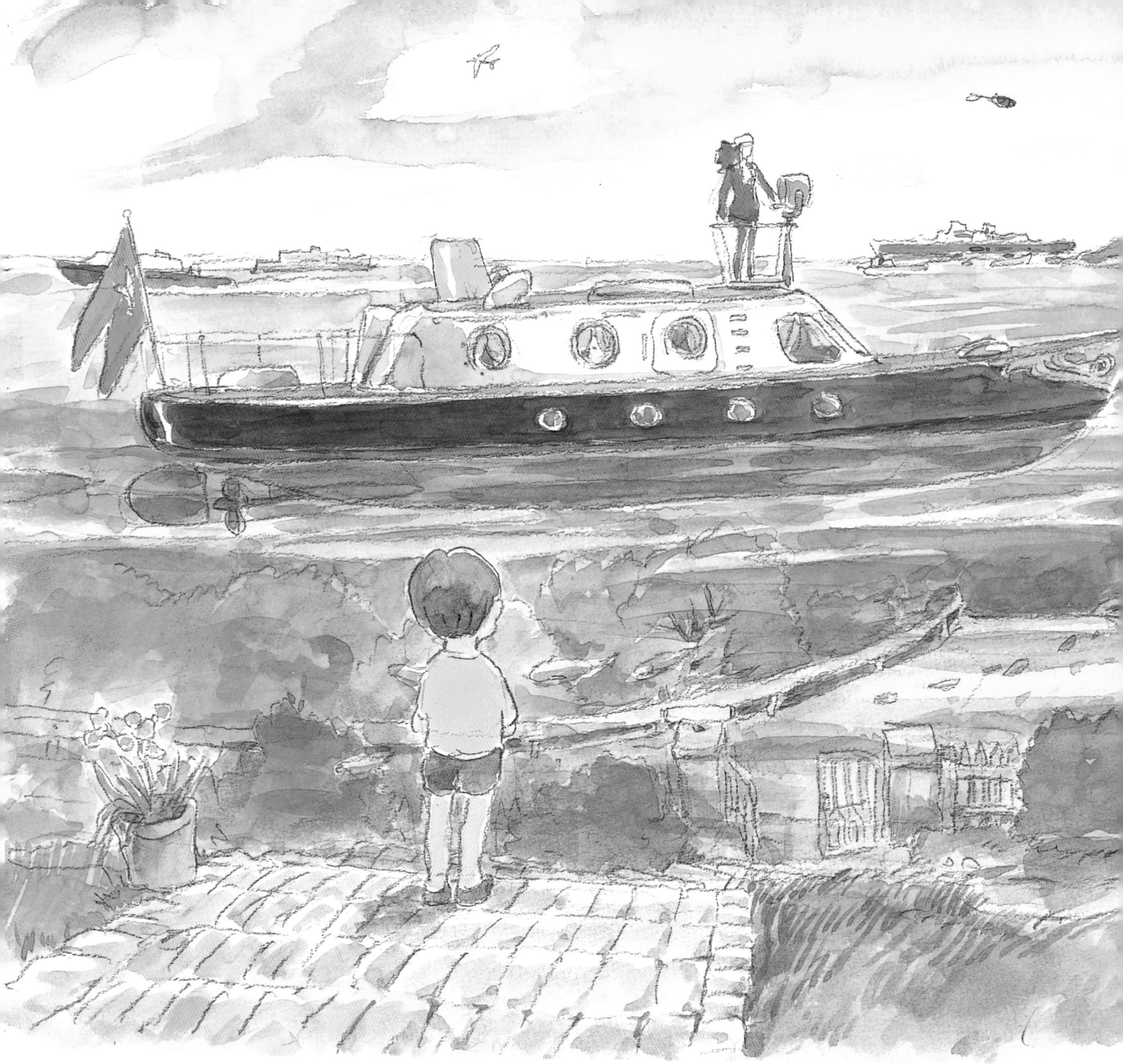

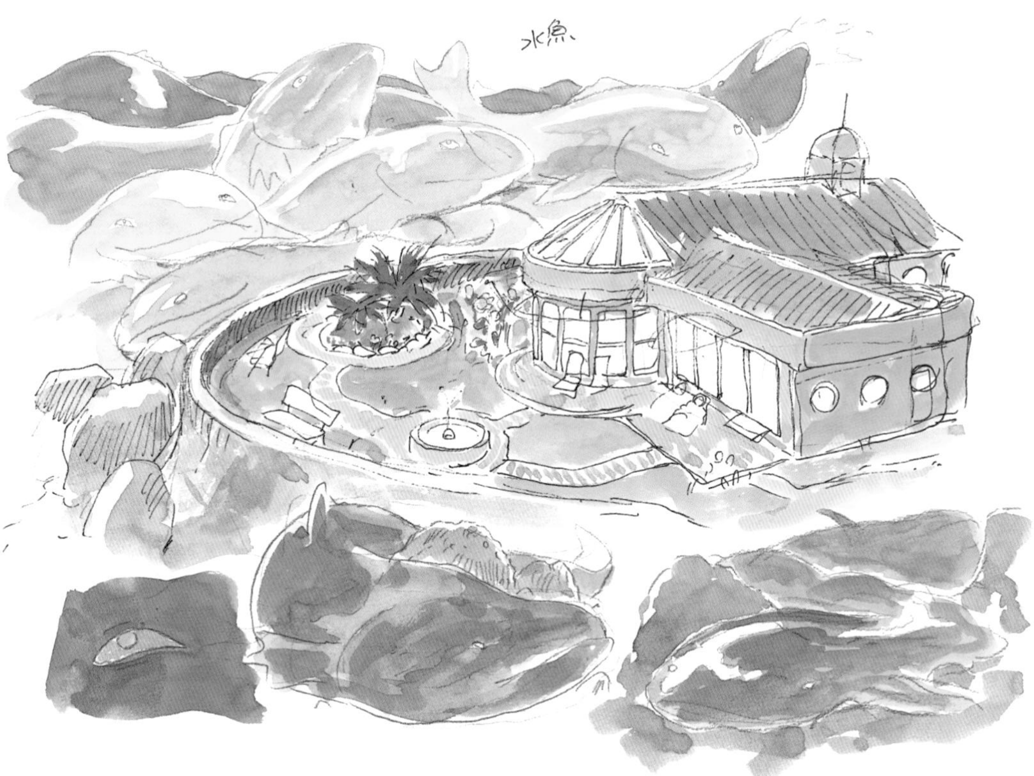
水魚

2

The Underwater Town

1 /Sosuke meets Fujimoto, who is visiting the flooded town, in a scene not in the film. Fujimoto's boat is also different from the *Basking Shark* in the film [Concept sketch].
2 /The Sunflower House surrounded by minions [Concept sketch].
3 /Prehistoric fish swimming in the floodwaters as if they have reclaimed the world [Concept sketch].
4 /Sosuke and Fujimoto [Concept sketches].

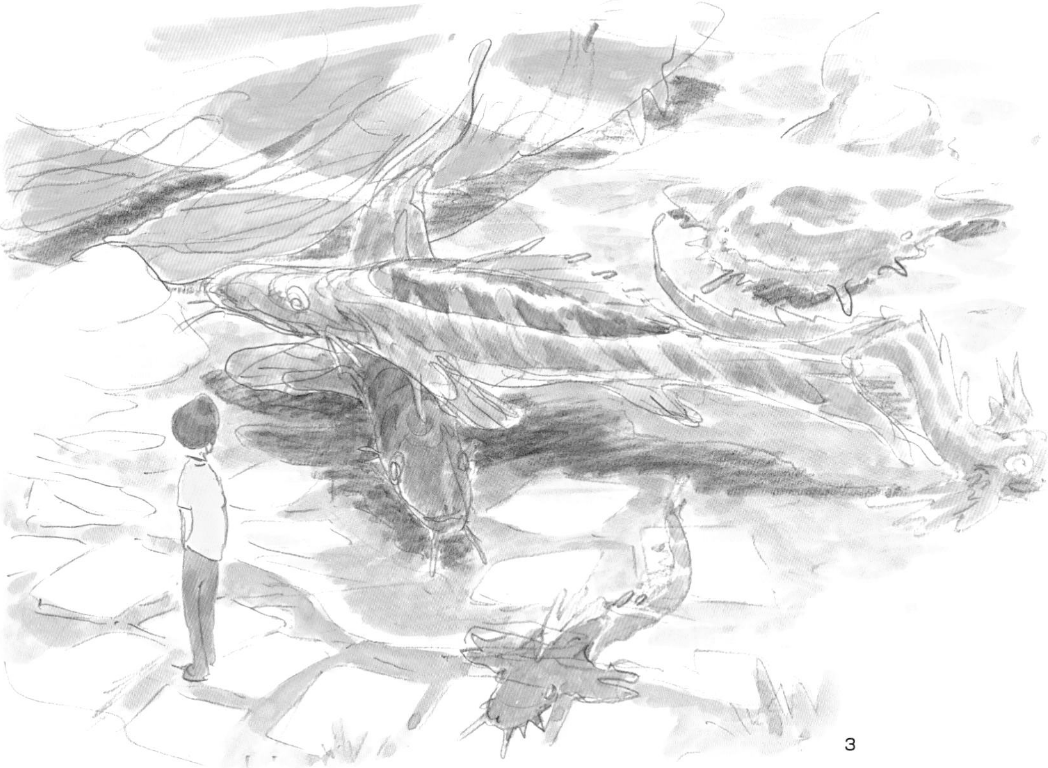

3

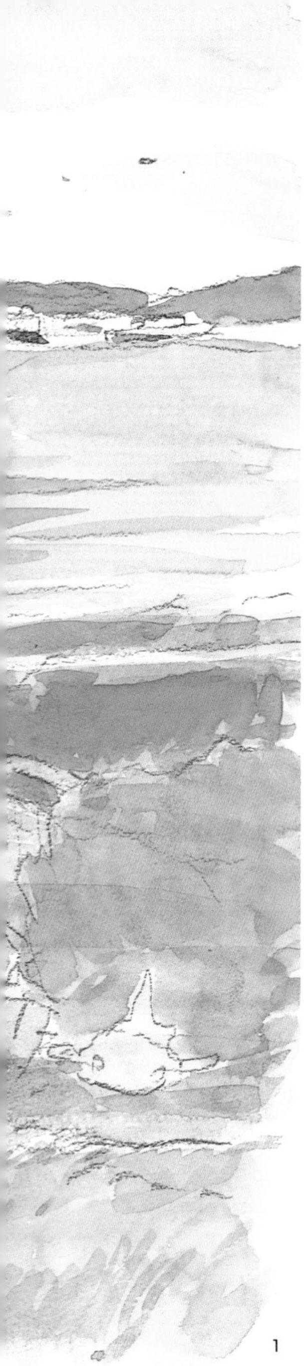

1

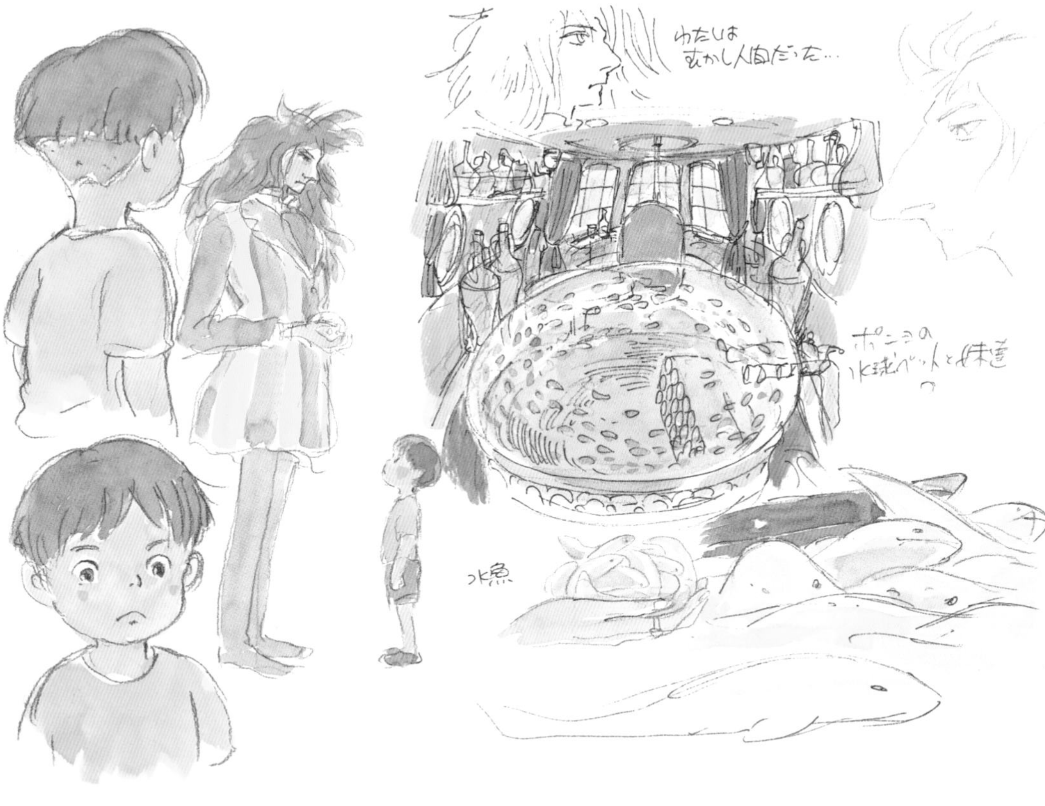
わたしは むかし人間だった…

4

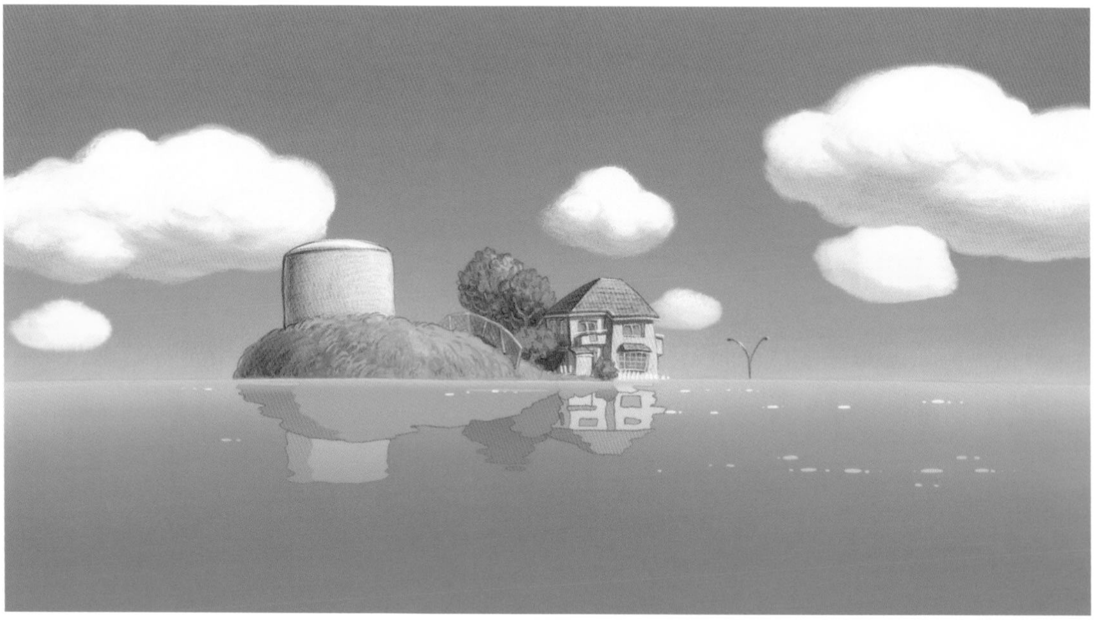

1

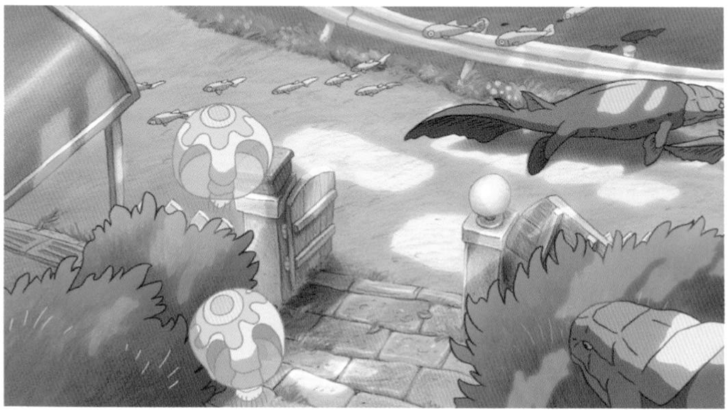

3

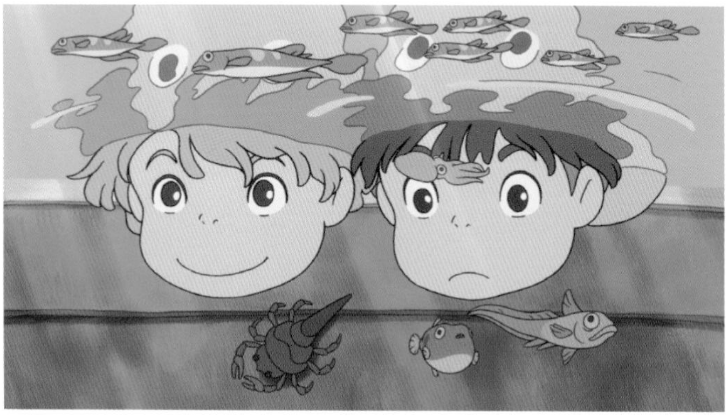

2

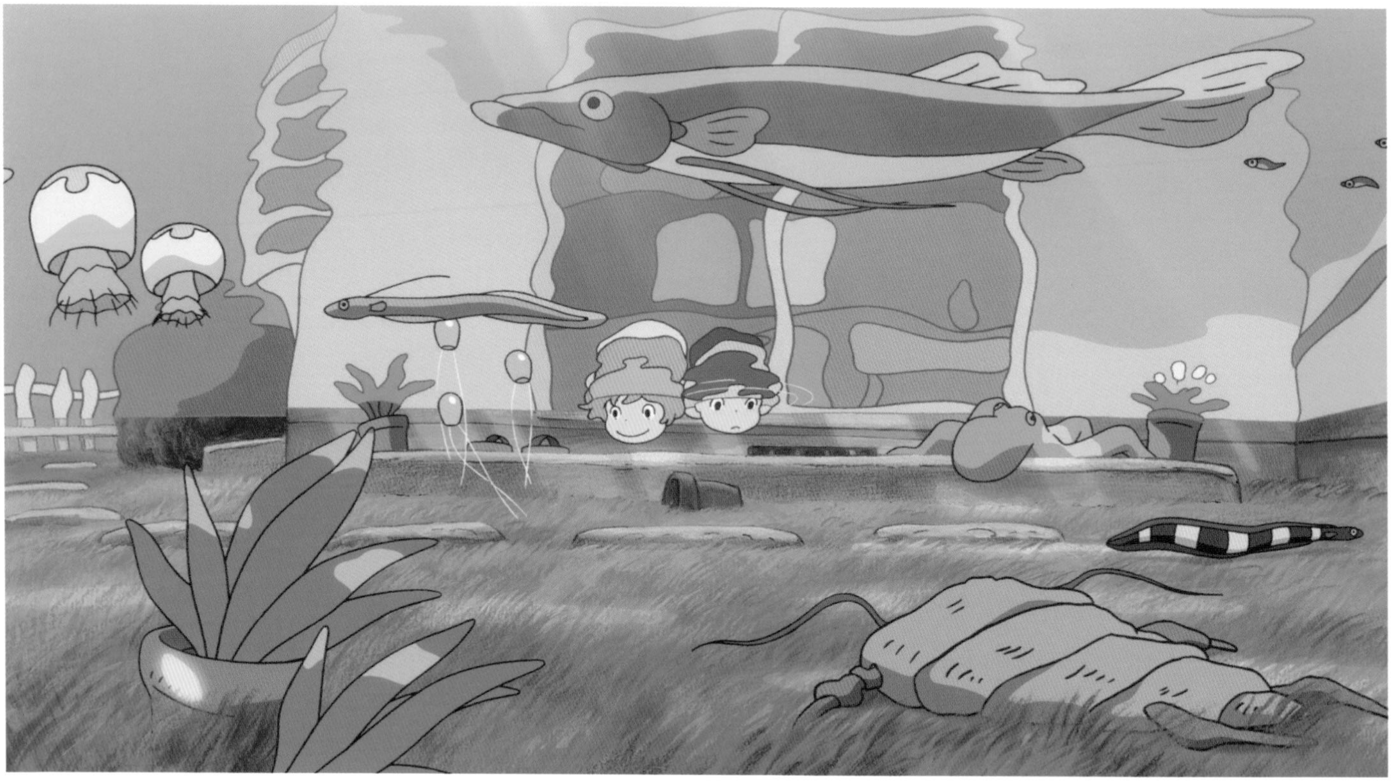

4

1 /Sosuke's house welcomes a new day after the storm. The promontory, almost completely submerged, is now an island.
2–4 /Sosuke and Ponyo admiring the prehistoric fish and various sea creatures swimming around the yard.
5–9 /Ponyo magically enlarges the toy steamboat for Sosuke, who wants to look for Lisa.
10 /Ponyo and Sosuke carrying the steamboat outside.

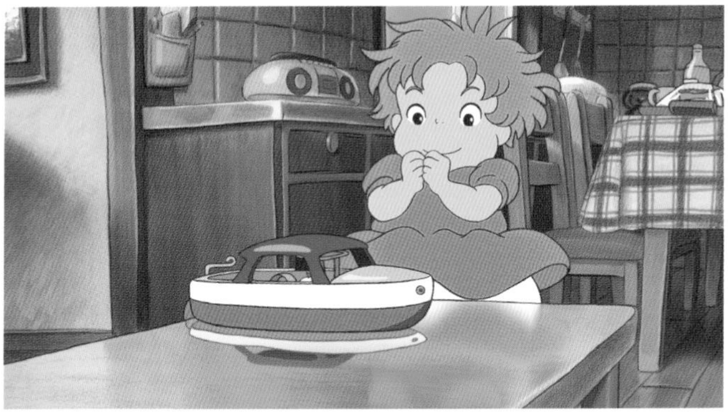

5

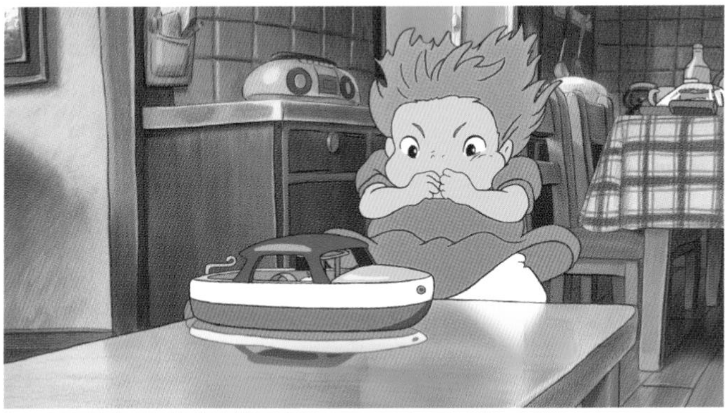

6

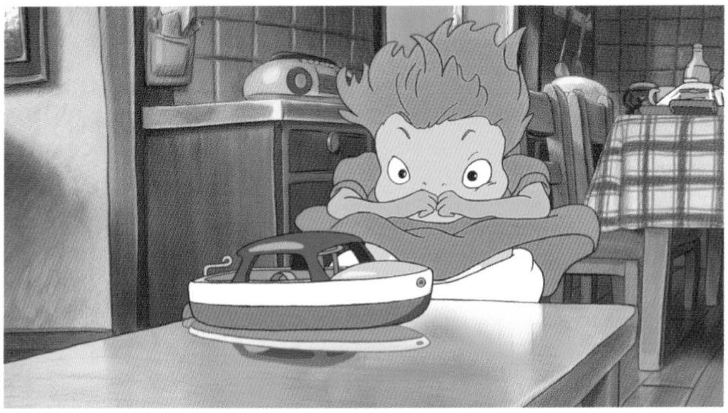

7

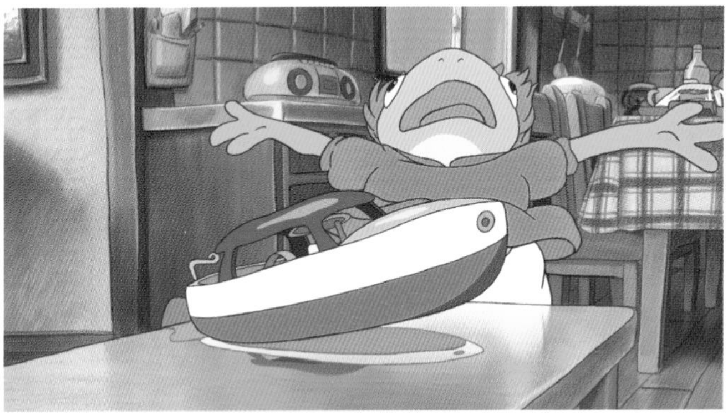

8

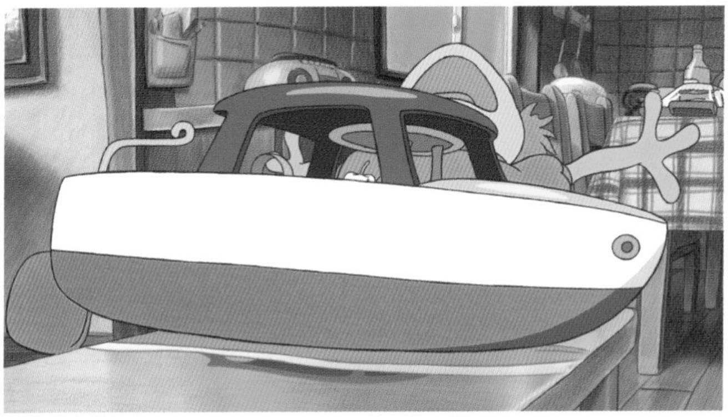

9

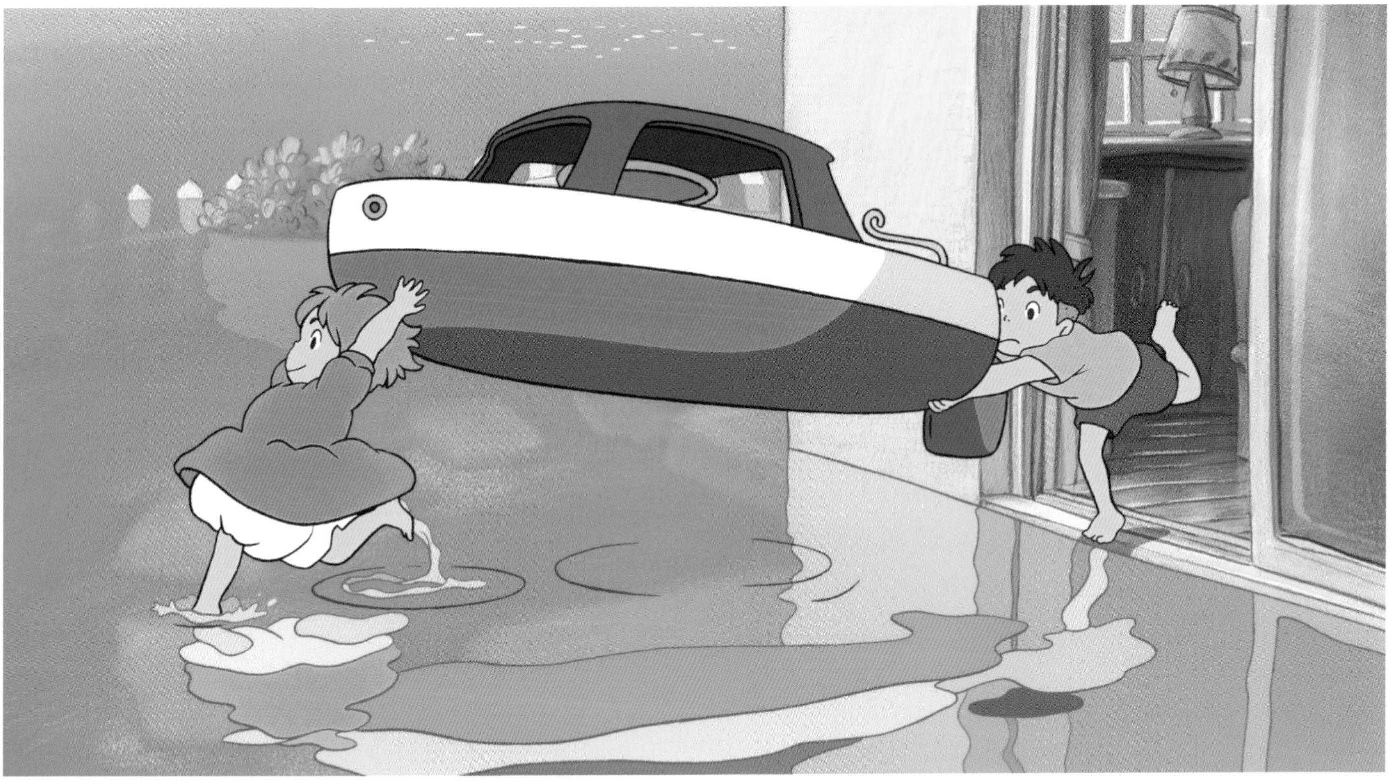

10

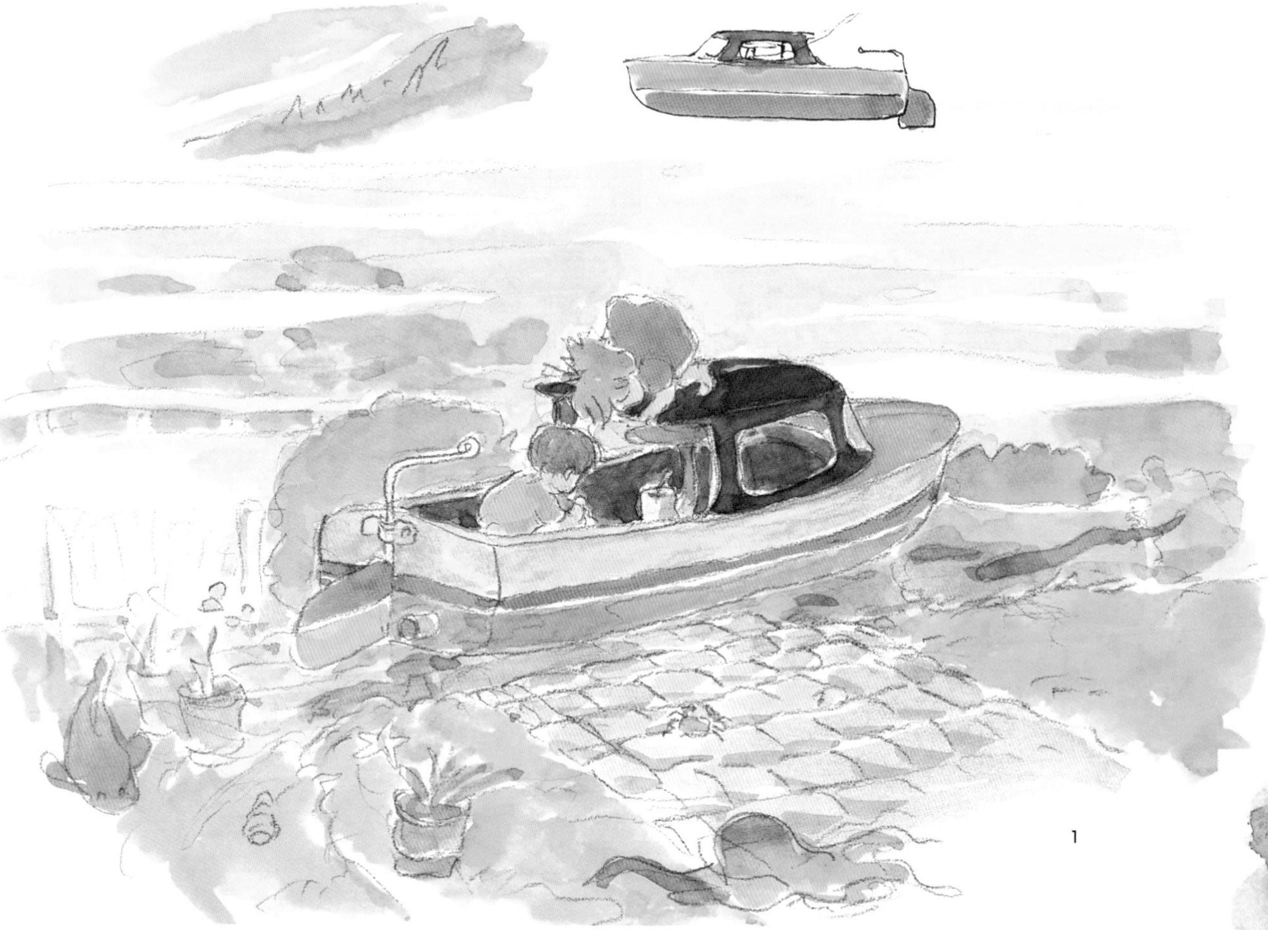

1

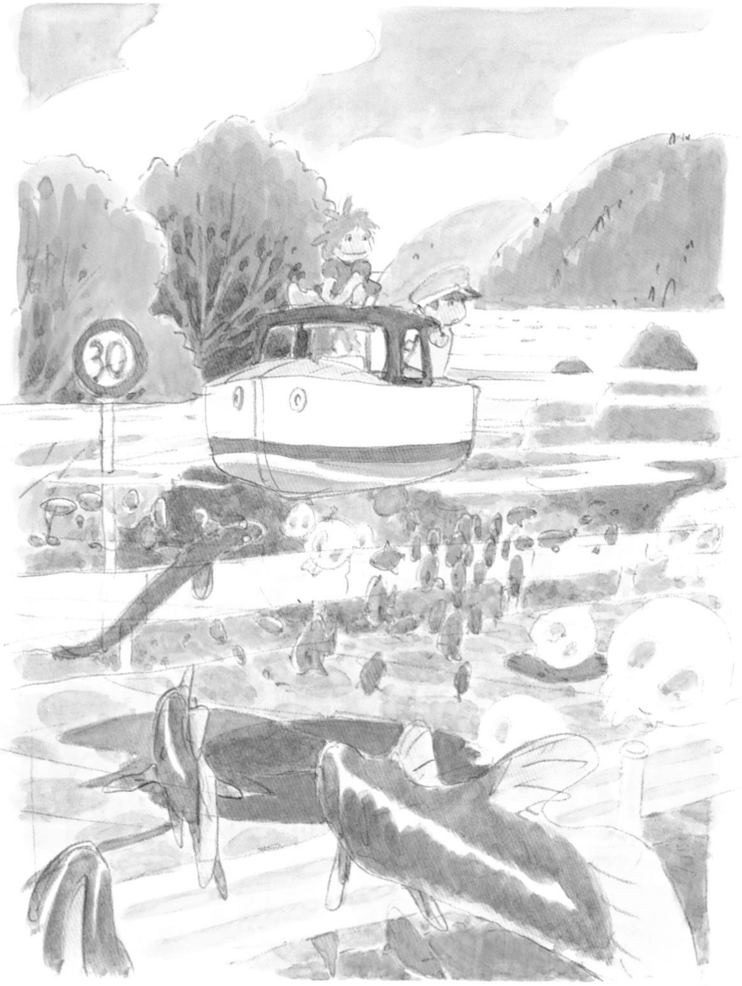
30

2

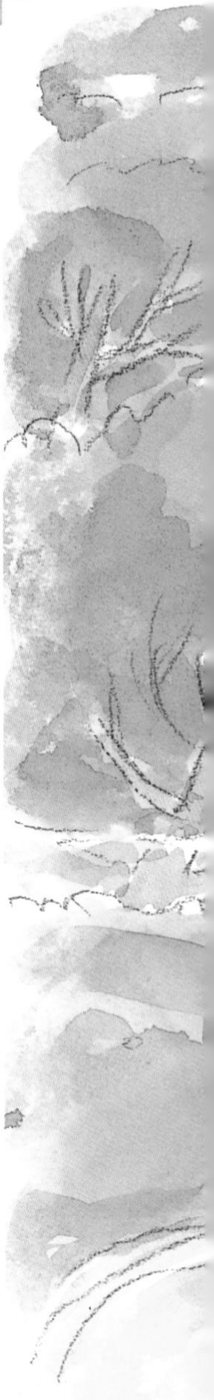

Aboard the Steamboat

1 /Sosuke and Ponyo getting the steamboat ready for launch [Concept sketch].
2 /The steamboat puts out to sea—a heaven unconstrained by time, teeming with fish, and full of vitality [Concept sketch].
3 /A sketch of Sosuke wearing a captain's hat [Concept sketch].
4 /In search of Lisa—full steam ahead! [Concept sketch]

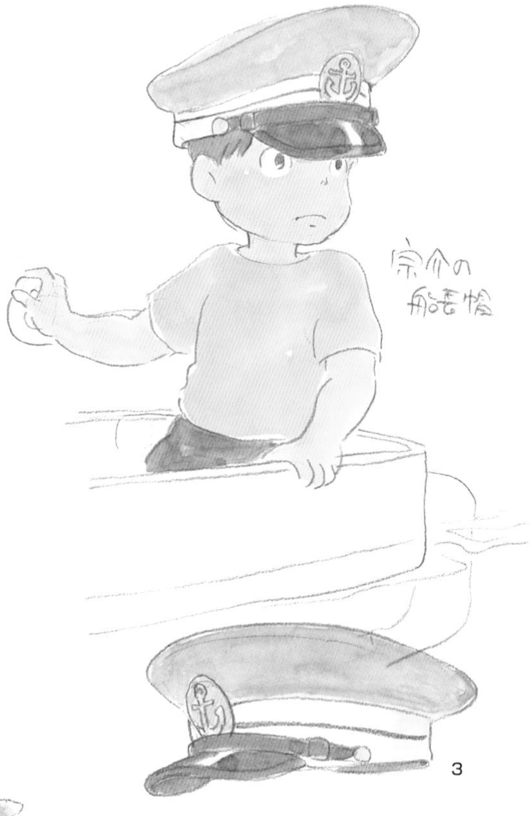
宗介の
船長帽

3

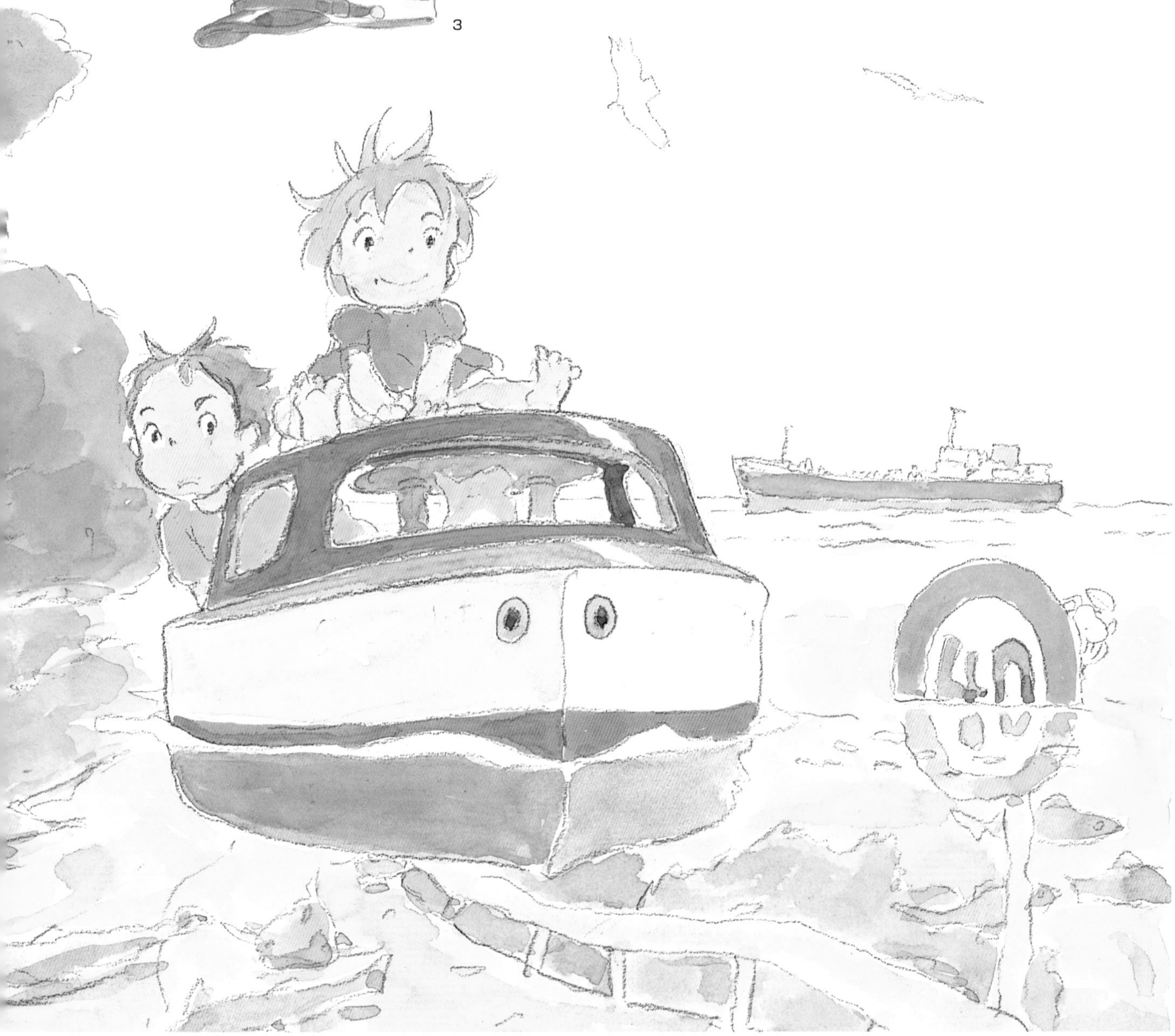

4

1, 2 /The road that Lisa's car raced down is now underwater [Concept sketches].
3 /A panorama of the submerged town [Concept sketch].

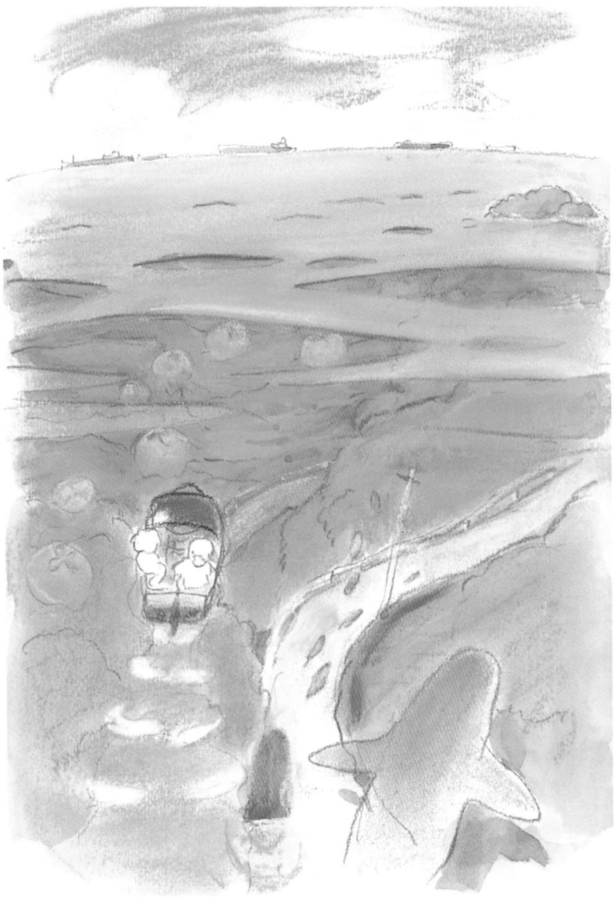

1

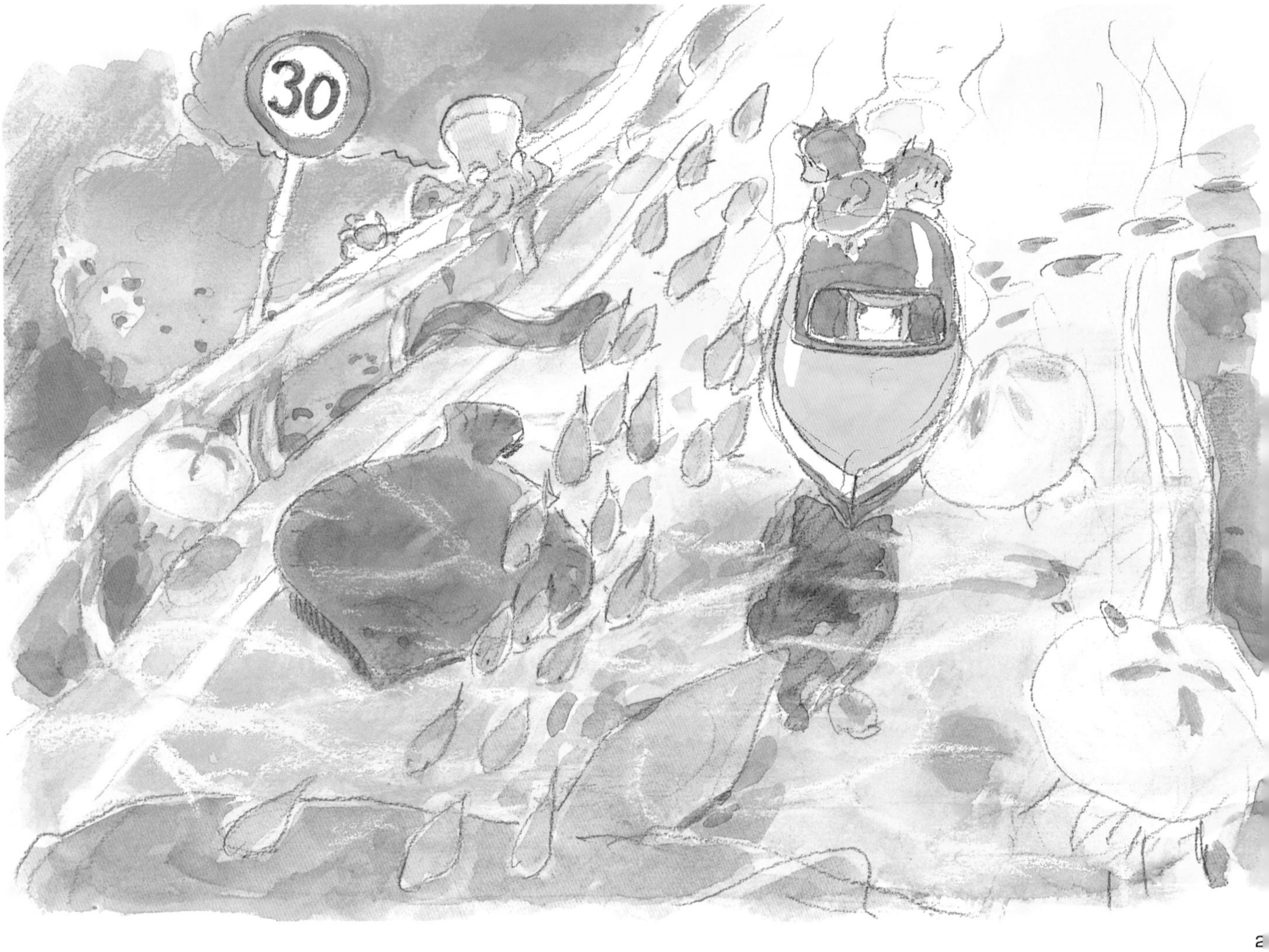
30

2

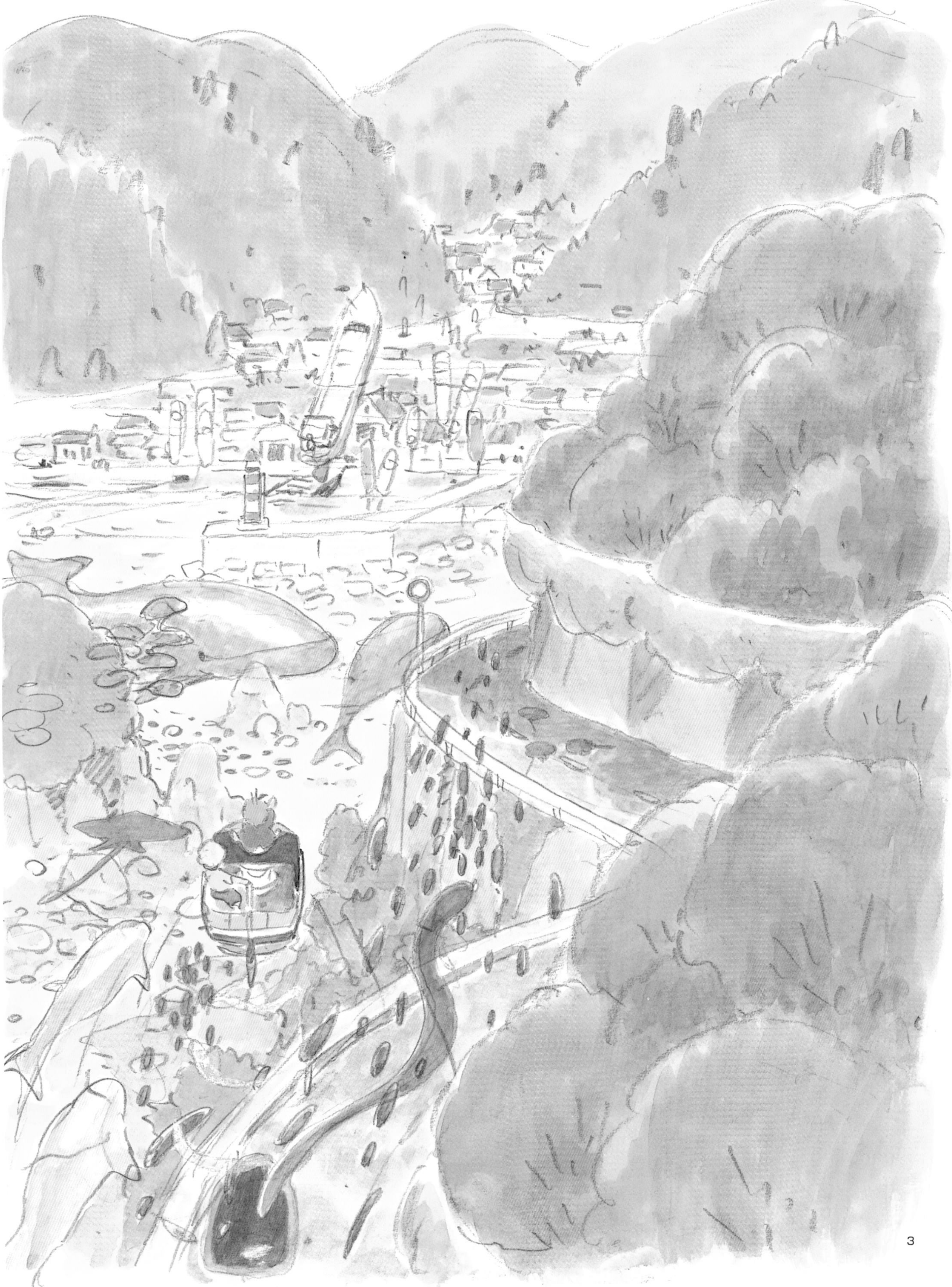

3

1 /Sosuke packs snacks and sandwiches prepared by Lisa.
2 /With his binoculars and captain's hat, Sosuke is ready to go.
3–5 /The steamboat moves out once the candle is lit and the boiler is warmed up.
6 /Sosuke gently tells Ponyo, who cannot contain her joy, "Ponyo, you be the boat's lookout. And I'll do the steering. Okay?"
7, 8 /Schools of Bothriolepis and Dipnorhynchus, and a giant Devonychus—fish of the Devonian period—swim past them.
9 /The steamboat speeding ahead after Sosuke quickly gets the hang of the rudder.

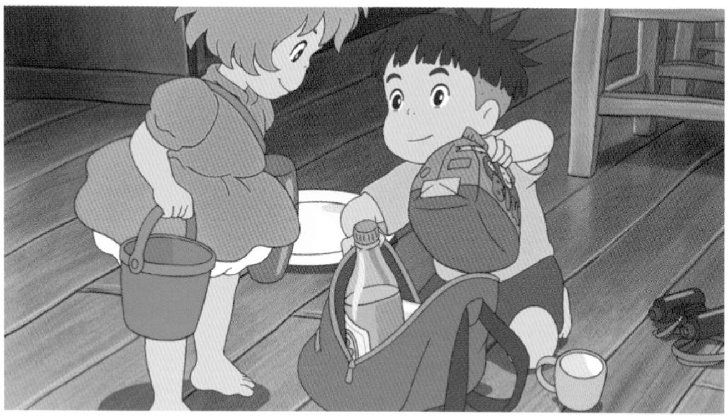
1

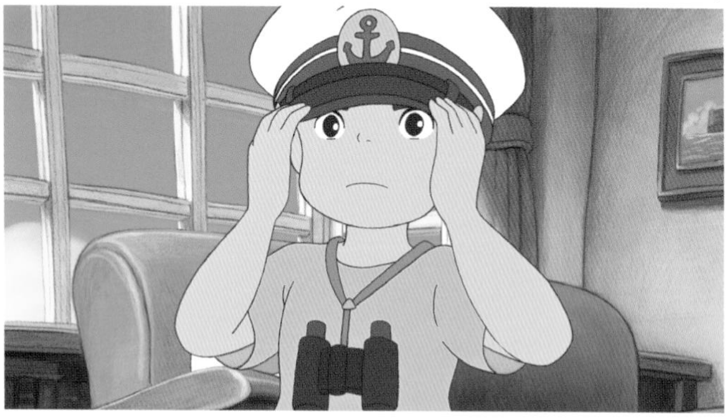
2

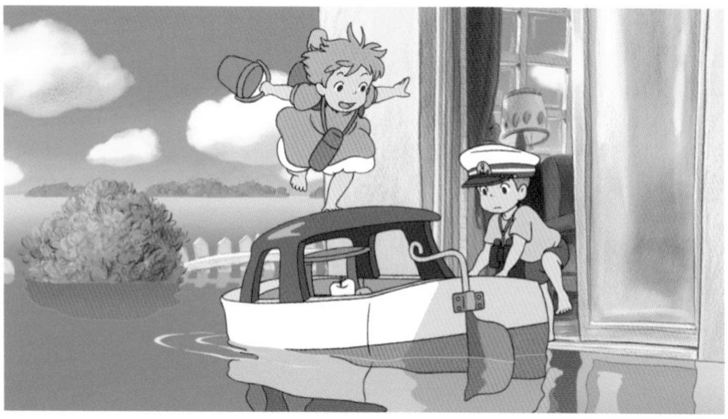
3

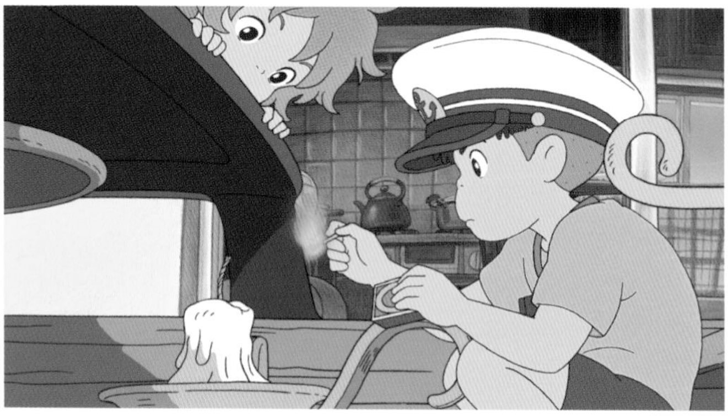
4

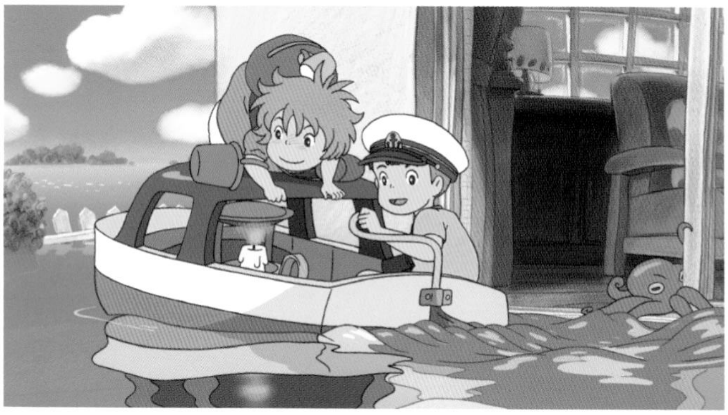
5

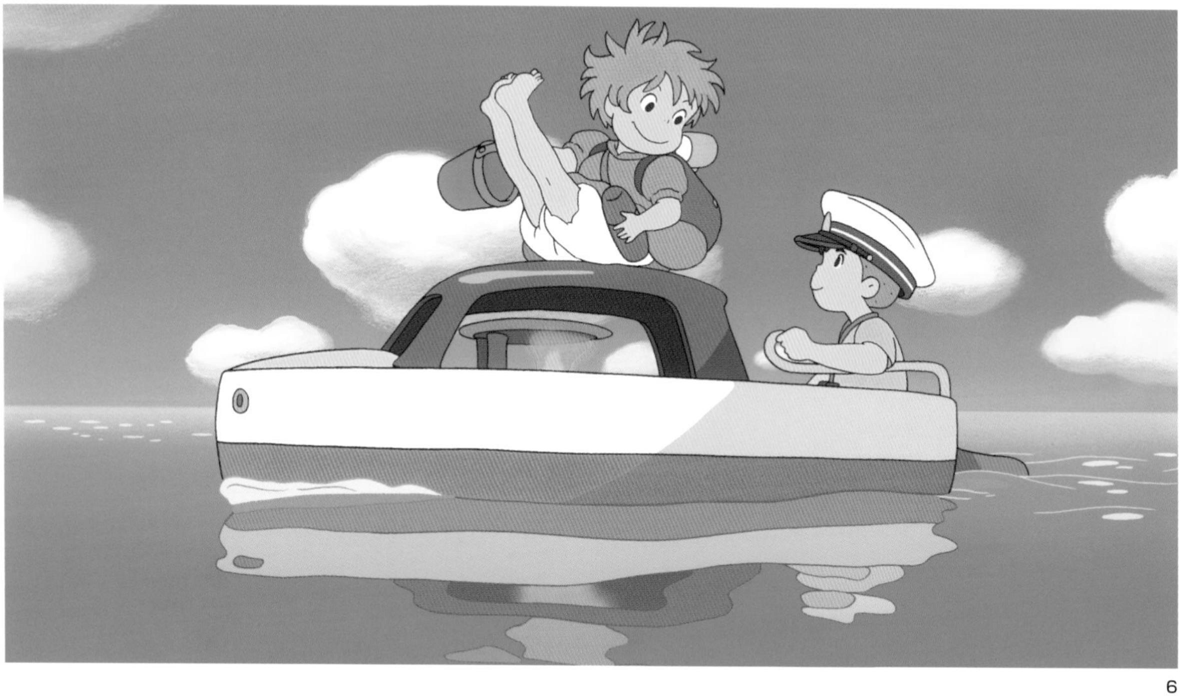
6

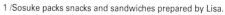

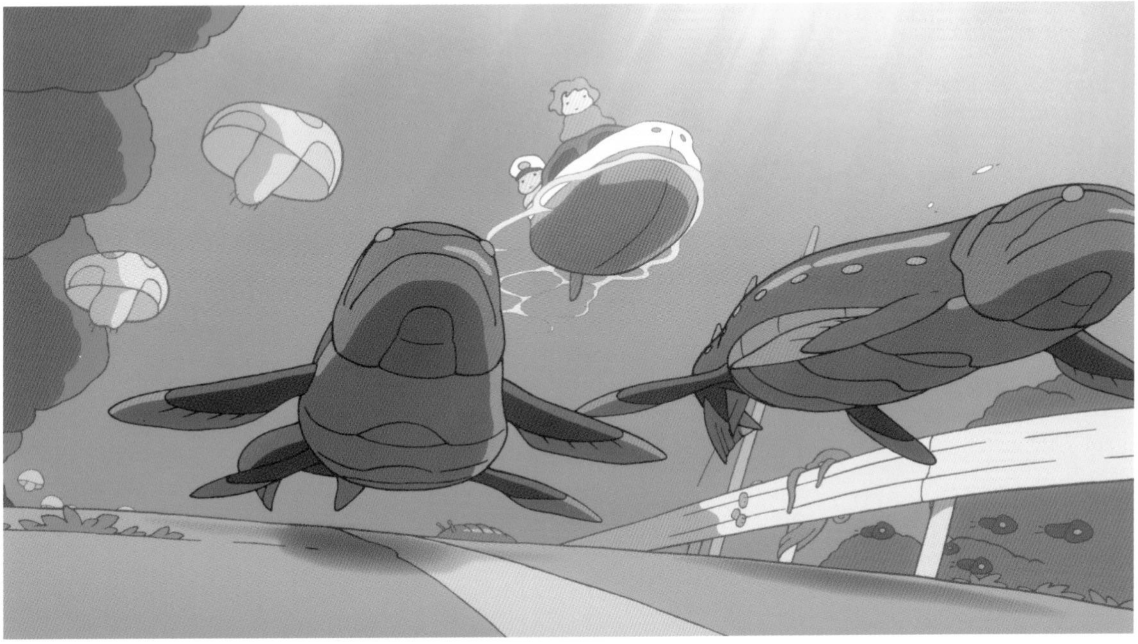

7

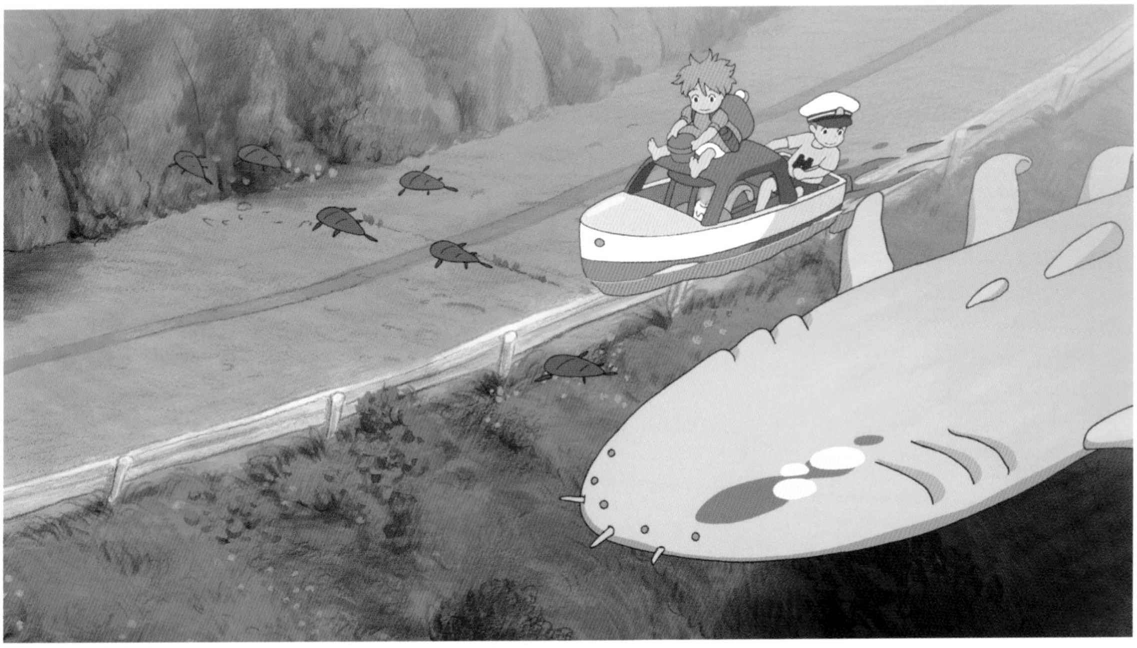

8

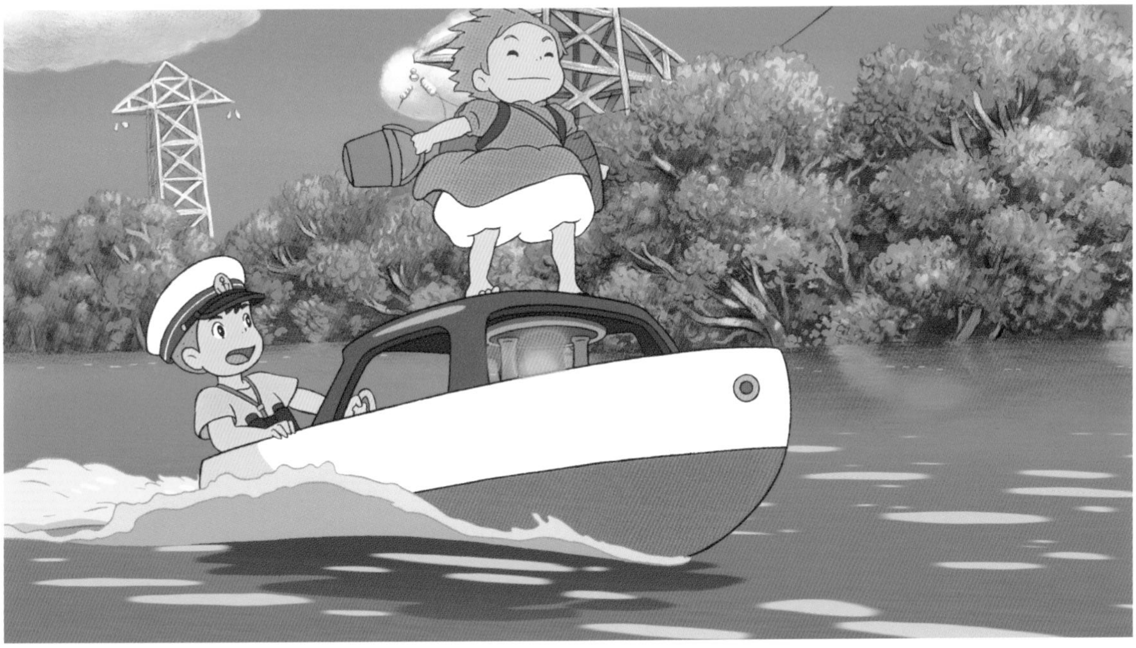

9

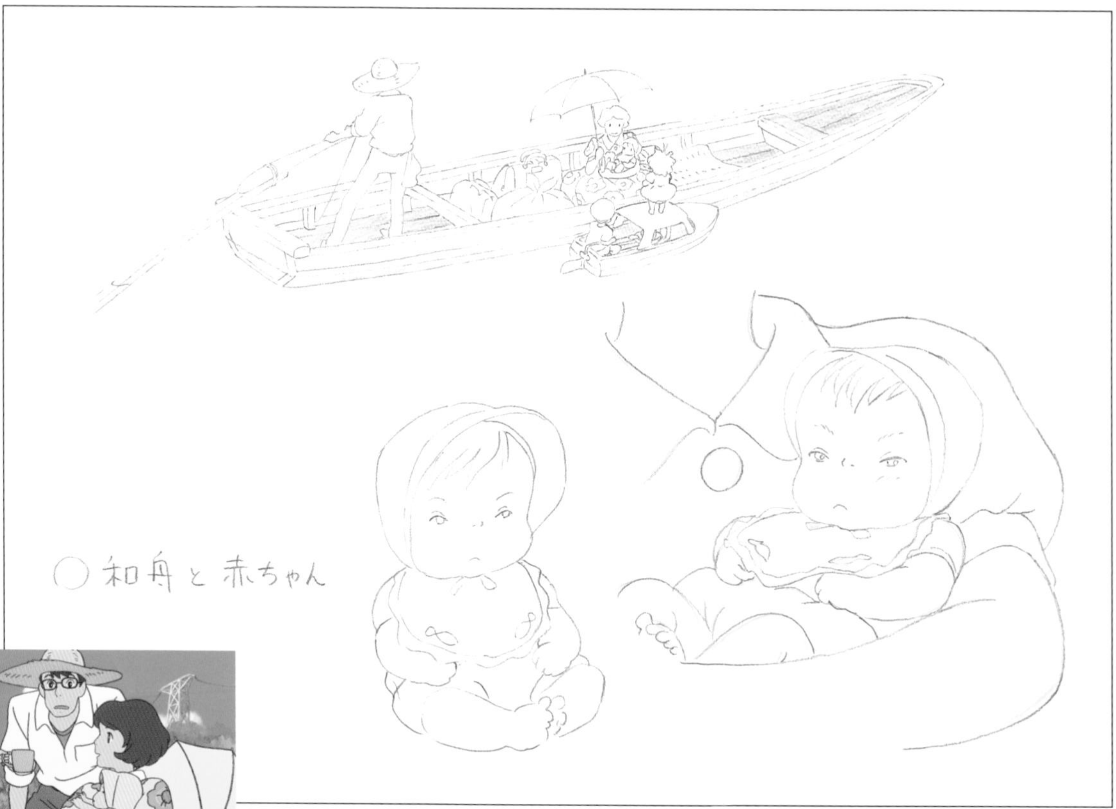
○和舟と赤ちゃん

1

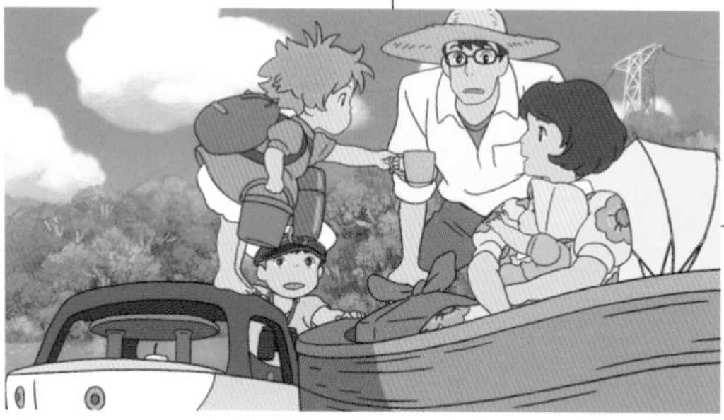

2

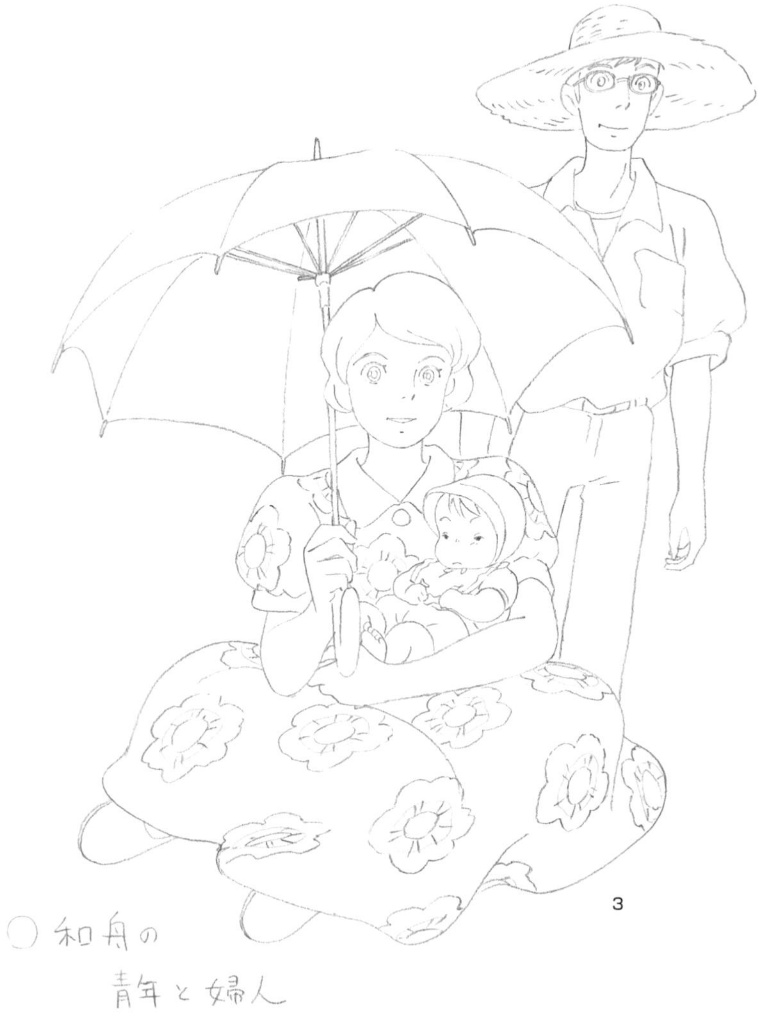
○和舟の
青年と婦人

3

For the part where Sosuke and Ponyo set out on the steamboat, Miyazaki added small details to the animation while looking at the backgrounds. He also wanted new backgrounds that the animation required. It was a scene that cleared one of the challenges of this film, which was to harmonize the cel animation with the backgrounds. We assembled each shot in terms of what would be depicted as background and what would be depicted as cel animation as we went along. We were also deliberate about showing the underwater landscape and switching from the background of the yard to one entirely of the water the moment Sosuke and Ponyo put out to sea. I was pleased with how this entire sequence turned out.

Also, the water is that luminescent color of bath powder familiar to kids, as the sea is a world enveloped by Ponyo's magic. And the forest they enter is generally of a darker color, as it is affected by Gran Mamare's spell to put Sosuke through a test.

—Art Director: Noboru Yoshida

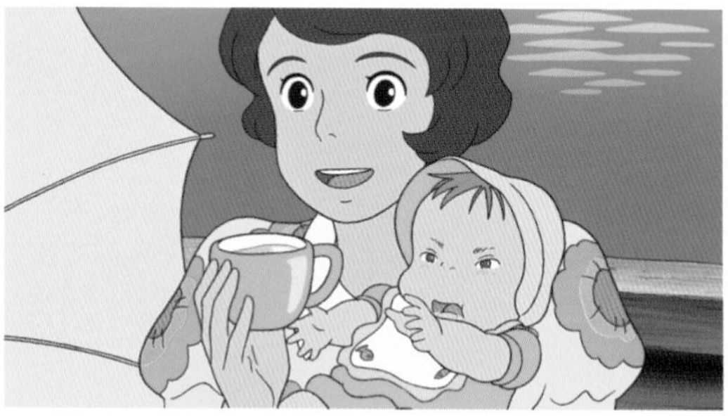

4

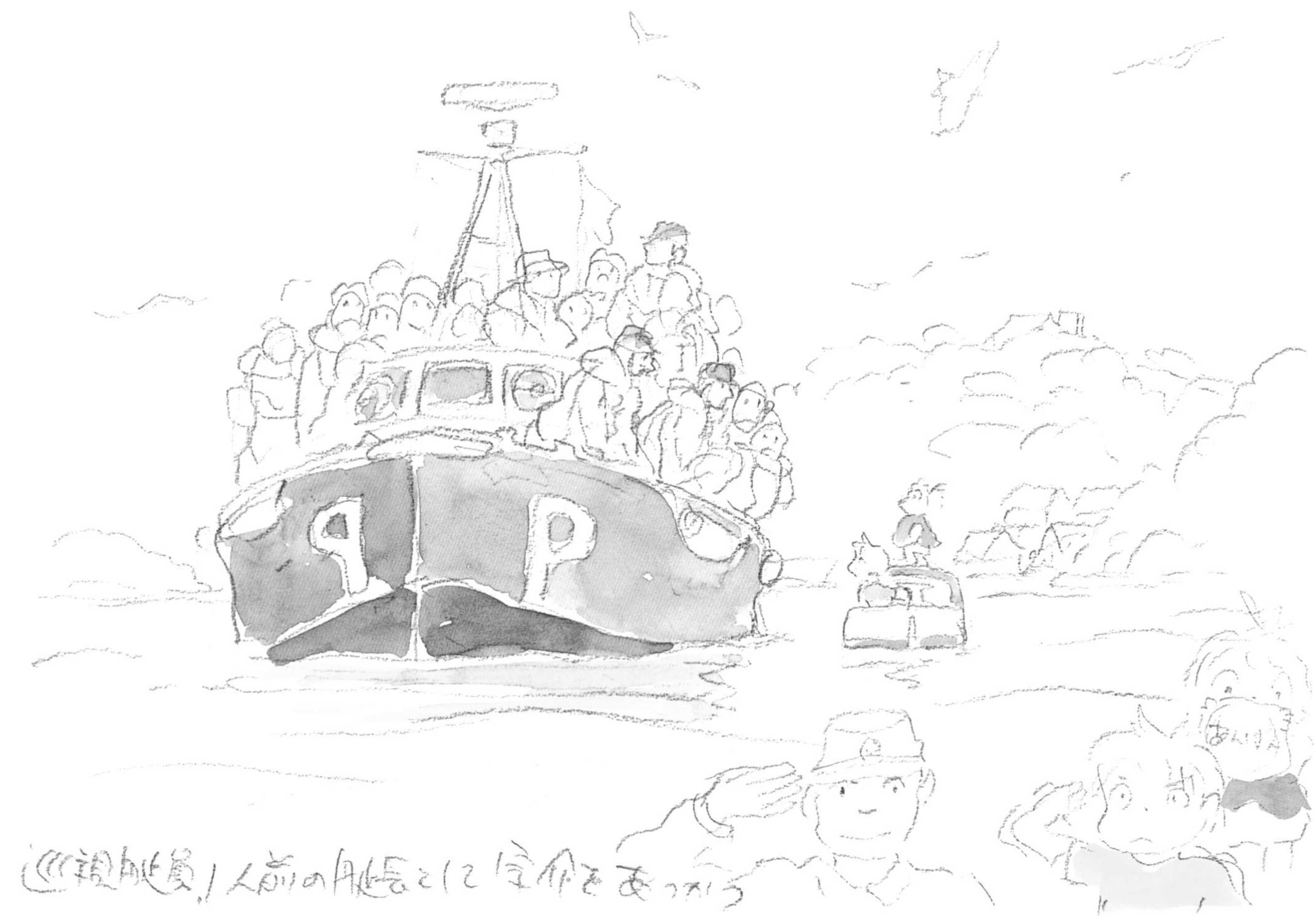
巡視艇員, 1人前の船長として宗介をあつかう

5

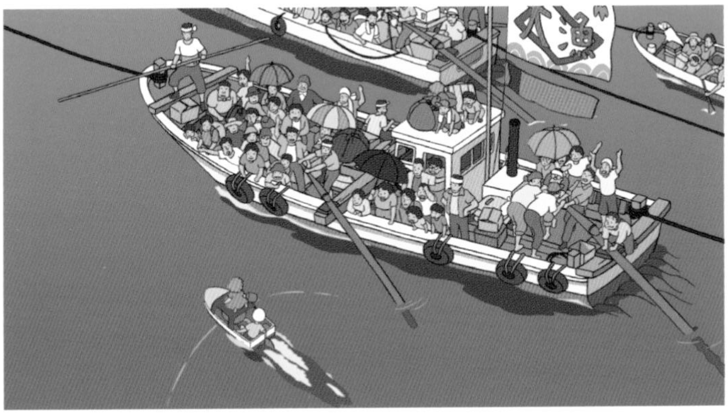

6

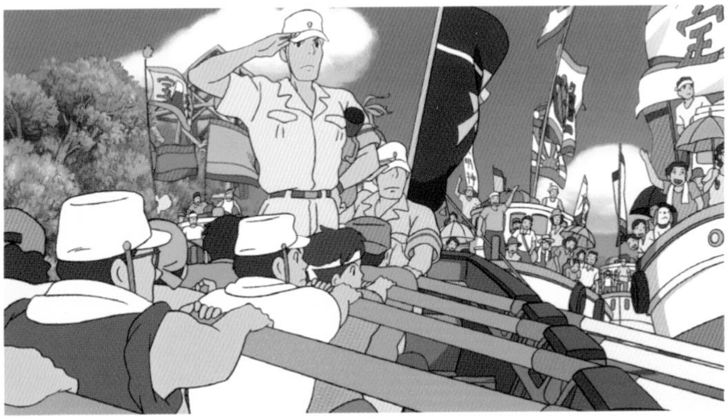

7

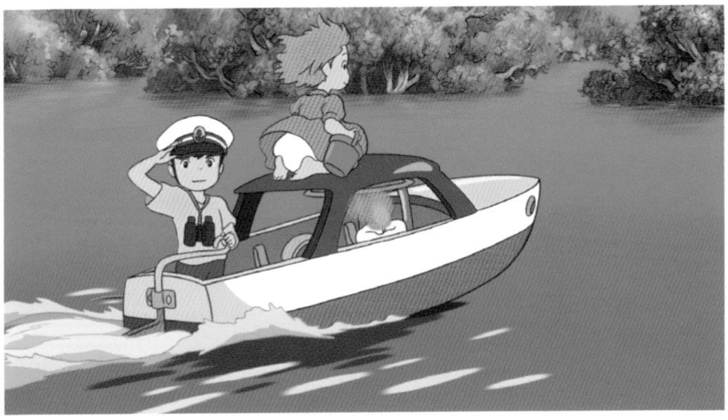

8

Encountering the Townspeople

1 /The Japanese-style boat, and baby, that Sosuke and Ponyo happen upon [Character design].
2 /Reading the baby's mind, Ponyo holds out a cup of Lisa's soup.
3 /The couple with baby from the Japanese-style boat [Character design].
4 /"He's a little too young, he can't handle soup yet. But I could eat the soup instead, and it would help me to make milk for him."
5 /A patrol boat headed for the mountaintop hotel that is now a shelter [Concept sketch].
6–8 /Sosuke and Ponyo continue on their way, sent off by the townspeople aboard fishing boats flying festive flags and cutters owned by the fishery's high school.

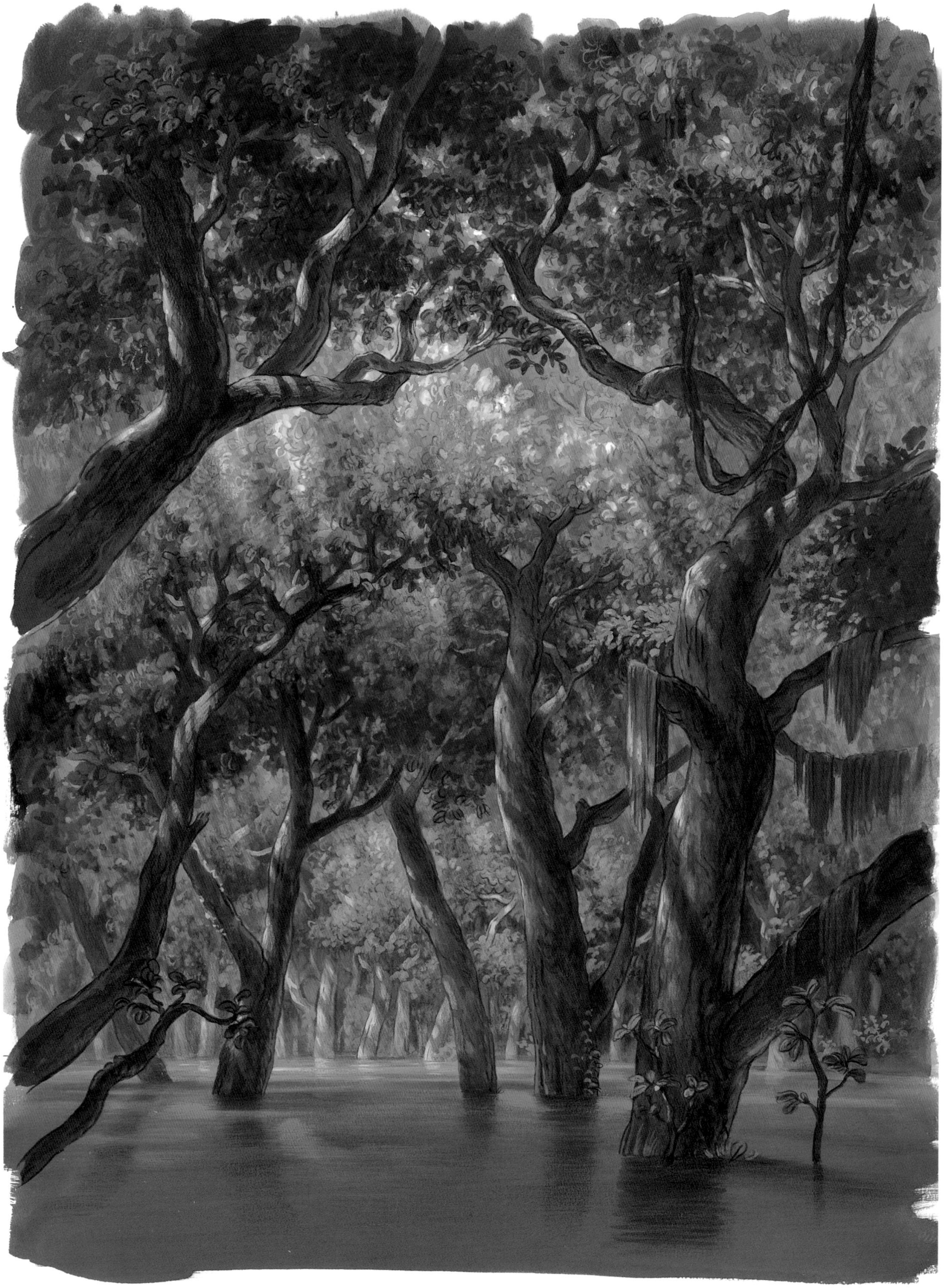
1

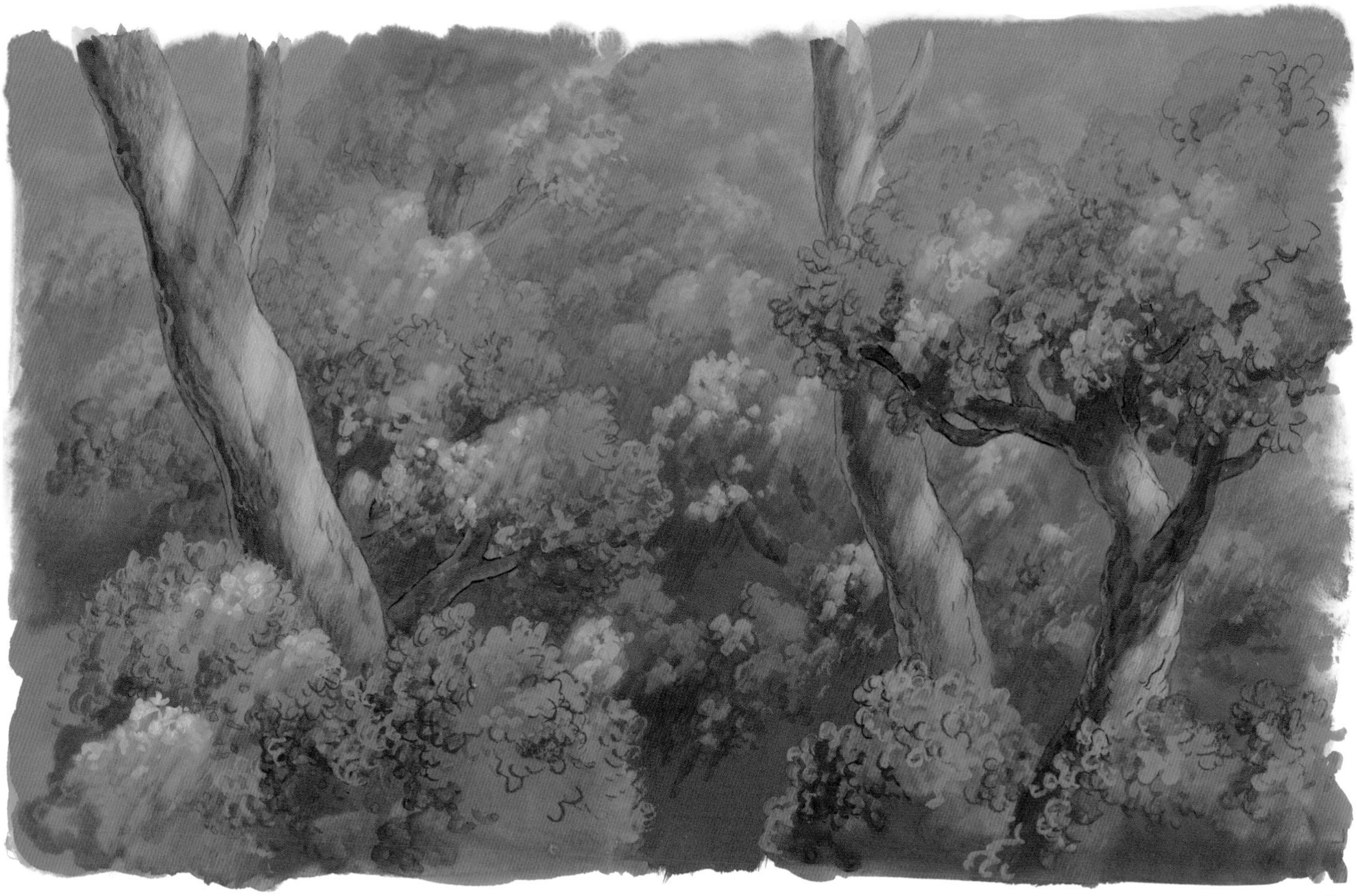

2

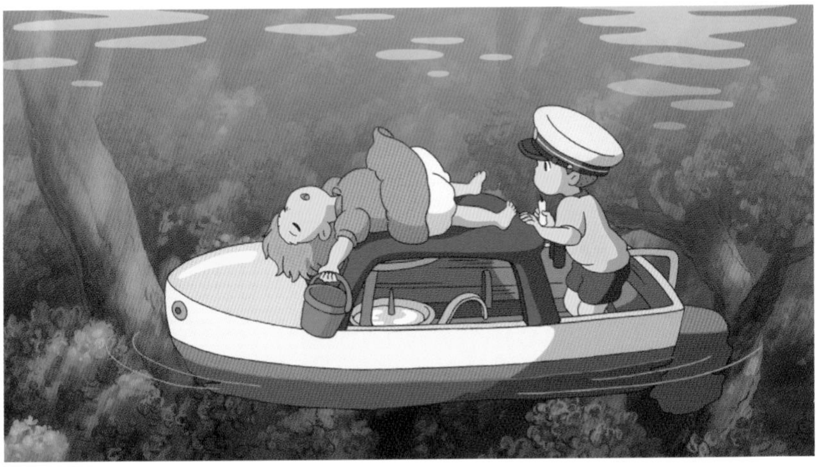

3

The Forest

1, 2 /The submerged forest through which the steamboat navigates. The sea of trees has become a paradise for the crowned pelican and other unusual creatures [Backgrounds].
3 /Ponyo falls asleep. Sosuke is unable to light a new candle.

Naoya Tanaka was in charge of creating the background and concept for each shot in the forest scene. Although there is the thrilling feeling of Sosuke going on a jungle expedition, it was also important to convey the stillness of the water, which is transparent and clear to the bottom. I asked him to use lines in areas where he would normally use a brush, to keep from rendering the background too realistically. Since Tanaka is a seasoned pro who has handled these types of demanding backgrounds in the past, he was able to deliver exactly what I was hoping for.

—Art Director: Noboru Yoshida

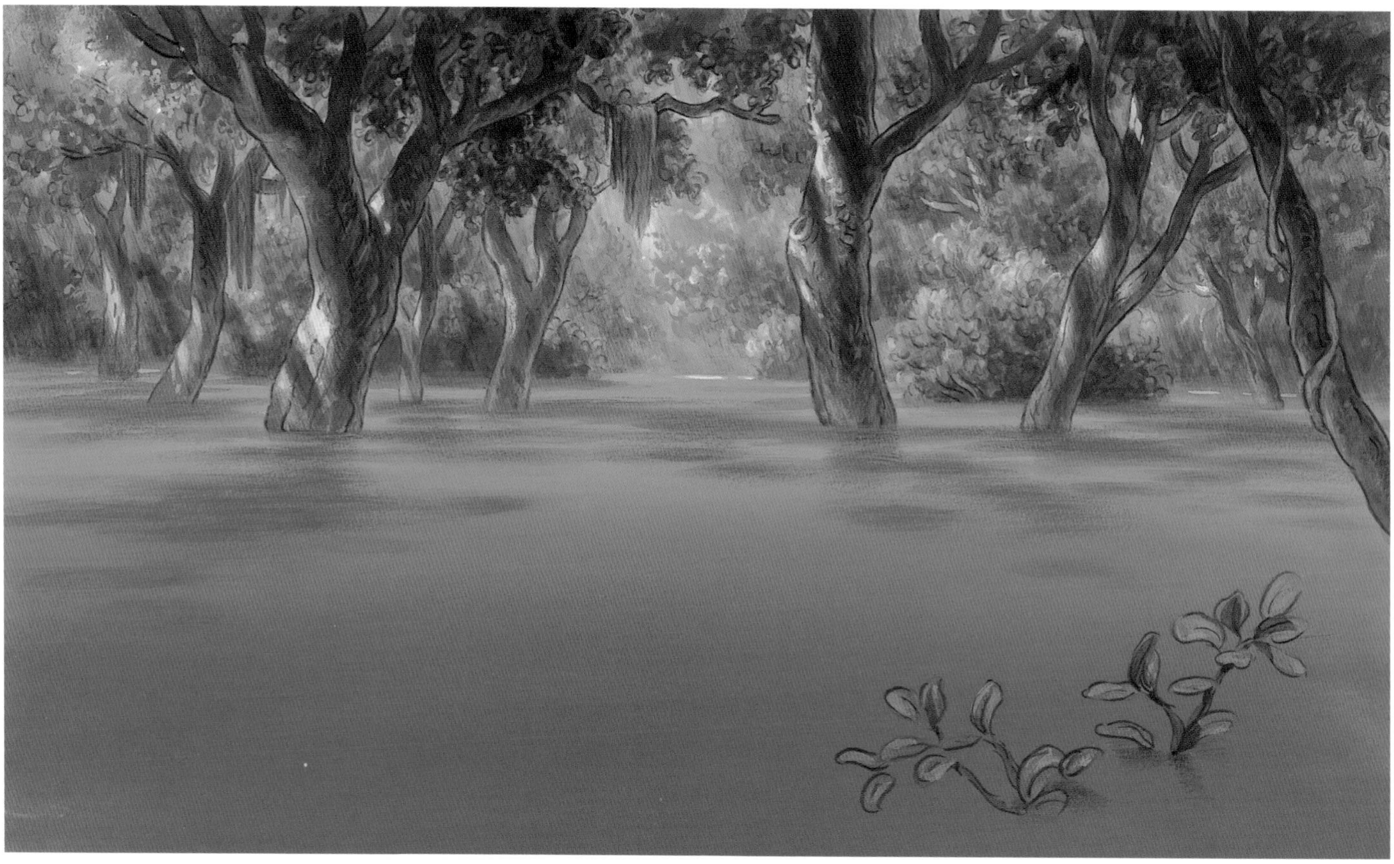

1

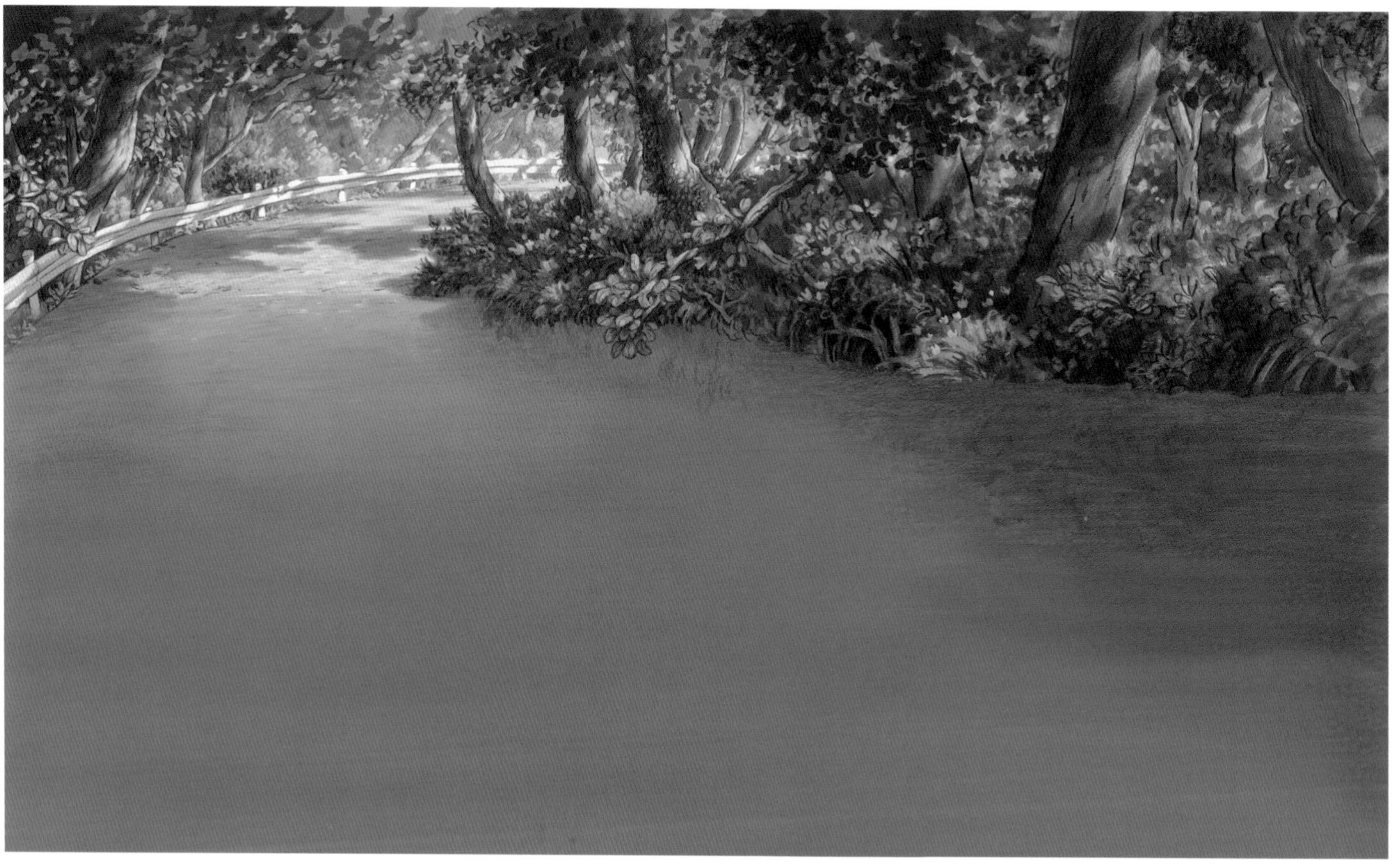

2

1 /The forest through which Sosuke pushes the stalled steamboat [Background].
2 /The road re-emerges up ahead [Background].
3 /The road where Sosuke and Ponyo come ashore. In the film, Lisa's car is visible up the road [Background].
4 /The forest where Sosuke finds Lisa's car [Background].

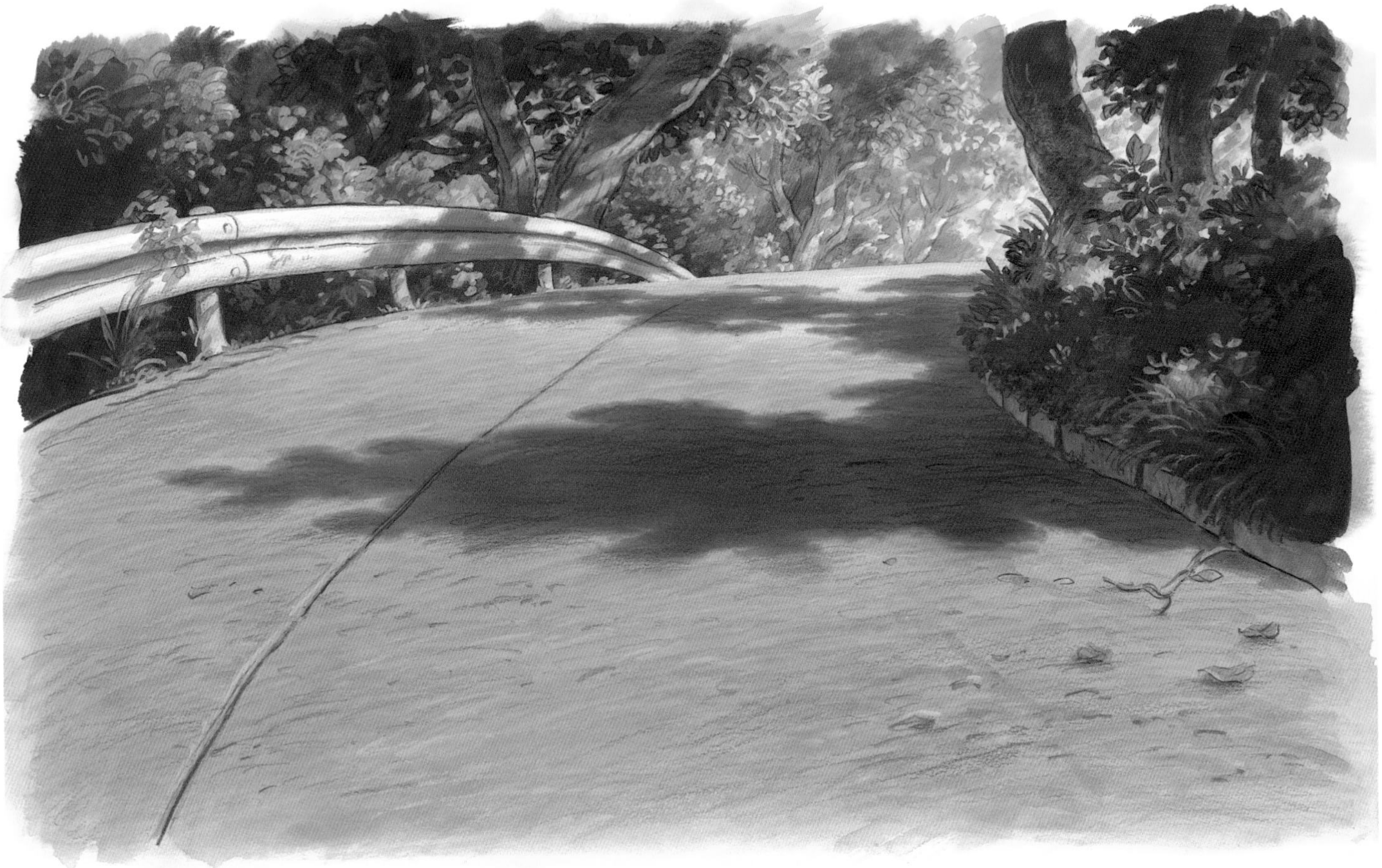

3

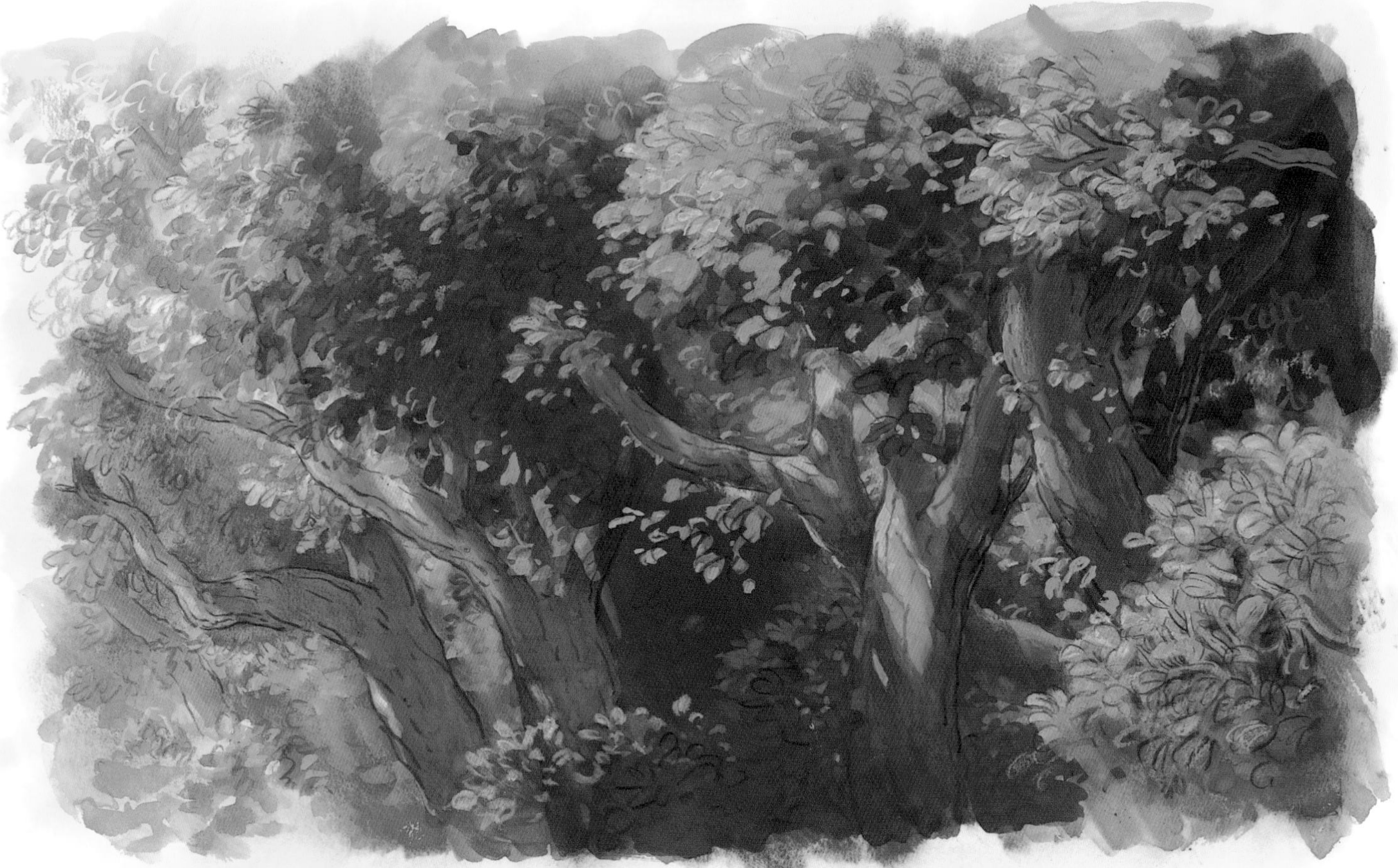

4

Sosuke Perseveres

1, 2 /Sosuke pushing the stalled steamboat.
3, 4 /Just before reaching the road, Ponyo's magic dissolves and the steamboat begins to shrink.
5, 6 /Sosuke pulling a sleepy-faced Ponyo to safety.
7 /Sosuke finds Lisa's car, but Lisa is nowhere to be found.
8 /Ponyo consoles a teary-eyed Sosuke [Concept sketch].
9 /Sosuke and Ponyo journeying deeper into the forest.

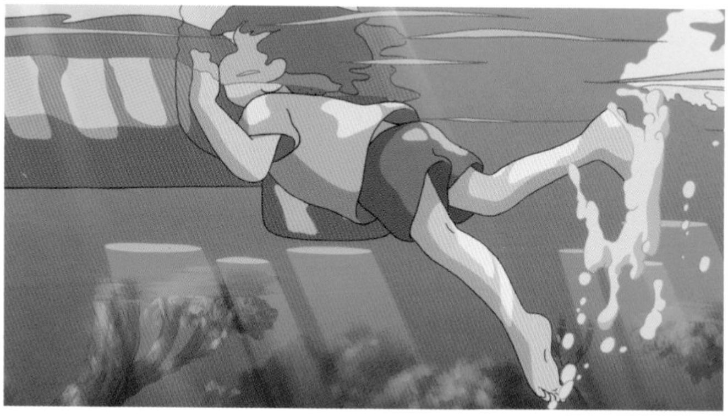

1

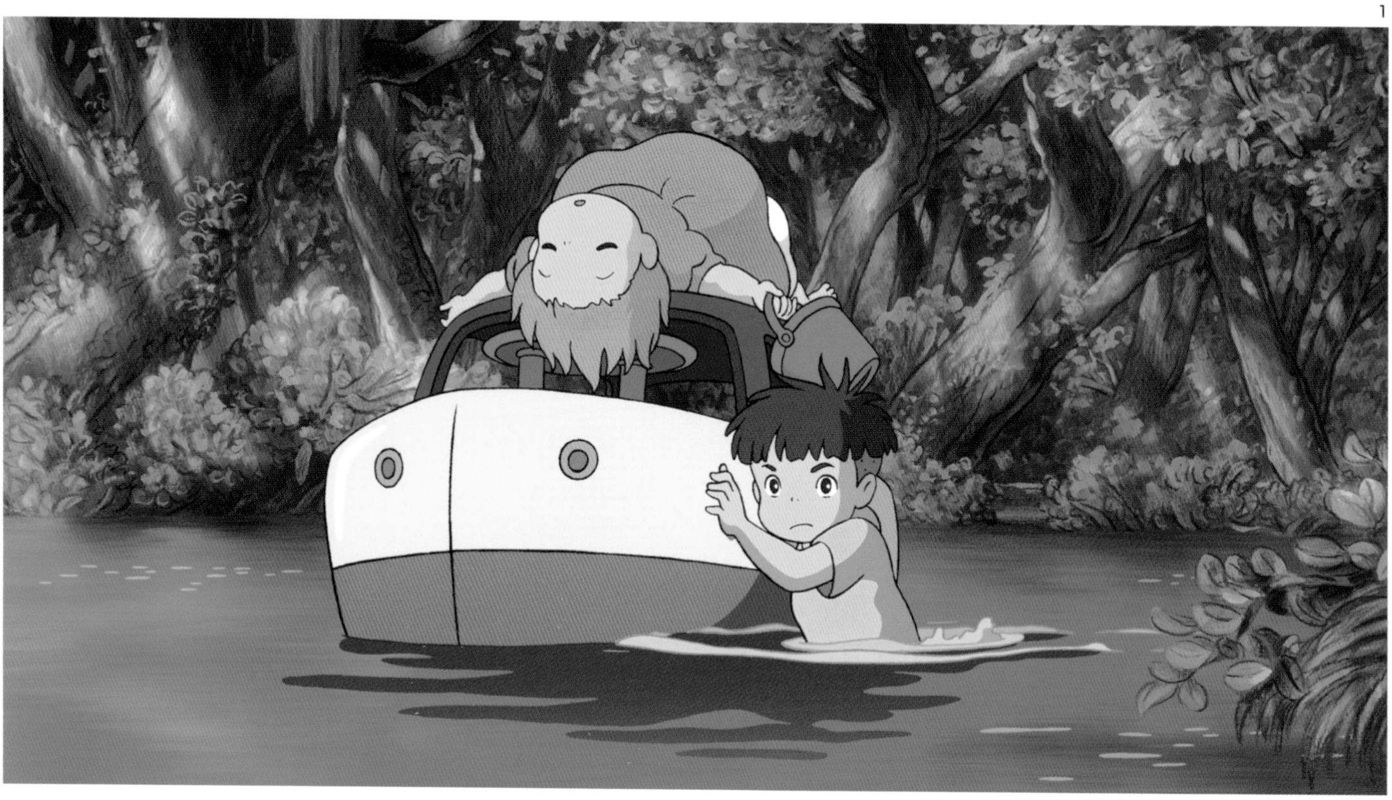

2

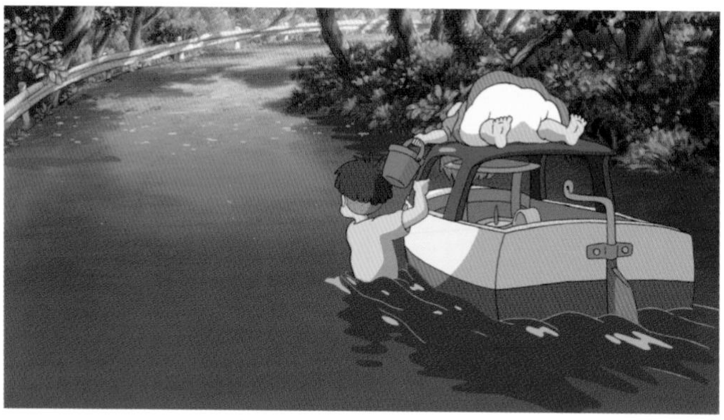

3

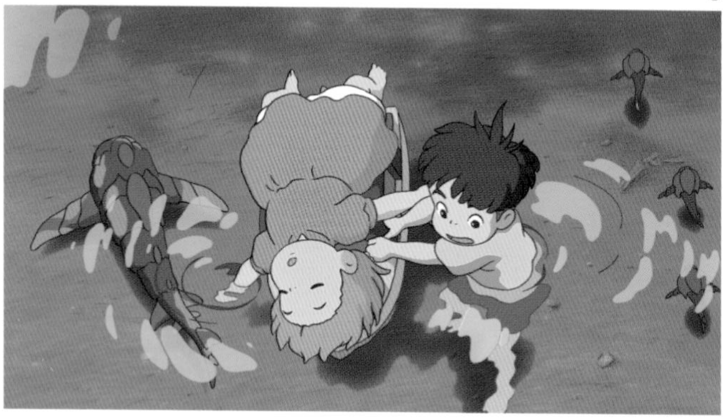

4

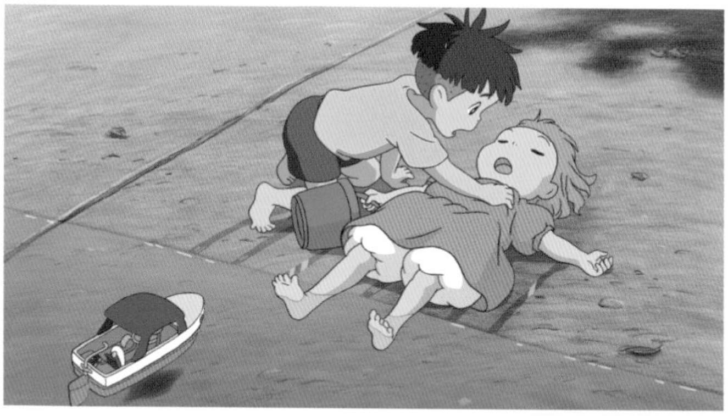

5

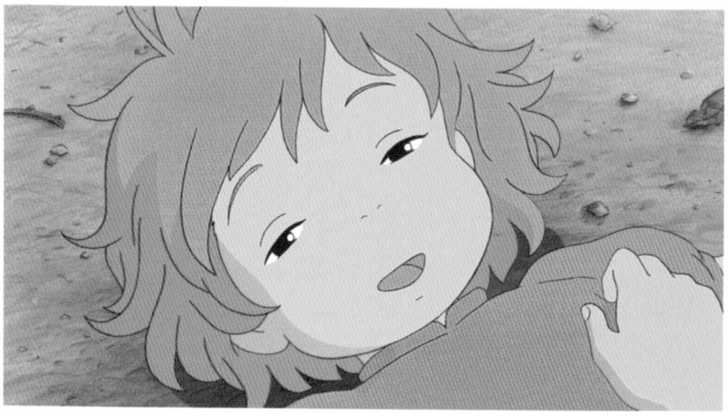

6

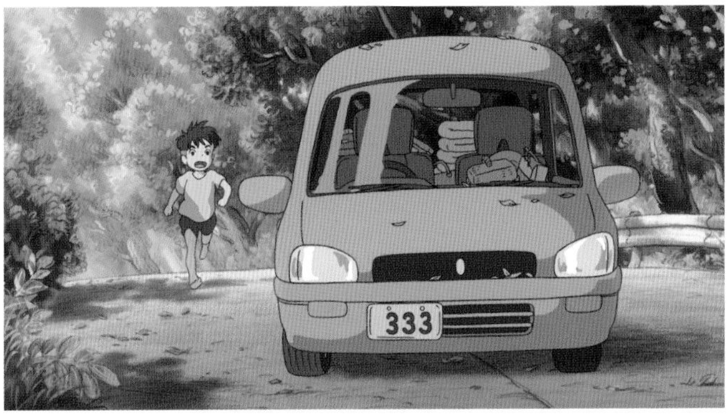
333

7

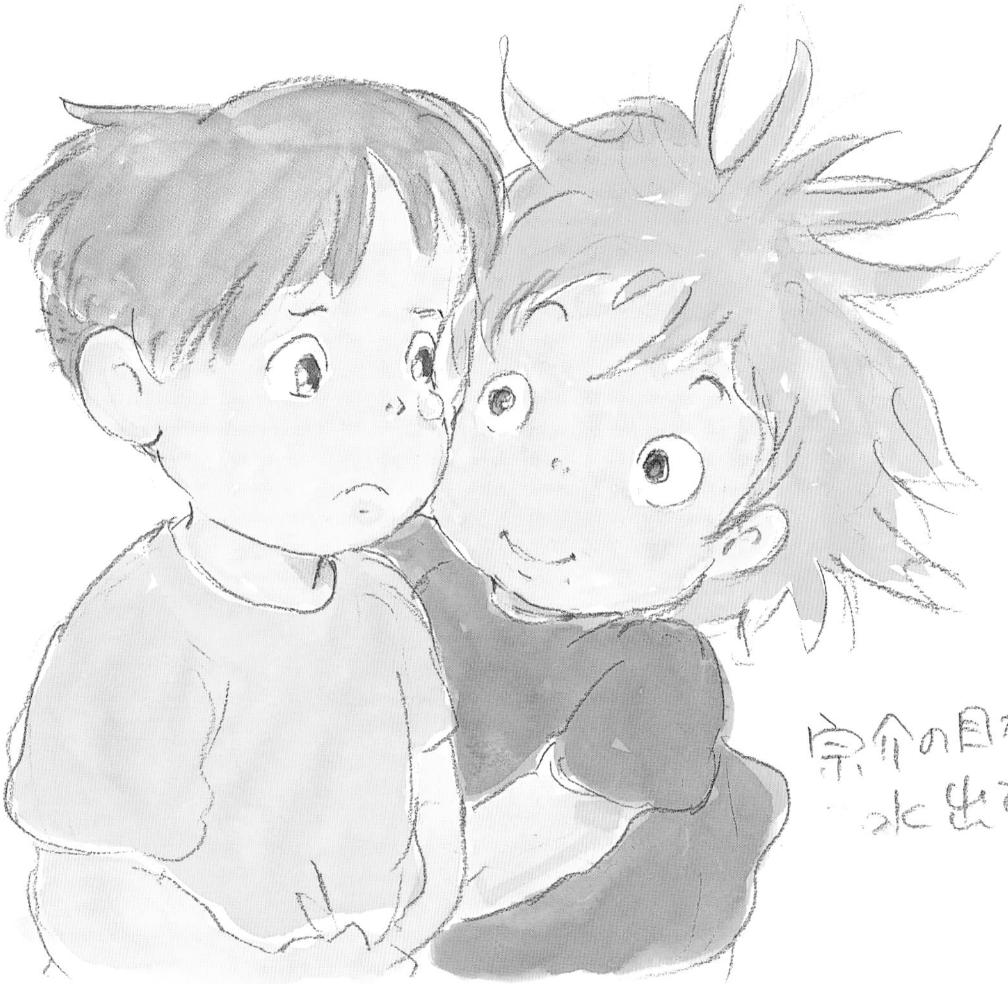
宗介の目から
水出てる!!

8

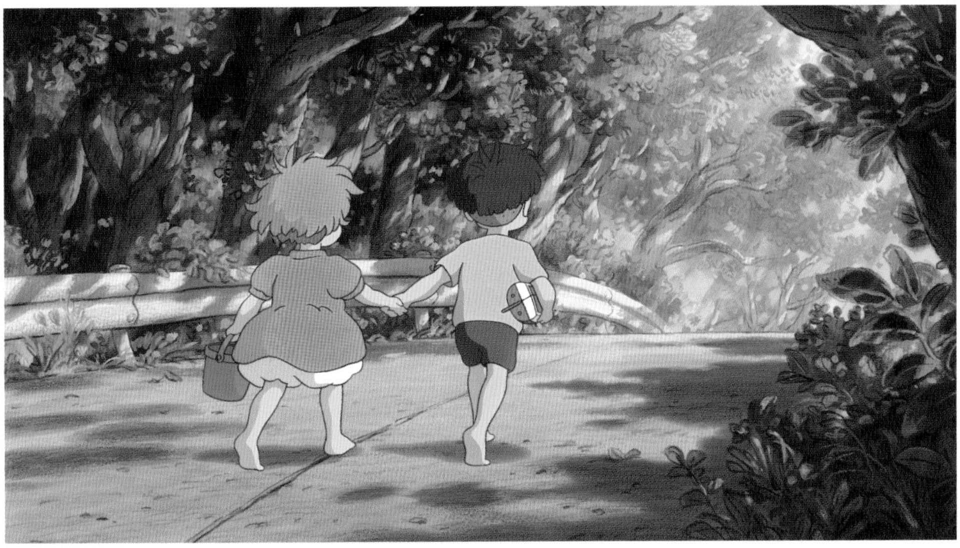

9

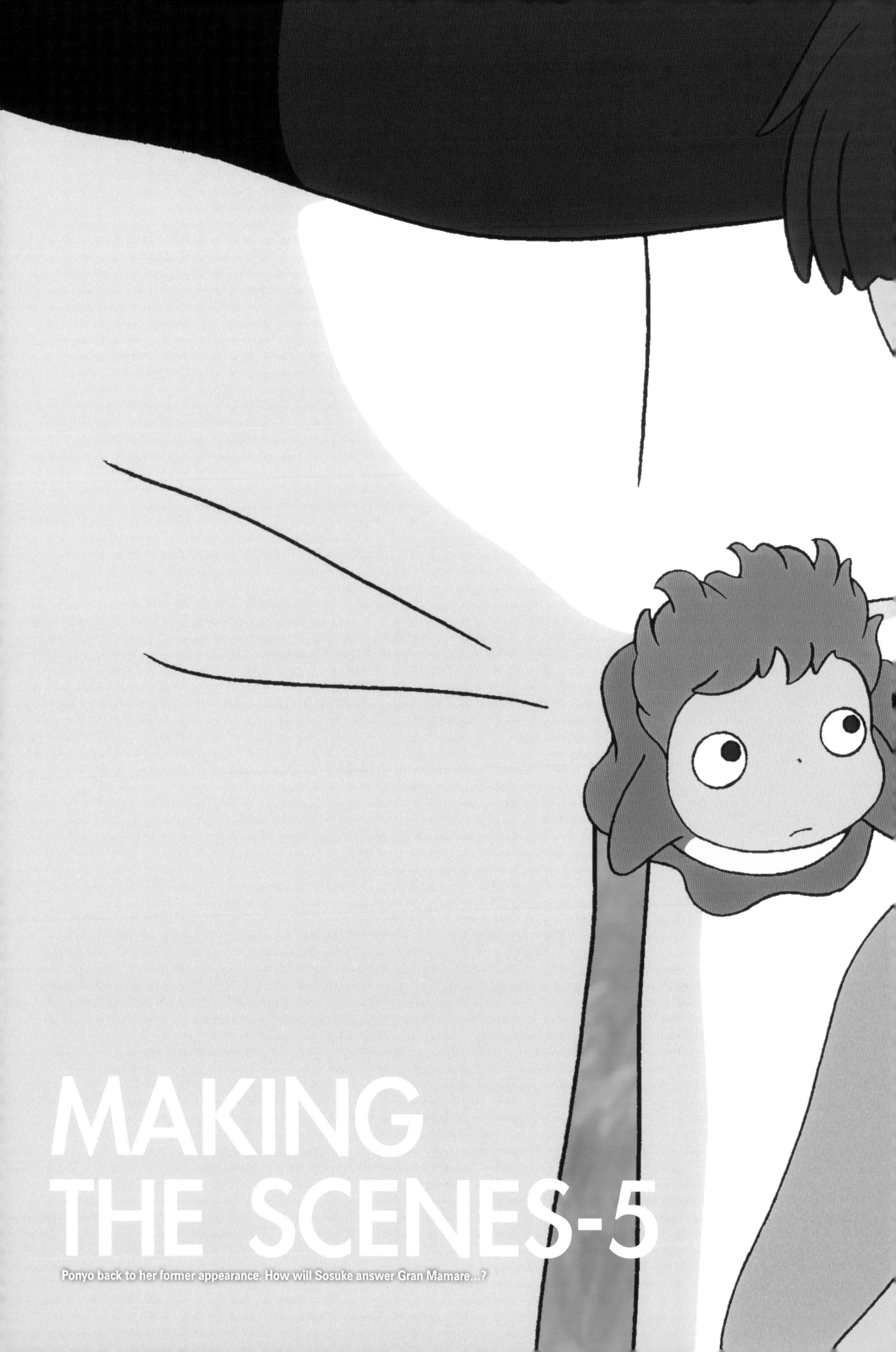

MAKING THE SCENES-5

Ponyo back to her former appearance. How will Sosuke answer Gran Mamare...?

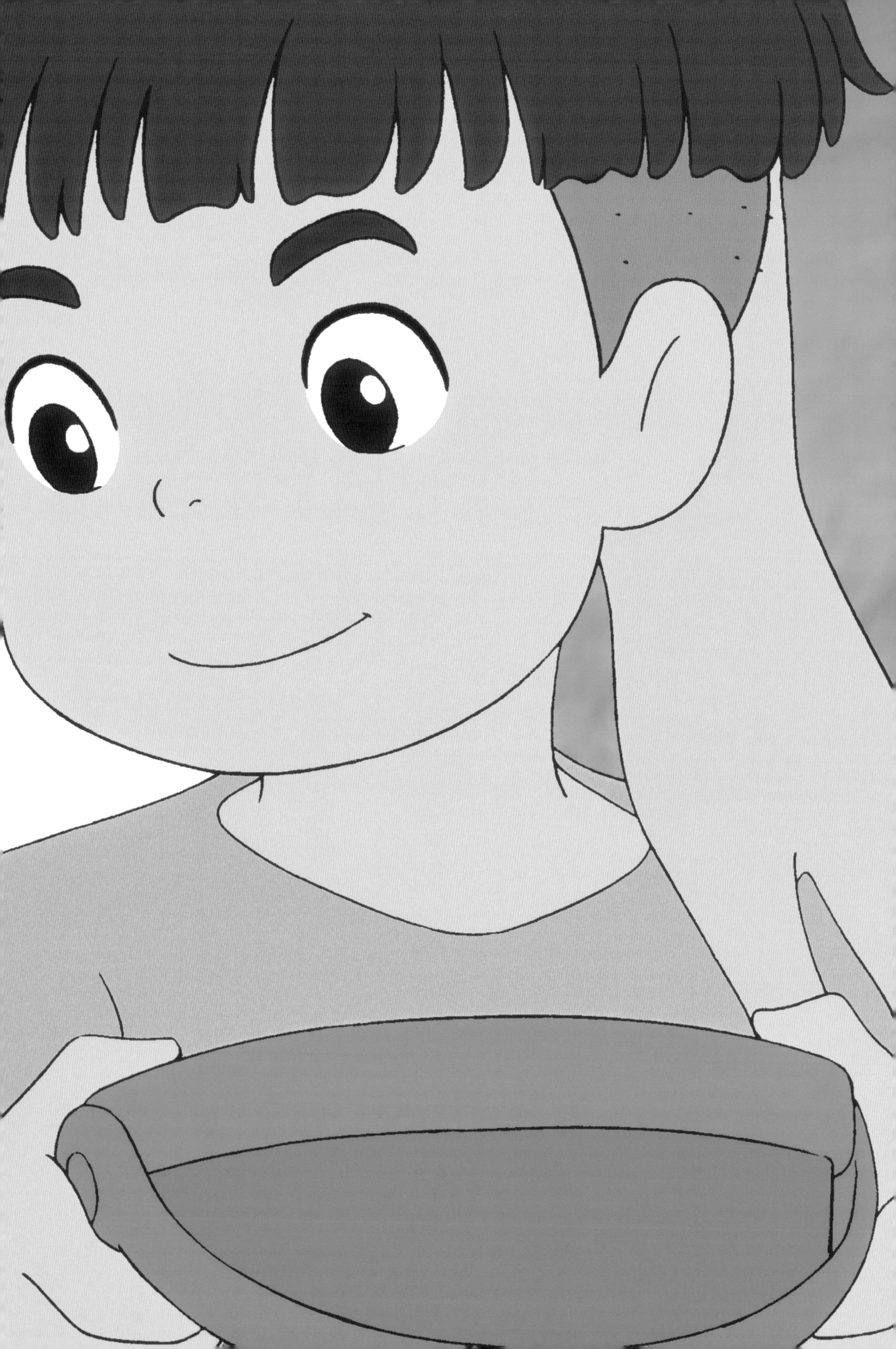

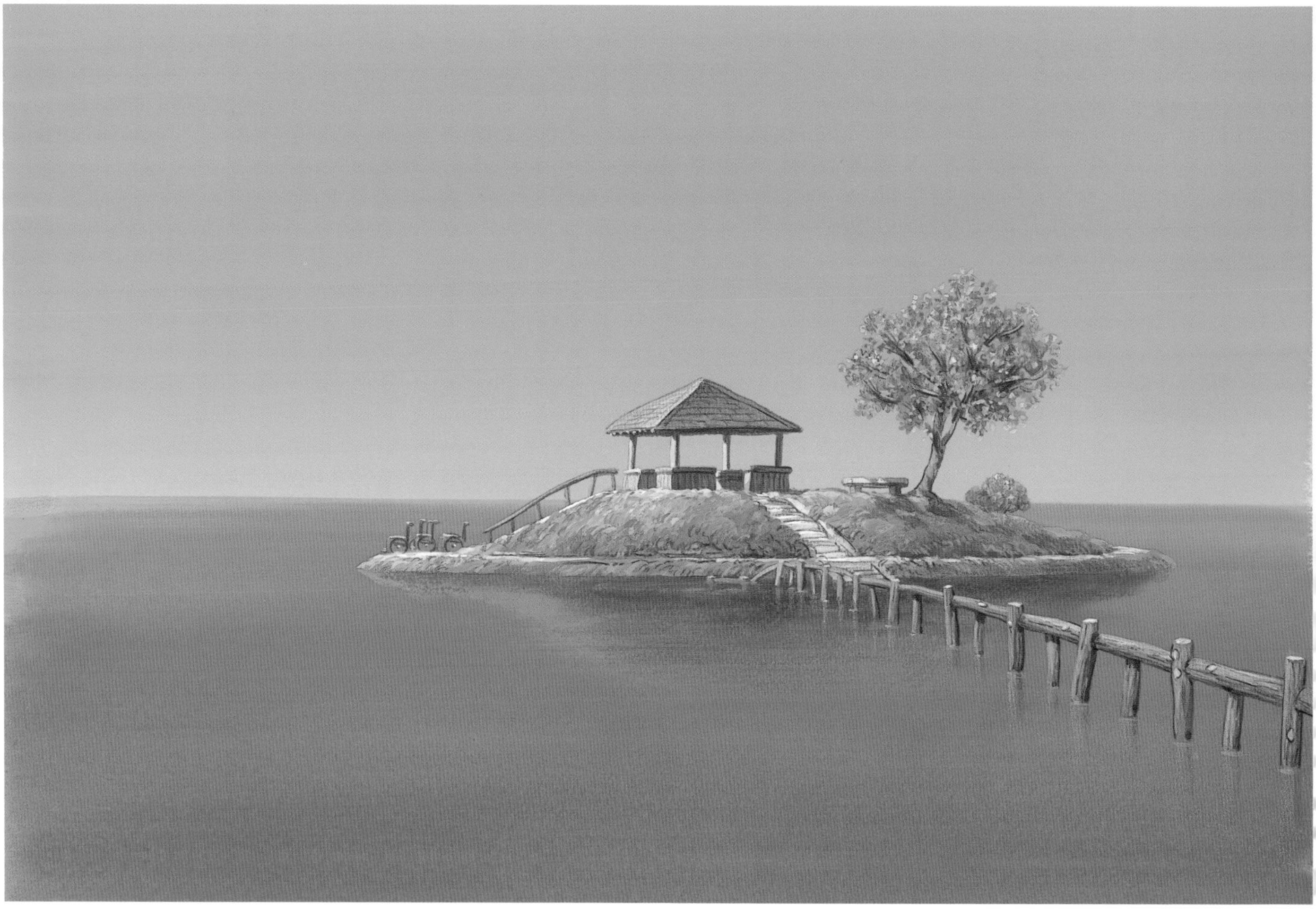

1

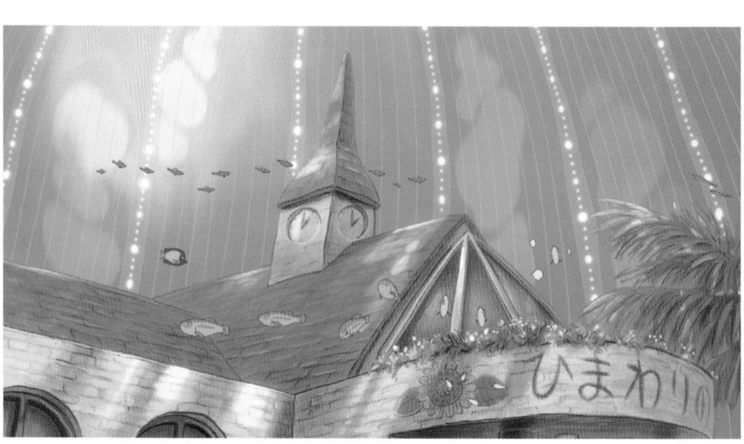
ひまわりの

2

The Town Under the Sea

1 /The park and gazebo on top of the mountain to which the people of the Sunflower House escape [Background].
2 /The Sunflower House enveloped by a giant jellyfish. Lisa and the elderly ladies are brought here by Fujimoto.
3 /The giant jellyfish covering the Sunflower House [Concept art].
4 /The Sunflower House inside the jellyfish [Concept art].

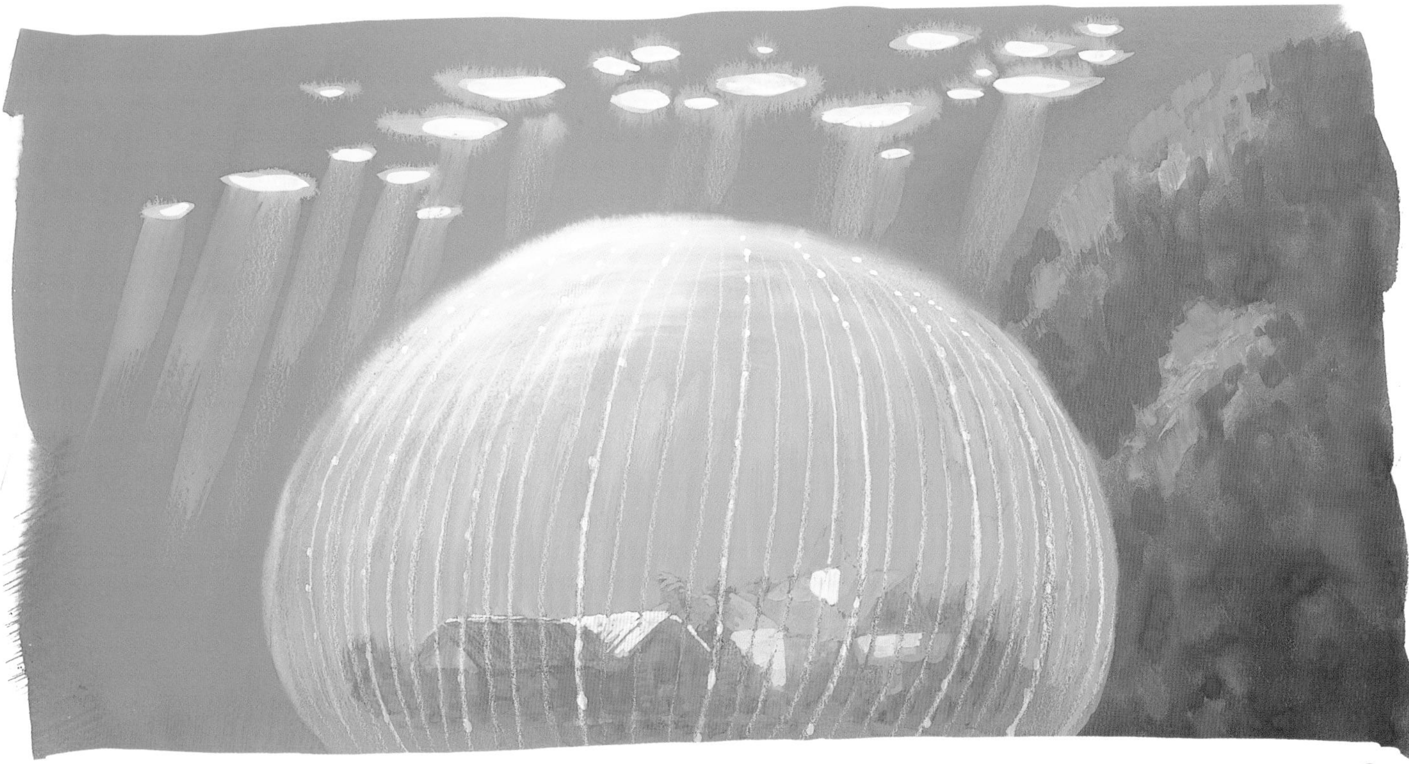

3

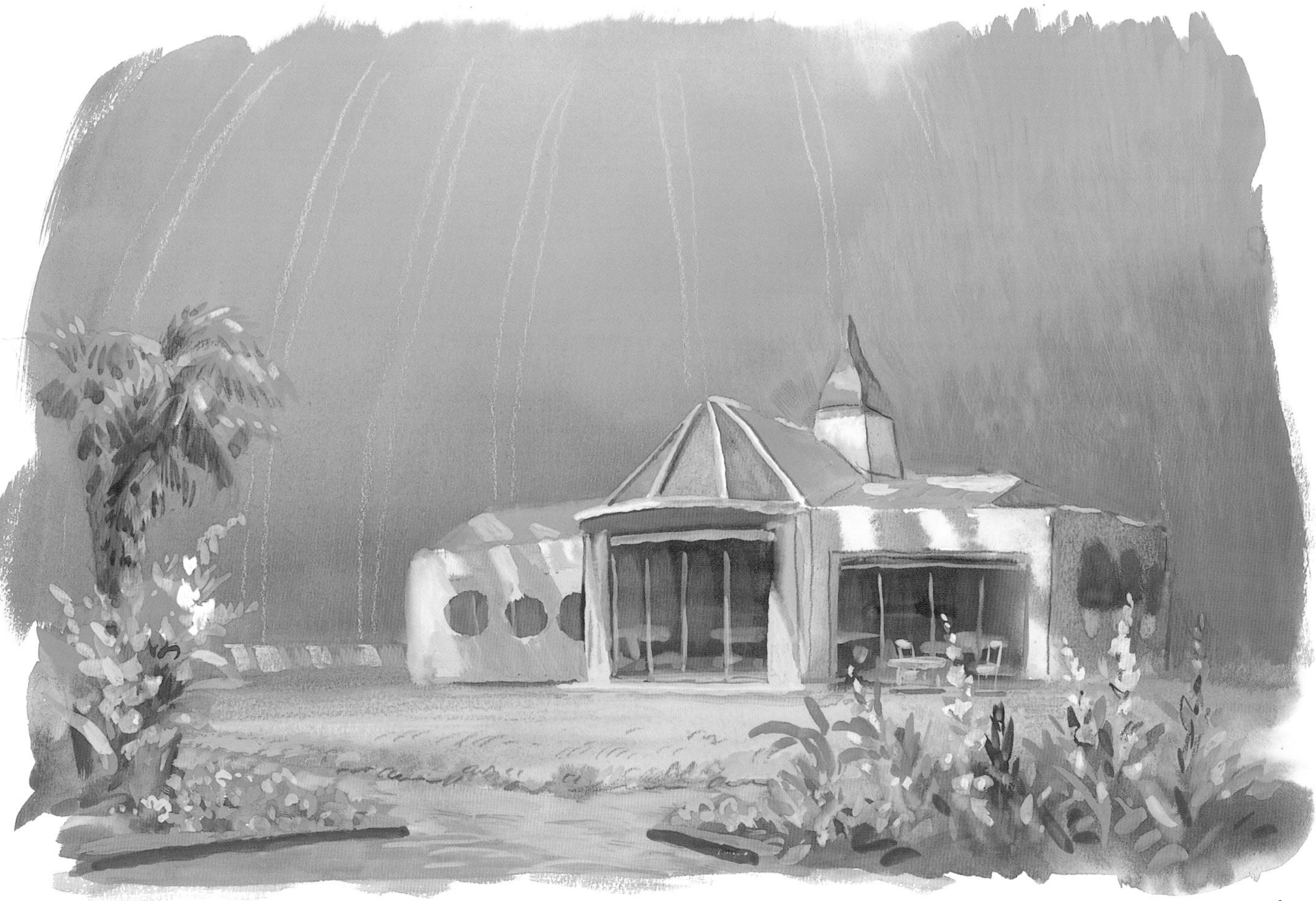

4

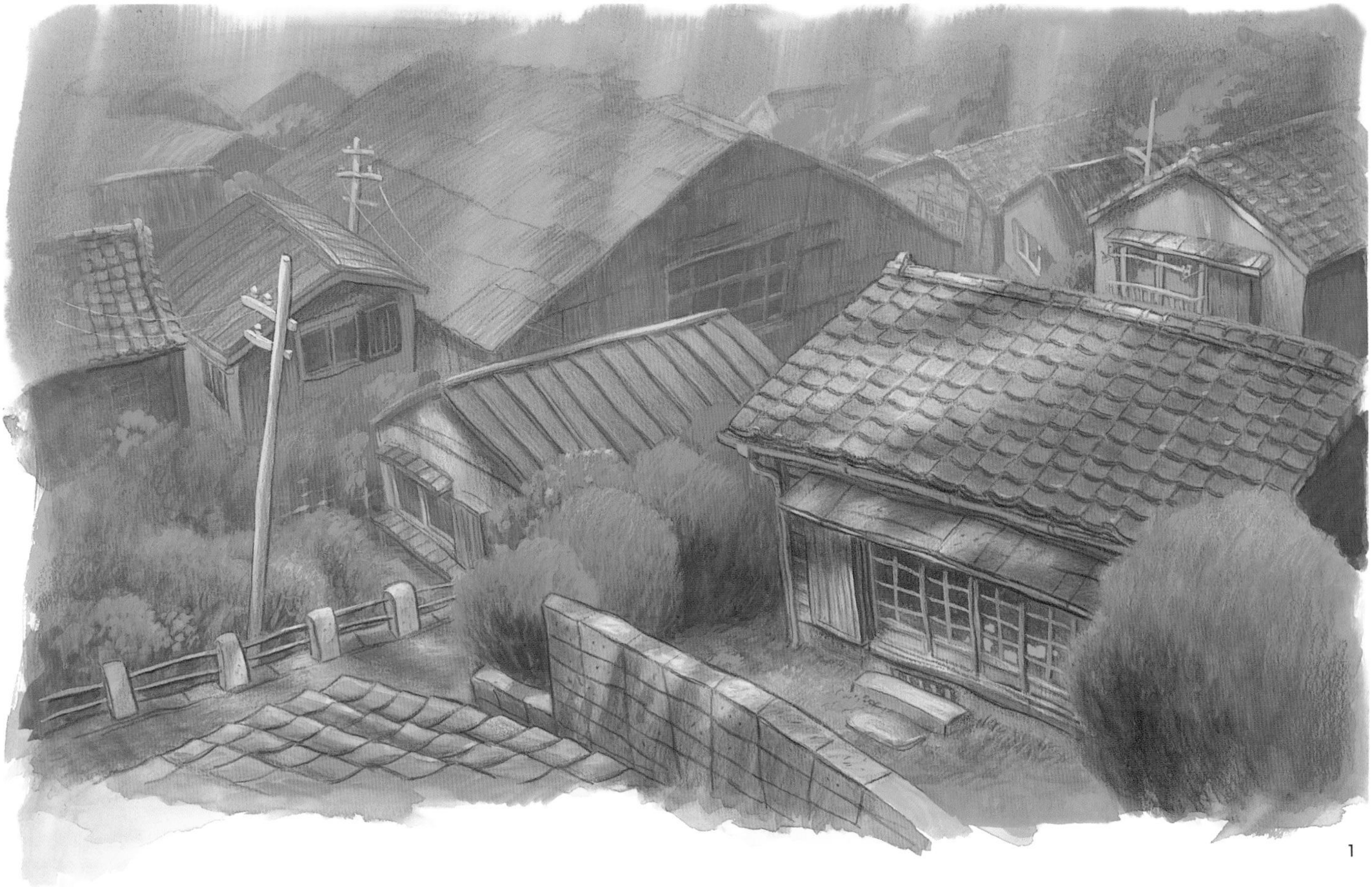

1

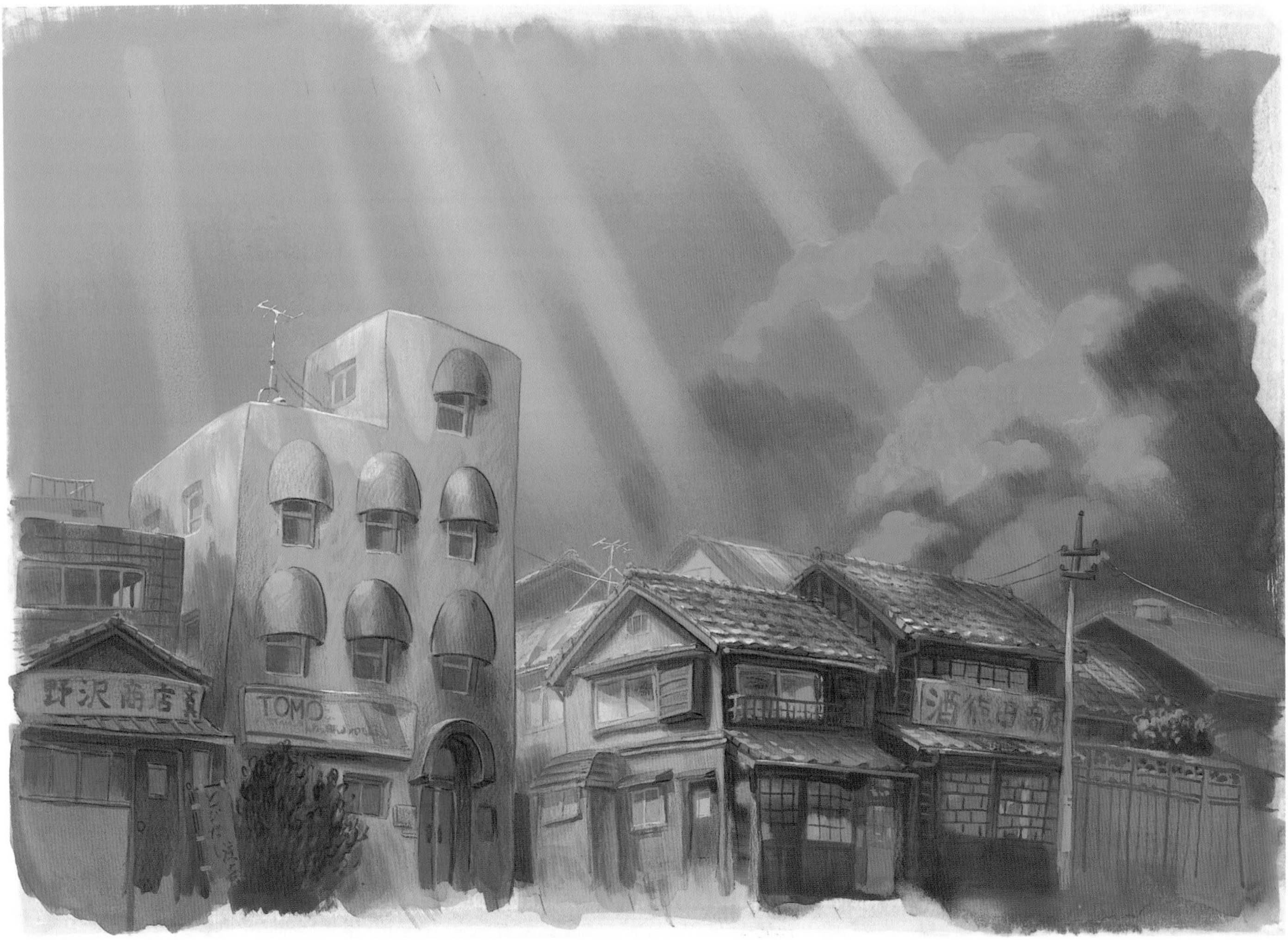
野沢商店
TOMO

2

1 /The sunken row of houses [Background].
2 /The shopping arcade along the embankment [Background].
3 /The actual picture created from Image 1. Cels of the boats, fish and clothesline were laid on top of the background.
4 /The Sunflower House under the sea. It is like Ryugu Castle from Urashima Taro.
5, 6 /Fujimoto goes off in the *Basking Shark* to retrieve Ponyo after asking the ladies to bear witness to the sacred test.

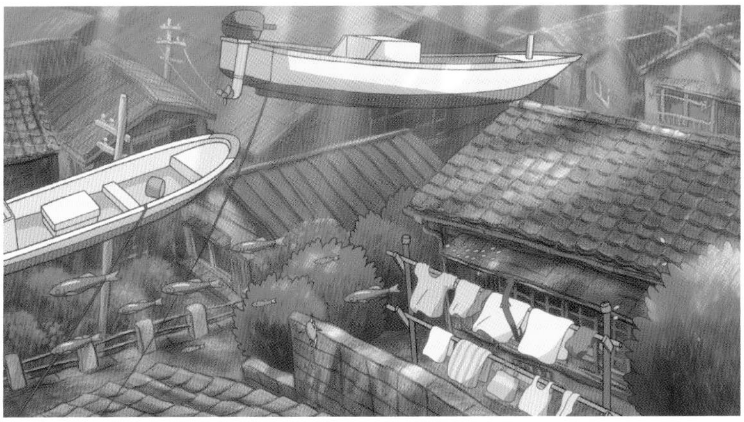

3

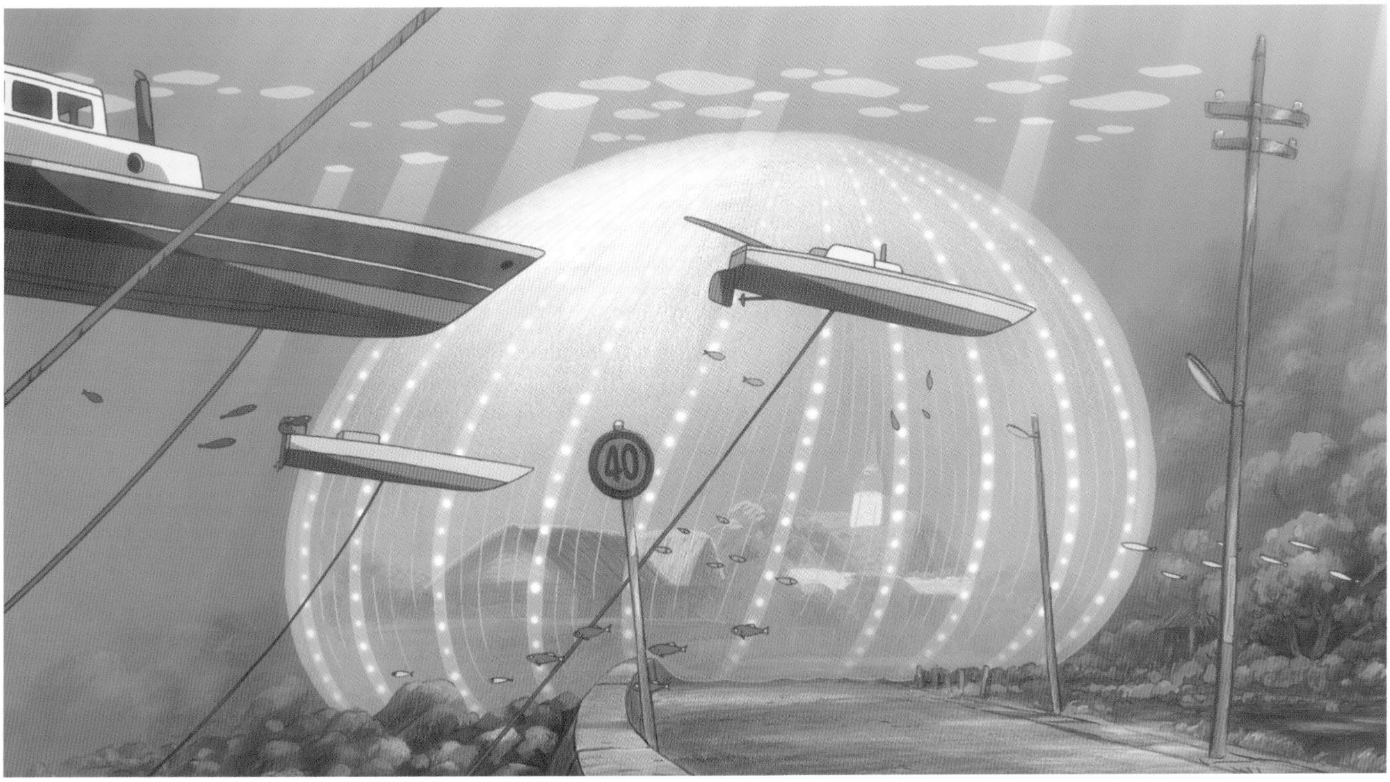
40

4

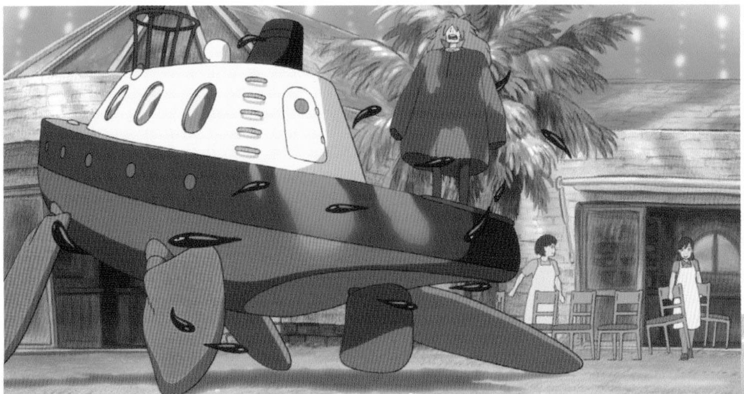

5

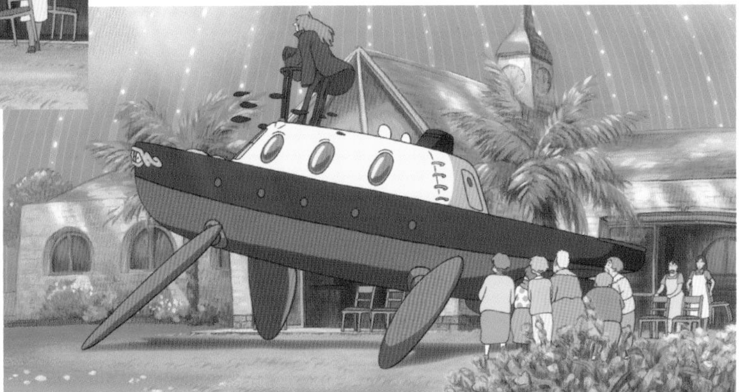

6

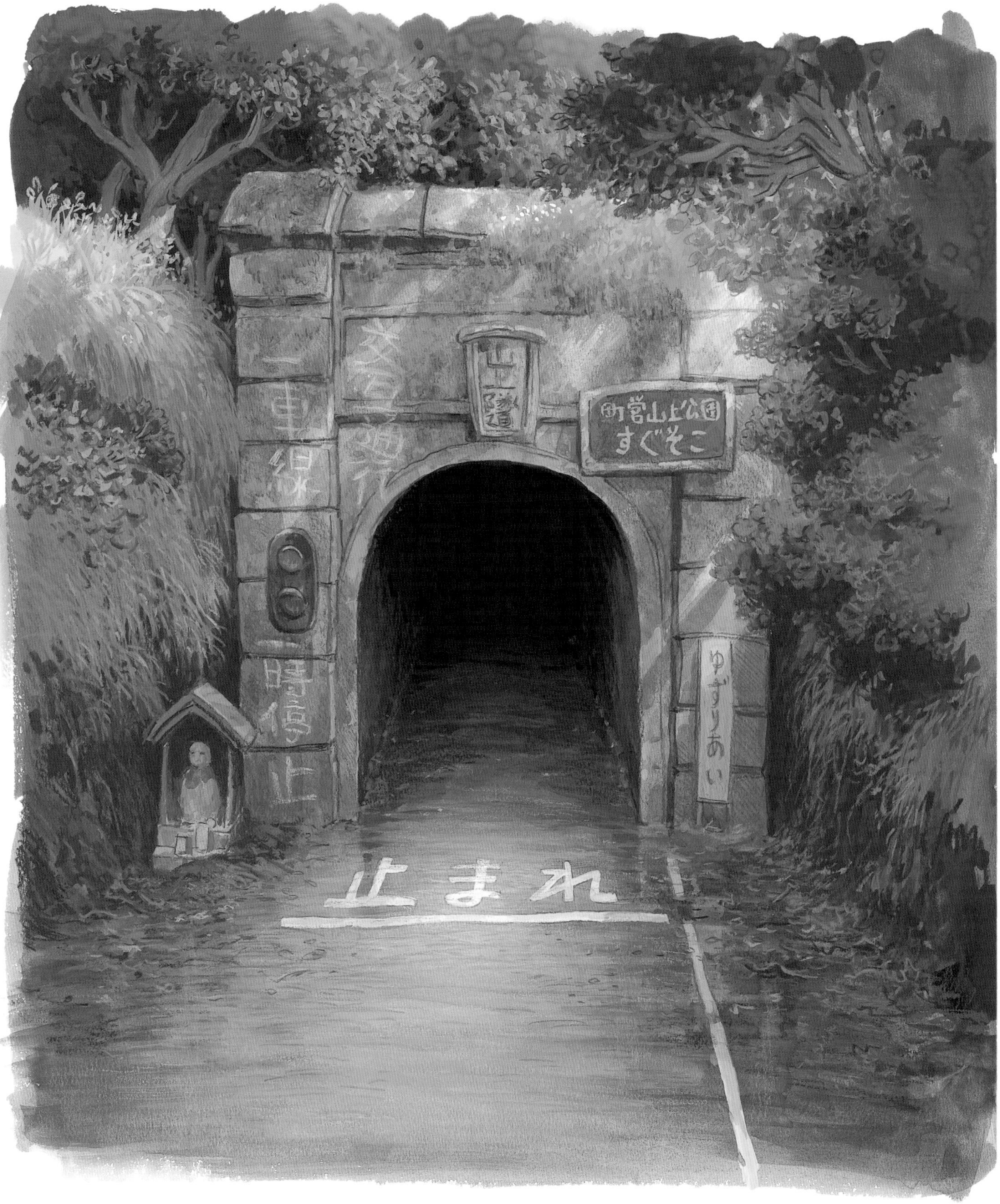
町営山上公園
すぐそこ
ゆずりあい
止まれ

1

Sosuke's Test

1 /An old tunnel in the forest. It leads to the park on top of the mountain [Background].
2 /They go inside as Sosuke encourages a frightened Ponyo, but...
3, 4 /Ponyo begins to turn back into her half-fish, half-human form.
5 /Sosuke dashing toward the exit with Ponyo in his arms.

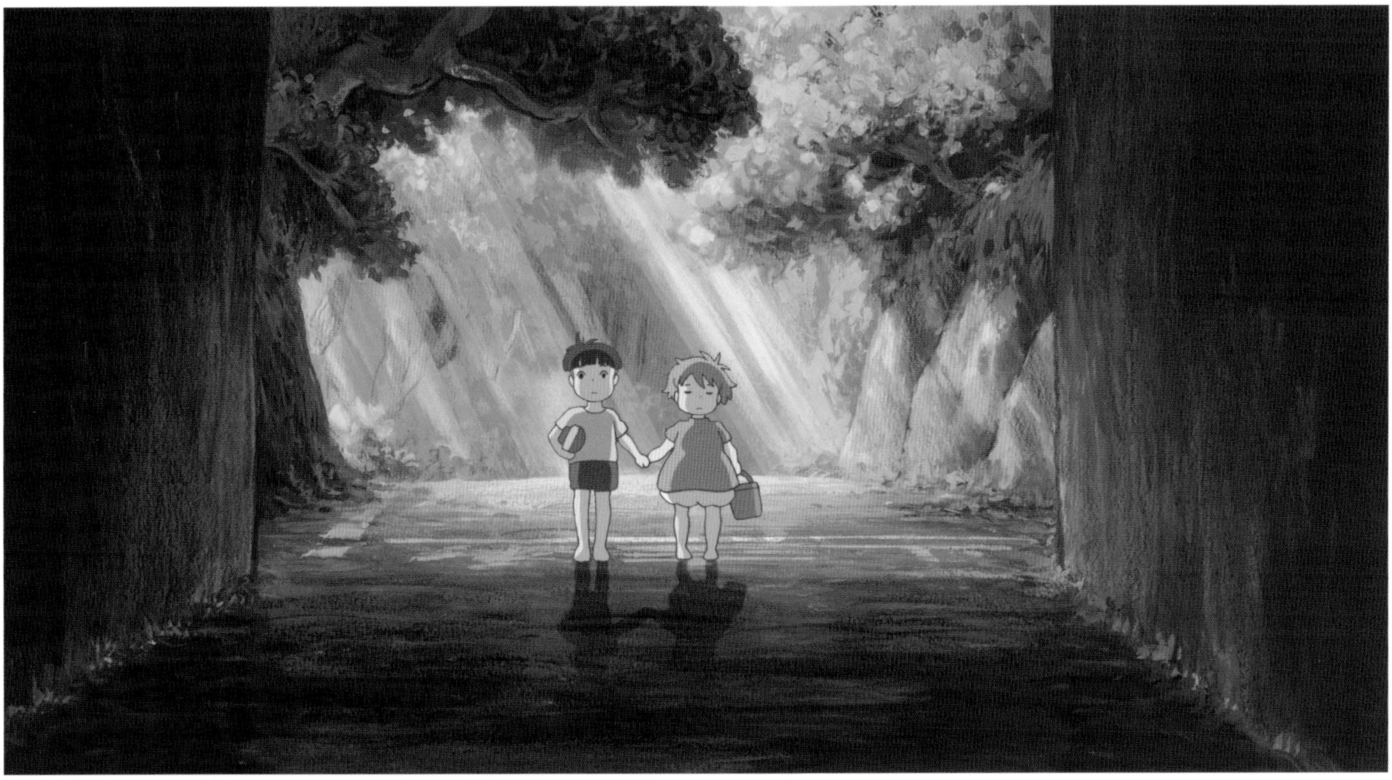

2

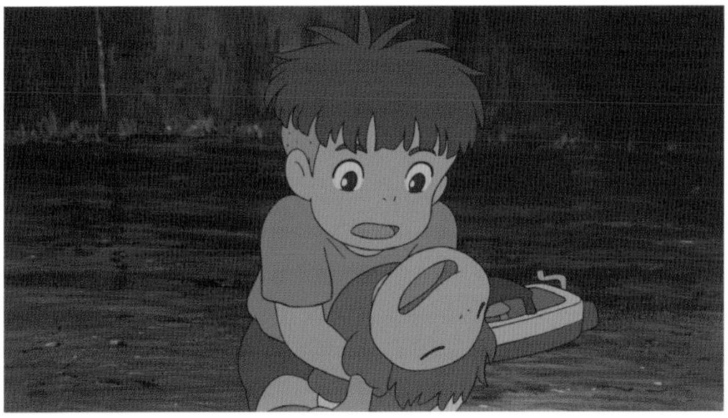

4

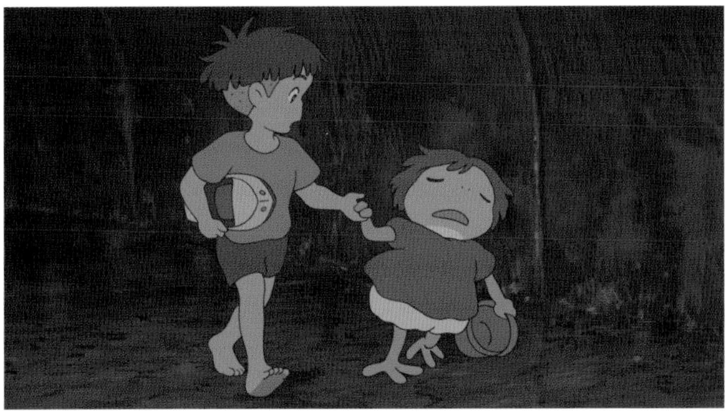

3

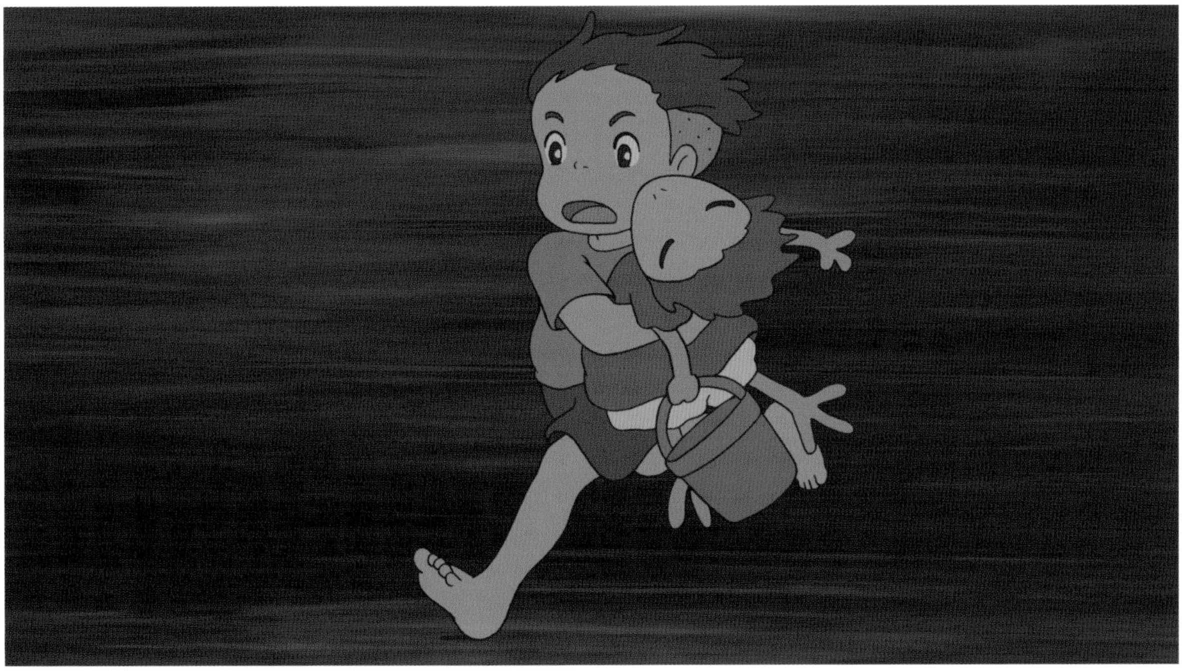

5

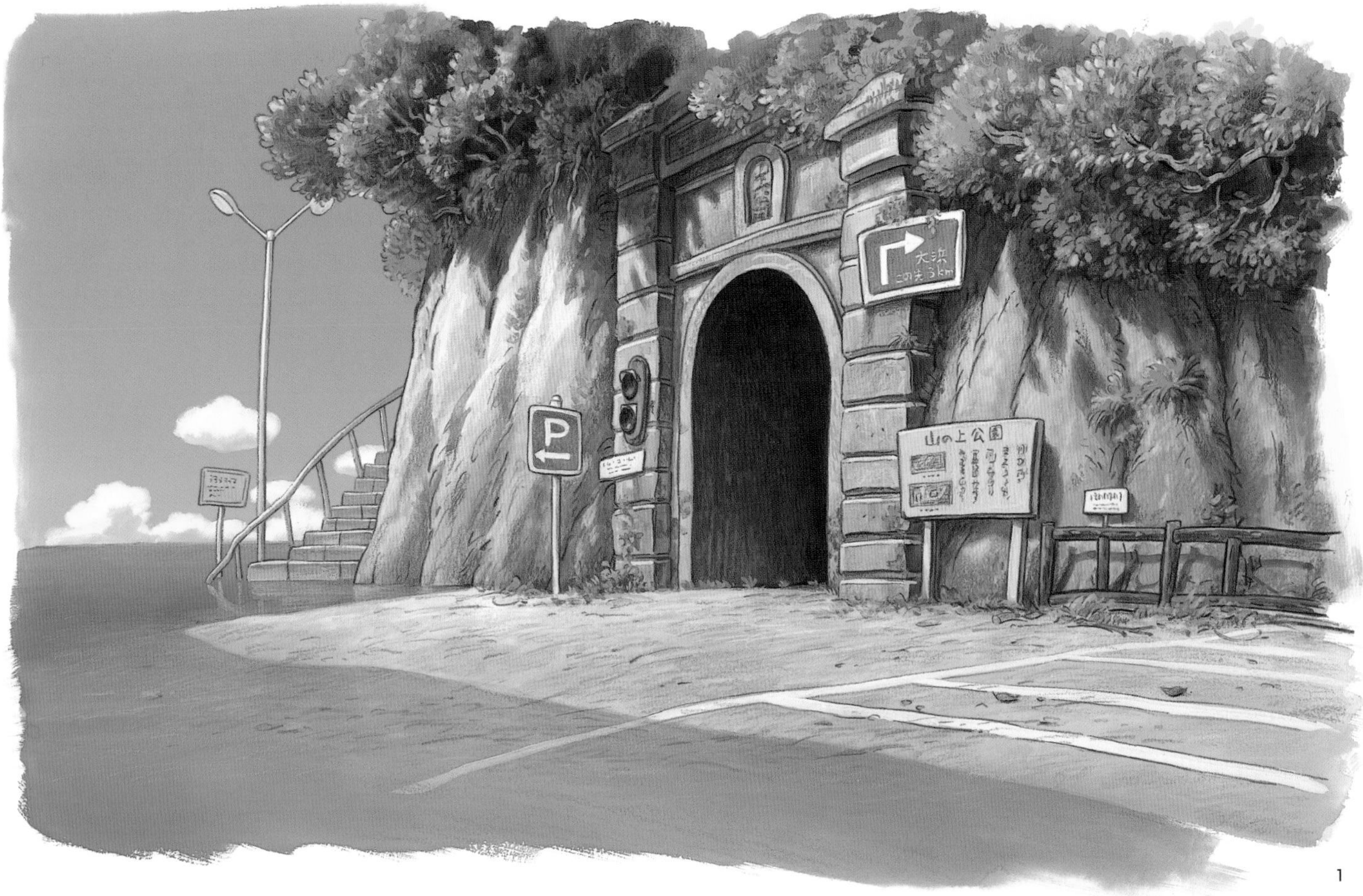

山の上公園
P

1

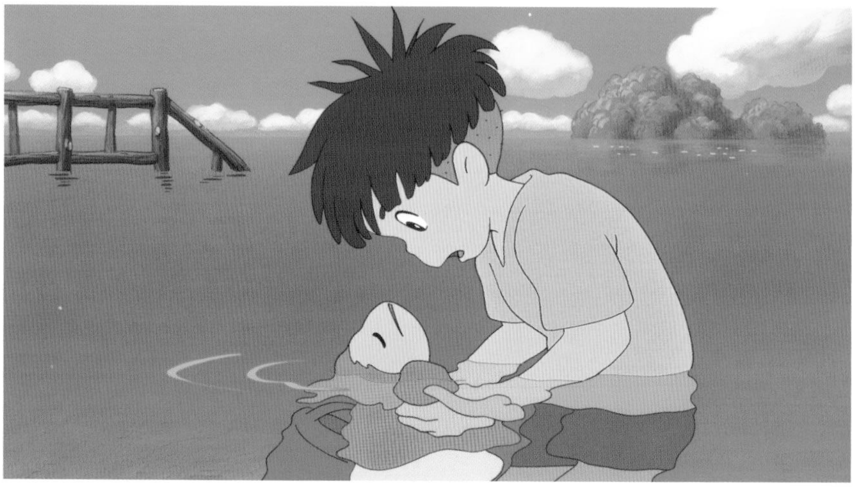

2

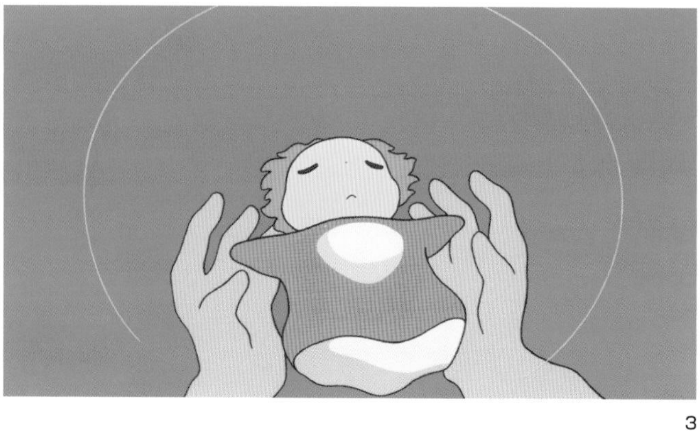

3

1 /The tunnel exit on the other side. The water is level with the parking lot [Background].
2, 3 /Sosuke dipping Ponyo in the water while calling her name. Ponyo transforms into a fish.
4 /Toki shouting for Sosuke. She is the only one who stayed behind at the gazebo.
5, 6 /At the same time, Fujimoto arrives to ask Sosuke and Ponyo to come with him.
7 /"If the moon comes any closer...we will be all underwater." exclaims Fujimoto.

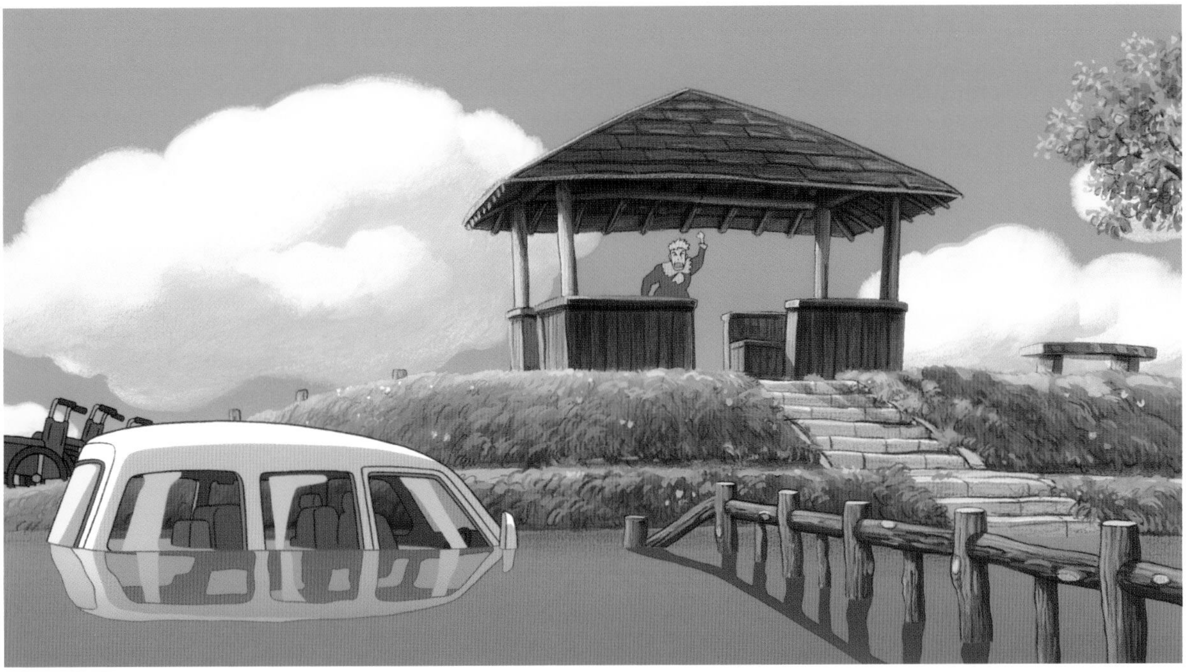

4

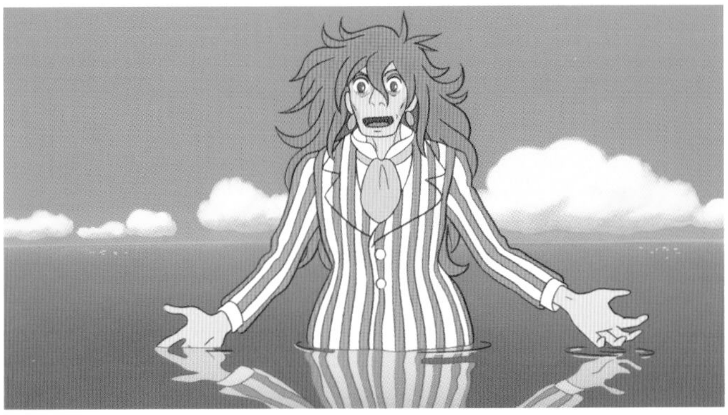

5

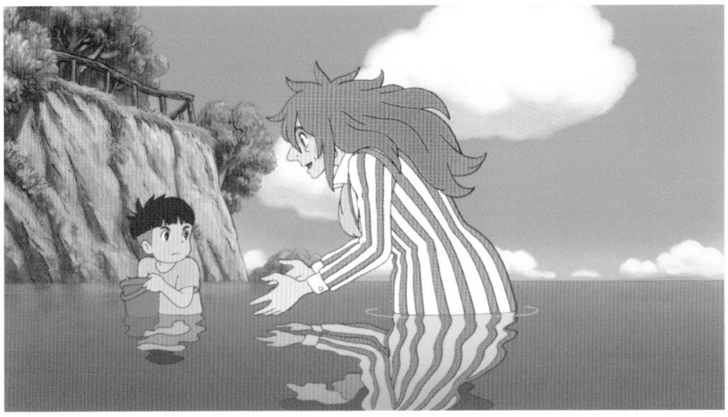

6

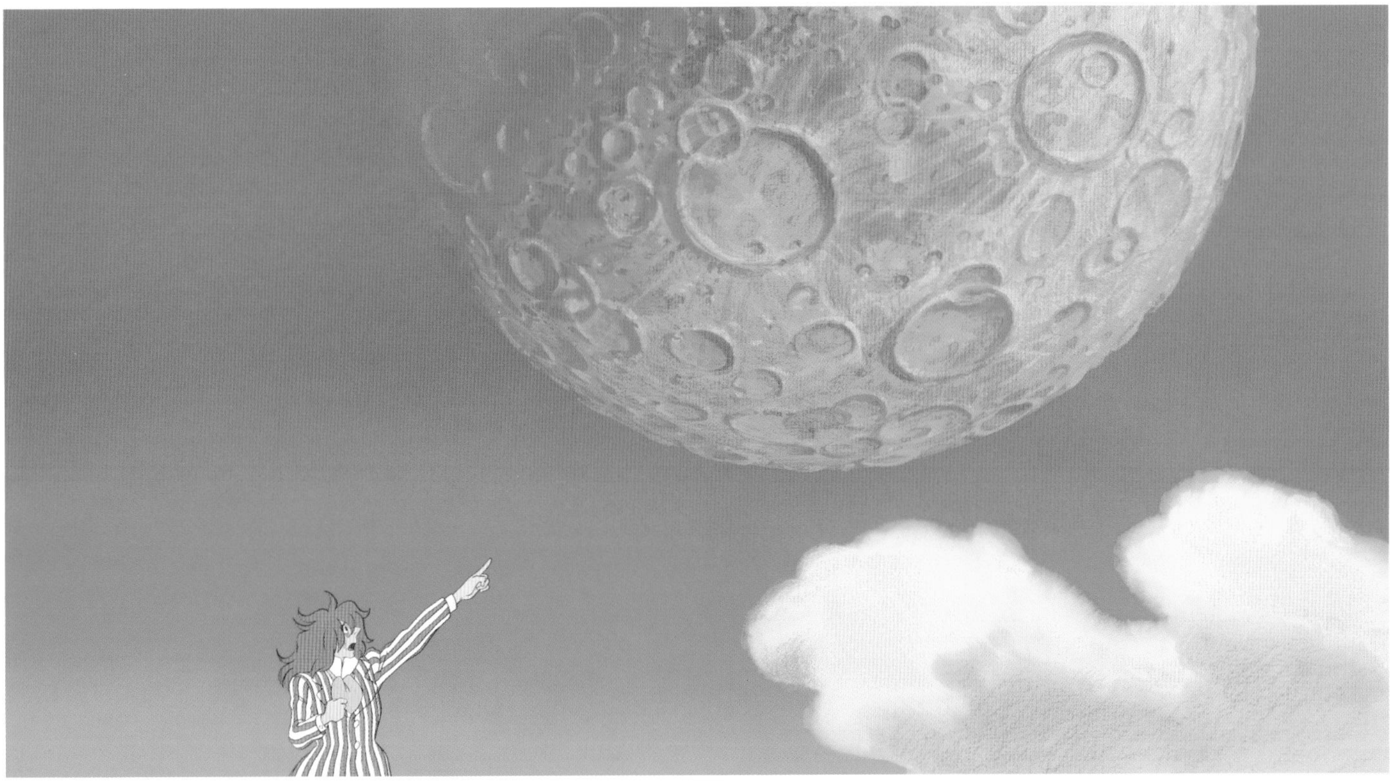

7

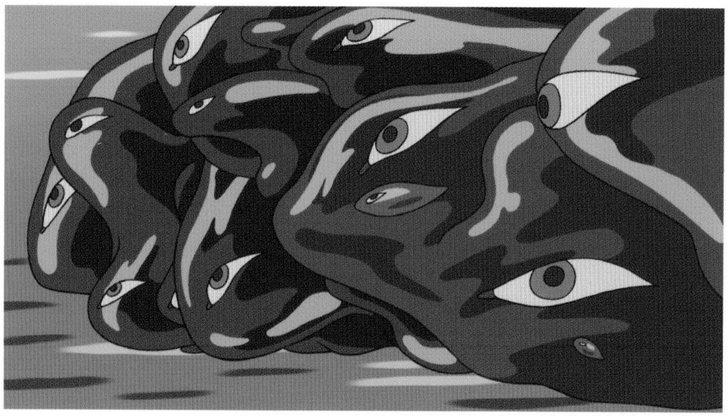
1

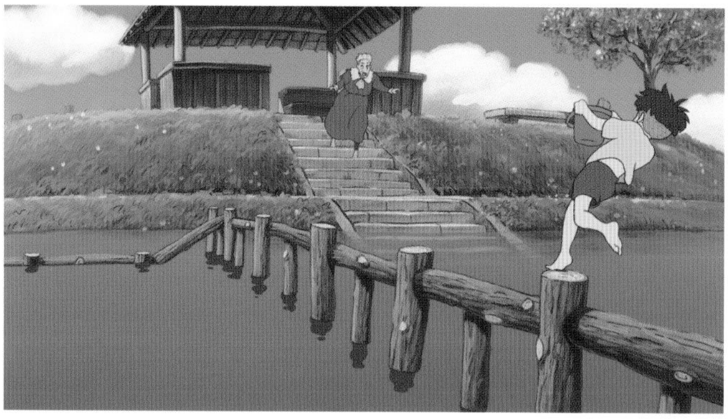
2

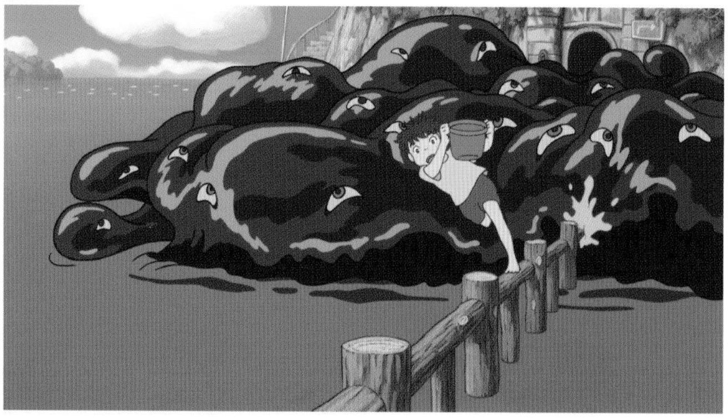
3

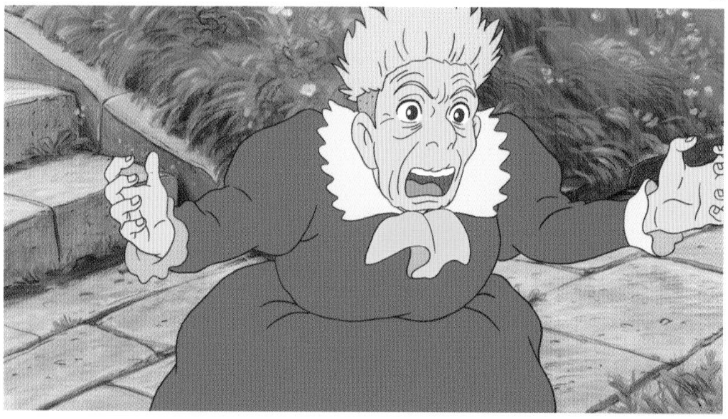
4

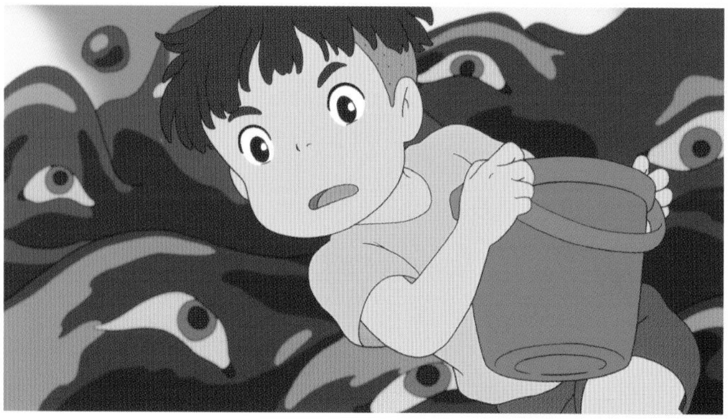
5

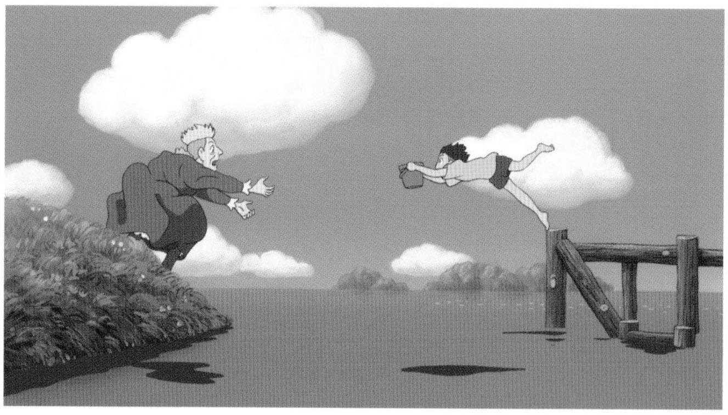
6

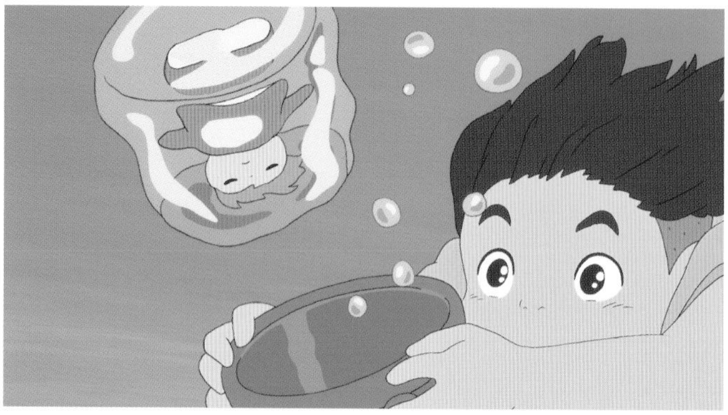
7

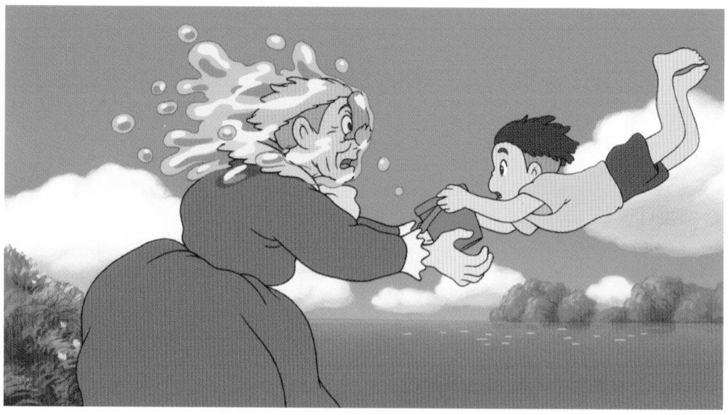
8

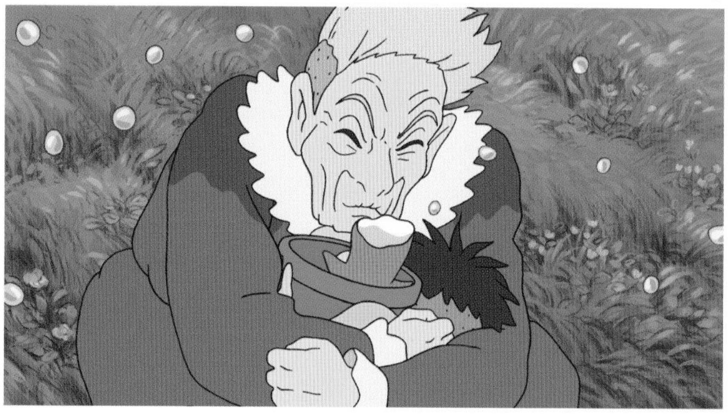
9

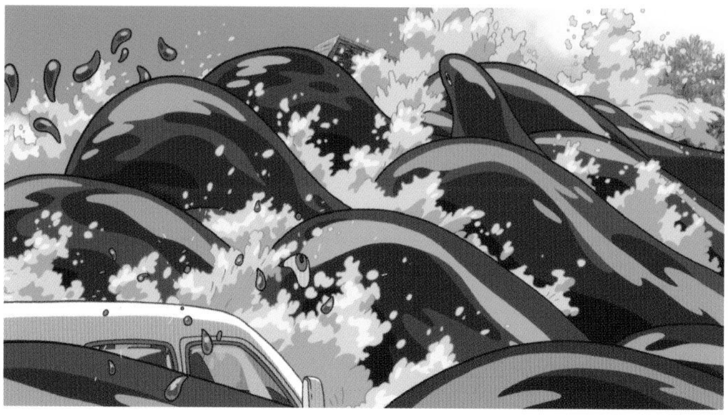
10

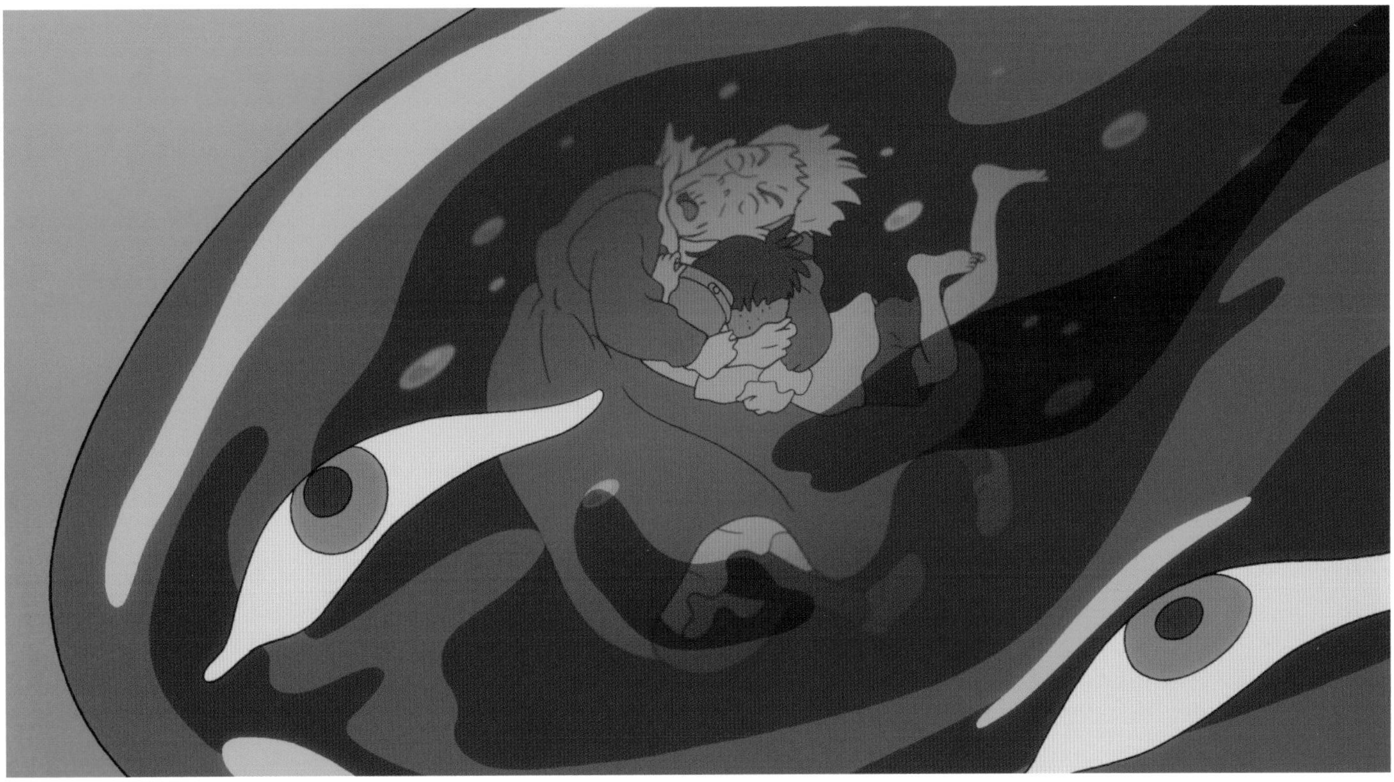

11

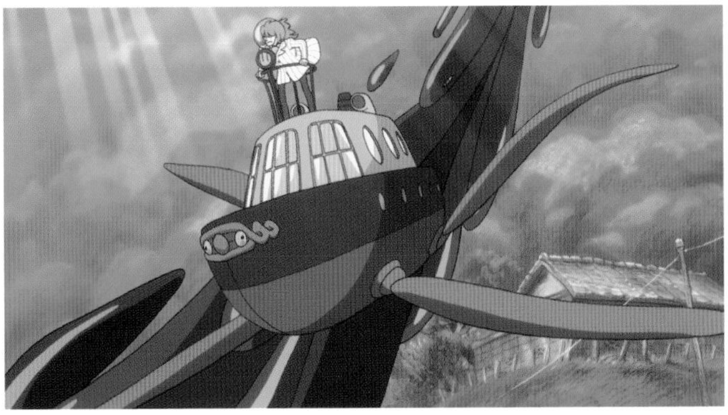

12

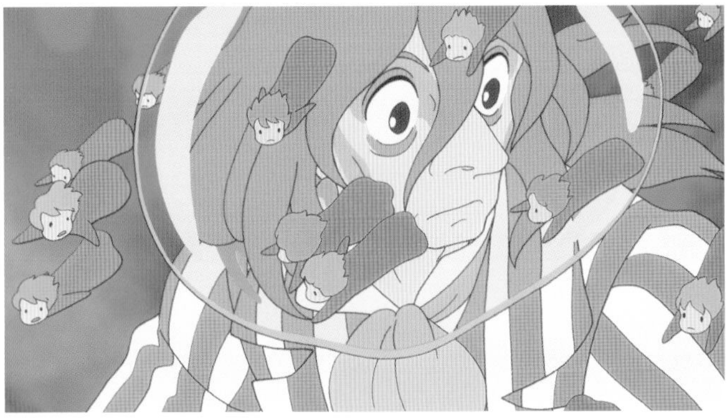

13

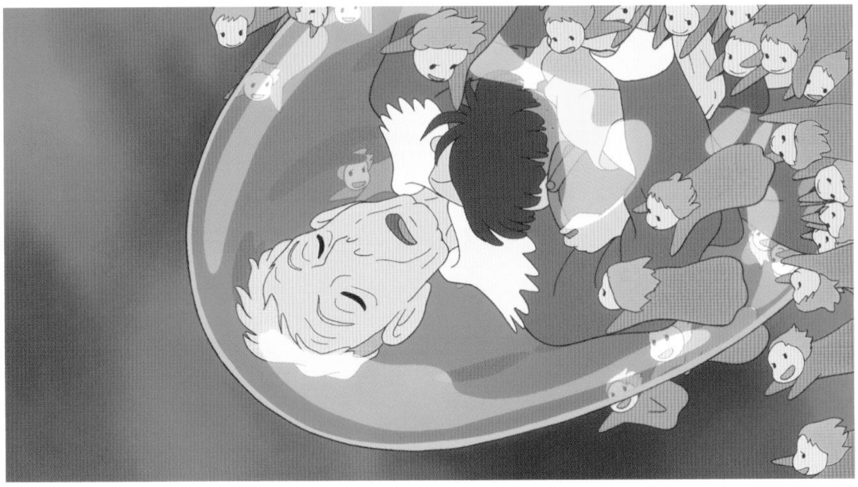

14

1–10 /Fujimoto dispatches the minions to fetch Sosuke and Ponyo, who refuse to listen. Sosuke runs across the fence toward Toki but…

11 /The minions swallow Sosuke and Ponyo, along with Toki, and bring them to Fujimoto.

12 /The *Basking Shark* following closely behind.

13 /Ponyo's little sisters rush in to persuade Fujimoto to let them return Sosuke and Ponyo to Lisa. Fujimoto reluctantly calls off the minions.

14 /The trio are led by the little sisters toward the giant jellyfish.

The Reunion

1 /The little sisters delivering Sosuke to Lisa's arms.
2 /Ponyo in the pail also makes a soft landing.
3 /Toki, caught by Yoshie and the others. She is surprised to find she's able to breathe underwater.
4 /Gran Mamare approaching Sosuke. She and Lisa appear to have already spoken mother-to-mother.
5 /Gran Mamare talking to Sosuke. The boy must accept Ponyo for what she is in order for her to become human.

Miyazaki seemed hesitant about showing Gran Mamare in human form at first, as she is a god-like presence in the film. Although there was an idea of making her a giant catfish that appeared in the form of a beautiful woman, he settled on depicting her as a goddess in the end. But once that was decided, I felt a responsibility to do my best to render her as a real existence in the world of the film.
—Supervising Animator: Katsuya Kondo

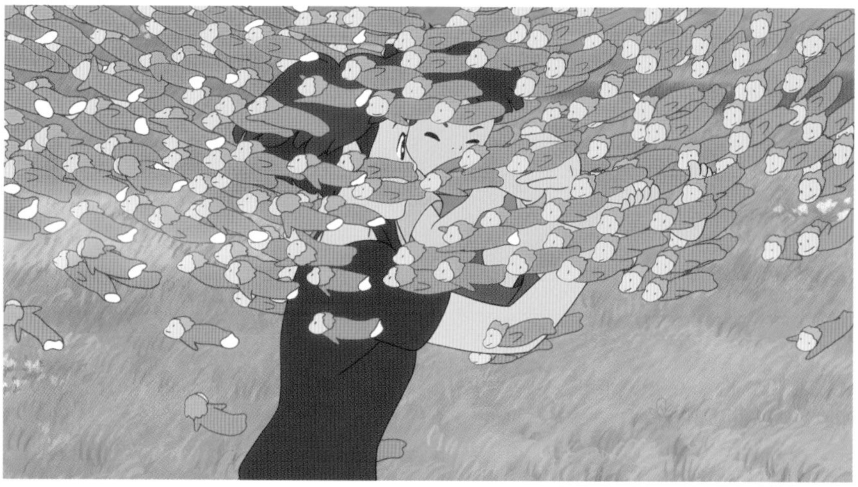

1

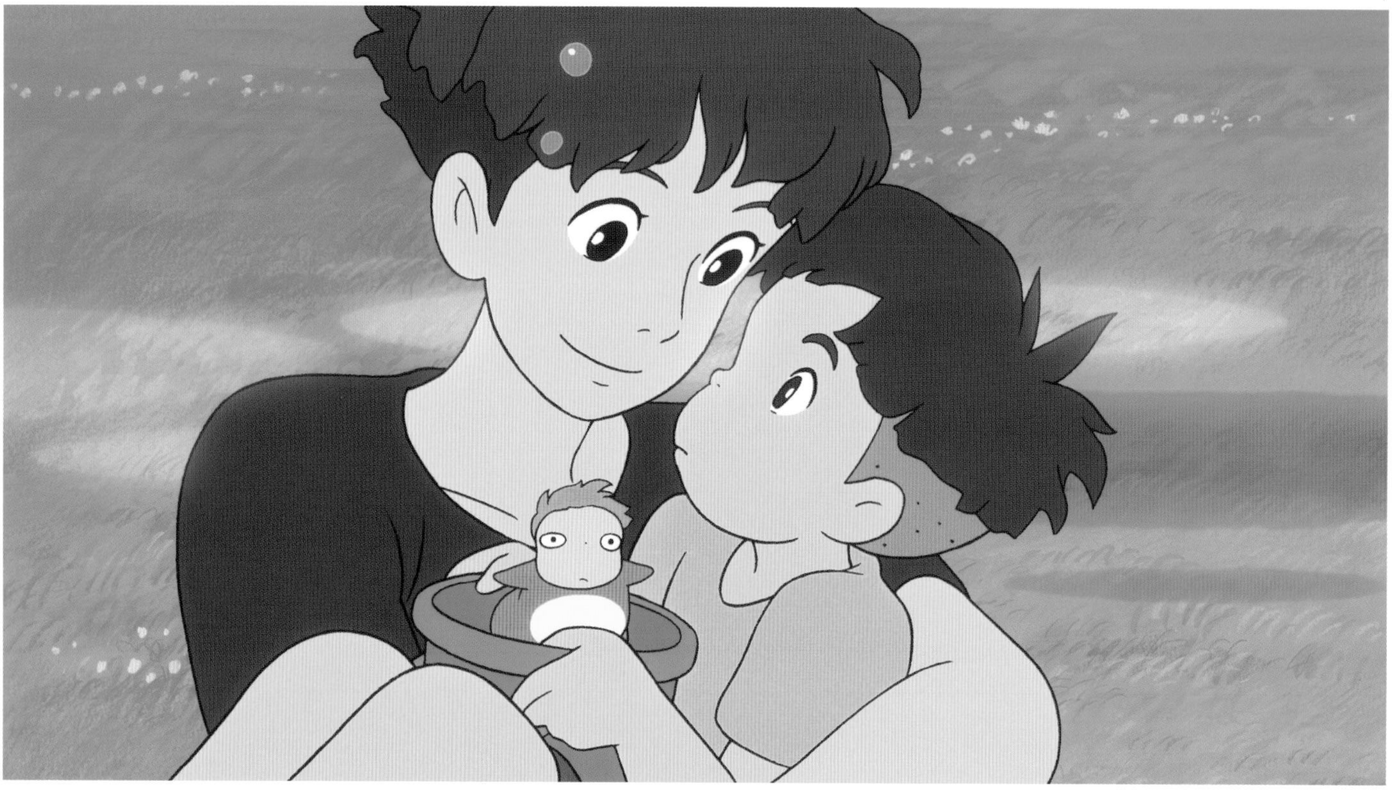

2

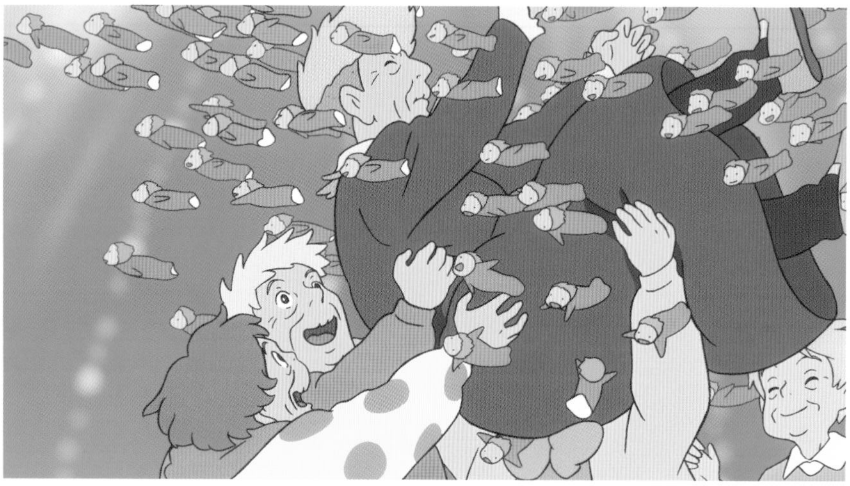

3

4

5

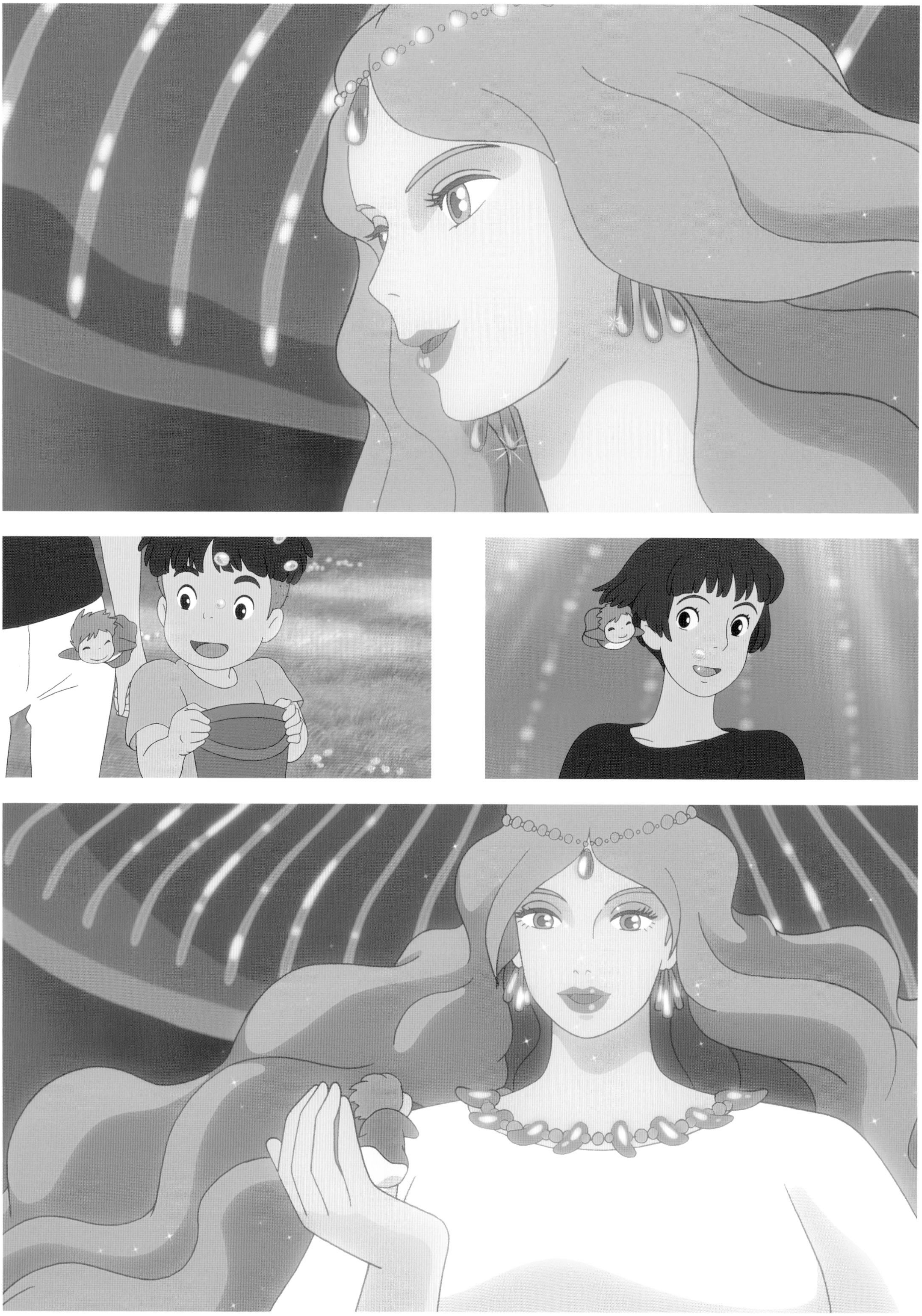

1 /"Could you love her even if she moved between two worlds?" "I love all the Ponyos. It's a big responsibility, but...I love that girl."
2, 3 /Ponyo overjoyed to hear Sosuke's answer. She also circles affectionately around her "mother-in-law."
4 /Mamare tells Ponyo that Sosuke will be her protector.
5–7 /Ponyo nodding as Mamare tells her she must give up her magical powers in order to become human.
8, 9 /Mamare enfolds Ponyo in a bubble and entrusts her to Sosuke. "Kiss the bubble, child, when you return to land... and Ponyo will become a girl, growing up, just like you."

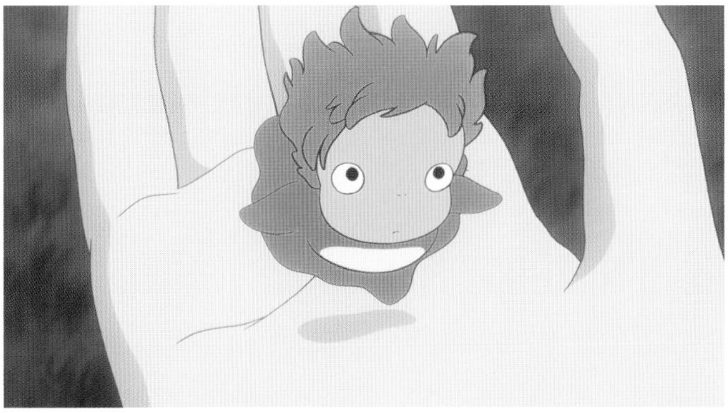

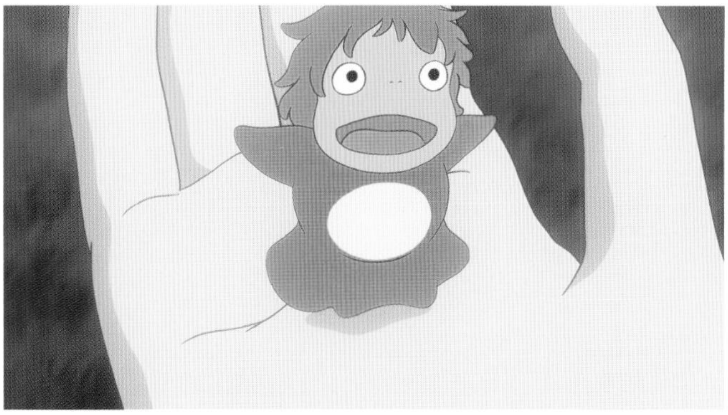

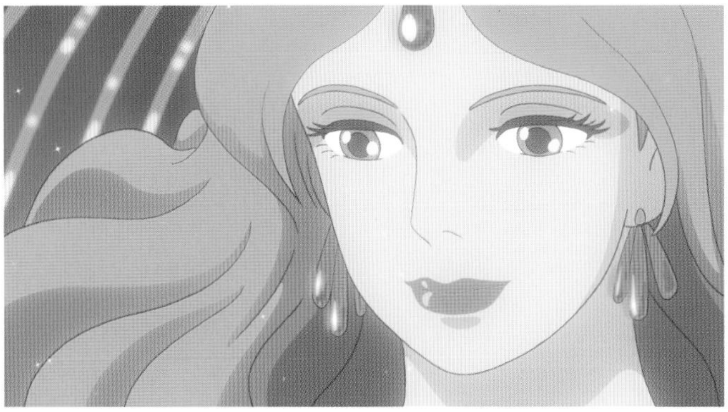

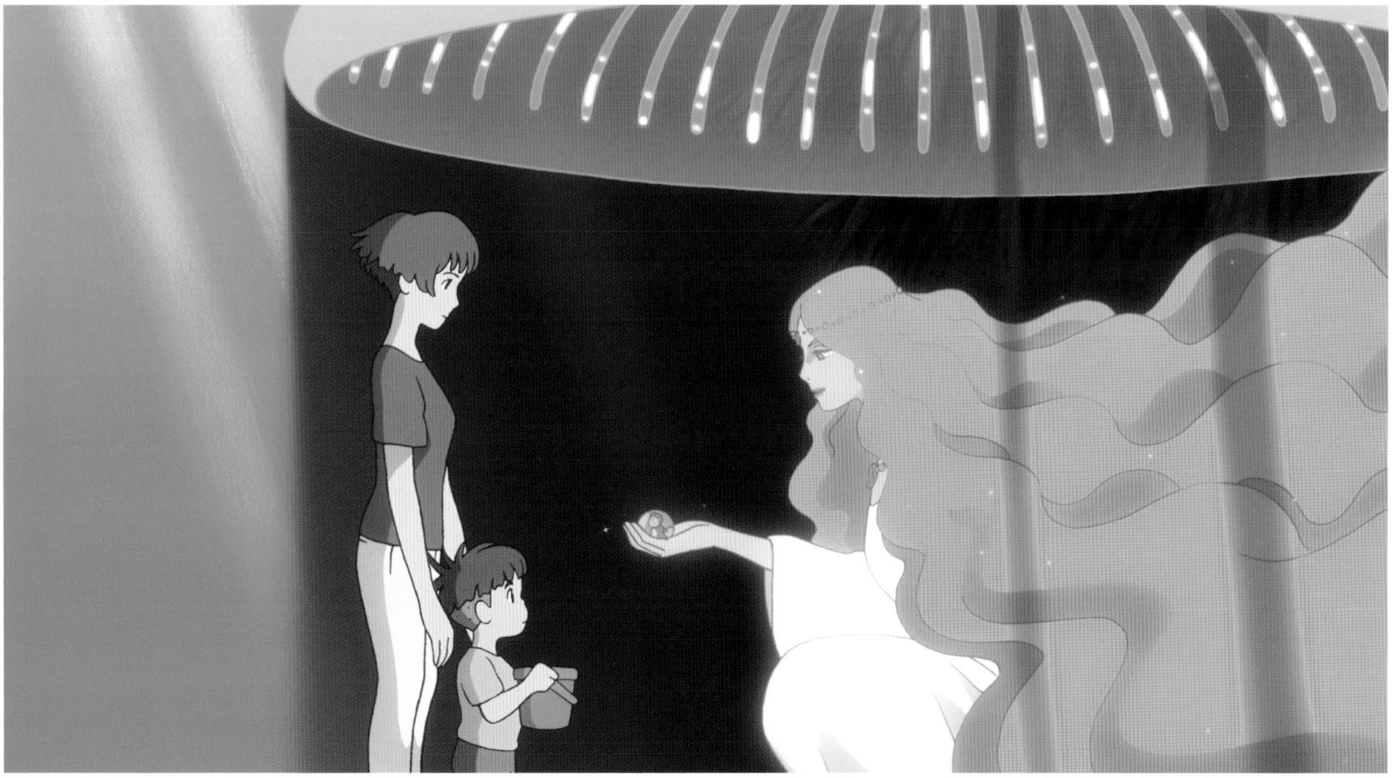

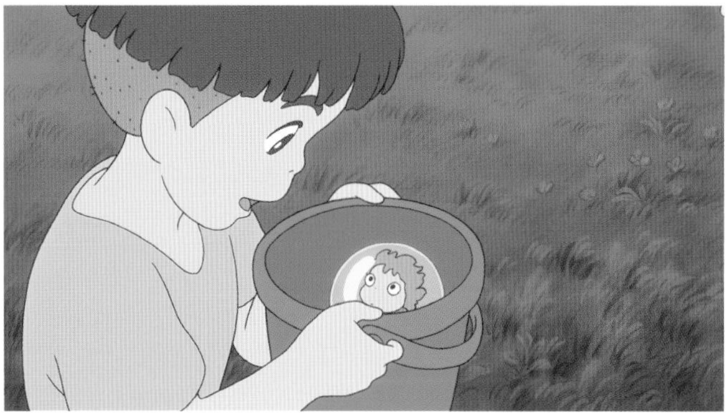

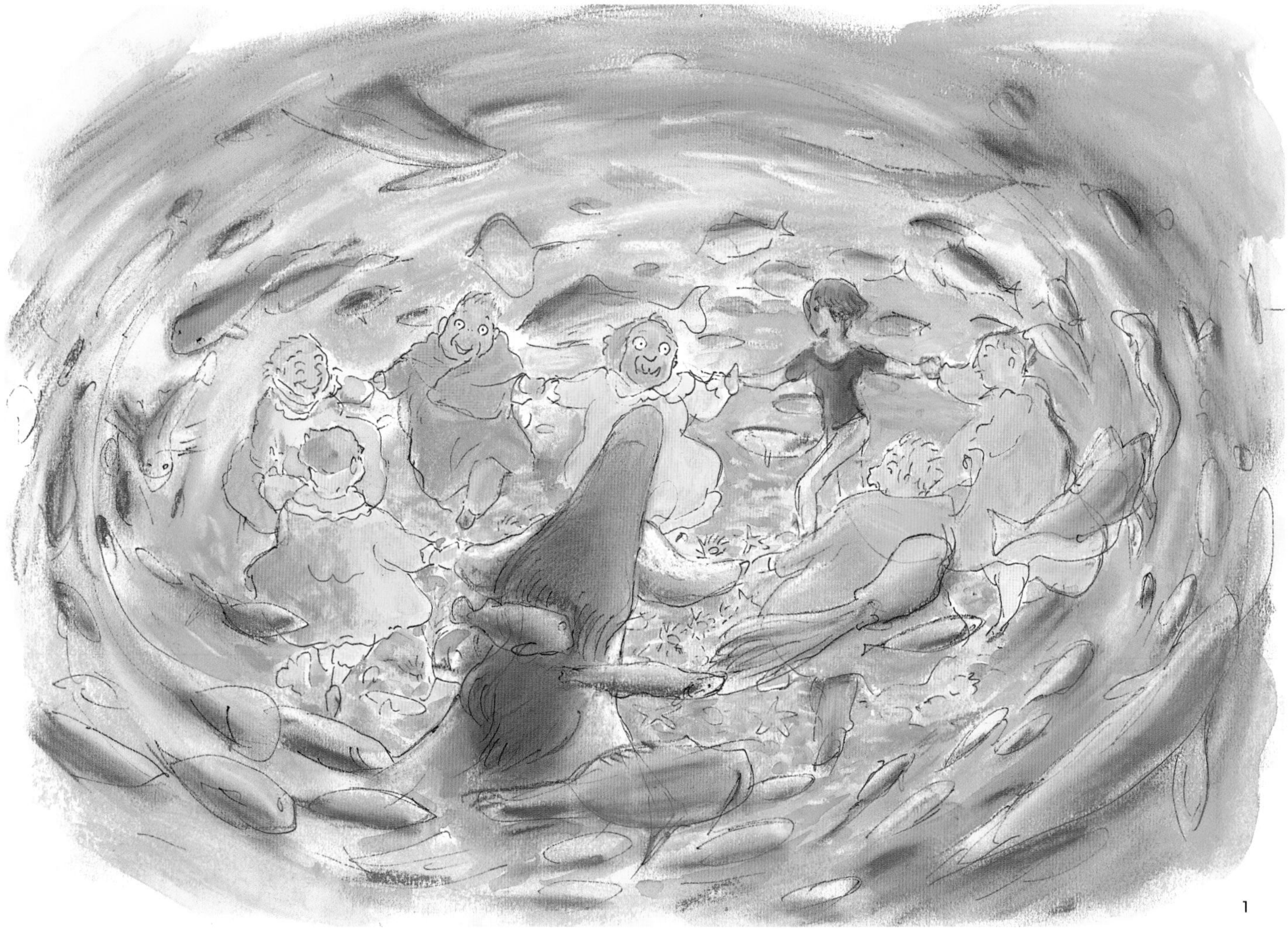

1

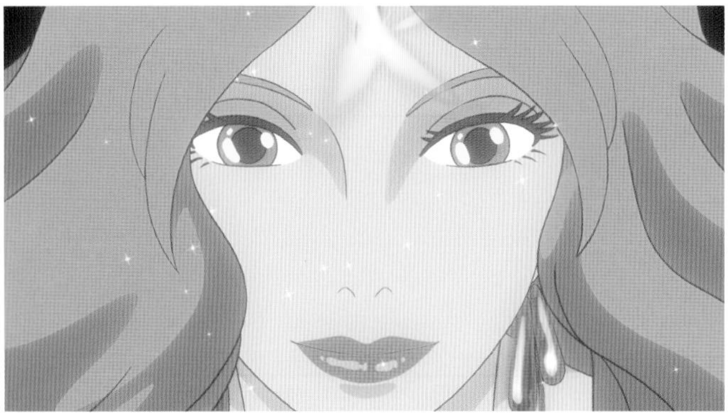

2

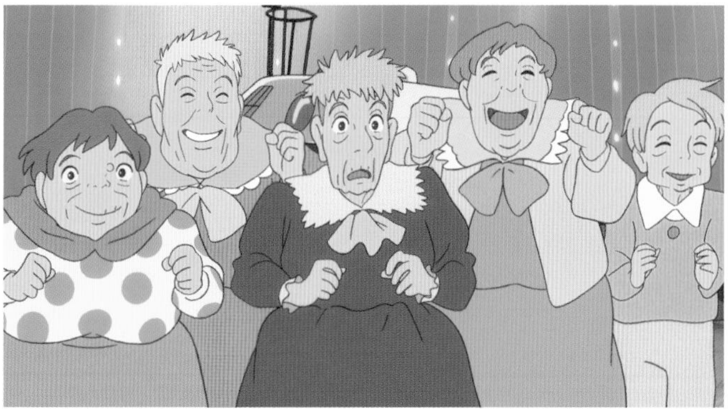

3

1 /Lisa, Mamare, and the elderly ladies dance [Concept sketch].
2 /Gran Mamare smiling as if to say, "You chose a wonderful boy, Ponyo." The balance of nature is restored by the union between Sosuke and Ponyo.
3 /The elderly ladies cheering.
4 /Toki hugging Sosuke. And then...
5–9 /Ponyo's little sisters saying goodbye and leaving. And then Mamare...
10, 11 /"Good luck, Lisa." "I'll need it."

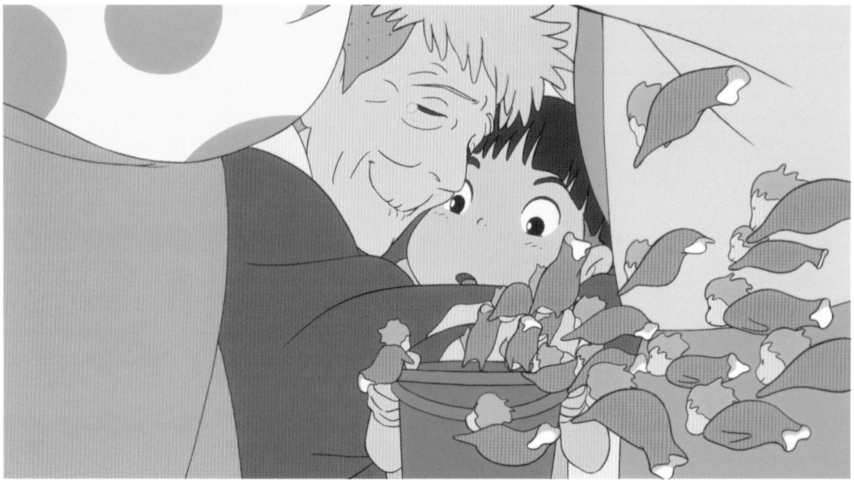

4

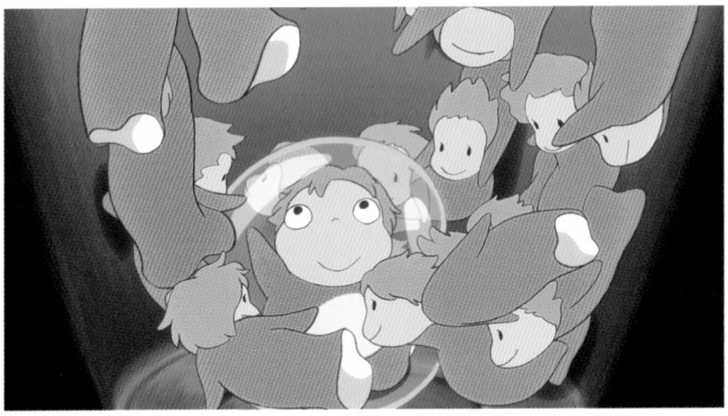

5

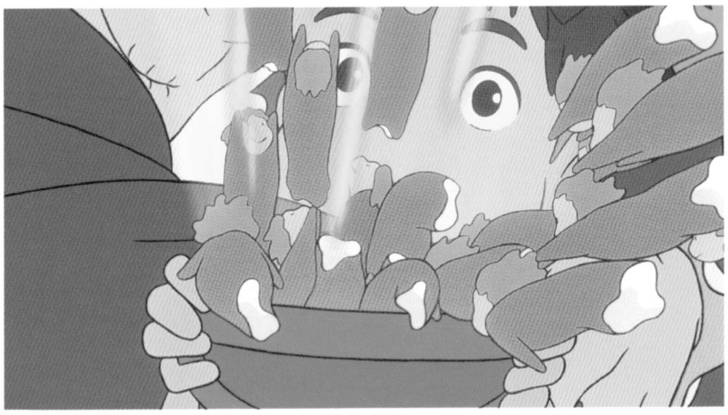

6

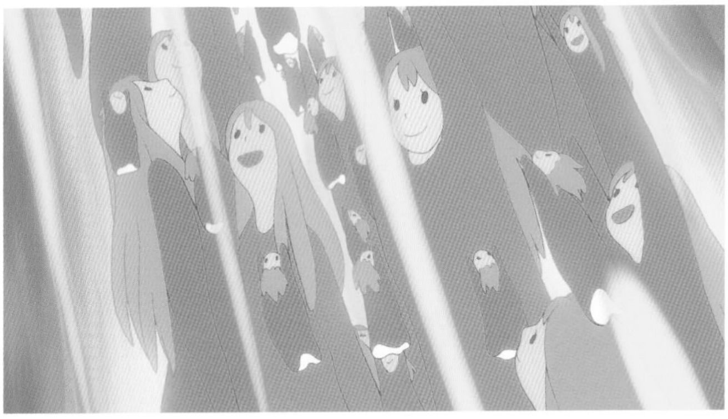

7

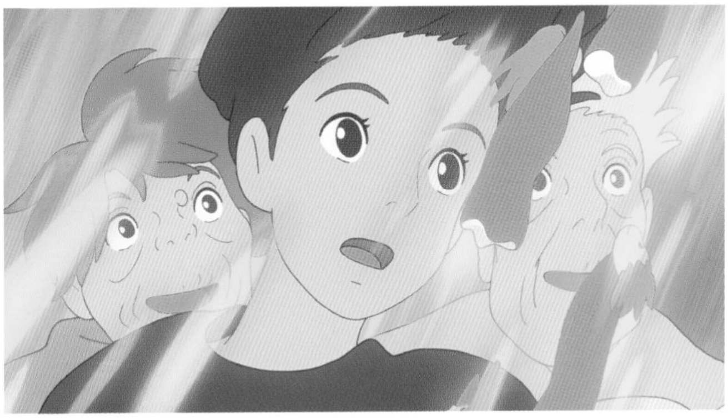

8

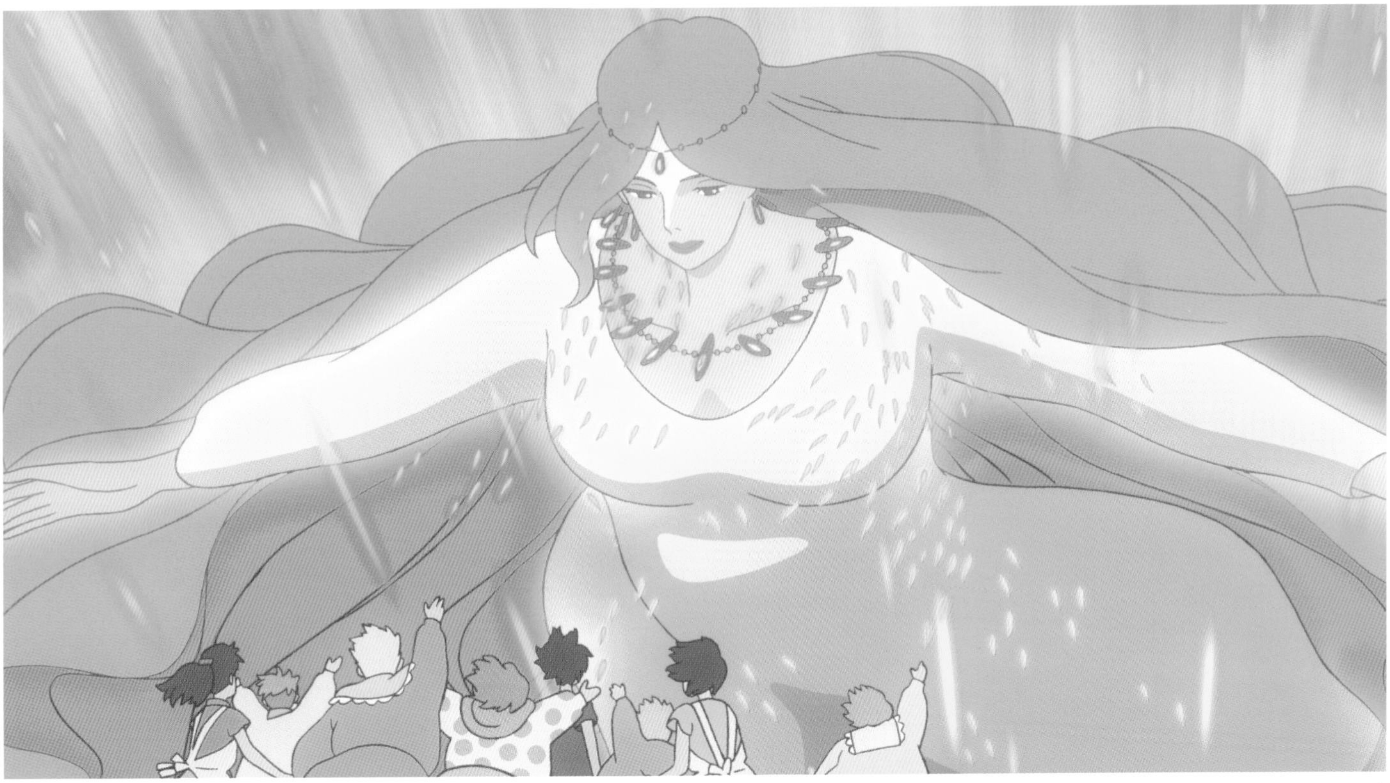

9

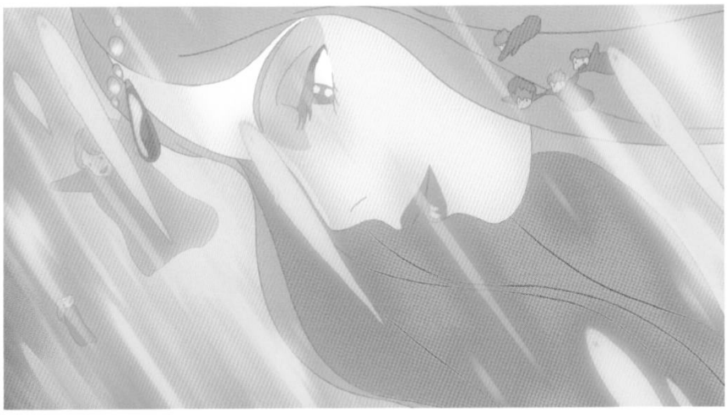

10

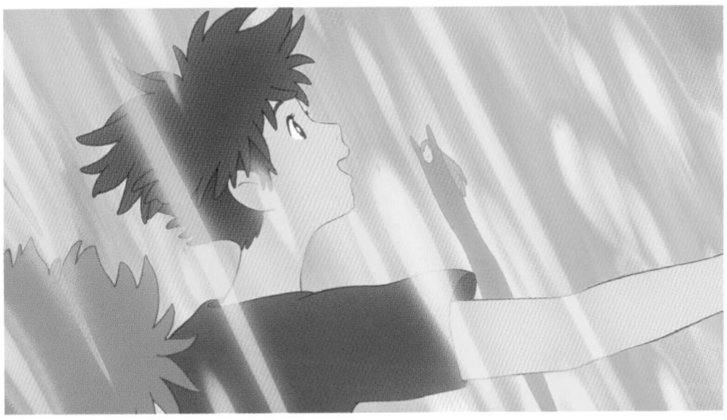

11

The Finale

1 /The sea and air are crowded with news and rescue planes, helicopters, and boats.
2 /The people of the Sunflower House brought back to the surface by the *Basking Shark*.
3 /The elderly ladies have completely recovered their health.
4 /"Care for Ponyo." Fujimoto shaking hands with Sosuke.
5, 6 /*The Koganei Maru* returns safely to port.
7 /"Look, Ponyo, there's my dad's ship," Sosuke tells Ponyo. And then...!

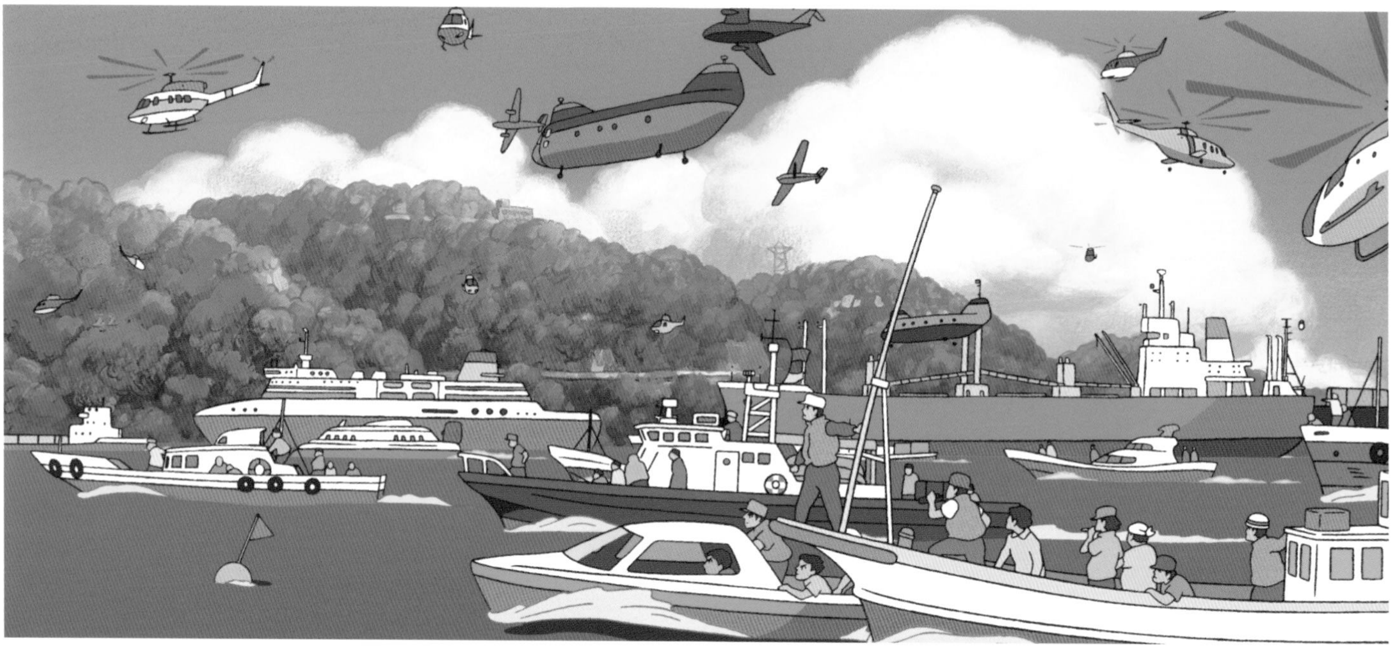

1

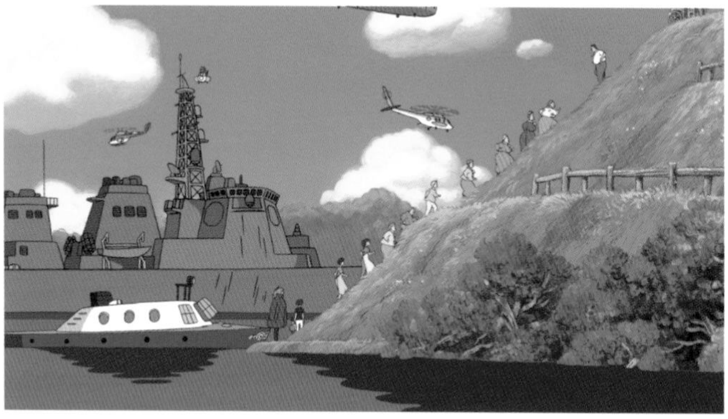

2

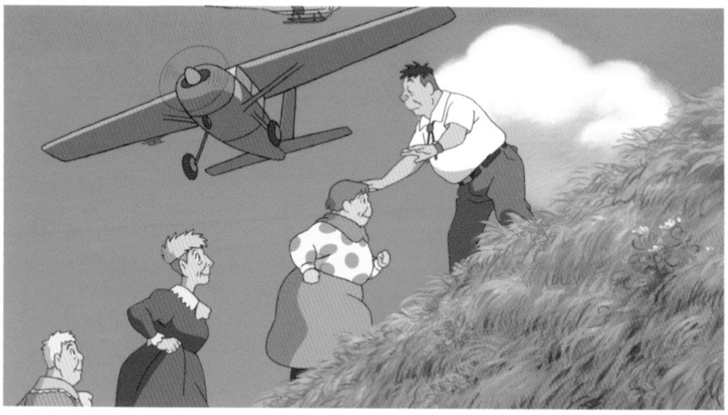

3

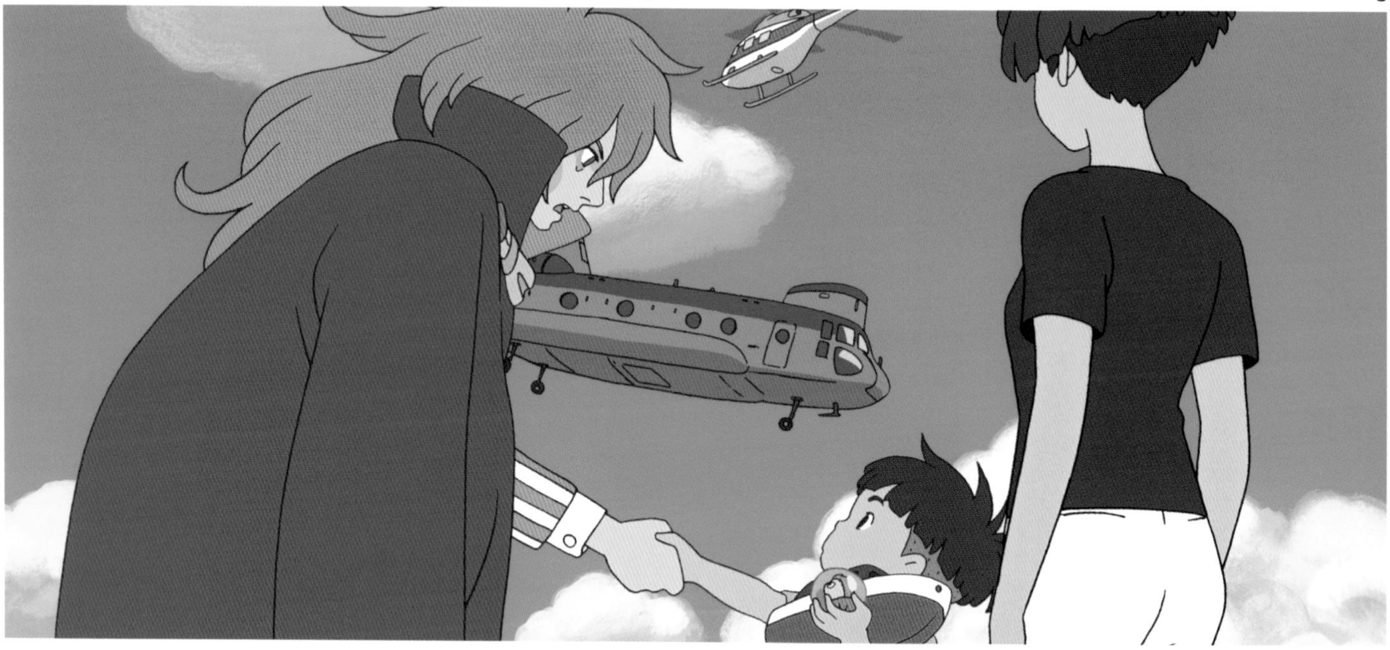

4

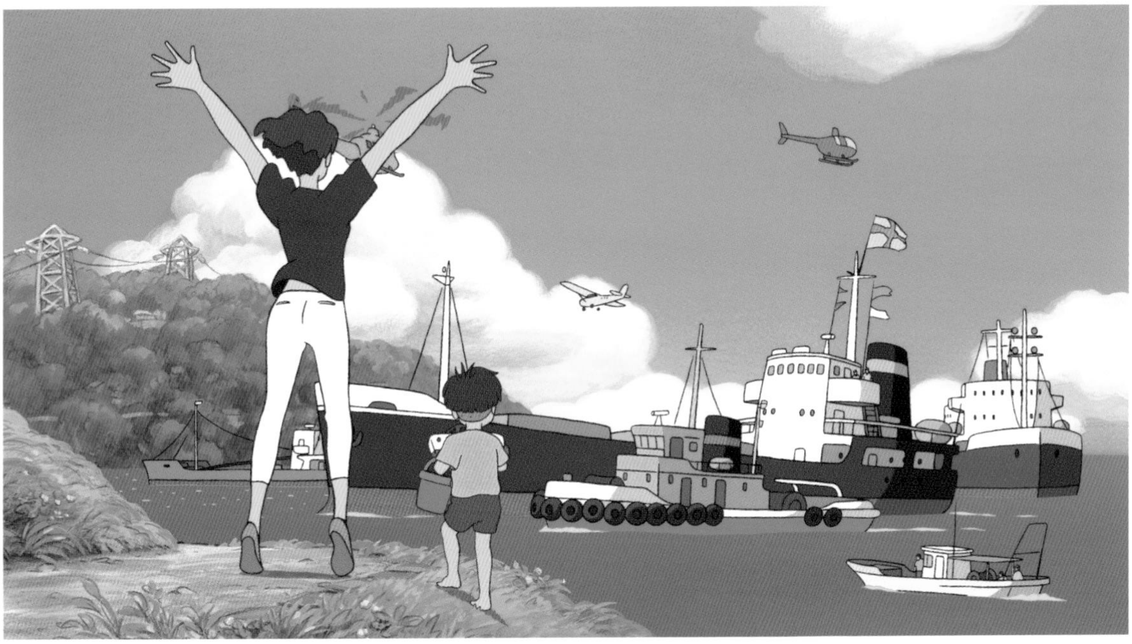

5

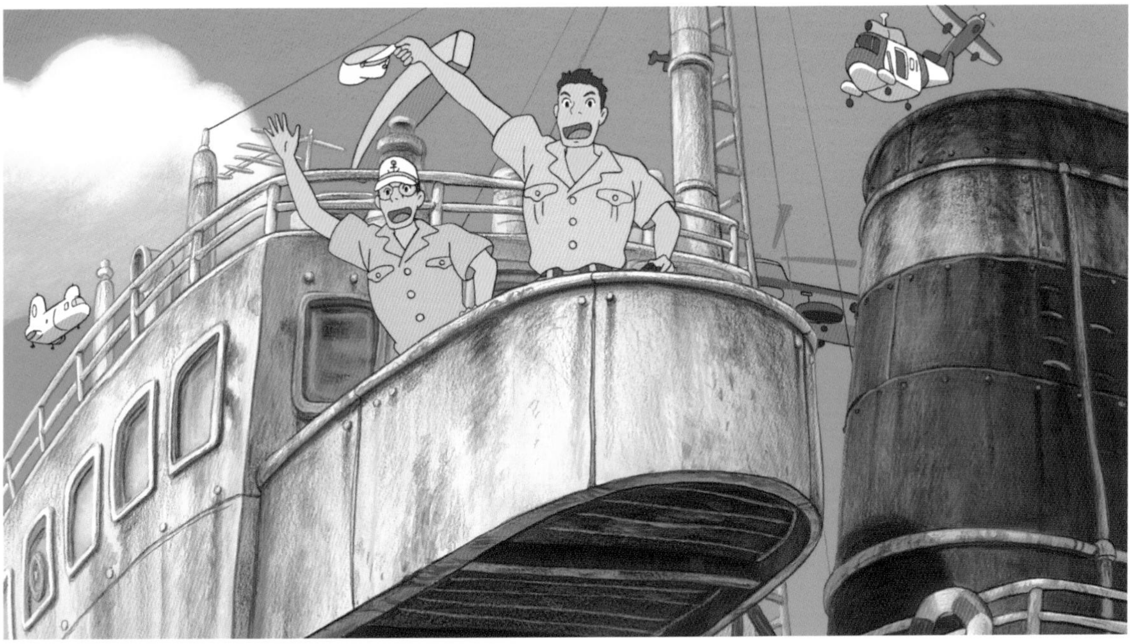

6

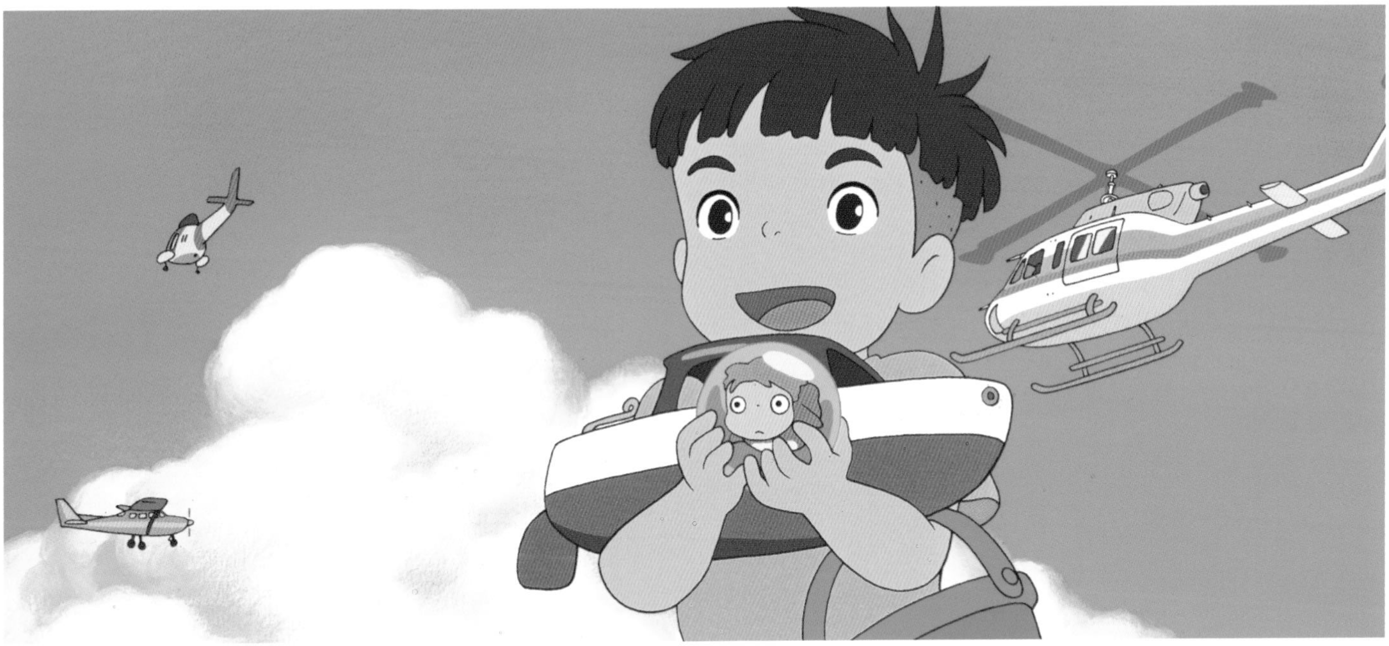

7

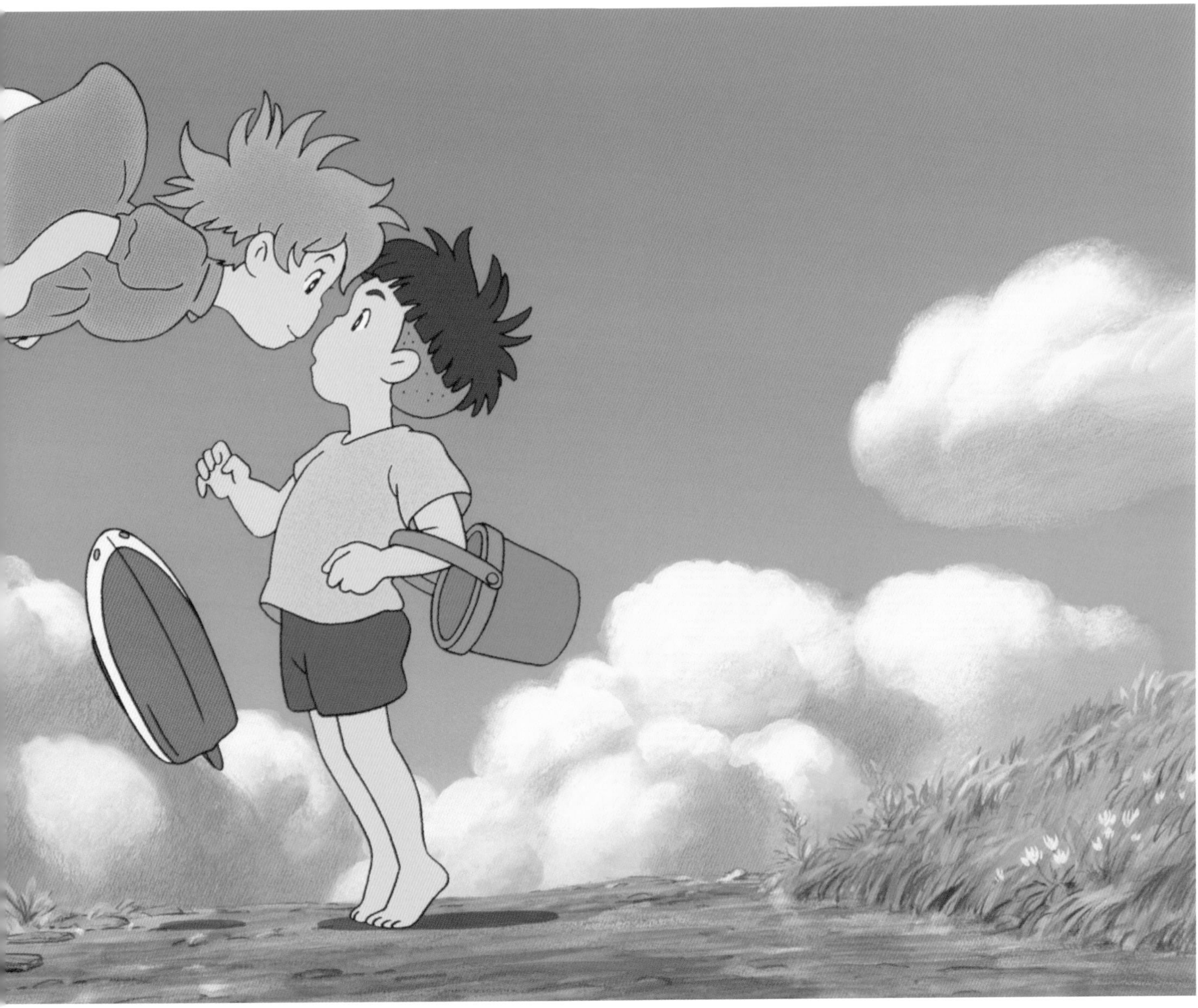
The bubble bounces up and kisses Sosuke. Out pops the girl Ponyo and...

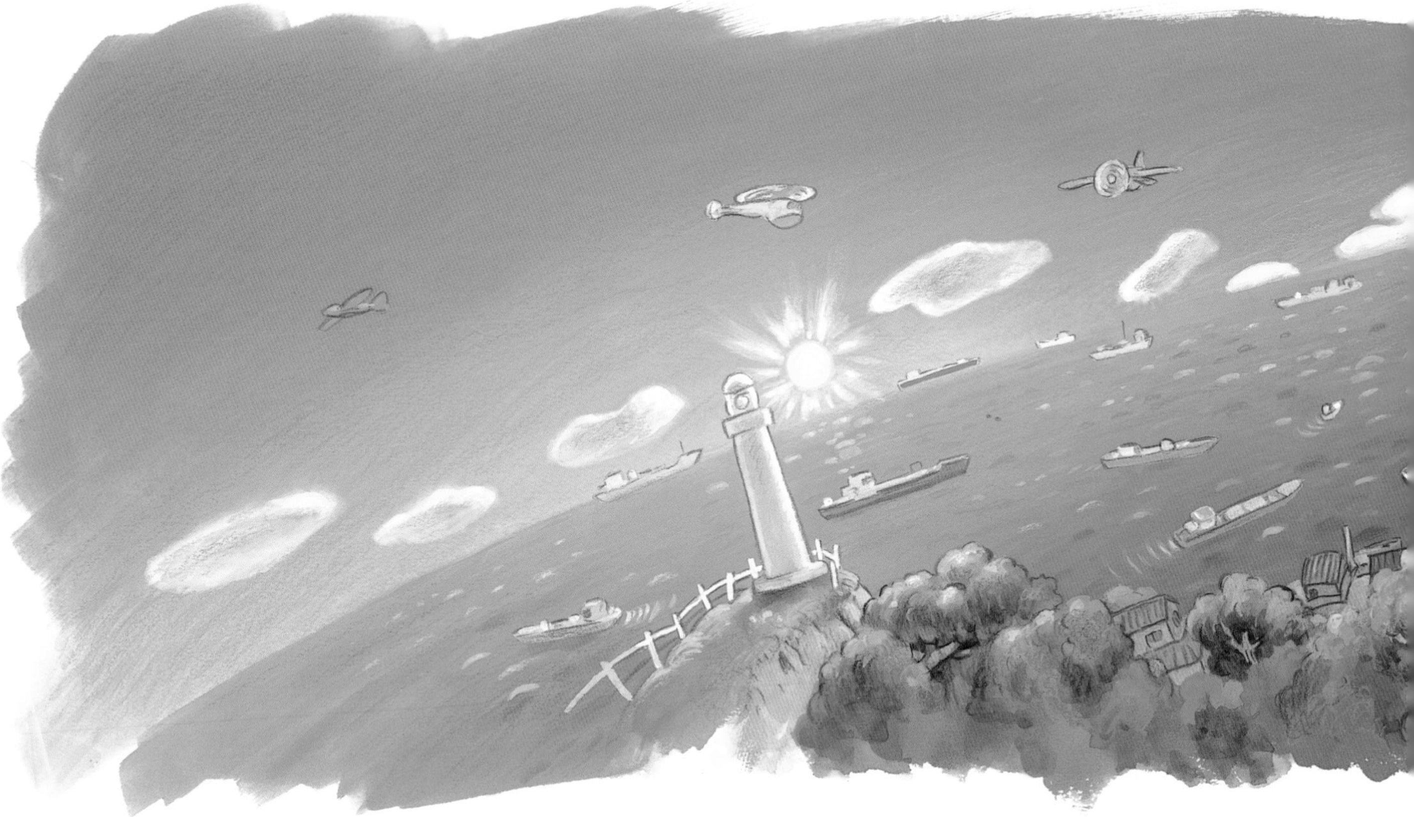

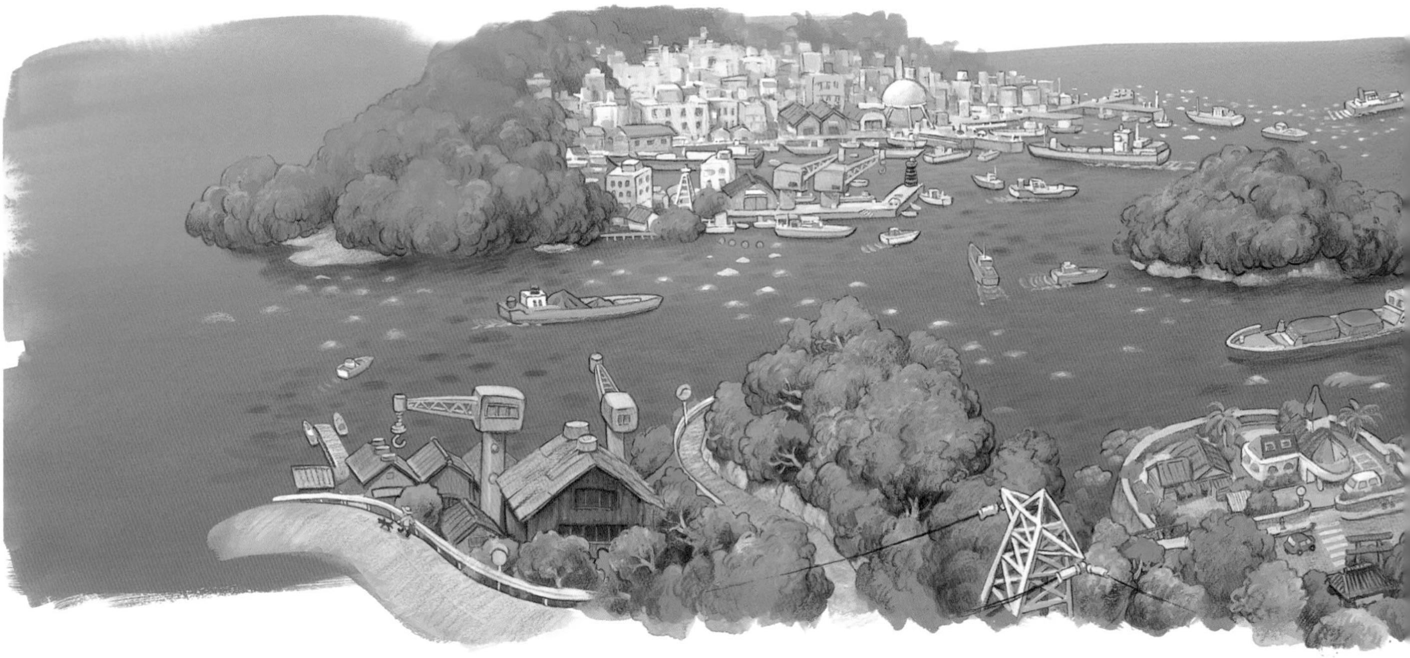

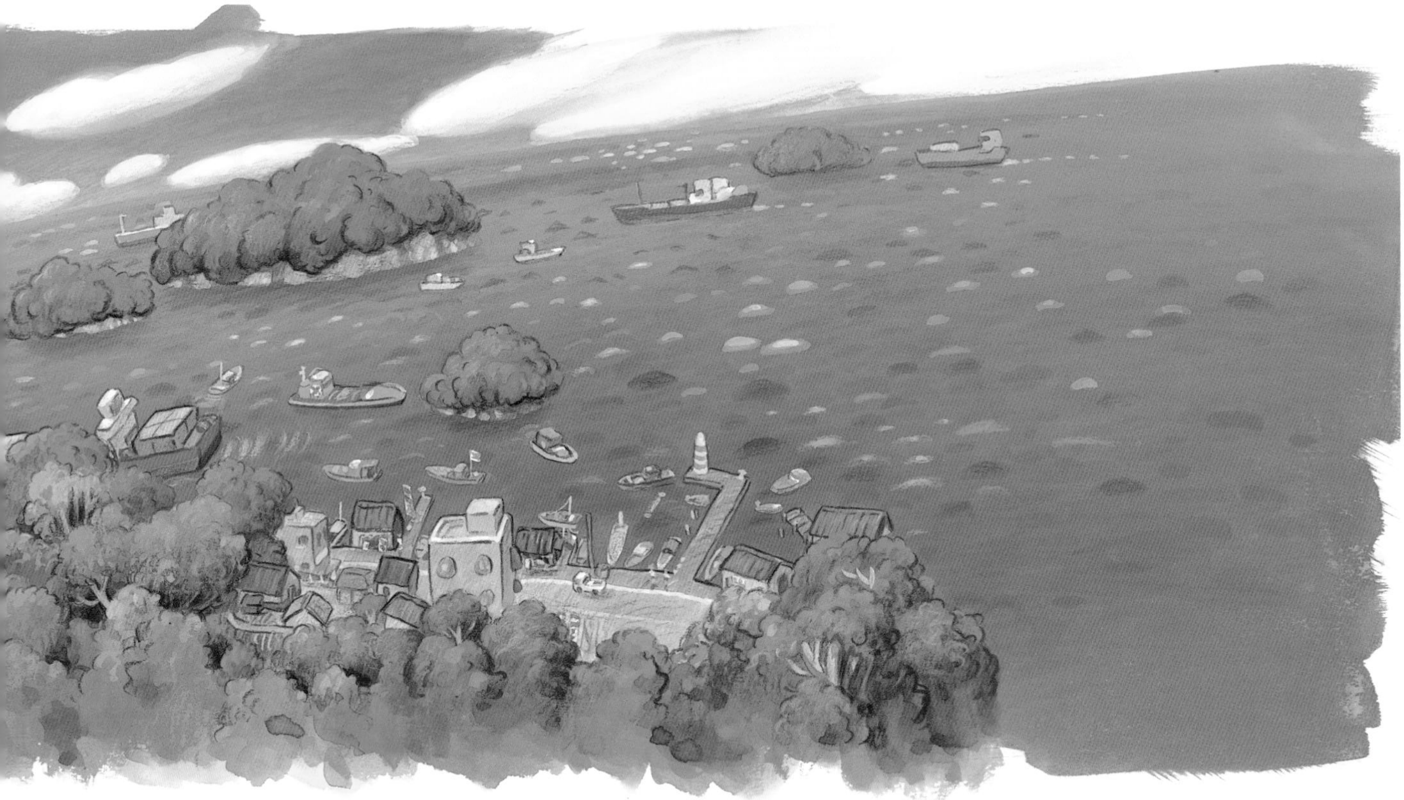

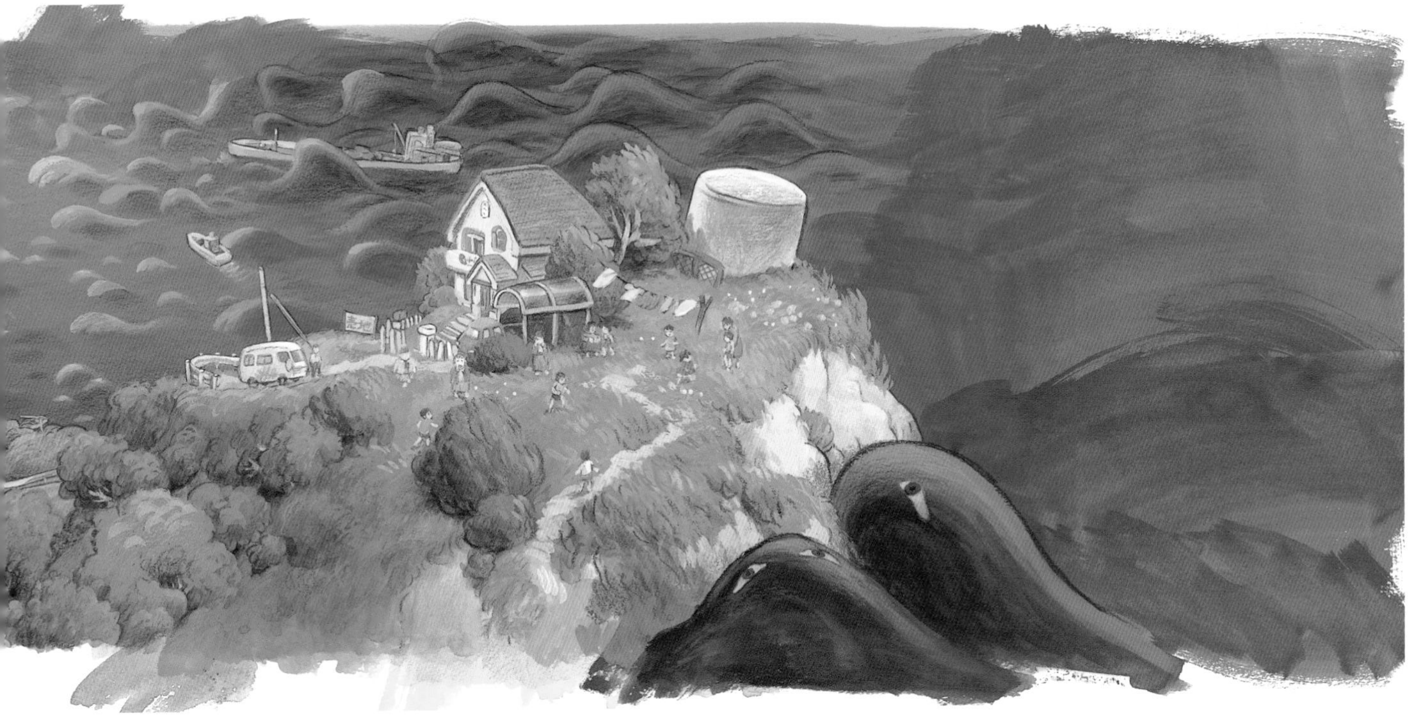

The Ending

P.214–221 /Background art of scenes drawn for the ending. In the film, they are connected to make one long picture.
P.222–223 /The actual stills, which include the end credits. The illustrations next to each name were drawn by Hayao Miyazaki.

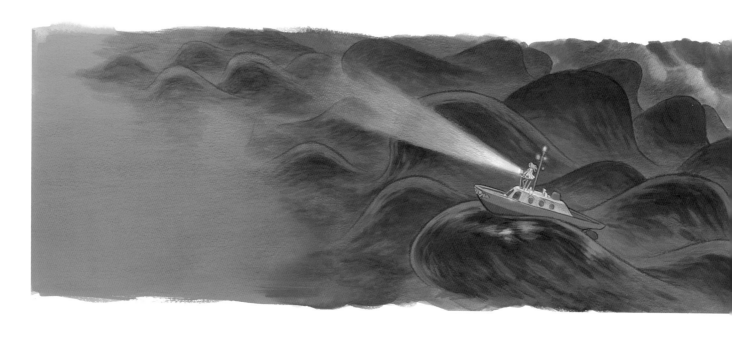

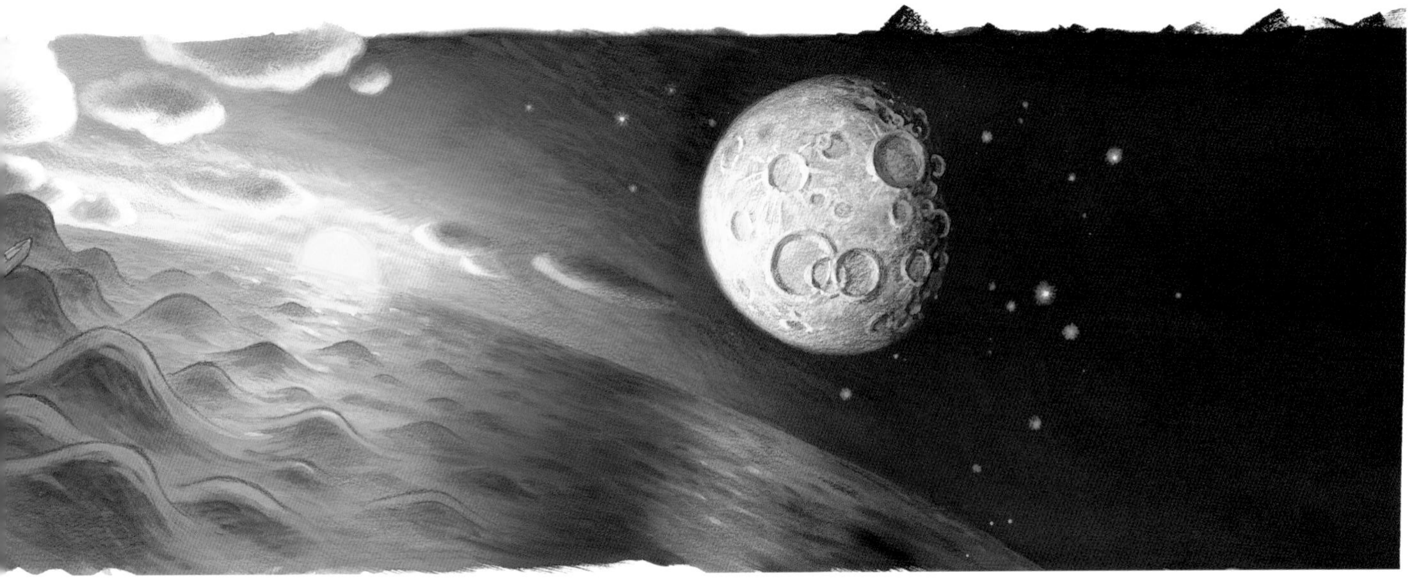

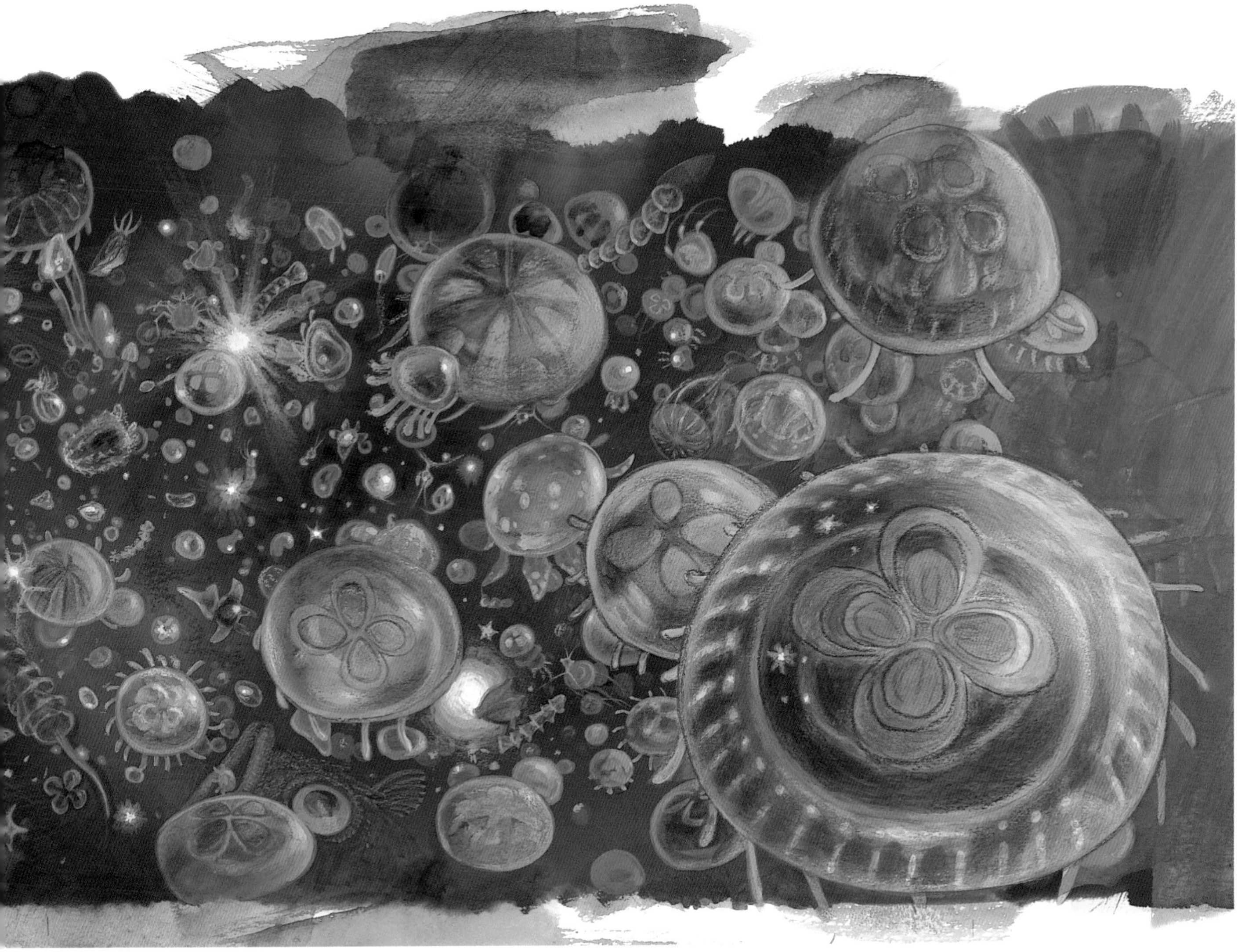

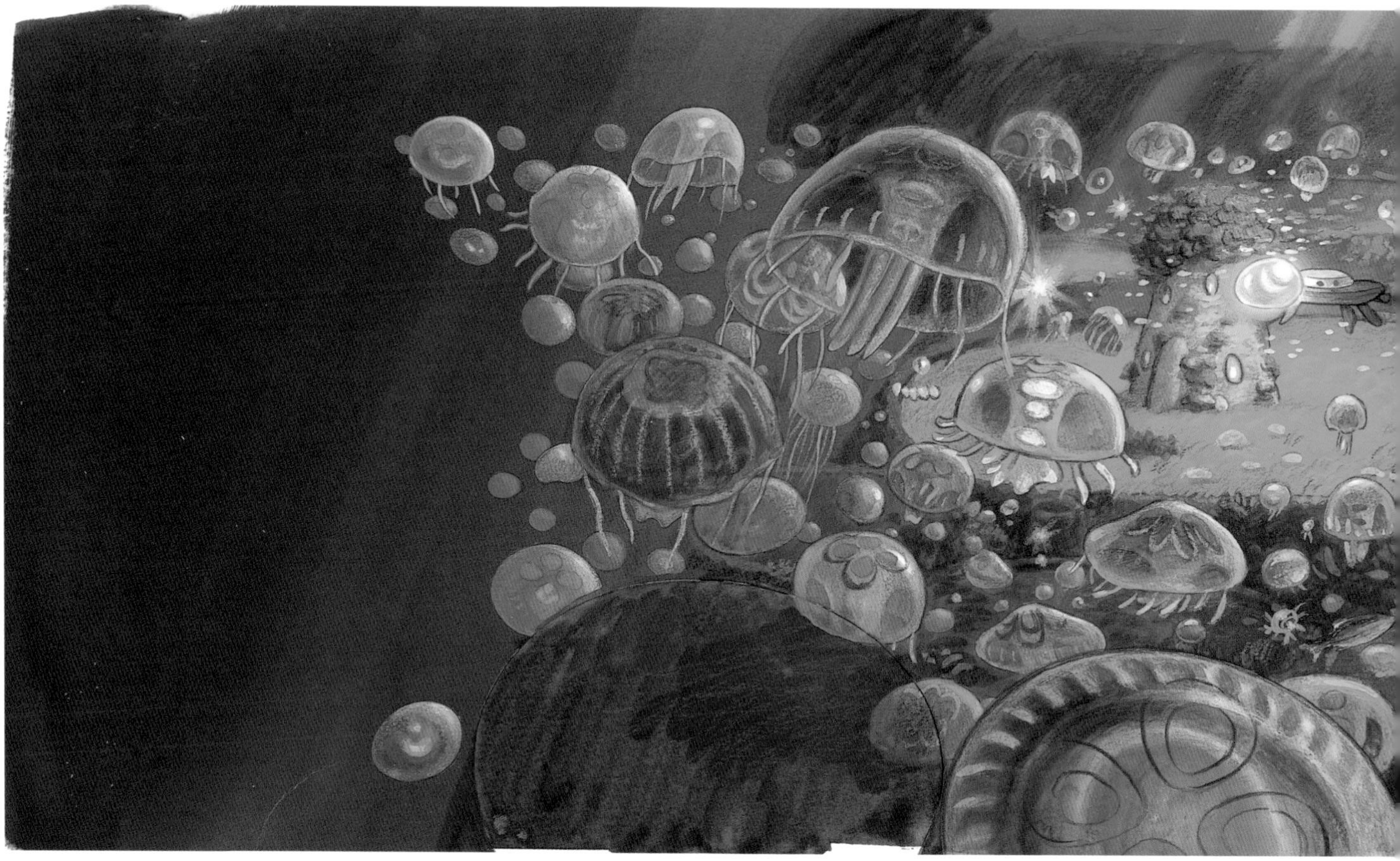

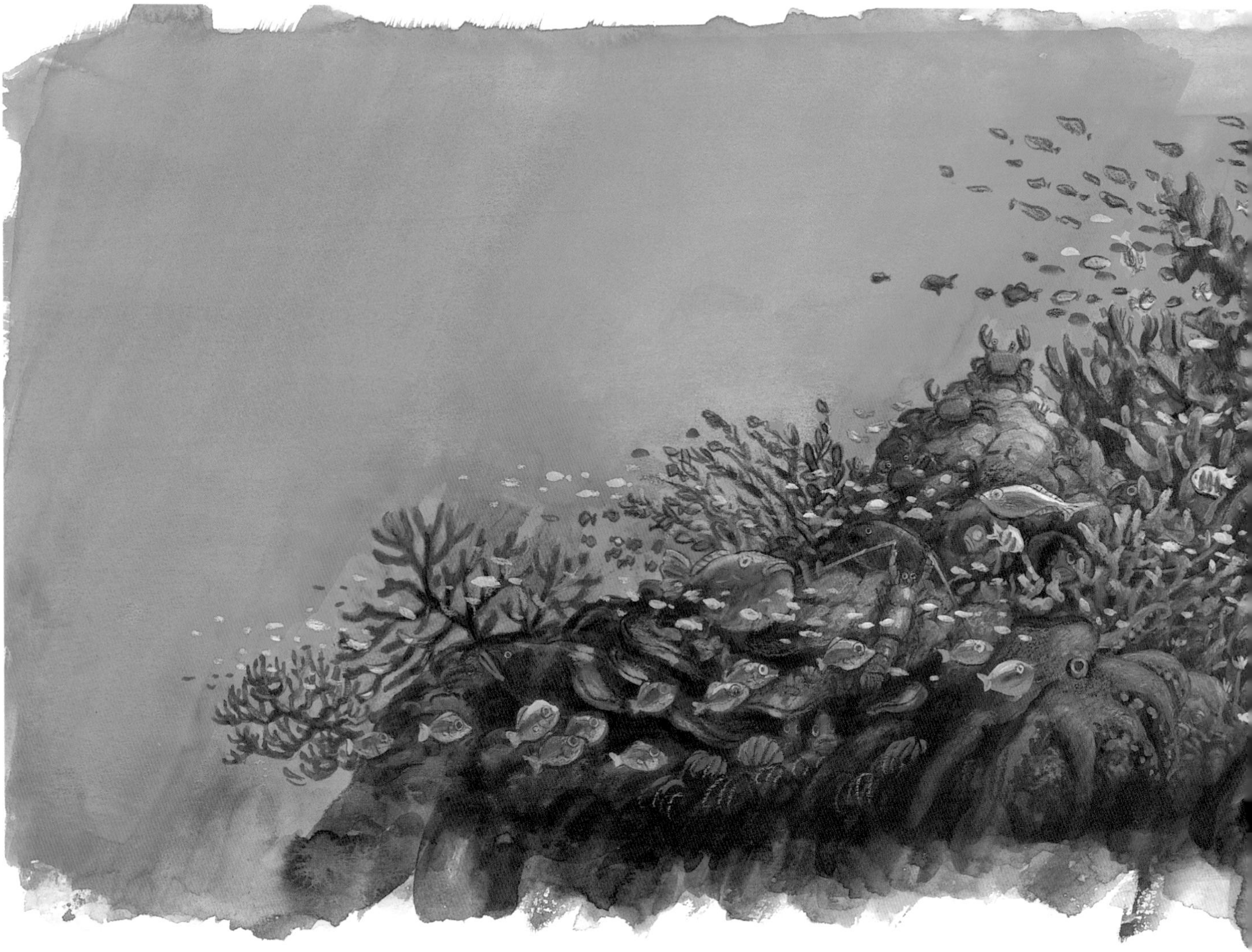

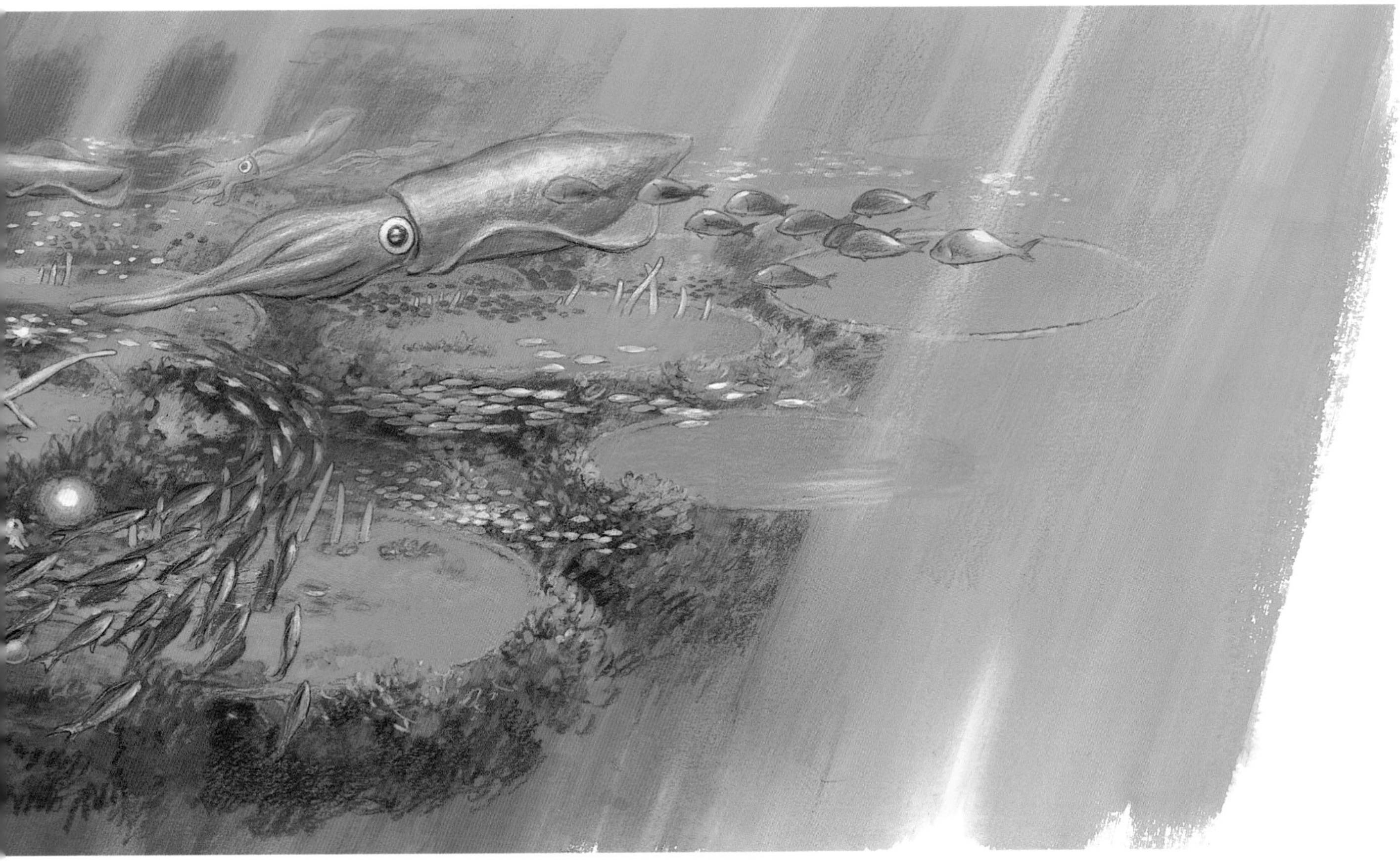

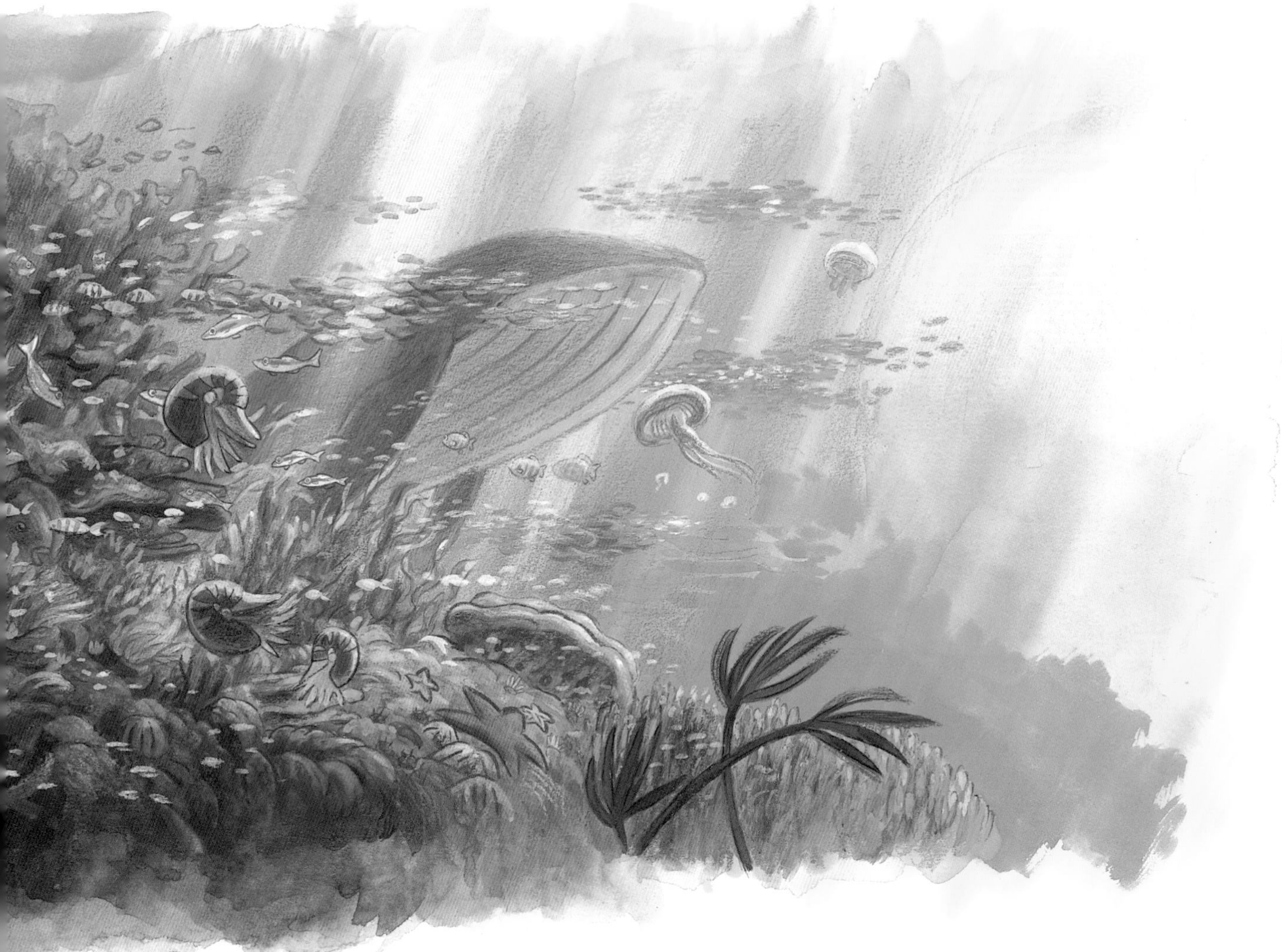

このえいがをつくった人

相川 敦	浅野宏一	東 誠子	熱田尚美
天海祐希	網崎 直	荒井竜吉	新神紀乃
荒川 格		粟田 務	石井邦俊
石井裕章	石角安沙美	市川 南	石住昭彦
伊勢伸平	磯前史子	板垣恵一	板橋 徹
一村晃夫	市村俊太郎	伊藤かおり	伊藤郷平
伊藤高康	伊藤 望	伊藤久代	伊藤純子
糸川敬子	稲城和夫	稲村武志	伊奈涼子
井上秀司	井上雅史	伊平容子	今泉 武
今井知記	居村健治	岩上由武	岩沢 駿

1

岩柳恵美子	上田太士	上田祐平	上野芳弘
氏家齊一郎	内田沙織	内田宣政	鵜木久徳
梅林画加里	エヴァン・マ	海老澤賢希	太田久美子
大谷 茜	大谷久美子	大塚伸治	大友康子
大橋のぞみ	大橋 宏	大原真琴	大村まゆり
大森 崇	男鹿和雄	岡田 健	岡田知子
沖田博文	奥井 敦	奥田誠治	奥山奈奈
小越 将	長田昌子	小野田和由	小野田 光
小見明子	新原裕之	賀川 愛	垣田由紀子
覚 和歌子	笠松広司	春日井直美	片岡冨枝

2

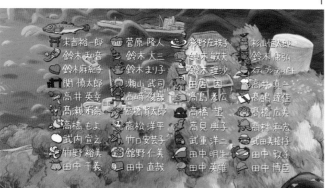

末吉裕一郎	菅原隆人	杉野左秩子	杉山恒太郎
鈴木和音	鈴木大三	鈴木敏夫	鈴木康弘
鈴木麻紀子	鈴木まり子	鈴木理沙	スティーブンアルパート
関 憤太郎	瀬山武司	田居 因	高井真一
高井英幸	高崎俊哉	高島孝広	高嶋達佳
高瀬有奈	高橋賢太郎	高橋 望	高橋広美
高橋もよ	高松洋平	高見典子	高村和宏
武内宣之	竹口安芸子	武重洋二	武田美樹子
竹野裕美	舘野仁美	田中明生	田中敦子
田中千義	田中直哉	田中英雄	田中博臣

5

田名部徹也	谷 香織	谷平久美子	田畑ゆり
玉川典行	田村 篤	田村 淳	田村智恵子
田村雪絵	千田 諭	千葉香代	塚越隆行
たかもと晶子	瓶 ちひろ	告 きよ子	津司紀子
土谷大輔	土屋 勝	筒井亮子	角川桂子
手島晶子	手塚裕介	寺田久美子	寺田貞佑子
土井洋輝	土居寿紀子	堂園佑子	土岐弥生
所ジョージ	冨沢恵子	内藤まゆ	長井 孝
中尾博隆	中込利恵	長崎佳子	中里 舞
仲澤慎太郎	長澤美奈子	長嶋一茂	中西 藍

6

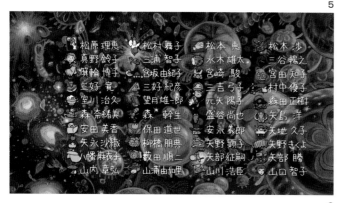

松原理恵	松村舞子	松本 恵	松本 渉
真野鈴子	三浦智子	水木雄太	三谷暢之
箕輪博子	宮坂由起子	宮崎 駿	宮田知子
三好 寛	三好紀彦	三吉弓子	村中優子
室川治久	望月雄一郎	元永陽子	森田正樹
森奈緒美	森 幹生	盛谷尚也	矢島 洋
安田美香	保田道世	安永義郎	矢地久子
矢永沙織	柳橋朋典	矢野顕子	矢野きくよ
八幡麻衣子	薮田順二	矢部征嗣	矢部 勝
山内章弘	山浦由加里	山川浩臣	山口智子

9

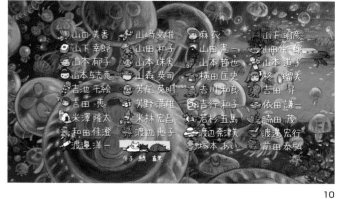

山口美香	山崎文雄	麻衣	山下明彦
山下幸郎	山田和子	山田憲一	山田伸一郎
山本郁子	山本珠実	山本哲也	山本道子
山本与志恵	山森英司	横田匡史	柊 瑠美
吉池千絵	芳尾英明	吉川和良	吉田 昇
吉田 恵	芳野満彦	吉行和子	依田謙一
米澤隆太	米林宏昌	若杉五馬	脇田 茂
和田佳登	渡辺恵子	渡辺奈津美	渡邊宏行
渡邊洋一		飯塚本 あい	前田泰弘

牛子 鮟鱇 高麗

10

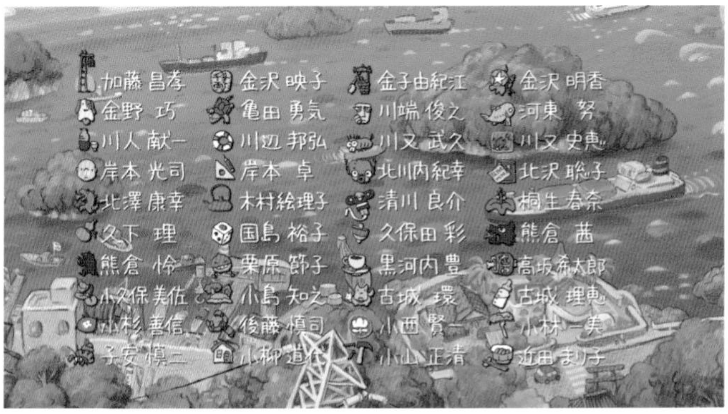
加藤 昌孝 金沢 映子 金子由紀江 金沢 明香
金野 巧 亀田 勇気 川端 俊之 河東 努
川人 献一 川辺 邦弘 川又 武久 川又 史恵
岸本 光司 岸本 卓 北川内紀幸 北沢 聡子
北澤 康幸 木村絵理子 清川 良介 桐生 春奈
久下 理 国島 裕子 久保田 彩 熊倉 茜
熊倉 怜 栗原 節子 黒河内 豊 高坂希太郎
小久保美佐 小島 知之 古城 環 古城 理恵
小杉 善信 後藤 慎司 小西 賢一 小林 一美
子安 槙二 小柳 道仁 小山 正清 近田 まり子
3

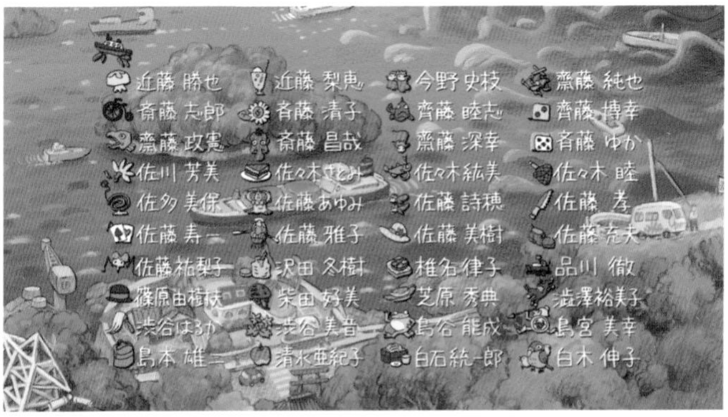
近藤 勝也 近藤 梨恵 今野 史枝 齋藤 純也
斎藤 志郎 斉藤 清子 齊藤 睦志 齊藤 博幸
齋藤 政寛 斎藤 昌哉 齋藤 深幸 斉藤 ゆか
佐川 芳美 佐々木さとみ 佐々木紘美 佐々木 睦
佐久 美保 佐藤あゆみ 佐藤 詩穂 佐藤 孝
佐藤 寿一 佐藤 雅子 佐藤 美樹 佐藤 充夫
佐藤祐梨子 沢田 冬樹 椎名 律子 品川 徹
篠原由樹枝 柴田 好美 芝原 秀典 澁澤裕美子
渋谷はるか 渋谷 美音 島谷 能成 島宮 美幸
島本 雄二 清水亜紀子 白石統一郎 白木 伸子
4

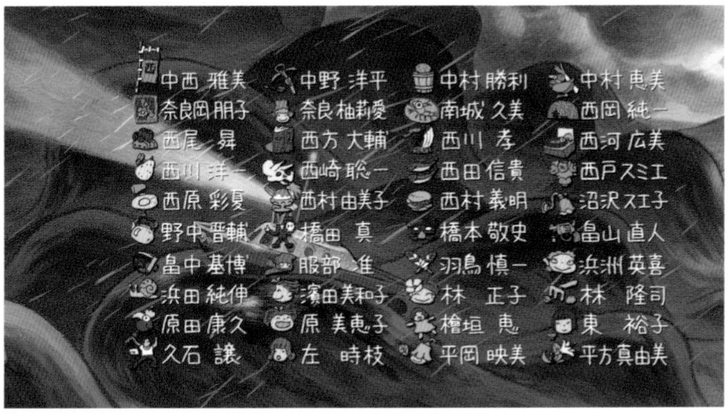
中西 雅美 中野 洋平 中村 勝利 中村 恵美
奈良岡朋子 奈良柚莉愛 南城 久美 西岡 純一
西尾 昇 西方 大輔 西川 孝 西河 広美
西川 洋一 西崎 聡一 西田 信貴 西戸スミエ
西原 彩夏 西村由美子 西村 義明 沼沢スエ子
野中 晋輔 橋田 真 橋本 敬史 畠山 直人
畠中 基博 服部 進 羽鳥 慎一 浜洲 英喜
浜田 純伸 濱田美和子 林 正子 林 隆司
原田 康久 原 美恵子 檜垣 恵 東 裕子
久石 譲 左 時枝 平岡 映美 平方真由美
7

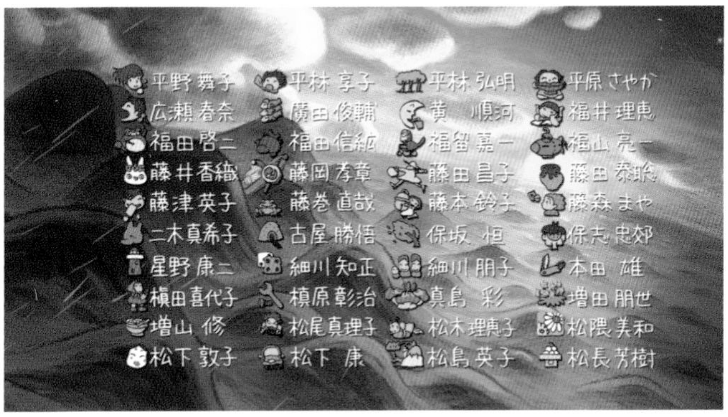
平野 舞子 平林 享子 平林 弘明 平原 さやか
広瀬 春奈 廣田 俊輔 黄 順河 福井 理恵
福田 啓二 福田 信紘 福留 嘉一 福山 亮一
藤井 香織 藤岡 孝章 藤田 昌子 藤田 泰昭
藤津 英子 藤巻 直哉 藤本 鈴子 藤森 まや
二木真希子 古屋 勝悟 保坂 恒 保志 忠郊
星野 康二 細川 知正 細川 朋子 本田 雄
槇田喜代子 槙原 彰治 真鳥 彩 増田 朋世
増山 修 松尾真理子 松木理恵子 松隈 美和
松下 敦子 松下 康 松島 英子 松長 芳樹
8

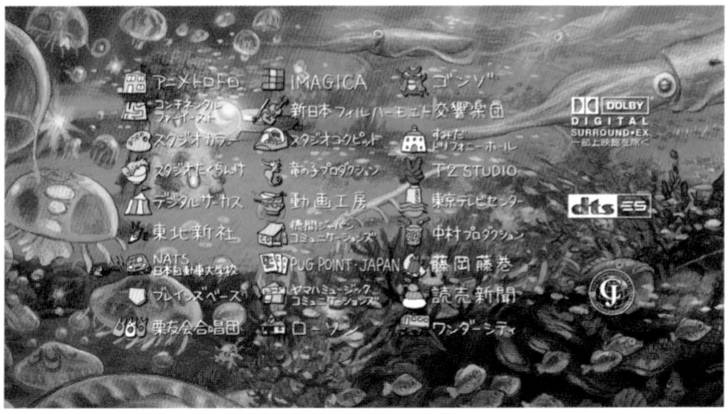
アニメトロフォロ
IMAGICA
ゴンゾ
コンチネンタル ファーイースト
新日本フィルハーモニー交響楽団
DOLBY DIGITAL SURROUND•EX
スタジオカラー
スタジオコクピット
すみだ トリフォニーホール
スタジオたくらんけ
竜の子プロダクション
T2 STUDIO
デジタルサーカス
動画工房
東京テレビセンター
dts ES
東北新社
徳間ジャパン コミュニケーションズ
中村プロダクション
NATS 日本自動車大学校
PUG POINT・JAPAN
藤岡藤巻
ブレインズベース
ヤマハミュージック コミュニケーションズ
読売新聞
栗友会合唱団
ローソン
ワンダーシティ
11

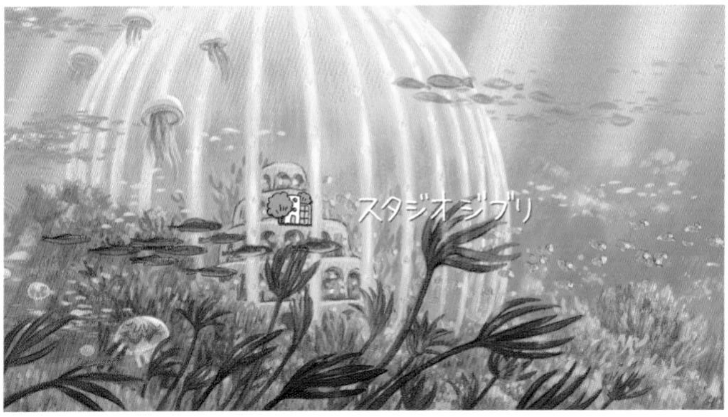
スタジオジブリ
12

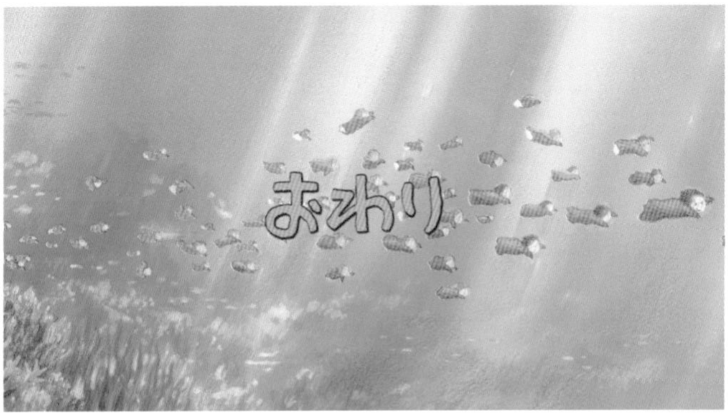
おわり
13

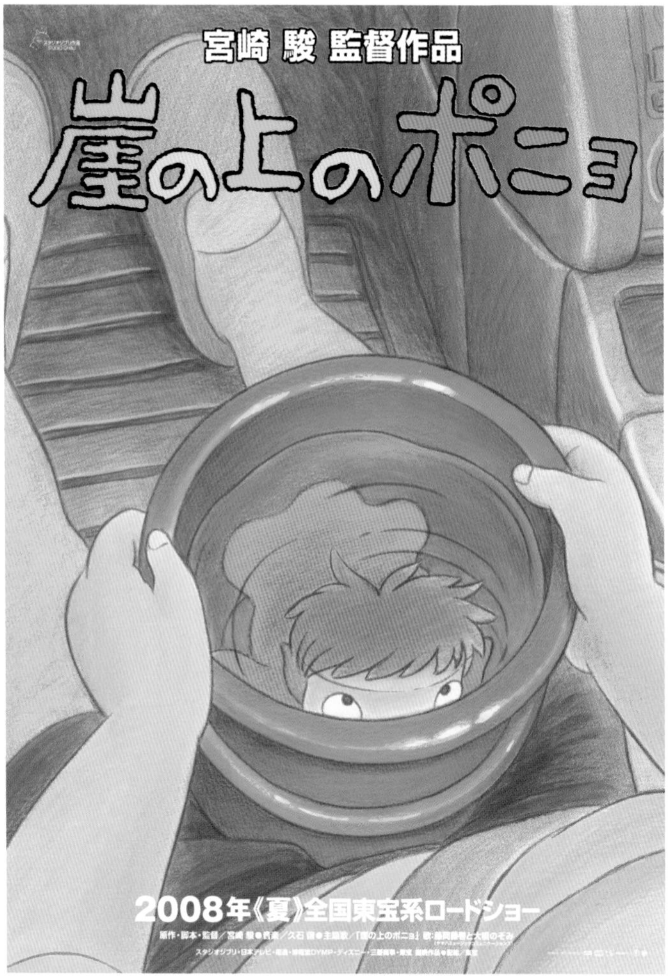
宮崎 駿 監督作品
崖の上のポニョ
2008年《夏》全国東宝系ロードショー

Poster No. 1.

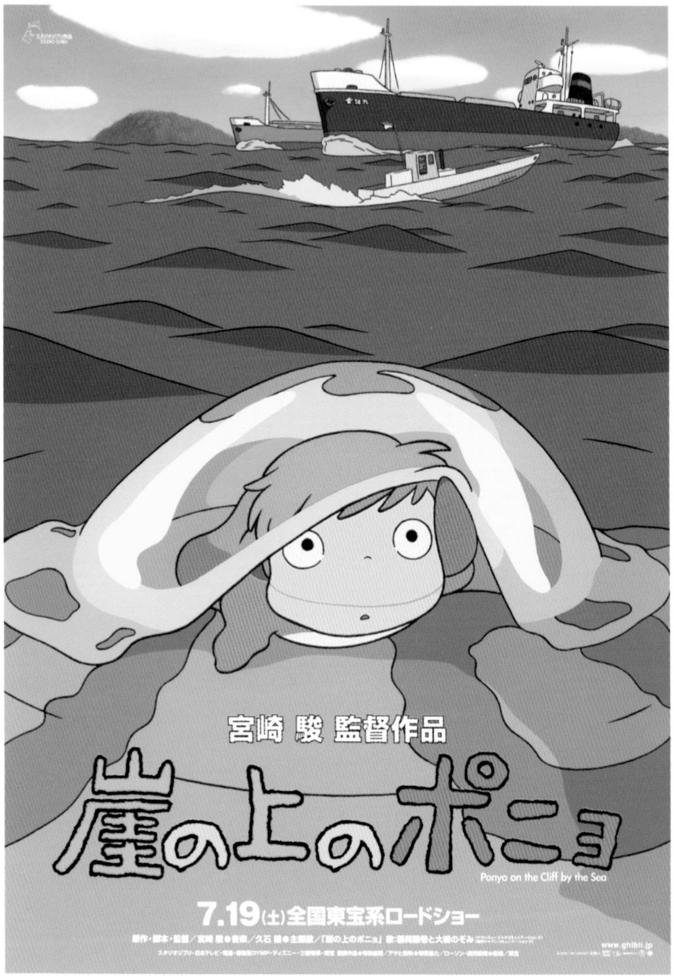
宮崎 駿 監督作品
崖の上のポニョ
Ponyo on the Cliff by the Sea
7.19(土)全国東宝系ロードショー
www.ghibli.jp

Poster No. 2.

From Hayao Mlyazaki's concept sketches. A sketch of the dry dock and town.

PONYO

The Complete Voice-Over Script

Screenplay by Hayao Miyazaki

Translated from the original Japanese by Jim Hubbert

English-language screenplay by Melissa Mathison

EXT. OCEAN - NIGHT
A rhapsody of fish life, every imaginable color and shape and disposition, transforms into a floating mass of pearly jellyfish. The jellyfish lead us to a transparent bubble and there we find a fantastic, mechanical-dream of a submarine and someone like Jules Verne himself—albeit with waist-length, auburn hair, a striped zoot suit, Beatle boots, and pearl drop earrings—standing on deck, feeding golden, life-creating droplets into the sea water.

This is FUJIMOTO. What follows is his daughter's story.

A plump goldfish with a girlish face—who will be named PONYO—emerges from a submarine porthole. She checks the skinny man brewing magic on the prow. Satisfied, she gobbles down one of the crustaceans her father has just created.

Little sister-fish—identical, but tiny—push their way through the porthole window in her wake, beseeching in soft, fish-baby voices:

SISTERS
Go, go, go. Go up.
Stay, stay, stay.

PONYO
(shushes her sisters)

Ponyo looks apprehensively toward her father. A wave and a wary big sister lift the tiny Sisters backwards:

SISTERS
Come back, come back, come back.

Fujimoto pauses in his work, looks behind him, sees nothing, and returns to his brewing.

Ponyo gestures for the wee ones to remain in place.

ONE SISTER
Sister, sister.
Ponyo kisses her sister on her tiny pink lips.

PONYO
(kisses sister)

SISTERS
Go up, go up, go up.

Ponyo slides aboard a passing jellyfish, stretching across its soft, opaque curves.

SISTERS (O.S.)
Go up, come back, go up, come back...

Ponyo tucks into a seductive membrane and falls asleep as she floats upward, toward the sunlight, leaving the submarine and the sisters, the father, and the magic, behind.

PONYO
(sigh)

TITLES
EXT. BAY - DAY
A Japanese seaside village.

EXT. OCEAN - DAY
Ponyo's jellyfish reaches the surface of the harbor.

Ponyo awakens and looks beyond the bay to see a Yellow House on a Cliff.

This is SOSUKE's house.

EXT. SOSUKE'S HOUSE - DAY
A five-year-old boy, SOSUKE, carrying a toy boat, runs down the steep, grassy path leading from his yard to the shoreline.

Sosuke's MOTHER, LISA, appears in a window.

LISA
Sosuke! You come right back up, okay?

SOSUKE
Okay.

EXT. OCEAN - DAY
The looming belly of an iron ship drags a dredging net across the muddy ocean floor of the harbor—churning up garbage.

Ponyo—surely out of her depth—becomes trapped in the net.

A bit more swirling debris and she becomes stuck in a flat-bottomed, glass jar.

EXT. SHORELINE, BELOW SOSUKE'S HOUSE - DAY
Sosuke has arrived at the shore, climbing over wet boulders.

SOSUKE
(efforts)

Sosuke sees something in the tide pool.

SOSUKE
Huh?

It is a fat goldfish. Face first, tail flopping, it is trapped in an open glass jar. It is Ponyo, arriving at his feet.

Sosuke lifts the jar.

SOSUKE
A goldfish.

He pulls and tugs, trying to free Ponyo.

SOSUKE
(efforts)

All his strength at call.

SOSUKE
Can't get it out.

Suddenly, a strange, dark, rogue wave comes racing toward Sosuke and his find. This is a MINION, servant to the sorcerer Fujimoto, searching for the master's runaway daughter. And, as befits a wave's nature, it must retreat.

MINION
(weird sounds)

Sosuke notices.

SOSUKE
That was weird.

Sosuke finally lays the jar on the gravel and hits it with a heavy rock—one time.

SOSUKE
(efforts)

Success. Sosuke has a cut finger, but a freed fish.

SOSUKE
Ow.

Sosuke peels away the broken glass.

SOSUKE
It looks kind of dead.

Ponyo makes a slurping sound and licks Sosuke's finger.

PONYO
(licking sound)

SOSUKE
It licked me!
(pause)
It's alive.
(end line o.s.)

Minion-waves rise in the near distance, watching.

MINIONS
(their sounds)

EXT. SOSUKE'S HOUSE - DAY
Lisa exits the house. A wind is rising.

LISA
Sosuke, I'm late!

EXT. OCEAN - DAY
The Minion crest rushes toward Sosuke as he clutches Ponyo in his palms.

MINIONS
(their sound)

Sosuke grabs his toy boat and races up the path to home.

SOSUKE
(over back of head)
Mom! A goldfish...

LISA
(o.s., over waves)
Sosuke!

EXT. SOSUKE'S HOUSE - DAY
Sosuke climbs.

MINIONS
(their sound)

Lisa is swept by a strange wind.

LISA
(to herself)
This wind is crazy.
(yells to Sosuke)
Sosuke, I'm starting the car now.

EXT. OCEAN - DAY
The red tresses of Fujimoto skim the surface of the blue sea and he rises. The watery minions approach him.

FUJIMOTO
You found my daughter?

Humbled, unsuccessful minions.

MINIONS
(moaning, revealing)

FUJIMOTO
What? She was captured by a human?

Fujimoto sees Sosuke nearing the top of the hill, the yellow house behind him.

FUJIMOTO
A boy. This is very bad.

A worried father shoos his minions away.

MINIONS
(moan)

EST. SOSUKE'S HOUSE - DAY
Sosuke fills a green pail with water from a garden tap. He places Ponyo in it.

The fish floats. Sosuke pokes.

SOSUKE
Is it already dead?

A few more pokes—this could become tragic—but with a gurgle and a suck...

PONYO
(sipping sounds)
...we discover...

SOSUKE
You are alive!

Ponyo squirts water in Sosuke's face.

SOSUKE
(laughter)

LISA
(o.s., over Ponyo)
Sosuke!!!

EXT. STREET OUTSIDE THE YELLOW HOUSE - DAY
Lisa is now in the car.

LISA
I have a job you know.

SOSUKE
Look, Mom...
(pause)
I found a goldfish.

LISA
(over back of head)
A goldfish?

SOSUKE
It was right down by the rocks.
(end line o.s.)

LISA
Yeah?

Lisa is a bit preoccupied. A strange, zoot-suited man is walking up the street. He carries a spritzer and a tank on his back and is spraying around him as he climbs the hill.

LISA
(a gasp of indignation)

Lisa gets out of the car and somehow successfully camouflages her son's arrival at the car as she confronts the spritzing Fujimoto.

LISA
I don't know who you are, but we don't use weed killer around here.

Fujimoto is shocked.

FUJIMOTO
(close mouth gasp)

He looks at his spraying apparatus.

FUJIMOTO
Wha...? This is not senseless weed killer. This is the purest ocean water.
(over back of head)
It keeps me from drying out when I'm on land.

LISA
Whatever, as long as it's not weed killer.

Fujimoto might see Sosuke...

LISA
Excuse us.

FUJIMOTO
(over back of head)
Wait...

Lisa speeds away.

FUJIMOTO
(open mouth gasp)

Fujimoto is left alone, staring at his predicament, spraying his skinny, drying-up bones.

FUJIMOTO
This is bad.
(pause)
This is very bad.

INT./EXT. LISA'S CAR - DAY
Zipping down the hill, around corners, hell on wheels—Lisa's late.

INT./EXT. LISA'S CAR - DAY
Zipping down the hill, around corners, hell on wheels—Lisa's late.

LISA
Gee, that guy was one wing-nut.

Re-thinks it.

LISA
(to Sosuke)
But don't you call people wing-nuts. We don't judge others by their looks.

SOSUKE
I know, Mom. I don't.

Lisa glances at the pail in Sosuke's lap.

LISA
Another experiment for school?

SOSUKE
Mmmm.

LISA
(o.s., over Ponyo)
Your teacher never likes show-and-tell.

SOSUKE
I think it'll be fine.
(to Ponyo)
Don't worry, I'll take good care of you.

LISA
(small laugh)
She sure is pretty.

EXT. HARBOR TOWN - DAY
Lisa drives like a wingnut. We can see freighters coming in to dock.

INT./EXT. LISA'S CAR - DAY
Lisa sees the inevitable spoiler up ahead.

LISA
There's a ship headed for drydock.

Lisa stuffs a sandwich in her mouth and hands one to Sosuke.

LISA
Sosuke, hurry up and eat your breakfast. Ham sandwiches.

SOSUKE
I wonder if she'd eat this.
(to Ponyo)
Want some?
Sosuke looks at his thumb.

SOSUKE
Hey!
(pause)
My cut is all gone.
(licks his thumb)
Sosuke turns to Lisa.

SOSUKE
Mom, I think I will call her Ponyo.

LISA
(mouth full)
Ponyo?

SOSUKE
She came to me.

[looks at Lisa]
She might be magic.
(o.s., over Ponyo)
I am going to have to be very careful.

Sosuke offers a crumb of bread to Ponyo who is not impressed.

SOSUKE
Want ham instead?

Sosuke tears off a small piece, but Ponyo grabs the entire slice and eats it.

SOSUKE
Oh, Mom.
(pause)
Ponyo likes ham.

LISA
So, she thinks she's human.

EXT. COAST ROAD - DAY
As Lisa races time, Fujimoto has returned to the sea. He follows the car, riding a fantastical yacht, sinking and rising, dodging freighters.

BENEATH THE SEA:
Fujimoto is headed for a ship's propeller.

FUJIMOTO
Whoa!
(pause)
Turn!
(efforts as he turns his yacht)
Clouds of grey muck and yuck fly into the sorcerer's face.

FUJIMOTO
(o.s., over boat)
Humans are disgusting!

EXT. DRY DOCK - DAY
A ship is being pulled onto the dock, inching forward, ready to settle. A CROSSING GUARD knowingly waves on Lisa.

CROSSING GUARD
Lisa, c'mon! Hurry up!

She makes it.

BENEATH THE SEA
Lost in the garbage and sewage, Fujimoto navigates muddy waters.

FUJIMOTO
All this waste. Filth.

EXT. COAST ROAD - DAY
Lisa hits ground level and spins past a minivan marked Property of the Senior Citizen Center.

LISA
Beat you there, ladies!

INT./EXT. LISA'S CAR - DAY
Sosuke looks out the window. He holds the bucket up for a fish-eyed view.

SOSUKE
Ponyo, you can see our house.

EXT. SCHOOL - DAY
Kids hanging out.

CHILDREN
(presence)

EXT. SENIOR CENTER - DAY
Lisa swirls into the parking lot.

LISA
Ask about the fish.

SOSUKE
(mouth obscured)
Yes.

LISA
Good luck.

SOSUKE
I will.

Lisa runs into the building as NAOMI, a female nurse, pushes an empty wheel-chair toward the minibus.

LISA
(over back of head)
Morning, morning. Seems I'm always late.

NAOMI
Help me with another wheel-chair?

LISA
(over back of head)
Sure.

Sosuke climbs out of the car. Green pail tenderly clutched in two hands, he walks past one of the old ladies, YOSHIE, as she is being helped from the bus.

YOSHIE
Good morning, Sosuke.

SOSUKE
Excuse me, I'm a little preoc-cupied, Yoshie.

YOSHIE
Is that so?

Shima lowers the second old lady, TOKI, from the bus.

TOKI
Sosuke, a moment...

SOSUKE
(o.s., over minibus)
Not now, Toki. I'm concen-trating.

TOKI
(exasperated sound)

EXT. SCHOOL YARD - DAY
Sosuke is concentrating as he approaches the school.

SOSUKE
Maybe she will get mad.

He looks around, has an idea.

SOSUKE
I got it.

Sosuke places Ponyo's bucket under a bush.

SOSUKE
(over back of head)
You'll be safe here, Ponyo.
(pause)
I'll be back soon.

Sosuke backs away from the bush, thinking...

SOSUKE
I wonder if there are any cats around here.
(end over back of head)
He grabs a large leaf and lays it across the lip of the green pail.

SOSUKE
That should do it.
(pause)
Stay put. I'll be right back.

EXT. SCHOOL - DAY
More mingling...

CHILDREN
(presence)

WOMAN
(over back of head)
See you later...
(pause)
Hello there, Toshi.

INT. SCHOOL - DAY
Sosuke stands hesitantly inside the doorway. A TEACHER holds a baby while talking to the BABY'S MOTHER.

TEACHER
(over back of head)
I'll call you if her cough gets worse, but she looks fine.
(to the baby)
You good, little sweetie?

BABY'S MOTHER
Oh, thank you. Good.
(to the baby)
Bye bye.

Sosuke is noticed.

SOSUKE
Good morning, Sensei.

TEACHER
(over back of head)
Good morning, Sosuke.

The Baby's Mother exits.

BABY'S MOTHER
(over back of head)
Bye, Sosuke.

One young and fabulous KUMIKO, the class terror, enters.

KUMIKO
Sosuke.

SOSUKE
Yes, Kumiko.

KUMIKO
Look at me! My mother made me a new dress. Isn't it unique?

Sosuke could not care less.

SOSUKE
(closed-mouth grunt)

KAREN, a more observant female, joins them.

KAREN
(over back of head)
Sosuke, let's go play.

SOSUKE
Can't. Not now. I'm busy.

KUMIKO
(mouth obscured)
You're not busy, you're five.

SOSUKE
I am too. I have a job.

KUMIKO
You are so... aloof.

KAREN
Yeah.

Kumiko and Karen walk away in a huff. Sosuke now makes his break, edging out the door and slipping away.

EXT. SCHOOL YARD - DAY
Sosuke lifts the oversized leaf and peers into the pail.

SOSUKE
(over back of head)
(gasps)

Again, Ponyo looks plump, round and dead. Sosuke nudges Ponyo, but she doesn't move.

SOSUKE
Ponyo!

Ponyo yawns.

SOSUKE
(relieved laugh, cough, choke...)

Sosuke wipes tears from his eyes.

KUMIKO
(o.s., over Sosuke)
Oh, Sosuke.

SOSUKE
(gasps)
Kumiko is leaning over his shoulder.

SOSUKE
Ah! Kumiko!

KUMIKO
What is that?
(pause)
There are rules about bringing things to school you know.

231

SOSUKE

I know. This isn't school.
(pause)
These bushes are on the
Senior Center's property.

KUMIKO

(over back of head)
Let me see.

Kumiko peers into the bushes.

KUMIKO

Oh, a goldfish.

SOSUKE

She's not *just* a goldfish. She's
Ponyo.

KUMIKO

Ponyo?
(pause)
Let's see her.

SOSUKE

(o.s., over Ponyo)
Okay, but don't tell anyone
she's here. The rules…

KUMIKO

(over back of head)
I know. I won't.

Sosuke pulls the pail
out of the bushes.

SOSUKE

Look at her. Isn't she pretty?

Ponyo glares at Kumiko
and turns away. Kumiko
is indignant.

KUMIKO

That's the most boring goldfish I have ever seen in my
entire life.
(line ends o.s.)

Ponyo sprays Kumiko
with her now trademark
fountain of water.

KUMIKO

(shrieks)

SOSUKE

(gasps)

KUMIKO

(looks at wet dress)
(cries)
(continues o.s.)

Sosuke thinks fast and bolts.

EXT. SENIOR CENTER - DAY
Sosuke sets down the
slopping bucket.

SOSUKE

That one was Kumiko's fault.
(pause)
We should never judge others
by their looks.

Sosuke sees a garden hose
handy.

SOSUKE

Let's get you some more
water.

Sosuke pulls on the
garden hose.

SOSUKE

(efforts)
While attempting to manhan-
dle the hose, Sosuke knocks
over the pail and the water
flows away and Ponyo is left
flopping on an outdoor drain.

SOSUKE

(gasps)

Sosuke fills the bucket
and plops Ponyo's chubby
body into the water.

Dead again?

SOSUKE

Ponyo!

Ponyo opens her eyes and
squirts Sosuke in the face.

SOSUKE

(startled, relieved, exhausted
laughter)
That was my fault.

Pony squirts her friend
a few more times.

SOSUKE

(closed-mouth laughter)

We hear:

YOSHIE

(o.s., over Sosuke)
There it comes again. I hear
old Sosuke's voice.

**EXT. OUTSIDE THE SENIOR
CENTER - DAY**
Yoshie and Noriko sit in their
wheelchairs, waiting for
something to happen as they
take in a view of the lawn.

YOSHIE

But, I know our boy is in
school right now, so it must
be only in my head.

Sosuke comes through
the brush, carrying his
precious green pail.

SOSUKE

Look, Yoshie.
(pause)
I'm right over here.

YOSHIE

Oh, that's a relief, I haven't
lost my mind quite yet.
(end over the back of her
head)

SOSUKE

Are you ready to see my big
surprise?

YOSHIE
(over back of head)
What is it?

SOSUKE
I'll show you. But first, guess what color she is?

YOSHIE
Hmmm, "she".
(pause)
She's red!

NORIKO
Red!

SOSUKE
That's right! How did you both guess that?

YOSHIE/NORIKO
(o.s., over Sosuke)
(together)
Let's see her, Sosuke, come on, show us.

SOSUKE
Okay.
The ladies peer into the bucket: something has happened today—a fish has come to visit.

YOSHIE
Well, look.

NORIKO
Oh, very pretty.

SOSUKE
Her name is Ponyo.
She likes to eat ham...
(Hear o.s. Ladies: "Ham? He said ham?")

SOSUKE (CON'T)
She might do magic. That's the secret.
(end with mouth obscured)
(turns head)
She likes to eat ham and she can do magic.
(end with mouth obscured)

YOSHIE
(open-mouthed gasp)

SOSUKE
I got a cut on my thumb, and it went away.
(pause)
Because she licked it.

YOSHIE
(open-mouthed gasp)
Wha...?

NORIKO
(open-mouthed gasp)

YOSHIE
My back and hips could use some of that magic... Maybe she'd fix my hips for me.

NORIKO
I'd let a fish lick me if it would get me out of this wheelchair.

SOSUKE
(mouth obscured)
Well, I don't know about all that licking, I'd have to ask Ponyo.

Toki drives up in her electric chair.

TOKI
Let me have a look in that green pail.

SOSUKE
Yes, Toki-san.

Toki peers at the fish and recoils with fear.

TOKI
Hawh... It has a real face on it!

Sosuke is shocked: Toki can see what he sees, but it frightens her.

TOKI
Hurry up and put it back in the ocean or we'll have a tsunami.

YOSHIE
With you it's all tsunami, tsunami, tsunami, day and night.
(end line o.s.)

TOKI
Fish with faces who come out of the sea cause tsunamis. That's what they always say.

Ponyo is ready—
she squirts Toki.

TOKI
Ah!
(o.s., over Sosuke)
It's the tsunami! It's here!
(on screen)
Help!

233

TOKI (CON'T)
(she flails her arms)
Sosuke, put her back where
she belongs!
(line ends o.s.)
Sosuke runs. Lisa enters.

LISA
(open-mouthed gasp)
She turns to Toki.

LISA
(over back of her head)
Toki, what's the matter?

TOKI
Ah!
(pause)
I'm soaking wet, my clothes
are completely ruined!

EXT. OCEAN'S EDGE - DAY
Pulled back to the sea, Sosuke
and Ponyo descend along wet
and slimy boulders through
the scampering of crabs and
mollusks, down to the edge of
the water.

LISA
(o.s., over Sosuke)
Sosuke!

Down and down.

LISA
(o.s., over Sosuke)
Sosuke!
(pause)
Sosuke!

Sosuke hides beneath
a dark, wet rock.

LISA
(o.s., over Sosuke)
Sosuke!

Lisa is leaning over the
road's concrete barrier.

LISA
Come back here and apolo-
gize.
(exasperated breath)

Back to Sosuke, curled tight.

SOSUKE
(to Ponyo, over back of head)
Don't worry, Ponyo.
(pause)
No matter what, I will protect
you. I promise.

Ponyo gazes at Sosuke.
She speaks.

PONYO
Sosuke.

It's like the hiss of a wave, is
it real?

SOSUKE
(gasp)

PONYO
Sosuke.

We hear Lisa calling his name
in the background, overlapping
Ponyo.

SOSUKE
(a gasp, a laugh)

PONYO
Ponyo.

That was real.

Sosuke nods his head.

SOSUKE
(whispers)
Ponyo.

Lisa's voice becomes
a soft echo. Sosuke
points to himself.

SOSUKE
Sosuke.

PONYO
Ponyo loves Sosuke.

Ponyo does a few back-
flips. She has arrived!

Sosuke pulls his skinny knees
tight to his chest, his head
bows low, as if praying, and
he says, with all humility and
responsibility and truth:

SOSUKE
I will love you, too.

PONYO
Ponyo loves Sosuke!

SOSUKE
(laughs)

And, as if to answer his
sweet, childish joy, Fujimoto
rises from the frothy sea.

EXT. OCEAN - DAY
Fujimoto releases a quiver
of slithering, wiggling fish
into the sea and they quickly
transform into his obedient
minions, swimming toward the
shore.

EXT. OCEAN'S EDGE - DAY
Sosuke sees those scary
waves coming toward him and
Ponyo. He grabs the bucket.

SOSUKE
(gasps)

MINIONS
(moan)

Sosuke is no match for the minions. Overwhelmed, he is pulled
under. As he loses his grip on
the bucket the minions grab it.
Sosuke is tossed and turned.

SOSUKE

(gasps)

(turns and gasps again)

Fujimoto sinks back
beneath the surface
with Ponyo in hand.

SOSUKE

Ponyo!

Sosuke pushes deeper
into the water.

SOSUKE

(over back of head)
Ponyo! Ponyo!
(pause)
Ponyo!

The bucket drifts by.
Sosuke pulls it to him.

SOSUKE

(gasps)
Ponyo! Ponyo?

Now, Lisa sees her son
drifting deeper into the
tumultuous water.

SOSUKE

Ponyo!

LISA

Sosuke!

She runs.

SOSUKE

Ponyo!
(pause)
Ponyo!

Lisa runs down the stairs
and over the boulders.

SOSUKE

(o.s., over Lisa)
Ponyo?

LISA

(breathes, gasps)

Sosuke submerges, green
pail in his outstretched arm.

SOSUKE

Ponyo!

LISA

(breathes, as she runs)
Sosuke re-appears, crying:

SOSUKE

Ponyo!

Lisa reaches him and pulls
him into her arms and
out of the rolling sea.

SOSUKE

(crying)

EXT. SENIOR CENTER - DAY

Lisa makes her way back
to the center, a sobbing
Sosuke in her arms. The Old
Ladies move towards them.

BENEATH THE SEA

Fujimoto speeds through the
ocean depths, Ponyo held
prisoner in a silky bubble.

EXT. COAST ROAD - DAY

Lisa drives to the market.

INT./EXT. LISA'S CAR - DAY

A tired, sad Sosuke
finds some comfort in
an ice cream cone.

LISA

Listen, Sosuke.

(pause)
You know this could be for the
best.
(pause)
I know you tried, but Ponyo is
a fish. She wasn't meant to
live in a bucket. The ocean is
home to her.
(pause)
Anyway, let's get home.

Lisa weaves past an oncoming
car.

LISA

(over back of head)
Hopefully, that spritzing weirdo
is gone.

Lisa leans toward Sosuke.

LISA

Can I have a lick?
(pause)
Hurry, it's starting to melt.
(takes a big lick)

Lisa careens a bit.

LISA

Yum. Dad's favorite. Me, too.

The tall grasses and weeds
shimmer alongside the road.

235

LISA

I'm really sorry, baby.

(pause)

Dad is finally home tonight.

(o.s., over house)

You can tell him all about Ponyo.

EXT. SOSUKE'S HOUSE - DAY

Lisa struggles through the front door with a load of groceries.

LISA

(efforts)

Her son is drooping.

LISA

No more ocean today, okay?

SOSUKE

(o.s., over Lisa)

Mmmm.

Sosuke stares longingly at the ocean.

LISA

(o.s., over Sosuke)

Sosuke?

Lisa shares his view of the sea.

LISA

Sosuke, time to come in now.

SOSUKE

Maybe if I leave the pail, Ponyo will know where we live when she comes back.

LISA

Do that.

(pause)

I think that's a lovely thing to do for Ponyo.

SOSUKE

Mmmm.

INT. SOSUKE'S HOUSE - NIGHT

Lisa is steaming big leafy greens. The phone rings.

LISA

Sosuke!

(over back of head)

Can you get that? It must be your dad.

SOSUKE

(answers phone)

Hello?

(pause)

Yep.

(pause)

She's fine.

(o.s., over ship)

Are you at the dock yet?

KOICHI (O.S.)

(over ship)

I caught a second run. I have to take it, so I won't be home tonight. I'll signal you when we pass. Can you help me out with Mom?

SOSUKE

(pause)

No, you should tell her.

Lisa takes the phone.

LISA

(o.s.,over her legs)

Hi, honey. Hmmm. What?

Sosuke sits with his toy boat. The temperature rises.

LISA

Too many in a row, Koichi. Let someone else take it.

(pause)

Go ahead, abandon your wife and child up here on the cliff all alone.

Lisa slams down the phone.

LISA

Jerk!

Lisa returns to the kitchen and slams the colander into the sink.

LISA

(frustrated sound)

Come on, Sosuke, let's get out of here.

(ends under apron)

SOSUKE

What if Ponyo comes back?

LISA

(closed-mouth inhale)

(frustrated grunt)

Men are impossible.

Lisa decides on a beverage. She pulls a beer from the fridge, pops it and is drenched in foam.

LISA

(startled reaction)

INT. SOSUKE'S ROOM - NIGHT

Sosuke scans the ocean with binoculars. Lisa lies on the floor, clutching a pillow. Sosuke sees a signal from a passing ship.

SOSUKE

There's Dad!

(turns to Lisa)

Turn off the lights, Mom. Don't you want to signal him?

LISA

(sighs)

Lisa is asleep on the floor. Sosuke turns off the house lights, then begins to work a ship-to-shore flashing lamp.

INT./EXT. THE KOGANEI MARU - NIGHT

Arai steers the ship while Koichi stands outside, signaling to Sosuke.

KOICHI
My son is working the signal all by himself!
(pause)
Can you believe that?

ARAI
Your wife must be very mad.

EXT. SHIP - NIGHT

A light flashes Morse code from the freighter.

SOSUKE
(o.s., over boat)
(reading)
S...O...R...

EXT. BALCONY OF SOSUKE'S ROOM

Sosuke translates his dad's signals.

SOSUKE
...R...Y.
(turns to Lisa)
Dad says that he's very sorry.

Lisa yells out a message for Sosuke to transmit.

LISA
B...U...G...O...F...F.

Sosuke sends the signal.

SOSUKE
B...U...G...O...F...F.

LISA
(o.s., over Sosuke)
B...U...G...O...F...F

Dad sends another signal.

SOSUKE
Dad says he loves you.
(o.s., over Lisa)
Now he says, "Lots and lots."

LISA
(angry closed-mouth sound)

The wife rises and takes control of the messenger, signalling "You are a stink bug." Dad responds with an impressive light display on the ship.

SOSUKE
Wow!
(pause)
Nice, Dad.

Lisa storms off. Sosuke signals, "GOOD LUCK," back to Dad.

Dad signals back, "THANKS," "LOVE AND KISSES."

Sosuke goes inside and turns on the light. Lisa is akimbo on the boy's bed.

LISA
(sniffles)
Sosuke strokes Lisa's whacky hair.

SOSUKE
(over back of head)
Don't cry, Mom. I know Dad

SOSUKE (CON'T)
breaks his promises sometimes.
(o.s., over Lisa's head)
But, he does his best for us. I promised Ponyo I'd take care of her, then I lost her.
(on screen)
I wonder if she's crying now.
Oooo. Lisa sits up and grabs her boy, squeezing him to death.

SOSUKE
(reacts to being squeezed)

LISA
You are so good.
(sings)
"When you wish upon a star, makes no difference what you are..."

She continues humming, not knowing the words, and squeezing.

SOSUKE
(grunts from being squeezed)

LISA
Don't you worry Sosuke.
(pause)
You did your best. Ponyo will be fine.

SOSUKE
Mmmm.

EXT. SOSUKE'S HOUSE - NIGHT

On the yellow house, caught in the moonlight.

LISA

(o.s., over house)

I say we start with dessert and go backwards. It's been a weird day.

INT. FUJIMOTO'S BASE - DAY

Inside Fujimoto's Nautilus, Fujimoto's enchanted cave, an underwater dwelling of sand and glass, marble urns and coral carvings—pan down to find the man himself standing next to a transparent spherical aquarium.

FUJIMOTO

(o.s., over ceiling)

It's all my fault, I exposed you to the magic and you are too young to understand.

Ponyo's sisters swim out of their aquarium dwelling to get a look at Ponyo—trapped in her solitary bubble.

FUJIMOTO

(o.s., over sisters)

I keep the sea in balance. It's a great responsibility.

Fujimoto spears an olive-like cube of green food.

FUJIMOTO

(mouth behind collar)

You will promise me this: you must never go back to the surface.

The toothpick pierces the bubble and the green substance is presented to an unwilling Ponyo.

FUJIMOTO

(o.s., over Ponyo)

Eat! Eat, Brunhilde.

PONYO

I want ham!

(spits the food away)

FUJIMOTO

(gasps)

Ham?

(pause)

Did you eat their food? What else?

(o.s., over Ponyo)

Did you... taste blood, Brunhilde?

PONYO

(begin over back of head)

My name is not Brunhilde.

(pause)

It's Ponyo.

FUJIMOTO

Ponyo?!

PONYO

Ponyo! Ponyo loves Sosuke!

(spins around)

I will be a human, too.

FUJIMOTO

Human?

(pause)

What do you know about humans?

(very slight pause when he grits his teeth)

They spoil the sea.

Ponyo's sisters watch, jaws dropped, scared.

FUJIMOTO

(o.s., over sisters)

They treat your home like their empty black souls.

Fujimoto stares off into the distance.

FUJIMOTO

I was once a human myself, Brunhilde.

FUJIMOTO (CON'T)

(pause)

I had to leave humans behind to serve the earth.

PONYO

Hands! I want hands!

(looks at feet)

I don't want these flippers any more!

(o.s., over Fujimoto)

I want feet like Sosuke!

FUJIMOTO

(closed-mouth grumble)

That's enough!

(startled reaction)

PONYO

(straining sounds)

PONYO'S SISTERS

(open-mouthed reactions)

Ponyo strains and strains —what's happening?—and strains, and then she sprouts appendages—inferior, scrawny little chicken-like three-toed legs. It seems inevitable.

PONYO

(efforts as legs pop out)

FUJIMOTO

(shocked reaction)

PONYO'S SISTERS

(open-mouthed gasps)

Ponyo puts her fish shoulder to the wheel.

PONYO

(efforts as arms pop out)

I made hands!

(pause)

I made feet, too!

(pause)

Look!

(begin with mouth obscured)

Look!

FUJIMOTO

What? Oh, no! Don't tell me you've tasted human blood.

PONYO

I'm going to Sosuke.

FUJIMOTO

Enough!
(pause)
You're making a terrible mis-take.
(pause)
Don't do it.
(pause)
Stop it, stop changing now!
(o.s., over his hands)
Revert! Revert! Revert!

PONYO

(sounds from being squeezed)

Ponyo's bubble squish-es and squirts through Fujimoto's gripping fingers.

FUJIMOTO

(reacts, o.s.)

The bubble gets bigger.

FUJIMOTO

(reacts, o.s.)
Giant drops of sweat are sprinkled across Fujimoto's desperate face.

FUJIMOTO

Stop, stop, don't change, don't change. Revert, obey, revert!
(squeezing efforts, o.s.)

Ponyo's bubble grows ever bigger. Again, as if inevitable.

FUJIMOTO

Ah!
(pause)
I need more power!

Fujimoto chugs some elixir from a long-necked bottle.

FUJIMOTO

(drinking sounds)

PONYO

(o.s., over Fujimoto)
Let me out, let me go. I want to see Sosuke! Let me go!

Fujimoto swallows and returns to Ponyo.

PONYO

Let...me out!

Fujimoto holds his hands over Ponyo, casting a spell.

FUJIMOTO

Be still. Be still, sweetheart.
(pause)
You can't be human and magic at the same time.

PONYO'S SISTERS

(open-mouthed whimpers)
Let her go, let her free.

Ponyo returns to her normal goldfish self and floats in her prison bub-ble; quiet, she sleeps.

FUJIMOTO

(sighs)
She's already so powerful. She is just like her mother.

Fujimoto gently lifts Ponyo in his long fingers.

FUJIMOTO

(o.s., over Ponyo)
She should remain innocent and pure forever.

PONYO'S SISTERS

(whisper to each other)
(yelps as Fujimoto approaches)
Let her go, let her go.

Fujimoto places Ponyo in the aquarium with her sisters. Her bubble—like Sleeping Beauty's tomb—rests solidly on the bottom. Close on Fujimoto.

FUJIMOTO

I don't have the power to hold her for long.
(pause)
I need her mother now.
(gasps)
(shakes head, gasps again)

A breech in the cavern has allowed a swarm of pink and blue CRABS to swarm in, sud-denly. Hundred of them—on a side-stepping mission.

FUJIMOTO

Ah!
(over back of head)
They're headed for my elixirs.
(shoos away crabs)
Shoo! Get out of here!

Fujimoto grabs his bottles of elixir and shoves them in an ancient freezer.

FUJIMOTO

(mouth mostly obscured)
That was very close. My shields are weakening. I must be careful not to upset the balance of nature.

Fujimoto runs back into the main room.

FUJIMOTO

(over back of head)
Calm. I must remain calm.
(he turns around)
When I think of meeting her again, my heart won't stop pounding. Hurry, hurry.

He turns out the lights.

FUJIMOTO

(mouth mostly obscured as he runs across room)
All right, focus on work. This batch should be ready.

Fujimoto runs down a flight of stairs.

INT. ANTECHAMBER/ FUJIMOTO'S HOUSE- DAY

A secret chamber. In the bowels of this coral cavern is a dark room filled with files and bottles and secret stuff. Fujimoto enters.

FUJIMOTO

At least there aren't leaks down here.

Fujimoto heads to a vault door. Like an old-fashioned Chicago bank, this door, marked "1907," has a spinning lock wheel and weighs a ton.

FUJIMOTO

(efforts)
(over back of head)
This door still won't shut tight.

INT. ELIXIR VAULT - DAY

Fujimoto opens the door.

FUJIMOTO

I shall fix that next.

He steps inside.

FUJIMOTO

If even one living creature got in here...

Fujimoto proceeds to prime the well. Into a deep, coral-walled well, glowing from its golden depths, Fujimoto pours an emerald liquid—the new batch of life force elixir. He drinks the final luminous drop.

FUJIMOTO

(reacts to the elixir)
Ah, yes. Superb.
(Pause)
I feel the power of the ocean in the furthest corners of my DNA.
(cut to wide shot)
When this well is full, the Age of the Ocean will begin again.
(leans forward)
An explosion of life to match the Cambrian Age.
(pause)
An end to the era of those abominable humans.

Fujimoto leaves, closing the vault door behind him.

FUJIMOTO

(o.s., over door)
Ach, this door...
(having trouble getting the door to shut)

EXT. FUJIMOTO'S BASE - DAY

Fujimoto takes off in his fantastical yacht.

INT. FUJIMOTO'S BASE

Ponyo's sisters start to chew on the rubbery bubble which entraps their big sister. They nibble and chew as the slumbering princess fish awakens.

PONYO'S SISTERS

(presence)
Come out, come out.

The prison bubble pops.

With incredible will power, the goldfish pulls and pushes and voila! She sprouts those bird-like arms and legs.

PONYO'S SISTERS

(gleeful sounds)
Sister, sister.

PONYO

(kisses a sister)
Look out—Ponyo grows teeth! Real chompers!

PONYO

Teeth!

PONYO'S SISTERS

(baby talk)
(laugh while hanging onto Ponyo's foot)
Teeth, teeth!

Her fate is revealed:

PONYO

I'm going back to Sosuke!

Ponyo willfully, but magically, creates a hole in the globe aquarium and water streams out.

PONYO'S SISTERS

Ah!

She now drills a passage in a porthole. Sea life rushes in.

INT. ELIXIR VAULT - DAY

Ponyo is swept toward the vault door, which—in her attempt to not be swept away—she inadvertently opens.

The aquamarine sea flows into the well and the elixir erupts in a golden stream, transforming Ponyo into a real little girl—with pudgy arms and legs and tummy and bellybutton.

EXT. OCEAN - DAY

Ponyo, her sisters, and armies of sea creatures burst from Fujimoto's sunken base and rush toward the ocean's surface.

PONYO'S SISTERS

(presence)
Teeth. Feet. Hands.

PONYO

(straining sounds)
Free!

PONYO'S SISTERS

(cheerful sounds)
Free!

Ponyo's sisters, like a tiny hurricane of gold, swirl and meld and transform into a school of giant fish.

EXT. THE SURFACE OF THE OCEAN - DAY

This leaping school of giant fish bursts from the water. They plunge back into the sea, rocking Koichi's ship.

EXT. KOICHI'S SHIP - DAY

Rocked and startled, out of nowhere this tumultuous wave comes.

KOICHI

A waterspout!

ARAI

Captain, look over there!

A mass of huge fish, rolling together in unison, race toward the ship.

ARAI

(o.s., over ship)
It's a rogue wave!

KOICHI

(o.s., over ship)
Turn her into the waves!

Koichi peers through his binoculars, he sees something strange.

KOICHI

(gasps)
What is that?

Ponyo—the girl—barefoot on her sturdy little child legs, with arms pumping, runs across the back of the diving fish. Koichi watches, incredulous.

ARAI

(begin with mouth obscured)
Captain! The radio and the radar just went dead!

KOICHI

It's a little girl.
(pause)
She looks like she's about Sosuke's age.

EXT. SCHOOL - DAY

Parents collect their children from school. The rain is coming down now, hard and cold.

SCHOOLKIDS

(presence)

INT. SCHOOL - DAY

A MOTHER leaves with her young one. Sosuke stands in the hallway.

MOTHER

Thanks again.

TEACHER

(over back of head)
Sure. See you tomorrow.
(to Sosuke)
It's raining so hard, Sosuke. Wait and I'll take you over myself.

SOSUKE

That's all right, I'll take the shortcut.
(pause)
Goodbye, Sensei.

TEACHER

Bye, Sosuke.
(over back of head)
Be careful out there.

EXT. SCHOOL YARD - DAY

Sosuke crosses the school yard to the senior center.

INT. SENIOR CENTER - DAY

Sosuke lets himself in through the heavy door. Rain is pelting, lights are out. Staff members run about, tending to the senior citizens in the dark.

SENIOR CITIZENS
(presence)

Lisa, hands full, enters the lobby.

LISA
Sosuke.
(pause)
I'm sorry.
(pause)
The door wouldn't open, right?
The power just went out.
(pause)
Everything okay at school?

SOSUKE
(over back of head)
Mmmm.

NAOMI passes by and speaks softly with Lisa.

NAOMI
Lisa.
(pause)
We'll be fine here. Go on home.

LISA
Are you sure you don't need my help?

NAOMI
(o.s., over Lisa)
Don't worry, we'll be fine.
(on screen)
We're thinking of spending the night here.
(pause)
If I were you, I'd get out of here now...
(pause)
...and get back home while you still can.

LISA
(over back of head)
Wait here, Sosuke, I'll be right back.

SOSUKE
Okay.

Lisa leaves the room and Sosuke approaches Yoshie and Noriko. The ladies are sitting in their wheelchairs, watching rain fall.

SOSUKE
Hi, Yoshie.

YOSHIE
Oh! Sosuke! Is that you?
(pause)
It's so dark, I can barely see you.

Sosuke hands Yoshie an origami goldfish.

SOSUKE
Here, Yoshie, I made this for you.

YOSHIE
Oh! What do we have here?

SOSUKE
There's one for you, too, Noriko.

NORIKO
Thank you, Sosuke.

TOKI
(o.s., over ladies)
I can't see a thing!

Toki enters in her wheelchair.

TOKI
I don't know why we're still here, it's just a little rain.
(o.s., over Sosuke)
I want to go back to my own house.

The lights suddenly come on.

YOSHIE
Ah, yes, that's more like it.

NORIKO
Now, let's see.
(looks at what she's holding)
Your goldfish!

YOSHIE
Maybe the lights came back on because Sosuke's here.

The TV is tuned to the weather, but there's a lot of signal interference.

TV ANNOUNCER
...They're now calling the bizarre event a "micro-typhoon."
(interference)
Ships in the affected area should exercise extreme caution...

The transmission is interrupted. Toki fiddles with the remote control.

TOKI
This stupid TV.
(cut to profile)
Nobody understands weather anymore. Might as well look at shadows or listen to crickets.

The TV announcer continues in the background.

TV ANNOUNCER
(o.s., Under scene)
Television and radio transmission are being affected, and viewers in some areas may experience poor reception. If you have been notified to evacuate, please give the authorities your full cooperation. The micro-typhoon is

TV ANNOUNCER (CON'T)

bringing heavy rain and high winds to some areas, with the possibility of landslides, flooding, and tidal surges. Remain tuned to this channel for further updates on the progress of the storm. And, as always, exercise extreme caution.

YOSHIE

(over back of head)
You should take your mom home now, Sosuke.
(on screen)
We've got our lucky goldfish to keep us company, so I'm sure we will be just fine.

SOSUKE

Mmmm.

Sosuke walks over to Toki and fishes another origami out of his pocket.

SOSUKE

This is for you, Toki.

TOKI

I can't tell what it is, it's all wrinkled. It's a...

SOSUKE

(unfolds it for Toki)
It goes like this.

TOKI

It's a... grasshopper.

SOSUKE

No, it's the *Koganei Maru*.

YOSHIE

That's the name of your father's ship, isn't it, Sosuke?

SOSUKE

(over back of head)
Mmmm.

TOKI

Still looks like a grasshopper.

Lisa appears at the door of the kitchen, wearing her coat.

LISA

Sosuke.
(pause)
We've got to get on the road. Let's hurry and say goodbye.

SOSUKE

Mmmm.
(turns to the ladies)
Ladies.
(bows)
Good evening.

YOSHIE/NORIKO

(over back of heads)
Good evening, Mr. Sosuke.

TOKI

Be careful the wind doesn't blow you away.

EXT. SENIOR CENTER - NIGHT

Lisa opens the driver's side door.

LISA

Hurry. Slide in.

INT./EXT. LISA'S CAR - NIGHT

It's a typhoon out here.

LISA

Now the phones are out too.

Lisa drives along the coast. The sea is boiling.

SOSUKE

The ocean looks all puffed up.

Sosuke sees a ship struggling in the waves.

SOSUKE

You think the storm could sink the ships?

LISA

Ships can handle a storm. They go out to sea. That's what your father's doing, right now.

Sosuke notices a lunging black fish, it's galloping behind them around the curve.

SOSUKE

I saw a fish!
(pause)
Did you see that, Mom?

LISA

Put your seat belt on.

EXT. DRY DOCK CROSSING

Lisa races towards the dry dock. The place is a river of rushing water; the two crossing guards wave her to a stop. They shout to be heard

above the wind and rain and waves crashing against the harbor's cement walls.

CROSSING GUARD A
(mouth obscured)
Hold on, Lisa. Can't cross here.

CROSSING GUARD B
Looks like they're going to evacuate this side.

LISA
Is it mandatory?
(tiny pause)
There are still a few people up at the senior center. You should get them out.

CROSSING GUARD B
The sea wall is high, they'll be all right.

LISA
OK, but right now I need to get home.

CROSSING GUARD B
Well, you can't cross here.

CROSSING GUARD A
Take the mountain road.

It's blowing and the rain is torrential, lights are out, tempers are short, nerves are frayed. Lisa is going home.

INT. LISA'S CAR - NIGHT
She straps on her seat belt and says:

LISA
Hold on, Sosuke.

SOSUKE
Mmmm.

Lisa begins inching the car toward the flooded crossing.

CROSSING GUARD B
Big one coming!

CROSSING GUARD A
Go back, Lisa!

The wave is building, stretching high, ready to break.

CROSSING GUARD A
Here it comes!

CROSSING GUARD B
Let's get out of here!

The men run. Lisa revs her engine. She waits for the water on the dry dock to be sucked back into the enormous wave and when it recedes, she guns it.

EXT. COAST ROAD - NIGHT
Sosuke stares out the window. The waves are like fish, they are enormous and black and shiny. But, now there are fish, too—black and shiny and enormous, rolling and leaping and moving close on the road and the car—one can barely tell the difference between wave and fish. Sosuke can.

SOSUKE
The fish are following us now.

LISA
(over back of head)
Seat belt, Sosuke! Seat belt!

And now, the most wonderful, incredible thing: Ponyo, running along the backs of the fish, leaping with them, above them, between them, her eyes on the prize—Sosuke. She is a laughing, red-haired little girl, tight-roping along the spines of giant sea monsters.

SOSUKE
(gasps)
Sosuke falls over as Lisa takes a sharp curve.

SOSUKE
Ah!

LISA
Hang onto something!

Ponyo sprints along the waves, chasing after Sosuke.

INT. LISA'S CAR - NIGHT
Lisa is a wild thing herself.

LISA
That wave is just after us!

Through the window, Sosuke watches Ponyo run. Lisa speeds around a corner and Ponyo can't quite keep up… she falls into the sea foam.

SOSUKE
Mom, the little girl just fell in!

LISA
What?

SOSUKE
She was running on fish and she fell!

Lisa slams on the brakes.

EXT. PROMONTORY ROAD - NIGHT
Lisa gets out of the car. Sosuke follows.

LISA
Where?

They look at the water, but all they see are massive waves.

LISA
(to herself)
I've never seen the ocean like

LISA (CON'T)
this.
(turns to Sosuke)
Sosuke, where did you see a little girl?

SOSUKE
She was out there, running on top of huge fish.

LISA
(o.s., over Sosuke)
Impossible.

A massive wave is headed toward them.

LISA
Sosuke... Let's go!

In an instant, the wind catches Sosuke and pulls him over the guard rail.

SOSUKE
Ah!

Lisa makes a leaping grab and pulls him back.

LISA
(efforts)

Lisa pushes Sosuke into the car with her, then hits the gas, escaping a tremendous rush of water.

INT./EXT. LISA'S CAR - NIGHT
Lisa tears up the hill.

LISA
Hold on, Sosuke, we're almost home.

EXT. SOSUKE'S HOUSE - NIGHT
Lisa speeds around the bend, toward the house. In the near distance, out of a flood of foaming, inky blue water, dances the green bucket.

SOSUKE
(gasps)
Now, Ponyo emerges from the water, taking the bucket, running with it, toward the car.

Lisa gets out of the car, staring.

LISA
There's a little girl...
(waving to Ponyo)
Come over here! We'll help you!

Sosuke runs toward Ponyo.

LISA
(mouth obscured)
Stay there, Sosuke!

PONYO
(gasps at the sight of Sosuke)

Ponyo runs toward Sosuke, ducking between Lisa's legs.

LISA
(breathes as she runs)
(reaction as Ponyo slips beneath her)
Ponyo leaps into Sosuke's arms and hugs him.

SOSUKE
(squeezed reaction)

Lisa runs up.

LISA
Sosuke, do you know this girl?

Sosuke looks Ponyo over.

SOSUKE
Ponyo?

PONYO
Mmmm. It's me, Ponyo!

SOSUKE
It is you!

PONYO
(laughs)

SOSUKE
Mom!
(pause)
Ponyo came back, and she's a little girl now.
(Reacts to Ponyo jumping on him)

LISA
Huh?

A huge waterspout rises into the night sky. Ponyo's tiny sisters ride atop it.

PONYO'S SISTERS
(hooting and hollering)
Sosuke! Sosuke!

PONYO
(to her sisters)
I found Sosuke!

Large golden raindrops fall from the sky. Lisa scoops up the kids and heads to the yellow house on the cliff.

LISA
(efforts as she picks them up, carries them to door)

INT. SOSUKE'S HOUSE - NIGHT
Lisa sets the kids down.

LISA
(efforts)
All right...
(turns to Sosuke)
Sosuke and Ponyo...
(turns to Ponyo)
Life is mysterious and amazing.
(turns to Sosuke)
But, we have work to do now.
(turns to Ponyo)
And, I need both of you to stay calm.
(pause)
Me, too.

Ponyo nods.

LISA
Good girl.

Lisa pulls a round emergency light from its wall socket.

LISA
You can take off your raincoat now, Sosuke.

(turns to Ponyo)
I've got a job for you, Ponyo.
(pause)
Will you hold the light?

The light is green and white and bright and heavy and altogether fabulous.

PONYO
(gasps)

LISA
Stay here while I get a towel.

INT. LIVING ROOM - NIGHT
Sosuke and Ponyo run into the room. Ponyo is here, she's there, she's everywhere.

SOSUKE
Here, this way!

PONYO
(reacts to going the wrong way)

SOSUKE
(laughs)

PONYO
(over back of head)
Smells like you in here!

Ponyo smacks into the sliding glass door.

PONYO
(over back of head)
Ow.

SOSUKE
(over back of head)
Ponyo!

Ponyo runs straight into the fluffy towel Lisa is holding.

PONYO
(reacts to being caught)

LISA
There! I gotcha!
(pause)
Now, let's rub you down and dry you off.

PONYO
(open-mouthed reactions to being dried off)

LISA
Look at that pretty red hair, it's almost dry.
(open-mouthed surprised sound)

PONYO
(open-mouthed confused sound)

LISA
(o.s., over Ponyo)
Your clothes are dry, too.

SOSUKE
That's because Ponyo was a fish, Mom.
(pause)
Water can't make her wet.

PONYO
Mmmm.

Ponyo buries her nose in the towel.

PONYO
(mouth obscured)
I really like this thing!

LISA
So.
(pause)
Let's calm ourselves down with a hot drink.

Lisa dons her apron and goes to the sink.

LISA
Ponyo, will you hold the light for me?

PONYO
(over back of head)
Coming!

Lisa holds up the kettle.

LISA
Okay, who assumes the water is working?

SOSUKE
I do!

PONYO
I do!

Lisa turns the tap and
yes, there is water.

SOSUKE
Water!

PONYO
Water!

SOSUKE
We have our own water tank
outside in the yard.

LISA
And, who thinks the stove will
light?
(turns knob)
And… light!
(the burner lights)
All right!

PONYO
All right!

SOSUKE
We have our own propane
tank.

Lisa goes to the refrigerator
and gets milk and honey.

LISA
Let's all sit at the table.

SOSUKE
Okay.

PONYO
Okay.

Ponyo, still clutching towel
and lamp, runs to the window.

SOSUKE
Ponyo, the table's over here.

Ponyo jumps onto her
chair and stands on it.

SOSUKE
Now, sit down, like this.

Ponyo plops into her seat.

PONYO
(happy sound)

SOSUKE
Now put your stuff down.

Ponyo shakes her head no.

SOSUKE
You need to use your hands.

PONYO
No, I'll use feet.

Ponyo wiggles her pudgy
pink toes like fingers.

SOSUKE
Look at that!

Lisa arrives with a
tray of drinks.

LISA
Mmmm.
(pause)
What are you doing?

SOSUKE
Look at her feet!
(pause)

They're just like hands.

Lisa sets a mug in
front of Ponyo.

LISA
(o.s., over Sosuke)
Ponyo.
(gives Sosuke a mug)
Sosuke.

Ponyo watches Sosuke
to see what to do.
Sosuke stirs his drink.

SOSUKE
This is the best!

Sosuke licks his spoon.
Ponyo stirs her drink
and licks her spoon.

PONYO
(closed-mouth yummy sound)

SOSUKE
(sound as he pulls spoon out
of mouth)
(blows on his drink)

PONYO
(blows on her drink)

LISA
(closed-mouth laugh)

PONYO
(downs her drink)
(sighs)
(hiccups)

Lisa finishes her tea.

247

LISA
(closed-mouth sigh)
(open-mouthed inhale)
That sure hit the spot.
(pause)
So, what would the two of you like to do now?

PONYO
Ponyo wants ham!

SOSUKE
All she thinks about is ham, Mom.

Ponyo nods.

LISA
I'll make some dinner, then.
(pause)
But first we should start the generator so we can call Koichi.

SOSUKE
(to Ponyo)
That's my Dad. We talk to him on the radio.
(pause)
He's out at sea right now, but he'll be fine.

PONYO
Is he an evil wizard?

SOSUKE
No, of course not.
(o.s., over Lisa)
He's the captain of a ship.

LISA
So, Ponyo.
(pause)
What's your dad like?

PONYO
He hates humans.
(pause)
He keeps me in a bubble.

SOSUKE
(surprised reaction)

PONYO
So I swam away from home.

SOSUKE
(even more surprised reaction)

LISA
So what's your mother like, then?

PONYO
Oh, she's big, and so beautiful...
(turns to Sosuke)
...but she can be scary.

SOSUKE
Just like my mom.

LISA
(laughs)

INT. STORAGE ROOM - NIGHT
Lisa enters and kneels down by the generator. Ponyo and Sosuke follow.

LISA
Ponyo, over here, please.

Lisa tries to start the generator.

LISA
(efforts)
(breaths)
Ach! Looks like something's wrong with it.

SOSUKE
Maybe it's clogged.

PONYO
It is clogged.
(points to the generator)
It's clogged right over there.

LISA
(efforts fiddling with the generator)

Ponyo focuses on the generator.

PONYO
(strained sounds)

SOSUKE
(gasps)

The generator grinds to life. Lights come on.

LISA
All right!

PONYO
It's light now!

Sosuke is stunned.

SOSUKE
Ponyo, you're enchanted.
(end over back of head)

EXT. SOSUKE'S HOUSE - FRONT YARD - NIGHT
Lisa sets up an antenna on the lawn.

PONYO
(mouth obscured)
Antenna! Antenna!

SOSUKE
Hey, Mom.
(pause)
Did all the ships out there sink do you think?

LISA
I don't see any light out there.

INT. SOSUKE'S HOUSE - NIGHT
Lisa gingerly turns the dial on a shortwave radio. Ponyo winces at the feedback.

PONYO
Too loud!

SOSUKE
What's wrong?

LISA
I can't get any reception, that's unusual.
(speaking into microphone)
Transmitting from JA4LL.

JA4LL
(o.s., over antenna)
Come in, Koichi. This is Lisa, Sosuke, and Ponyo. We wanted you to know that we're all doing fine.

Lisa moves the microphone toward Sosuke.

SOSUKE
(yelling into microphone)
I am taking care of everyone, Dad.

PONYO
(into microphone)
Ham!

INT. SOSUKE'S HOUSE - COFFEE TABLE
Sosuke and Ponyo, sitting at the low living room table, eagerly dump instant noodles into their bowls. Ponyo crushes hers.

SOSUKE
(laughs)
Lisa enters with the kettle.

LISA
(over back of head)
Got your noodles ready?
(kneels to pour water)
Be careful, it's really hot.

Lisa pours water into each bowl and places a lid on top.

LISA
(over back of head)
It's not ready yet.

SOSUKE
It takes three minutes.

The children wait patiently, then Lisa returns.

LISA
(o.s., over Ponyo)
Okay! Close your eyes.
(kneels)
Keep 'em shut.
(leans forward)
Ponyo.
(o.s., over Ponyo)
No peeking.

PONYO
(gasps)
Lisa puts something in the bowls and replaces the lids.

LISA
Get ready to look now.
(touches the lids)
Abracada...
(removes the lids)
...bra.

SOSUKE
Ah!

PONYO
Ah!

The bowls now contain slices of ham.

PONYO
It's ham!

SOSUKE
Careful, it's hot.
(Sees Ponyo stick boiling hot ham in her mouth)
Ah!

Ponyo dances around with her mouth open.

PONYO
Hot! Hot! Hot hot hot!

LATER
Ponyo slurps her noodles, drowsy.

PONYO
(sleepy sounds)

First her eyes droop, then her eating slows, and then Ponyo rather elegantly topples over, fast asleep under the table.

SOSUKE
Hey, Mom, Ponyo fell asleep.
(end with mouth obscured)

PONYO
(snoring)

Lisa puts Ponyo on the couch and tucks a blanket around her.

SOSUKE

(mouth obscured)

Do you think Ponyo came from far, far away?

LISA

I'm sure of it.

(pause)

But, where?

EXT. SOSUKE'S HOUSE - NIGHT

Lisa looks out the window.

LISA

Look outside, Sosuke. The waves have calmed down.

SOSUKE

Maybe because Ponyo fell asleep?

LISA

See that light?

A light flickers far off on the mountainside. It almost looks like a signal.

INT. SOSUKE'S HOUSE - NIGHT

LISA

It's moving.

(pause)

There's somebody over there.

SOSUKE

That's the senior center.

The light disappears.

SOSUKE

I don't see it now.

LISA

(over back of head)

Did they evacuate? The seniors might be in trouble.

EXT. SOSUKE'S HOUSE - NIGHT

Lisa goes outside for a better look.

LISA

(over back of head)

Sosuke, stay here with Ponyo.

Lisa looks at the water covering the road.

LISA

(to herself)

I've got to go help them.

(pause)

I could get there if I took the mountain road.

Lisa goes back to the house.

LISA

Sosuke, I should go to the senior center.

SOSUKE

I'll go with you.

LISA

I'd feel better if you stay here.

INT. SOSUKE'S HOUSE - KITCHEN

Lisa prepares emergency food.

SOSUKE

But, why can't we come?

(pause)

We'll wake up Ponyo and take her with us.

You can do it, I'll be back.

SOSUKE

Promise?

LISA

I promise.

SOSUKE

You *promised*.

LISA

(mouth obscured)

I love you, Sosuke.

EXT. SOSUKE'S HOUSE - NIGHT

Lisa gives Sosuke a thumbs-up, then drives off.

INT. SOSUKE'S HOUSE - NIGHT

Sosuke pulls the door shut. He sits at the foot of the couch, next to Ponyo. Quietly.

PONYO

(snoring)

EXT. THE KOGANEI MARU - NIGHT

The sea is frightening. The ship rocks violently. Waves crash against the sides. Arai yells down to Koichi from the bridge.

ARAI

Captain, I can see the lights of a city up ahead.

(end over back of head)

KOICHI

(over back of head)

Finally.

(cut to front)

We can get our bearings again.

ARAI

We're someplace I've never seen before.

Cut to a shot of the moon over a band of twinkling lights.

ARAI

(o.s., over lights)

Did the storm blow us to China?

Koichi looks at the "city" through binoculars. He pans up to the moon.

KOICHI

(o.s., over water and clouds)
That's a huge wall of water.
(o.s., over the moon)
Why is the moon so close?

Cut to a two-shot of Arai and Koichi. Koichi grimaces.

KOICHI

(grimacing sound)
That's no mountain we're looking at.
(pause)
And, that's no town, either. Those lights are ships.

Beneath the moon, we see a massive wall of water with hundreds of ships piled at its base. Koichi and Arai stare from the bridge.

KOICHI

(over back of head)
The moon's so close, its gravity is forcing the ocean to rise.

ARAI

(over back of head)
The ocean is rising?
(pause)
What's going on here?

BANG! Something hits the ship, shakes it.

KOICHI

(gasps)

ARAI

(gasps)

The propeller stops.

HELMSMAN

The engine stopped!

KOICHI

Try to hold her steady.
(Turns to Arai)
Arai, drop the sea anchor.

ARAI

Aye-aye, captain!
(end over back of head)

Koichi turns to see a triangle, a dome of light heading toward the ship at high speed.

KOICHI

Something's coming.

It takes a moment to make out the form, but then there is a form. It's a woman. We make out a beautiful, enormous face, with long, flowing pink hair, a jeweled forehead and eyes so stunning and kind. This is GRAN MAMARE, Ponyo's mother. Yes, she is **big**. And, she looks right at Koichi. The Goddess passes directly under the ship, filling its shadow with her flowing robes and lightly undulating body. She leaves a wake as she passes.

KOICHI

Ah!
(gasps)

Koichi looks over the side of the ship and sees Gran Mamare's face. She looks directly at him. Koichi is left holding a fish.

KOICHI

I just saw the Goddess of Mercy.
(gasps at fish in hands)
(startles at sound of engine)
Suddenly, the ship's propeller starts to turn.

ARAI

The engine's working.

HELMSMAN

It was her.

ARAI

So, you saw her too?
(pause)
I thought I might be hallucinating.

HELMSMAN

Thank you for protecting us, Goddess of Mercy. Thank you for protecting us, thank you for protecting us...

Arai claps his hands twice and bows. In the distance we see Gran Mamare pass under the tangled mass of ships—that mountain in the distance—as she frees them from their fate. She swims up, over the wall of water, and out of sight.

EXT. OCEAN SURFACE - CLIFF BENEATH SOSUKE'S HOUSE

Fujimoto teeters on the heads of his fishy minions. He motions for them to rise higher.

FUJIMOTO
Higher. Higher.

MINIONS
(efforts)

Fujimoto is lifted, rising to the level of the grassy cliff and the yellow house. He peers in the window. He's about to be lifted over the fence and tries to get a grip on a picket when he receives a jolt.

FUJIMOTO
(gasps)

He puts his hand near the fence again and the fence zaps him again.

FUJIMOTO
(gasps)
That's got a real barrier spell on it.
(looks up)
How did she learn to do something like that?

EXT. SOSUKE'S HOUSE - NIGHT

The minions heave Fujimoto toward the window and he peers through the glass— spotting Ponyo and Sosuke asleep on the couch.

PONYO
(sleeping sounds)
Fujimoto looks in through the window.

FUJIMOTO
(shocked reaction)
I can't believe it! No! She's turned into a human!

The minions suddenly begin to sway violently.

MINIONS
(laugh from being tickled)

FUJIMOTO
(yells as he loses his balance)
Hold still! What are you doing?
(gasps as he looks down)

We see Ponyo's hundreds of little sisters nibbling at the base of the minions' tower of water.

FUJIMOTO
Girls! Stop! Please!
(yells o.s., over legs)
(on screen)
Respect your father!
(yells as he falls)
Fujimoto plunges into the sea.

PONYO'S SISTERS
(giggling)

FUJIMOTO
(frustrated gasp as he surfaces)
This is serious! I want to save your sister!
(gasps as he turns)

Suddenly, as he is about to tumble in an avalanche of water, Fujimoto sees Gran Mamare's aurora borealis of brilliant light approaching. He gets a little giddy.

FUJIMOTO
Finally here.
(pause)
She has come.

As the Sisters scurry toward their mother, Fujimoto swims back to his vessel. Gran Mamare surfaces in front of him. She fills the screen with her serene beauty. Her voice is an angel.

GRAN MAMARE
Fujimoto.

Fujimoto is shy around the Goddess, a little flummoxed. She is quite formidable.

FUJIMOTO
You've come, my beloved.

GRAN MAMARE
Look at my ocean.

She swims onto her back.

GRAN MAMARE
(one run-on sentence)
Something has changed. It's like my ancient Devonian seas, full of magic and power.

Fujimoto rushes through the bad news.

FUJIMOTO
You're going to be very upset, my dearest.
(pause)
Ponyo got into my elixirs. And she drank human blood.

GRAN MAMARE
Ponyo?
(little laugh)
What a lovely name.

FUJIMOTO
(Closed-mouth gasp as Gran Mamare approaches)
It's all my fault really.
(over boat and Gran Mamare)
She's so powerful, she's opened a hole in the fabric of

FUJIMOTO (CON'T)

reality.

(cut to his face)

She doesn't understand, but she wouldn't listen to me.

(over back of head)

She became a little girl and she loves a little boy and the world is out of balance.

(cut to his face)

Please remove the human in her or the planet is doomed.

Fujimoto sees satellites glitter across the skyline, falling like shooting stars.

FUJIMOTO

(two gasps)

Fujimoto looks up. The moon looks enormous.

FUJIMOTO

Already!

(pause)

The earth is pulling satellites from the sky. The moon pulls the sea...

Gran Mamare encloses Fujimoto in her enormous hand.

GRAN MAMARE

Be calm, dear.

She closes her eyes, scanning Fujimoto's mind.

GRAN MAMARE

Sosuke.

(pause)

The boy's name is Sosuke?

Ponyo's sisters cling to their mother's fingers.

PONYO'S SISTERS

(giggling)

Sosuke. Ponyo.

GRAN MAMARE

(to Ponyo's sisters)

You love your sister and we all want her to be happy.

Gran Mamare swims to Fujimoto.

GRAN MAMARE

Listen, my darling, why don't we let Ponyo become human for good.

FUJIMOTO

(startled reaction)

GRAN MAMARE

We must test the boy. If Sosuke's love is true, Ponyo will be permanently transformed and the balance of nature will be restored.

FUJIMOTO

But, if his love isn't real, then Ponyo will turn into sea foam!

GRAN MAMARE

True, that is where we all originated, my darling.

FUJIMOTO

(over back of head)

The boy's so young, so innocent. Consider, darling... If he fails...

GRAN MAMARE

Shh!

(waves hand over Sosuke's house)

Let them sleep. They'll need their rest.

EXT. SOSUKE'S HOUSE - DAY

The water level has risen so high, Sosuke's house appears to be perched on a tiny island.

INT. SOSUKE'S HOUSE - DAY

Ponyo gets in Sosuke's face.

PONYO

Sosuke!

(cut to wide shot)

Sosuke!

Sosuke startles awake and bumps heads with Ponyo.

SOSUKE

(pained sounds)

Sosuke looks to Ponyo, concerned.

SOSUKE

Ponyo! You okay?

PONYO

Goooood morning, Sosuke!

EXT. SOSUKE'S HOUSE

The sea outside is almost level with the floor of the house.

PONYO

(gasps)

SOSUKE

Look at that, the ocean is at our door.

The children put their heads under water. Ancient sea life has come to the cliff. An incongruous mix of small and large, odd and some-how familiar creatures swim past toys and rocks and grass and stone steps.

PONYO
How come your mom's not here?
(end over back of head)

SOSUKE
The water's so high, she must be stuck.
(open-mouthed sigh)
Too bad we don't have a boat.

Ponyo points to Sosuke's toy boat, which is sitting on the table.

PONYO
There's a boat right there.

SOSUKE
(deadpan)
It's a little small.

PONYO
No, it's not.

Ponyo runs to the boat and concentrates.She turns into her middle stage, her bird-like self, her half human/ still magic self, as she pre-pares to deliver the goods.

PONYO
(strained sounds)
Ah!

The boat grows. Still chubby and soft-edged like a toy, it is now big enough to carry them.

SOSUKE
(gasps)
(inhales while smiling)
Thank you!

Sosuke inspects the boat.

SOSUKE
Wow.
(End with mouth behind arm)
You even made the candle bigger.

PONYO
(over back of head)
We can fit!

SOSUKE
This is fantastic.

PONYO
(over back of head)
Fantastic!

Sosuke points to the bow.

SOSUKE
Grab that end, please.

PONYO
(over back of head)
Okay.

SOSUKE
Ready?

PONYO
Let's go!

Ponyo lifts up her end before Sosuke's ready.

SOSUKE
Whoa!

Ponyo dashes outside, Sosuke scrambles to keep up.

SOSUKE
(over back of head)
Whoa, whoa, whoa, whoa, whoa!

EXT. SOSUKE'S HOUSE
Sosuke and Ponyo fall into the water.

SOSUKE
Ah!

Sosuke checks out the boat.

SOSUKE
It actually floats!
(Delighted laugh)
Doesn't look like it has any leaks.
(Over back of head)
Now we have to fill the boiler.

Sosuke shows Ponyo the submerged inlet/outlet pipes at the rear of the boat.

SOSUKE
The water gets sucked in through this pipe.
(points to boiler)
Then it gets heated up here in the boiler.
(takes a deep breath)

Sosuke ducks underwater and starts blowing water into the opening.

SOSUKE
(surfaces, takes a few breaths)

Ponyo submerges and blows on the other end of the pipe, shooting water in Sosuke's face. The boat moves forward.

SOSUKE
(laughs)
Well, that worked!

Ponyo, clutching her green pail, climbs aboard.

PONYO

(laughs)

SOSUKE

(over back of head)
Looks like every-
thing's shipshape.

PONYO

Shipshape?

SOSUKE

(over back of head)
Yep.

PONYO

Shipshape!

SOSUKE

(over back of head)
Shipshape.

Ponyo dances around
the roof of the boat.

PONYO

Shipshape! Shipshape!
Shipshapeshipshapeshipshape!

INT. SOSUKE'S HOUSE - DAY
Sosuke packs provisions
then dons his captain's cap.

EXT. SOSUKE'S HOUSE - DAY
Sosuke pulls out a match.

PONYO

Is it hot?

Sosuke lights the match.
Ponyo startles.

PONYO

(mouth obscured)
It's hot!

Sosuke tries to light the candle, but the match burns his
fingers.

SOSUKE

Ow!

PONYO

Ow!

While Sosuke gets out
another match, Ponyo notices
that the candle has lit.

PONYO

(gasps)
Look at that!

SOSUKE

It's burning!

He puts his matches away.

PONYO

It's hot! It's hot! It's hot! It's hot!
(end line o.s.)

Sosuke slides the candle under
the boiler.

PONYO

It's hot, isn't it?

SOSUKE

(mouth obscured)
Hmm...

Finally, the water in the boiler
starts to boil. The boat lurches
forward.

PONYO

It works!

The boat chugs past the

front yard fence...

PONYO

Sosuke, we're shipshape,
right?

SOSUKE

(mouth obscured)
Yep.

PONYO

This is a good boat.

SOSUKE

Mm-hmm.

...And smoothly sails away
from Sosuke's house.

PONYO

(gasps)

EXT. SOSUKE'S BOAT - DAY
Sosuke steers the boat
across the placid ocean
spreading out in every direction. They sail at treetop level,
with octopus and eels swimming in such odd contrast to
the landscape, it appears as
if they are flying. Ponyo sits
on the roof of the cabin.

PONYO

Hey, Sosuke, look at me!

SOSUKE

Mm-hmm.

Ponyo turns upside down
and looks at the boiler.

PONYO
Sosuke, we're moving, aren't we?

SOSUKE
Mm-hmm.

PONYO
Sosuke, it's really hot isn't it?

SOSUKE
Ponyo, you be the boat's look-out.
(pause)
And I'll do the steering. Okay?

PONYO
(closed-mouth affirmative sound)
I'm the lookout!

BENEATH THE SEA - DAY
The submerged landscape is a dreamscape. So many fish, so many shapes, sizes and colors—as rich a tapestry as Fujimoto could ever imagine. The ancient creatures swim over asphalt roads, past stop signs and over guard rails—it's like vertigo. Quiet. An enchanted, unbalanced, peaceful world. Ponyo and Sosuke pass overhead, moving on the surface of this surreal, watery valley.

EXT. SOSUKE'S BOAT - DAY
Ponyo and Sosuke look down into the water.

PONYO
There's the road.

SOSUKE
That's the road my mom took last night.

PONYO
(over back of head)
I don't see her anywhere.

SOSUKE
(over back of head)
We'll see her. She promised me she'd come back.

Huge prehistoric fish cruise the highways and byways beneath their boat.

SOSUKE
Those are ancient fish... they lived during the Devonian age.

PONYO
That's a Bothriolepis.

They spot another unbelievable fish.

PONYO
(over back of head)
And that one is...

SOSUKE
(over back of head)
Dipnorhynchus!

PONYO
(over back of head)
Dipnorhynchus!

A whiskered, flat-headed sea monster swims right beneath their boat.

SOSUKE
Wow.
(over back of head)
That one's really huge.

PONYO
That's Devonynchus.

SOSUKE
(mouth obscured)
Devonynchus.

EXT. SUBMERGED TREES - DAY
The dreamy journey continues.

MAN IN SKIFF
(o.s., over trees)
Ahoy there!

A wooden skiff comes into view with a MAN and a WOMAN in it.

WOMAN IN SKIFF
Ahoy!

MAN IN SKIFF
Ahoy!

SOSUKE
There's a boat!

WOMAN IN SKIFF
Ahoy!

PONYO
I'm gonna say that.
(pause)
Ahoy!

Sosuke pushes the candle closer to the boiler. He burns his hand.

SOSUKE
Ow!

The boat zooms forward.

PONYO
Whoa, that's fast!

Ponyo spreads her arms, enjoying the speed.

PONYO
(delighted sound)

SOSUKE
I'm getting the hang of this.

They speed toward the skiff.

SOSUKE
Prepare to stop, Ponyo.

PONYO

(takes a big breath)

(blows out candle with lots of spit)

SOSUKE

(reacts to spit in his face)

They pull up to the skiff. The woman is holding a baby.

WOMAN IN SKIFF

Hello, you two.

SOSUKE

(over back of head)

Hello.

MAN IN SKIFF

That's quite a boat you've got there.

WOMAN IN SKIFF

(peers at Sosuke)

You're Lisa's little boy, aren't you?

PONYO

He's not a little boy, he's Sosuke.

SOSUKE

That's Ponyo.

PONYO

I used to be a fish.

WOMAN IN SKIFF

Is that right?

(laughs)

I like your name, Ponyo, it's cute.

PONYO

(closed-mouth affirmative sound)

SOSUKE

By the way,

(pause)

have you seen my mom?

MAN IN SKIFF

(o.s., over Sosuke)

Your mother?

(on screen)

Why isn't your mother with you?

SOSUKE

She went to the senior center.

MAN IN SKIFF

Oh, did she?

Ponyo stares curiously at the baby.

WOMAN IN SKIFF

My baby likes you.

The BABY has a big, sniffly face and doesn't look all that friendly. Ponyo stares at him fixedly. They seem to be communicating.

BABY

(coos twice)

Ponyo nods. She reaches for the cup on her backpack.

BABY

(cries)

WOMAN IN SKIFF

Oh, sweetheart.

(mouth obscured)

What's the matter?

Ponyo holds out the cup. The baby reaches for it.

BABY

(babbling)

WOMAN IN SKIFF

Oh, is that for us?

The woman takes the cup from Ponyo. The baby chews on its handle.

BABY

(sucking on mug)

Ponyo uncaps her Thermos.

WOMAN IN SKIFF

(to the baby)

Let me have the cup, sweetie.

Ponyo empties the Thermos into the woman's cup.

BABY

(cries)

WOMAN IN SKIFF

Yum, is that soup?

(cut to close-up)

It smells good.

(slurps the soup)

It's delicious, Ponyo, thank you.

SOSUKE

My mom made it from scratch.

Ponyo shakes her head
at the woman, angry.

PONYO
The soup's for him.

WOMAN IN SKIFF
Oh,
(pause)
I'm sorry.
(Pause)
He's a little too young, he
can't handle soup yet. But I
could eat the soup instead,
and it would help me to make
milk for him.

PONYO
(gasps in awe)

SOSUKE
(to Ponyo)
My mom made milk for me,
too.

WOMAN IN SKIFF
Ponyo, what do you say? Is it
all right if I eat this soup?

PONYO
That's fine.

WOMAN IN SKIFF
Thank you, sweetheart.

MEN IN BOATS (O.S.)
Stroke!

Sosuke turns to see a small
flotilla of boats approaching,
crowded with people from the
town and flying colorful flags.

SOSUKE
(gasps)

MEN IN BOATS
Stroke! Stroke! Stroke!...
(continues under)

BOAT PASSENGERS
(presence)

SOSUKE
People from the town.
(pause)
It's like a parade.

COMMODORE calls out from
one of the boats.

COMMODORE
(through bullhorn)
Ahoy!
(pause)
Are any of you in need of
assistance at this time?

MAN IN SKIFF
(shouting back)
We're all good here.
(pause)
But thanks for checking on
us, Captain.

COMMODORE
(mouth obscured)
We're ferrying everyone to
the Mountain Peak Hotel. For
your safety, we'd request that
you follow us.

MAN IN SKIFF
Aye-aye, will do.

SOSUKE
(over back of head)
Looks like the whole town is
here.

WOMAN IN SKIFF
I don't see your mom.
(pause)
I hope she's okay.

Remembering his mission,
Sosuke urgently preps the
boat.

SOSUKE
Ponyo, it's time for us to cast
off.

MAN IN SKIFF
Hold on a second.
(over back of head)
Let's see...

Ponyo hands some sand-
wiches to the woman.

PONYO
Here, have some milk.

WOMAN IN SKIFF
Oh! Uh...

PONYO
It's for milk!

SOSUKE
She already ate all the ham
off those sandwiches.

WOMAN IN SKIFF
(to Ponyo)
Thank you.
(Pause)
That's very generous of you,
Ponyo.

MAN IN SKIFF holds out
half a candle to Sosuke.

MAN IN SKIFF
Here, Sosuke.
(over back of head)
I brought you our biggest
candle.

SOSUKE
Thanks.
(pause)
Ponyo will make it bigger.
(pause)
See you later!
Sosuke and Ponyo motor off.

MAN IN SKIFF
Take care!

WOMAN IN SKIFF
Be careful!

Ponyo stares at the baby.

BABY
(coughs and cries)

WOMAN IN SKIFF
You have a cold.
(o.s., over baby)
Ssh, it's okay...

Ponyo considers. Her limbs change to middle-stage. On three-toed bird feet she runs across the glassy surface of the ocean and over to the skiff.

SOSUKE
(startled reaction)

Ponyo grabs the baby's face in her birdlike paws.

WOMAN IN SKIFF
(startled reaction)

BABY
(sounds as Ponyo squishes his face)

SOSUKE
Ponyo!

Ponyo runs back to Sosuke's boat and they motor off.

A girl again.

BABY
(laughs - Cold gone?)

WOMAN IN SKIFF
(gasps)

Sosuke sails over to one of the rescue boats, crowded with people.

BOAT PASSENGERS
(presence)

WOMAN A (by the farthest left tire strapped to the boat)

Calls to him:

WOMAN A
Sosuke!

WOMAN B (waving arms, near stern)
Hey, Sosuke!

WOMAN A
Where's your mother?

Cut to reverse angle. WOMAN C (in front, holding hands by her mouth) yells to him.

WOMAN C
(over back of head)
You shouldn't be out here alone.

SOSUKE
She went to the senior center last night, we're on our way to find her.

Crossing guards A and B beam at Sosuke.

CROSSING GUARD B
I can't believe your mother beat that wave!

CROSSING GUARD A
Yeah, that's Lisa!

Kumiko shoves her way to the front of the boat.

KUMIKO
Sosuke!
(pause)
Can I ride with you?

SOSUKE
I can't. I'm busy. I have a job.

A POLICEMAN (near tire in front of boat) yells to Sosuke.

POLICEMAN
Check the park, the seniors should have evacuated to there.

MAN ROWING WITH STICK
Good luck, kid!

WOMAN WITH SCARF
You'll find her!

COMMODORE
(through bullhorn)
We'll send a boat for the seniors as soon as we drop this group off.
(pause)
Good luck, Captain!

Sosuke salutes the commodore and sails off.

EXT. HOTEL ON THE PEAK
Bird's eye view of boats pulling up to the hotel.

EXT. DROWNED FOREST

Sosuke's boat chugs through a half-submerged forest of tropical trees and evergreens and mossy limbs, dripping green. Ponyo begins to look very sleepy.

SOSUKE
Ponyo.
(pause)
Our candle is about out.

Sosuke looks below deck.

SOSUKE
We'll be okay.
(pause)
The fisherman gave me another one.

Sosuke touches the candle dish.

SOSUKE
Ow!
(pause)
It's still pretty hot.

Ponyo sleepily waves at the candle as it goes out.

PONYO
Bye-bye.

Sosuke holds out the new candle to Ponyo.

SOSUKE
(over back of head)
Here, Ponyo. Can you make this bigger?

PONYO
All right.

Ponyo starts to nod off.

SOSUKE
Hey.
(Pause)
Are you okay?

PONYO
(startles awake)
Mm.

Ponyo touches her fingertips together, then nods off.

SOSUKE
(o.s., over Ponyo)
Ponyo?

PONYO
Hm?

She focuses, tries to work her magic. Tired, in her young girl's body.

PONYO
(efforts)

She can't. She falls asleep.

PONYO
(snoring)

SOSUKE
Ponyo! Ponyo!

With Ponyo fast asleep, Sosuke jumps in the water and pushes the boat along. Soon his feet touch bottom.

SOSUKE
Oh, good, I can walk from here.
(Reacts to slipping)
(efforts pushing boat)
(gasps)
(more efforts)

Sosuke sees a forest road climbing, leading out of the water.

SOSUKE
(over back of head)
There's the road.

As they near the road, the boat suddenly starts to shrink.

SOSUKE
(gasp off screen)
(gasp on screen)
It's shrinking!
(grabs Ponyo)
Ponyo!

Sosuke pulls Ponyo from her lookout perch as the boat shrinks to toy size beneath her. He pulls her safely out of the water.

SOSUKE
(efforts)
(panting)
He shakes Ponyo.

SOSUKE
Ponyo!
(pause)
Ponyo, wake up!

PONYO
Sosuke...
(yawns)

SOSUKE
You scared me.
(pause)
Don't turn into a fish again, I'd hate it.

Sosuke suddenly notices his mom's car a short distance up the road.

SOSUKE
(gasps)
My mom's car!
(turns to Ponyo)
Ponyo, come on, she might be there!

Sosuke runs up to the car.

SOSUKE

(breaths)

Hey, Mom!

(mouth obscured by rearview mirror) Mom?

He opens the car door. The car is stocked with supplies.

SOSUKE

Mommy!

(cut to inside car)

Mom?

(cut to outside car)

Mommy!

(runs to front of car)

Mom!

(runs to side of car)

Mom!

(looks inside car)

Mommy?

Sosuke walks farther down the road.

SOSUKE

Hey, Mom!

(turns around)

Mom!

(soft crying off screen)

Ponyo picks up Sosuke's boat and walks over to him. Tears stream down his face.

PONYO

Here, I've got your boat.

(sees he's crying)

There's water coming from your eyes.

SOSUKE

(sniffles as he wipes eyes)

PONYO

Let's go find your mom.

Sosuke nods.

Mm-hmm.

Sosuke tucks the now ordinary boat under his arm. Ponyo carries her ordinary green bucket tightly in her fist and the two walk off, hand in hand.

EXT. PARK ABOVE THE SENIOR CENTER - DAY

The park is nearly submerged. A gazebo stands on a little island with a row of empty wheelchairs at the foot of the steps.

BENEATH THE SURFACE

The town's senior center is now underwater. But it is safe, air-tight, enclosed in a skin membrane—a pink and blue jellyfish dome. It becomes apparent that the inhabitants are safe, sound and... rejuvenated. Our familiar ladies, Yoshie and Noriko, are up and out of their wheelchairs—on their feet! They are joined by other seniors: Hana, Ritsuko, Hina, Kayo—joyous and ambulatory all—all not believing their luck.

Running across the grass:

OLD LADIES (O.S.)

(Laughter)

HANA

It's so beautiful!

RITSUKO

You forgot your cane!

HINA

Who needs it?

A giant blue sperm whale swims by.

YOSHIE

Here comes the whale, again!

Hana runs toward the protective jellyfish skin.

HANA

(over back of head)

His eyes are so gentle.

KAYO

I think he sees us.

HANA

(begin with mouth obscured)

The "Other Side" is nice, isn't it.

RITSUKO

(over back of head)

And, my knees don't hurt.

Ritsuko bends her knees.

YOSHI

We didn't need to be afraid.

NORIKO

(over back of head)

You mean this is the Other Side?

261

RITSUKO
Where do you think we are, Las Vegas?

OLD LADIES
(laughter)

RITSUKO
It's like a dream.

Fujimoto stands on the deck of his yacht—now dry-docked on the senior center lawn. He'd like to get the women's attention.

FUJIMOTO
Ladies!
(pause)
Gather round, please!

YOSHIE/KAYO/NORIKO
Coming!

YOSHIE
(starts to run)
It's so nice to run.

OLD LADIES
(laugh)

Kayo cups her hands by her mouth.

KAYO
(yells to Hina)
Run!

Hina turns from the sea view and runs to join the ladies.

YOSHIE
(to Noriko)
Speed!

Kayo comes speeding by.

KAYO
Beat you there.

YOSHIE
(startled reaction)
(running efforts)

NORIKO
(strains to run faster)

Kayo makes it to Fujimoto's yacht first, touching the side.

KAYO
Gold!
(laughs)

OLD LADIES
(laugh)
Hina shows up last.

HANA
Kayo, who knew?

OLD LADIES
(laugh)

FUJIMOTO
Everyone quiet please.
(cut to close-up)
The time has come for you to bear witness.
(o.s., over old ladies)
To a sacred test of love.

NORIKO
Oh! Exciting!

YOSHIE
It's a trial of love.

RITSUKO
(to Kayo)
Are we too old?

OLD LADIES
(laugh)

KAYO
Are they in danger?

FUJIMOTO
Please, ladies.
(exasperated)
The children are coming now

FUJIMOTO (CON'T)
and this is a very important moment.

YOSHIE
Fujimoto,
(pause)
You won't let any harm come to Sosuke or Ponyo, now will you?

NORIKO
It's not in his nature.

OLD LADIES
(o.s., over Fujimoto)
He might. I believe in him, don't you? He's a wingnut. We can protect them, if he...

Fujimoto becomes enraged with the old ladies' incessant chattering.

FUJIMOTO
Of course I wouldn't!
(exasperated)
I hope Ponyo will stay asleep.
(pause)
Excuse me.

Fujimoto departs in his yacht.

KAYO
Now, I don't believe him.

YOSHIE
What does Lisa think?

RITSUKO
She's with that woman.
(pause)
They've been talking all night.

Lisa stands a short distance away, talking to Gran Mamare.

YOSHIE
Poor Lisa.
(pause)
A burden on his little shoulders.

NORIKO
I wish we could hear what
they're talking about.

KAYO
Why don't we just ask?
(calls out)
Lisa? Are you all right?

OLD LADIES
Lisa! Lisa! Do you need us?

Lisa raises her hand in
acknowledgement. The ladies
shout simultaneously.

KAYO
(overlapping)
Please don't worry.

RITSUKO
(overlapping)
Sosuke is a strong boy.

HANA
(overlapping)
That's right.

NORIKO
(overlapping)
He is an old soul.

Lisa leaves Gran Mamare
and walks over to the ladies.

YOSHIE
My dear!

RITSUKO
What's going on?

LISA
I wish his father was here.

OLD LADIES
(over backs of heads)
Of course you do. We're here.
We love him.

EXT. FOREST ROAD
Sosuke and Ponyo walk along
the road. Sosuke seems to
know where he is headed.
Ponyo is almost asleep again.
But, this is odd. They see
the entrance to a tunnel.

SOSUKE
Look, it's a tunnel.

The children reach the tunnel's entrance and stop.

SOSUKE
I think I've been here before.

Ponyo is weak and faltering
and losing ground rapidly.

SOSUKE
Ponyo?

PONYO
Don't like this place.

SOSUKE
Don't let go of my hand.

PONYO
Mm.

The children walk further
into the tunnel. Step by
step, instant by instant, the
girl begins to change. Her
limbs revert. There seems
no magic left in her.

SOSUKE
(startled reaction)

Ponyo collapses.

SOSUKE
Ponyo!

Sosuke shakes her. She
doesn't wake up.

PONYO
(snores)

SOSUKE
(gasps)

Ponyo clings to her bucket—
her skeletal, loose little body
is growing weaker. Sosuke
clutches her to him and runs.

SOSUKE
(breaths)

**EXT. PARK ON THE
MOUNTAIN**
Sosuke runs into the water,
and knowingly submerges the
morphing Ponyo into the sea.

SOSUKE
Ponyo!

PONYO
(snores)

SOSUKE
(gasps)
Ponyo!
(cut to close-up)
(gasps twice)
Ponyo turns back into a fish.

263

SOSUKE

(gasps)

Sosuke puts Ponyo in
the green bucket.

SOSUKE

Ponyo!
(pause)
Please don't die!
(o.s., over bucket)
Ponyo!
(cut to wide shot)
Ponyo! Wake up, Ponyo!

Fujimoto rises from the water
a short distance away.

FUJIMOTO

(over back of head)
Shhh. Don't wake her.
(cut to front)
I'm glad to meet you, Sosuke.
(pause)
We've all been waiting for
you—your mother, those old
ladies, your friends.

SOSUKE

(shocked)
My mom?

FUJIMOTO

Won't you come with me and
join them? Ponyo, too.
(pause)
Come with me.

Sosuke shakes his head no.

FUJIMOTO

I'm not going to take Ponyo
from you. Come with me.

We hear:

TOKI (O.S.)

Sosuke!

FUJIMOTO

(startled sound)
Toki is on the hill above the
senior center, standing in the
gazebo.

TOKI

Sosuke, don't listen to that
wacko.
(cut to close-up)
He tricked all the others into
going with him.

SOSUKE

Toki!

TOKI

(o.s., over Sosuke)
But he couldn't fool me
though.

FUJIMOTO

There's little time. A choice
must be made.

Fujimoto points to the moon,
which now looks enormous.

FUJIMOTO

If the moon comes any
closer...
(pause)
I won't be held responsible
if we're all swimming
underwater.

TOKI

So, that's the best you can
come up with? A falling moon?

Fujimoto pulls at his hair,
he's at his wit's end.

FUJIMOTO

(frustrated sounds)
Humans!

TOKI

(o.s., over Sosuke and underneath Fujimoto's following
speech)

TOKI (CON'T)
Sosuke, come to me!

FUJIMOTO

Sosuke, please listen to me.
(grabs Sosuke's shoulders)
You're the only one who can
save the planet!
(o.s., over Ponyo's pail)
If I have to, I'll...

Ponyo wakes up.

FUJIMOTO

(gasp)

SOSUKE

Ponyo!

Ponyo shoots a stream
of water at Fujimoto.

FUJIMOTO

(reacts to being squirted)
Brunhilde!? Respect your
father

Sosuke runs off.

SOSUKE

(breaths)
Ponyo!

TOKI

Hurry! Come to me!

FUJIMOTO

You don't understand!

Fujimoto raises a hand, gives
a look, and the minions rise.

TOKI

Faster!

The minions are right
on Sosuke's heels as he
races, bucket in hand.

TOKI

Jump for it!

The water from the bucket lifts into the air and Ponyo splashes into Toki's face as Sosuke leaps into Toki's arms. Just as quickly, the minions engulf them all and sweep them down, under the sea.

BENEATH THE SEA

Fujimoto follows in his yacht as the minions carry Sosuke and Ponyo and even Toki to the jellyfish dome. Ponyo's sisters swim alongside Fujimoto's head.

PONYO'S SISTERS
(complaining sounds)

FUJIMOTO
(gasps)
Oh, what now?

Fujimoto decides to call back his minions. He allows Ponyo's sisters to place a protective bubble around Sosuke, Ponyo and Toki.

EXT. UNDERWATER SENIOR CENTER
The sisters carry Sosuke and Ponyo—still in the green bucket—into his mother's waiting arms.

PONYO'S SISTERS
(cheerful sounds)

The old ladies catch a tumbling Toki. Sosuke opens his eyes.

SOSUKE
Mama.

LISA
Sosuke.

Ponyo peeks out of her bucket.

SOSUKE
Ponyo!

Toki thinks she should be swimming, not quite grasping the rules of the environment she's in. Yoshie sees something in the distance.

YOSHIE
Toki, look at a real woman!

TOKI
I'm confused.

Gran Mamare approaches Lisa and Sosuke.

GRAN MAMARE
So this is Sosuke.

SOSUKE
How do you do?
(he bows)
Are you Ponyo's mother?

GRAN MAMARE
Yes.
(o.s., over ladies)
You brought my daughter safely here. Thank you.

TOKI
(overlapping Gran Mamare)
Do we know that woman?

OLD LADIES
Shh!

GRAN MAMARE
Sosuke, Ponyo opened a magic well because she wants very much to be human.
(o.s., over Sosuke)
To become a real girl she needs you to accept and love her as she truly is.
(cut to close-up)
You know that Ponyo was a fish, don't you?

SOSUKE
(closed-mouth affirmative sound)
Mm-hmm.

GRAN MAMARE
(o.s., over Sosuke)
And, you know her as a human. Your drop of blood did that.

SOSUKE
Oh, that's it?
(pause)
I cut my thumb.
(looks down)
Then Ponyo licked it and made it better. (looks up)
So that's how she changed into a human.

GRAN MAMARE
Could you love her if she moved between two worlds?

SOSUKE
Mm-hmm. I love all the Ponyos. It's a big responsibility, but...

SOSUKE (CON'T)
I love that girl.

Ponyo swims joyously
around Sosuke's head.

SOSUKE
(laughs)
Ponyo swims by Lisa's head.

LISA
(laughs)

GRAN MAMARE
Ponyo, come here, please.

Ponyo swims to Gran Mamare
and sits in her palm.

GRAN MAMARE
Ponyo, Sosuke has promised
to accept you as you are.
(over close-up) To become
human you must choose to
abandon magic.
(o.s., over Ponyo)
Can you do that?

PONYO
Hm-hmm.

Gran Mamare closes her hand
around Ponyo. When it opens,
Ponyo sits encased in a
simple bubble. Gran Mamare
kneels before Sosuke.

GRAN MAMARE
Kiss the bubble, child, when
you return to land...
(pause)
...and Ponyo will become a
girl, growing up, just like you.

Gran Mamare gives Ponyo
to Sosuke, who puts her
in the green bucket.

SOSUKE
I accept, Ponyo.
(to Gran Mamare)
Thank you, Ponyo's Mother.

Gran Mamare swims
before the old ladies.

GRAN MAMARE
Everyone, the balance of
nature is restored.
(pause)
Life begins again.

The old ladies cheer.

NORIKO
He did it!
(laughs)

YOSHIE
Of course he did!
(pause)
So proud, so proud.
(everyone runs off, cheering)
The ladies run to Sosuke and
Lisa and embrace them.

OLD LADIES
(laugh and cheer)

LISA
(laughs)

Toki squeezes Sosuke.

TOKI
Mr. Sosuke!

Ponyo's sisters swim into

Sosuke's bucket and surround
Ponyo's bubble.

PONYO'S SISTERS
(laugh)

The sisters swim rapidly
upward. They swirl in a school
of gold and morph into a
cluster of beautiful females,
swimming together, upward.

LISA
(gasps)

Gran Mamare glides upward
with the sisters. She hovers
over Lisa.

GRAN MAMARE
Good luck, Lisa.

LISA
I'll need it.
(pause)
She'll be fine.

Gran Mamare glides
up and away.

**EXT. PARK ON THE
MOUNTAIN**
Rescue helicopters hover
around the gazebo. Shima
—the male nurse—sees
something below and runs
down the hill. The water is
withdrawing, the dream is
over and the ladies are ready
to go home.

SHIMA
There you are! Are you all
right?

The old ladies exit Fujimoto's yacht and begin to climb up the hill.

OLD LADIES
(presence)

SHIMA
Wait, I'll get the wheelchairs!

TOKI
Don't bother, Shima-san, we like to walk.

YOSHIE
Life begins again.

Lisa and Sosuke stand together with Fujimoto at the base of the hill. Fujimoto hands Sosuke his boat.

FUJIMOTO
This is yours I believe.

SOSUKE
(gasps)
Thank you.

FUJIMOTO
Remember me kindly, hmm? May I?

Fujimoto extends his hand. Sosuke, the bubble in one hand, extends the other to shake Fujimoto's.

FUJIMOTO
Care for Ponyo.

A ship's horn sounds in the distance.

LISA
(gasps)
It's your dad!

Lisa sees Koichi's ship sitting in the harbor and begins waving frantically.

LISA
(over back of head)
Koichi! Hi! Over here!

On KOICHI: Koichi looks through binoculars from his ship.

KOICHI
(gasps)
Lisa! And Sosuke!
(waves to Lisa)
Ahoy!

BACK on the Hill:

Sosuke balances Ponyo's bubble in his hand.

Enjoy it, it's the last time you will see her as a fish!

SOSUKE
Look, Ponyo, there's my dad's ship.

Ponyo leaps out of Sosuke's hand.

SOSUKE
(startled reaction)
The bubble falls and lands on Sosuke's upturned face. Ponyo kisses Sosuke and turns into a little girl. Song begins over beautiful pictures of this enchanted village and the harbor and the yellow house on the cliff. If you look carefully, you might see Fujimoto's minions loitering as waves on the shoreline—keeping an eye on the red-haired girl.

Ponyo, Ponyo, Ponyo
Tiny little fish
A tiny little fish
From the deep blue sea
Ponyo, Ponyo, Ponyo
She's a little girl
A tiny little girl
With a round tummy
Pitter-patter
Hip-hop and jump
Look, I have legs
I'm gonna run
Squeeze squeeze
Wave them around
Look, I have hands
Let's hold hands now
Whenever I'm skipping with her
My heart starts to dance
Munch munch, kiss hug
Munch munch, kiss hug
Oh she's my favorite little girl
Rosy red
Ponyo, Ponyo, Ponyo
Tiny little fish
A tiny little fish
From the deep blue sea
Ponyo, Ponyo, Ponyo
She's a little girl
A tiny little girl
With a round tummy

THE END

MOTHER SEA

The sea lilies sway
In a world of blue
To brothers and sisters uncountable
We spoke in the bubbly, watery language of the sea

Do you remember when
So very, very long ago
We dwelt there together

Deep in the blue, blue sea?
The jellyfish, the sea urchins, the fish and the crabs
Were our family

LYRICS	WAKAKO KAKU AND HAYAO MIYAZAKI
MUSIC COMPOSITION AND ARRANGEMENT	JOE HISAISHI
PERFORMANCE	MASAKO HAYASHI
TRANSLATION	RIEKO IZUTSU-VAJIRASARN

THE BIRTH OF A NEW SONG ABOUT THE SEA – BASED ON THE POEM "SAKANA" BY WAKAKO KAKU

For *Ponyo*, director Hayao Miyazaki wanted to make a song that captured the sea in a totally new way. Existing songs in Japan depicted the sea as a landscape or a setting, such as in the song "Umi"* taught to Japanese school children, in which it is sung that "the sea is so wide and open."

For his work, Miyazaki somehow wanted to make a song that sang of the sea itself.

One day Miyazaki was struck by a poem by Wakako Kaku. In the poem, the sea was represented in the way Miyazaki had been imagining. Based on this poem, Miyazaki wrote the lyrics for "Mother Sea".

Later, in the director's music notes handed to the film's music composer Joe Hisaishi, the following message was written along with the lyrics: This is based on Wakako Kaku's poem "Sakana" (Fish) in her poetry collection "Umi no Youna Otona ni Naru"**.

Thus, a completely new song of the sea, *Umi no Okaasan* ("Mother Sea"), created by Hayao Miyazaki, Wakako Kaku, and Joe Hisaishi was born.

*Lyrics written by Ryuha Hayashi, music composed and arranged by Takeshi Inoue.
**"Umi no Youna Otona ni Naru" (Becoming a Grownup Like the Sea), published by Rironsha.

GAKE NO UE NO PONYO
(PONYO ON THE CLIFF BY THE SEA)

Ponyo Ponyo Ponyo tiny little fish
She's a little fish from the deep blue sea
Ponyo Ponyo Ponyo she's a little girl
She's a little girl with a round tummy

Pitter-patter, hop-hop and jump
Look, I have legs! I'm gonna run!
Squishy-squeeze, wave them around
Look, I have hands! Let's hold them now!

When I'm skipping with her, my heart does this dance
Munch n'munch, kiss-hug! Munch n'munch, kiss-hug!
O he's my favorite little boy, rosy-rosy red-red

Ponyo Ponyo Ponyo tiny little fish
She's a little fish from the deep blue sea
Ponyo Ponyo Ponyo she's a little girl
She's a little girl with a round tummy

Sniff-sniff-sniff, this smells so good
I'm so hungry, I'm gonna eat!
Take a look around, very carefully
I'm sure he's there looking too

When we laugh together, my cheeks feel so hot
Happy happy kiss-hug! Happy happy kiss-hug!
O he's my favorite little boy, rosy-rosy red-red

Ponyo Ponyo Ponyo tiny little fish
Came to the house on the cliff by the sea
Ponyo Ponyo Ponyo she's a little girl
She's one happy girl with a round tummy

LYRICS	KATSUYA KONDO
ADDITIONAL LYRICS	HAYAO MIYAZAKI
MUSIC COMPOSITION AND ARRANGEMENT	JOE HISAISHI
PERFORMANCE	FUJIOKA FUJIMAKI & NOZOMI OHASHI
TRANSLATED BY	RIEKO IZUTSU-VAJIRASARN

ENDING CREDITS LIST OF *PONYO*

Studio Ghibli, Nippon Television Network, Dentsu, Hakuhodo DYMP, Walt Disney Studios Home Entertainment, Mitsubishi and Toho PRESENT

VOICES

Lisa	Tomoko Yamaguchi
Koichi	Kazushige Nagashima
Gran Mamare	Yuki Amami
Fujimoto	George Tokoro
Ponyo	Yuria Nara
Sosuke	Hiroki Doi
Young Woman	Rumi Hiiragi
Ponyo's Sisters	Akiko Yano
Toki	Kazuko Yoshiyuki
Yoshie	Tomoko Naraoka

Tokie Hidari	Akiko Takeguchi
Yoshie Yamamoto	Tomie Kataoka
Yuri Tabata	Mutsumi Sasaki
Eimi Hiraoka	Nozomi Ohashi
Shinichi Hatori	Michiko Yamamoto
Eiko Kanazawa	Shiro Saito
Akihiko Ishizumi	Akio Tanaka
Shigeru Wakita	Keiko Tsukamoto
Ikuko Yamamoto	Fuyuki Sawada
Haruka Shibuya	Kunihiro Kawabe
Yusuke Tezuka	Tomonori Yanagibashi
Ai Tsukamoto	

PRODUCTION STAFF

PRODUCER
Toshio Suzuki

ORIGINAL STORY AND SCREENPLAY WRITTEN AND DIRECTED BY
Hayao Miyazaki

EXECUTIVE PRODUCER
Koji Hoshino

MUSIC BY
Joe Hisaishi

THEME SONGS

"Mother Sea"
LYRICS	Wakako Kaku
Hayao Miyazaki	
Based on the poem "Sakana" by	Wakako Kaku
MUSIC COMPOSITION AND ARRANGEMENT	Joe Hisaishi
PERFORMANCE	Masako Hayashi

"Ponyo"
LYRICS	Katsuya Kondo
ADDITIONAL LYRICS	Hayao Miyazaki
MUSIC COMPOSITION AND ARRANGEMENT	Joe Hisaishi
PERFORMANCE	FUJIOKA FUJIMAKI
	Nozomi Ohashi

(Yamaha Music Communications)
(Tokuma Japan Communications)

SUPERVISING ANIMATOR
Katsuya Kondo

ASSOCIATE SUPERVISING ANIMATORS
Kitaro Kosaka	Megumi Kagawa
Takeshi Inamura	Akihiko Yamashita

KEY ANIMATION
Atsuko Tanaka	Kenichi Yamada
Hideaki Yoshio	Eiji Yamamori
Kazuyoshi Onoda	Mariko Matsuo
Shogo Furuya	Makiko Suzuki
Atsushi Tamura	Hiromasa Yonebayashi
Masafumi Yokota	Masako Sato
Fumie Konno	Shunsuke Hirota
Makiko Futaki	Shinji Otsuka
Hideki Hamasu	Kenichi Konishi
Tsutomu Awada	Sachiko Sugino
Hiroko Minowa	Nobuyuki Takeuchi
Hiroomi Yamakawa	Yuichiro Sueyoshi
Takashi Hashimoto	Takeshi Honda

ANIMATION CHECK
Hitomi Tateno

ANIMATION CHECK ASSISTANTS
Rie Nakagome	Kaori Fujii

IN-BETWEEN / CLEAN-UP ANIMATION
Akiko Teshima	Masaya Saito
Mayumi Omura	Katsutoshi Nakamura
Alexandra Weihrauch	Mariko Suzuki
Minoru Ohashi	Shinichiro Yamada
Moyo Takahashi	Asami Ishikado
Megumi Higaki	Satoko Miura
Yuko Higashi	Maiko Matsumura
Yasuyuki Kitazawa	Reiko Mano
Sumie Nishido	Seiko Azuma
Kiyoko Makita	Yayoi Toki
Ritsuko Shiina	Kumiko Otani
Keiko Tomizawa	Maya Fujimori
Yasuko Otomo	Hisako Yaji
Yukari Umebayashi	Tomoko Miyata
Keiko Watanabe	Kumiko Ota
Emiko Iwayanagi	Atsuko Matsushita
Masako Terada	Hiroko Kunishima
Kumiko Tanihira	Yukari Yamaura
Mai Nakazato	Takahito Sugawara
Yukie Kaneko	Masami Nakanishi
Masakiyo Koyama	Rie Fukui
Risa Suzuki	Akane Otani
Setsuya Tanabe	Yoshitake Iwakami
Yohei Nakano	Yoshimi Sagawa
Kazuhiro Takamura	Ko Hosaka
Hiromi Nishikawa	Kumiko Terada
Kaori Ito	Rie Kondo
Soonha Hwang	Tomoyo Masuda
Aya Kubota	Rena Okuyama
Makoto Ohara	Kunitoshi Ishii
Hirofumi Okita	Megumi Matsumoto
Nobuyuki Mitani	Yoko Motoya
Yuna Takase	Shuntaro Ichimura
Saori Yanaga	Kazune Suzuki
Megumi Nakamura	Takahiro Takashima
Yuka Saito	Tomoyuki Kojima
Mitsuo Sato	Yuhei Ueda

SUPPORTING ANIMATION STUDIOS
Anime Tororoto	Nakamura Production
Studio Takuranke	Studio Cockpit
Doga Kobo	Gonzo
Brain's · Base	Tatsunoko Production
Studio Khara	

ART DIRECTOR
Noboru Yoshida

ART DIRECTOR ASSISTANTS
Naoya Tanaka	Naomi Kasugai
Takashi Omori	

BACKGROUNDS
Ryoko Ina	Mitsuo Yoshino
Sayaka Hirahara	Yoshikazu Fukutome
Masako Osada	Yoichi Watanabe
Kikuyo Yano	Yohei Takamatsu
Yoichi Nishikawa	Shiho Sato
Osamu Masuyama	Yoji Takeshige
Kazuo Oga	

COLOR DESIGN
Michiyo Yasuda

COLOR DESIGN ASSISTANTS
Kazuko Yamada	Yukie Tamura
Akane Kumakura	

DIGITAL INK AND PAINT
Naomi Mori	Hiromi Takahashi
Rie Kojo	Sumiko Saito
Hiroaki Ishii	Junya Saito
Eiko Matsushima	Makiko Doi
Hiromi Takeno	Kaori Tani

T2 Studio
Kumi Nanjo	Haruna Kiryu
Kasumi Wada	Akiko Shimizu
Natsumi Watanabe	Yoshimi Shibata
Yukiko Kakita	Fumie Kawamata

DIRECTOR OF DIGITAL IMAGING
Atsushi Okui

DIGITAL CAMERA & COMPOSITE OPERATORS
Junji Yabuta	Atsushi Tamura
Hidenori Shibahara	Norihiko Miyoshi
Miki Sato	

DIGITAL SPECIAL EFFECTS
Keiko Itogawa

PROGRAMMER
Masafumi Inoue	Shun Iwasawa

RECORDING & SOUND MIXING
Shuji Inoue

SOUND EFFECTS
Koji Kasamatsu

DIRECTOR OF AUDIO RECORDING
Eriko Kimura

SOUND EFFECTS ASSISTANT
Yoshiki Matsunaga

FOLEY
Mika Yamaguchi

RECORDING & SOUND MIXING ASSISTANTS
Takeshi Imaizumi	Yumiko Shibusawa

OPTICAL RECORDING
Futoshi Ueda

DIGITAL OPTICAL RECORDING
Noboru Nishio

DOLBY FILM CONSULTANTS
Tsutomu Kawahigashi	Mikio Mori

DTS MASTERING
Mariko Konta	Atsushi Aikawa

CASTING COORDINATION
Motohiro Hatanaka	Ayumi Sato

SOUND PRODUCTION SUPPORT
Tokyo T.V. Center   digitalcircus
Tohokushinsha Film   NATS Nihon Automobile
                          College
PUG POINT · JAPAN   Continental Far East Inc.

CONDUCTOR & PIANO
Joe Hisaishi

MUSIC PERFORMANCE
New Japan Philharmonic
Concert Master   Munsu Choi

VOCAL
Mai

CHORUS
Ritsuyukai Choir

RECORDING & MIXING ENGINEER
Suminobu Hamada

MUSIC RECORDING
Sumida Triphony Hall

MUSIC PRODUCTION MANAGEMENT
Wonder City   Nobumasa Uchida
Kayo Chiba   Yasuhiro Maeda

EDITING
Takeshi Seyama

EDITING ASSISTANTS
Rie Matsubara   Keiko Tsunokawa
Hiromi Sasaki

PRODUCTION MANAGER
Hiroyuki Watanabe

PRODUCTION DESK
Kyohei Ito   Yuichiro Mochizuki

PRODUCTION ASSISTANTS
Shintaro Nakazawa   Yumiko Miyoshi

POST PRODUCTION
Tamaki Kojo   Noriko Tsushi
Ayaka Nishihara

ASSISTANTS TO THE DIRECTOR
Kenji Imura   Ryosuke Kiyokawa

PRODUCTION ADMINISTRATION MANAGER
Shinsuke Nonaka

PRODUCTION ADMINISTRATION
Shokichi Arai   Toshiyuki Kawabata
Daisuke Nishikata   Tetsu Shinagawa
Minako Nagasawa

MUSIC COPYRIGHTS
Takashi Nagai

PRODUCER SUPPORT STAFF
Nobuko Shiraki   Kazumi Kobayashi
Yoshiaki Nishimura   Mayu Naito

ASSISTANT TO THE PRODUCER
Yoko Ihira

PUBLIC RELATIONS
Junichi Nishioka   Setsuko Kurihara
Yumiko Nishimura   Chieko Tamura
Chihiro Tsukue   Nozomu Ito
Akiko Omi

MERCHANDISING DEVELOPMENT
Tomomi Imai   Kazumi Inaki
Koichi Asano   Mika Yasuda
Naomi Atsuta

PUBLISHING DEVELOPMENT
Yukari Tai   Kyoko Hirabayashi
Satoko Kitazawa   Chikashi Saito
Taku Kishimoto   Mine Shibuya

SPECIAL EVENTS MANAGEMENT
Shin Hashida   Kazuyoshi Tanaka
Kan Miyoshi   Ryoko Tsutsui
Noriko Takami

FINANCE & PERSONNEL MANAGERS
Miyuki Shimamiya   Noriyoshi Tamagawa

GENERAL ADMINISTRATION
Akio Ichimura   Hisayo Ito
Tamami Yamamoto   Junko Ito
Takayasu Ito   Hisanori Unoki
Hiroyuki Saito   Yukiko Miyasaka
Natsuki Ebisawa   Misa Kokubo
Miyuki Saito   Saori Uchida
Eiko Fujitsu   Sueko Numazawa
Masako Fujita   Kiyoko Tsuge

SYSTEM MANAGEMENT
Noriyuki Kitakawachi   Satomi Sasaki
Shoji Makihara

OVERSEAS PROMOTION
Stephen M. Alpert   Mikiko Takeda
Nao Amisaki   Evan Ma
Yasuaki Fujita

AUDITOR
Hirotaka Nakao

SPECIAL THANKS TO
Kaku Arakawa   Fumiko Isomae
Tomoko Okada   Masataka Kato
Asuka Kanazawa   Takumi Kaneno
Yuki Kameta   Kenichi Kawahito
Yutaka Kurokochi   Shinji Goto
Shinji Koyasu   Masanori Saito
Miho Sata   Toshikazu Sato
Yasuhiro Suzuki   Shintaro Seki
Shinichi Takai   Kentaro Takahashi
Hideo Tanaka   Hiroomi Tanaka
Daisuke Tsuchiya   Yuko Dozono
Soichi Nishizaki   Jun Hattori
Miwako Hamada   Ryuji Hayashi
Yasuhisa Harada   Haruna Hirose
Keiji Fukuda   Takaaki Fujioka
Tadahiro Hoshi   Masaki Morita
Naoya Moritani   Maiko Yahata
Fumio Yamazaki   Chie Yoshiike
Kenichi Yoda   Ryuta Yonezawa

PROMOTIONAL SPONSOR
Asahi Soft Drinks

SPECIAL MEDIA SUPPORT
Lawson   The Yomiuri Shimbun

ADVERTISING PRODUCERS
Shimpei Ise   Tomoko Hosokawa

Toho
Nobuhiro Fukuda   Nobutaka Nishida
Ai Nakanishi

Toho Ad
Masaru Tsuchiya   Masaru Yabe
Yuta Mizuki   Rieko Matsuki
Michiyo Koyanagi   Yukio Shinohara
Mieko Hara   Hiroshi Yajima
Hiroyuki Orihara

FILM PREVIEW PRODUCTION
Keiichi Itagaki

PONYO PRODUCTION COMMITTEE

Nippon Television Network
Seiichiro Ujiie
Noritada Hosokawa   Haruhisa Murokawa
Yoshinobu Kosugi   Yoshiko Nagasaki
Suzuko Fujimoto   Nozomu Takahashi
Naoto Hatakeyama   Miwa Matsukuma
Mayumi Hirakata

Dentsu
Itsuma Wakasugi   Tatsuyoshi Takashima
Kotaro Sugiyama   Yasushi Matsushita
Toichiro Shiraishi   Yuji Shimamoto

Hakuhodo DY Media Partners
Takashi Sato   Kazuyoshi Yoshikawa
Takashi Nishikawa   Yoshiro Yasunaga
Megumi Yoshida   Masatsugu Yabe

Walt Disney Studios Home Entertainment
Takayuki Tsukagoshi   Maiko Hirano
Koji Kishimoto   Yuko Muranaka
Yukio Yamashita

d-rights
Daizo Suzuki   Toru Itabashi
Tetsuya Yamamoto   Toshiya Takasaki
Kino Arai

Toho
Hideyuki Takai   Satoshi Chida
Yoshishige Shimatani   Minami Ichikawa
Akihiro Yamauchi   Hikaru Onoda

ASSOCIATE PRODUCERS
Seiji Okuda   Ryoichi Fukuyama
Naoya Fujimaki

FILM DEVELOPING
IMAGICA
TIMING
Hiroaki Hirabayashi   Yoshihiro Ueno
FILM RECORDING
Sho Ogoshi   Satoshi Kumakura
COLOR MANAGEMENT
Wataru Matsumoto   Aya Majima
DIGITAL CINEMA MASTERING
Ken Okada
LAB COORDINATION
Yuriko Sato
LAB MANAGEMENT
Takehisa Kawamata   Osamu Kuge

PRODUCTION   Studio Ghibli

THE ART OF

PONYO

BASED ON A STUDIO GHIBLI FILM

ORIGINAL STORY AND SCREENPLAY
WRITTEN AND DIRECTED BY
HAYAO MIYAZAKI

English Adaptation/Takami Nieda
Design & Layout/Carolina Ugalde
Editor/Nick Mamatas
Editorial Director/Masumi Washington

Gake no Ue no Ponyo (Ponyo on the Cliff by the Sea)
© 2008 Studio Ghibli - NDHDMT
All drawings and image art © 2008 Studio Ghibli - NDHDMT
All rights reserved.

© 2008 Studio Ghibli - NDHDMT
First published in Japan by Studio Ghibli Inc.

Printed in China

Published by VIZ Media, LLC
P.O. Box 77010
San Francisco, CA 94107

First English edition printing, August 2009

10 9 8 7 6 5
Hardcover edition first printing, September 2013
Fifth printing, January 2020

Visit www.viz.com